JESUS ~~WAS~~ IS INVOLVED IN POLITICS! WHY AREN'T YOU? WHY ISN'T YOUR CHURCH?

THE ONLY WAY TO A HAPPIER, HEALTHIER, SAFER, AND MUTUALLY PROSPEROUS AMERICA

JESUS ~~WAS~~ ^{IS} INVOLVED IN POLITICS! WHY AREN'T YOU? WHY ISN'T YOUR CHURCH?

THE ONLY WAY TO A HAPPIER, HEALTHIER, SAFER, AND MUTUALLY PROSPEROUS AMERICA

NEIL MAMMEN

RATIONAL FREE PRESS

JESUS ~~WAS~~ IS INVOLVED IN POLITICS!
REVIEW EDITION

This limited review edition has been created for reader, reviewer and endorser comments, corrections, recommendations, and disagreements. The final version will incorporate your suggestions, recommendations, and clarifications. It will also include professional editing to improve the style as well as correct grammatical, factual, and formatting errors that were missed. Email addresses provided are current but all web pages may not exist yet. Distribution and publisher inquiries are welcome. Christian organizations who wish to resell or purchase bulk copies of this book for their use are encouraged to contact us.

Please review and forward any comments and corrections to
review@JesusIsInvolvedInPolitics.com

The author's biography is listed in the back of the book.
Neil Mammen is available as a speaker on this and other topics
speaking@JesusIsInvolvedInPolitics.com

Special Thanks and Gratitude

To Peter Sprigg, Vice President and Senior Fellow for Policy Studies at the Family Research Council (FRC) who in between appearing on TV news shows and debates and doing research, spent much of his limited free time reading early versions of this manuscript, correcting facts and suggesting better ways of phrasing things. Thank you, Peter. *www.FRC.org*

To David Sawkins, Senior Pastor of South Valley Christian Church/Venture Christian Church and Founder & Chairman of the Values Advocacy Council; for showing me how a pastor can be involved in politics; know both the local and national politicians personally; display integrity at all stages; and still pastor a growing thriving church.

To Gil Mertz, Regional Director of Development at the Family Research Council (FRC). Teacher of the Forgiveness Seminars. For your friendship and encouragement and for teaching me more about forgiveness during one casual dinner than I've learned in 10 years. *www.ForgivenessCoaching.org*

To Frank Turek, Businessman, Apologist, Author, Radio and TV Host, Friend. Thanks for your encouragement and for the opportunities. You are a man who does not suffer from the fears of scarcity. *www.CrossExamined.org*

DEDICATION

To my Daughters

Caroline Lois
from *your* father's arms to *our* Father's arms
when I see you next, you will no longer be a baby
but you will always be *my* little girl
You reminded me of my future and why I exist
and
that this is *not* our final destiny

and to
Mary-Katherine
who *daily* reminds me
why despite my final home
I cannot give up the fight for a Godly America *today*!

I love you both

Contents

Appendix and Notes

The guns are silent in this war but frontiers fall while those who should be warriors prefer neutrality.

Not too long ago two friends of mine were talking to a Cuban refugee. He was a businessman who had escaped from Castro. In the midst of his tale of horrible experiences, one of my friends turned to the other and said, "We don't know how lucky we are."

The Cuban stopped and said, "How lucky you are? [At least] I had some place to escape to."

And in that sentence, he told the entire story. If freedom is lost here, there is no place to escape to.

A TIME FOR CHOOSING, October 27, 1964
Ronald Wilson Reagan[1]

Preface: Setting Fire to the Straw Men

Have preconceived objections about this book? Read this.

There was an explosion behind me. Not one caused by gun power, (you'll have to wait a couple of chapters for *that* story). But this was an explosion of air. "Harrumph!" it went. I was standing in the dinner line at a Christian conference chatting about this book, when I heard the loud exclamation behind me. I glanced at the lady behind us. I could tell by the disapproving look on her face that she thought I was completely misguided. I turned to her, smiled, and gave her an opening. She laid into me. She'd had it up to her teeth with all those Christians in politics, the huge hypocrites, claiming to be Christian and then having affairs or ending up in prison. "Christians should stay out of politics and focus on loving people! Our job is to just preach the Gospel. You can't legislate morality!" she exclaimed to everyone who had turned to see what the commotion was all about.

A few months later there was another similar explosion. I was teaching a junior high Sunday School class. The topic: How to defeat abortion arguments *without* using the Bible.[2] In the sermon, I explained what each of the political parties platforms were on abortion. Suddenly, one of the counselors exploded from his seat and stormed out of the room in a huff. I found out afterwards that he wasn't upset about my talking about abortion. He was upset that I'd tied it to politics and that I'd had the *gall* to name a party, i.e. the Democratic Party as the pro-abortion party *in church*.

Whenever we deal with divisive issues like Christians in politics, not

---

[1] www.reagan.utexas.edu/archives/reference/timechoosing.html By the way this entire speech with at least 15 quotable and memorable lines was written by Reagan *himself* before he had speechwriters.

[2] If you are interested in this, please go to www.JesusIsInvolvedInPolitics.com and look up "Abortion."

only do we need to be sensitive to those who may disagree with us, but we also need to clarify certain points, for often they presume we are proposing things we are not proposing. I call this preliminary discussion "Burning the Straw Men," after the well-known flaw in logic.[3] I have had folks like that lady, hear the topic, and immediately conclude that I'm advocating something that I am not.

What is "politics" anyway?

One person objected when I stated, "John the Baptist got involved in politics."

"When?" came the incredulous retort.

"When he condemned Herod, a political leader, for committing adultery with his brother's wife." I said.

The person immediately shot back, "John was *not* getting involved in politics; he was *just* speaking out against evil."

This made me realize that while most of us have an understanding of what many politicians do, we seem to forget what it is they are *supposed* to do. Thus, when I say we as Christians should be involved in politics; they think I am suggesting we get involved in the cult of personality; posturing for position; making ourselves out to be better than others; seeking favored positions in the eyes of men; taking illegal contributions; bribing people and all sorts of other vain and pompous things.

But, as you will find out, I am not talking about *that*. In fact, I agree with the objection, *if* that's what politics is about, we should all stay far away from it. Yet, when I say Christians should be involved in politics, I am talking about what politicians *should* be doing, not what they *have* been doing. We and they should be speaking out against evil actions that affect us all. You will see later in this book how Herod's very actions are at the root of our nation's problems *today*. Furthermore, I'm talking about pastors and lawmakers, not *just* speaking out against evil men and their evil laws like John did, but *also* taking *action* against evil men and eliminating evil laws. Making just laws, appointing impartial judges, ensuring that justice is served, making sure that people are not oppressed, ensuring that true equality in opportunity is given *without* the state equalizing results. That every person is free to work towards achieving their greatest potential. That they are not enslaved, i.e. the product of their labor is not forcibly taken away from them.

I'm talking about lawmakers who look towards the future and realize how a law today could damage an entire nation by undermining the family structure. I'm not talking about a popularity or self-promotion. I'm talking about getting involved as "servant-leaders," *not* "leader-kings."

You see, if that's what politics is about, surely, you can agree with me that not getting involved in politics it's no longer an option for us who love the Lord, and have compassion for those who suffer unjustly. In fact, it's because we love people that we *have* to get involved in politics.

---

[3] The Strawman or Straw Man Fallacy is created when the opposing side misrepresents your position and then argues against it. From the concept of building a straw man and attacking it instead of you. Then saying, "See I won." I've tried to avoid Strawmen in this book, but do let me know if I accidentally created one. It was not my intention.

Neil Mammen

The Straw Man List

Over the years, I have compiled a list of these objections, concerns, and comments, I've listed them here, and I address them individually in the appendix:

1. You are arrogant to think you have all the answers on this issue.
2. Aren't you suggesting that we should create a United States with the Christian equivalent of the Muslim Sharia Law – that is, interpret biblical laws and legislate from them? This would just be a Theocracy, a Christian Taliban.
3. Christians talking politics will scare non-Christians away from the Gospel.
4. Right wing Christian involvement in politics has created a backlash.
5. You are implying that politics is the most important issue facing the world or our country today.
6. All politics is nasty and dirty, the Church should not be involved in it.
7. You are recommending involvement in politics as a way of evangelization; or you are suggesting that we use political legislation to attempt to change the wickedness of man instead of preaching the gospel to achieve that end.
8. You are recommending using laws as a way to force people to convert.
9. Christians should focus on changing themselves and their churches, not on changing the world or the culture.
10. When I meet non-Christians, should I really be talking to them about politics? Shouldn't I be witnessing to them?
11. All politicians are human, if we endorse one candidate and he turns out to be a bad apple, loses, or messes up, then the church will be marred.
12. God is not a Republican or a Democrat.
13. When people come to church, if the pastor is talking about a political issue that they disagree with, they won't come back.
14. You are promoting Liberation Theology.

If you have any of these objections, let me assure you that most of them are a mischaracterization of my view. If you feel they will prevent you from understanding or accepting the biblical and logical case that I am about to present here, please *first* turn to the appendix titled "Burning the Straw Men" and read my responses to these objections. It is my hope that this will allay your fears. Chances are we actually have a lot more in common than you think.

One way to engage that is successful

I've found that when we talk to people, if we seek common ground first (without compromising our true values), we can usually achieve a lot more than if we seek to differentiate ourselves. I was recently at a Tea Party demonstration at my liberal representative Mike Honda's Health Care Town Hall . There wasn't much of a discussion because the hall was stacked with union employees (wearing their Safeway union T-shirts) and very few *conservatives* were able to get in. But *outside* the meeting place, there were a few outnumbered non-union liberals, those who hadn't been able to get in. One had an Obama T-shirt. I was wearing a T-shirt my wife had given me. It said "Old School Conservative" and had a picture of Ronald Reagan.

Somewhere in all the hubbub, the guy, (I'll call him Hans), turned to me, looked at my shirt and said something to the effect of, "Ah, what's the use, there's nothing we'd agree on."

My sister-in-law responded, "So you think that that's a good reason never to talk? I'd think that would be a good reason *to* talk."

Hans was a bit taken aback. I guess he thought we conservatives hated talking about things we'd already been "brainwashed" about.

I said, "Why do you say that? I think there's lot we agree on."

"Like what?" sneered Hans.

"Like Iraq" I said.

"Iraq? Are you saying that we shouldn't have gone into Iraq?"

"Yes," I nodded, "I think we agree that if there were *no* Weapons of Mass Destruction, we should have never gone in? Now we can argue whether there were WMDs or not, but we both agree that if there weren't any we should not have gone in."[4]

He seemed surprised. I continued, "Can we agree on the other hand, that if Saddam *did* have WMDs he probably would not have used them on us, but he *would* have sold them to Al Qaeda who would have had no compulsion *not* to use them on us, and in that case we *should* have gone in."

Hans responded, "Well yes, but they didn't have any."

"We can discuss that later, but can we agree that if we *honestly* believed they had any,[5] we should have gone in."

Hans nodded. "Okay," I said, "so there's something we do agree on. Let me tell you what else we agree on."

"What?"

"Healthcare, we both agree it would be wonderful for everyone to have access to good affordable healthcare."

"Huh? I thought you were here to object to healthcare."

I smiled, "Well, you see while I'd love for everyone to have access to *good and affordable* healthcare, I don't think that Universal Healthcare is *good or affordable*, because it has never worked well and has always ended up having to be rationed. Look at Medicaid, it's a nice idea, but it costs about 100 times more than they said it would and it's going bankrupt. Oh, and I don't think I should force people who don't want to pay for another person's health care to pay for it. I don't think it's the government's job."

Hans looked at me quizzically "Then who pays for it?"

"We Christians will. You, Hans, shouldn't have to pay for it."

That blew his mind. "How are you going to do that?" he demanded.

I said, "Christians have been paying for the healthcare for millions in almost every country in the world. Reduce our taxes and we'll take care of the poor like we used to."

"Are you serious?"

"Yes, have you heard about missionary hospitals? I grew up going to them. Send us your poor and sick, we've always taken care of them. Do you agree that if that is a better solution, then wouldn't you rather we did that? Have you ever heard of Medi-Share (www.medi-share.org) where people

---

[4] It turns out that Saddam had indeed been buying Yellow Cake Uranium, despite what Valerie Plame's husband Joe Wilson lied about. www.washingtonpost.com/wp-dyn/articles/A39834-2004Jul9.html and slate.msn.com/id/2103795. But is this evidence of WMDs? I hope we find out one day for sure.

[5] Like Bill and Hillary Clinton said they did. The Snopes site has a number of these verified quotes. Note however that liberal Snopes also argues that the Clinton administration did not want to invade Iraq, the key is that they admit that Iraq had WMDs. www.snopes.com/politics/war/wmdquotes.asp

voluntarily share each other's medical costs?"

Hans wasn't sure, "Would it work?"

"Ah" I said, "It *is* currently and I think it would work better than unfeeling uncaring entitlement healthcare. Also, let's let doctors who want to, take a certain number of pro-bono cases and get a tax write off for their time. But, that's what we could discuss. That and outrageous lawsuits, which force doctors to send people for unnecessary testing to cover their own hides, why there's a government cap on the number of medical students a college can accept, why every other government health system is bankrupt. So you see it's not that we don't agree who should get healthcare, we just need to figure out the best solution. I think I can prove Universal Healthcare is not the best solution."

Hans thought for a while. "Okay I guess I can see that."

"We also both agree that schools should not be in the business of brainwashing kids."

"We do?"

"Yes, imagine if one day conservatives took over the public schools, would you like us brainwashing your kids to be conservatives?"

Hans agreed, "That would not be nice."

"In fact, take anything you guys are doing now, like the unions using dues money to promote the Democrats and imagine that one day we take over the unions and do the same thing to you. Would you like it?"

"That is scary," nodded Hans, his eyes widening.

"My name is Neil. What's your name? Why don't we do lunch and I'll show you more of where we do agree."

"Yes, that may be interesting." We exchanged email addresses.

You see once you start focusing on where you *do* agree many people will listen. Then we can look at the specifics of what we disagree about.

In conclusion

To finish the stories I started, in the first case I was fortunate that the dinner line was a long one and I was able to give the lady some gentle assurances and explanations of her objections before we were separated, all of which are in the appendix. Her parting comment was "Okay, maybe you can send me your book when it's out."

In the second case, the youth pastor, Josh Keller, explained that this particular counselor thought politics had no place in church. Josh added, "But he knows that *I* think that it's ridiculous to try and divorce the two. What's the use of talking about abortion if we can't change the laws? That's like making a big fuss about slavery but never going the next step to make it illegal."

I encouraged him to have the counselor talk to me.

The counselor hasn't approached me yet.

Maybe he'll read this book.

One

California allows anyone born in California to change the gender marker on a California birth certificate with an appropriate court order.
California Health and Safety Code sec 103425
A California law today. Will this be a Federal law soon?

I re-visited some Muslim countries this year, they have no old pastors, their pastors have a short lifespan. They keep being murdered. Pastors are the first in line.
Muslim Convert

When they came, they came for the pastors first. They targeted them.
Hindu Convert (but could have been said by a Muslim convert or a Chinese Christian or even a Swedish Christian)

It All Begins

One Sunday morning, your pastor reads aloud the passage in Leviticus that includes, among other things, a section on homosexuality. On Monday morning, someone files suit, calling it "hate speech." The ensuing legal struggles drain money from your church accounts and forces your pastor to focus on the church's financial survival instead of preaching (the Hate Speech Law, HR1592 introduced to the House by Representative John Conyers, Jr. in March of 2007[6]). Whether they win the suit or not, those who file the suit have been as effective as they were with Pastor Ake Green in Sweden who suffered in the same way for the same reason.

You swat your child's hand one day in a supermarket. You are arrested and put in prison for one year for "spanking your child" (AB755 introduced in the California Assembly by Assemblywoman Sally Lieber, in February of 2007, reissued as AB2943 in 2008[7]).

Judges who admit that they will acknowledge God and consider His Natural Law[8] in their rulings and interpretations of original laws[9] are fired

---

[6] Some have argued that this will not be the automatic result of this law. However, it seems to me that we have evidence of this sort of oppression in Canada and Sweden from laws similar to these. In addition, history has shown us that many pastors, lest their churches lose tax-exempt status, shy away from political issues even when they are legally allowed to make certain comments on politics. They throw the baby out with the bath water, a result of a law forced through by Lyndon Johnson to muzzle non-profits. We will discuss this in detail further.

[7] Lieber has since had to make many modifications to her bill, but with a fully liberal house, senate and president those who wish to pass this at the federal level would probably not need to do so.

[8] Referred to as "The Laws of Nature and of Nature's God. They are referring to the nature of God and how his laws necessarily manifest themselves in His creation. We'll discuss this in this book.

from their posts (Judicial Inquiry Commission, Alabama 2003).

Same-sex marriage is legalized by five California Supreme Court Justices and self-identified homosexuals become a protected minority. These Supreme Court Justices were appointed or elected to office because of the passivity of Christians. A constitutional amendment to the California Constitution to protect marriage and limit it to one man and one woman passes with a majority but results in the same Supreme Court threatening to overthrow it despite the will of the people. Another judge goes on a witch hunt to over throw it, even reading emails trying to determine if the authors of the proposition are anti-gay bigots, (as if that's relevant *after* the people have voted on it). Yet another judge, forces the release of the names and addresses of all donors to the amendment. These individuals are harassed, and receive death threats. Eventually the courts override the people's vote and homosexuality becomes a civil rights issue not a behavioral choice.

Shortly thereafter, your cousin's church refuses to hire a gay man as the Youth Pastor at their church. Days later they are slapped with a civil rights discrimination lawsuit and they see their church bankrupted by legal fees.

Your parents have been attending a small church in a prime downtown location for almost 30 years. Suddenly, their church is sued for not allowing a gay couple to attend their annual married couples' retreat. Besides the cost of the suit, the church loses its tax deduction. The congregation wakes up one morning to find out that since their tiny downtown church property is worth millions of dollars, they now have to come up with tens of thousands of dollars each year to pay property taxes. To make matters worse, Church members find out that they all owe back taxes on deductions they've already taken on their tithes and offerings. The IRS, run by a Treasury Secretary, appointed by the president has no compassion. Your parents can't come up with the back taxes and have to declare bankruptcy.

A judge rules that home schooling is illegal unless the parents are 'state credentialed tutors.' This unconstitutional ruling is not overthrown by the state senators (elected due to the non-involvement of Christians). As a result, parents who refuse to send their kids to a state approved school risk losing them to child protective services (the Second Appellate District, Los Angeles County, 2008).

Yet, when you send your child to the very same state approved public school, another judge rules that your parental rights cease once your child has passed through the public-school doors, especially when it relates to sexual values and the teaching of homosexuality and sexual matters (Fields v. Palmdale School District Ruling 2005).[10]

The definition of gender is expanded to include any gender an individual chooses for himself or herself. It becomes illegal to insist that a person's gender be determined biologically. School kids are given the freedom to choose the girls' restroom or the boys' restroom depending on whether they view themselves as male or female that *day* (SB777 passed by California, the

---

[9] That is laws that were written by men and women who acknowledged God's natural laws in their codification of those laws.

[10] www.citizenlink.org/FOSI/abstinence/education/A000001079.cfm

Neil Mammen

California Health and Safety Code sec 103425 and an actual attempt by a Los Angeles School to adhere to this).[11]

Oh, you are over-reacting!

Am I being an alarmist?

Unfortunately, I don't think so. We have already seen examples of people in the United States and Europe persecuted and suffering under such laws.

Here in the "free" United States, Christians have been thrown in jail for distributing Bibles on public property. They have been slapped with huge lawsuits; churches and Christian organizations have lost leases or have had to spend millions on legal fees just to be able to build on property they own.

In Philadelphia, a 70-year-old African American great grandmother and ten other Christians were thrown into *jail* for having the audacity to stand on a sidewalk during a gay parade and preach a loving message about salvation. They were simply preaching the gospel. They were not condemning homosexuality. These peaceful men and women were arrested and faced 47 years in prison and fines of $90,000 each.[12] Forty seven years! Am I really over-reacting? You tell me. This is happening in America. What happened to free speech? Why are Christians being targeted? Why do you think you won't be next?

At 8:30 p.m. on October 31, in Salem, Massachusetts, police officers arrested an evangelism director preaching the gospel to a crowd of rowdy Halloween partiers.[13] The police arrested him for *disturbing* the peace. Yet alarmingly, he was but one of many *other* just as loud "street entertainers" that night. Do you think he was being targeted? That could be your church high school group being arrested.

A pastor in Phoenix, AZ was sentenced to jail for 10 days and 3 years of probation because a judge forbade their church bells to chime except for 2 minutes on Sundays. It's important to note that the bells were lower in volume than an ice-cream truck.[14]

In Alameda California, Superior Court Judge Frank Roesch yelled at parents who had sought to excuse their elementary kids from a controversial pro-homosexual curriculum forced on them by their school board. The judge called the parents bigots and refused to let them pull their kids from class *despite* a federal law that says parents can do this.[15] Why weren't there

---

[11] "Legalizing" Gender: California allows anyone born in California to change the gender marker on a California birth certificate with an appropriate court order (California Health and Safety Code sec 103425 et seq). Equitable jurisdiction has been found to give courts authority to grant change of gender for people born outside of California. See also www.transgenderlawcenter.org

[12] www.covenantnews.com/repent051013.htm

[13] Watch the video here: www.youtube.com/watch?v=eYuaOenys60 the city proceeded to discriminate against him and judges ruled against him despite the fact that the city law specifically allowed what he was doing. Watch the video and decide if our reaction should be one of passivity as the tide turns against us. Or should we change those who make, judge & enforce our laws to be those with Godly Worldviews?

[14] Defended by the Alliance Defense Fund www.telladf.org/UserDocs/PainterOrder.pdf

[15] The Pacific Justice Institute is continuing to defend the parents legally. www.PJI.org
http://www.wnd.com/index.php?fa=PAGE.view&pageId=117841

Christians on that school board?

The organization MassResistance, has documented the changes in Massachusetts after their Supreme Court merely indicated that same-sex marriage was not banned. A willing Governor Mitt Romney and a liberal legislature led to elementary kids being forced to be brainwashed with homosexual curriculum.[16] Scarier still, parents who confronted the school to object, were arrested.

In Oakland, California, my friend, the mild and gentle Pastor Walter Hoye, a member of the National Black Pro-Life Union was standing outside a Planned Parenthood clinic with a sign that said, "Jesus Loves You, can we help." The manager of the Planned Parenthood accused Walter of aggressive behavior towards her and had him arrested. Coincidentally, Walter had video tape of the *whole* day with no gaps and no aggressive behavior. Walter even meekly backed off whenever he was approached by her. They showed the judge that the manager was committing perjury. Yet despite the video tape that proved he was innocent, Walter was told he could not come within 100 feet of the clinic. When he stood on his constitutional rights, he was thrown into jail for 30 days. What value were his constitutional rights? They were only on paper, with no elected official to defend him. What value was the physical evidence? It is of no value if the authorities have decided to make America a corrupt 3rd world nation. The Planned Parenthood manager was not even held to account for lying under oath. Why? Because the DA was anti-Christian![17]

With changes like this, do you think Christian free speech and free worship will last long? All of these actions reflect a specific strong anti-Christian and anti-God bias by those in control. All of these actions against us were taken by people that *we* Christians have the power to appoint or dismiss.

Yes, someone *is* over reacting; but it's not us, may I suggest that it's those with an anti-Christian bias? If Christians don't at least *start* reacting soon, perhaps it will be too late.

Christians in other countries also thought this could never happen to them. In Canada, parents had their kids taken by child protective services simply for refusing to *agree* that they would *abstain* from spanking their own children.[18] Focus on the Family Canada, is not allowed to broadcast any radio shows that are either critical of the homosexual political agenda or disclose the physical consequences of the behavior even if that data is taken from a medical source like the Centers for Disease Control.

In Sweden, Pastor Ake Green was thrown into jail for reading a Bible passage on homosexuality; he was not on some street corner. He was reading this while in his *own* pulpit.

In Britain, a Christian was arrested for merely handing out pamphlets at a rally. A spokesman for the police said the campaigner had *not* behaved in a violent or aggressive manner, but that officers arrested him because "the

---

[16] What same-sex "marriage" has done to Massachusetts
www.massresistance.org/docs/marriage/effects_of_ssm.html

[17] Defended by Life Legal Defense Foundation. Read Pastor Hoye's story and watch the video
www.lldf.org/articles/WalterHoyeVsOakland contact his organization here www.issues4life.org

[18] www.cbc.ca/news/story/2001/07/09/parents_spanking010706.html

leaflet contained biblical quotes about homosexuality."[19]

Politics?

All the laws I mentioned earlier are genuine currently proposed laws, proposed by senators and representatives, some waiting to be passed. All these laws and all the oppression of Christians could have been stopped by Christians and the Church.

Yet people in your church and your pastor do not think they should be involved in politics.

---

[19] www.annointed.net/Article1040.html

Two

Congress never reflects the values of the nation; ...it only reflects the values of those who voted in the last election.

David Barton, www.wallbuilders.com

*Based on voting statistics, it's apparent that Christians could stop **all** abortions in **one** election cycle. The fact that we haven't, indicates that we don't know, don't care or don't wish to. Either way, the blood of innocents is upon our hands.*

My response on FaceBook to a debate

We Can Win This Battle

I want to set the tone from the beginning. The battle for America can be *won* without ever having to convince a single non-Christian or non-conservative about anything. The battle for America begins and ends with Christians and conservatives. The task is well within our reach:

> *Aside from the fact that more than 55% of the country agrees with most of our beliefs, there are more than 60 million evangelical Christians of voting age in America. Some 24 million of them are not even registered to vote. Of the 36 million who are registered to vote, not all do.*
>
> **David Barton**[20]

In 2004, 122 million[21] people voted in the general election. George Bush won that year by 3 million votes. In 2006 only 96 million people voted.[22] Karl Rove even noted that the Republican majority in the house was lost by only about 3000 votes.[23]

As a result, we see these trends:

In 2004, almost 28.9 million evangelicals voted and voted biblical values, and consequently 78% of the new senators and 63% of the new representatives who came to Washington that year were pro-life.

In 2006 *only* 20.5 million evangelicals voted (8.4 million less than in

---

[20] From a power point presentation by David Barton, the facts and sources are documented on his web page at www.wallbuilders.com/LIBissuesArticles.asp?id=3930 see also www.reuters.com/article/domesticNews/idUSN0741145420070207

[21] http://www.washingtonpost.com/wp-dyn/articles/A10492-2005Jan14.html

[22] https://www.census.gov/prod/2008pubs/p20-557.pdf

[23] Personal conversation with Karl Rove in 2007. That sounds impressive, but it really isn't. I met him at an FRC.org briefing in WA DC and asked him what he thought about their 2006 thrashing in the polls.

Neil Mammen

2004), and that year only 10% of the new senators and only 31% of the new representatives were pro-life (see the same Barton reference above for details).

In the two years following the 2004 election most of the key pro-family propositions passed in many of the states.

In the years after the 2006 elections, some of the worst anti-family and anti-biblical laws were passed by the U.S. Senate and House.[24] With 24 million of us sitting on the sidelines,[25] presidential and senate races were being won or lost by a few hundred thousand votes here or there in key states or a paltry 200 votes in Florida in 2000. *Chances are that we could have changed every one of those outcomes.*

Lest you forget, it's only because of those 200 votes that President Bush was able to appoint the correct judges and a pro-life congress with a pro-life platform was able to legislate and then defend the constitutionality of a ban on partial-birth abortions. A procedure, which partially delivers a baby that could live outside the womb, and then sucks its brains out.[26] A procedure, mind you, that Barack Obama believes should remain legal.[27]

These pro-life senators and presidents and state congressmen went on to pass over 500 state and federal pro-life bills, causing one of the greatest decreases in abortion since it's height of 1.6M abortions a year (which destroys the liberal lie that electing pro-life representatives have no effect on abortion or abortion laws).[28] But as we will see, abortion is only the tip of the iceberg.

In many elections, Christians vote for representatives, judges, senators, and even presidents who have moral beliefs and Worldviews that are specifically and clearly *condemned* in the Bible. They seem to forget that the President of the United States does far more than act as a cheerleader for the country. He leaves a legacy of hundreds of judges (not just the Supreme Court, but every federal judge in every district). Sadly, most of the setbacks that Christians have seen in the last century have been due to judges with anti-Christian Worldviews. With his bully pulpit and a compliant legislature the

---

[24] American Voters and the Abortion Issue, David Barton, wallbuilders.com/libissuesarticles.asp?id=6449

[25] While the ratio of those who voted in 2004 to 2006 reduced by the same amount the fact remains that if those Christians were encouraged by their pastors and got out and voted it would not have reduced amongst us and we'd be winning every single race.

[26] For a diagram showing this despicable procedure go to www.JesusIsInvolvedInPolitics.com and do a search for Partial Birth Abortions.

[27] Despite his own claimed dislike of it. We'll eviscerate this excuse in a later chapter.

[28] This just shows that they are ignorant of the facts and are blindly buying the pro-abortion propaganda. Others have tried to argue that the decrease in abortions is only due to other things like ease of access of contraceptives, but numerous studies show this to be untrue. "Since 1992, approximately 17 states have enacted parental-involvement laws. Twenty-eight states have adopted informed-consent laws, which give women seeking abortions information about fetal development, sources of support for single mothers, and potential health risks incurred by obtaining an abortion… Twenty-four states have enacted waiting periods. Articles published in peer-reviewed academic journals (and studies released by the Heritage Foundation and the Family Research Council) have found that many of these pro-life laws succeed in reducing abortion. … According to data from the Centers for Disease Control and Prevention, the number of abortions performed in the United States peaked in 1990 and has declined nearly every year since that time. Among the 47 states reporting abortion data in both 1990 and 2005, the number of abortions had fallen by 22 percent. Many states that passed pro-life legislation have experienced even larger declines." www.article.nationalreview.com/?q=OTExMGJkZGMzMDI3ODY0YWU0ZDA2ZWVmOGRjNmRkZDg=

president effectively holds the purse strings to billions of dollars that *can* go to causes that actively grieve the heart of God and destroy our society from within. [29] He also appoints men and women with incredible power to push their personal agendas, and when those people do not feel kindly to evangelicals or God's moral laws, their agendas and their rulings directly affect churches, the dissemination of the Gospel and our freedom to witness to others. A simple example was Obama's appointment of Kevin Jennings, the founder of the Gay, Lesbian and Straight Education Network to be the School Czar. His organization since 2000 has had an agenda in the public schools to recommend a pornographic reading list for underage students. A reading list that includes the glorification of adult on minor homosexual sex,[30] books that your kids will be forced to read. Still think a president's Worldview does not matter?

With so many Christians *not* voting, do you see that this battle is actually just among Christians? If Christians can educate and encourage enough others to vote and that too, to vote morally and biblically, we can change this country in a single election cycle. And if we do, the dire trends we see will be stopped and reversed. But this must start in our churches. For if churches and pastors do not teach how God's moral values should affect our political appointments, all will be lost. If they do, we can move mountains.

Pastors, do not worry, I'm not going to be asking you to tell your congregation which individual to vote for. I'm just going to be asking you to teach them oft ignored biblical principles. This will automatically teach them *what* to vote for and what to look for in the character and moral values of anyone they vote for. That should be sufficient for them to discern *whom* to vote for.

Social Justice? Aren't those bad words?

In this book I occasionally use the words "true social justice." Many may imagine I am referring to socialism or economic justice," I am not. Socialism is theft as we will prove, and economic justice is communism (an oligarchy that practices theft). There is truly only one type of justice that has any value, "Moral Justice." However I will use the words *true social justice* to take these words away from their abuse, to reuse them to refer to laws that protect our unalienable rights; *not bring equality of results or grant us goods.* The fight to free the slaves was a battle for *true* social justice because it was moral justice the fight for God given rights. The misguided fight for universal healthcare was a battle to give "goods" to people. We will cover this in detail in the chapter titled: Who Gives Us Our Rights?

The obvious goal of this book

This book is written to help you convince enough others to get out there and be involved biblically. It is written to mobilize the Church, the very people who will suffer needlessly if they don't get involved. These are also the

---

[29] He has the veto power as well as the ability to set the direction of government spending like Obama did with the trillion dollar deficits in 2009. This includes amongst other things, government funding of abortions as well as things like the National Endowment of the Arts that has repeatedly used that money to produce anti-Christian art.

[30] www.massresistance.org/docs/issues/fistgate/handouts/index.html

Neil Mammen

very people who have the power to easily turn the tide around to help the poor and oppressed, with solutions that work.

This is a battle for **True** *Moral Justice. Will you join in the battle?*

Three

If I see a madman driving a car into a group of innocent bystanders, then I can't as a Christian simply wait for the catastrophe and then comfort the wounded and bury the dead. I must try and wrestle the steering wheel out of the hands of the driver.
Dietrich Bonhoeffer, German Theologian, and Pacifist[31]

How To Use This Book

I want to get your attention – not by sensationalizing facts, offering half-truths or over spiritualizing things. While you may disagree with the long-term effects, all the pending laws in the first chapter were real attempts at legislation.[32] I want to get your attention the same way Paul got the attention of the people on Ares Hill in Athens. I want to get it by using logic, facts and reasoning,[33] all of which are biblical principles.

I hope you will allow me to work towards persuading you, your pastor, fellow Christians,[34] and God-fearing Jews[35] about the critical need for all of us to be involved in politics. Many Christians think politics should be barely tolerated by Christians. They think that it should be avoided by pastors and never discussed in church. People will quote the Bible in defense of this position. We will look at those passages in context and see if they truly say what people claim they say.

Once that is done, I hope you will work with me using this book to motivate and train pastors; to first start training their congregations to think biblically and rationally about these moral issues, then to start encouraging and discipling key people in their congregations to run for office. To run for school

---

[31] www.christianhistorytimeline.com/GLIMPSEF/Glimpses/glmps063.shtml

[32] Will they be as terrible as I suggested? If we fall asleep at the wheel, I believe they will.

[33] Isaiah 1:18 "Come now, let us *reason* together," says the LORD. "Though your sins are like scarlet, they shall be as white as snow; though they are red as crimson, they shall be like wool.

[34] This book presumes the reader is a Christ follower or God fearing Jew who believes the validity of the moral values taught by the Bible. While I will try to prove the validity of these moral values, I have not attempted to justify or validate the accuracy of the Bible or provide the historical evidence for the resurrection of Jesus. This proof is readily available in the writings of William Lane Craig, Lee Strobel, Josh McDowell, and many others. For more information go to www.NoBlindFaith.com.

[35] When I use the phrase "God fearing Jew," I intend to imply any Jew who honors and loves God and believes in the Law and the Prophets (i.e. the Christian Old Testament).

Neil Mammen

boards, city boards, county boards, local and national offices. You may not think this is the role of the church, and I understand that. Yet, I hope to show you how and why it is indeed the role of every Christian who cares about the poor and the suffering.

Yes, I know you are a busy parent with lots of kids, a dog, two cats and a demanding job. Or, you are an unbelievably busy pastor and the last thing you need is one more hassle that you don't consider biblically mandated. I hope you will let me show you how it *is* biblically mandated, and thus it is your moral duty. Don't feel overwhelmed, as I think I can show you how easy it is to do if we all work together (see the chapter titled "Conclusion: We can *indeed* win this battle!)"

Pastors, I would like to show you why your "everyday" job of ministering and preaching the gospel will be *easier* if you do this and we change America. I believe the best incentive for participation is success and the growth of your ministry, and I am convinced that we can achieve that.

Third, and perhaps most important I want to explain to you how *not* participating will hurt the very people whom you were called to help; the lost, the poor, the helpless, the widows, and the children.

In the end, I hope to show you that Christ's call for *true* social justice can only be ignored by a hardened heart.

The way to a Happier, Healthier, Safer and Mutually Prosperous America

I make this audacious claim in the subtitle of this book, yet as you read more, I pray that you will see how this is the logical, rational and natural result of a majority of Christians and churches becoming politically active in the *biblical* way. Statistics and studies show that if we do this effectively, Americans will be happier, they will be healthier, our society and streets will be safer, our prisons will be emptier, we will need fewer law enforcement officers,[36] and our mental institutions will be under-populated. Not only that, but poverty and hunger within the United States will be reduced, our schools will be more effective, and we will all be mutually prosperous. But just as important, I hope to show you how a healthier America will result in more outreach, more missionaries, more financial and medical aid to the rest of the world and most importantly, more true social justice and less taxes.

Can we get there? The solution will be up to us Christians and our pastors. Sadly, if we don't try, we will continue to spiral down and the consequences will be dire. Meanwhile, be encouraged that many of our goals are shared by non-Christians. It's the methodologies that we disagree on; I hope to equip you to be able to show others why our methodology actually works, and to point you to information that shows this rationally, logically and statistically.

Pastors are the key to the solution

Our most difficult challenge will be gently helping pastors see the crucial role they play in informing their people about God's heart on existing, future and pending laws. Pastors are the key to equipping and preparing their

---

[36] But don't worry, the free market will find lots of alternate productive and rewarding jobs for them.

congregation to respond to the moral ramifications behind current cultural issues. They cannot endorse candidates, but they can change the nation if they teach the logical and rational basis of God's Moral Law. If they encourage their members to run for office, write letters and educate their representatives. Our representatives need to know what Christians view the heart of God to be regarding laws that are affecting the country. Pastors are the best conduit for this.

We need to convince pastors to do their part in getting the entire Church, the Bride of Christ in America, to throw its mighty weight behind the legislative direction of our country. By doing this we can change our nation spiritually, politically, legally and culturally. Let me prove this to you step by step in this book.

It may be a lofty goal, but it is attainable if we focus on common goals, remove misperceptions, and talk winsomely with pastors.

I intend to show you that not reaching the goal will exact a grave cost in our children's lives and worse, have ramifications for the *eternal* salvation of billions of people outside this country. Not trying to reach this goal will be violating our Lord's second greatest commandment: Loving your neighbor as yourself.

My Journey

In many ways, this book describes my journey which started as a young foreign student in the 80's who, though a Christian, was liberal, pro-choice, despised Ronald Reagan and was not interested in politics. This book shows you what I've learned since then about politics, the law, and morals. It explains the thinking, growing and maturation process I went through. It is thus a way to talk others through the same learning dynamic. I didn't want to write a dry technical explanation because there are plenty of those out there, and frankly, I can't sit through many of them.

The knowledge I will present to you changed me, and if I can change, perhaps you can change. And if you can change, I know America can change. And as I want to show you, if we change America, we change the world.

What were my opinions based on?

Everywhere we look, we see opinions based on ignorance or misinformation. I am the prime example. As that young liberal Christian student just off the "boat" from the Middle East, I bought into what I was hearing in the media, watching on television and seeing in movies. I wasn't thinking for myself. Nor was I doing my *own* research. I accepted all of liberal dogma and assumed that the other side – that is you, the conservative fundamentalist Christians in America were selfish and either stupid or evil. I did not realize I was grossly misinformed and misguided until someone challenged me to look at the statistics of what worked, to consider historical analysis and to dig for the truth on my own. As a "left wing Christian," I did not want to admit that I was wrong. Why? Because this would have implied that I had been fooled or, worse, had been fighting the wrong battle. It would have shown my passions to be misplaced and misdirected. In those days, the consequences of my logic were forcing me to abandon my logic.

Neil Mammen

So, our battle is twofold. First, we must correct misinformation.

Second, and just as important, we must do it gently so people they don't hold their old positions out of spite, pride or a sense of loss. We need to assure them that the years they held other views were not wasted as long as they remember why they held those positions and figure out how to reach out to people who think exactly as *they used* to think. I hope my recollection of why I held those positions is helping *me* to understand the way my liberal friends think these days.

If, as you go through this you see that my logic is sound and realize that perhaps you've been mislead or misinformed, it's okay. Perhaps God was preparing you as he did me to reach others like you. We all came through a similar journey, so you can plainly see that it isn't that I am smarter or wiser than you in figuring out this stuff. I just learned a few things and had patient – very patient -- teachers and coaches.

A personal note - I could be wrong

I believe that I have made every attempt at historical and factual accuracy and have earnestly tried to avoid any sense of self-righteous ego in writing this book; but it is important that I clarify that I do believe I could be mistaken in my arguments or details of various historical events or their interpretations. So, if someone can show me that I'm wrong, I am willing to correct things and even change my mind if that follows. Only a fool would say he could not be wrong. Only an irrational person refuses to change his thinking when presented with compelling evidence. If I'm wrong, be kind enough to email me at: *Idisagree@JesusIsInvolvedInPolitics.com.*

You may change my mind, or in dialog, I may be able to clarify my points better.[37] At the end of the day, we seek understanding, but most importantly, we seek the truth, the reality of what really is; even if that is not what we wish it was. As such all corrections and updates will be posted regularly on www.JesusIsInvolvedInPolitics.com.

If you agree with this book

I ask that you work with us to implement these ideas in your church and help spread this message by getting this book into the hands of your congregation, your elder board, your pastors and, just as important, pastors, priests, rabbis and bishops[38] in neighboring churches and synagogues. We also have resources available to enable you to teach Sunday school using the concepts in this book. We need to convince as many Christians as possible that they have a biblical responsibility to be involved in politics. And do feel free to send us a note of encouragement at

---

[37] We ask that before you do so, you read entire book and fully consider all the arguments presented; we also ask that you use standard hermeneutical principles in interpreting the Bible and provide us with rational rebuttals. This is not an attempt to avoid hearing your disagreements. Rather, it is an attempt to put discussion on the playing field of truth and logic, not emotion.

[38] I'll use the word pastor most of the time instead of saying pastors, priests, bishops, rabbis and teachers every time. Similarly I may default to using the word Christians when I intend most times to indicate not only Christians but also God fearing Jews who hold to the divine inspiration of the Torah and Old Testament. I will also default to writing "Church," but please know I intend to include synagogues in that word as well.

I agree, but my Pastor doesn't

If you attend a church where the pastor does not agree with the idea of Christians being involved in politics and you know him personally, we ask that after you have read this book; give him a copy and ask him to *refute* it. Give him a few weeks, and then invite your pastor out to lunch, telling him that you'd like to go over some of the points raised by this book. In a relaxed setting, start by clarifying to your pastor that you will abide by his decision whatever it maybe. Then go over the salient points[39] of the key chapters in a non-confrontational way. If your pastor disagrees, that is fine. Do not hit him over the head with it. You will fail and he'll just despise this book. So instead, just ask that he consider reading the entire book – even if it is so that he can explain to you how he thinks I've misguided you in what I've said. (After all, I could be wrong. I don't think I am, but I open to the possibility and always try to correct my errors.)

We ask that you then do the same with members of your elder board.[40] Do it one elder at a time so the odds are even and you can focus due consideration for each individual's honest questions and objections. Keep it friendly and respectful. Remember in some churches the pastor is unable to take any decisive action without the consent of the elder board. Send any observations you think will help our cause to:

Feedback@JesusIsInvolvedInPolitics.com.

If on the other hand you are in a big church and the pastor does not know you personally, I'd recommend multiple people give and/or recommend this book to the pastor over the period of a few months. It may finally pique his interest.

Pray that God uses you to change minds, but be respectful of people's decisions. Do not be a pest. Remember, at the end of the day, as long as you are a part of your church, you are under the authority of your pastor and elder board.

You may wish to do what I try to do. Whenever I talk to people whom I think may disagree with me, I try[41] to point out that this was how *I* came to my personal conclusions, and I'm only presenting this to them so they can evaluate it and use it if it helps them. I mention that while I don't think I'm wrong (after all, who runs around thinking they are wrong); I do know that I could be wrong and constantly strive to correct any of my own false beliefs.

A note to Laypeople and Lay Leaders

Once you understand the arguments in this book, I, those in this type of ministry, as well as pastors, priests, rabbis and others who have endorsed this book ask that you talk with others about what this book has to say. We also ask that you give copies of the book to your church lay leaders, so they too can prayerfully consider what is here and act on the challenge we make to followers of Christ. See if you can teach a Bible study or lead small groups

---

[39] An index will be provided at JesusIsInvolvedInPolitics.com with pages numbers to easily find things.

[40] Pastors are going to hate me for that suggestion.

[41] This does not mean I'm always successful, sometimes my pride and my eagerness get in the way.

using this and the associated small group guide. We will also cover many important biblical concepts and ideas we have found to be great witnessing tools. Even atheists engage when Christians present rational arguments.

A note to Pastors, Priests, and Elders

Pastors, rabbis, priests and elders, if a member of your congregation has given you this book, I ask that you prayerfully consider what I have written and diligently compare it to your understanding of the Bible. If you are a pastor and think some points in this book could be made more winsomely, please do contact us with your suggestions. We want to be effective.

Not limited just to Christians

While this book's primary target audience is Christians, I believe that those of the Jewish faith who believe the Law and the Prophets i.e. the Old Testament will find much to agree with. When I say "Bible Believers," I intend to include Orthodox, Protestants, Catholics, Jews, Evangelicals, Coptics and such.

If you are not a Bible believer, while this book is not directed at you, I still think you will gain some understanding of the rational basis for many of our beliefs. However, may I recommend that you first read the appendix chapter titled "Afterword: This is an Argument Not an Opinion." I believe it will place the arguments I present in the proper context.

Liberal? Conservative?

I also use the word "Conservative" in this book when in fact I really mean Laissez-faire Liberal. You see, 200 years ago we Conservatives would have been considered Liberals. Classical Liberalists believed in a form of liberalism in which the government does not provide social services or regulate industry and banks and who believe in strict constructionism. I'll explain what this is later. Obviously, the language has changed so I've chosen to use the common vernacular of today.

Topics

The topics in this book bounce around a fair amount; I do this primarily because there are times when I need to switch to a new topic to introduce and explain a specific concept before I can continue with studying the evidence at hand. I pray that the reader will bear with this.

A Reference Manual

May I also suggest that you view this as a reference manual. Once you've read it, look through the contents occasionally to address issues that people hit you with. To learn it the best though, I suggest teaching from it.

Resources

Free slide presentations and sermon outlines of this book are available for download. You may personalize them and use them freely for presentation to your church or Sunday school. We also have a booklet[42] you can use as a

---

[42] Additional resources will eventually include the "Jesus Was Involved In Politics: 20 Reasons" booklet, an easy to read book that you can hand to your friends.

Small Group Bible Study or as questions for a book club to discuss. This will help you to take Christians systematically through a series of steps to a logical understanding of why they have what may amount to a divine ordinance from God to be politically involved. It will also help you teach morality and the law in such a way that people will be able to witness more effectively. The junior high and high school versions of this Bible Study allow you to introduce these concepts to kids at an early age and facilitate discussion around the family table and on car trips.

The presentation and notes can be found at
www.JesusIsInvolvedInPolitics.com.

You can also contact us by email at
ChurchesTogether@JesusIsInvolvedInPolitics.com for help and support in this battle.

Neil Mammen

Four

Islam has no concept of the separation of Church and State.
A Muslim scholar, to my father.

We Get Kicked Out Of the Yemen Arab Republic

I was born in Ghana.

Some of you may be asking yourselves, "Isn't that a town in Texas?" It's actually a country just off the West Coast of Africa. I was born in the town of Cape Coast, Ghana, to East Indian parents. By the time I was two, my dad moved us all to Jamaica and kept traveling from there. Over the years, we've lived in Sudan, Ethiopia, Eritrea, India, and Yemen. I mention all of this to indicate my experience and exposure to multiple cultures and various political structures and to introduce a story.

Though my family traveled all over the world, I spent the largest part of my childhood in Sudan. Now I know some of you are thinking that unlike Ghana, Sudan really *is* a town in Texas, just off Highway 84. Turn left at the Dairy Queen. That is true, but that's not *the* Sudan where I grew up. The Sudan where I spent a large part of my youth is an Arabic speaking country just south of Egypt on Africa's east coast.

Today when I say "Sudan," some may know of the current genocide and murder of Christians by the Muslims in Darfur. But, when I was young, Sudan used to be one of the most beautiful places in the world. The great rivers of the Blue Nile[43] and the White Nile merged about three blocks from our house before heading out to Egypt and the Mediterranean Sea. We lived in Khartoum, the capital. At that time, there was no persecution of Christians. In fact, there were churches of all kinds and Christians of all denominations and traditions, from Coptics to Syrian Orthodox to Greek Orthodox to Church of England to the church we attended, the SIM (then known as the Sudan Interior Mission) Church.

---

[43] Yes, I really did grow up in de-nile. It's just not funny when you write it out, is it? Actually, in the interest of full disclosure, I need to mention that I never actually went swimming in "de Nile." There were occasional crocodile sightings there, so my mom forbade me to hang out on or fish from the banks.

The Jesuits ran one of the best schools in Khartoum. I was fortunate (though I didn't think so at the time) to end up going there. It was called Comboni College, and the headmaster was a stern faced priest named Father Goromino. We called him "Father Grow Meaner - Day by Day," especially if any one of us was unfortunate enough to be punished by him for an offense. (Yes, I was – but I was innocent…no really.)

Being a brown-skinned kid, darkened by the sun with jet-black hair, I looked just like my friends and neighbors, the local Arab and African Sudanese kids. I spoke enough Arabic to get around but unfortunately forgot all of it once I made it to the U.S. and started watching Star Trek in English.

Baby Traveler

You may wonder why we traveled so much. No, my dad is not an international thief nor spy. At least that is what he claims. Dad is a professor of physics, who taught at universities all over the world, till he settled in the U.S. Some of these universities were in Islamic countries. This was what made me the jet setter and international traveler by the age of two. Every year we would travel, from wherever my dad was teaching, to see our extended family and cousins in India. My father has nine brothers and sisters in his family, and my mother has seven in hers. Each time we traveled my dad would find the most creative route to take us home, allowing us to visit and enjoy many countries, cultures, and cuisines. We've vacationed in Syria, Egypt, Jordan, Dhahran, Abu Dhabi, Kuwait, England, Spain, Italy, Aden, and Lebanon. Believe it or not, at one time both Aden (Yemen) and Beirut (Lebanon) were thriving affluent free ports similar to Monte Carlo.[44]

However, don't imagine this was the plush life for us. Along with the good, we experienced wars and evacuation from wars. When my dad moved us to Yemen, there were no British schools there, so as was common at that time amongst ex-pats;[45] we went to a British boarding school in Asmara. I was 12.

War

I remember the lions. Asmara was still part of Ethiopia then, and we lived about half a mile from Emperor Haile Selassie's palace.[46] At night, we could hear his pet lions roar. Despite what your image of Ethiopia may be today, the land is the most fertile of all the countries in which I have lived (yes even more fertile that California). The weather was always around 40 to 77 degrees, and we could literally walk out of our classrooms and pluck plums, berries and other fruits. The area seemed lush with farms. No one was starving. We got there, had six months of peace then politics made its presence known.

---

[44] These are two examples of killing the Golden Goose. Aden fell to the communists and was never the same after that. Lebanon used to have a majority of Christians and was the jewel of the Middle East, but it was taken over by Muslims fundamentalists and in a matter of months tourist trade stopped, it ceased to be of any economic value and the standards of living were destroyed.

[45] Short for "expatriate" meaning those who live outside their country and not to be confused with "ex-patriots," which would either be football players who no longer play for New England or people who do not like their country any more.

[46] Born Prince Tafari Makonnen, the Ethiopian word for Prince is "Ras," so he was Ras Tafari Makonnen, yes the very same "Messiah" to the Rastafarians. Now you know where the word comes from. Although I think Haile Selassie would have been saddened to think that he was being used to replace his *true* Messiah, Jesus Christ.

One quiet night in the middle of chapel, gunfire erupted outside the walls of our boarding school. I didn't recognize it at first, it was different from the movies. It echoed around the buildings. The gunfire was followed by an huge explosion. I recognized that. I remember diving for cover under the benches – not that they would have stopped any bullets – and huddling in fear. The next morning, BBC radio told us that we had gotten ourselves caught in the civil war between Ethiopians and Eritreans.[47] For four traumatic days, we heard bombs and machine gun fire and mortars going off as we hid under our beds in fear that a wayward shell would hit us or that some soldiers would decide to raid the school for supplies or hostages. Finally, on the fourth day, we were driven to the Asmara Airport and put under the protection of the U.S. Marines. Then, under their safe and watchful eye, we were evacuated from the city on a PAN AM jet.

Can you imagine the security we felt, the relief that came over us when we caught sight of that first Marine? This was when I started to admire the U.S. Marines and the United States and decided that one day I wanted to come to America. I wanted to be a part of a great nation that even today is the first to come to the aid of others.

Indian Christians?

You may also be wondering why I'm a Christian and not a Hindu. It is a little known fact (little known to most Americans, that is) that there are many Christians in India. Sure, we are a minority, but even 2% of a billion is a bunch of people. In fact, our family hails back to the church in India founded by St. Thomas in 51 A.D. My father tells me that there has been a lay preacher in our family in each generation right from the first conversion of our ancestors.

While India as a whole has a very low percentage of Christians, our particular state, called Kerala, is almost 20% Christian. It also happens to have 100% literacy and, strangely, the highest population of communists. One of my uncles was even a leader in the early communist movement and had a price on his head right after the Indian Independence. I rationalize this as having something to do with taking the Christian ideal of equality and sharing too far.

Lest you think this is a book about my life, it isn't. As I said at the beginning of this chapter, I'm giving you my background for two reasons. First, I want to show, with no credit to myself, how I have been blessed to have lived in, traveled to, visit and experience multiple cultures. Relevant to the topic, I have personally lived and experienced various political regimes, from fascist and military dictatorships to emperors to kings to communism to democracies and finally to a real republic.[48]

The second reason I provide you with my background is to introduce this brief but important story of my *first* attempt to come to the U.S.

---

[47] It was during this time that Mengestu Haile Mirrium took advantage of the situation and took control of Ethiopia and put it under fascist communistic rule. This resulted in the massive starvation that most Americans associate with Ethiopia. It's important to note that the starvation was not a result of un-farmable land but of man's inhumanity to man.

[48] As opposed to North Yemen, a fascist state called the Yemen Arab *Republic*, or South Yemen that was communist and called the "People's *Republic* of Yemen." Everybody seems to have jumped on the "Republic" bandwagon with no idea of what it really means. Note by 1989 both Yemens had reunited.

The Yemen Arab Republic

My father was teaching at the University of Sana'a in the Yemen Arab Republic at the time. Yemen is an Islamic country controlled by a military dictator. My father had worked at the university for about six years and planned to continue working there for quite a while longer.[49] When I was 15, he determined that since I had completed all 12th grade level mathematics and science classes as a sophomore, I was ready for college. He decided that I didn't need to spend two more years in high school just to take English lit, so he asked me if I felt ready for college. Imagine my glee as I told my disbelieving classmates that I was not going to 11th grade but straight to college. Initially, they mocked me for thinking I could skip ahead, but they changed their tune when I came back to visit as a college freshman.

For the next three years, I studied at the University of Sana'a, majoring in physics with a minor in mathematics. My classmates were mainly Egyptians, Palestinians, and Yemenis with a few Syrians thrown in for good measure. I was now 18, and since my evacuation from the war zone in Eritrea by the Marines five years earlier, I had dreamed about coming to the U.S. to finish my degree. America was the land of my dreams. It was the land of my destiny. It was the land of my heart. It was the land of very beautiful women. Or at least it seemed so on the movies that I saw on Yemeni TV (with all the even slightly suggestive scenes like kissing, short skirts and swimsuits edited out).

A professor's pay in Yemen was not enough to pay out of state tuition and room and board in the U.S. However my parents talked about it for a while, and I did a lot of research, and we were finally able to find a school in Oregon (Eastern Oregon State College) that we could just barely afford. So, with great excitement I planned my future. Of course, it was conditional on my dad continuing to work at the university making the same salary. But, we saw no reason why he would not do that.

I vividly remember that afternoon, two months before I was supposed to leave for the USA. Dad came home from work and sat us all down. He told us that his contract with the university had been terminated. We were shocked.

We soon found out what had happened. It turned out that my dad's colleague, a fellow professor who suffered from constant migraines, had committed suicide. When the police went into his house, they found a Bible that belonged to my father on the nightstand. My Dad hadn't even lent him the Bible; the professor had taken it from my dad's desk at work. In effect, my dad was telling me that, because they thought he had given a fellow worker a Bible, we had to leave Yemen and my dreams of coming to the U.S. were shattered.

Why?
***Because it is illegal to give a Bible to a non-Christian
in the Yemen Arab Republic.***

---

[49] During the latter years of the Clinton administration, just after the USS Cole had been attacked in Yemen and Bill Clinton had bombed a factory in Sudan claiming that they'd been producing WMD gases; my brother and I half expected a visit from the CIA since my family had lived in both of those countries just prior to us coming to the U.S.

Five

But Jesus didn't get involved in politics. He didn't try to change the Roman laws. He said, "Give to Caesar what is Caesar's and give to God what is God's." If Jesus didn't do it, then we shouldn't.
    College Coed

Jesus Was Involved in Politics!

It was a candle lit room full of college students – a typical emerging[50] type church setting. I had been invited to speak to the young adults. Many had tattoos and weird hair, yet after spending three weeks with them, teaching apologetics and the dangers of blind faith[51] and seeing positive responses, I decided to venture into uncharted waters and try to help these students understand why Christians need to be involved in politics. I was doing well, feeling good about the impact I was having on this particular topic, when suddenly out of the darkness a coed interrupted. "That's all well and good, but Jesus didn't get involved in politics," she declared. "He didn't try to change the Roman laws. He said, 'Give unto Caesar what is Caesar's and give unto God what is God's.' If Jesus didn't do it, then we shouldn't."

There seemed to be a stunned silence in the room.

Was this a valid objection? Let's see if we can respond to it.

If Jesus did not do something, does that mean we should not do it either?

Just because Jesus did not do something does not mean it is a bad or unwise thing to do. Though the Romans killed and massacred people, Jesus never said or did anything about that. He didn't condemn them for it.[52] He could have stopped their evil practices with a wave of his hand. But he did not.

---

[50] By this, I mean the good evangelical kind, not the heretical emergent kind. Confused? I know - everybody is. For more information go to www.str.org and look up "emergent church."

[51] See www.NoBlindFaith.com for more information on a Rational Logical approach to Faith.

[52] You cannot arbitrarily attribute our Lord's many statements on love as a vague fuzzy condemnation of the Romans' cruel practices. After all He was not reluctant to let loose specific condemnation on the Pharisees. Why then would he be reluctant to condemn the Romans specifically for slavery or abuse. Yet we know He did not condone it.

Does this mean we should allow people to massacre others? Of course not! There were slaves[53] everywhere in the ancient world. Jesus never fought for their freedom. He did not even say they should be freed. Was he condoning racism and slavery?[54] No, that's ridiculous.[55]

Obviously, just because Jesus didn't do something doesn't mean we should *also* not do it.

The clincher here is marriage. Jesus never got married,[56] yet we don't hear the same people arguing that because He was not married, no one else should be. That would clearly be invalid and illogical.

What if Jesus did do something?

The reverse of an invalid argument, however, may be valid. I hope we can agree that if Jesus *did* do something, that is probably a good indication that we should do strive to do likewise. Keep this in mind as we investigate this further.

German and U.S. Politics

Many people seem to be confused about who the "politicians" of Jesus' day were and how laws were enacted in Judea.

For perspective, let's compare the relationship between Judea and Rome in 33 A.D. to a more recent situation, the lengthy U.S. occupation of Germany after WWII.[57] Suppose a German citizen living under American occupation at that time started calling for change in American laws. How effective would that be?

Not very.

Why would a citizen of Germany under U.S. occupation not be allowed to get involved in American politics? Obviously because he could not vote in the United States, nor did he have any rights of U.S. citizenship.

Similarly, it would not make sense for an Iraqi citizen today to petition

---

[53] Do note that as far as I can tell the Jews never had slaves the way we think of slaves. The Old Testament allowed what would be called indentured servitude or those of prisoners captured during a war. The former was a system in which a person could pay off his debt by becoming and indentured servant of the person to whom he owned money. When the debt was paid, he was free to leave or become a bondservant, someone who loved his master so much that despite the fact that he was legally free, he chose to remain under the master's protection and providence. This was far different from the U.S. version of slavery. The latter was a side effect of the wars of conquest and aggression. But one was never allowed just to kidnap a person and make him or her a slave.

[54] By the way, the response, "Well, Jesus didn't drive a car either" doesn't work. Because the answer would be, "Well, that doesn't apply because cars hadn't been invented."

[55] Interestingly in light of the fact that He never spoke out against slavery, my atheist friends say he approved it. But we know that is ludicrous. There are multiple passages in the Bible that condemn slavery e.g. Ex 21:16 Anyone who kidnaps another and either sells him or still has him when he is caught must be put to death.

[56] Don't start me on absurd claims of the novel, *The DaVinci Code*, which tries to claim that Jesus was married. If you want a rebuttal, see www.str.org and do a search for DaVinci. Or see *The DaVinci Code: Fact or Fiction*? Hanegraaff, Maier, Tyndale House Publishers, 2004.
Of course, you could argue, "But Paul says we can get married later, so the analogy is not a good one." However, what that merely shows is that just because Jesus didn't do something it's not a sufficient reason for us not to do it. Obviously, Nicodemus's involvement in politics and Paul's approval of and Peter's involvement in marriage can be shown as equivalent valid examples of this.

[57] It took a long time to train a nation of people under submission to fascists to become good democratic citizens.

U.S. senators to change American laws – say, for example, to allow a man to have four wives. Although Americans are administering Iraq as this book is being written, Iraqi citizens are not to influence American politicians or even donate money to them. It would be illegal and a waste of time for an Iraqi citizen to try.

Jesus and Roman Politics

So when we look at Jesus, His comment about Caesar and His non-involvement in Roman politics, we first have to ask, "Was Jesus a Roman citizen?"

No, he wasn't!

What *was* His citizenship? Well, obviously, He was Jewish. He was a Jew living in a country *occupied* by Rome. Yet He and his countrymen were not Roman citizens. They were a conquered people, but they *were* Jewish citizens.

So would the Romans have allowed Jesus to be involved in their legal system? No. In fact, would it make any sense for Him to confront Caesar or any Roman politicians in an attempt to alter their laws (never mind that they were physically about 1,422 miles away)?[58] No again.

Jesus was Jewish, so we should look at the Jewish political structure, not Caesar's minions. Who wrote the Jewish laws? With whom would Jesus have had to be engaged with if He wanted to affect public policy? Who were *His* senators, representatives and judges?

Before we answer that, let's look at the structure of Israel in Christ's time. In doing so, maybe we can dispense with commonly held misconceptions.

Did the Romans run Israel and make all their laws?

The biggest misconception most people seem to have is that the Romans ran Judea, treating it like an extension of Rome. While it is true that they conquered the nation and renamed it Judea (from Judah), they did not run all of it, nor did they legislate or create all of its civil laws. Most people today seem to have the idea that the Romans were the civil police force, the army, the lawmakers and the judges in territories they controlled. However, even from our own nation's experience we know that this is not the case. It's just not practical.

We did not run occupied Germany and Japan immediately after World War II and more recently Iraq. We occupied these countries and administered them, but many local government functions were retained. In cases where there was no local structure, a local one was created as soon as possible. And while

---

[58] But guess who was a Roman citizen? Paul the apostle! And though he did not directly get involved in their political system, did Paul get involved in the Roman legal process? You bet he did. He appealed to Caesar, and since he was a dual citizen, he met with both his Jewish representative, King Agrippa, and his Roman representative, Governor Felix. When organizations like the Alliance Defense Fund (ADF), Pacific Justice Institute (PJI), the American Center for Law and Justice (ACLJ) use the legal system to bring about God's moral law and to find new witnessing opportunities, they are emulating Paul's example. As we know, if Paul hadn't appealed to Caesar, he might have gotten out of his imprisonment earlier. Yet, he knew that if he wanted to witness to Caesar, his best bet was to work within the political and legal process and gain an audience with Caesar.

certain overriding laws were enforced based on U.S. law, it was locals who legislated.

Similarly, Judeans in 33 A.D. had a fully functioning political system that included their *own* executive, legislative and judicial powers. Not only were Jews self-governing in many ways, but the Romans actually gave them a level of self-governance above what they gave most other conquered nations. The Jews had control over their laws and were allowed to pass their own sentences on most crimes. The only punishment the Jews could not exact was the death sentence, and that was a limitation that had been enacted recently.[59] By Jesus' day, the Jews had to get the local Roman governor's permission to pass the death sentence.

Most people these days imagine that the Romans policed Jewish society. This could not be further from the truth. The Jews had their own police officers, public jail (see Acts 5:17-29) and temple guard, and King Herod had an entire army of his own. Dr. Paul Maier,[60] a well-known author and historian has translated the works of the 1st century historian Josephus. He has indicated[61] that there is a high degree of probability that the soldiers who killed Jewish babies in Bethlehem after the birth of Christ were not Roman soldiers but *Jewish* soldiers or possibly hired mercenaries working for the "*Jewish*"[62] King Herod.

So, contrary to widely held views, Judea had a fully functioning political system. This was a political system in every sense of the word. Not only was there a lot of infighting to get to be a lawmaker, but even the post of High Priest was often contested and occasionally bought through money and favors.

If Jesus had wanted to become involved in this Jewish political system, he would have been able to do so. But did he? That is, did He engage the official powers of his culture in trying to bring about desired change? Who

---

[59] A great historical "faction" novel (i.e., fiction based on facts – unlike *The DaVinci Code*, which was fiction based on false facts) – to learn the Jewish and Roman political structures and tenuous relationships is *Pontius Pilate: A Novel* by Paul L Maier. It's an easy read and allows the reader to learn much about the Roman and Jewish relationships in the days when Christianity began. It covers many of the facts about the Roman and Jewish legal systems. While I'm at it, let me pitch one of the best Christian mystery novels ever written. It's *A Skeleton in God's Closet* by Paul Maier. But beware. Don't start reading it unless you have plenty of time. I was so engrossed that I was loath to put it down, so I missed out on much of my sleep for two days.

[60] For more information on Dr. Maier www.wmich.edu/history/facultystaff/facultyprofiles/maier.html.

[61] Personal email correspondences dated December 2006. Paul is a friend.

[62] Actually, Herod was not a true Jew. He was an Idumean (i.e., an Edomite, a descendant of Esau). Idumea, or Edom, was south of Judea and the Dead Sea. John Hyrcanus, who was both king and high priest during the tumultuous years between the Old Testament and the New Testament conquered the Idumeans and "converted" them and the northern Galileans into Jews by the sword. A century later King Herod's father Antipater become friendly with the Roman general Pompey and later with Caesar, managing to get himself appointed as administrator of Judea. After Antipater was killed, his son, Herod, ingratiated himself with Octavian and convinced him to appoint him as "King of the Jews." Thus in 4 B.C., when the story and prophesy of Jesus being born in Bethlehem came up, Herod, not a true Jew and not from any line of kings, who had merely been appointed by Rome to be king, was triply scared. Baby Jesus would be, first, a real Jew and, second, one who was from the actual line of King David and, third, one whose kingship had been foretold by the prophets. This puts Herod's fears of baby Jesus into better perspective; here then was a true contender to his purchased and manipulated throne.

were His senators and representatives? Who were His lawmakers?

Well, at this point you are probably precisely 30 seconds ahead of me. Yes, the Jewish legislators were known as *the* – exactly – *the Sanhedrin*.

The Sanhedrin

Here's the definition of the Sanhedrin and their role in Judea:

The Sanhedrin (Hebrew: סנהדרין, Greek: συνέδριον, synedrion, meaning "sitting together," hence "assembly") is the name given to the council of seventy-one Jewish sages who constituted the supreme court and legislative body of Ancient Israel. The make-up of the council included a chief justice (Nasi), a vice chief justice (Av Beit Din), and sixty-nine general members who all sat in the form of a semi-circle when in session.[63]

We see that the people of Judea had a legislative system similar in many ways to our system,[64] except they had combined their judicial and legislative arms. The members of the Sanhedrin were not democratically elected – yet one can still be "politically active" or engaged with powers that be, even though he or she is not elected.

Thus, the Sanhedrin was a legislative body, with lawmakers similar to *our* lawmakers (our senators and representatives). But who were its members? Who were these guys that were the senators and lawmakers of the Jews? Do we ever hear about them in the Bible? Did Jesus ever talk to them? Or, in line with what many Christians claim, did He stay far away from "all that stuff" because it was too worldly?

I am sure that by now you are again precisely 30 seconds ahead of me. Exactly! The politicians, the senators and lawmakers of the Jewish governing body, the Sanhedrin, were the scribes, *the Pharisees and the Sadducees.*[65] In fact, some translations of the New Testament use the word "lawyer" instead of "scribe."

Wait now, besides the apostles, with what leaders did Jesus interact? Whom did He advise, admonish, condemn and chastise? Whom did He warn about corrupt laws and incorrect or twisted interpretations of the original Hebraic law? Whose execution of the law did He consider evil?

Why, it was the members of the Sanhedrin, of course. They were his senators and lawmakers.[66] They were His politicians. Jesus was so involved in

---

[63] www.123exp-read.com/t/00284113926/ Also see www.thesanhedrin.org/en/main/organization.html and www.thesanhedrin.org/en/index.php/The_Re-established_Jewish_Sanhedrin for a full organizational structure and information of the ancient and re-established Sanhedrin.

[64] Actually this is because we based our legislature on theirs, including the semi-circle seating.

[65] At one point, someone actually tried to argue with me, saying that the Pharisees and Sadducees were *not* members of the Sanhedrin. I'd never heard that before, but Acts 23 destroys that assertion completely. Acts 23:6 says, "Then Paul, knowing that some of them were Sadducees and the others Pharisees, called out in the Sanhedrin, 'My brothers, I am a Pharisee, the son of a Pharisee. I stand on trial because of my hope in the resurrection of the dead.' 7 When he said this, a dispute broke out between the Pharisees and the Sadducees, and the assembly was divided." See also John 11:47, Acts 4:1 and Acts 5:29-41. It seems hard for the assembly of the Sanhedrin to be divided among themselves if they weren't part of the Sanhedrin!

[66] Recall, they did not have a democratic system, so they were not elected, they were appointed. However, they *were* the people who made and interpreted the secondary lesser laws, and that is the function in which we are interested. Jesus was involved with His lawmakers though he did not get to vote for them.

the politics and with his politicians that one can't even teach about Jesus without including his politicians. In fact, the most quoted biblical passage in history, John 3:16, was made specifically to a politician, Nicodemus.

Objection: Civil or Religious?

"Ah but" you may complain, "Members of the Sanhedrin were in charge of the *religious* laws only." But this is simply false. As the Jewish historian, Reifmann tells us:

> "[A]ll religious matters and all **civil** matters not claimed by Roman authority were within [the Sanhedrin's] attributions; and the decisions issued by its judges were to be held inviolable."
>
> **Reifmann, Sanhedrin, Heb. (Berdichef, 1888) xi, 2-4.**[67]

Historian David Breed says:

> "[W]e know that Paul was a Pharisee, and a member of the Sanhedrin, and that the Sanhedrin had **legislative**, executive, **judicial, civil, criminal** and ecclesiastical power under the Romans, only Roman Citizens having a right of appeal to Rome. Paul's writings abound in references to Roman Law which, judging from their content, he must have[also] known considerable about; see Acts 25:8; Gal. 3:15; I Tim., Chap. 1; and Wilfley."[68]
>
> **The Trial of Christ, by David K. Breed, [1948], Appendix A pg 79**[69]

Thus, we see that the Sanhedrin determined not only religious laws but also legislative, executive, judicial, civil, criminal and of course ecclesiastical – that is, religious laws. Now except for the ecclesiastical part of that, does this not reflect exactly what our politicians and judges are responsible for? In other words, the members of the Sanhedrin were the lawmakers and *politicians* of Judea.

In the correct historical light now, we see that Jesus was always talking to various members of the Sanhedrin, trying to influence them, calling them to account, showing them that many of their laws, both civil and religious, were wrong and overly numerous. So we see:

Jesus was involved in Politics!

Pharisees

Please note that this was not an outright condemnation against *all* the Pharisees, as we know of God-fearing Pharisees who had Jesus' approval and blessings. Jesus' admonitions were targeted at just those *particular* Pharisees[70] who were hypocrites, who were into power and publicity, who were looking not at the intent of the law but only at the letter of the law and manipulating it to oppress people. Jesus was chastising the bad politicians and working with

---

[67] As quoted in www.newadvent.org/cathen/13444a.htm

[68] Xenophon P. Wilfley, Esq., *St. Paul the Herald of Christianity.*

[69] From www.sacred-texts.com/chr/toc/toc13.htm

[70] Over the years Christians have unfortunately used the word Pharisee, or Pharisaical, in a generic derogatory way. This is an inaccurate use of the term. There were numerous *righteous* Pharisees like Nicodemus, Joseph, Gamaliel (see Acts 5:34-40), and many of those were purposely not invited to the trial of Jesus. It's like saying that all lawyers are sharks. Yet, we all know godly lawyers. May I suggest that we be more technically accurate in the use of this word from now on?

the good ones. Why does this sound familiar?[71]

Jesus persisted in telling those Pharisee lawmakers who were hypocrites that their laws or their interpretations of laws were unjust (for example, the woman caught in adultery). Then, in addition to being involved politically by calling out these leaders, He also used civil disobedience to show the injustice and bankruptcy of various laws[72] when He and the Apostles went about picking and husking wheat on the Sabbath, and later when he and the Apostles healed on the Sabbath.

Jesus and the Apostles were working with, lobbying their lawmakers, and showing them they were unwise and their laws were wrong and needed to be changed. Though He did not get involved in their political system by running for office (remember too that this was not possible as no one was elected), we could say that Jesus was among other things a lobbyist with a personal staff of twelve aides.

What would Jesus do?

Another common misunderstanding is that Jesus would never call his political leaders names. But the Bible shows Jesus even goes as far as calling Herod the political ruler of all Israel, a fox.[73]

> **Luke 13:31** *At that time some Pharisees came to Jesus and said to him, "Leave this place and go somewhere else. Herod wants to kill you."*
> *32 He replied, "Go tell that fox, 'I will drive out demons and heal people today and tomorrow, and on the third day I will reach my goal.'"*

Jesus was not saying that Herod was *clever* like a fox; it was actually a direct insult. In the Middle East, a fox was considered a varmint. These animals lived in the ground and were pests, running away and hiding after raiding your chickens. Jesus meant to imply that His own earthly ruler, Herod, was a slinking slimy cowardly, wicked, thieving, dirty *rat*. Jesus was telling the truth about Herod's character. Surely then it is also our job to do that with our leaders. But that was just the start. We all know that He not only calls those of His senators, the Pharisees who deserved it, hypocrites, but He also calls them putrid rotting white washed tombs and slimy snakes.

> **Matt 23:27** *"Woe to you, teachers of the law and Pharisees, you hypocrites! You are like whitewashed tombs, which look beautiful on the outside but on the inside are full of dead men's bones and everything unclean...*
> *33 "You snakes! You brood of vipers! How will you escape being condemned to hell?"*

What an appropriate description of many of our current day politicians. Snakes, if you recall, were symbols of evil and the devil. No, the romantic notion of Jesus as this sweet non-confrontational "speak love only" kind of person is not only unbiblical and historically inaccurate, it's just plain silly.

---

[71] Please note very carefully here that you cannot attribute to Christ the requirement to force others to pay for the poor. In other words, there is no way you can attribute socialism to Christ. We will deal with this in some detail later.

[72] There are specific guidelines on how civil disobedience was carried out in the Bible that are not in the scope of this book.

[73] My gratitude goes to George Bettisworth for reminding me about this example.

What would Jesus do? He'd call an evil man an evil man. He'd call a hypocrite a hypocrite. He'd admonish evil or immoral politicians and call them out. He'd speak out against evil and immoral laws. He'd be harsh when He needed to. We need to do likewise. Jesus was involved in political commentary *and* informed people if they were at risk of going to hell. What would Jesus do? Speak out against evil politicians and correct them – that's what He'd do!

Objection: But Judea was not a democratic nation

You are correct that Judea was not a democratic nation, but that does not change its political nature. It is important not to confuse the existence of democracy or democratic elections with politics. After all, if a person were to get involved in influencing the king of Spain to create or change laws to help the poor, help the merchants or even to help himself by being granted a dukedom, that would still be considered politics, though one did not get to elect the king or the nobles. In truth, politics is usually much more prevalent and much worse in a dictatorship or a monarchy. And, to their detriment, some of the companies I've worked at have had more politics than a small country, and yet nobody got to elect anyone there.

So, while Jesus and most Jews did not get to elect any of the members of the Sanhedrin,[74] they could still attempt to influence them on how they legislated and ruled. Politics, judging and lawmaking were all involved.

Objections: Jesus was dealing with their religious laws, not their civil laws.
Jesus was only addressing their mistakes in theology.
Jesus was only addressing their hypocrisy.

Now one might try to fall back on this position and argue that while the Sanhedrin *did* deal with civil laws, Jesus on the other hand was *only* dealing with them on *religious* laws or theological issues, not *civil* laws. But this is simply not accurate. Jesus was not *only* concerned about our spiritual destiny; He was also concerned about oppression and true social justice. Politics has a direct effect on the suffering of innocents. Jesus addressed both kinds of laws. As we've pointed out, the woman caught in adultery, the moral or legal basis of divorce, even the ethics of paying taxes to Caesar – all of these issues were also civil moral issues, not only religious theological issues.[75] He didn't ignore the paying taxes issue; He answered it by explaining both the theological and civil aspects of it. Had our Lord not been interested in the civil aspects, He could have simply said, "Why do you ask me questions about taxation? That's not religiously relevant, so I won't answer that."

Moreover, Jesus was constantly castigating these politicians, saying "Woe to you, teachers of the law and Pharisees." Remember again that what He was referring to here were the Levitical laws, which were not just religious

---

[74] Of course, I say this knowing that God the Son had full power to put whomever He wanted into leadership of the Sanhedrin, but then again that wouldn't have been an election but an appointment, and by the same argument, He could have forced them to interpret the laws correctly. Why bother to argue with them then?

[75] I know you are about to object, saying that the incident of the woman caught in adultery involved a moral issue, not a civil issue. You will see why this objection is invalid when we deal with whether we can legislate morality.

Neil Mammen

but also civil and concerned justice and mercy.

> **Matt 23:23** *"Woe to you, teachers of the law and Pharisees, you hypocrites! You give a tenth of your spices—mint, dill and cumin. But you have neglected the more important matters of the law—justice, mercy, and faithfulness.*

Jesus obviously wasn't talking only about spiritual justice here, since that would mean he didn't care if the Pharisees were oppressing people. He was obviously *also* talking about *true social justice* – the kind these particular Pharisees were *not* dealing out. This would be a civil issue, wouldn't it? He was not talking only about the mercy of *God* here, was He? He was talking about the mercy of the *human* judges. These were moral issues, not theological issues.

Remember, to say that Jesus never addressed civil laws, true social justice, human mercy and human faithfulness would imply that He didn't care about these matters. But we see in the Bible that He and the apostles did care about the suffering, the poor, the oppressed as well as the widows and orphans. They always did.

Finally, saying that Jesus was addressing religious issues only is even more meaningless because, as we will prove shortly, *all* laws are based on moral values, and *all* moral values are affected by one's religious paradigm.

Religion and Politics

It's important to note that while morality is not religion, one's morality is invariably affected by one's religious values and beliefs. Even "not believing in organized religion" is a belief system and thus, in effect, a religious paradigm. Even atheists have religious paradigms. Thus, I've found that *all politics is personally religious at its base* because, whether you believe that God exists or not, your personal politics will immediately reflect that.[76]

Now, if all politics is religious at its base, and if politics affects lives and can create or prevent suffering, does it not make sense that Jesus would be involved with his senators, representatives and judges, calling them to godly justice, godly mercy, godly morality and godly wisdom? If Christ cared about the suffering and told us that the second great commandment was to love our neighbors – that is, care about true social justice – does it not make sense that He would demonstrate this in His time here on earth? Does it then not follow that pastors and churches should also be similarly involved? Should they not be intrinsically involved with legislation? Should we not emulate that? Should we not stand before our senators and judges and call them to be just, merciful, moral and wise? Jesus did it. He even called them names! Pastors, why aren't you doing it?

And from that follows naturally that if we are the ones who get to elect those very same senators, should we not be electing senators who are just,

---

[76] Note, however, that morality itself does not need to come from any single religious value. We will clarify this when we show that while morals come from our religious values, people from multiple religious backgrounds can arrive at the same moral values.

One of the greatest Christian debaters and philosophers of our time, William Lane Craig, debates atheists on the topic of whether one can logically claim that moral absolutes exist without God. It's important to note that he wins all of those debates according to audience polls.

merciful, moral and above all wise?

Objection: But the Sanhedrin didn't get to make the law. They already had God's law, so what could they legislate?

This is a very common objection and sadly a misconception of the law and of the Judean government. You see, the Jews though a theocracy had many similarities to what we would call a republic. That is, they were a representative government based on a Primary Law. This Primary Law was the transcendent unchanging Law from God. Yet, the Sanhedrin could and would legislate in all *secondary and minor laws* (note that none of these new laws could violate God's original Primary Law). When we talk about the difference between a republic and a democracy in a few chapters this will become glaringly clear and you will see how the founding fathers closely modeled *our* government after theirs. The Sanhedrin were always legislating new laws both Civil and Judicial. They were the executive, legislative and judicial branches *all in one*. For now, think of how our legislature *still* creates laws even though we *already have* an overriding law, i.e. our Constitution.

Did the followers of Christ get involved in politics, and did Christ influence them when they did?

Let's take it a step further. Who among the *followers* of Jesus were politicians and lawmakers? Who were the Christian Sanhedrin "senators?"

Those would be Joseph of Arimathea and Nicodemus, of course. Jesus hung out and hobnobbed with these politicians, yet once they started to follow him, He never told them to leave the Sanhedrin or abandon politics. We also know that at our Lord's burial, Joseph of Arimathea was still involved in the Sanhedrin. Joseph also went to the Romans and used his cross-governmental political influence to get permission to bury Jesus' body. This would be similar to a high-ranking Iraqi politician going to see the U.S. Commander of Iraq to ask for a favor.

Of course, some still say, "Well, we never see the apostles trying to run for office." But therein lies the rub. They couldn't run for office because there was no democracy. You only got into positions of power by buying it or schmoozing yourself into those positions. Remember again that we can't make a decision on what not to do just because the apostles happened not do it. Recall our example of Jesus not getting married.

Objection: But Jesus *would* have never run for office

Even if I grant you that, what can you conclude from that – that nobody *else* should? All we can say is that *He* didn't do it, and as we have shown, that is not a condemnation of it. In fact, it's obvious that He had a few *more* important things to do while here. He also didn't interview for a job, try out to be a firefighter, design any technology, invent anything new, go to college, start a hospital, free the slaves or provide end of life hospice care. Do I need to go on? If you cannot condemn Christians for being engaged in such activities, then I hope you see why you cannot similarly speak authoritatively from our Lord's silence on this matter of running for office. And as we will see shortly, if Christians aren't involved in political leadership, there is going to be a lot of suffering for all, including the oppressed.

Moreover, as we saw, Jesus never asked those of his immediate followers who were political leaders to resign from office. If he didn't do that but was content to let them remain enmeshed in "dirty" politics, why would we assume that it would be wrong for *us* to be involved in politics?

So what does this mean? Well, it means that if I can provide a rational case as to why you as a Christian or a pastor should be involved in politics or even run for office, then unless you can *prove* that it is immoral, that argument would have to stand.

Did Jesus influence politicians?

Finally, can we not imagine[77] that Jesus, in spending time with and in teaching Nicodemus and Joseph, influenced both men to cast votes and act differently in the Sanhedrin? Is it reasonable to think that these men, who met with Jesus many times, were attracted to His teaching, trusted Him, risked their lives and reputations for Him, would have never asked our Lord's opinion of the life changing laws they were making or interpreting on a daily basis? Let me ask this: If you were a senator and were in the presence of someone whom you thought was not only a great moral teacher but was also someone who had claimed to be God[78] and was someone whom you trusted and followed, would you not consider asking him for advice on issues of state? How about advice on a current piece of legislation? How about questions regarding civil laws?

Obviously, if you really had the person you considered the wisest man in the world, and the greatest teacher of all time, you would ask him for advice. Have kings, rulers and politicians in history asked wise, learned, or religious men for advice? What if it was advice for a serious moral issue that was facing the Sanhedrin, an issue that could have generational consequences? And would our Lord *not* give advice when asked and as a result let unjust laws be made? Would He say, "I'm sorry, Nic; I know I stopped them from stoning that woman caught in adultery, but I have nothing to say about any other issue of the law to you"? Would He not care if Nicodemus was about to pass a law that would cause suffering to the poor?

You may wish to disagree with this last point since the Bible never indicates that Jesus *did* talk to Nicodemus and Joseph about legislative issues. But all you could say is that Jesus did not work with politicians in an *agreeable* way. You cannot say that He did not try to influence them at all. The Bible is full of examples of how He influenced politicians by chastising and reprimanding them.

What about Caesar?

Don't worry I won't leave you hanging. Let's address Jesus' statement that one should "render unto Caesar what is Caesar's and render unto God what is God's." Let's look at the passage. What does it say?

> **Matt 22:17** *[The Pharisees said] tell us then, what is your opinion? Is it right to pay taxes to Caesar or not?" 18 But Jesus, knowing their evil intent, said, "You hypocrites, why are you trying to trap me? 19 Show me the coin used*

---

[77] I submit that this is the only speculative part of this argument.

[78] Yes, it's true that perhaps not all His followers realized His claim to divinity until later, but they did at the least perceive Him to be a prophet and a direct messenger of God.

for paying the tax." They brought him a denarius, 20 and he asked them, "Whose portrait is this? And whose inscription?" 21 "Caesar's," they replied. Then he said to them, "Give to Caesar what is Caesar's, and to God what is God's."

But wait! Where in this passage does it say do *not* give to Caesar what is Caesar's? If you are interpreting "Caesar" to be the symbol of our involvement in politics, then just replace the Caesar phrases with the phrase *involvement in politics* and you get this:

[The Pharisees said] Tell us then, what is your opinion? Is it right to be involved in politics or not?" ... Then he said to them, "Render unto the involvement in politics what is due involvement in politics,' and to God what is God's."

If Caesar is politics, then Jesus is saying "Render unto 'politics,' and do *it* in the *same* enthusiastic way *you* are to give to God what it is God's." It doesn't say *don't* give to Caesar, does it? [79] It doesn't say you should *not* be involved in politics. It says you *should*. And it certainly doesn't say "separate the things of God from the things of this world." This passage does not talk about separation; it talks about participation. By the way, if you were still to insist that it says do not give what is Caesar's to God, you'd immediately be stuck with the realization that this would then lead to you not being able to give any money to the church. After all, that was the topic of the discussion, wasn't it? And what about coins with Caesar's head imprinted on them? Should coins with our country's seal on them *not* be given to the church? Pastors are you sure you want this interpretation as the prevailing one?

The truth of the matter is that we cannot logically read separation into it any way we try. However we interpret this passage, we are stuck with the logic that says *you* are to be involved with the government *and* with politics in the same way as you are to be involved with God. This includes pastors.

You may disagree that this verse is even talking about politics, but there is no rational way that this verse could be used to argue that we should *not* be involved with politics. If this verse was the basis for your objections, I hope that I've shown that that objection has no basis in fact.

Who is Caesar today?

Author Gary DeMar adds this:

"It might also help to realize that we do not live under Caesar. Our civil rulers took an oath to uphold the Constitution, which is the "supreme law of the land." Neither the president nor the members of Congress are Caesar. If we have a "Caesar," it is the United States Constitution. But even the Constitution recognizes its own limits and the right of the people to (1) express their grievances, (2) vote corrupt and oath-breaking rulers out of office, and (3) change existing laws." [80]

This makes logical sense, so in our case when it comes to "giving" to

---

[79] Anytime anyone quotes a part of a verse to you, ask the person for the reference and then go read it in context. You may find it actually says something different. I encourage you to do so for all the references I've provided in this book.

[80] www.americanvision.com/establishmentandlimitsofcivilgovernment.aspx.
Another excellent source, Dave Barton, suggests that with a representative democracy Caesar is the "people" of the United States.

Caesar and submitting to the authorities, the supreme authority is not the president or the judges or the Congress, but the Constitution of the United States of America. In reality for Americans this verse now reads:

Render unto the Constitution what is the Constitution's and unto God what is God's.

Please remember this the next time you imagine that it is not your place to speak out against injustice or immoral laws because it involves contradicting an elected official. Your "Caesar" – that is, your "God appointed authority," your Constitution – has commanded you to speak out and act against elected officials who violate it. Our God appointed authority has ordered us to vote out of office and reject those who violate the Constitution. And God orders us to work to reduce the authority of evil men to protect the weak. If you wish to "give unto Caesar" then you must do so by voting, being involved and protecting Caesar (the Constitution) from those who would destroy it and this country. Notice how our Constitution even prescribes the forcible removal of those in power if they violate its provisions.

Jesus was involved in Politics, and He still is!

Having discussed our Lord's involvement while He was on earth physically, we should at least spend a few sentences determining whether our Lord is *still* involved politically. I think that's easy to answer. Do you think our Lord was involved in or cared about the political activities of William Wilberforce[81] when he (Wilberforce) worked for 47 years to end England's involvement in the slave trade? How about when racism was made illegal? Do you think it grieved Christ when abortion was made legal in the United States? Do you think He cared? How about when Hitler took power in Germany and many true Christians[82] stayed out of the political process? Can we agree that whenever a society legislates on a biblical moral issue, our Lord cares? Whenever a society passes a law that would hurt the poor or the innocent, I believe Christ cares. If Christ was concerned with the least of us, can He *fail* to be involved in politics?

Now do we think that Christ through the Holy Spirit guides His own children to enact these laws, or do we think Wilberforce acted without any prompting from the Holy Spirit? And if Christ *is* involved in politics, what makes us think that His Moral Will *will* be brought about by those who reject Him?[83] Isn't it more likely that His Moral Will will be brought about by those who love and follow Him – pastors, elders, churches and Christ-following lay people like you? Or do you think He's expecting us to be passive and take no active role?

When the Israelites were told to take the land of Canaan and refused to do so, what was their punishment? Did God really need them to go to war

---

[81] There are so many great sources for information on William Wilberforce, so I'll just refer you to a concise one: www.christianitytoday.com/ch/131christians/activists/wilberforce.html

[82] Not all. The Confessing Church did not, and it was persecuted as a result of not having enough support from the rest of the Christians.

[83] On the other hand, God's Sovereign Will is often brought about by those who hate Him, a perfect example being Christ's crucifixion. God's Moral Will is that which would be in line with His Moral Laws. God's Sovereign Will is what actually happens.

before He could vanquish the Canaanites? Does God really need you to act politically? No, of course not, but when the Israelites backed away, God gave them forty years in the wilderness. I don't know about you, but I don't want forty years in my own personal wilderness.

Is Jesus involved in politics *today*? I would have to say yes. Does he want us to be involved today? I can only logically conclude that the answer is also yes.

In summary

The Pharisees were Jesus' politicians. They were the lawyers, the lawmakers, the judges and the executive branch of their society. He was involved in their activities. He hung out with and influenced some politicians and castigated and confronted others. He called them names and was extremely harsh with them or, where necessary, when talking about them with others.

Getting involved in the law making process, civil disobedience, condemning politicians publicly and attempting to influence lawmakers politically is modeled for us in the New Testament by Jesus and Paul. Jesus evidently saw working with and correcting politicians as part of his earthly ministry. In addition, being part of a legislating body is modeled for us by the believers Nicodemus and Joseph of Arimathea. So there *is* a New Testament precedent for pastors and Christians to be interacting with the lawmakers. There is also a tradition of Christians being lawmakers from the very beginning of Christianity. Moreover, Christ continues to be involved in the politics of the world to this very day, leaving His mark on the great true social justice laws of all history.

Jesus IS involved in politics!
Why aren't you?

Neil Mammen

Six

*The wicked shall be turned into **hell**, and all the nations that forget God.*
Psalms 9:17 KJV (emphasis added)

This is what the LORD Almighty, the God of Israel, says: Listen! I am going to bring a disaster on this place that will make the ears of everyone who hears of it tingle. 4 For they have forsaken me and made this a place of foreign gods;... they have filled this place with the blood of the innocent. ... 9 I will make them eat the flesh of their sons and daughters, and they will eat one another's flesh during the stress of the siege imposed on them by the enemies who seek their lives.'
Jeremiah 19:3

What Happens When God Judges A Nation?

With a final bloody push, the kings of Assyria brought their charioteers and men to the heart of Israel and camped right outside her walls. They'd already laid waste to every town in their path. God had allowed an *evil* king to come right to Israel's door.

After spending 40 years in the wilderness building up a ragtag group of cousins into a fighting force, 800 years building up the nation of Israel and 50 years building Solomon's kingdom into this immensely rich and influential empire; within a few generations, God sends the Assyrians to crush Israel. A few years later, He sends the Babylonians into the lone surviving nation of Judah to destroy it and burn it to the ground. The Babylonians do this so completely that the Ark of the Covenant disappears *forever*, Solomon's great Temple is razed to the ground, and the gold in the Holy of Holies melts and runs into the dirt.

The horrors of these sieges are seen in events that fulfilled the horrific prophesy of Jeremiah:

2 Kings 6: 26 [During the siege] as the king of Israel was passing by on the wall, a woman cried to him, "Help me, my lord the king!" 27 The king replied, "If the LORD does not help you, where can I get help for you? ..." 28 Then he asked her, "What's the matter?" She answered, "This woman said to me, 'Give up your son so we may eat him today, and tomorrow we'll eat my son.' 29 So we cooked my son and ate him. The next day I said to her, 'Give up your son so we may eat him,' but she had hidden him."

This woman was not complaining that she had to eat her own son; she was complaining that she did not get to eat her neighbor's son *as well*.

Why?

Why did God do this to His people? Weren't these His children, His chosen? Why did God abandon them like that? Why did He let them be so horribly tortured and destroyed?

Why? We know why, don't we?

What was usually happened in Israel, just before a foreign nation came in and attacked it? What was slowly happening in the years before the destruction of the temple? What was happening to the heart and the culture of Israel and Judah?

> *Judges 2:11 Then the Israelites did evil in the eyes of the LORD and served the Baals. 12 They forsook the LORD, the God of their fathers, who had brought them out of Egypt. They followed and worshiped various gods of the peoples around them.* **They provoked the LORD to anger 13 because they forsook him and served Baal and the Ashtoreths.** *14 In his anger against Israel the LORD handed them over to raiders who plundered them. He sold them to their enemies all around, whom they were no longer able to resist.*

And

> *2 Kings 17:1 ...Hoshea son of Elah became king of Israel in Samaria, and he...did evil in the eyes of the LORD. 3 Shalmaneser king of Assyria came up to attack Hoshea, [and] seized him and put him in prison. ... 5 The king of Assyria invaded the entire land, marched against Samaria and laid siege to it for three years...7* **All this took place because the Israelites had sinned against the LORD their God...** *They worshiped other gods 8 and followed the practices of the nations the LORD had driven out before them, as well as the practices that the kings of Israel had introduced.*

So, what was the routine? Well quite simply, prior to most attacks and sieges we see the Israelites abandoning God. This was primarily reflected in their abandoning His law, doing things like sacrificing their children and disobeying His guidelines. We see that He then punished them, because they turned away from Him, because they abandoned His principles and did not fear Him anymore. In fact, the history of Israel is littered with stories of their abandoning God and being punished (and for some reason never learning). But if you look at that passage above, you notice that it wasn't just the people of Israel and Judah that turned away from God. It was their kings in particular.

> *2 Kings 17:7 All this took place because the Israelites had sinned against the LORD their God...8* **and followed ...the practices that the kings of Israel had introduced.**

In other words, God punished the people because of their *leaders* whom they followed.[84]

When we read the first-century historian Josephus's history,[85] we see again how certain leaders of the Jews rebelled against Rome, bringing the wrath of that mighty empire down on everyone. As a result, Jerusalem was completely destroyed; hundreds of thousands of Jewish families slaughtered

---

[84] This will be of special importance when we get to the part where we discuss our submission to authority and the founding fathers.

[85] For an easy to read version of Josephus' historical account, please see Paul Maier's excellent translation of this fulfillment of prophecy, documented by an eyewitness. Go to www.JesusIsInvolvedInPolitics.com and do a search for 'Maier Josephus.'

Neil Mammen

and only one stone wall was left of Jerusalem, as a warning sign to all who dared to defy the Roman army. An event predicted by Jesus 37 years earlier.

What about the good people?

During these sieges and attacks, God obviously saved a few people like the widow who helped Elisha.[86] But here's the real question: Did *all* the "innocent" people – that is, all who still loved God – get spared? Oh sure, we'd like to think so. However, the Bible never says they were saved. In fact, we know that the good were taken into exile along with the bad. For instance, Daniel, Shadrach, Meshack, and Abednigo,[87] good men taken from their families and most likely castrated into eunuchs. Women raped, babies smashed and, as we have seen, cooked and eaten. Are you telling me those babies disobeyed God?

No, of course they didn't. The good suffered along with the bad. The good experienced the terrible judgment of God just as the bad did. The good were raped, beaten, kidnapped, and orphaned, and they had their heads smashed *just* as did the wicked.

What's my point? My point is that when God judges a nation for the behavior of certain people in that nation or because of its leaders; you and I, the followers of Christ *and our children* will also suffer the physical consequences!

Let me repeat that. When God judges our nation because of others, or because of our leaders, you and I, the followers of Christ, and our one- and two-year-old children will also suffer the physical consequences! True, *we personally* will never suffer the spiritual consequences, but as you will see later, I will make the case that our grandchildren may not only suffer the *physical* consequences but they may *also* suffer the spiritual consequences. Do we want their blood on our hands? Remember too, Exodus shows us that not only do our kids suffer because of our evil choices but succeeding generations will also suffer for what we do, or allow to happen.

> ***Exodus 34:7** Yet he does not leave the guilty unpunished; **he punishes the children and their children for the sin of the fathers to the third and fourth generation.**[88]*

When did we stop believing that this passage was true? Or that it didn't apply to us? I believe this means our kids will suffer the physical consequences of our folly and not the spiritual consequences. As far as the physical consequences for the sins of the fathers, such as divorce, there are *natural physical, emotional, and psychological consequences* of abandoning the moral laws of God, and these will affect children to the third and fourth generations. Divorce has measurable effects.

Are you confused at this point? "What does divorce have to do with politics?" you ask. "Divorce is only due to sinful people and their free choices." That is actually not true, and I hope to open up your eyes to this in a

---

[86] 2 Kings 4:1-7

[87] Sadly we never remember their real names: Hananiah, Mishael, and Azariah

[88] It is of value to note that the Jewish Rabbi "Rashi" (AD 1040-1105) indicates that the punishments were only to the children who hated God themselves. Of course, parents can influence children to hate God.

few chapters, so stay tuned. If it's not obvious to you, I hope to prove to you that true social justice begins with moral laws.

But the question at this point is: Do you think we deserve to be judged for the way we are today? Do you think this judgment from God is going to fall upon our great nation? Perhaps not in the guise of a lightning strike or a flood, but surely as the natural consequences of our behavior and of our following our leaders.

Objection: But *only* the Children of Israel were to be judged, not run of the mill nations

"Ah" you object, "but that was only for Israel, they were special." Yet, that's not true either, because we can easily see in the many historical accounts like those of Daniel and the handwriting on the wall, where both Babylon and Assyria were also judged severely by God. Remember Nineveh, the capital of Assyria? (Yes, that was the answer to Monty Python's question at the Bridge of Death). Nineveh was destined to be destroyed, yet when her people turned away from evil, they were saved. None of these were "godly" or "chosen" nations. Were they special? Were they any *more* special that *we* in America are? If not, how much more will we be judged?

Psalms 9:17 says: *The wicked shall be turned into hell, and **all the nations** that forget God.* This is saying that *all nations* who forget God will be turned into hell.[89] The author of the Psalm is obviously including Israel *and other* nations here.

Has God judged us in the past?

In the early days of my research, I ran into an acquisitions editor who, upon reading my summary of arguments, tried to argue something to the effect that God won't judge our nation. At least I think that was his point. He wrote in the sidelines of my summary: "Did God judge our nation due to slavery?"

The implication was that since God did not send the equivalent of modern day Assyrians and the Babylonians into America to destroy us, He therefore didn't judge us and won't. But there are many ways God judges us. Most often, it is by allowing us to suffer the natural consequences of our evil choices.

We have paid the price

My wife and I recently had the solemn privilege of visiting Gettysburg; it was a cold day, and thus completely deserted. We had the entire field to ourselves. Standing up there alone on the ridge where one of the bloodiest battles occurred, looking down on the valley where brother marched upon brother in a war that eventually took the lives of 620,000 Americans, it struck me that God did indeed punish us. We have borne the price of the evil of slavery in our blood. And not only did the unjust die, but in tragic

---

[89] It would have been handy if we could take this to mean "all nations will become like hell" which would allow us to say any nation that does not obey God's laws will become like hell on earth. But to be true to the context we have to realize that this is most probably talking about salvation and eternal damnation, not hell on earth.

consequences, the just, and the merciful also paid the price for the centuries of sin.[90]

I would suggest that God did indeed judge and punish America for slavery. And we paid that price in blood.

Of course, knowing the standards of education these days, perhaps this person was never taught that history lesson. Not only that, but the cost of the war and its destruction was so great that any financial benefits, the years of slavery may have brought, were erased in those years of destruction and "reconstruction" as almost every slave owner went bankrupt and the economy of the South was systematically destroyed. In the end nobody and I repeat nobody benefited from slavery, everyone suffered even the just. God judged us and punished us and in some ways is still punishing us as the rifts are not healed yet.

Are we overdue for another judgment?

So look around you, look at the way this nation is acting. Do we deserve to be judged and punished similarly *again*?

Of course, we deserve to be judged. What's worse, as I intend to prove, is that many times God's judgments end up being the *natural* consequences of our foolish decisions and immoral laws. You see many people, like that editor, don't seem to realize that there are natural

---

[90] Some have tried to argue that the Civil War was not about slavery but about States rights vs. keeping the Union intact. Others argue that Lincoln was not so much interested in abolishing slavery as he was interested in centralizing power and so merely used slavery as a tool to rally the minority abolitionist Christians, ensure the now anti-Slavery England would support the North over the South and sow the seeds for a slave uprising in the South. This may be true, but if you read the Southern States "Declaration of Causes for Secession" they do state that one of their reasons is the northern states' refusal to uphold their southern laws regarding slaves that they saw themselves as released of their obligations to the Union.

See www.sonofthesouth.net/leefoundation/Confederate_states_America.htm to read the Declarations of the Causes of Secession. Included in this are statements like:

> *"Our position is thoroughly identified with the institution of slavery -- the greatest material interest of the world. Its labor supplies the product which constitutes by far the largest and most important portions of commerce of the earth. These products are peculiar to the climate verging on the tropical regions, and by an imperious law of nature, none but the black race can bear exposure to the tropical sun. These products have become necessities of the world, and a blow at slavery is a blow at commerce and civilization. That blow has been long aimed at the institution, and was at the point of reaching its consummation. There was no choice left us but submission to the mandates of abolition, or a dissolution of the Union, whose principles had been subverted to work out our ruin.*

> *It [the Union] advocates negro equality, socially and politically, and promotes insurrection and incendiarism [sic] in our midst.*

> *It refuses the admission of new slave States into the Union, and seeks to extinguish it by confining it within its present limits, denying the power of expansion.*

> *Utter subjugation awaits us in the Union, if we should consent longer to remain in it. It is not a matter of choice, but of necessity. We must either submit to degradation, and to the loss of property worth four billions of money [i.e. slaves and slave based commerce], or we must secede from the Union framed by our fathers, to secure this as well as every other species of property. For far less cause than this, our fathers separated from the Crown of England."*

Sadly, there is good reason to believe that given time, slavery could have been abolished peacefully in the US as it was in England years earlier and subsequently in much of Europe. Many times God uses another *unjust* entity to bring a *just* punishment to people. So any way we interpret our history, we see God punished us dearly for our sin of slavery. The question is: Should God be judging us today for something else?

consequences to disobeying God's laws. God doesn't have to step forward to smite us for us to suffer, in fact I would say that most of the time He has to choose to actively *protect* us from the consequences of our own current foolishness. This changes the scenario from God, deciding to punish us as a nation; to God just letting us learn through the school of hard knocks and not protecting us from our just desserts.

We have to change our nation, even if it's just for the sake of the unsaved folks who have not yet heard the gospel message in a way that resonates with them. The longer we can stave off the judgment, the better for the lost.[91] The more time they may have to repent.

We have to change our nation, but we have to see it change not only from the bottom up in the people, but also top down in its leadership and culture. That means we have to be *involved* in its leadership to change its leadership, we have to be *involved* in its laws to change its laws, and we have to be *involved* in its culture to change its culture. If we do not, our children, the poor, the widows and the oppressed are all doomed to suffer the consequences of our inactivity.

If you care about the weak and the oppressed and bad political policies that create more suffering, notice that God has placed you in a country where you can glorify Him by *doing* something about it. Take advantage of that.

Pastors and Elders

Therefore, pastors, elders and lay leaders may I ask this, "Is it not our duty as the leaders, protectors and shepherds of our flock to at least try to ensure that the natural or supernatural judgment of God does not fall upon our people."

Pastors, like the prophets of old, shouldn't you be involved in the moral direction of this country? When did that stop being your role? Shouldn't you be worried about the consequence of ignoring one of the most effective opportunities that you have, to influence your church to get involved and redirect the decline of this nation's moral laws and values? If you can influence a politician or, better still, encourage members of your churches to *be* those politicians, could you not effect positive change for mankind and perhaps delay the coming judgment of God? Is that not your job as well?

As compassionate leaders, do we care about the poor and weak? If we have a heart for the poor, then it seems we need to pay attention.

When God judges our nation because of others or because of our leaders, you and I, the followers of Christ, and our children and the poor will also suffer the physical consequences!

---

[91] This sentiment works for both reformed and non-reformed views.

Neil Mammen

Seven

We hold these truths to be self-evident, that all men are created equal, that they are endowed by...
Declaration of Independence, 1776

Countries die, history is littered with their bones.
My on-line debate response to someone who thought fears that America could fall apart were extremist and unrealistic. I think I stole this saying from Newt Gingrich.

"Maybe your college professor taught that the legacy of colonialism explains Third World poverty. That's nonsense as well. Canada was a colony. So were Australia, New Zealand, and Hong Kong. In fact, the richest country in the world, the United States, was once a colony. By contrast, Ethiopia, Liberia, Tibet, Sikkim, Nepal and Bhutan were never colonies, but they are home to the world's poorest people."
Walter Williams[92]

*"It is not for kings ... to drink wine, not for rulers to crave beer, lest they drink and forget what the law decrees, and deprive all the oppressed of their **rights**.*
Proverbs 31:4-5

Who Gives Us Our Rights?

Iwas in a bind. I was 21 years old, I'd be getting my Master's Degree in Computer Engineering and Solid State Physics in 6 months and nobody would even interview me. If I didn't get a job offer, I'd have to leave the country that I thought was the greatest nation in the world. At the university Student Recruiting office, you could sign up to interview with companies. Yet each interview signup sheet said, "US Citizenship required." I'd already mailed about 200 resumes to companies and only gotten a form letter basically saying "Thanks but we are only interviewing US Citizens". I was doomed. Then someone said, "Why don't you try and talk to the recruiters in between their interviews." Intimidated, I put it off for months. Finally, I went down and hung out at the office. I ran into an engineer who was sent to interview candidates for Advanced Micro Devices. I said, "Are you with AMD? I can't sign up to interview with you officially, but I was wondering, can I buy you lunch?" *He* bought me lunch. A few weeks later they flew me down to Sunnyvale, CA, interviewed me, and made me a job offer on the spot. Apparently if they really want you, they can make things happen. Using my

---

[92] www.capmag.com/article.asp?ID=3770

new tactic, I soon had interviews with six other major companies and ended up with job offers from four including Intel and Tektronix. I chose AMD.

With all that, it still took me almost 12 years to *earn* my US Citizenship. I finally had all the right qualifications and got all the right paperwork filed. Still, in order for me to get my actual citizenship, I had to learn about the constitution and the history of the US and be tested. I set about it with zeal. At the end of the interview, the immigration (INS) officer[93] said, "You know more about America than most Americans. We need more citizens like you. Welcome. I am proud of you." Then he shook my hand. I thought he was going to hug me.

I was proud too, proud to be an American. My friends were happy and threw me a big party. The theme was Phil Collin's song, "It ain't no fun being an Illegal Alien" (you should note I'd never been illegal, but there weren't any songs about *legal* aliens apparently).

But, looking back at what the INS officer told me, I grow alarmed. If Americans do not understand our Constitution or where our rights come from, the free exercise of those very rights will be in jeopardy. While not the exact focus of his statement, Reagan said something very applicable about this:

> ..history will record with the greatest astonishment that those who had the most to lose did the least to prevent its happening...[94]

To explain how important it is for pastors, churches and Christians to be involved in politics, we must first understand (or be reminded) of important *biblical* concepts in our Constitution and the Declaration of Independence. Concepts that the INS official indicated, were not even known by most Americans. We not only need to learn what they say, but also to understand how fragile they are and why pastors and Christians are critical to their survival. Bear with me now as we go through a little history. I'll make it interesting.

The Declaration of Independence and the Constitution

How many of us have read our Declaration of Independence and the Constitution lately? May I recommend that our kids and we read these great documents at least once every three years? We should read these historic documents from end to end,[95] from the Declaration of Independence all the way to the 27th amendment, which was passed in 1992. Do you know what that amendment was by the way?

The preservation of the Constitution is a noble trust and generations will suffer if it does not survive. We must honor and keep that trust. We cannot do that if our kids, or we, don't even know what it is.

Almost every other constitution of every other country has been abandoned, overthrown or rewritten numerous times. The United States is the only over 200-year old country that still has its original constitution. There is good reason for this. It is based on biblical principles and it works.

---

[93] Now they are called HHS officers.

[94] Ronald Reagan, Televised Nationwide Address on Behalf of Senator Barry Goldwater, Oct 27, 1964 www.ronaldreagan.com/sp_23.html

[95] It's really easy to read on-line, just do a Yahoo Search for it.

Neil Mammen

As I recounted earlier, I was born and raised in multiple cultures and countries. Throughout my stay and visits there one thing became apparent to me, though it has problems, the United States is the most prosperous, ethical, stable, and opportunity filled country in the history of the world. While many people believe that the United States is where it is economically, because of its natural resources, I can honestly say that after living in all those countries, across four continents, natural resources are not the reason why the U.S. is doing so well. Many nations have greater natural resources. Take India, China, or the old U.S.S.R. as obvious examples. Consider Kenya, South Africa or Nigeria for lesser known examples. Take the most fertile of all lands I have lived in: Ethiopia, where fruits were so plentiful you could pick and eat them in the wild. Both Asmara[96] and Addis Ababa are situated with perfect Silicon Valley-like weather with fruit trees in abundance. Still, we associate Ethiopia with starvation and tend to think instead, of sunny California as the place where orange, plum, and apricot trees grow in abundance along with cultivated grape vines.

You may argue that colonization by the British or other empires caused these nations to fall behind. Yet, as the quote at the beginning of this chapter shows, perhaps you forgot that the United States and Canada were *also* colonies, and Hong Kong was one until 1997. Colonization is not an automatic condition for poverty. Having lived in some of those colonized countries after their independence, I can attest to this fact, Sudan was a great place to live for both Sudanese and ex-patriots, post colonization. Yet as the Sudanese got further away from colonization and Christian influence, the worse the country seemed to become. Till today, the word Sudan is synonymous with starvation, suffering and persecution.

I believe one of the main reasons we Americans are where we are today is of the soundness of our governmental system. Can anyone argue that the primary reason Africa is still in poverty and suffering and oppression is so great is because of the political structure of each of its nations? Change their constitutions and you start to reduce suffering.[97]

A second reason America is so great is our Christian heritage.

This Christian heritage has done two important things for us. Most Christian denominations hold to the belief that people are saved by God's grace through repentance and faith in Christ, not by works. This instills within us a realization that we are personally responsible to God for our actions. That is, it requires a personal relationship, and there is no way anyone can work or earn his or her way to salvation without genuine repentance.[98] It follows logically then that in countries where most people have this belief, corruption would be less than in other places where people do not have this heritage. Our salvation is *not* dependant on a scales-of-justice system – that is, we can't

---

[96] Asmara was part of Ethiopia when I lived there. After various wars, it has become part of the country of Eritrea.

[97] I know you are wondering why India and China are catching up now. Because they are copying us. But oppression is still great in those countries and corruption is pervasive. Their growth will be slow till they can deal with this.

[98] If you are interested in the Theology behind all this, go to www.NoBlindFaith.com and lookup "Why Christ HAD to die & Why God HAS to punish sin."

accept a bribe on Friday, go to Church on Sunday, say a hypocritical prayer, give money, and expect God to forgive us unless we are truly repentant and desiring to change.[99] It is just God and us, a straight relationship with no intermediaries.

Forgiveness does not depend on us doing good deeds to make up for bad deeds, but genuine repentance. Sure, many people did get confused about the Gospel and hypocritically try works, but Christ's true followers have a hard time doing so, and historically they have passed their spiritual understanding and these Christian ideals on to their kids. As secular as Northern Europe is, it too has a powerful Christian heritage.[100]

You see of course, that a political structure like the one we have in America cannot last without the Christian heritage. It will slouch towards oppression and corruption.

Secondly, our Christian heritage helps us realize that humankind has a basic sin nature, and any systems of government that do not take this into account – i.e. systems like monarchism, fascism, communism, or socialism – are doomed to failure.[101]

If you are familiar with our Constitution, you will realize that all these are critical pieces of our Constitution.

Imagine now, as America moves forward *without* a strong Christian influence, where we will be. If we continue to slide away from our Christian principles, who will maintain our fragile Constitution? Disorder will reign. Is this the legacy you wish to leave to your children?

Don't be arrogant

Having said all of this, I also want to say, despite the benefits of our Constitution, let's not become arrogant. Countries die, history is littered with their bones. Remember that Rome fell after 1000 years of power, sacked by the Vandals. (Yes, that's where the word came from.) But, *before* the Vandals destroyed Roman cities, Roman civilization had been weakened from within, due to apathy. Thus when the Vandals showed up there was no strong army, no strong determination and in fact no desire to defend its culture or its principles. Rome had lost its identity. This can happen to our great nation as well. Don't be fooled.

---

[99] And depending on Christ for the capacity to change.

[100] You may wonder why Northwestern Europe, which is secular, has such low corruption while South Korea, which is predominately Christian, has a high corruption rate. I believe it's mainly because Northwestern Europe has a few centuries of Christianity in their past, setting up these moral concepts as part of their culture and tradition. However, if my theory is correct over the next few generations we will see corruption start to grow in Europe – assuming, of course, that they remain secular and don't become Muslim. If they do become Muslim, they will have a culture of corruption for sure; as Islam is a religion with a scales-of-justice system based on good works. Similarly, South Korea is a recently Christian nation (after the Korean War), and as it becomes more Christian and these principles of personal responsibility to God are instilled in their young, corruption should go down in a few generations. Time will prove or disprove my thesis. Others have argued that corruption is lower in Europe because it is wealthy and corruption is a by-product of poverty, but this doesn't hold under scrutiny because many extremely rich Muslim countries have widespread corruption and during the depression in the US, crime did *not* in fact increase.

[101] This second part also ensured that we had a stable political system that enabled us to have a stable environment in which to grow and develop, unlike countries like Ethiopia, which moved constantly through various political structures, the last few, from being under an emperor to being under a dictator.

I was at an engineering seminar one day and met an old colleague of mine. He'd made a few million as a founder of one of the startup companies that I had worked at, and was now retired, working on some of his pet projects. We started talking about our current trend towards big government and socialism and what was happening to the United States.

He said, "Come on Neil, this is America, we'll never do that. We'd never let that happen."

I said, "Yes Dave, it may not happen with *our* generation, but are you sure about the next generation?"

He stopped shocked and said, "Wow, I hadn't thought of that. You are right. That is really really scary."

And maybe it will happen one day. But let's just make sure it does not happen on *our* watch, and let us pray that we can at least slow down and retard the existing decay, so we can protect our children and the young of our nation.

Freedom is never more than one generation away from extinction. We didn't pass it to our children in the bloodstream. It must be fought for, protected, and handed on for them to do the same, or one day we will spend our sunset years telling our children and our children's children what it was once like in the United States where men were free.
Ronald Reagan[102]

Few bother to read and understand the Constitution

When I was in Asmara, being evacuated by and admiring the U.S. Marines and feeling grateful to a nation that would airlift people from an unrelated country who could never pay them back, I knew nothing about what the Marines stood for. In fact, even after I came to the States and talked with my new American friends, I still didn't really understand the Constitution. Why? Because nobody was teaching it. And you can't make a plea to the fact that I had not grown up in the U.S. because apparently none of my American friends understood it either (unless they were home schooled).

Do we get our rights from the Government?

As Proverbs 31:45 quoted in the chapter heading indicates, the Bible *is* concerned with rights. It would seem that thus we Christians and pastors should be too. So let me ask you this: Who gives us our rights? Do we get our rights from our own government? Do we get our rights from other people, i.e. the masses? If we do get our rights from the government, what could happen to those rights? What if instead we got our rights from the people (in a democratic fashion), what could go wrong in *that* scenario?

Does the Constitution grant us rights?

While the Constitution of the United States and the Bill of Rights presume that we all have rights, many make the terrible mistake of thinking that the Constitution *grants* us those rights. This could not be further from the truth. To understand where the rights spoken of in the Constitution come from, we have to look to the Declaration of Independence. This vital document was written for multiple purposes. Here are three that I've derived, that I think are

---

[102] Address to the annual meeting of the Phoenix Chamber of Commerce, March 30, 1961.

critically important to our case:

The first purpose I surmise was to justify separation from the British Empire – to prove that this cause was just. The founding fathers knew that they could not convince their fellow colonists to join the fight to separate from England unless they had a just and moral reason to do so.

The second purpose was to rally the colonists around this cause.

The third purpose was to explain to the world and future generations where our rights come from and thus to set the basis for our moral constitution.

The first and second purposes are clear and straightforward. So let's look at the third purpose in detail.

To explain where we get our rights from and set the basis for our moral constitution.

Do you remember this from the Declaration of Independence?

We hold these truths to be self-evident, that all men are created equal, that they are endowed by their Creator with certain unalienable Rights, *that among these are Life, Liberty and the pursuit of Happiness – That to secure these rights, Governments are instituted among Men, deriving their just powers from the consent of the governed.*

Hopefully you were able to finish it on your own when you read it at the beginning of this chapter. First, let's notice: Who gives men their rights? Is it given to them by government? Let me ask you that again. Are your rights given to you by the government? No. Absolutely not! According to the Declaration and thus our founding fathers, our rights are given to us by God, the Creator. They are *unalienable*. The word was purposely chosen. You can't give them away, lose them, or abdicate them, they are an inherent part of you. Note though, that evil people may *unjustly* prevent you from exercising them.

Why do rights *have* to come from a Creator?

We should all recognize that rights can't be self-assigned. Nor can they be assigned by the majority or the state. Why? Well, rights cannot be self-assigned because that would be meaningless. There has to be some logic or reasoning, something to back the claim that you have rights. Or I could just stand up and say, "I have the right to be Emperor." That is sheer silliness, of course.

You could appeal to fairness, but then who says anyone needs to be fair when it comes to rights? In fact, we should ask where the concept of fairness comes from. Where does even the concept of equal rights come from? Who says that a brown Indian immigrant born in Ghana is equal in value to a white American-born man? This is not something that comes out of evolutionary instincts.

One person tried to argue with me saying "we get our rights from a social contract." But do you think the African slaves contractually agreed to be slaves? How silly. They had no contract; it was oppression and violence that kept them there. Are you trying to suggest that they thus had no inherent rights? What rot!

What if rights were assigned by the majority or by the state? If that were true that would again mean the African slaves really had no rights before the majority and the state arbitrarily gave them those rights. That makes no sense. African slaves always had God-given rights, but these rights were constantly being violated until the majority and the state finally realized this and recognized the rights the slaves always and *already had*.

But, if they always had those rights, where did they get those rights to begin with. Rights have to be given by an authority.

Who could that authority be? Well, obviously there is only one Being with authority over mankind. It is their Creator.[103]

What if the government gave us our rights?

If the government gave us rights, then it could chose to take them away. It would also mean that in times when the government chose *not* to give rights to slaves it was *not* morally wrong in doing so.

Don't gloss over that. It is an important point. You see, if rights come from the government, then there is no inherent moral value that says that everyone must get the same rights. Government can arbitrarily hand out rights just as a king could hand out dukedoms or knighthoods. And in the same way, government can arbitrarily *take* away those rights just as the Soviets and the Nazi's did.

This is insidious if you take it to its logical conclusion. If government were the giver of rights, this would mean that you could only call what the U.S. did during the slavery era a *preference*. You could not say it was wrong since in this scenario the slaves had no inherent rights. Again, this is key. You cannot place any moral value on rights if the very basis of those rights is decided by the *preference* of a group of men or women who feel a certain way at a certain time.

The truth is that slaves on American soil and worldwide have always had rights, those given to them by the Creator, but they were being immorally and unjustly oppressed by the government and the people of the United States.

In the same way, if the government had been the granter of rights, then the slaves received rights that weren't theirs previously; they just got some *new* rights, and the whole battle for their God-given rights was a farce. Worse yet, if popular opinion should shift one day, those rights could be just as "justly" taken away.

The only way any person could claim he *already had* rights, which could never ever be taken away from him by any other human, is if someone who was in charge of *all* humans were to give that person those rights. Then regardless of majority ruling or culture or change in attitudes or economic standing, that human would always have those rights.

Now of course, people can illegally and unjustly violate your God given rights, but no one truly has the authority to take them away. A king cannot justifiably take them away because who gave him his right to be king, he got it by force or by genetics. The majority cannot justifiably take them away. Powerful evil men may repress you, but they cannot change the fact that

---

[103] If you are not a theist and are reading this, please do not mistake this as a proof that God exists. For a proof that God exists, please go to www.JesusWasInvovlvedInPolitics, register and do a search for "Agent X." In that paper we present a Scientific Logical Argument that shows that it is more reasonable and rational to believe God exists while it requires Blind Superstitious Faith to believe he doesn't. See also www.NoBlindFaith.com.

you have those rights. Your economic status cannot change them. Culture cannot change them. Attitudes cannot change them. Time cannot change them.

Only a Being who has authority over the entire human race can change them. And there is only one such Being.

One of the major concerns of politics is rights, which is directly tied to true social justice. But rights come from God; therefore politics **must** *be concerned with God.* There is no way to avoid this connection. Moreover, this works both ways, because the minute anyone argues that rights are not granted by God, they are in the unenviable position of trying to argue that African slaves never really *had* rights. It is just that a bunch of nice white people decided out of the kindness of their hearts to give these poor black slaves and brown Indians some rights. Of course, this is a despicable racist position, but it is the logical conclusion of the faulty premise. As we know and believe, the rights of the slaves were given to them by God, and contrary to that, the government during the 1800's violated these human beings' pre-existing God-given rights. We all recognize the immorality of it. Even my atheist friends believe it was immoral,[104] though they are being illogical in this, for at the end of the day they cannot define slavery as anything but a preference, or a less modern approach to social engineering, or a less socially acceptable practice, since they believe no authority over all mankind exists.

What if there is no God?

Technically we can argue that if there is no God, then morality is merely the preference of those who are in power i.e. might makes right. This immediately has a very unpalatable consequence as it means that if Hitler had won World War II, it would have been morally acceptable to kill Jews since the victor – that is, the mighty – determined the morality of that situation. Similarly, had the South managed to succeed and secede after the American Civil War, slavery would have been "morally correct" for the South. This is obviously completely abhorrent to all of us today, but how do we *determine* that, if there is no standard and no standard giver?

What happens if you take the Creator out of the equation?

Now since we've determined that these rights are not given to us by the government but by the Creator, what happens if you take the Creator out of the U.S. Constitution? That is, what if you now claim that the Creator does not exist anymore, or that His existence is not valid, or that His existence in the Declaration or in the laws of the nation violates the U.S. Constitution.

Well, if you take away the Creator, you take away what? You take away those very same rights.

Let me say that again: If you say there is no Creator, you are saying that we have *no* unalienable rights.

This is actually a logical dilemma for atheists. Atheists may hold to

---

[104] One of course I argue that if there is no God then the atheists in the 1800s would not have known this intrinsically since all cultures around them had slaves. As to the where the intrinsic knowledge of morality comes from? If you are a Christian, the Apostle Paul says it's all inherent in us and if we reject it, it's in spite of our conscience. But we'll leave that debate for later when we discuss how to determine moral law without appealing to the Bible.

Neil Mammen

slaves having rights prior to the emancipation, but they can't logically defend that view. They can't claim that those slaves always had or deserved those rights. The best they can say is, "We, as atheists, *prefer* that those slaves had had rights." Or they may say, "Society now prefers that those slaves have rights." And these preferences may change with the tide or popular opinion (as the rights of the Jews changed in Germany over time).

So, if there was no God, one could never appeal to a right or a wrong about "rights." In other words, no atheist could ever argue that humans have a priori rights or that it is wrong to take those rights away from them. Sure, they could argue that it is *now* not normative or legal to take their rights away, but before the Constitution of the United States was ratified, they would have no rational or legal basis for it. And in truth, there is no precedence in history for *any* nation to give all men equal rights. Look at the history of humankind. It took the United States, even with its sound Constitution, many years to come to awareness of its application to slavery and eventually give all humans equal rights.

> "God who gave us life gave us liberty. And can the liberties of a nation be thought secure when we have removed their only firm basis, a conviction in the minds of the people that these liberties are of the gift of God? That they are not to be violated but with His wrath? Indeed, I tremble for my country when I reflect that God is just: that His justice cannot sleep forever."

Thomas Jefferson[105] **(who does not sound very deistic here)**

Atheists have a problem

There is another perhaps more important conclusion that we can arrive at. Since atheists don't believe that God exists, they cannot rationally or logically agree with the Constitution when it comes to the rights people already have. They may emotionally agree with it. They may *feel* that it is right that everybody has equal rights, but they cannot rationally arrive at that. It is merely irrational belief, an unsubstantiated feeling – that is, a preference.

And the danger is that if someone merely *prefers* that people have rights and has not come to it logically, then maybe one day he could be persuaded to change his preference. Perhaps that change will be for a noble cause, such as imposing fascist rule for the protection of the nation from an invading force or to protect it from economic collapse like Hitler did. However, a believer in God can never justify the removal of anyone's rights, since those rights derive from the existence of God. This is even more powerful if he has derived the existence of God from facts and not from feelings or from traditions. And it would be illogical for a rational Christian to suddenly to think that God changed His mind about equal rights for all mankind.

Why is this so important to this topic?

If you haven't figured out why this is important to this topic, it's quite simply this: Without a godly and Christian moral foundation, our Constitution is meaningless and our Country would never have been founded. In other words pastors, I'm showing you how important religion was and is to the very

---

[105] Panel Three on the Jefferson Memorial in WA DC. From Notes on the State of Virginia.

foundation of our country. Remember that shortly after Americans declared their independence, France tried the same experiment without God and it had resulted in a massive bloodshed and failed.

Without our constitution, our laws, our rights and any concern for true social justice would be meaningless.

What rights are we talking about though?

The editor I mentioned earlier, also tried to argue at one point that governments can and do take away our rights all the time. His example was "being forced to wear seat belts." Presumably, he feels that driving without a seat belt is a right, but his statement showed that he misunderstood not only the Constitution but also the very concept of a "right."

Driving is not an unalienable right. God gives you certain rights. Driving a car on government-funded roads any way you wish to, is not one of them. Drive all you want in your own driveway or your own property without hurting others. That's a right. But, if the public decrees that they wish you to wear a seatbelt while driving on the public roads, which *they* made for you with combined funds, then you may disagree and I may even agree that the government maybe overstepping its correct boundaries, but you can't claim that God gave you that right. The only "right" you can insist on, is that they treat you as fairly as everyone else on that same road (equal rights).

So if driving is not an unalienable right, what is? The Constitution and the aptly named "Bill of Rights" enumerate some rights. Here is a brief list to give you an idea: Life; liberty; the pursuit of happiness;[106] justice; freedom from unreasonable search and seizure; freedom of religion;[107] freedom of speech; freedom of the press; the people's right to keep and bear arms; the freedom of assembly; the freedom to petition; the right to be free from cruel and unusual punishment; freedom from compelled self-incrimination; the right to a speedy public trial with an impartial and local jury; habeas corpus; freedom to move around the country;[108] equality under the law (derived from equal rights) – and so it goes.

For more information on our rights as penned by Jefferson, you may wish to refer to www.etext.virginia.edu/jefferson/quotations/jeff0950.htm

But how do I determine what a right is? Don't get confused between rights and goods

Many people confuse "rights" with "goods." It's critical to differentiate the two. Here's an easy way to look at it[109]: If a 'right' depends on

---

[106] "The evidence of [the] natural right [of expatriation], like that of our right to life, liberty, the use of our faculties, the pursuit of happiness, is not left to the feeble and sophistical investigations of reason, but is impressed on the sense of every man. We do not claim these under the charters of kings or legislators, but under the King of Kings." --Thomas Jefferson to John Manners, 1817. ME 15:124 as quoted in //etext.virginia.edu/jefferson/quotations/jeff0100.htm

[107] "The constitutional freedom of religion [is] the most inalienable and sacred of all human rights." --Thomas Jefferson: Virginia Board of Visitors Minutes, 1819. ME 19:416 as quoted in
http://etext.virginia.edu/jefferson/quotations/jeff1650.htm

[108] Wait...is this really a right or just a Southwest Airlines commercial? And do you have to wear a seatbelt when you *move* around the country?

[109] My sincere thanks to Judge Andrew Napolitano of Fox News. I was looking for an easy way to articulate this when he explained it so well, while hosting the Glenn Beck show. I have elaborated a bit.

someone *else's* service, work, or money, it's not a right, it's goods, and it's certainly not a God given or Constitutional right.

FDR for instance, tried to create a second bill of rights. In that bill, he wanted to include things like the right to a good education, the right to healthcare, the right to your own house, the right to a good paying job, and the right to adequate food, clothing and recreation.[110]

But, if you have your thinking hat on, you'll immediately realize that while these are nice things, they all violate the very concept of God given unalienable rights. Why? Because while you may have the right to *not* be *prevented* from having an education, you don't have a right *to* that education. Why? Because that education will be dependent on someone else providing the labor to give you that education. Same for the food, someone had to grow that food. Someone had to harvest it and clean it. As soon as something is a product of someone *else's* work, it becomes a good, not a right. You always have a God given right to your *own* goods, but you have no right to someone *else's* goods. That's called stealing. And if goods are what you are promising to someone, however noble those goods are (like healthcare or a home), eventually you'll have to enslave *some* men to guarantee those goods to *other* men. Our founders were not idiots. They understood quite well, why rights were not goods and why they could not write a constitution that guaranteed goods to anyone, unless they were the fruit of your *own* honest hard work.

Notice the difference. The right to bear arms is not a right to be given a free firearm. The right to free speech is not the right to be given a free printing press or radio station. The right to the pursuit of happiness is not the right to a guarantee of happiness. I hope you see the great difference. This is critical, anytime you vote on something, ask yourself, "Is this law acknowledging a true right or is it mandating goods that are a result of someone *else's* hard work?"

Notice too, that the constitutions that *have* a bill of rights for education, jobs, healthcare and homes and other such "goods" are all communist and socialist constitutions. And we all know how successful *they've* been. Why? Because goods that are granted as rights, require men to be forced to provide those goods to others and will most likely eventually result in a totalitarian state. Goods that are granted as rights require you to enslave men fiscally or physically to ensure a continuous supply of the goods that you have promised to others.

So when people or even your church talks about social justice, ask them what they consider to be a 'social justice cause' that we should fight for. If they name "government provided goods," like government healthcare, state subsidized housing, medicine, food, or welfare, or even a guaranteed minimum wage, *run away* from their twisted thinking. If they talk about "economic justice," flee. Why? Because unlike rights, those are goods that must come from *some other human.* Any church that fights for the government to mandate this is fighting to enslave everyone. That's not social justice. If they say,

---

Some people use the concept of negative rights and positive rights, but I got confused by that. This is much simpler to understand it seems.

[110] www.worldpolicy.org/projects/globalrights/econrights/fdr-econbill.html

"unalienable rights," like the "right to life, liberty and the pursuit of happiness," or if they talk about freeing child prostitutes, stopping abortion, stopping the modern slave trade and helping those living in communist countries from enslavement, then they are on the right track. *True* social justice starts with respecting and protecting people's unalienable rights.

Remember, if the government starts giving you things that aren't rights and calling them rights, they will soon start taking *real* rights away from you.[111]

But what is the church's political role then?

One of the Church's roles is to be the conscience of the government. In fact many people imagine that Jefferson and the founding fathers came up with all these concepts, but that is based on an ignorance of history. If you look at the sermon archives of centuries before you'll see hundreds of sermons, preaching the source of the unalienable rights of man (*including* freedom for the slaves), freedom of worship, just war, Lex Rex, freedom from tyranny and many others.[112] The Church was the source of most of these ideas. And the Church must continue to fight for laws that protect men's *real* rights. We'll see shortly how they've done that throughout history. The Church is *not* to fight for laws that supply men with goods. We'll talk more about the churches' and Christians' role in this later, (see "Is Jesus a Socialist?").

Some governments take away rights

Remember that silly acquisitions editor, and his comment about seatbelts? His third misunderstanding was that he presumed that if government takes away a right that shows that it is acceptable. But that is far from true. Just because a government somewhere takes away a right, that does not make that action acceptable. In fact, this was the exact focus of the Declaration of Independence. The British Government had taken away our rights, which didn't come from King George, and this travesty needed to be corrected.

Remember, atheists cannot appeal to a de facto authority who has given mankind rights. Why? Because there are no unalienable rights in a world without God, the strong determine what rights the weak have. The concept of unalienable rights is ludicrous for atheists. In the atheistic case, the only justice is a bigger stick or gun. The Declaration of Independence and its dependant Constitution set about identifying that injustice and correcting it. Rights were from God, not from might.

But the Declaration is not part of the Constitution

Now at various times when I've discussed this issue, some people have claimed that since the Declaration is not part of the Constitution, we are not bound by it. Others have argued that I'm overstating the purpose of the Declaration. Others say, "Well, Jefferson, who wrote the Declaration, did not participate in writing the Constitution[113], so there is no connection." Still others

---

[111] Note, technically, no one can *take away* your rights; they can only prevent you from the free exercise of those rights. However, that statement is bulky so I've defaulted to saying "take away your rights" when I really mean the latter.

[112] Defending the Declaration, Gary T. Amos, Providence Foundation (1996)

[113] Madison was the primary author of the Constitution.

Neil Mammen

have asserted that the first part of the Declaration is purely symbolic, like a greeting.

But this is quite irrational and is merely parroting Woodrow Wilson[114] (one of the worst presidents we've ever had). You see, though the Constitution was not written until much later, the Constitution is logically connected to the rights that are declared in the Declaration of Independence. Remember, the Declaration argues for the morality and legality of separation from the Crown and the creation of the future Constitution to the colonists. In fact, if you look at the Declaration, you will recognize most of the items in it *are* realized in the Constitution. These include this laundry list taken directly from the Declaration: 'a Government instituted among Men which deriving its just powers from the consent of the governed';[115] the Bill of rights; Representative Houses; Laws for the accommodation of large districts of people; legislative bodies that meet at convenient places to their public Records; Naturalization of foreigners; established Judiciary powers; the elimination of Standing Armies; having the military under the control of the civil authorities; requiring consent for taxation; and requiring a trial by jury, and so it goes.

In addition, read the Ninth Amendment. It says, "The enumeration in the Constitution, of certain rights, shall not be construed to deny or disparage others retained by the people." What is this talking about? It's talking about rights. Well, where did these rights come from? If they came from government, this Amendment just took them away from the government's greedy clasping grabbing hands.[116] So where do these rights come from *now*? This leaves a void and clearly indicates that even the Constitution and the Bill of Rights requires a giver of rights. Who is that? Well it has to be who the Declaration told us it was. The Creator. So the Bill of Rights clarifies that rights don't come from government, and thus they have to come from God.

Let me say that again: It's irrational for the constitution to say that individuals have rights, right after saying that the government and the people en masse don't have any say in those rights, unless those rights come from something other than the government and other than the masses.

Anyone who says the Declaration is inconsequential or not related to the Constitution or not the justification of the future Constitution misses the logical and obvious connections (or has not read the entire Declaration but stopped after the preface, as many do).

Logically, if you sever the Declaration of Independence from the Constitution, you cut away the rationality of all the rights in the Constitution. Think about this. If our rights do not come from our Creator as stated in the Declaration, then the Constitution is conferring rights that were given to mankind by the government. In that case, why was slavery wrong?

---

[114] Wilson gave us income taxes and the Federal Reserve boondoggle.

[115] Even this sentence is loaded in the presumption of justice and the rights of men to consent to be governed.

[116] Those rights can't come from the "people" because you can't grant yourself rights (remember I can't just say "Hey, I'm emperor") and the people can't vote themselves rights because the minute they do that they are what? The government taking that action. So where do our rights have to come from for the Ninth Amendment to make sense? It can't come from our culture or our DNA as I'll show in a later chapter "Where Do Our Moral Values Come From?"

It's the foundation and the house will fall without it

If rights are not immutable and unchanging as the Declaration claims they are, then the founding fathers were speaking gibberish when they tried to claim that since the king was violating our God given immutable, unchangeable rights, they had the 'right' to fight for independence. They were also fooling themselves when, much later, they enumerated those rights in the Bill of Rights. Where did those rights come from? Why stop there? Why not make themselves all emperors? It's just as silly.

And if the Declaration of Independence is inconsequential or meaningless, then the rights in the Constitution are also illogically granted to us and are only "there" because the government decided to give them to us. We have already talked about the danger of that.

So if we separate the Declaration of Independence from the U.S. Constitution, the Constitution loses its moral and objective validity, becoming merely a document of the current preference of society – that is, it becomes a majority rule moral.

One problem with majority rule morals is that if the majority of society suddenly decided to deem that Jews were not persons, we could not logically call that decision immoral. Yet, we all know that the National Socialists, i.e. the Nazis were being immoral when they did precisely that.[117]

So remember, the Constitution of the United States would fall apart like a house with no foundation if it had no objective moral basis.[118]

Now you may say "But the Declaration has no legal founding!"

Well, yes, I agree. The Declaration was not ratified by the states (though it was signed by all the representatives of the states). Yet, that's not the issue here is it? The question on hand is if the Constitution could logically make sense without the philosophical foundations that are in the Declaration of Independence. We have logically concluded that it doesn't.

Objection: The original Constitution never said slavery was illegal

Yes, it didn't specifically do so, but the principles that it was based on logically proved that slavery was wrong because it violated man's God given rights. In truth, Jefferson and others wanted the slaves to be freed but the founders realized that they would not be able to get the southern states to join the battle if this became an issue. So, they postponed the issue. One can argue if that was the right decision or not, we can even agree that the *application* of the valid God-given unalienable rights principle was faulty, but one cannot invalidate the logic and reasoning behind the principle, because it stands on its own.

---

[117] Of course, one can argue that the Nazis were a minority. But they fact that they got a majority of Germans to allow them to round up and kill the Jews indicate that they had compliance from the majority.

[118] You can only be morally obliged to a being; you cannot be morally obliged to an accident or a piece of paper. For instance if a box of scrabble accidentally spilled and spelled out: "Take out the Garbage, Mom." Are you morally obliged to take out the garbage? Of course not. But if your mom spelled that out then you *would* be morally obliged. You are not morally obliged to an accident i.e. evolution. We expand on this later in this book.

Neil Mammen

A quick summary

If you disagree with the source of our rights – the idea that they come from the Creator – and you are a U.S. citizen, you render the fundamental premise of the Declaration of Independence false. If the fundamental premise is false, then the Declaration of Independence is false. If the Declaration is false then, because of its subsequent justification of the Constitution, you render the entire Constitution an erroneous illogical document based on a house of collapsing cards.

Christianity

By the way, in case you are wondering, Christianity is the source of the idea that all men have equal rights.

There is neither Jew nor Greek, there is neither bond nor free, there is neither male nor female: for you are all one in Christ Jesus.
Galatians 3:28

There is no other major religion or culture[119] that predates Christianity that ever had the concept of equal rights for *all* mankind. Many religions had equal rights for their sect or caste members, but no religion had the concept of equal rights for all men and women regardless of race, economic status, or national origin. Though it took years for mankind and even Christians to grasp it, it is a purely Christian concept that originates from the Bible.

What then is the purpose of governments?

Well then, you may ask, if the government doesn't give us our rights, what is their purpose? Well let's go back to the Declaration of Independence:

That to secure these rights, Governments are instituted among Men...

So, what is government's purpose? To give us these rights? Obviously not. The government is there to *secure* the rights that we *already have*.

Governments are instituted among Men to secure and protect these rights that we what? Already *have*. Let me repeat that: The government's job is *not* to *give* rights to people but to protect the rights they *already* have from God.[120]

The government is force and they require compliance at the point of a gun (whether it be an IRS agent's gun or a sheriff's gun). We *should* enforce *rights* with force (government) as the Constitution states, and we should protect a person's goods with force, but we should never assign *goods* to another with a gun. Why? Because as we said, those goods must come from somewhere, unlike the rights. Any government that does this will eventually enslave everyone.

---

[119] No, the Greeks had democracy but not equal rights. Their democracy only extended to male Greeks. A racist, ethnocentric, sexist system is not a system of equal rights is it? While it maybe true that over time various persecuted minorities in the past envisioned such a system, it was only through Christianity that such a system ever started to become more of a reality.

[120] I was once arguing with a very close Israeli immigrant friend of mine who was an atheist. He said, "Well I don't think that's right," referring to God giving us rights and the government being the one to protect them. I said, "You should note two things, first that's the way the United States was founded so you are currently stuck with it. Second, if you really believe that then how can you argue that Hitler was wrong? He was the government and he took away your grandparent's rights."
He responded, "I'll have to think about that."

On as side note: I find it tragic and ridiculously illogical that many liberals are so twisted in their thinking that they want government to enforce goods, like healthcare or our labor but want government out of the way when the issue is if a baby should have rights, like the right to life. This is the opposite of what the Declaration said, and the opposite of why America was founded. Do you see that? America was founded because we had an oppressive government & king that were taking away our God given rights and taking away our personal goods and assigning them to others. Yet, today we have people who want to do the same, take away our rights, and assign our personal goods to others. One is oppression, the other is stealing. There is only pain on this path.

Now let's keep going.

When is it right to replace a government?

"That to secure these Rights, Governments are instituted among Men, deriving their just Powers from the Consent of the Governed,
that whenever any Form of Government becomes destructive of these Ends,
...it is..."

it is the what?

"...the right of the People to alter or to abolish it, and to institute new Government, laying its Foundation on such Principles..."

Why did I bring this up? Because I think it is crucial that we realize that our founding fathers wrote into the Declaration, that whenever a government started doing the *wrong* thing —that is, the *immoral* thing – and violated their unalienable rights, it was then the right of the people to alter the government. Which meant to change the law at the least, and if that didn't work to replace those in government, and if that didn't work, to abolish the government and start a new one. The last option was precisely what our forefathers were doing in breaking their bonds with England and creating their own government. We should be exercising the first two options through our elections every few years – changing the people in government if they aren't doing what they should. Pastors and elders, our very constitution says that when our government starts to violate our rights we should get involved and at the least vote them out.

So, our Declaration insists that we use moral judgment to run the government and alter its laws or to change the government itself if it ever becomes immoral. The founding fathers then used this very same document as the basis for the Constitution.

The just reasons to split from England.

While writing this book, I ran into yet another acquisitions editor for one of the major Christian publishers. We were in the preliminary stages, and I was interested in knowing what he thought of this book idea and if he thought there would be any commercial interest. Yet, rather than discuss the commercial viabilities of this controversial idea, he started to argue with me that Christians should *not* be involved in politics. I had already related information about Jesus' involvement in politics and had mentioned that if someone thought that we should not be involved in politics, then a natural conclusion would be that our founding fathers were stupid for founding the

USA. Now I'm always ready for an argument or a debate (no... really), but as many people are prone to do, rather than deal with the entire argument, this editor picked on this latter point alone. He said something to the effect of "Well, I've always thought that not wanting to pay taxes was a stupid and invalid reason for wanting to start your own country."

Now you have to understand that I was shocked speechless. Here was I, an immigrant to this great nation, listening to a young editor who had obviously never read or studied his *own* Declaration of Independence. Aren't people who choose books for publishers supposed to read books for a living and have a well-rounded knowledge? For anyone to imagine that the USA was founded *only* to avoid paying taxes is just baffling.[121]

Of course, we could blame our educational system as well.

The next time I saw him, I thanked him for "incentivizing" me to write this next section explaining the real reasons. He responded with. "I'd better stop talking to you lest you get more ideas."

Okay so now, let us look at what the *real* reason was for us to split away from Mother England.

This was not an attack on the British people

As I present this, I want you to remember that nothing in this discussion should be taken as disparaging toward the British people. In fact, many of the colonists at that time *were* British common folk who had just moved to the colonies. The focus of the Declaration was specifically King George. This was *not* a referendum on the British worker or farmer or common man. It was directed at one man and those who did his bidding without regard to moral values.

Let's take a look:

The history of the present King of Great Britain is a History of repeated injuries and usurpation, all having in direct objection the establishment of absolute Tyranny over these States. To prove this, let Facts be submitted to a candid World.

He has refused his Assent to Laws, the most wholesome and necessary for the public Good.

...He has plundered our Seas, ravaged our Coasts, burnt our Towns, and destroyed the Lives of our People. He is, at this Time, transporting large Armies of foreign Mercenaries to complete the Works of Death, Desolation, and Tyranny, already begun with the Circumstances of Cruelty and Perfidy, scarcely paralleled in the most barbarous Ages, and totally unworthy the Head of a civilized Nation.

This is a far cry from merely not wanting to pay taxes isn't it? What were the founding fathers saying? They were saying that King George was what? That King George was *immoral!* That he was unjust. That he was killing people, being cruel, tyrannical, and evil. That he was *wrong.*

Just taxes? I don't really think so.

---

[121] If you reread his words, you'll see that that's precisely what he is suggesting.

A slap in the face to relativists[122]

It's also important to note that the Declaration of Independence, and thus the justification for the foundation of our country, was based on the fact that there were objective truths and also that someone was wrong and someone else was right. In other words, the revolting colonists declared not only that there is an objective morality, but also declared that King George was at the wrong end of it!

Note that they didn't say King George was right for *himself* and wrong for us. They said King George is wrong for *everyone*! And they were submitting the facts to whom?

Let the facts be submitted to a candid world.

To the world. In other words, to everybody. They were saying King George was wrong *even* for himself! The Declaration of Independence was no friend of relativistic morality. Those who adhere to syncretism, the New Age, or what is sometimes called "the eastern way of thinking" should recognize the slap in the face.[123] In fact, may I be so bold as to say that relativists are lucky that the rest of us aren't relativists? If we all were, we could argue that if one day someone decides to take away all rights those particular relativists have, they wouldn't be able to make a single valid argument against it.

Are there objective moral truths?

This reminds me of an event narrated by Walter Martin, the founder of the Christian Research Institute (CRI – www.equip.org). Martin was on a show arguing against a liberal rabbi and a liberal priest. Somewhere during the show, the argument turned to relativism, with the rabbi, of all people, claiming that there was no objective right or wrong. [124]

Just moments before the break, Martin turned to the rabbi and said something to the effect of, "Rabbi, assume it is 1942, and you have just been brought before the Gestapo. The Gestapo captain turns to you and says: 'Rabbi I am about to kill you. Is there any reason why I shouldn't?' What do you say to him? Do you say 'No you shouldn't because it's what? ... Wrong?' What do you say to him if there is no right and wrong? – Commercial break."

As Martin put it, "all purgatory broke loose in the studio and the lines lit up. But for the rest of the debate, the rabbi was strangely muted." Why? Probably, because for the first time in his life, someone had the guts to show him the consequences of his ideas.

It's easy to live a theoretical relativistic life of irrationality in a cocoon. But when the rubber meets the road, there is a price to pay for irrational relativistic thinking. Sadly, some of the consequences may take generations to be seen. It is important that we help train the world to think

---

[122] Much of this material was summarized from Frank Turek and Norm Geisler's great book, "Legislating Morality: Is it Wise? Is it Legal? Is it Possible?" Bethany House Pub (July 1998). I heartily recommend this book as a good resource. www.impactapologetics.com/product.asp?P_ID=249

[123] Go to www.NoBlindFaith.com and look up "Suicide Statements" to easily refute the claim of inclusiveness in "eastern thinking."

[124] Not to be confused with "my Rabbi" Rabbi Daniel Lapin. www.RabbiDanielLapin.com. Rabbi Lapin says even Christians need a Rabbi. Once you meet him or read his books, I think you will agree with him. The depth of knowledge one can gain about the Old Testament from a true Rabbi provides a deeper richer understanding of the Jewish culture, the New Testament, and the early church.

rationally.

Remember the Gestapo captain in the scenario was *also* a relativistic thinker. He thought that whatever the powerful decided, or whatever he preferred was good. Relativistic thinking leads to immorality and injustice.

Is what we do for God good?

However, we would be just as relativistic if we blindly thought that whatever we did for God was good too. Why? First, because unless we can logically prove that it is more rational to believe God exists[125] we are being relativistic as well (and it is relativistic to think that God exists just because we *feel* God exists). Second, we have to prove that what are doing for God is really what God wants and not some subjective selfish desire (i.e. we have to be able to verify that the communication from God is objectively real). Third, we should realize that an act is not good because we do it for God, the act must be objectively good in itself for it to be good. This does not make God separate from good. Good is good because of who God *is* and what his nature *is*. To clarify, we will discuss this and the capriciousness of God in a later chapter and provide guidelines to determine a firm logical moral basis.

So yes, we hope relativists will realize their irrationality, but more often than not when I talk with relativists they believe *rationality* is relative as well. So, they never seem to get the picture. Still, we keep trying with occasional glimmers of hope.

Back to the Declaration

Thus, we can see that our Declaration of Independence was based on the concept that there is an objective morality that applies to the *entire* world. And as a result of that Declaration; and on the basis of that Declaration, and on the *moral* foundation of that Declaration, a few years later our country's founders created our Constitution.

Eliminate the Declaration and you have in the Constitution an irrational, meaningless, and random document based on the momentary personal preferences of some dead ancient white guys. And this is precisely why relativists have concluded that the Constitution needs to be changed as often as our society changes. After all, if the Constitution is not based on unchanging principles, on unchanging Natural Law, it merely reflects the preferences of those in power. This means that whenever they do have power, the relativists act towards weakening the constitution with laws based on relativistic values. As a Christians or pastors do you not think it's our responsibility to stem the tide?

The Supreme Court is in some sense the keeper and protector of the Constitution, Presidents appoint Supreme Court Justices. So, whom we elect as president will determine greatly how long we can preserve our Constitution.

What else follows?

Sometimes when I discuss these things with friends who are not believers, they try to claim that there is no objective morality. "Morals have no

---

[125] To prove this, please go to www.NoBlindFaith.com and look up "Who is Agent X: Proving Science and Logic show it's more Rational to think God exists."

place in politics," they claim. Some even say, "You can't legislate morality."

I'll show you how to destroy both these illogical claims later on in this book. But for now, we can see that the Declaration of Independence strikes a nail into the coffins of both claims. How could anyone decide that even though the purpose and incentive for the Constitution was based on the idea of morality, that from then on no moral laws would be constitutional? Let me rephrase that so you understand clearly. Does it make sense that after basing the Declaration and the Constitution on objective moral principles, they would make the Constitution ban the concept of legislating morality or ban the requirement of morals in the political arena?

Obviously not. That would be not only self-defeating but it would be illogical and incompetent. So, we see that not only do the Declaration of Independence and the Constitution support objective moral values, they apply the same moral standard to everyone in the world, and *both* support the concept of *legislating* moral values.

A danger to the Constitution

But this all means that there is a danger that we need to watch out for. As more and more Americans abandon objective morality, the Constitution will be in peril. This is simple to prove. As we said, the Constitution is based on a sense of an objective God-given morality. Yet, if a majority of people stop believing that God exists or stop believing that moral values come from God, then we will rapidly tend towards a civilization that believes that anything is acceptable as long as the mob decides it. So at some point the Constitution will have no basis, no foundation, no rational footing and no acceptance by people in general. When this happens, the document will be abandoned or modified beyond recognition. The masses will decide what morality means to them according to relativistic whims of the moment, and we may go back to the arbitrary and traditional morality of the Aztecs or the Vikings or the Romans.

So, fellow Christians, does it not worry you that we have a fragile Constitution that at any moment in time could be eviscerated, torn into and gutted? Once that happens, entire classes of people may lose their rights and their lives. If human tragedy upsets you now, imagine what will happen to our nation when our Constitution no longer protects rights from God, just those granted by government – think immediately of the Chinese Government. It is clear, or it should be, that this Constitution has validity and stability only if it is maintained by people who have three primary convictions:

All rights come from God and are immutable and unchanging.

There is a non-relativistic objective truth, and we don't get to vote on it.

Assigning goods to others as a right will oppress all.

Do you see that if at any point the majority of legislators (i.e. our politicians) start to disagree with those two points, our entire government and Constitution will crumble? Do you see how we as Christians are needed to bolster and maintain this Constitution? Can we fail to be involved on a daily basis?

"In this age there can be no substitution for Christianity... That was the

Neil Mammen

religion of the founders of the republic, and they expected it to remain the religion of their descendants."

House Judiciary Committee, 1854[126]

"Our Constitution was made for a moral and religious people. It is wholly inadequate to the government of any other."

John Adams, 1798

On a side note, never forget that the Federal Government did not make the States. The States made the Federal Government. So, the Federal Government should always be seen as the servant of the states. The primary power should always lie in the hands of the individual states. A shift of power will jeopardize the federation.

Pastors and Elders

So pastors and elders, do you see how our very Constitution and laws depend on the belief system of those who execute and legislate them? The very existence of the U.S. Constitution required the foundational beliefs and teachings of Christianity. While it in itself is not a "biblical" or Christian statement, hopefully you've seen in this chapter, and in the years leading up to the Constitution, that such a document could not have ever come into being apart from Christian influence. No society of Muslims or Hindus or atheists or Baha'is or Buddhists or Aristotelians or pagans or even Wiccans could have ever created such a document. If you argue that they could have, then why didn't they do so in history past? All except the Muslims and the Baha'is have been around much much longer than us. In the same way, it was atheists who gave us the bloody massacres of the French Revolution and atheists who gave us the 120+ million dead under communism within 40 years.[127] By the way, if you buy Christopher Hitchens' weak argument that atheism didn't cause the massacres, but communism did, read the footnote.[128]

Pastors, if God-fearing Christ followers stop being politicians, what do you think will happen to our Constitution? What will happen if we find ourselves with a majority of legislators who are syncretistic, believing everything is relative? Our laws and system of government will fall apart and become an illogical and irrational shamble. What if we end up with legislators

---

[126] Reports of Committees of the House of Representatives Made During the First Session of the Thirty-Third Congress (Washington: A. O. P. Nicholson, 1854), pp. 6, 8. As quoted by David Barton.

[127] Since the great example of the U.S. Constitution, many nations have adopted similar guiding documents. But, they are not the originators of the concepts codified in the Declaration of Independence or the Constitution. The Bible is the source of these ideas.

[128] Atheists like to claim that the 120 million dead were consequences of communism not of atheism, but that statement shows simple ignorance of history and of communism. The French Revolution was based on atheism and resulted in a pure bloodshed. Encarta says over 40,000 were executed with or without trials or died in jail. No communism was involved there. As far as communism, in Kerala, my home state in South India, most of my family were communists. And yet, many of them were Christians and yet there was no violence. Why is it that you don't see Christian communists going around killing people but we see atheist communists doing just that? The only difference between the two is Christianity. It's because atheism can logically have no objective morality and proscribes only the relativistic morality of those in power. In other parts of India, atheistic communists like the Naxalites are still killing people. Similarly, if you compare all the Christian empires, even the evil ones, you will not find any of them to have killed any in those numbers. It took atheism to kill people in the hundreds of millions.

that think *goods* are God given *rights*? We will devolve into a nation of oppressed laborers. Do you see why Christians need to be in office? Can you imagine what would happen if we Christians were to shirk from it? If you, dear pastor, are not involved; if you do not encourage your flock to be involved; if you do not guide them as they engage with it; if you do not enable them to be involved; if you don't inform them about the moral issues of the law, and the need for moral character in our representatives; what will become of our Constitution in a few years? God has put you in a place that allows you to influence the future of our nation. What kind of Constitution would *you* leave to our grandchildren?

Conclusions

1. Rights do not come from the government. They come from God. If they came from government, then government could just decide to take them away. Governments are there to protect our God given rights. If they violate that function, we are to replace them.
2. If you remove God, you remove any God given rights and are left with merely self-granted rights.
3. If Christians aren't involved in legislation, the Constitution will lose meaning and crumble.

Find out More

In this chapter, I discussed some major concepts of the Constitution and Declaration of Independence. If you'd like to teach this material in a high school or to adults in a Bible study setting you can get the special student guide that we have created for this. Go to www.JesusIsInvolvedInPolitics, register and do a search for "Declaration of Independence." You can also download a free Power Point presentation and notes for use with it.

Eight

We have now sunk to a depth at which the restatement of the obvious is the first duty of intelligent men.
George Orwell 1934[129]

Dennis: *I told you. We're an anarcho-syndicalist commune. We take it in turns to act as sort-of-executive officer for the week.*
King Arthur: *Yes.*
Dennis: *But all the decisions of that officer have to be ratified at a special biweekly meeting...*
King Arthur: *Yes, I see.*
Dennis: *...by a simple majority. In the case of purely internal affairs...*
King Arthur: *[getting bored] Be quiet.*
Dennis: *...require two-thirds majority. In the case of old ladies...*
King Arthur: *Be quiet! [shouting] I order you to be quiet!*
Dennis' Mother: *Order, eh? Who does he think he is?*
King Arthur: *I am your king!*
Dennis' Mother: *Well, I didn't vote for you.*
King Arthur: *Don't be stupid, you don't vote for kings.*
Monty Python: The Holy Grail

Obvious Connections:
Politics plus Lawmakers equal Laws

What is the job of a politician? Should we as Christians even care about what they do? Is being a politician just a worldly esteem thing, like becoming prom king or prom queen or athlete of the year?

I teach and speak in a number of churches and gatherings and as a result have the privilege of interacting with kids and adults all the way from junior high age to empty nesters. What I've found is that many of the younger folk do not really understand what politicians actually do or what politics is all about. Many equate electing a politician to something like electing a homecoming queen, just a popularity contest. Once elected, they think politicians just get to schmooze with rich people and get quoted on television or show up on Fox News to argue with or against Sean Hannity.[130]

When asked about what they think politicians actually do, they mutter something about wage war, waste money, raise taxes, and be corrupt. Unfortunately, they are correct. But, when I ask them what they think politicians *should* do, they look at me blankly or spout some socialistic ideas like "feed the poor," or "provide housing for the homeless."

---

[129] http://thinkexist.com/quotation/we_have_now_sunk_to_a_depth_at_which_the/196027.html
[130] Let it be known that I'd be happy to debate any of them personally, on any moral issue.

Now obviously *you* know that when we elect politicians we are electing them to make or administer the laws of our land. If you don't know this, then let me say that again. ***Politicians are the ones who make our laws. That is why we call them lawmakers.*** These laws could vary from something as obscure as when you are allowed to call chicken fresh vs. frozen to whether the death penalty should be a punishment.

Why were Governments formed?

Many people seem to have forgotten why we form governments. Let's look at this briefly. Years ago when hunting and gathering tribes entered the agricultural age, they found that rogue males and roving gangs would attack their farms and homes and rape and pillage. Farmers realized that if they had to spend most of their energy just guarding their farms, they and their families would starve. So they banded together to create governments for the purpose of preserving their property and protecting their families. This way they could pay individuals to protect them, to build their roads and to ensure that commerce took place. Governments were originally formed to protect and preserve our families, our culture, our property, and our values and to support trade and commerce.

Note carefully, that they did *not* form governments to feed or take care of the poor. They formed *voluntary* charities for that.

Every thinking person realizes that it is in the interest of society to ensure that they have a stable place for their children to grow up. I want my daughter to have a safe comfortable self-fulfilling life, and I want to elect only politicians who will ensure that through the laws they make. Thus, it is the interest of any society to elect people who will make laws to protect their own culture and ensure the longevity of their own society.[131] In fact, one of government's primary roles is to ensure a continuation of its society. Any government that does not observe this soon dies along with its culture; sadly, its death is usually accompanied by extreme suffering and social injustice.

For a civilized society to function smoothly and survive, laws have to be codified.[132] As technology advances and new issues arise, new laws have to

---

[131] One of the best examples of this happens to be the Mayflower Compact. This document was composed by the Mayflower pilgrims when they ran into problems with some "strangers" who refused to abide by the pilgrims' rules. The compact gives a clear explanation of why any government should be formed. I've quoted just the relevant portions here.

"In the name of God, Amen. We whose names are underwritten...do by these presents solemnly and mutually in the presence of God and one of another, Covenant and Combine ourselves together into a Civil Body Politic, *for our better ordering and preservation and furtherance of [our goals]*; and...*to enact, constitute and frame such just and equal Laws, Ordinances, Acts, Constitutions and Offices,* from time to time, as shall be thought most...convenient for the general good of the Colony, unto which we promise all due submission and obedience."

Mayflower Compact (1620) Bradford, William, 1590-1657.

In other words, they combined themselves into a civil and political body to preserve, and better order their goals and for the good of the colony, i.e. their families. To achieve these they would create laws, offices, ordinances etc. However, do note, that for the first few years after this compact, they implemented a socialist community and almost all starved to death. It wasn't till they resorted to free market principles that they became prosperous. So, you need good economic principles on top of it all.

[132] Note that I did not say new laws need to be "created." I try to use the words "codified" or "identified." This is because the principles behind good laws are immutable and unchanging. The basics

be identified and some of the old more specific laws that are not relevant anymore (e.g. no hitching horses to the street signs) may as well be taken off the books.

However, I would argue that the main reason we find more and more laws being needed today is that we have abandoned the concept of objective morality. The fact that so many people believe that morality is achieved by consensus (i.e. what the majority decides is moral). This requires us to legislate every single thing we can think of, because the consensus of the masses need not be logical or rational or fixed, it's just their preferences, and preferences can change over time. As result, people believe that you cannot logically or rationally derive one moral law from another, and so every situation has to be specified.

The bad way many governments formed

The other way governments came to be, was when the local farmers were unable to defend themselves and marauding bandits took over the communities and setup themselves as kings, emperors, or chiefs over the conquered people. The history of the old world is littered with these examples. In this latter case, the rulers ensured that all power was centralized and representation by the people was minimized.

The Basics of the U.S. Government

We looked at the Constitution and how important it is for Christians to protect it. Now let us focus on our laws and nation's structure to see whether Christians should be involved in making these laws to protect us and whether pastors should be in the business of advising politicians which laws they should be passing or not.

The U.S. Government was formed to be closer in structure to a corporation rather than any of the previous nations in history.[133] The founding fathers, the framers of the Constitution, understanding the sin nature[134] of man, wanted to form a government that did not allow one person to have too much authority or control. Recall, "Power corrupts, absolute power corrupts absolutely." Yet, they knew that the government still had to have some sort of a centralized system.

So, to accomplish this, the framers wrote the Constitution to provide

---

are already there. We can only identify them as we come up with specific applications of them. In the horse-hitching example it wasn't that horse hitching was inherently bad, but rather than perhaps the horses hitched to the street sign was impeding traffic and could be dangerous. In the same way, when we now say don't drive faster than 65 mph, it wasn't that going faster than 65 was evil, it is just that with the current technology and human response times driving faster than 65 mph may be dangerous. The underlying value here is that life should be protected. In a few years when cars are controlled by microprocessors, perhaps 65 mph will not be dangerous anymore and while the underlying value to protect life continues, it is not applicable to driving over 65 mph due to the advances of technology.

[133] In fact, if you take the analogy to its logical conclusion, the U.S. president should really be called the CEO (Chief Executive Officer) of the USA. In most companies, the CEO is the idea man while the president or the COO (Chief Operating Officer) is the person who runs the day-to-day operations. In some companies, the same person does both, but then the title is "CEO and President."

[134] It is important to understand that the Christian concept of man's sin nature is that he is totally depraved but not absolutely depraved. The implication of this is that, though we have a sin nature it does not mean that we will always do the worst possible thing. We are capable of good but we need to be encouraged to do that good.

for a separation of powers. They did this by creating three separate branches of government. Each branch has its own responsibilities, and at the same time, the three need to work together to make the country run smoothly, to protect the rights of citizens and to ensure the citizens are not suppressed. This is done through something we call "checks and balances." Any branch may use its powers to hold in restraint the powers of the other two in order to maintain a "balance "of power among the three branches of government.

Please don't skim over this - even though you know all this, as I have a very important point to make here.

As we see, the U.S. government has three branches. They are the Executive, Legislative, and Judicial Branches. James Madison proposed this breakup based on Isaiah 33:22

> *"For the LORD is our judge, [judicial] the LORD is our lawgiver, [legislative] the LORD is our king; [executive] He will save us."*

The Legislative Branch

This branch consists of the Congress – the Senate and the House of Representatives. These are the only folks who are allowed to make the laws.

The Executive Branch

The Executive Branch consists of the president and the vice president and now includes a bunch of departments, like the Department of Defense. Their job is to *execute* and uphold the laws passed by the legislative branch.

The Judicial Branch

The Judicial Branch consists of the Supreme Court and lesser federal court judges. Note that the Supreme Court is unelected and is appointed by presidents. Their job is to interpret the intent of the laws passed by the Legislative Branch.

Equal Branches?

Here's the important point: it's a common fallacy that the three branches were created to be three co-equal branches with regard to law making. Yet, if we study our nation's foundational documents, we immediately see that the branches were not co-equal when it came to law *making*. While it is true that the branches could co-equally *prevent* bad laws (the checks and balances) through vetoes or judicial rulings,[135] it is not true that the branches can co-equally codify new laws. In fact, the *only* branch that is allowed to identify and codify new laws is the Legislative Branch, thus the name Legislative – (the definition of Legislative is: Of or relating to the enactment of laws).

So remember that only one branch of the federal government is allowed to codify laws: i.e. the Legislative Branch. This is important. The President (i.e. the Executive branch) is *not* allowed to make laws (except for Executive Orders, which apply only to the departments under him).[136] He is

---

[135] Actually even the idea of judges ruling against a law may not have been an original intent. It turns out that one of the earlier judges claimed this right for the bench after the Constitution was ratified.

[136] Presidential Executive Orders seem to be laws the President can legislate. But Presidential Executive Orders are not laws to the public. In order to implement the laws of the land, Presidents can give

responsible for upholding laws created by the Legislature. And when he does not do this, he is to blame.[137] This is important because even if the Legislature passes laws, if the Executive Office does not enforce them, they are of no use. A good example of this is what happened during Bill Clinton's two terms in office. He refused to uphold pornography laws already on the books in America, thus contributing to the spreading of hard core and up until then, illegal, pornography. Another example is what happened during G.W. Bush's terms, when he chose not to focus on protecting our southern border, resulting in the thriving of MS13 and other cross border gangs who have murdered thousands.

The Judicial Branch is also *not* allowed to create laws. It is responsible for interpreting the *existing* laws and passing judgment based on that interpretation. The Judicial Branch is also at the mercy of the Legislative Branch.

Note too, that it makes sense that the Legislative Branch is the only branch that is allowed to identify and articulate laws because it is the only branch that is *directly* elected by the people. Both other branches are either elected through the Electoral College or appointed by the president. Today, only the Senate and the House are directly elected by us.[138]

At this point, it is worthwhile to reemphasize that these judges are not appointed to create laws. They are there solely to *interpret* the law based on what they believe the original intent of the law was by the *original* legislatures and pass judgment based on that interpretation. I really wish we could stop calling them judges and instead call them Interpreters.

The Senate and the Supremes

It is a little known fact that the Supreme Court actually serves at the pleasure of the Senate. The Constitution barely even mentions the structure of the court or any of the lower courts, and the Constitution doesn't say anything about the size of the court. Jefferson thought that a strong Supreme Court was very dangerous.

> *To consider the judges as the ultimate arbiters of all constitutional questions [is] a very dangerous doctrine indeed, and one which would place us under the despotism of an oligarchy. Our judges are as honest as other men and not more so. They have with others the same passions for party, for power, and*

---

direction and guidance to (only) Executive Branch agencies and departments. They do not require Congressional approval to take effect and have the same legal weight as laws passed by Congress. But note that these orders are limited to the departments within the Executive Branch and not to the general public. In other words, these are very limited laws *only* for the employees of the President. The President's authority to issue Executive Orders is authorized in Article II, Section 1 of the Constitution is also the one that grants to the President the "executive Power to enforce laws."

[137] Yes, unfortunately guess who is to blame for not enforcing all those immigration laws or all the gun control laws that we already have. It is the president. This is important because the less the current gun control laws are enforced, the more laws the legislative branch dreams up to supplement them creating more restrictive measures that stifle our freedoms.

[138] Interestingly it wasn't until the 1900's that the people got to elect the Senate. Until then, the individual State Legislatures would appoint the Senators. And in the original conception of the Senate, it was supposed to be very passive and basically review legislation crafted in the House of Representatives. Note that while some judges at the local level are indeed elected, they are not elected to make the laws.

the privilege of their corps. Their maxim is boni judicis est ampliare jurisdictionem [good justice is broad jurisdiction], and their power the more dangerous as they are in office for life and not responsible, as the other functionaries are, to the elective control.

Thomas Jefferson to William C. Jarvis, 1820. ME 15:277[139]

In line with that, Congress could at its will decide to eradicate all the Supreme Court justices, close down the Supreme Court for a season and have the president reappoint just a single judge or even 20 of them. In fact, this very thing happened in December of 1800 when Jefferson shut down the Supreme Court.[140]

What kind of judge do we want on the Supreme Court?

Over the years Supreme Court judges have decided that it is their role to mould the American people to bring about change by the way they interpret the law. They've abdicated their role as "Interpreters" and feel that it is their duty to update the laws to reflect the current culture or the current moral values. In fact, two of the laws Christians think are the most damaging of all have been imposed on this nation by these types of judges, i.e. Abortion and same-sex marriage. Most of these laws would have had no chance had they been offered to the populace and legislators to vote on. This is not what judges were *ever* supposed to do. Judges were supposed to be what we call strict constructionists. A strict constructionist[141] is a judge who interprets the law as it was *originally* intended by the *original* lawmakers, leaving the molding of society to the lawmakers. I'll explain why this is so important and why it's of great interest to pastors, Christians and even liberals shortly.

A few years ago, President George W. Bush nominated a lawyer named Harriett Miers to the Supreme Court. She was a wonderful lady, a great lawyer and from all reports a very committed evangelical Christian. However, as soon as the president made this nomination, a large number of evangelical Christians and Christian organizations like the Family Research Council (www.FRC.org) strongly objected. They resisted the move even though as far as they knew Harriet Miers was a Christian and biased *toward* their viewpoint. Christians and conservatives objected to Harriet Miers because they knew little about her attitude toward the Constitution. Was she a strict constructionist? They weren't sure. And as far as they knew, she was not well versed in the Constitutional law. They wanted someone who was going to *interpret* law, not make judgments based on his or her views of what the country should become, even if those views were the same as theirs. And as we saw, President Bush went on to appoint a Catholic and strict constructionist, a person whom most evangelicals felt was a better choice than even a fellow evangelical.

We have standards, they work both ways, and they are worth

---

[139] www.landmarkcases.org/marbury/jefferson.html

[140] Go to www.JesusIsInvolvedInPolitics and do a search for keywords, "Jefferson Supreme Court" to find out more.

[141] Sometimes also called strict construction*al*ist or originalist. There is some question of the exact definition of the former term, as it seems that Antonin Scalia, one of the current Supreme Court Judges says he really isn't a strict constructionalist. However, he does adhere to the definition that I am using, so regardless of the optional definitions, when I say Strict Constructionist or Strict Constructional*ist*, I imply the definition that I have provided here.

Neil Mammen

"standing" up for. But lest you think we were being extra noble, remember that judges who make decisions based on their personal views are dangerous for everyone. Why? First, as Jefferson said, we didn't elect them. They were appointed. Second, as Jefferson emphasized, the Supreme Court is a *lifelong* appointment, so we can't easily get rid of them (short of a lengthy impeachment process). Thus, the last thing we want is to be stuck with a judge who makes decisions based on personal views or personal experiences and who cannot be taken off the bench. Why is this significant? Because even if their views mesh with ours today, they can change over time. What then? This has happened to us with a number of Supreme Court justices who are not strict constructionists. Naturally we are thinking of some appointed by President Reagan who ended up voting for issues Reagan opposed.[142]

Given all this, we will see that it was a sad day when a person who was elected President of the United States thinks that while he was a legislator he was *not* supposed to pass legislation based on his own conscience, but instead believes that Supreme Court Judges *should*.

We are fools if we think we are safe

Let's use an unlikely but possible scenario. Imagine that a socialistic fascist (someone who wants an extremely strong controlling central government) pretended to be a moderate and managed to convince people to ignore his previous associations and became president. Imagine too that he managed to ensure that five of the sitting Supreme Court judges had tragic fatal accidents, and was able to put in five of his own cohorts in there because Congress who has to approve these judges, were ignorant of the need for them to be strict constructionalists (evidenced by all their past rulings). Without strict constructionalism to limit them, these judges could immediately 'reinterpret' the Constitution based on 'penumbras[143]' (which is what the Supreme Court used to create a right to abortion). They could give this new president dictatorial powers and make him essentially an emperor. What could stop them or him? Absolutely nothing legal. Unless the citizens were in the habit of being watchful, realized the danger and stopped it. Which sadly does not seem to be the case today.

Is this too alarmist? Don't be foolish or ignorant of history. Similar things *have* happened in other countries where existing laws have been reinterpreted by the whims of the oligarchy. It is ignorant, arrogant and naïve to think it can't ever happen to us.

But this cuts both ways

Note that this can work both ways and hurt liberals. Let me show you a scenario as to why even liberals should want strict constructionalists. Imagine that after many years of hard work and billions of dollars spent by

---

[142] Of course, one could argue that a judge could start out with a personal view that it's good to be a strict constructionist and "change their mind about that" after a while– but that's human nature and we have to live with that possibility. I wish that when this happens the country would recognize the danger and we could simply impeach those judges.

[143] A penumbra is that hazy shadow around the moon during an eclipse. Go figure.

pro-Gay millionaires like Tim Gill,[144] and Peter Lewis, chairman of the well advertised Progressive Insurance company, liberals finally take over the house, the congress *and* 2/3rds of the states and finally a new amendment to the Constitution legalizing same-sex marriage is passed.

However, imagine that sometime thereafter, a conservative president is elected and manages to tip the Supreme Court balances such that there are five conservatives and four liberals. Let's further imagine that all five conservatives are not strict constructionists but, like the liberals today, believe they have the right to interpret the law the way they themselves saw fit. That is by their personal experiences and by the way they think the culture "should be" or by the way they perceive the culture to currently be.

In this scenario imagine if some state decided to *still* ban same-sex marriages and the case went to the Supreme Court. Now despite the liberal congress and states, these new Supreme Court judges could still say, "We are going to decide on this law according to our *personal* biases and experiences and our biases say that the new constitutional amendment[145] has a penumbra in it that indicates that this amendment really means something different." Then they come up with a new interpretation of this law that completely contradicts the original intent of the amendment. In short, despite even a constitutional amendment legalizing same-sex marriage, the Supreme Court rules you can't have same-sex marriage and it's banned everywhere in the U.S.

Nobody could stop them if this was the case. Liberals, is this what you want? Similarly, this same court could in a heartbeat change all the gun laws to force every state to force the legalization of arms for everyone and anyone. They could immediately change the abortion ruling to make abortion illegal in all states under any condition. They could change the immigration laws, and of course repeal all taxation laws. Who could stop them?

In fact, they wouldn't ever really need to fully justify themselves or even use precedent to prove it. They could give any reason even it if was logically false – who could argue? It's a personal preference. And they could then go further and change all the other laws they did not like. Where do we draw the line? Who draws the line? At this point, the people have abdicated their power to an oligarchy as Jefferson said. Liberals, are you sure this is what you want? It's what you *will* get if you aren't careful. This is one way the Nazi's took power. At some point we should ask ourselves, why even elect representatives to make our laws, why not just let the Supreme Court make the laws any way they wish. It is functionally no different except by degree. Why not return to a king or an emperor? The end result may be the same.

Why is this important to you pastors and Christians? Because what if we get a group of anti-Christian judges in there who feel that it is time to change America to the America they think it should be, an America that

---

[144] http://citizenlinkelectioncentral.com/2008/10/17/tim-gill-and-like-minded-donors/

[145] One cannot say this is not possible, after all the excuse used by the judge to justify the "right to an abortion" was that there was a 'penumbra' in the constitution that indicated that the right to privacy about killing what was until then considered a human baby. Can we think of a more force fed twisted justification? Radio Host Mark Levin has an excellent history of the Roe v. Wade law at: www.nationalreview.com/levin/levin200503140754.asp

persecutes Christians and imprisons pastors. How do you stop them? You can't un-elect them?

If you start to change laws according to the common culture or someone's own personal opinions, you do injustice to the original intent of the law. Worse, you end up not really having a law to begin with; all you have is some mushy guidelines that rely on the most creative manipulative minds to twist it for their personal gain. Clearly, all laws should be interpreted according to the intent in which they were *originally* written and not left to the personal whims or biases of unelected individuals. Otherwise, the laws have absolutely no value.

In case you think I've made this up, let's see what one of our founding fathers thought about it:

> *"On every question of construction [of the Constitution] carry ourselves back to the time when the Constitution was adopted, recollect the spirit manifested in the debates and instead of trying what meaning may be squeezed out of the text or invented against it, conform to the probable one in which it was passed."*
>
> **Thomas Jefferson to William Johnson, 1823. ME 15:449**

But how do we know what the original intent was?

This is actually a question that shows the dire need of improving our educational system. Any home schooled student can tell you that we have almost every comment, every argument that was said in favor or against each and every line in our Constitution. Why? Because they argued about it for days and at times got stuck on single words. And guess what, the minutes of each of these discussions were written down for you and I to read by James Madison the "father of the constitution" (see the reference in the footnote[146]). We should read what they were arguing about if we are confused about their intent.

What if the original intent was bad, as in racial discrimination?

"But," you argue, "what if we don't like the original intent, or what if the cultural values have changed or we've learned more about the moral laws. Or what if we need to change an immoral law?" After all, the law used to allow for discrimination. And in fact, the Dred Scott decision, which allowed a slave to be classified as only 2/3rds of a person, did stem from a valid strict constructionalist interpretation of the law. Surely, I'm not suggesting that Dred Scott was a good decision. Wouldn't this mean that judges are forced to uphold bad immoral laws?

Yes, unfortunately, that is true. And as I've shown it's necessarily for judges to uphold even bad laws, or we end up not having a law to begin with. We didn't appoint those judges to fix the law. But surely, that's not the end of the story?

Then how do we change those evil or bad laws?

We all agree that bad laws must be changed. But we should not

---

[146] memory.loc.gov/cgi-bin/ampage?collId=llac&fileName=001/llac001.db&recNum=223 or memory.loc.gov/ammem/collections/madison_papers/mjmser5.html or books.google.com/books?id=A8Y4AAAAIAAJ&dq=%22congressional+records%22+1789+Madison &source=gbs_navlinks_s This is a free abridged version.

change bad laws using judges. It is not the job of the judges to change existing laws.

Whose job is it? And you should be about 30 seconds ahead of me at this point.

Exactly, it's the job of the legislature; it's the job of your senators and representatives, politicians, who were personally elected by you, to change the law. So there *is* a way to change a bad law but unelected, lifetime judges are not the ones to do it. Our elected senators and representatives must change bad laws under pressure from us. What should happen is that enough concerned citizens have to write their representatives or send political action committees to them to talk to them. Then politicians get the idea or their conscience kicks in, then they submit a bill to change the old bad law or to identify and codify a new good one. Or the states get together to pass a new amendment. That's how it's supposed to happen. If that doesn't happen, we just elect a new set of representatives the next cycle with whom we agree. We aren't supposed to use the judiciary to change laws. It violates all the principles of elected representation and is just dangerous. Remember again, the Supreme Court is not elected and should never be allowed to become an oligarchy.[147]

Look at what is happening today where powerful groups and rich people have figured out that if they can get judges into office that share their viewpoint and who share their desire to bypass the Constitution, these judges can change laws without the consent of the people. This is called a tyranny or the word I've used repeatedly, i.e. oligarchy. It violates the spirit of our representative government.

An oligarchy by definition is a form of government where most of the political power effectively rests with a small segment of society (typically, the most powerful, who got there by their wealth, military strength, ruthlessness or political influence). The word oligarchy is from the Greek for "few" and "rule."

So to ensure that the judges always *just* interpret the laws (in as much as we can control it) we want judges who have a long history of being strict constructionists. Ignore that and we get the tyranny of an oligarchy.

Now some of you may still be thinking that I have not dealt with the fact that if it hadn't been for judges who imposed their personal views against racism on the country, we may still have racist laws being upheld. First, that is not totally accurate but it *is* precisely the point. Remember as we've said, according to the Constitution, the *lawmakers* are supposed to write new laws, not the *judges*. And anytime you mess with something even for a *good* reason, you open the door for someone else to decide to mess with it for a *bad* reason and make it very tough to shut the stable door again – because the precedent has been set. Here's another example to press home the point; would we want some judges someday to decide to legalize racism against some group or race because they personally felt that a cultural shift had occurred in the population? Impossible you say. Yet, it happened in Germany in 1936 when their supreme court determined Jews were *now* not fully human.

---

[147] Note we do elect some local and even State Supreme court judges, but not the US Supreme Court, and again we elect these local judges to interpret the law not to create the law.

Neil Mammen

Remember as I said, the right way for 'good' changes to occur would be for the *elected* representatives to take action and amend the law or the Constitution. This is what happened with the Civil Rights Act in 1964.

The great danger is using precedence in Law rather than original intent

There's been a terrible move in recent years to look at what judges have ruled as law in the past (precedence) and use that to influence what the law means and not go back to what the law was originally intended to mean. This is very dangerous in my opinion. If you want the law to be different, change it. Don't reinterpret it. And judges knowing that other judges may have had a tendency to twist the law to their own meanings should always go back to the original intent and never to the intent that some other judge may have "deciphered." Precedence is only applicable in areas that are new (e.g. technology) and only in the lesser laws that we are discovering, never in the primary moral code and never if a law has already been established by the legislators. Let's stop letting judges get away with precedence. We will lose our rights that way. Imagine if an oligarchy got hold of the three branches and gradually changed the "meaning" of our constitution without ever "changing" it. They could "precedence" us into tyranny and oppression.

But isn't the Constitution supposed to be a living document?

Al Gore, in his debate with George W. Bush in the year 2000, stated that the Constitution should be a "living document," and that's why he didn't want strict constructionists on the Supreme Court. But what's funny is that this shows us that Al Gore was either completely ignorant or he was being disingenuous. I am not sure which is worse.

You see, when we say the Constitution is a living document, it doesn't mean courts can interpret it willy-nilly. It means the Constitution can be amended through the amendment process by the *states* to reflect their desires. Al Gore was either a complete idiot or confuses this point, saying judges can reinterpret the Constitution any way they like. What nonsense! If Gore would stop to think about this rationally for even a moment, maybe he would realize how dangerous a notion it is. For as we showed, that would mean that the unelected Supreme Court could then decide what all laws mean *today* even if some of them been passed just a day ago. Al Gore has divorced himself from reality.

If this is true, how can Gore complain about the 2000 elections?

Given this foolishness on his part, it's ludicrous that Gore and his supporters said that the presidential election had been stolen from him by the Supreme Court. If they think the Supreme Court is allowed to interpret the laws any way they seem fit, why are they crying foul when that same Supreme Court decides to do that *very* thing and hand an election over to his opponent? Using their logic, the Supreme Court merely decided to interpret or create a new law regarding elections the way they saw fit. They were merely deciding to manipulate the country to their liking. This knife cuts both ways Mr.

Gore.[148]

Even liberals should want strict constructionalists.

What even funnier is that liberals keep saying the founding fathers, did not want to merge church and state, but then go on to say constitution should mean whatever we want it to mean today. In which case, why are they complaining if we say that merging church and state is the *new* meaning of the old constitution?

So what does a "living constitution" mean?

A living Constitution does not mean it is one that is controlled by the oligarchy of the Supreme Court, by the biases of unelected men and women. It means it can only be amended by the people using a tedious but carefully prescribed process. And we've done precisely that 27 times so far. *We* the people make it a living document, not a bunch of un-elected lifetime judges with an agenda.

The law *has* to mean what legislators originally understood it to mean, not what a group of black robed idealists feel it should mean. Otherwise, calling the U.S. a republic is meaningless.

The Constitution becomes capricious and has no meaning if judges can interpret it at their whim. It becomes useless.

"What, then, is the Constitution? I will tell you. It is no vague, indefinite, floating, unsubstantial, ideal something, colored according to any man's fancy, now a weasel, now a whale, and now nothing. . . . The American Constitution is a written instrument full and complete in itself. No Court in America, no Congress, no President, can add a single word thereto, or take a single word therefrom. It is a great national enactment done by the people, and can only be altered, amended, or added to by the people."
Frederick Douglass, Ex-Slave, Glasgow, Scotland, March 26, 1860

Not every part of the constitution is ethical

Yet, there are certain amendments to the Constitution that aren't ethical. For instance when the 16th amendment was passed in 1913 (this is the one that allows us to be taxed), it was sold as a tax only on the rich. All the folks who voted for it were told, "If we pass this, it will force the rich to share with everyone else. It'll never affect the middle income folks or the low income folks."[149]

Yet within four short years, middle-income folks were taxed and within a few decades not only was every hard-worker paying taxes, but those who were entrepreneurs and job creators were paying taxes as high as 90%. Meanwhile the real rich merely went offshore or used tax shelters. They aren't stupid. Do you see the danger of ever voting for something that will "stick it to someone else?" Besides being unethical, (can you imagine passing a law that will *stick* it to the Chinese or Indians or plumbers or farmers and thinking it was ethical), it will come back to bite you or your descendants. It is first of all, not the job of the government to equalize results and second it is not moral to

---

[148] Obviously, I don't think the Supreme Court did do anything illegal or unjust, but liberals don't have a leg to stand on in either case.

[149] http://www.crf-usa.org/bill-of-rights-in-action/bria-11-3-b.html

take away from anyone what they legally and ethically earned, especially if the difference is *just* that they earned more. "Ah," you may be about to object, "But many rich people did not get that money morally or legally."

In that case, you don't tax the good and the bad indiscriminately in a biased mean-spirited way; you fix the law to prevent immoral actions and prosecute the immoral ones. You don't punitively punish the good as well as the bad for the actions of some. Is this moral? Is this fair? Is it godly? Never!

Note this does not mean all taxes are evil. Taxes can be ethical and have some purposes but only when severely limited.

We do need to amend the constitution again

And so, in line with our *living* constitution, there are certain things about the Constitution that do need to be fixed. There are other things that need to be clarified, like the right to bear arms and what the establishment clause (freedom of religion) really means, how our government should never exceed a tiny portion of our population or GDP, how we are never to be socialists, the difference between rights and goods and how the government is forbidden to assign goods to people as though they were rights. *We the people* should clarify it in the proper way.

Similarly, we need a Marriage Amendment to limit marriage to be between one biological male and one biological female. The founders would never have thought we needed to clarify this, but it's apparent that we do now.

In addition, as we saw from the introduction to this book, there are many attempts to strip Christians of the right to preach the gospel in public. So, we need amendments to protect and defend our moral laws and to protect Jews and Christians. If Christians don't set about ensuring that we are protected, we will lose the ability to protect ourselves and others, like the weak and poor.

Here are some more laws and amendments that we should consider:
1. To ban "precedence" and require original intent and Natural Law in judicial rulings.
2. To require all representatives to read each entire bill and answer a test on the bill before being allowed to vote on it. Their answers are made public.
3. To require all bills to be fully funded before being able to pass.
4. To require that any president who declares war without the approval of congress be impeached and convicted.
5. To require all laws to indicate what part of the Constitution validates that law.
6. To disallow any unrelated riders on any bill.
7. To require the legislature to be only a part time legislature (say 3 months a year).
8. To require the legislature's salaries to be voted on by the public.
9. To require all legislators to be subject to every one of the laws that the rest of us are subject to. No retirement programs, no special healthcare, no special exceptions. Any future changes for this have to be voted on by the people.
10. To require all taxes on profits to be based off the increase of the original price only *after* it is indexed for inflation and the increase in the money supply and debt.[150]
11. To ban the government from colluding with industry, i.e. to ban the creation of regulatory laws designed to prevent small businesses from competing with large business. Usually large businesses can afford to "buy" representatives.

---

[150] If you buy a business for $500K and sell it for $900K after 10 years, you pay taxes on that 400K profit even though due to inflation that original $500K would have been worth $1.2M. You lost money and still had to pay taxes.

12. I was also thinking that it maybe a good idea to allow voters to vote for first and second choices in any given election. If the first choice does not make the top two contestants then their votes are applied to the second choice.

These should be added to the suggestions that Milton Friedman provides in the last chapter of his book "Free to Chose", Mariner Books (November 26, 1990). We could go on and on. Years ago we'd have never thought we'd need this. But now we've come to the point that we are forced to clarify each and every detail and explain why we made that decision, lest some future fool of a judge tries to subvert the will of the people. As George Orwell said in the opening quote, we've come to that time when the obvious has to be made explicit.

Local Political Offices: City, County, Aldermen, Water Boards

Christians need to be very concerned about local politicians, especially as this is the level at which most Churches and pastors would be impacted. An antagonistic local politician can destroy your church and even ban home Bible-Studies without a permit, like the city of San Diego did.[151]

City council members, aldermen or supervisors and such are elected to legislate for their towns, cities or counties. Similarly, school boards are elected to legislate for their schools. Water boards determine water policies for their constituents. Note too, that most of these roles are combinatorial in that they include a judicial role as well. However, in most these situations, any citizen who disagrees with councils or boards can still sue, taking the case to an independent judge who will interpret the law and decide for justice. What is critical is that these council positions can eventually lead to higher office. This means the person you ignore today may be running for mayor tomorrow, governor in four years and president after that.

City Councils decide if your Church can mark as many parking spots as you need on your *own* property, they decide if you can buy that lot next to the Church to expand into. They get to decide if that Evangelical Russian Church in California, meeting in a garage is an "illegal" church (which they did). They decide if you can close down the streets to have your Christmas Parade, or if you *have* to include that gay group in your church parade. Pastors and Elders and church members, if you don't think your church or other Christian Churches will be affected by your city council, you may have your head in the sand.

School Boards and PTA

School Boards are very powerful positions. Why? Because they have the authority to mould the minds of millions of impressionable kids. Boards not only determine curriculums, school agendas and how text books treat each topic, but they also hire and fire principals and school supervisors. Remember the parents in Alameda who were forced to send their elementary kids to pro-homosexual brainwashing classes? That was the agenda of their School Board.

Why aren't more Christian parents running for School Boards and the PTA (Parent Teacher Association)? Pastors, why aren't we encouraging and enabling them to do so?

By the way, do remember that you can run for School Board even if

---

[151] www.wnd.com/index.php?pageId=98895

you have no kids in school or your kids are home schooled. You just need the votes. We'll discuss how easy it is for pastors and churches to work together to help godly school board members win races in a non-partisan way.

Pastors and Christians

Why is all this relevant to Christians and their spiritual shepherds? Well, for one, if we Christians aren't involved in politics and don't return our Supreme Court back to a strict constructionist body in short order, it will just be a matter of time before the nation's courts turn against Christians and not only remove God, from the Pledge of Allegiance but slowly and surely take Him out of public life altogether. Please don't assume I'm being an alarmist. It's already happening. Atheists like Michael Newdow have already sued to remove God from the pledge *and* our national motto; you can bet that they are going for the deletion of God everywhere, in all public venues. How safe do you feel about the Supreme Court making decisions about such things if they are not strict constructionists? How safe do you feel if a liberal president appoints these black robed men and women? You'll get what judges *feel* should happen to America. That's how abortion was legalized.

Similarly, if Christians don't start taking over school boards and putting in morally founded principals and supervisors, who will we have to blame when our young kids get brainwashed? Many school boards positions are decided by fewer than 50 to 100 votes. Pastors, one or two small churches in a community with all of their members voting can make the difference. Are you concerned enough to move out of your comfort zone to do something?

I will propose an easy solution for this later in this book.

What can we conclude in this chapter?

1. Politics is really about the laws of the land.
2. Only elected senators and representatives are allowed to make the laws.
3. Judges are supposed to interpret laws, not make them.
4. A judge who interprets the law according to what he or she thinks it should be is abusing power and violating the Constitution.
5. The interpretation of the law should be based on the original intent, not trendy cultural values.
6. If a law needs to be changed for any reason, whether it's a bad law or values have changed, it should be done only by elected legislators, not judges.
7. The definition of a living Constitution is not that judges can reinvent it, but rather that the people can propose and vote on amendments.
8. Local offices lead to state offices and to federal offices. You can't ignore them.

Nine

I said that we live in a pluralistic society, that I can't impose my own religious views on another, that I was running to be the U.S. Senator of Illinois and not the Minister of Illinois.
Barack Obama,[152] 2006

A just law is a man-made code that squares with the moral law or the law of God. An unjust law is a code that is out of harmony with the moral law.
Dr. Martin Luther King, Jr.

Politics is nothing more than the practical application of our most deeply held beliefs.
Rabbi Daniel Lapin[153]

But You Can't Legislate Morality?

I was sitting in a Thai restaurant with an engineering colleague arguing about abortion. He was one of the best and the brightest, a liberal Christian with a Ph.D. from a very prestigious university, an author of multiple patents, with a deep analytical mind. I was presenting him arguments from a sermon that I use in churches titled "How To Win Arguments Against Abortion, Without Appealing To The Bible Or Religion."[154] Halfway through the conversation and after a bite of red curry chicken, he looked at me and said, "But you know, you can't legislate morality." I almost choked on my rice.

I use this highly learned and achieved man to show that this opinion is held at all levels of education and intelligence. I've heard it from a great many people. In fact, just recently, a well-known liberal politician said that he didn't want to be in the business of legislating morality for others. People spout this at me all over the place. It's usually the first objection. Sad to say, it often comes from Christians. I even had a Christian criminal attorney spout it at me. I usually try to give them a way out, and I always ask, "Is that something you've thought about at length, or is it just something you've heard someone else say and are merely repeating."

Now, if we can't legislate morality then indeed Christians may not have any overriding justification to be involved in politics. But what if we do and must legislate morality? If we do legislate morality, Christians, would you agree that you might indeed have a vested responsibility to be in politics? After all, if politics is about legislation and legislation is about morality then surely

---

[152] This quote is taken directly from Obama's 2007 campaigning website:
obama.senate.gov/speech/060628-call_to_renewal_keynote_address/index.html Visited 3/23/2007.
[153] American Alliance of Jews and Christians, www.RabbiDanielLapin.org
[154] Available at www.NoBlindFaith.com

Neil Mammen

there is a tie there between the source of our moral values and our religion and faith in God. Especially so, if as we've said the consequences are severe punishments from God and increased pain and suffering for the poor, defenseless and minorities.

So can you legislate morality or not?

"You can't legislate morality." If you think about it, that statement is one of the silliest and most illogical statements in the world. Why is it illogical?

Exactly! Because if we don't legislate morality, what on earth are we legislating? Platitudes? Fuzzy feelings? What? Cultural values? What are our representatives and senators legislating? Traditions?

What *are* they legislating? Well generally, they legislate things like, "Rape is against the law." "If you are a child predator, we will put you in prison!" "Killing is against the law."

But why do they legislate things like this? Because it's what? It's *wrong* to kill. It's *immoral* to kill.

We have laws that say things like "stealing is illegal." Isn't stealing a moral issue? In fact isn't it also a commandment of God, as in "Thou shalt not steal!" How about the laws that said that slavery was illegal? Was that just because it was economically bad to have slaves? On the contrary, it was economically *good* for the landowners to have slaves. After all what could be better than free labor? And at the time, there was a social and societal value that said owning slaves was acceptable. If fact, it was a social and status symbol. So, we couldn't appeal that slavery was wrong on social grounds or on tradition. But we *know* it was wrong to have slaves. We know it was *morally* wrong to have slaves. The new law against slavery was solely based on the concept that slaves are human and have rights and that it was what? It was *immoral* to take away their rights.[155] Moreover, this was a *religiously* based moral value.

Are you saying even the minor laws are moral values?

Even when we legislate things like "Do not litter," why are we legislating it? Because we think that littering destroys property. And we think that destroying property is a what thing? A bad thing. Would that make destroying the environment an *immoral* thing perhaps? Of course, it would. It's also a beauty thing, but that then moves into the issue of the fact that you are defacing public property. That's a moral issue again because you are spoiling something that also belongs to many people not just you.

Even tax laws are based on moral issues. Most tax codes are based on basic moral principles – it's good to educate all kids, for example. It's good to give single mothers money for food. So to pay for that we made a law that says "it's necessary to take money from people and give to these good causes." You may argue about the morality of taking money from one person and giving to another, but at the root of it, it may not by your moral value but it is *someone's*

---

[155] I always like to put it this way: In the 1870s when they said slavery was wrong was it wrong because it was against man's law? No, it was wrong because it was against God's Law. That's a moral issue solved by a political action. That is, a moral issue solved only when Christians got involved politically.

moral value.

So, as you can see, our legislation is about *someone's* moral values most of the time. While it's true that a few times we write laws on matters that have no obviously strong moral content, such as celebrating Thanksgiving Day on the third Thursday in November and Mother's Day on the second Sunday in May. The day on which Mothers Day falls is not really a moral issue, but the concept of honoring mothers *is* a moral issue. And in reality when Thanksgiving was first made a day of giving "thanks to God," that was a moral matter.

But is this the same? Is there really a punishment associated with that? I mean, let's say one Mother's Day I actually forgot to send my mom a card in time, for being the best mother in the entire world, (which she is by the way).

Will the ATF-MDEs – the Bureau of Alcohol, Tobacco, Firearms and Mother's Day Enforcers –come charging through my door? Throw me to the ground, hog tie and handcuff me, shove me into a police car saying "Please mind your head" and then haul me to off to jail for three years until I learn to respect and love and make my mother a priority? "Call your mother, you naughty boy," says the judge as she passes down my sentence.

Absolutely not. Or what if I celebrated it two days later? Do I get stuck with a $15,000 fine for being late? Nonsense! Right?

So when we *do* legislate in less important moral areas, we don't punish in connection with them, do we? We just declare them and recommend that people follow them (remember this when we get to Old Testament Ceremonial and Judicial Laws). But as we've said, if you think about it, why do we declare Mother's Day in the first place? Because we think it's what? We think it's *good* to honor our mothers. And the opposite? *Bad* to ignore her. That's a moral value, isn't it?

In the same vein we don't have a Hitler's Day, do we? No. Unless it's to recall all the *bad* things he did, so we never forget that and do it ourselves. Again, a moral issue is present.[156]

So we *do* legislate morality all the time, and most of the time and over and over again, and we punish people who violate moral laws.

But aren't we just legislating social values?

Now some people may argue that we are just legislating social values, not moral or religious values. But that argument fails immediately. Take slavery. It was *always* immoral to have slaves. It didn't suddenly become immoral to have slaves only after American society woke up to the evils of slavery. In fact, it was still socially *acceptable* and desirable to have slaves at the time that they were fighting against it. American – and in fact African, Asian, Native American and almost all societies have approved of slavery (as long as the dominant groups in those cultures were not the slaves – in other words "as long as I'm not *the* slave, slavery is okay"). The immorality of slavery was really a Christian religious concept. No religion before Christ had

---

[156] Of course, one could argue that Nazis had a Hitler's day. But this merely supports my argument because the Nazis were making an a priori moral assumption that Hitler was good and that having the Third Reich control the entire world was a good thing. This leads to: How do we know whose morals are good and whose are bad? This will be discussed later in this book.

ever proposed that all men were created equal, as the Bible teaches, and many religions that started after Christianity, like Islam, didn't teach it either. In fact, Mohammed gave his favorite wife at least 40 slaves.

So you can't use social or cultural values as the sole basis for moral values.

No, the American and British idea that slavery was wrong was a *religious* value right from the start. Slavery was against whose law? Not man's since slavery was legal. Slavery was only against God's law. And that's a religious value. And if we can't impose our religious values on others, then are you going to argue that the emancipation proclamation, which freed the slaves, was a religious law and so we have no right to hold people to it? As you can see this is quite ridiculous when taken to its logical conclusion.

What's worse, if you don't think Christians should be involved in politics; you are also claiming that the *political* battle to free the slaves was wrong. Are you sure, you want to be making this statement?

I was teaching an Apologetics class in Sunday School at our church a few weeks before the 2008 election in California. I started by talking about the upcoming ballot to define Marriage as being between only a man and a woman in our Californian Constitution. One gentleman raised his hand and said, "I thought we were here to learn about Apologetics, I don't think we should bring politics into church."

I'm always mindful that though some people call me out on this issue, as the teacher, I still have to give them grace and avoid embarrassing them in public. So, I asked him if he thought it was wrong of our country to free the slaves and later grant every person their God given civil rights. He said "No."

I then explained how those movements started in the Church, not in the Parliament or Congress. I explained that it would have been considered "apologetics and theology" to *prove* that the slaves were fully humans with equal rights in the 1800s just as I had done with fetuses. "But," I said, "what if I'd spent time proving the slaves were human, but then ignored the fact that we could actually do something about their plight. What sort of a teacher would I have been? What was God's heart regarding that? Does God want us to just *know* the truth but not make it a reality?"

When we teach Apologetics, we have to teach the *solution* to the problem as well as the *facts* of the problem. In the case of slavery, abortion, and same-sex marriage, the solution is to change the law. So when I talk about same-sex marriage, I also have to teach the solution, i.e. change the law to protect it.

If anyone says the Church should not get involved in politics they are immediately saying, the Church should never have gotten involved in the battle against slavery or civil rights. Thus implying that slavery and legal discrimination should *still* continue. I think you are treading on heartless cruel wicked dangerous ground here.

The next logical question is: If the church cannot or does not address these *moral* issues that result in political action, then who will?

What do we call laws not based on moral values?

Think about this fact, any law that is *not* based on a moral value is considered tyrannical. Imagine if a legislative body suddenly created a random law that had no purpose other than the whim of some person like a king or emperor, or even a judge. We'd call that tyranny and fight against it. In fact as we saw earlier, that's exactly what the Declaration of Independence was claiming – that King George of England was a tyrant, and his laws and actions were immoral and thus tyrannical.

Oh, and we should add that most people who complain about legislating morality want to legislate against a host of things based on their *own* moral values, especially their *own* politically correct values.[157]

So, in my opinion anybody who says we can't legislate morality is really ignorant or lying.

Yet, don't feel bad if you also bought into the "you can't legislate morality" platitude. As a young liberal, I accepted it myself until I started thinking about it, and many intelligent people, like my Stanford Ph.D. and criminal lawyer friends, had also bought into it. All this goes to show that even educated people can be ignorant about things and buy into liberal lies if they've never spent the time to think through issues carefully. What happens is that you hear this phrase over and over and over again, so you just take it as truth. This is usually called propaganda. So I heartily recommend that you always ask, "Why is that true? Why do you think that?" before accepting anything you hear.

Apply this principle to this book and me

I would be misleading you if I didn't ask you to ask yourself that about what I have written as you continue to read through this book. If you find logical errors, please do notify us.

Okay so you can legislate morality, but you can't enforce it

Now in response I've heard people say, "But just because you *can* legislate morality doesn't mean you can enforce it. So it's a waste of time."

But even that argument fails. First, as we've shown, we do legislate morality all the time. Second, even if we were unable to enforce certain laws every time, that fact would not invalidate legislation. For instance, it is difficult to enforce the law against murder. For some reason in all murder cases, we seem to get there too late,[158] and many times, we never ever catch the murderer. But that's not a reason to eliminate laws against murder. This is an important concept to grasp. The inability to stop an immoral act every time is

---

[157] Occasionally when I'm feeling ornery and having this discussion with one of my liberal friends, I say, "So if you think we can't or shouldn't legislate morality, does that mean that if some extremists pass a law that says the country should execute green eyed people, that would be acceptable to you?"

Of course, they think that's ridiculous. I ask them, "Why is that unacceptable?"

They mutter something about "executing someone just because they have green eyes is wrong."

"Aha" I say. "So you agree that we should not be legislating people's random opinions especially if they are wrong or immoral."

Then I ask, "So what *should* we be legislating other than moral values?"

They never had a good alternative.

Of course, if they suggest cultural or social values I beat them about the head with my napkin while asking them if they have a preference between Nazi cultural and social values or the Taliban's.

[158] Okay this is a joke, obviously, if we knew about it and got there on time (to stop the murder) it wouldn't be a murder case would it? It would be a conspiracy to murder case.

not a valid reason to *avoid* legislation against it. We wouldn't consider our legislature very highly if tomorrow they eliminated all laws against stealing and extortion because we frankly have a hard time catching crooks. We have a tough time stopping *most* crimes when you think about it.[159]

The point I am making is that we *do* legislate morality and just because you can't prevent a law from being broken does not mean that you shouldn't legislate it. As we will find out later, there are many other reasons to legislate even those laws that we cannot easily enforce.

Religious Values, Religious Views and Barack Obama

At the beginning of this chapter, I quoted Barack Obama. He had made that statement in a response to Alan Keyes, his opponent during an election. Keyes had maintained that a Christian could not in good conscience vote for Obama because Obama would not take a stand in moral issues like abortion or same-sex marriage. Keyes was specifically talking about the stance that Obama took, that an infant born *alive* in a failed abortion should be thrown in the dustbin to suffer and *die*. Obama responded to this on his website:

> *Unwilling to go there, I answered with what has come to be the typically liberal response in such –debates – namely, I said that we live in a pluralistic society, that I can't impose my own religious views on another, that I was running to be the U.S. Senator of Illinois and not the Minister of Illinois.[160]*

He later said that while he personally may believe otherwise (which I doubt since he attended one of the most pro-abortion church denominations in the U.S. for more than 20 years), he can't impose this law unless he can give people a non-biblical defense of his supposed anti-abortion stance.

Obama makes two embarrassing mistakes here. The first is that it is very easy to give people a non-biblical defense of the pro-life position (as we've mentioned before go to NoBlindFaith.com and look up "Abortion"). The second, which is more embarrassing, is that he says he does not wish to impose his religious views on others. But for an African American to say this is ironic and shows sheer ignorance. We have already shown that the law to end slavery was not based on man's laws, nor was it based on social values, nor was it based on economic values. The law and indeed the fight to end slavery was based purely on the fact that *Christians* (yes, religious people) believed that slavery was an abomination to *God* (a religious entity) and that all men were equal (another *religious* concept never codified before the United States Constitution, except in New Testament scriptures).

What was the anti-slavery movement? It *was* a purely *religious* endeavor based on the moral and religious convictions of religious people (Christians). As we've mentioned before, there is and was no secular precedent to abolish slavery or to ban racism in history. Not a single nation prior to the 1800's had any concept of equal rights for all men and women regardless of creed, color or culture.[161] Atheists have no compelling "theology" to believe

---

[159] Now you *could* argue that what you *really* mean is that we shouldn't make laws if we can *never* catch the people who break them. But that is not the issue I am trying to argue. All the laws we are talking about are enforceable in some way.

[160] obama.senate.gov/speech/060628-call_to_renewal_keynote_address/index.html Last visited 3/23/07.

[161] And even in our great country it took years for it to be implemented.

that all men are created equal. In fact, since they are forced to believe in evolution, they have very compelling reasons to believe that some races or groups or cultures are more evolved than other races. In fact, any evolutionist would have a hard time arguing that if evolution is true; all races of man are indeed created with equal rights.[162] The emancipation of slaves only occurred because religious people realized that they had to *impose* their *religious* views on others and legislate those self same views. So for an African American like Obama[163] to make the claim that religious views should *not* be made into law or should not be imposed on others who aren't convinced of it, indicates he of all people is ignorant of the origin of the very law that allowed him to run for office, showing us his ignorance of lawmaking. There's a lot more to be said about this. We will revisit Obama's statement again.

Same-Sex Marriage, Slavery and Equal Rights

It is also interesting to note that the very book – that is, the Bible – that claims that all people are created equal with equal rights *and* was the fundamental moral basis for freeing the slaves in America is also the book that declares homosexuality as immoral and damaging to the body. So when people try to use the idea of human rights to justify same-sex marriage, the first question I ask is "Why do you think all humans have equal rights? That idea only comes from the Bible. If you invalidate the Bible on the same-sex marriage issue, you invalidate the concept of equal rights. You can't have your cake and eat it too."

Of course, they may respond that equal rights are a modern concept, not a biblical concept. Yet history plainly refutes that. Why didn't all those older philosophies ever fight for these rights? The burden is upon them to show us the evidence. There would have been no equal rights for all mankind without the Christians fighting for it (and that too politically).

Does this mean we should legislate all moral values?

Not at all. We should not legislate *every* moral value, just certain carefully chosen ones. The methodology of how to select them deserves and has a chapter of its own in this book.

Does this mean we should legislate from the Bible?

Be at ease everyone, we are certainly *not* proposing that we legislate from the Bible. We do not wish to have a Christian version of the Taliban; however, we still have to legislate our moral values from our spiritual convictions. And as Christians, our moral values come from the Bible; otherwise, we can't really call ourselves Christ-followers. How do we separate the two? Keep reading.

Rather than just trying to legislate morality, we should work to change

---

[162] Note that atheists would argue that the concept of "better" does not apply here, just that some species adapt better to their ecosystem than other species. But this assessment comes with no moral values, so they can't say it's wrong to discriminate. Who makes the rules if there is no standard and no standard giver?

[163] Now of course no one can argue that he really meant religious views as in how often to take communion or if you should be dunked or sprinkled. He was talking about the controversial same-sex marriage and abortion issues. These are religious views and values similar to being against slavery.

the situations that create the "immoral" behavior?

Debating on-line is an interesting hobby of mine. One argument that gets play on the Internet is this, "Rather than just trying to legislate morality, Congress needs to try to change the social situations that create the 'immoral' behavior. Society can't just be ordered to change; instead, it needs to be helped into whatever change will eventually happen." Whenever I hear or read this, it cracks me up. Why? Because if people who put forth this argument had any sense of history and tried to apply what they were saying to what has happened in the past, they would see the lack of logic that they are so desperately trying to hang on to. For instance, imagine we were back in 1961 before the Civil Rights Act was passed and someone had gone up to Martin Luther King and said, "Dr. King, rather than just trying to legislate equal rights, you and Congress need to try to change the social situations that create racism.[164] Society can't just be ordered to change; instead, it needs to be helped into whatever change will eventually happen."

What do you think his response would have been? How about this:
"The other familiar cry that we will hear is that freedom riders, the federal government and no other agency can force integration upon the South. Morals, they argue, cannot be legislated. To this we must answer, it may be true that morals cannot be legislated, but behavior can be regulated. It may be true that laws and federal action cannot change bad internal attitudes, but they can control the external effects of those internal attitudes. The law may not be able to make a man love me, but it can keep him from lynching me. The fact is that the habits, if not the hearts of men, have been and are being changed every day by federal action."
Statement Delivered at a Rally to Support the Freedom Rides.
May 21 1961, Montgomery, AL[165]

To show more of the silliness of this idea – that rather than legislate morality we should change social situations that create "immoral" behavior – let's start with something as severe as murder.

How exactly does Congress change the social situations that cause murder? If you think murder is too severe, consider seatbelts. How do we change the social situations that lead to people not wanting to wear seatbelts?[166] How about slavery back in the 1800's? Should the government have allowed slavery and instead focused on changing the social situations that induced people to want free labor for their farms? Meanwhile slaves were dying in the thousands on the slave ships. It's pure nonsense and idiocy.

I used to spend a lot of time vetting my arguments on an email list with a bunch of disillusioned missionary kids. It seems that there is no lack of

---

[164] Ah, you say, "but racism affects other people, we are talking about actions between consenting adults." "Yes," I say, "like seat belts?" Also, as we will show shortly, most things people claim are done by consenting adults and thus harmless will actually affect society in general.

[165] Don't get hung up here that MLK said that "maybe" morals can't be legislated because he goes on to prove that they can and are when he talks about the habits of men being changed by federal action. The idea that lynching is bad is a moral value that was subsequently legislated against -- though to be accurate, lynching was already against the law. The courts and police were just a bit racist about who they allowed to lynch and who were lynched and who was prosecuted as a result of a lynching.

[166] I know, I know. You are thinking about movies and TV shows where only the cool people wear seatbelts. But it's just not as effective.

hate for God greater than that of a kid who was put into a boarding school while his parents were on the Indian mission field. They don't openly hate their parents, but sadly they do hate their parents' evangelical fundamentalist God. Sadly, many of them have embraced Universalism and would go into conniption fits when I asked them, "Now let me get this straight, your parents abandoned you in a boarding school to tell a bunch of *my people* (the Indians) that Jesus was just *another* way to God? Why waste their time and your lives? My people already had 3 million *other* gods, why would they have needed yet another named Jesus? And why would the apostles sign up to be persecuted, tortured and killed if they thought that *all* roads led to heaven. Why not stay at home and fish? Why go out and get massacred?"

I remember arguing with one such person about abortion (we'll call him Junior). Junior has bought massively into relativism. Junior said, "If you wish to prohibit abortion, then ethically, I believe you must also stop being pharisaical and take responsibility also for the fact that people end up choosing abortion." i.e. Rather than banning abortion, we should eradicate the reasons why women choose abortions."

I then showed Junior that 98+% of all abortions are performed for convenience (using data from a pro-choice source[167]). The number one and two reasons for abortions (21%) is that the woman has inadequate finances, or she is afraid the baby will affect her career. The next two most common reasons given are that her relationship with the baby's father has ended or having to raise a child would change her life too much. I asked Junior what he suggested the government do to address something like the woman's relationship with the baby's father or the fact that her career would be affected. I even quoted MLK's comment to him.

His response? "You are using sophistry." I had to look up the word (see footnote[168]), but when I did, I saw that I was not using sophistry. For everything I had said made *logical* sense. His argument had been refuted completely, and his response was to call me names. Sure, we should work towards changing the conditions that we *can* change, but it's silly to expect us to change basic human nature like selfishness, and it's even sillier to insist that *nothing* be done until that point.

This is also important to pastors. We can work all day to preach the gospel and change men's hearts, but should we merely let evil continue unabated until sufficient men's hearts are changed? It hasn't happened in the last 2000 years. It didn't help the slaves, to preach the Gospel to their slave owners?[169] How do you remove the conditions for people to want to sin? How long do we wait and let evil continue when we could create healthy laws to

---

[167] Physicians for Reproductive Choice and Health®
www.prch.org/resources/index.php?pid=123&tpid=5. I have used 2002 data here.

[168] **soph·ist·ry:** *subtly deceptive reasoning or argumentation.* **soph·ism:** *an argument apparently correct in form but actually invalid; especially: such an argument used to deceive.* But if I was doing that, he just needed to show me where I was wrong. Since he couldn't find the flaw, he resorted to calling me and my argument names.

[169] Of course, I can't say the same for Slave Ship Captains like John Newton. But when he got saved and became a Christian, somebody else merely took his place as captain. You have to change the *law* for real and effective change to take place.

hamper it? Will God hold us responsible for doing nothing? If he held the Jews, the Babylonians, the Assyrians, the Canaanites and the Midianites, responsible, why would he not hold the "Americanites" responsible too?

Pastors and Elders

So pastors and elders, if all laws are based on moral values and all moral values stem from religious convictions of some sort,[170] then who better to have in political power than a God-fearing man or woman? Who better to advise them, than a man or woman of God? And perhaps this is why during the foundation of this great country and for years after, most of the politicians were either ministers or theologians.

If all Christians get out of politics, can you envision what a United States will look like? What would become of the moral basis of our laws?

So, what can we add to our argument?

We can and must legislate morality. Anyone who tells you otherwise is ignorant or disingenuous. If someone running for office says this, you shouldn't vote for that person.

Inability to enforce a law fully is not a reason not to pass it. We enact laws that we can't enforce fully all the time. The law against murder is one example.

All laws have moral foundations, and all morals have religious foundations. Politicians are in the business of making laws, so in a way politics is religious in nature. A politician's religious views are just as critical as his economic views. A politician who does not understand this is not going to be a good lawmaker, and you should never vote for him or her.

Religious values have played a significant role in the laws of our land. The abolition of slavery is a grand example. If religious people were not active in politics on a daily basis, then England and the United States might still have slavery.

Find out More

In this chapter, I discussed a manual that I wrote to train people how to argue the conservative position on abortion. The title is, "How to win Abortion Arguments without appealing to the Bible or Religion." If you are interested in obtaining the manual and/or the accompanying PowerPoint presentation, please visit www.NoBlindFaith.com. Then do a search for "Abortion." Feel free to give this paper to your pro-choice friends and ask them if they agree with it. Better still; use it to train junior high, high school, and college kids how to win arguments in the struggle against abortion. That's a battle that we are winning, as over 51% of the US now considers themselves pro-life.

---

[170] Don't forget that even atheists have morals. Yet, since they cannot logically support a moral standard, they invariably have to borrow those standards from other religions.

Ten

*Infanticide, which might seem contrary to human nature, was almost universal **before the rise of Christianity**, and is recommended by Plato to prevent over-population. [Notice how this is the same cry by today's pro-abortionists].*

*..."In antiquity, when male supremacy was unquestioned and **Christian ethics were still unknown**, women were harmless but rather silly, and a man who took them seriously was somewhat despised.[171]*

Atheist Bertrand Russell (emphasis added)

*"Speak up for those who cannot speak for themselves, ...defend the **rights** of the poor and needy." [Notice it speaks of rights not goods]*

Proverbs 31:8-9

*Blessed are they who **maintain justice**, who constantly **do** what is **right**.*

Psalms 106:3.

But The Church Should Stay Out Of Politics! Besides, Christian Involvement In Politics Always Fails!

Look how we've failed every time we've tried to get involved in politics! What good has the Moral Majority done? How useful was the Christian Coalition? The Church should stay out of politics! We should focus on changing the culture and hearts, not laws!" A pastor friend of mine was attacking every Christian organization which had ever dared to become politically involved.

On another occasion, a lady on FaceBook come on to my profile after I'd condemned those in leadership (yes, I was just taking the lead from Jesus and calling them snakes and rats). This lady was one of those who though a Christian, seemed to spend more of her time attacking fellow Christians who had the "gall" to stand up for righteousness than to speak out against sinful people who were really hurting others. When I suggested that "just praying" was not an option she went ballistic. "Just pray!" she hollered (electronically), "Just pray! You think petitioning the Almighty creator is 'just' praying."

But this is a common Strawman fallacy. I'd said "we can't *just* pray, we have to speak out against evil *and* change the law as well." It's true, we can't "just" pray. We have to take action. James is quite clear about this.[172]

---

[171] Bertrand Russell, *Unpopular Essays*, 1950, New York: Simon & Schuster.

[172] James 2:26 *As the body without the spirit is dead, so faith without deeds is dead.* What sort of deeds is James talking about? He's talking about justice. James 1:27 *Religion that God our Father accepts as pure and faultless is this: to look after orphans and widows in their distress...*

Neil Mammen

Same with all the Israelite battles like Jericho. They had to go out there and obey God's commandments before God acted. Not because He couldn't, but because He has chosen to allow us to participate with Him. Imagine if they'd just prayed and sat tight despite God's commandments to them?

What has God commanded us to do with regards to justice? What does Psalms 106 in the chapter heading quote say? We are to *maintain* justice and *do* what's right, not *just* pray about it!

Notice however, that both the lady and the pastor's biggest gaffes were thinking that Christians had always failed whenever they've tried to use politics to change things. To put it kindly, they are completely ignorant about history.

Sadly, they are not unique in this view. And to tell the truth, it's natural that many of us would believe this. After all newspapers and TV are always too willing to show us the failure of Christian leaders, and the U.S. seems to be getting worse not better despite the many attempts by Christians to change laws.

What we easily forget is that not only does the media *not* report *all* the news, but most of us also have a very sparse knowledge of history. Let's take a brief look at what Christian involvement in politics has *actually* done in the last 2000 years for the causes of true social justice.

Has Christian involvement in politics really always failed?

This idea is simply false. I'm tempted to ask people who state this if they would have tried telling that to the *Christian* William Wilberforce who stopped slavery in England almost six decades before it was stopped in America? Yet, even *he* had to try every year for almost 47 years before he was fully successful in achieving true social justice. Imagine telling Wilberforce not to get involved in politics and to "just pray." What hypocrisy? Compared to that, the battle against abortion, another battle for true social justice, has yet another 11 years to go.[173] How about complaining to Rev. Martin Luther King that Christian[174] political involvement wasn't effective in changing the civil rights laws? But that's just looking at the big successes, how about all the little successes, like laws that said the king was not above God's law, laws the British Christians imposed on India that prohibited sati, the killing of Hindu widows on their husband's funeral pyre (again true social justice). We mustn't forget too the original laws to limit marriage to one man and one woman that over rode the native traditions that allowed leaders and chiefs to have multiple wives. How about the Church influenced law in Northern Europe in the 1200s that insisted that the wife had to consent to marriage, [175] rather than the customary marriage by capture and kidnapping that had prevailed until then. I kid you not!

---

[173] And we are gaining much ground; we've succeeded in turning a majority of Americans *against* abortion on demand. Gallup in May 2009 showed 51% of Americans identify as "pro-life" and 42% as "pro-choice." www.gallup.com/poll/118399/more-americans-pro-life-than-pro-choice-first-time.aspx
[174] Yes, the first people to rally to this cause were Christians and pastors, not New Agers or atheists. The Civil Rights cause was first preached in the churches across America. Sadly, some churches preached the resistance to this movement as well, in full violation of the Scriptures.
[175] stason.org/TULARC/travel/nordic-scandinavia/2-5-6-Christian-and-pre-Christian-laws.html

Don't forget too, the laws that outlawed social injustices like:

1. Infanticide
2. Child marriage
3. Temple prostitution
4. Forced prostitution
5. Child prostitution
6. The superstitious killing of twins[176]
7. Women as second class citizens
8. Abandonment of elderly in the wild
9. Revenge killings[177]
10. Honor Killings
11. The abuse of children
12. The purchase of wives
13. Animal cruelty[178]
14. Sale of children to pay family debts[179]
15. Killing special needs/deformed children.
16. The abuse of prisoners[180]
17. Child labor[181]
18. Gladiatorial combat
19. Death games
20. Bribery
21. Selective gender abortions
22. Cruel and unusual punishments
23. The restriction of a man's right to divorce his wife for *any* reason.[182]

All these were stopped by laws that came about due to Christian political action. We could go on, as there are thousands of laws in all Christian and post Christian cultures that were based on just the moral values of Christians. Notice that all of these battles were for actual *rights*, not goods. This was not "economic" justice. But true moral social justice. People's God-given rights were being violated and the church stepped in to stop that injustice. They didn't step in to equalize results and bring about socialism.

What's more relevant to pastors and Christians is that most of the changes in these laws started because of a sermon from the pulpit of a church. It wasn't something that the Church shied away from. Christians and churches who were involved in politics took it upon themselves at great costs to change the law and their societies. The same societies that now assume that all those values are self-evident and forget the very people and the very religion, which brought those *just* and *moral* laws into existence. All these laws took years and years and numerous heartbreaking tries to implement and they only came about because Christians and their pastors took a stance publicly, politically, legally and judicially and just as important financially. Don't forget that all these laws were fought and rejected over and over again by those very same societies that later embraced these ideals. And in each case, there was a huge backlash of unpopularity and malice against these particular pastors and their churches.

Are you sure you want to go back to the old days?

What is even scarier is that if the Church retreats from lawmaking, many of those laws will be changed back eventually. Do you doubt me? What happened when Christians retreated, and pastors and churches capitulated to Hitler's socialists and Lenin's communists?

---

[176] www.dundeecity.gov.uk/slessor/
[177] This and the next two from: www.newadvent.org/cathen/09066a.htm
[178] The Royal Society for the Prevention of Cruelty to Animals was started by William Wilberforce.
[179] Cod. Theod., lib. III, tit. 3, lex 1
[180] Cod. Theod., lib. IX, tit. 3, lex 1
[181] Alvin J Schmidt, How Christianity Changed the World (formerly called "Under their Influence") Zondervan, 2004 pg 142.
[182] Cod. Theod., lib. III, tit. 16, lex 1; Cod. Just., lib. V, tit. 17, leg. 8, 10, 11

Neil Mammen

For a list of all the places and ways Christians have used politics to change society see Alvin Schmidt's book, How Christianity Changed the World (formerly called "Under their Influence" Zondervan, 2004.)

So, just because you've seen some recent attempts to bring about a more moral society fail on occasion, that does not mean that it does not work. That view is myopic, ignorant and *not* based on historical facts. It is natural for us to try and try and try and fail many times. It took Wilberforce decades of multiple failures to stop slavery in England, and he was only successful because he decided to first attack it indirectly. He started by just passing a law that said that no British could trade with slave ships which were owned by France or America with whom they were at war. Since most slave ships were French or American, this bankrupted the slave traders and stopped money coming in to pro-slavery politicians. Eventually the slippery slope helped him win.

So, if someone tells you that Christian involvement in politics *never* works, ask them why it worked for William Wilberforce and why it worked to stop marriage by capture and the myriad of other such laws that we take for granted today? Then ask them why they think it worked to pass over 500 laws restricting abortion in the last few years, which reduced abortion by over 22%. And then finally ask them if they think all those laws should never have been made, because that's exactly what they're suggesting by saying that we should not be involved in politics today.

By the way if any atheist or secularist says, "Read your constitution, it says religion doesn't mix with politics" or something ridiculous like that. Just respond with "Ah, I guess that means that you wish all these things were still legal." Then read that list above and wrap up with "After all, all those *horrible* things became illegal because of those stupid religious Christians who forgot to stay out of politics. No, we'd never want *that* to happen."

OK, OK, you should probably say it less sarcastically and more kindly.

Our history of stopping infanticide

As the quote in this chapter's heading shows, even atheists like Bertrand Russell, recognized the value of Christian involvement in lawmaking and politics. Russell, unlike many today, realized that infanticide was common in many ancient cultures like Greece, Rome, India, Japan and China. Historian Rodney Stark says "Not only was the exposure of infants a very common practice, it was justified by law and advocated by philosophers."[183]

Even when Roman society turned Christian in 313AD with Constantine, it was *still* legal to kill any baby you didn't want especially if it was a baby girl. It took a full 61 years until 374AD, before a pastor, a preacher, a man of God named Bishop Basil of Caesarea was able to convince a politician, Emperor Valentinian to outlaw infanticide.

Don't tell me that Christian involvement in politics always fails.
Go tell Bishop Basil and his church!

---

[183] Rodney Stark, The Rise of Christianity, page 118, as quoted by Christopher Price in his article "Pagans, Christianity, and Infanticide" www.christiancadre.org/member_contrib/cp_infanticide.html

Eleven

I said that we live in a pluralistic society, that I can't impose my own religious views on another, that I was running to be the U.S. Senator of Illinois and not the Minister of Illinois.
Barack Obama's quote again, 2006[184]

*It's a sad day when a person who was elected President of the United States thinks that while he was a legislator **he** was **not** supposed to pass legislation based on his **own** conscience, but instead believes that **Supreme Court Judges should.***
From an earlier chapter

Our Founders had an opportunity to establish a democracy in America and chose not to. In fact, the Founders made clear that we were not, and were never to become, a democracy.
Dave Barton[185], www.wallbuilders.org

The United States Is A Republic, Not A Democracy

You may have heard people say this over and over again. In fact, the first time I heard it, I asked, "What on earth does that mean? How are they different?"

Let's see if we can quickly clarify this, because it holds a very important lesson about *who* needs to be making our laws, *how* they should make them, and *why* this is so critical to the Church and Christians who care about the innocent.

What's a republic? I'm glad you asked. A republic is a government that:

1. Bases its primary laws on a *fixed primary moral code*. This is unlike a democracy. (In a democracy there is no fixed moral code, the *majority* gets to decide what the law is to be and thus the law has no fixed basis).

2. In a republic, secondary or *day to day lesser* laws are determined by a group of responsible *representatives* who legislate according to their conscience. These new laws and the conscience of the representatives are expected to be in submission to *the* fixed *primary* moral code. The representatives are personally responsible for their decisions. (In a democracy there are no representatives. The *majority* decides to legalize or criminalize whatever they wish. All responsibility is shared by the group, which means no one is responsible).

---

[184] obama.senate.gov/speech/060628-call_to_renewal_keynote_address/index.html
[185] www.wallbuilders.com/LIBissuesArticles.asp?id=111

A Fixed Primary Moral Code

But you ask, *what* is the Fixed Primary Moral Code and were did we get it from? Great question, and important, we will deal with it in a later chapter.

The Bible's view of Governing

So first let's look at that second point; the representatives and the lesser laws. Right after the "Exodus" of the children of Israel from Egypt, Moses with God's laws in hand, finds himself really busy being the judge, lawgiver and chief executive for the emerging Jewish nation in the desert.

So Jethro, his father-in-law, suggests the following in Deuteronomy 1:9-17. I'll quote two key verses here:

Deut 1: 13 [Jethro said] Choose some men from each tribe who have wisdom, understanding, and a good reputation, and I will appoint them as your leaders.' ...15 So I [Moses] took the wise and respected men you had selected from your tribes and appointed them to serve as judges and officials over you. Some were responsible for a 1000 people, some for a 100, some for 50, and some for ten.

This biblical system was part of the model for the Republican form of government we have today. These men were appointed to officiate based on the Law given by God, a law also written on their hearts. Any derivative issues required them to legislate new laws based on their own conscience. Notice how this is *not* a democracy. In fact, as Dave Barton of Wallbuilders says so eloquently in the quote at the beginning of this chapter:

Our Founders had an opportunity to establish a democracy in America and chose not to.[186]

Dave goes on to quote many of our founders. I've included a few:

[D]emocracies have ever been spectacles of turbulence and contention; have ever been found incompatible with personal security, or the rights of property; and have, in general, been as short in their lives as they have been violent in their deaths.[187]

James Madison, "father" of the Constitution

Remember, democracy never lasts long. It soon wastes, exhausts, and murders itself. There never was a democracy yet that did not commit suicide.[188]

John Adams

[T]he experience of all former ages had shown that of all human governments,
democracy was the most unstable, fluctuating and short-lived.[189]

John Quincy Adams

---

[186] www.wallbuilders.com/LIBissuesArticles.asp?id=111

[187] Alexander Hamilton, John Jay, James Madison, The Federalist on the New Constitution (Philadelphia: Benjamin Warner, 1818), p. 53, #10, James Madison.

[188] John Adams, The Works of John Adams, Second President of the United States, Charles Francis Adams, editor (Boston: Charles C. Little and James Brown, 1850), Vol. VI, p. 484, to John Taylor on April 15, 1814.

[189] John Quincy Adams, The Jubilee of the Constitution. A Discourse Delivered at the Request of the New York Historical Society, in the City of New York on Tuesday, the 30th of April 1839; Being the Fiftieth Anniversary of the Inauguration of George Washington as President of the United States, on Thursday, the 30th of April, 1789 (New York: Samuel Colman, 1839), p. 53.

Pure democracy cannot subsist long nor be carried far into the departments of state, it is very subject to caprice and the madness of popular rage.[190]
John Witherspoon, Signer of the Declaration

But what's so bad about a democracy?

So, what is the difference and why were the founding fathers so vehemently against democracies? After all, democracies seem like a great idea – one man, one vote, every person gets a say, power to the people and so on.

Well, the problem is mob-rule. Remember the stories of mobs who would gather and in a frenzy, lynch innocent men for crimes committed by unknown persons? What happens in a pure democracy is that the masses start to legislate as mobs, creating laws based on the whims of the group. All it takes is one charismatic Hitler or one influential Robespierre (the evil French dude who sent probably 40,000 innocents to the guillotine during the French Revolution) to manipulate people and convince them to allow him to start executions. Or all it takes is 51% of the poor people to choose to kill 49% of the rich people and take all their goods.

Dave Barton of Wallbuilders says:[191]

*A pure democracy operates by direct majority vote of the people. When an issue is to be decided, the entire population votes on it; the majority wins and rules. A republic differs in that the general population elects representatives who then pass laws to govern the nation. ...A democracy is the rule by majority **feeling** (what the Founders described as a "mobocracy"); a republic is rule by law.*

The Golden Calf of Democracy

A great example of a democracy vs. a republic is the story of the Golden Calf. Moses goes up into the mountains to talk to God. While he is gone, the masses camped below get bored. So they convince Aaron, a man of weak convictions that they want to create a physical image of God. We all know what happens next. They create a calf of pure gold and start to party. Moses shows up, and puts an end to the partiers and then later God punishes them with a plague[192] (Exodus 32).

But, back to the story. Had Aaron been a man of strong convictions, he would have said, "I know that you want a physical representation of God in the form of a calf. But as your responsible leader, my *conviction* is that this is not only a very stupid idea; but a cow is also very bad and insulting representation of the living God. So as your representative, I refuse to allow you do that."

Instead, Aaron, being a man who took polls rather than stand on conviction, let the mob have what it wanted. Perhaps he wanted to be popular or "compassionate." In any event, because of his cowardice, the Israelites sinned and many people who were influenced by their leader and moved by the

---

[190] John Witherspoon, The Works of John Witherspoon (Edinburgh: J. Ogle, 1815), Vol. VII, p. 101, Lecture 12 on Civil Society.

[191] See Benjamin Rush, Letters, Vol. I, p. 498, to John Adams on January 22, 1789. As quoted by Dave Barton in http://www.wallbuilders.com/libissuesarticles.asp?id=111

[192] Earlier editions referred to an earthquake until a friend, Ed Garr, reminded me that that was the Hollywood version not the Biblical account.

emotions of the moment, suffered and died under God's justice.

Aaron's weakness destroyed the people.

Thus, the Bible shows us that leaders who go along with the masses are dangerous for all involved. Compare this to Joshua and Caleb, the two Israelite spies who, despite public opinion, stood by their convictions that they were supposed to go into Canaan.

As we all know, mobs and masses are dangerous since they are easily swayed by bad ideas, charismatic leaders, and smooth talkers. It's simply peer pressure. We all know how influential and damaging that can be. We know too the stupid things peer pressure can make people to do.

British statesman Edmund Burke said:

> [Your representative's] unbiased opinion, his mature judgment, his enlightened conscience, he ought not to sacrifice to you, to any man, or to any set of men living. These he does not derive from your pleasure; no, nor from the law and the constitution. They are a trust from Providence, for the abuse of which he is deeply answerable. **Your representative owes you, not his industry only, but his judgment; and he betrays, instead of serving you, if he sacrifices it to your opinion.**[193]

Let's do what the people want us to do?

When I first came to the U.S., I wondered why representatives and senators did not just poll people in their districts and then vote according to their wishes. That would make sense, I thought. It is what I would do.

But now that I think about that, knowing human nature, I realize it would be a terrible thing to do. Even if an elected representative, in the quiet of his rational thoughts, believed a certain "mob action" was evil, he would still go along with it. There's no difference between this and mob rule, is there?

No! Representatives must have their personal convictions and stand by them. They must know that at the end of the day they are responsible for their decisions. They must be able to look into a mirror and look themselves in the eye and say, "I made the right decision." The buck stops with the representative, and he or she should never say, "Well, the masses wanted that, so I gave it to them." That is what Aaron did. That's also, what Adam did.

Does it not follow, then, that we should vote for representatives based on what we know about their convictions and whether we agree with those views? Yes. And we should also vote for representatives who will stick to their guns – unlike some pro-life candidates like Al Gore who became pro-choice because their party wanted that. Was being pro-life their real conviction? Or were they pressured by the masses? Were they an Aaron representative or a Joshua representative? Joshua was looking at God's laws and promises and his own conscience, not popularity.

An electorate-polling leader is the worst thing we can have because it takes us back to mob rule. And in those scenarios who is responsible at the end of the day for bad decisions? Where does the buck stop?

So to review: A republic is a governmental system in which groups of citizens elect representatives, and these representatives make laws based on

---

[193] "Speech to the Electors of Bristol" in 1774
http://press-pubs.uchicago.edu/founders/documents/v1ch13s7.html

personal convictions and a fixed moral code. A democracy is a system in which the masses vote to do something. Democracies can become mob rule and thus are dangerous.

What kind of convictions do we want in our lawmakers?

What is the role of our representatives and the legislatures? It is to codify lesser secondary laws based on their what? *Their convictions*, which should be based on that *fixed primary moral code*. And this naturally leads to the question: What kind of men and women do we Christians and Jews want creating our laws for us? And which moral code should they be using? Do we want men and women of godly character and beliefs or men and women of ungodly convictions? As Christians do we want godly men and women creating the laws that our children will live under. Or do we want ungodly or godless men and women doing this? This is not meant as a slur against those who are not religious. It's just a frank question that pastors and Christians need to ask themselves. As Christians, what is our desire for *our* society?

It is also the question we should ask ourselves every election cycle. As Christians, whom do we want writing the laws this year? Whom do we want deciding what is legal and what is not? Which moral compass should they be basing the laws on? Whom do you want deciding whether your church can expand or park cars on the street? Whom do you want deciding if the age of sexual consent should be lowered to 13? It's being considered! Whom do you want deciding if same-sex marriage should be legal? Whom do you want deciding if spanking should be *illegal*? How about home schooling or holding a Bible Study in your home (outlawed in Arizona).[194] Whom do you want deciding if Planned Parenthood should be forced to reveal (to Social Services) the identity of underage girls who have become pregnant by an adult, so that law enforcement officials can protect the girls and capture the habitual molesters, who made them pregnant?

I would say this is just as important an issue for you whether you are a layperson or a pastor or priest, though I believe pastors need to be more concerned than others about the welfare of their flock. We will talk more about the source of that primary moral code soon. But for now, don't you agree that our representatives need to be strong, principled men and women of moral convictions, unswayable by the feelings and emotions of the masses? As Martin Luther King said:

> Most people...are thermometers that record or register the temperature of majority of opinion, not thermostats that transform or regulate the temperature of society.[195]

Then what about calling our representatives?

Why then, some may wonder, do we waste time calling our representatives and sending them letters? I would idealistically say the purpose of those letters should be to explain to the representatives *how* they should come to the correct moral conviction. To reveal to them new information or correct their illogical thinking *and* if they *claim* to be Christian like Obama,

---

[194] theundergroundsite.com/index.php/2010/03/at-home-bible-studies-outlawed-in-arizona-city-11205
[195] Martin Luther King Jr. Strength to Love. http://books.google.com/books?id=errxX4tzSMcC

Neil Mammen

show them that they have a duty to base their moral convictions and thus laws on the Bible – not to pressure them to vote the way we want them to just because we want them to side with the masses. The other reason we contact them is to let them know that there are people watching what they do, holding them accountable, and encouraging them to do what is morally right, not what is only politically expedient. This is even more critical if a politician has *no* core beliefs and is thus easily manipulated by money or the promise of power and status. Of course, once we realize this we need to work diligently to get them out of office.

This means that Christians and Pastors need to do more than vote.

Why this history and civics lesson? There is a *very* important lesson here. Many Christians fallaciously think that it is enough to vote, and that ends their civic duty. But as we've seen in our republican form of government, when we vote, we are *not* voting in laws.[196] We are voting in men and women, who will, in turn, *write* our laws.

You see the problem, don't you? This means that the men and women that we elect had better have godly consciences and a godly or Christian Worldview so we can have godly moral laws. Laws that are going to protect us and more importantly, protect those who are *unable* to protect themselves. But our lawmakers won't have godly consciences and convictions unless they are godly people. And it won't be godly people making those decisions unless godly people run for office.

What does this mean? It means Christians had better be running for office.[197]

Samuel Adams said,

"Neither the wisest constitution nor the wisest laws will secure the liberty and happiness of a people whose manners are universally corrupt. He therefore is the truest friend to the liberty of his country who tries most to promote its virtue, and who...will not suffer a man to be chosen into any office of power and trust who is not a wise and virtuous man."
    The Life of Samuel Adams, 1:22.

Does this make sense? Let me reiterate. Samuel Adams and many of the founding fathers believed that a republican form of government *requires* godly men and women as representatives because in a republic we don't vote for laws, we vote for representatives who *make* the laws for us. So, Christians

---

[196] Being a resident of California, I realize that we actually do get to vote for laws directly, but this "propositional" system arose because the will of the people was being stifled in Congress by political games. Perfectly viable bills proposed by the minority party, which may have passed, were never given a chance to be voted on by our representatives. Instead, they were being stifled by a few individuals. In other cases, our legislators were too afraid to have their votes tallied for or against controversial issues, so they punted to the people rather than take a stance and alienate part of their constituency. The propositional system was an attempt to fix a legislative methodology problem.

[197] Note that this requirement is not one that we have for judges since they just need to interpret the laws and their personal beliefs (except for one) should not enter the equation. The one belief that should enter the equation is that they must *not* create law. Of course Christians may argue that Christian judges may uphold this tradition more astutely than non-Christians, but this is not a given, and it is a tougher argument as we all know people of questionable character who claim to be Christians or are young in their faith. And we know many non-Christians who are of good character. Meanwhile, non-Christians could argue that Christian judges may be just as prone to impose a theocracy upon us.

need to do more than vote. They must run for office and *become* the *ones* making the laws.[198]

A republican form of government that affects Christians (and God-fearing Jews) *requires* Christian and God-fearing men and women to *be* the lawmakers. There is no way out.

And if you can't be the lawmaker, then you need to help make these kinds of men and women the lawmakers, by working actively to get them elected to office.

So your choices are:

- Run for office; remember I'm also talking about things like school boards.
- Help someone *else* run for office through funding or by direct involvement or by providing them the needed exposure and publicity. You can open your home to local school board candidates and politicians, inviting your friends over to meet them.
- Teach the law and the reasons behind it. Guide other people in how to vote morally and biblically. Glean the statistical research from groups like FRC (www.FRC.org) and pass it along to your friends and family.
- Be involved in guiding politicians who are in office.
- Vote; this is the minimum and, as we've shown, it is certainly not enough.

Pastors

So pastors, priests, elders and deacons, are we taking the lead here? Are we encouraging Christians to run for office? Why not specifically encourage your members to be on a local school board? They don't even need to have kids. Do you have any singles in your church that may have some time? How about empty nesters? Identify them and ask them privately. Remember, most school board members are decided by a difference of a few hundred votes. With just the support of your congregation, they might easily be elected. All you would need to do is for the few weeks before the election invite each person who is running to give a 5-minute talk to your congregation, followed by some direct questions from you about their faith in Jesus Christ.[199] Do one a week. This would allow *all* candidates to be heard and would give your church member who is running the exposure within your church. You could team up with local churches to do the same thing. Call up some of your neighborhood pastors and pass along the names of those whom you trust and the offices they are running for. See an upcoming chapter for what you can and can't do in order to preserve your non-profit status. School board positions are

---

[198] This reminds me of a conversation I had with a friend while Bill Clinton was in office. There was a lot of talk going around that Clinton was not a man of character because he cheated on his wife and had had some shady dealings in the past. The friend of mine (not to be named to save him the embarrassment) actually said this to me about Bill Clinton, "Why does his character count? We didn't vote for him to do anything but manage the country."

Now to be fair to my friend, the entire liberal media was saying this same stupid thing. "Why do we need to worry about the character of the president? He just needs to be a good manager or executive." My friend, influenced by the media, was merely spouting what he'd been brainwashed with.

But that's the whole point as we saw a few years later with Clinton; character counts in every single thing, as any Boy Scout will tell you. Remember Samuel Adam's quote too about virtuous men?

[199] I like: Do you believe that Jesus is the only way to salvation? Or for Jews: Do you believe the Bible is the Divine Law of God and plainly understood? It quickly clarifies to your Christian or Jewish congregation who is or isn't God fearing and what the source of their moral values are.

Neil Mammen

strategic for Christians who want to be positive influences in their communities.

Why not encourage members of your singles group to run for city council or even Water District. Small roles lead to big roles.

Barack Obama

In the last chapter, we quoted Barack Obama in regards to moral laws. Let's look at that quote again.

I said that we live in a pluralistic society, that I can't impose my own religious views on another, that I was running to be the U.S. Senator of Illinois and not the Minister of Illinois.

Barack Obama, 2006[200]

Now I hope you can see the bankruptcy of this statement. In the original context, Obama was discussing moral issues like abortion and same-sex marriage. Recall, he was referring to a debate with Ambassador Alan Keyes. Keyes had said that Jesus would not vote for Obama because Obama sanctioned killing babies who had been born *alive* after a failed abortion. Look up the article in the footnote by Jill Stanek if you want to see how sick this action is. It will break your heart.[201] There's *no* debate here that these *are* babies even by pro-choicers. Yet, Obama was implying that he was personally against murdering these babies, but would *not* vote his moral conscience because his electorate did not share his values. He went on to explain that until he could show a non-biblical reason to stop killing these babies, it was not his place to do so.

Now as I mentioned before, I believe I can easily show a non-biblical reason to stop *abortion*, even more so to stop killing *delivered* babies. So that is pure ignorance or disingenuousness on his part, and second as we mentioned, it's only because *someone* imposed *their* religious values on Americans, that he Barack, an African American was even able to run for senator and president.

There's a third mistake he was making, Barack is mistaking the United States of America for a "Direct Democracy" like Switzerland.[202] He's in the wrong country. This also shows the moral and logical bankruptcy of any senator or representative or executive who claims to hate abortion but votes pro-choice because he doesn't want to impose his moral values on others.[203]

---

[200] This quote is taken directly form Obama's website: Last visited March, 23rd, 2007 obama.senate.gov/speech/060628-call_to_renewal_keynote_address/index.html

[201] Why Jesus would not vote for Barack Obama, Jill Stanek www.wnd.com/news/article.asp?ARTICLE_ID=51121

[202] Actually, Switzerland adopted a "double majority" process in the late 1800's to copy the U.S. Even they decided that too much "direct democracy" was dangerous.

[203] The other question we need to ask people who make this ridiculous statement is: Why do you think abortion is bad? Is it because it's killing a human being? Because if it's not about killing a human but about removing a lump of flesh why are you saying it's bad? Let me get this straight. You either really think abortion is killing a human being but you won't stop it because you think that people should be…what? Able to kill other humans? Or you think it's not human and you feel that removing a lump of flesh is terrible? Either you are a Nazi or you are an idiot or you are lying.

Okay, you may need to say it nicely.

This great argument (the nice version of it, of course) was first presented by Scott Klusendorf of the Life Training Institutewww.prolifetraining.com.

What Obama was really implying here is that while he was in the Illinois legislature he would not be the kind of representative who would vote his moral convictions but will rather vote the will of the masses. He would not be a Joshua type of representative but an Aaron type of representative and give us a Golden Calf if we ask for it, *even* if he thinks it's a bad idea. That would be disastrous. As we saw, the founding fathers specifically warned us about having mob rule, which is why they formed a republic and not a democracy. This further indicates that Obama does not have a deep knowledge of the constitution or of the writings of the founding fathers, nor of the basis of our representative government. I find this interesting since he is supposed to have been a professor of "Constitutional Law."

The dangers inherent in ignorance

What is scary is if you take Obama's logic to its natural conclusion, a Christian in Hitler's government could then have justified voting for the extermination of the Jews. Because, while his *own* personal and religious convictions which were based on the Bible said the Jews were human; German society's values at that time (and in fact its Supreme Court in 1936[204]) said the Jews were *not* human. Thus, using this logic, he would not be responsible for that. When asked why he didn't vote *against* exterminating the Jews. He could *also* merely say, "I said that we live in a pluralistic society, that I can't impose my own religious views on another, that I was running to be the *Legislator of Berlin and not the Priest of Berlin.*[205]

Don't get turned off by the Nazi reference; as the then Speaker of the House, Nancy Pelosi justified using Nazi and Holocaust references to refer to Tea Party members in their battle against Universal Health Care.

But we don't have to go to the extreme. Obama was saying that despite the fact that *he* thought a baby born alive should be left alive, his electorate wanted *him* to let *them* kill the baby, so he was going to let them.[206] Is this anymore acceptable to you? Can you say lynch mob? The sheriff says to the mob, "Oh, you want to lynch him? Sure!" Do we even need to bring up Hitler? And the excuse that he needed a non-religious reason to stop the murder of already born babies is so bereft of reason and compassion that one doesn't know where to begin. Look, even an atheist, with no religion could determine that we should not kill a baby if it was born alive in a botched abortion. Why can't Obama?

Obviously we see a very large disconnect and perhaps a breakdown in logic when applied to real life. If a man or woman will *not* vote according to their deeply held faith convictions, then what sort of a person is that? What is the character of that person that against all odds will not stand up for what they

---

[204] "The Reichsgericht itself refused to recognize Jews as persons in the legal sense," German Supreme Court 1936.

[205] Then of course there is that extremely hilarious case where someone says: There should be a law against legislating morality. You should immediately ask: Why? If they say it's because "it's wrong," ask them if that's their morality. Note too that I'm not comparing Obama to a Nazi; I'm comparing him to a non-Nazi surrounded by Nazis who weekly *capitulates* to the Nazis.

[206] Jill Stanek, Why Jesus would not vote for Barack Obama, wnd.com/news/article.asp?article_id=51121

Neil Mammen

believe? What is the meter of a man or woman who will not stand up for injustice in the face of opposition or unpopularity? In fact, when that happens, we can justly argue that they don't believe what they claim they believe. They are lying. It is at this point that one can validly question the faith claims of leaders. It is very dangerous to have any legislators who are ignorant of these critical American foundational premises.

Sadly, while I have picked on this particular individual (it was not my intent to pick on a sitting president, but in my defense he was elected as president almost two years after I wrote much of these chapters), our Senate and House are rife with representatives ignorant of our constitution. It is a sad day when an foreign born immigrant and full time FPGA,[207] System Architect and printed circuit board design engineer like me seems to have a better handle on parts of my adopted country's constitution than they do. If America is going to fall, ignorance of our own constitution, by our own representatives and our own presidents will play a large part in its disassembling.

The Theocracy

Some think Christians want a theocracy. To tell the truth, a theocracy is just as bad if not worse than a dictatorship. There are many reasons for this. The first and most familiar is captured simply and briefly in the famous Monty Python statement, "No one expects the Spanish Inquisition."

What I mean is that, a theocracy can result in an Inquisition-type event, which would be *very* bad for everyone. Many non-Christians don't realize this, but the last government any Christian, especially a Protestant evangelical, wants is a theocracy. Remember we are the "protestors," the rebels. There are umpteen different protestant denominations. We don't want to be controlled. This would be like being forced to believe in and follow laws ordained by people who insist on their own interpretation of the Scriptures. It would be like being forced to go to one church even if you disagreed with it. A theocracy would be like Catholics being in England after the creation of the Church of England during Henry VIII's time or Protestants being under the Inquisition. It is a little known fact that first the Inquisition was run by the government, not the church, and secondly, through much of the Inquisition period, it was not unbelievers who were being persecuted but people whose beliefs were slightly different from those of the government. After all, unbelievers could merely pretend to acquiesce to the government's beliefs. They don't believe anything anyway, so who cares if they lie about it? But the true Christ followers couldn't do that because their belief system says if they denounce Christ, they will go to hell. So we can see that theocracies are worse for believers than non-believers. A Christian theocracy would be no different than the Taliban or living under Muslim Sharia law in Iran.

Finally, it was because of theocracies that the pilgrims came to America. They wanted to be free of theocracies and state ordained religions. So, it's not a great way to live, and it's not great form of government, and

---

[207] That's FPGA for Field Programmable Gate Array. It's a chip that can be programmed to do multiple things. If you need consultants to design your FPGAs or PCBs or systems for your company please go over to www.TentmakerSystems.com

Christians do not want anything to do with one while on earth.

In closing

So in summary: We elect politicians to establish laws according to their convictions and a moral standard. That is their function. This is a crucial concept to keep fresh in your mind whenever you think about politics.

In closing, don't ask yourself "Is this a messy business?" Of course, it is messy. Humans with a sin nature are involved.

Don't ask "Is it corrupt?" Again, of course, there are going to be corrupt politicians. Are there corrupt police officers? Yes. Is this a reason to say Christians should *not* be police officers? No. Of course, they should. Are there corrupt pastors or priests? You get the point.

So when someone says, "Christians should stay out of politics because politicians are corrupt and always have to compromise," you should respond. "You are right, so are pastors, many of them have to compromise what they really believe and have to they soften it in the pulpit, and many of them are corrupt, so no Christian should be a pastor and we should stay out of churches." Of course, in places like Canada and Sweden, all pastors are forced to compromise and not speak out on the dangers of homosexual behavior. Which is what will happen here, if we *don't* get involved *now*.

Again, don't ask yourself "Is it worldly?" Of course it is. Politicians are going to be dealing with worldly people every day – just as you do at your job, by the way.

Instead, ask yourself this: As a Bible believing Christian or Jewish father or mother, what kind of person do I want making the laws that will affect my culture and my children? What kind of person should be governing? What kind of moral values do I want made into law? Since laws are based on people's convictions, ask yourself, "What kind of convictions do I want our laws to be based on, godly or worldly? The need for godly men and women to be making the laws and rules is clear – just as clear as the need for strict constructionists to be in judge positions. If we Christians are not directly and intimately involved in politics, how will this happen?

Pastors, are we to instruct our flock about this? If we care about the poor, those who cannot defend themselves and children, can we abdicate caring about who is going to make the laws that will affect those *very* people?

A reminder

Yet, after all this discussion, if we think our country is great, just because it is a republic we'd be missing something. After all, both Rome and Nazi Germany were *also* republics. There's obviously something else very important that we need to understand. We'll deal with that, shortly.

Twelve

All laws have moral foundations, and all morals have religious foundations. Politicians are in the business of making laws. Thus, all politics is religious in nature. A politician's religious views are just as critical as his economic views. A politician who does not understand this will not be a good lawmaker, and you should never vote for him.

Objective Morality & Politics,
No Blind Faith Sunday School Class

Train a child in the way he should go, and when he is old he will not turn from it.

Proverbs 22:6

I've never known a man worth his salt who in the long run, deep down in his heart, didn't appreciate the grind, the discipline. There is something good in men that really yearns for discipline.

Vince Lombardi

But Laws Don't Change Hearts

How many times have you heard it said, "Ah, but laws don't change hearts!"

The idea here is that we should *not* focus on changing the laws of the land because that doesn't work; instead, we should just witness to people, and *Christ* will change their hearts. We just need to preach the Gospel. Then over time we'll see social change and social justice. When people say this, I ask them if this is an idea that they came up with on their own after much research or if they are blindly repeating what they heard someone else say.

Note that we are not talking about changing your heart to accept Christ, only the Holy Spirit can do that. We are talking about if laws can influence your views and change your beliefs and thus bring about behavioral and social change?

So let's look at this carefully. Is it true that laws don't change hearts?

As you know, I am from India, yet for many years I kept refusing to do the Indian thing, which is, have my parents arrange a marriage for me with a rich beautiful lady doctor from India. My roommates would look at all the pictures my mom sent of these pretty, young and rich doctors or scientists and tell me that I was an idiot. Yet, I could never bring myself to allow them to arrange a marriage for me. I wanted to fall in love first.[208]

---

[208] Note that I am not in any way saying that arranged marriages are a bad idea. My sister had an arranged marriage and couldn't be happier. She and her husband are now completely in love and they both and we all feel that they are perfect for each other.

Then one day I met a very young, very gorgeous redhead. Yes she is all of that – very young, very gorgeous and a redhead. I knew she was young because after a few dates I asked her, "Where have you been all my life?"

"In grade school," she answered.

But here's the point, lest you think I've lost my train of thought, distracted by the vision of my lovely wife. Her maternal grandfather, though a very godly man with a loving heart and a deep and powerful faith would probably have had a hard time accepting me, a person from another culture, into the family. (Of course, if you think this is bad, you should see the attitude of many Indian Christians when *their* kids want to marry Americans. The racism can be even more extreme on *my* ethnic side. At times Indian kids have been disowned over this. Fortunately, my parents did not feel this way).

You see, years ago cultural and ethnic separation and indeed racism were the norm here in the United States. Young kids were born into a system of laws and regulations that encouraged separation. They grew to believe that racism or separation was acceptable or at the minimum, a necessary evil.

But then the Civil Rights Movement gained momentum, borne by the people who suffered and groaned under its ungodly weight and by Christians who cared about justice and got involved politically (again don't tell me that Christian involvement in politics never works). Finally, the legislature was convicted or replaced, and laws were changed.

As a result, almost all kids grow up today observing and believing in the new law and value – that it is wrong, immoral and wicked to discriminate. In fact, this law of the land is so prevalent that even in families in which the parents are ethnocentric or racist, the kids frequently grew up rightfully believing racism is wrong. So, when my wife's parents met me, they accepted me without hesitation, even though I am not white. Why? Because they had grown up under the new Civil Rights laws.

The law is a teacher

Consider what Scott Klusendorf,[209] a fascinating and globally recognized speaker on ethics, says (www.prolifetraining.com):

> *The purpose of the law is not to change hearts (though it often does just that), but to restrain evil acts by heartless individuals... As MLK Jr said, "the law cannot make the white man love me, but it can sure stop him from lynching me." Furthermore, it's simply false to say that laws cannot change public behavior or public opinion. **As history shows, the law is a moral teacher that can help change hearts.** Prior to the 1964 Civil Rights Act, popular opinion in the southern states overwhelmingly opposed desegregation and anti-discrimination efforts. Within five years of passage, however, public opinion had shifted dramatically, with better than sixty percent favoring the new laws. Again, the law served as a moral teacher that helped model public opinion.*
>
> **Scott Klusendorf, Taking Abortion Seriously, 2000.**

Britney Spears

We recently had an excellent example of this in action. Britney Spears, the troubled pop singer, was on the front page of every magazine and

---

[209] Scott is also an excellent teacher with an easy to understand message. Invite him to train you and your youth. www.prolifetraining.com

newspaper. Her crime? Holding her child in her lap while driving. Oh, you should have heard the talk about how horrible it was for her to do that. What a heartless evil mother she was. Bloggers wanted Social Services to take her children away from her. People I know personally were commenting in this way on the incident. Yet, if you stop and think about it, less than 15 years ago everyone carried their babies in their laps while driving. Car seats were available everywhere, but there wasn't a car seat law back then. How else was a mom supposed to go to the store? Nobody would have cared if Britney had done this back then. In fact, they might have admired her for wanting to spend extra time with her child despite being a busy rock star.

So here's a law that once it was in the books not only changed our children's hearts but *also* changed many adults hearts. And it did so in less than 15 years. Now that previously moral act was "evil."[210] People's moral attitudes had changed. Society had changed. Behaviors had changed.

My point is that laws *do* change hearts. And while in some cases it may not change *your* heart, it sure will change the hearts of your children and their children. You see the law may not change the hearts of the ones under whom it was first legislated, but it will certainly change the hearts of the ones that grew up knowing *only* it.

Abortion Laws have changed hearts and society

But what's even more relevant is that laws not only change hearts, but they change societies. Take even the law on abortion. In 1973 when abortion was legalized a majority of the country was against it. It was forced on the public by the Supreme Court. In fact two years before Roe V. Wade passed, 33 states debated abortion and voted against it. Once Roe V. Wade passed, it forced all states to legalize abortion. What is more tragic is we see the consequence of the slippery slope. Roe V. Wade only forced legalized abortion in the first trimester; states could limit abortions anytime after that. Yet, within a few years, the law had changed the heart of the people and most states legalized abortion, such that today it is legal to kill a baby till the moment before the baby's head leaves the birth canal.

Divorce Laws have changed hearts and society

Let's look at divorce. The following chart[211] shows the number of divorces over the years. Guess when the "No Fault Divorce" became law?

---

[210] You can't argue that "now" we know that car seats save lives. We knew that for years before the law was passed, while it was being debated, and nobody thought it was "evil" or worthy of taking someone's child away if they didn't use a car seat before the law. Nor did they for the first few years *after* the law.

[211] http://www.cdc.gov/nchs/data/mvsr/supp/mv43_09s.pdf

Divorce rates

Source: Monthly Vital Statistics Reports

If the number of divorces went up only because there were a large number of couples that wanted to get a divorce but couldn't before the law changed, then the rate of divorces would have gone back down after an initial peak. But the fact that the rate stayed high indicates that it has nothing to do with pent up demand. The law changed how people felt about divorce. It used to be a shameful thing; it used to be something we didn't speak about. Yet, look at how you yourself view it now. Many people view it as unfortunate, but socially acceptable. The law had changed their heart. We'll come back to this chart later.

Colleges and Universities think that Laws change Societies

Lawyers, academia, and many liberal organizations think laws can change hearts and thus entire societies. Do a web search for "law and social change" and you will find a few hundred thousand listings, ranging from activist papers to legal briefings. There are universities like the Harvard Law School[212] that will give you an entire Law degree (J.D.) in this specialization. There's even a journal put out by the University of Pennsylvania Law School, called "The Journal of Law and Social Change."[213] Colleges and universities seem to think that laws change hearts and effect social change and is worthy of a degree. They believe it's a valuable skill to teach. As you can imagine most of these are ultraliberal. So why don't Christians believe that laws change hearts? Why don't pastors? What statistical or analytical studies have you done to prove that laws don't change hearts and thus societies?

Of course, we all know that changing the law is not a full proof method, but it is certainly a very effective method. Harvard Law School thinks so.

Now, we should note that sometimes what really happens is that the Law, rather than changing your *heart*, changes your *behavior* and the behavior of those around you, and *that* is what eventually changes your heart.[214]

---

[212] www.law.harvard.edu/academics/degrees/jd/pos/lawsocchange/index.html

[213] www.law.upenn.edu/journals/jlasc/

[214] Thanks to Frank Nemec for noting this.

But the law won't make you accept God

Yes indeed, we know, of course, that the law will not change a heart to repentance. Only the Holy Spirit can do that. Our objective with laws is not to lead people to Christ, but surely we have other responsibilities as citizens of this country. How about the responsibility to help create a safe and healthy society? How about the responsibility to reduce oppression and suffering? How about the responsibility to kids, to try and ensure they have a healthy family? How about true social justice? If we care about those things we will care about the law.

Laws *will* move hearts in the direction of good actions and good habits. Why do we think that regular discipline in our lives is healthy even if we chafe against it? The Bible says:

Ps 119:97 *Oh, how I love your law! I meditate on it all day long.*

Does this mean the psalm writer loved the law first and then meditated on it? I believe it is more of a symbiotic relationship. We are attracted to His law, and the more we meditate on it, the more we realize its value and the more we learn to love it. And the more we love it, the more we obey it.

Boys will be boys

Now let's think closer to home. Why do you have laws in your home? Why do you teach your child rules? "No Billy, you are not to hit little Timmy over the head with the Thomas the Tank Engine. That is wrong, immoral, wicked, not nice, bad, evil, unjust, and naughty."

Are you hoping to terrorize your children into obeying only when you are around to catch them? Or are you hoping that the rules you teach them today will change their hearts and cause them to embrace those guidelines and internalize them? Don't we see this happen with our kids as they get older? Take brushing teeth for example. As a child I saw it as a big pain and avoided it at all costs. Yet today I have trouble sleeping unless I've brushed my teeth. Kids grow up and start to love being clean. They start to desire the safety of discipline. They begin to love getting things done. The laws, the rules, the regulations, the discipline changes them. Remember Lombardi's quote about discipline at the beginning of this chapter?

How about Proverbs 22:6?

Proverbs 22:6 *Train a child in the way he should go, and when he is old he will not turn from it.*

How would we train a child? By teaching him the moral law. And what will that do to a child when he grows up? Well, he won't turn from it. What is it talking about? It's talking about the law having a lifelong influence on a child. The Bible it seems thinks laws will change the heart of your child.

Do laws and rules and discipline change hearts? Of course!

Remember that 1961 Martin Luther King letter: [215]

The fact is that the habits, if not the hearts of men have been, and are being changed everyday by federal action.

---

[215] Martin Luther King, Statement Delivered at a Rally to Support the Freedom Rides, 21 May 1961, Montgomery, Alabama. also quoted from
www.stanford.edu/group/King/publications/speeches/unpub/610521-
000_Statement_Delivered_at_a_Rally_to_Support_the_Freedom_ Rides.html last visited 5/4/07

And we know that as the habits change, the heart will change.

Caution: It works both ways

But here's the tragedy. Just as a good law changes the hearts of kids who grow up under it to good, a bad law can change the hearts of the generations of children in elementary school today towards *immorality*.

Today the good laws say same-sex marriage is illegal and immoral. If the law of the land changes, our own children, despite what we tell them that God says and despite the physical and statistical evidence, will reject the moral laws of God and have their hearts changed by the immoral laws of the land. They will come to believe in, embrace and celebrate same-sex marriage and as some of the statistics indicate, to assume that the institution of marriage is meaningless.

They will ignore the fact that the law given by God was given for our safety and health. So we must ask: Are we going to sit by and let an immoral concept become the law of our land? Are we going to let our children be brainwashed by bad laws? Or are we going to draw the line in the sand and say, "Enough! I will exercise my right as an American!" The decision you make today will impact your children, your neighbor's children, and your children's children.

Does the law save you?'

Again, it is vital that you understand that we are *not* talking about laws directly changing hearts to accept Christ or be saved. But as we have seen, laws will incline hearts toward moral values. As I will shortly prove, all laws were given by God because they are good for us. A nation that adheres to God's laws will have a better physical well being because God's laws set forth the best ways to live our lives. Recall if you will that it's like someone who buys a car and adheres to the manufacturer's manual about how to keep the car running well. Disregard the manual, and the car breaks down; follow it, and the car runs smoothly. In fact, even if you despise and hate the manufacturer of the car but *still* adhere to instructions, your car will run better than if you blindly violated the instructions.[216]

Our laws can have some effect on salvation though!

But I want to go a step further. While I just noted that laws won't change a heart to Christ, what I did *not* say is that this same law couldn't *prevent* someone from hearing about Christ. Earlier in this book we discussed what happens when God judges a nation. At that time I said I will make the case that our grandchildren may suffer not only the *physical* consequences but also the spiritual consequences of a nation abandoning God's laws. Let me explain.

If we allow the laws to change in such a way that they turn people's hearts away from godly values, we will end up losing the right to preach the gospel. Do not think this is alarmist or an unlikely prophecy? It is already

---

[216] In fact, and this is a very important point, even if people say the manufacturer does not exist yet adhere to the instructions, the car will run better than if they didn't. Apply this truth to our culture and our country.

happening with hate speech laws and restrictions on Focus on the Family transmissions in Canada. They have to edit out any disapproval of homosexuality on air, or their affiliates will be fined or have their licenses revoked. Remember the men who were arrested for handing out Gideon's Bibles in the United States? Even preaching the Gospel is being suppressed in what used to be the "Free" United States. As I often say, if the culture changes and they start to "come" for us, they will start with you *pastors* first. Do not be fooled into thinking this will never happen. They thought it would never happen in the land of the Protestant Reformation either (Germany). Do not be arrogant. If we lose the right to preach the gospel in the United States, do you not think that this will have spiritual consequences on millions of kids who will be prevented from hearing the Good News? Do you not think that it will have spiritual consequences on the billions of people in the rest of the world? People who currently have American Christians and churches funding their outreaches and compassion ministries? When churches cease funding, the only religious funding will be Muslim fundamentalist funding. Sure, the Word of God will still go forward, but do we seriously want to be part of the generation that killed one of the primary sources of missionary and humanitarian outreach – the American people? We will talk about how enormously large this amount is shortly.

In other words, yes, laws may not be able to change your heart towards God; but bad American laws may have the effect of damning billions around the world by restricting the proclamation of the gospel and restricting compassionate outreaches to the oppressed and poor. This, as I will show, is funded in large part by Christians in America. Is this not a concern for every pastor or elder?[217] Should this not appeal to the heart of every Christian, man, woman and child? Can we say, "We care about true social justice," and then ignore this?

Forcing our values on our kids

My wife is a public school teacher. I was talking to one of her fellow teachers one day, and the teacher said this, "Well, we decided that we didn't want to force our morals onto our sons. We wanted them to develop their own moral values."

At this, I responded dryly. "Oh well, either from you or MTV, right?"

Her jaw dropped as the implications of what she and her husband were doing dawned on her. "Oh my!" she said.

But wait. What is the difference between what she said, and what most of us say? "We don't want to impose our laws and values on others by getting involved in politics." To that I say, "Oh, okay, I guess the U.S. will just have to get its morals, values and laws from Bible despising lawmakers, Hollywood, and TV." Wait, isn't that exactly what is happening today?

Pastors

For years, we Christians fought against abortion and same-sex marriage until we were blue in the face, but it was forced upon us by a few

---

[217] Note that you cannot claim that we should not worry about this and leave it up to God in His sovereignty. Because that logic would lead to not needing to ever witness either.

lawyers and the courts; by a minority. Why do you think they did that? The minority forced this on us because they realized that laws change hearts, culture *and* society. Meanwhile many Christians and pastors blindly repeat the mantra "laws don't change hearts" while we live and suffer the reality of it changing hearts on a daily basis in the *wrong* direction.

Pastors, are you weary from the battle, watching the culture degrade around you despite the 100 hours a week that you put into it?

We cannot stop preaching the Gospel message, but if our moral values determine our laws and our laws determine the heart of our nation, if the soul of our nation determines its course in history, then who better to be directing that course than you pastors? Who better to be codifying laws that determine the heart of our nation than those who *know* the laws of God? Why are pastors not on the forefront of this battle? Elders in every church should be thinking, "What we decide to focus on this year will affect not only the people in our congregation but the people down the street, the child in the other state, and truly the lost soul in that other country. What we focus on this year will affect if we can *even* preach the Gospel. We should therefore focus on the laws of the land and the people who make those laws."

Yes, but you are really busy, and most pastors, I know, are booked solid. But shouldn't we be focusing on the future as well as the present? Can we mortgage the future to gain some momentary relief for the present? Shouldn't this be made a priority?

Why do you think so many pastors and preachers saw fit to be involved in politics when our country was first founded? Why and when did we let worldly people tell us we should back off and leave the lawmaking to them?

Is this not the heart of God concerning this?
Jesus was involved in politics on a daily basis, why aren't you?
Why isn't your church?

Neil Mammen

Thirteen

One thing I hate about those d*** right-wingers is that they want to force their moral values on others.
Engineer griping to me after the Republican Senate tried to pass a ban on partial birth abortions.

We know that the law is good if one uses it properly. We also know that law is made not for the righteous but [it is made] for lawbreakers and rebels, the ungodly and sinful, the unholy and irreligious; for those who kill their fathers or mothers, for murderers, for adulterers and [sexual] perverts, for slave traders and liars and perjurers—and for whatever else is contrary to the sound doctrine that conforms to the glorious gospel of the blessed God...
1 Timothy 1:8-11

It's Wrong To Force Your Moral Values On Others! Suicide Statements!

I am an electrical and computer engineer, I design printed circuit boards, integrated circuits and FPGAs. I consult at various companies. I wear a badge (okay, okay it just lets me into the building). One day I was working in the laboratory of a well-known international semiconductor company in Silicon Valley. I was working on a high-speed video printed circuit board that I had designed and built for them. In the course of our development of this board, I found that I needed to solder a few wires to give us some additional low speed test points. So I was doing that. Next to me, at another bench was one of the company's engineers – normally a sour, angry chap. Most of the other engineers gave him a wide berth, but he and I seemed to have hit it off. We had some rapport at least.

Partial birth abortions were in the paper that day. The Republicans had passed a ban on it. Of course, the liberal San Jose Mercury News called them "late term abortions." Looking momentarily at the write-up, this workmate of mine said, "One thing I hate about those d*** right-wingers is that they want to force their moral values on everyone else."

I turned to him and asked, "Are you saying that it's wrong to force your moral values on others?"

He said, "Yes."

How should I have responded to this? Is it true? Is it really wrong to try to force your moral perspective on other people?

Suicide Statements

Before I address this objection, let me first tell you about a subject I love teaching about. It's something that Gregory Koukl of Stand to Reason Ministries (www.STR.org) calls a Suicide Statement.[218]

"What is a suicide statement?" you ask.

Well, it is an assertion that kills itself. That is, it is *self*-refuting. For instance, if I say, "I can't speak a word of English" and I say that in English, it is a suicide statement because as I utter it I refute it. The two most famous[219] suicide statements are "Never say never" and Uriah Heep's "I am well aware that I am the 'umblest person going."[220] The latter really meaning, "Hey there, look at me! What do you see? None other than the world's humblest person."

Forcing Morals?

Okay, why go through all of this? Well obviously it's because the first objection my engineer friend came forth with, was a suicide statement. Did you catch it? Let's look at it again:

"It's wrong to impose your morals on others."

If someone ever says this to you, you should immediately ask him or her, "Why not?"

To which they will say something to the effect of, "Because it's not right?"

Then you simply say, "But wait, isn't that *your* moral value? Why are you imposing *that* moral value on *me*?"[221]

You see, whenever someone tells you that it is *wrong* to do something, what they've just stated *is* a moral declaration. The person who says, "You shouldn't force your moral values on others" is doing exactly what he or she is saying you should *not* do.

I pointed this out to my engineering friend. There was a look of consternation on his face – not because he didn't understand what I said. He understood fully. It was the consequences of this realization that threw him for a loop. He turned to me and said, "Oh…" There was a long pause. Then he asked, "So what, then, is the answer?"

I was happy to respond, (imagine that). "You see, of course it's all right to impose moral values on other people – if they truly *are* moral values. In fact, you can't fail to impose moral values on others. All laws are *someone's* moral values. The issue is, *whose* moral values do you impose. Hitler's or

---

[218] Stand to Reason: Tactics in Defending the Faith. Audio and Video Series. STR.org. I recommend getting this entire CD series. Gregory goes into detail about the various kinds of "Suicide Statements" that exist. He identifies multiple variations of them, while I tend to be lazy and treat them as a common group.

[219] One can debate whether the Liar's Paradox i.e. "This statement is a lie." is a suicide statement or not.

[220] David Copperfield by Charles Dickens.

[221] Someone may say, "But I'm not imposing my moral value on you, I'm just telling you what I wish." But that is simply not true. Any time you say something is **wrong** that's a judgment call. Do you wish to rephrase it as in I wish that others would not impose their model values on me? Wish away, no one cares.

Mother Teresa's (or someone else's)?"[222]

While the law that allowed partial birth abortions existed, that law was based on *someone's* moral values, and it was being imposed on those who opposed that law based on *their* moral values.[223] You can't get away from this.

The irrationality of that Silicon Valley engineer's statement is made even clearer the minute we apply it to real life. For example, in any society, there are people who feel they are justified in stealing from anyone who has more than they have. Do we say, "How dare we impose our moral values on these thieves?" Do we legalize theft? Let's take this to the next logical level. Outlaw and "gangsta" organizations like the Mafia or the Bloods or Crips feel it is morally right for them to exterminate traitors to their causes, and they have similar sentiments toward rival gang members. Now, if we can't force our moral values on others, then are we saying we don't have a right to impose societies' moral values on the Mafia? Of course we do. It would be absurd to think otherwise. The question is not *whether* we should force moral values on others. It is *whose* morals should we be trying to make dominant? Do we force Mafia "values" upon ourselves or *our* values on the Mafia? Or is that the wrong approach? Perhaps the reality is that we should try to get everyone to adopt God's moral measurements.

We will answer that question later in this book.

Other Suicide Statements

By the way, another famous suicide statement is, "There is no absolute truth."

To which you respond, "I'm sorry, is that true?"

You see, if what you say is true, then there is at least *one* absolute truth. And if there is one, who's to say that there aren't more?

I encourage you to become an expert at recognizing suicide statements. We hear them every day. Many an illogical argument can be defeated in a single sentence, *if* you can recognize them as a suicide statement. In fact, the advantage of teaching everybody about suicide statements is that it even helps our opponents to think clearly. Once they start thinking clearly, *everyone* is better off.

Here are a few more suicide statements, for fun, try to detect the fallacies and craft a quick rebuttal. For answers go to www.NoBlindFaith.com.

1. You can't know anything for sure about God.
2. The problem is that you think you are right about this.
3. Everything we know about reality is based on facts; everything we know about faith is based on feelings or is unknown.

---

[222] Often in discussing topics like this, I try to get people to a place of neutrality – where they abandon invectives and mean-spiritedness and are willing to converse with an open mind. I want them to realize that we Christians are not close-minded blind faith fanatics, but that our beliefs are rational and logical, and even if they don't agree with us, if they can just understand how we go to our value system we'll all be ahead of the game. It's amazing how the conversations change once this has happened. I recommend it to everyone who cares about the lost. If you wish to find out more about this non-blind faith Christianity please go to www.NoBlindFaith.com

[223] Lest someone argue that abortions are no one else's business, I recommend my free downloadable manual entitled "How to win Abortion Arguments without appealing to the Bible or Religion" Go to www.JesusIsInvolvedInPolitics.com and do a search for Abortion.

4. Who are you to judge people?
5. From a Christian: You are using human reasoning to come to that conclusion and you are taking away from God's word.
6. It makes good practice to avoid values like – 'never', 'always', and so on, including avoiding use of modals like 'should,' 'need to,' and if at all possible, avoid other dictates, like 'make sure.' (I was seriously told this).

But we can't hold non-Christians to biblical principles

A Christian friend who is claims to be a libertarian, used to keep trying to argue with me, saying that we should not try to force our *biblical* moral values on non-Christians.[224] For instance, she said she just doesn't think that we should ban same-sex marriage. However, a quick review of the I Timothy 1 passage (quoted above), shows us immediately that Paul by inspiration from the Holy Spirit and by unity, our Lord Jesus Christ says the contrary. God says, "The law is *not* made for the righteous, but it *is* made for murderers, adulterers (sex outside of marriage), perverts (the Bible includes homosexuality in this), slave traders, liars and perjurers—and for whatever else is contrary to sound doctrine." Since we are all sinners, God's laws apply to *everyone*, believers and unbelievers. Now of course, unbelievers won't be easily convinced of this, but Christians have no excuse to think otherwise.

And what's more: God's laws are there to bring true social justice (not economic justice, but moral justice) equally to all mankind. If you care about the poor and the defenseless, you *will* care about imposing God's moral values on issues like slavery and liberty on society.

Pastors and Elders

Pastors and elders, I hope you can see the implications. If all laws impose *someone's* moral values on *others*, and the Bible tells us that God's laws are precisely for the unrighteous, who better to be deciding *which* values are to impose than persons with morals patterned after God's heart. Can you as a shepherd shirk from this responsibility? If it is your job to speak God's truth into the lives of people, is it not *also* your job to speak His truth into the laws of the nation? What is the heart of God concerning this?

Imagine the consequences on our nation if we relinquish this responsibility! We will describe some of these consequences in the next few chapters.

Find out More

In this chapter, I discussed Suicide Statements. If you'd like to learn to recognize these and find single statement rebuttals, please go to www.NoBlindFaith.com to the Sermons page. Those notes are also useful for leading a Bible study or college group about these concepts. May I encourage you to do so?

---

[224] But presumably, we can force non-biblical moral values on non-Christians? Huh? It's pure silliness.

Fourteen

You ask me why I don't believe in god, I'll tell you. Last week there was an earthquake, and over 100 little children died. What sort of a mean evil god lets that happen?

Paraphrase of an atheist's opening argument in a debate with William Lane Craig. www.williamlanecraig.org

It's a sad day for us all, for even today in an age of enlightenment, 50% of all humanity has a below average education. 50% of the people in the world earn below average paychecks, 50% of the world is heavier than the average and half of the entire world has a below average intelligence i.e. their IQs are below 100.

My introduction to a talk titled "Christians need to start thinking critically again"

*When in the Course of human events, it becomes necessary for one people to dissolve the political bands which have connected them with another, and to assume among the powers of the earth, the separate and equal station to which the **Laws of Nature and of Nature's God** entitle them, a decent respect to the opinions of mankind requires that they should declare the causes which impel them to the separation.*

The Declaration of Independence of the United States of America

Where Do Our Moral Values Come From? What is the source of our Republic's Law? Defusing The Most Common Complaint About God and Evil

I am pro-life. Don't get me wrong," said the youth pastor, "I just don't think we should be forcing biblical values on non-Christians." I was so shocked at this, that my jaw dropped (yes, it was…groan… 'shock and jaw').

We've discussed and hopefully convinced you that the main job of politicians is to codify laws. And I hope I've been able to convince you that despite what my Stanford PhD friend *used* to think, in any government, one *must* legislate morality. We also said that the United States is a republic based on a *fixed primary moral code*.

We've also seen that the types of laws we make are *critical* to a nation. They have the capacity to change people's hearts, especially the hearts of children who grow up under them. *The moral fabric of any nation is reflected in its laws.*

I also hope you're convinced by now that, logically, one group *has* to force its moral values on other groups. So now we need to decide *which* group gets the upper hand. If we care about the poor, the orphans, the widows and all kids, which is the group that we should want to *get* to do the forcing? Whose law is that "fixed primary moral law" that our republic should be based on. And just what is Natural Law? How is it different from biblical laws or pro-life laws.

Remember, I said earlier, "If we think our country is great *just* because it is a republic and not a democracy we'd be missing something. After all, both Rome and Nazi Germany *were* republics also." Yet, we can clearly see what happened there. Why did those systems destroy themselves? Well, if you study history you'll see it was because the rights of certain people eroded over time and their governments started allocating goods as rights to others; both lead to oppression. How did this happen? It was because their primary moral law was not fixed or was not really moral to begin with. Remember, Hitler did nothing illegal; every act he took was fully *legal*. They were all just horrendously *immoral*. In most cases the German legislature passed a special law to allow Hitler to do what he wanted to do. In others, the Supreme Court reinterpreted the law for Hitler's agenda. Many communist countries claimed to be republics too, yet most fell apart in less than 40 years; because in addition to their unfixed moral law, their economic systems were un-maintainable.

So, what is the primary difference between the U.S. and Nazi Germany and Rome? As indicated in the Declaration of Independence, the founding fathers intended our fixed primarily moral law to be what? …It was to be the *unchanging* "Laws of Nature and of Nature's God."

The Laws of Nature and Nature's God: What are these laws? How did we get them?

There are three sources of the laws.

1. Revealed Laws: To protect us from pain (and show us the path to Salvation), God supernaturally revealed many of the laws through the Bible. We believe these revealed laws are far superior and fuller than the next two sources.
2. Conscience Laws: Other laws are written in our conscience. We all have them, though over time we can learn to harden our hearts to some of them.
3. The Laws of Nature: The third set of laws, are laws that we can logically derive just from nature. And if you think about that, it makes sense. After all, if God exists, He would have created an orderly universe based on a system of laws, laws that we believe are part of His very Character. If we study Creation we'll learn how it works. Just like physics.

Let's look at the third set, the discoverable laws. As mentioned, in this last group, are laws that even if we didn't learn them from God, we could eventually figure out by rational thought. Even before Christ, men like Cicero (a contemporary of Julius Caesar), figured out that there *was* a Natural Law and it was ordained by *the* Supreme God or gods (Cicero just didn't know *which* God that was). Cicero realized that if you keep evaluating what prevented pain and worked and what caused pain and thus *didn't* work, you'd eventually be able to come up with an objective rational system of moral laws. They wouldn't be complete, but they could each be valid. As we'll see in the chapter titled "Why The Law Was Given: Introduction," moral laws are what keep us safe, they are the instructions for reducing pain. These were also called

"The Natural Law." Obeying the Natural Law would allow any civilization to advance rapidly, be the most productive and reduce the causes of pain and suffering. When we violate these laws, our society learns from the "school of hard knocks" what they are and why those laws exist.[225]

So we see, it follows logically then that even atheists[226] could derive the Laws of Nature and choose to obey them and prosper. But do note that just because you derived the Laws of Nature, that did not mean you were *obligated* to obey them. After all, it there was no ultimate authority and this was all a big accident, why would you as an individual care about the rest of civilization, as long as *you* personally had it good?

Germany and Rome

Why is all this so critical? Well, quite simply, in the German and Roman republics, over time, they changed *what* the Primary Moral Law *was*. Why did they do that? Well, in Rome it was because the law was not really based on an Authority who was unchangeable and it was not fixed. In Germany, those in power had ceased to believe in this Authority. So, it became easy to arbitrarily classify a group of humans as *sub-human*, which is what the German Supreme Court decided to do, to allow Hitler to kill the Jews *legally*. Their Supreme Court decisions were built on precedence and current majority consensus and no more on a *fixed* moral code. So over a relatively short period of time, they merely changed the moral codes that their republic was based on. This is what will happen here, *if* we let our Supreme Court use precedence and current consensus and we elect politicians with shifting moral values. They will then come up with *new* laws and change the existing standards.

As Christians we logically and rationally think *only* God's laws will work. Man's laws will fail and hurt many innocents in the process, as we've seen so clearly in history. So as Christians, we naturally hope that more of *our* godly moral values would become the law of the land. If you are a pastor or elder reading this, surely you must be hoping that in your daily preaching and teaching, the biblical values you work so hard to instill in your flock will eventually find their way into the moral fabric of the culture and this nation. If you care about the young, your grandchildren, the poor immigrant child or the child next door, you must care that our nation has moral laws. But how will the values you teach and the things the Holy Spirit convicts us of become part of the moral fabric of our nation if *none of us* get involved in making those very same morals into laws? Are we praying that God will strike fear into the hearts of non-Christian legislators so they will suddenly legislate godly values when they've been so consistently doing the opposite? Surely this is sheer folly.

The only way to have a nation with a godly moral fabric is to ensure that biblically grounded men and women of faith are *weaving* it. Did God ask the children of Israel to sit around eating manna burgers and slurpees in the shade while He dropped the walls of Jericho? No! They had to get themselves

---

[225] Sadly for Cicero, Mark Anthony found Cicero's moral concerns to be dangerous to men with ambitions of supreme power, and had him assassinated.

[226] As you see most atheists can be "moral" based on the last two groups. Their consciences and the laws of nature. But as we will find out shortly, there is no logical obligation to *keep* those laws.

out there on the front lines and work before He made it happen. In the same way, *we* must be on the front lines of legislation. As a pastor or elder, you need to encourage your flock to be these legislators, to be on the front lines.

The Source of the Law

Okay, so, the founding fathers believed that all basic laws were based on a fixed moral law. Let's go back to this quote by Dave Barton[227]

> *A democracy is the rule by majority feeling (what the Founders described as a "mobocracy"); a republic is rule by law. If the source of law for a democracy is the popular feeling of the people, then what is the source of law for the American republic? According to Founder Noah Webster:*
>
> > *"[O]ur citizens should early understand that the genuine source of correct republican principles is the Bible, particularly the New Testament, or the Christian religion."* [228]

The transcendent (unchanging) values of biblical *natural* law were the foundation of the American Republic. Consider the stability this provides; in our *republic*, murder will always be a crime, for it is always a crime according to the Word of God. However, in a *democracy*, if majority of the people decide that murder is no longer a crime, murder will no longer be a crime. This unchanging law, the founders claimed is the "The Laws of Nature and of Nature's God" and that only in areas where God had not already spoken were they allowed to codify new *lesser* laws – the 1771 Blackstone's Commentaries tells us:

> *To instance in the case of murder: this is expressly forbidden by the Divine... If any human law should allow or enjoin us to commit it we are bound to transgress that human law... But, with regard to matters that are... not commanded or forbidden by those superior laws such, for instance, as exporting of wool into foreign countries; here the... legislature has scope and opportunity to interpose.* [229]

Similarly, James Wilson, a signer of the Constitution and U.S. Supreme Court Justice said:

> *All [laws], however, may be arranged in two different classes. 1) Divine. 2) Human... But it should always be remembered that this law, natural or revealed, made for men or for nations, flows from the same Divine source: it is the law of God.... Human law must rest its authority ultimately upon the authority of that law which is Divine.* [230]

Divine law is what our primary moral law is; *human* law is what our secondary laws are. Do you remember when we claimed that Jesus was interacting with his legislators on *both* moral and religious laws? Remember too how we indicated that while the Sanhedrin had God's Primary Law, they

---

[227] See Benjamin Rush, Letters, Vol. I, p. 498, to John Adams on January 22, 1789. As quoted by Dave Barton in http://www.wallbuilders.com/libissuesarticles.asp?id=111

[228] Noah Webster, History of the United States (New Haven: Durrie & Peck, 1832), p. 6.

[229] Sir William Blackstone, Commentaries on the Laws of England (Philadelphia: Robert Bell, 1771), Vol. I, pp. 42-43. Note too that this does not mean that morality is not an issue with wool exportation, but rather that human wisdom must be applied here based on God's superior laws.

[230] James Wilson, The Works of the Honorable James Wilson, Bird Wilson, editor (Philadelphia: Lorenzo Press, 1804), Vol. I, pp. 103-105, "Of the General Principles of Law and Obligation." As quoted by Dave Barton at www.wallbuilders.com/resources/search/detail.php?ResourceID=4

Neil Mammen

still were responsible for making the lesser laws, *just like our politicians*? Some people get confused and claim that because the Jews already *had* the revealed law they didn't need lawmakers. But this is simply not true as we now see.

Continuing on where our Primary Moral Code was supposed to be, these quotes show that the founders of our Republic believed that all laws, both moral and religious flow *"from the same Divine source: [they are] the law of God."* In other words, there is no rational justification to imagine that God, the church and religion are only concerned with religious laws. And this is why my jaw dropped while talking to that pastor who said we should not impose biblical laws on non-believers. If we don't impose the Laws of Nature and of Nature's God on non-believers, *whose* laws should we impose? Random tyrannical laws?

So now, let's look at the involvement of pastors and Christians again, in light of these facts. If the law is based on "the Divine law," the Laws of Nature and of Nature's God, who better to legislate it than a pastor who seeks the heart of God, who better to be involved in politics than a Christian who is a godly man or woman? Who better to be in politics than one who knows and loves "Nature's God"? Who better than the one who loves that "Divine Law."

"The founders were close-minded old white males! Why should our current laws be based on their made-up God?"

But, in doing this we will be challenged, as I was with that statement. Strangely enough spouted at me by no other than a *middle-aged* white male (who was also an atheist). As Christians we will be asked what right we have to impose *our* thinking on others and why we believe our values are in fact *moral*. Despite the founder's convictions, why is the Christian God the right source of the supernaturally revealed laws of our republic? Why not Thor or the Greek gods of mythology? Or the Muslim Allah's Sharia laws? Or what is wrong with the *majority* making up the primary laws? Why is the Constitution *still* applicable today?

Determining the Source

To rise to this challenge, the first step is to determine the origin of our moral values. Then we need to decide which of those values should actually become a law and which values should just be kept as suggestions. We godly Christians and godly Jews, believe all true moral values come from God, but we need to be able to defend our ideas in the public square. Why? Because we need to justify to both believers and unbelievers why we need to impose these moral values on everyone, including unbelievers. (Please do not confuse legislating morality with legislating from the Bible; we will clarify the difference later.) So, I want to show you how we can rationally prove this concept to atheists and other non-believers.

Let's start by proving that moral values do indeed come from God. In so doing we will actually also answer the atheist's age-old question about the existence of God and presence of evil. We will also answer some more pastors' objections as to why we need to be involved with the lawmaking of our nation.

This chapter is very complex and I've been told that is has been difficult reading for some. So can I ask you dear reader to do me a favor? If you find yourself bogged down. Rather than quit reading, please mark this page then skip to the end of this chapter and review the summary of conclusions; then continue to the next chapter. You can always come back to this chapter at a later date to find the backup logic for the conclusions.

How can God exist when there is so much evil in the world?

As shown in this chapter's heading quotes, a well-known atheist starts an attack on Christianity by saying something to the effect of:

You ask me why I don't believe in god, I'll tell you. Last week there was an earthquake, and over 100 little children died. What sort of a mean evil god lets that happen?

His premise is that if God existed, He would not allow death, suffering or evil to exist. What this person is really asking is: How can there be a *good* God when there is so much evil in the world? After all, if one was just arguing that God existed, we could try to argue the existence of a "bad" god who enjoys seeing people suffer, could we not?[231]

So, the atheist claim is that, because there is evil and suffering, no good God could possibly exist. This, they say, means that either He is *unable* to stop the evil, meaning He isn't powerful; or that He is *unwilling* to stop evil, meaning He isn't good.

Problems for Atheists

Now whenever someone argues these points, the first thing I ask is: So you agree that evil exists?

If they say, "No I don't," then the conversation is over. They have asked a meaningless question. i.e. "How can God exist when there is so much evil which doesn't exist?" Mock them and move on (okay I'm kidding, be nice).

When they say, "Yes, evil exists," then I ask, "What is your definition of evil?"[232]

Their reply is usually "Hitler" or "when someone is raped" or more recently "Karl Rove and George W. Bush." I have to be disciplined to not take the bait when the latter happens. "Stay on task" I tell myself. The issue is God, not a past administration of the United States.

---

[231] Note later in this book we will prove that in actuality, a bad god cannot exist. Which reminds me of a story: Once in a college debate I had our team say, "We are just arguing about the existence of a supreme being, not on his character or nature, so presume for all intents and purposes that 'the being' we are arguing for, enjoys torturing you personally." We then defined the basis of the debate on the Big Bang and the need for a non-mechanistic free will extra-dimensional first cause. This immediately eliminated 80% of the other side's argument, we literally saw them peel off the top 20 pages of their debate and toss it aside. They then had to scramble for points to debate us on. Naturally, we wrapped up the debate with a disclaimer saying we do believe that God is good and anyone who wanted to find out why was encouraged to talk to us afterwards. Of course, if the atheists had tried to argue that a bad God could *not* exist they'd have defeated their own argument.

[232] I wish I could claim to have come up with these arguments, but to give credit where credit is due; I first heard these from Ravi Zacharias (www.rzim.org) and then saw them fleshed out by Gregory Koukl of Stand to Reason (www.str.org). I recommend that readers consider avail themselves of the resources provided by the ministries of these two scholars to equip themselves in the defense of the faith. Both men are excellent and dynamic speakers as well.

Neil Mammen

So then, I say, "I didn't ask for an example of evil. I asked for a *definition* of evil. Can you give me a definition?"

Well, they usually try a few more times, most often throwing in a few more examples, usually inflammatory ones like: Right wing fundamentalist Christians, the Crusades. In the end, however, they never seem to have a definition, just more of their own examples.

So I ask, "How can you ask a question about how evil can exist if you can't define it? And how can you provide an example of evil if you don't have a standard for it? Is a child accidentally stepping on an ant evil? If a child does this on purpose, is that evil? Is eating meat evil? Is eating humans evil? What if you are very very hungry? What is your standard of evil? Just because you can come up with good examples, it does not mean you know what all evil is and that God is party to it.[233] And if you don't know what the basis of evil is, how can you make a judgment call? Aren't you being arbitrary?"[234]

More often than not, people are stumped. Sometimes they say, "Well Hitler! Hitler is the standard."

That's when I hit them with:

If there is no objective morality, why was Hitler wrong?
If there is an objective morality, why do you get to decide what it is and not Hitler?

Sometimes I shout it. (I really have to stop doing that).

But let me repeat what I just asked, because it's important.

If there is *no* objective morality, why *was* Hitler wrong? If there *is* an objective morality, why do *you* get to decide what it is and not Hitler?

And yes, this works just as well with "Bush" when talking to a liberal.

Do you see the problem people face? First, by asking the "God" question – how can a god exist when there is so much evil in the world? – they acknowledge the existence of evil. When they do this, they must admit that there is a difference between evil and good. If that is true, there must be a standard of good. Otherwise, you can't really know the difference. You can't define a quality unless you have standard on which to base it.

What do you mean by 'tall'?

Have you ever been to Starbucks and wondered why their coffee sizes start with "tall." It makes no sense. It bothered you when you first saw it. After all, you can't really say someone is tall unless there is someone you are comparing him to, who is shorter, or to a standard that tells you what tall is. Tall is a meaningless word, unless there is an understanding of short or normal

---

[233] On the other hand we can define "good" on it's own terms. E.g. Beauty is good. Wisdom is good. Truth is good,

[234] Now at this point atheistic relativists will go off and still say, "Well, there is no evil."

To which I then say, "In that case what is your question? Because you've just asked a completely meaningless question -- how can there be a good god when there is evil – which is an imaginary thing that does not exist in the world?" Or "how can there be a god because imaginary things exist?" It's a meaningless statement.

To which some have said, "But *you* believe evil exists."

To which I reply, "In which case my definition of evil stands, not yours. After all, if you have no definition of evil and are relying on mine, my definition allows for babies dying in earthquakes to not be an evil thing, just a sad thing."We will deal with relativism more fully in a later chapter.

or unless there is a "tall standard."

Similarly, to say something is evil, there must be a standard of good or a standard of evil, and if there is a standard, it must have come from somewhere. Some authority must be the standard giver or some mutually agreed upon standard must be set. It's meaningless to have a standard coming from nowhere.

Is the average or the norm the standard?

So the next question is, "Does the standard for evil come from other humans? Is the average the standard?"

This is a trick question.

Clearly, this is meaningless, for if the mean or average determines the standard, you are claiming that 50% of the world is evil and the other 50% is good. Yes, the quote at the beginning of this chapter is a joke; an IQ score of 100 is based on the average score of the population so of course half the population will score below 100. It shows that you can't just go around randomly using the average as a "good" or "bad" standard.[235]

Okay, so the average cannot be the standard. Still, can the standard come from specific humans? This doesn't help us either because the next question is: Which humans set the standard of *good*? Mother Teresa or Hitler?

Certainly not Hitler. Maybe Mother Teresa. But why her? Why not Hitler? Who's to say he wasn't good? In fact, in Hitler's view, Mother Teresa was evil; she was committed to the "slave morals of the Christian God[236]," which would have weakened the human race. Hitler, on the other hand, wanted to purify the race of man and create Nietzsche's superman. He thought *that* was a noble goal.

The standard is what is "best for the Human Race"

In fact, if someone claims that morals are "whatever would be best for the human race," tell them they have two problems. First, how do they know that Hitler's "species refinement" plan was not the *best* for human kind? Similarly, how can they prove for sure that killing babies is also *not* best for the human race? Population alarmists and gullible "anthropogenic global warmists"[237] think killing fetuses and thus babies is good for everyone including the climate. Second and this is what will destroy this argument: How do they know *who is* human. Hitler thought the Jews were not human. They (the person suggesting this) probably thinks fetuses are not human. It all seems rather random for them to be making such absolute judgment calls without a standard.

Further if Hitler is the standard of evil, is someone who slightly less evil than Hitler still evil? Or don't you become evil until you hit the depths of Hitler's depravity. What's your standard? Obviously, you can't just arbitrarily

---

[235] You could argue that I should have used median instead of average, but for some reason it's not as funny. When it was designed, by definition the median IQ of the population as a whole was 100.

[236] Friedrich Nietzsche, Daybreak, Campaign Against Morality. Hitler was a fan of Nietzsche and based his ideal of creating the super race from Nietzsche's Übermensch (superman/overman) concept.

[237] Make sure you get Brian Sussman's book Climategate: A Meteorologist Exposes the Global Warming Scam, WND Books (2010).

pick whom you think is a good or bad person. Remember this is all about the atheist's complaint about God being good. Why does the atheist get to set God's standard?

Societies set the standard?

Okay, what about societies? Perhaps we have to use the consensus of each society to determine good and evil. We could argue that what a majority, of each society thinks is good is good for that society. But this is no help either because if we decided to use societies as the standard for the consensus, which society do we use? Do we use Mother Teresa's co-workers, the Sisters of Charity, or Hitler's National Socialists, the Nazis for our consensus? After all, in Hitler's Socialistic society, killing Jews was the "moral" thing to do to purify the Aryan race and help the "people" and the economy.

We just spiraled back to "If there is no objective morality, why were the Nazis wrong? If there is an objective morality why do *you or Mother Teresa's society* get to decide what it is and not Hitler's society?"

But some might argue that we're taking the societies apart individually and that we have to take the entire race of mankind and all societies as the norm and look at the consensus of the majority.

This tack is worse for them because before the 1800s the majority of mankind would have indeed said that slavery was acceptable. Most Europeans thought it was acceptable. So did most African tribes when they defeated other tribes or sold other tribes to the slave traders. Muslims, Hindus, and Native Americans had slaves. Are they trying to argue that until the majority decided that it was wrong to enslave anyone, it was morally acceptable to kidnap, kill, maim, torture, and then enslave Africans? Nobody seriously thinks or believes that.[238] So you can't take what the entire race of mankind believes at any given time as a standard.

You see, if tomorrow some society decided that it was acceptable to torture babies for fun or that it was all right to enslave my next door neighbors and best friends from my birthplace (Ghanaians, that is), does that make those acts suddenly good? No! Not only no, but no way! Could enslaving anyone against their will or torturing babies for sport *ever* be good regardless of what most people think?

Clearly, unlike the tall or short example, when it comes to moral values, you cannot use society, the average, or the norm as the standard.

Characteristics of the Standard

What this shows is that to be valid, a standard of good and evil, and thus for morality, must be both timeless and non-cultural. Another way of saying this is to use the word transcendent. Any argument brought against the standard, which *isn't* timeless and above culture or nation, can be defeated soundly with simple examples.

Is it just a preference?

At this point, I've had people suddenly back away and say, "Well

---

[238] Okay, except perhaps the KKK, but we note that the KKK, like the Nazis, never argued that there is no objective morality, just that they were the ones who had the right to define it.

there's no standard. Good and evil are just our personal preferences." The minute they say this, their statement that "I can't believe God exists because there's so much evil in the world" becomes equivalent to "I can't believe God exists because I don't like honey melons."[239]

Let me explain. You see, without a standard giver who has authority over all of humankind, regardless of whether they are National Socialists or Christians or atheists or nuns, the definition of good is merely a *preference*. And if it is just that, then your preference of what is good has as much validity as your preference of what is tasty. It merely becomes your *personal* preference. In that case what you are saying is similar to saying, "I can't believe God exists because I personally don't prefer killing people or eating honey melons, I prefer watermelons."

You like good watermelon. Hitler likes killing Jews. I, an Indian immigrant, like spicy chicken curry. Before the Emancipation Proclamation, farmers liked having slaves. The Taliban, Iranian mullahs and Muslim law like killing homosexuals. The Christian God according to atheists allegedly prefers killing babies in earthquakes. With just 'preferences' as a standard, who's to say any of them is wrong? Can you honestly argue that my preference for spicy chicken curry is wrong or that your preference for watermelons is good? It's a preference,[240] not a standard or objective moral value. We all intrinsically see that there is a vast moral difference between liking watermelons and liking to kill Jews. Preferences like taste are subjective.[241] We know Truth is objective.[242] Morality as we are proving must also be objective.

Only with an actual objective moral *standard* can one make a moral statement that evil, death and suffering are bad. Clearly, humans can't set the standard. Remember again:

If there is no objective morality, why was Hitler wrong?
If there is an objective morality, why do you get to decide what it is and not Hitler?

Isn't the logical conclusion that there is a standard, and neither you nor Hitler has the authority to set it?

Then who sets the standard?

The standard can *only* come from someone who has the *authority* to set it for mankind. But who has that sort of authority? Well that could only be a Being who created mankind (if He existed that is),[243] and the standard must have some inherent timeless and non-cultural qualities. Again, the word is

---

[239] Gregory Koukl of Stand to Reason www.str.org has an excellent example of this using Brussels sprouts, see www.str.org/site/News2?page=NewsArticle&id=5264

[240] Never confuse preference or perception with truth. Never confuse subjective truths with objective truths. For more on this difference see www.truthnet.org/Christianity/Apologetics/Truth2/

[241] Note that it may be an objective *truth* that you like watermelons. But, your liking watermelons more than honeydew melons is not an objective *moral value*.

[242] Oh and don't even try to say, "Truth is not objective." Because the minute you say that, you've made an objective truth claim and refuted yourself. And even if you disagree with what I just said, you are making *another* objective truth claim.

[243] We could argue that God, the creator of life, has the authority to destroy life. Though true, that's a harder concept to sell to atheists, some who hate the thought of a God rather than merely disbelieve one exists.

Neil Mammen

"transcendent." And the standard cannot be a preference. More importantly, it cannot be a preference *even* for the Standard Giver.

That means the Standard Giver has to be some*thing* or some*one* who created man. That thing must be transcendent, timeless, outside of culture and possesses authority over all men. This automatically makes the standard giver God, doesn't it?[244] But, isn't that God exactly whom you are trying to disprove?

Your question makes no sense.

Now that you have the gist of this complex argument, let me repeat it concisely. The atheist asked, "How can God exist when there so much evil in the world?"

Your response should be this: When you say there is no God, you are saying there is no absolute moral authority. But if there is no absolute moral authority, that means there can be no objective moral standards. If there are no objective moral standards, then there is no difference between good and evil. If there is no difference between good and evil, that means there is no evil. If there is no evil, then evil is *nothing*. But if there is evil is nothing, then your original statement, "How can God exist when there so much evil in the world" becomes meaningless. It becomes "How can God exist there is so much *nothing* in the world."[245] Is this what you really meant to ask?

Any atheist who is rational will immediately realize they've made a nonsensical complaint. The statement is self-refuting and makes no sense. It's a suicide statement. The statement kills itself the minute they say it. When you say evil exists, you *must* presume that God exists. Anything else is irrational.

Thinking atheists agree

Few atheists can effectively counter this. Most are forced to agree and back away from any such claim. For example:

> *The modern age, more or less repudiating the idea of a divine lawgiver, has nevertheless tried to retain the ideas of moral right and wrong, not noticing that in casting God aside, they have also abolished the conditions of meaningfulness for moral right and wrong as well.... Thus, even educated persons sometimes declare that such things as war...or the violation of human rights, are 'morally wrong,' and they imagine that they have said something true and significant.*

> *Educated people do not need to be told, however, that questions such as these have never been answered outside of religion.*

> *Richard Taylor, Ethics, Faith, and Reason, pp. 2–3.[246]*

Taylor is an atheistic professor who has taught philosophy at Brown

---

[244] Or an alien who created the human race, if you are Erich Von Daniken. But that can be refuted easily go to www.NoBlindFaith.com and read the paper titled "Who is Agent X" which provides a rational argument for the existence of a free will, non mechanistic, omniscient, omnipotent, omnipresent extra dimensional first cause that exists outside and prior to time and space and the universe, which eliminates aliens.

[245] Thanks to Ravi Zacharias for this brilliant example. Ravi Zacharias, Can Man Live Without God? (Nashville: W Publishing Group, 1994), pg 182.

[246] Richard Taylor, Ethics, Faith, and Reason (Englewood Cliffs, N. J.: Prentice Hall, 1985), pp. 2–3. As quoted by William Lane Craig in Craig's easily won debate against Taylor. www.leaderu.com/offices/billcraig/docs/craig-taylor2.html#text2

University, Union College, the University of Rochester and Hartwick College.

A little mental break here

This stuff can be heady, so I want to take a quick pause here and remind you why we are going through this. I'm trying to show you that true morals cannot exist without God. And in the same way the *discovery* and *comprehension* of those true morals is best done by those who *acknowledge* God.

Now since I've already shown that all laws are based on moral values; and that these laws are going to be critical to your children and grandchildren's well-being; and that laws change hearts. I hope you can see that if you care about society you will care that men and women of God *are* the ones making the laws of your society. Pastors, this must include you.

Refuting the atheist's claim

If you recall the atheist's claim was that, a good God does not exist because evil and suffering exist. This, they said, meant that either He is *unable* to stop the evil, indicating He is not powerful and thus not God, or that He is *unwilling* to stop the evil, indicating He is not good.

As we see from the logical refutation provided, neither of these conclusions necessarily follows because their very premise falls apart. In reality, there can be many valid reasons why evil exists,[247] and these do not eliminate God. ***What we do conclude instead is that, if evil exists, then God exists.***

What then is the answer?

In a brilliant article entitled Sixty Second Theodicy, Gregory Koukl articulates one of the best ways to respond to this. He suggests that you ask a few questions. (I have provided a brief summary in my own words here, but I recommend reading the entire article at the Stand to Reason website www.STR.org[248] to be prepared yourself.)

Question 1: "Would you like to see laws prohibiting all homosexuality?"
Naturally, they will say "No."
Question 2: "So do you think it's a good thing that you have the freedom to make moral choices?"
They will answer, "Yes, of course."
Question 3: "So having moral freedom means that you have the option to choose either good or evil, not just a range of good?
Answer, "Yes"
Question 4: "If you are forced to choose one kind of path all the time, would that be bad"
Their answer, "Yes."

---

[247] Of *course*, one could try to argue that God created man and does exist, but he is not *all-powerful*. But this lends itself to the God is a spaceman silliness, which is refuted when we start looking at the rational argument for necessity of the existence of a God who is *outside* of the universe as described in www.NoBlindFaith.com/whoisagentx.pdf. See also my response to the age-old college question: Can God create a stone so big that he cannot move it? It addresses the question of whether there can be more than one all powerful being. (Simple set theory proves that there cannot.)
www.NoBlindFaith.com/writings/CanGodcreateastonesobigthatHecannotmoveit2.pdf
[248] www.str.org/site/News2?page=NewsArticle&id=5629

Question 5: *So does having absolute power have anything to do with the removal of moral choices if someone has genuine moral freedom?*
The answer there is "No."

As Gregory concludes:

"Having genuine moral freedom entails the notion that you might choose evil, as we just said. And being strong can't change that. You can have all the power in the entire universe and you can't create a being who has moral freedom and at the same time has only one thing he can choose: good things, not bad things. Moral freedom requires that a person be capable of choosing evil and having moral freedom is a good thing."[249]

God can't be contradictory. If you truly have moral freedom, you must be able to do evil. God being powerful won't change that.

Now the atheist may try to argue, "Why can't God give us moral freedom but stop us when we start to hurt others?" But that is quite silly. If God said, "you can do anything evil you want," but the instant you start to do it, he makes sure it doesn't hurt anyone. Then you'd never be doing evil would you? Evil is evil only because there are real consequences as we showed earlier. In fact, such an action on God's part would make Him capricious. He'd be punishing and oppressing you for something you'd only wanted to do but had never done and in fact never *could* have done.

What if an atheist argues that moral Laws are only preferences?

At this point, some atheists will abandon the "God doesn't exist because of evil" argument and instead argue that all moral values are merely our *current* preferences and there is no objective morality. And in truth, if there is no God, then all our moral values really *are* just preferences. But here's the catch for the person who tries to argue this. Any atheist who tries to argue that moral values are merely preferences will be forced to admit that it *was* morally acceptable to enslave Africans in the past because it was society's choice back then to do so. So whenever I run into an atheist who tries to argue this, I introduce him to an African American friend and ask him to look into my friend's eyes and repeat his claim that the enslavement of Africans was morally acceptable in the 1800s because it was just the preference of the *majority* of society in those days. Needless to say, the stark cruelty of this claim has an instant effect on them. It was *never* morally acceptable to enslave anyone, especially on the basis of skin color alone. And what's more important is that is this obviously clear to thinking people. So, current preferences cannot logically determine objective morality!

In the end, if there is no God, there is no objective morality and all moral claims are unfounded, baseless and merely preferences.

But atheists have morals too

Of course they do! Don't get me wrong. I'm not *ever* saying that atheists have no morals or are bad people. This is a Straw Man. I know atheists who are *far* more moral than some hypocritical Christians are. I have atheist friends whom I'd trust with my life and property over Christians I have known. Remember, the Bible clearly says that *everyone* has a moral compass inside

---

[249] Please note that this applies regardless whether you hold to a Calvinistic or Semi-Pelagian theology.

them (recall, this was the second source of the law). They may not always follow it, but God has put the concept of right and wrong in their hearts. But, my atheist friends cannot *logically* claim that they are being morally good because, as we have shown, if God does not exist, then the words good and evil have no standard meaning.[250] My atheist friends are unknowingly borrowing Christian philosophical and moral capital from us (and some are doing a better job at it than we are).

So while we theists can determine that atheists are good people based on our logical understanding and standards of good; at the end of the day the atheist's own "moral" values are not based on any transcendent, immutable truths. They are *illogically moral*. I call them "emotionally moral" atheists because there are no objective reasons for their morality. They believe in moral values, and they are still trustworthy with my life, but they have no rational basis for this belief. It is merely a preference or a blind, unsubstantiated belief system. They have *blind faith* in their moral system.

What about claiming that the standard of morals simply come from "The Golden Rule?"

One could argue that the Golden Rule is the standard for morality, so we don't need God. After all, it seems to make sense that one should treat others they way he or she would like to be treated. Atheists may claim that they are moral because it is logical to be moral and love your neighbor so that society can live peacefully.

If you look at this argument carefully, however, it too falls apart – not on the basis of actions, but on motivations. Why should I "prefer" to treat *others* as I want to be treated? I would only need to do that if I were afraid that one day the tables would be turned. But if I was sure the tables would never be turned, why worry?[251] The Golden Rule falls apart when you realize that it is a reciprocal agreement. For instance, there is no compelling reason for a slave owner to give up slavery or discrimination based on the Golden Rule as long as he maintains control. If slaves are not allowed to revolt, owners will always be in control, and some careful precautions could prevent that. In fact, when you think it through, this would mean that there was no reason for any of the white Americans (even the non-slave owners) in the U.S. to ever care if slavery was abolished. After all, they couldn't ever conceive of a scenario in which they, the whites, would ever become slaves as long as they remained in power and kept slaves uneducated and unable to congregate. History has precious few examples if any of slaves becoming the masters, so there was no precedence for this either.

---

[250] When atheists or relativists claim that many Christians are hypocrites, I merely ask them this: If there is no objective good or bad, why is being a hypocrite bad? What are you complaining about? You don't like hypocrites? So? Why do you get to decide that hypocrisy is bad? *I* think it's bad, but what's your basis for saying it is?

If they say, "Well it's good for society for people not to be hypocritical."

You respond (tongue-in-cheek): But why do I care what is good for society; if I can get away with being a hypocrite and nobody every finds out, how can you say it's bad? It's good for me. It works for me. You have no basis for being so judgmental.

[251] Or if I believed in some sort of Karmic law. But atheists don't believe in this. In fact, the desire for a Karmic law indicates in some sense the need for a final judge, an authority that cannot be fooled.

So we see that while it makes sense to observe the Golden Rule, there is no compelling reason for ruling class members, powerful people, sadists and others like that to adhere to it. Hitler, after all, felt that the National Socialists would *always* be in power, so who cared what happened to the Jews, gypsies, mentally disabled, Christians and homosexuals. He did not apply the Golden Rule to them. He didn't feel he needed to. He would never need the reciprocity that the Golden Rule awarded him. As far as Hitler was concerned, killing the Jews *was* the Golden Rule. What say Golden Rulists to that?

In addition, the Golden Rule is valid only as a truly moral law *if* it is applicable to the entire human race and everyone has equal rights. In ancient Rome, they believed that women (and slaves) were not as valuable as men and not entitled to the same rights. They felt that it would be unthinkable to treat women the way men were treated and that they would never be at the mercy of women. So they applied the Golden Rule only to male Roman citizens and certain free men. Of course, outside of science fiction novels it is improbable that women could someday revolt and take over the culture and dominate men. So the Romans had no reason to give women rights.

Thus, we see that merely claiming that the Golden Rule is the source of morality fails in the area of authority and motivation, leaving large gaps to be filled. Even if the Golden Rule is observed, there is no compelling reason to do or uphold what we know is moral today. There is no compelling reason to believe that anyone has any of the inherent rights that are described in the Declaration of Independence or the Bill of Rights.

If the Golden Rule were all that counted, then anything you did to someone just before you killed them would also be 'morally' acceptable. Or anything that you did that nobody ever found out about would also be 'morally' valid. Why? Because there is no reciprocity possible and no one is keeping track, it won't affect anything.

What about the claim that it is all relative?

One might argue that morality is relative. In other words, people could say that while killing Jews was bad for us, it was not "bad" for National Socialists because that was the Nazi's morality. I've had various New Agers and atheists say, "Well I *personally* think that killing Jews is bad, but I don't think it's objectively bad. Who am I to judge anyone else?"

Whenever I run into people like this, I know that my argument is going to go nowhere. Unfortunately, these people choose not to think logically. However, if I have a Jewish friend handy, I may recruit him to do what I do with atheists. Ask the person to look into my friend's eyes and say, "I can't condemn Nazis because while it may be wrong for *me* to kill Jews like you, who am I to say it was wrong for them?" Really?

So where do moral values come from? Who is the standard giver?

To summarize, we believe there is a standard of good and evil, and it can be given to us only by a Moral Law Giver or Standard Giver who has authority over all mankind. Who is such an authority? Obviously, the only Being who has authority over all mankind would be the *Creator* of mankind. So logically and rationally, we are arguing that the *only* possible standard giver is God.[252] And this is why it makes sense for the United States to take its primary moral law that we *founded* our nation on, to be the one *found* in the Bible. Pastors and Christians, do you see that any other source of the law will be dangerous, lead to more death, more pain and as we've seen throughout history, to tyranny.

Why can't it be our DNA?

Some atheists like Michael Shermer, have argued that our morality comes from our DNA. It is objective, he claims, because it evolved that way. There are multiple problems with this.

a. You could then determine that slavery was not immoral when it existed; it only become immoral *after* we 'evolved' that way. Tell that to the descendant of a slave.
b. Those who didn't get that particular morality gene are not being immoral when they torture babies for fun.
c. You can't be morally obligated to a thing. You can only be morally obligated to a person.

The first two are self evident, so let me prove the third one to you.

You can't be morally obligated to a *thing*

Let's say we are back in high school and one night you invite me over to play scrabble. As we start, you take the box of letters and throw them on the table. Amazingly, they fall making a complete sentence.[253] It spells: Take out the garbage.[254] Are you morally obligated to take out the garbage?

Of course not! Why should you be obligated to one random event or a million random events?

But now let's say we finish playing but don't put the pieces away. The next morning as you come down for breakfast you notice that your mom has arranged the letters in a sentence. It spells: Take out the garbage.

Now, are you obligated to take out the garbage? Yes! But what changed? It's the exact same sentence. Two things changed didn't they? First, it was a *person* who asked. Second that person had *authority* over you. In the same way, if a thing (especially a random thing as the atheists think), i.e. our DNA asks us to do something; we are not being immoral by ignoring it. We are not obligated to things. But if a *person* with *authority* i.e. God asks us to do something, we *are* being immoral if we ignore Him.

But whose God?

The next natural question is: Okay, but *whose* God is the standard

---

[252] Of course, some atheists I've debated with have argued, "Just because God created you why does that give him the right to tell you what to do. If Satan had created you, would you think you had to do what he told you to do."

My answer is quite simple. First, Satan can't create anything out of nothing, and even if he had, who created *him*? That's the authority you are responsible to in the end; you are responsible to "the uncaused first cause." Secondly, the issue is precisely that I think that the Supreme Creator *does* have the authority to demand my obedience, and you don't, and therein lies the rub. You rebel, I obey. Rebellion was the first sin in time, it is as witchcraft.

[253] Don't be skeptical, this is a far simpler and more likely event than some amino acids randomly coming together to create life. An event that had to happen millions of times before life was able to make a foothold on earth but an atheist has to accept by faith.

[254] Thanks to Brett Kunkle of www.str.org for this great example.

giver? Which god are we obligated to? Is this moral lawgiver the god of the Muslims or Hindus? How about the god of the Thagees? The Thagees were a cult of Hindus who believed that their goddess Kali required them to strangle people to allow them to achieve Nirvana. Whose god is the standard giver? And how do we know what His Law is, what His moral values are?

I believe the only God anyone should trust, is the one true God. That's nice, you say. But who exactly is that *true* God and what is His law? Well, I believe the "Standard Giver," the only true, factually and logically provable God, is the God of the Bible. The complete proof of that is indeed available *but* outside of the scope of this book, but it is worth a brief overview especially as you may be called upon at some point to prove that the source of your moral and legislative ideas are sound.

The only rational faith

First, we note that all the religions have concepts of God and heaven that differ to the point of contradiction. They all have different ways to get to God and different gods and different ideas of what heaven is. Religions like Islam and Christianity are exclusive in that they say everyone else is going to hell or something like a hell. Hinduism and Buddhism are exclusive as well, they say there is no hell, or that life is hell and heaven is becoming nothing and merging with the Brahman, – that is, heaven is when you finally reach Nirvana and get to stop the endless cycles of reincarnation.

Thus to try and claim that they are *all* true is sheer nonsense. It violates the law of non-contradiction.[255] This means we are left with only two options. Either *one* religion's concept of God is true, or *no* religion's concept of God is true.[256]

The only way to move forward from there is to then evaluate each religion based on facts, history, archeology, and scientific evidence. I believe that only one religion is able to withstand this scrutiny, and that religion is Christianity. A careful study of all religions shows that all religions are founded on blind faith, except for Christianity. All other religions claim to be based on un-provable beliefs, and that, they say is healthy. Christianity is the only religion that condemns blind faith. In our ministry, No Blind Faith, we teach Christians a five step non-confrontational non-awkward way to prove this.

1. We prove that Blind Faith is dangerous (and if you are a Christian or Jew, that Blind Faith is condemned by God in the Bible).
2. We prove that Science and Logic show it's more rational to think that God exists. We also prove that science confirms the existence of supernatural dimensions lending credence to the concept of multidimensional beings and souls.
3. Using history and documentary evidence we prove that we know 100% of the content of the original New Testament documents and that they have not been

---

[255] If you run into someone who tries to reject the law of Non-Contradiction repeat this quote to him "Anyone who denies the law of non-contradiction should be beaten and burned until he admits that to be beaten is not the same as not to be beaten, and to be burned is not the same as not to be burned." Avicenna, an Arabian Medieval Philosopher, Metaphysics, I; commenting on Aristotle, Topics I.11.105a4-5.

[256] Remember even religions that say all other religions are true are contradictory with religions that say no other religions are true.

and can *not* have been corrupted or changed over time.

4. Without using the Bible, we prove that history shows that Jesus was a real human being who claimed that He was God. Then *using* the Bible, we prove the Apostles believed that Jesus claimed He would die and rise from the dead to prove this. He also claimed to be the only way to God.

5. Using the minimal facts that are agreed upon by 75% of New Testament scholars and historical experts, many of whom are skeptics, we show that history, science and forensic techniques show that the most reasonable conclusion of the evidence is that Jesus Christ *physically* rose from the dead. Thus, proving that His claims of Divinity and of being the only way to God, is true. If point 2, that God exists is true, then point 5 is logically possible, because any Being that can create an entire universe, surely can bring someone back to life.

To prove this to yourself (and everyone should do so), may I recommend you visit www.NoBlindFaith.com. I would also recommend that you read the following books:

- Who is Agent X, Proving that it is more reasonable to Believe God exists. Neil Mammen, Rational Free Press, 2009.
- I don't have enough faith to be an Atheist, by Norman L. Geisler and Frank Turek, Crossway Books, 2004.
- The Case for a Creator: A Journalist Investigates Scientific Evidence That Points Toward God, Lee Strobel, Zondervan, 2004.
- The Case for Christ: A Journalist's Personal Investigation of the Evidence for Jesus, Lee Strobel, Zondervan, 1998.
- Any of William Lane Craig's debates on the resurrection of Jesus. www.williamlanecraig.org
- The New Evidence That Demands A Verdict, Josh McDowell, T. Nelson, 1999.

Consider visiting these websites as well:

www.CrossExamined.org and www.STR.org

But look at all the evil Christians have done

Now the minute we say Christianity is the "right" answer, we will be hit with this argument. But this doesn't work either. Just because Dr. Mengele, the Nazi doctor was an evil doctor, that does not make medicine or all doctors evil does it? Just because fire can be used to kill people, that does not make fire evil. Of course Christians have done very many stupid things in the name of God. I'm one of them. And don't forget Christians had slaves and it took yet *other* Christians to stop that evil. You have to judge Christianity on the teachings of its founder, not on the misguided actions of some of its followers. Is the core teaching of Christianity consistent with slavery or oppression or the hatred of entire races of people? In fact this entire book is to *Christians* precisely about stopping or changing many of those twisted actions or inactions by *Christians*. Remember too, that the very teachings of Christ indicated that we all have a sin nature, the very thing the atheists are confirming when they complain about us "sinning" i.e. doing evil. The fact that they recognize our evil as we've shown indicates they *and we* need a Moral Standard Giver. That same Standard Giver and Creator said that we will never be able to be fully sanctified (i.e. sinless) in these bodies. And that logically follows from our being free agents. God could no more create a group of people who *freely* did not choose to sin than He could create a round square in 2D space.[257] Being a free agent means that some may freely sin and logically their sin must be allowed to have an effect and affect the rest of us, if it didn't then sin would have no consequence (God would be punishing you for not doing anything bad, but just *wanting* to do so).

Furthermore, as C.S. Lewis says, you can't just look at Christians and see how bad they are. You have to look at how Christianity has changed them. Look at a sour Christian and see how much more sour he was before being a Christian, look at a nice atheist and think how much nicer and kinder he would become if he were a Christian. Look at how Christianity has changed the world. Look at its core teachings.[258] When studied in context, it makes sense and withstands scrutiny. (The atheist will naturally disagree so we'll always have to go over it point by point. But that's why our ministry No Blind Faith exists.)

But I'm only pointing out the holes in your logic

Now the atheist may argue, "I personally don't think there is an absolute; I'm just showing that you Christians are hypocrites." But first, why is being hypocritical wrong if there is no standard? So what if I'm a hypocrite in that case? I know *you* don't *prefer* it, but who cares. Second, we already know that we Christians are hypocrites. Why? Because we know the standard exists and we fail miserably at trying to keep it perfectly. Christianity explains precisely why Christians are hypocrites and it's part of the *very* need for Christ (our sin nature).

The Skimming Atheist

OK, I have to note something here. I say this with humbleness as I'm sure I do the same thing with their arguments. But I can't count how many times I've carefully articulated this argument with each of these points by email, only to have an atheist friend come up with an objection that I've *already* covered. It's endemic. The most recent was a few days ago as I completed this last revision of this chapter. The only thing I can think is that they never fully read and follow the argument. They just skim over it, thinking they've either heard it all or they think that there's no way I could anticipate their preconceived objections. So if someone objects, chances are I've already dealt with it and they are failing to understand the argument. Ask them to go step by step over it.

Death is not our final destiny

In closing out this chapter, I want to refute one last misconception that the atheist presented when he argued about God and death. I was once having lunch with a group of engineers. When one of them, a very vocal person, found out that I was a Christian, he hollered out in front of the entire group, "I'm an atheist, last month in Italy, many kids died in an earthquake, how can you say God exists when innocent children are killed all the time!"

---

[257] Remember, God cannot be illogical or irrational. Nor can He die, or stop being God. For more details see www.NoBlindFaith.com and look for "Can God creates a stone so big that He cannot move it?" Also note a 3D round square is a very squat cylinder.

[258] Note if someone could explain and justify the core teachings of the Koran and explain why Mohammed's adherents have gotten it wrong we would afford it the same conclusion.

I turned to him and said, "Let me ask you this. If there is a God, where did those kids go when they died?"

He paused. Long silence. Everyone at the table stopped eating. I could sense the wheels churning. After a while he offered very timidly, "With God?"

"Yes" I said, "and in fact they went to a far greater place than they'd ever been before. If there is a God, then the death of a child is not a terrible thing, is it? If there *isn't* a God, then death *is* a terrible thing. So saying that if there is a God, death is a terrible thing is illogical. It's only because there *is* a God that death is *not* a terrible thing."

I expected an argument back. But to my utter surprise, after an even longer pause he said very quietly, "I understand."

I'd never had that happen before. We became friends.

It's one thing to have the head knowledge of this; it's another when it is your own child who dies. If you would like to find out how my wife and I responded to the death of our own sweet daughter Caroline Lois, and how God used it to glorify Himself, please go to www.NeilMammen.WordPress.com.

Death is not extinction to God

You see, death is simply a moving from a temporal 3-dimensional space into an eternal multidimensional space (that science indicates does exist) to be in the presence of the most beautiful Being ever. It's like me leaving a horrible suffering life to go live in the most luxurious of all palaces. Sure, you can be sad for the family and friends who are left behind, but you can't complain about it being a terrible thing for the person who died.[259]

In fact, look at the starving kids in Africa. Look at the poor raped Darfur refugee – she had a terrible life, was displaced from her home, lost her family and finally was raped. If death is her final destiny, it would indeed be the worst thing ever. It's precisely because there *is* a God who will right all wrongs, bringing justice, and who takes us to a place of comfort – where there will be no pain, no sorrow, and no tears – that we have hope. I'm not saying this proves that there is a God, but you certainly cannot use it to refute the existence of God.

What does this all mean?

If you recall, at the beginning of this chapter, we stated that there were two important questions that we still had to resolve. Where do *our* moral values come from, and what is the source of *our republic's* law? As we have seen, the only logical, viable, provable source for *all* moral values and *our* republic's *fixed moral law* is the Judeo-Christian God. This means that the only hope of maintaining a healthy, mutually prosperous nation is to keep our *primary moral code* as "the Laws of Nature and of Nature's God." Everything else will result in death, destruction and pain. If you care about the innocent and care about protecting your kids and preventing suffering you *must* care about this.

---

[259] Obviously not everyone goes to Heaven, although most of our theology indicates that children will. I have not discussed pain or hell in this context due to space limitations but I encourage the reader who is interested to investigate this further at www.JesusIsInvolvedInPolitics.com. Search for "How can a Good God exist if there is so much evil in the world."

Neil Mammen

Here's one more important point, there is no "official" way to insist that every elected official recognize the Bible as the source of our moral values. *Any* citizen is free to run for office. That means there can come a day when our nation changes from a republic built on the *unchanging* truth to a republic built on the *changing* opinions of our leaders or of the masses. Then death and pain are at our doorstep. If the former, this rule by few is called an oligarchy. If the latter, it is a mobocracy equivalent to the bloody short lived French Revolution. The only way to ensure this does not happen is for pastors and churches to be the educators of this noble trust. Not to tell them *whom* to vote for, but to inform Americans the *principles* on which to base their votes. "Why pastors, and not teachers or even parents?" you ask. Teachers and parents *do* need to teach this as well, but do you not see that at the very core, this is a *religious* issue. It's about *morality*, the law of Nature and Nature's God. Who better to teach it than you dear pastor? Imagine if every Christian could explain to others how to get here from *there*. The future and stability of our constitution lies not in the hands of the elites; maintaining the freedom to worship, to witness, to send out missionaries lies *not* in the hands of some political action committee, but in the hands of each pastor each and every Sunday morning.

Pastors, the future of your freedom to preach the Gospel lies today in *your* hands.

It would take only *a few* election cycles to destroy America if we fall asleep at the wheel. And when we do, *history will note with the greatest astonishment, that those who had the most to lose, did the least to prevent it.*[260]

Summary of this chapter

1. Republics are not based on majority rule but on the rule of a *fixed primary moral code*.
2. But, being a republic is not a guarantee of a successful government. The moral code that they are based on will make or break them.
3. Any *fixed primary moral code* must come from an authority, this authority needs to be morally good.

But how do we determine that authority and its code?

4. Christians and Jews claim that authority can only be God. A majority of people or DNA as an authority fails logically and practically.
5. The fact that we recognize evil exists, is strong evidence that God exists. Here's how we got there:
   a. You need a standard of good if you are going to call something evil.
   b. If you have a standard, you have to have a standard giver.
   c. The standard giver can only be someone who has authority.
   d. That authority can only be someone who created mankind, i.e. God.
   e. Therefore if you say evil exists, God must exist.
6. But this doesn't prove that *we Christians* have the privilege of knowing God's Law or that the God that exists is the Judeo-Christian God.
7. To prove this we have to: Historically, logically, scientifically and forensically, prove that God exists; the Bible is accurate; Jesus rose from the dead proving that He is God; and thus what we have is the one and only true

---

[260] Ronald Reagan, A Time for Choosing, 1964.
//reagan.utexas.edu/archives/reference/timechoosing.html

Word of God. (This information is available at www.NoBlindFaith.com). Naturally the Jewish version of this proof is slightly different and not within the scope of this book.

8. Once we prove all that, we can show that the only true fixed primary moral code must be the Laws of Nature and of Nature's God; and that we Christians and Jews have that Law, in the Bible.

9. This is a noble trust, and pastors must be the teachers.

Find out More

In this chapter, I have said the presence of evil actually proves that God exists, rather than the contrary. If you'd like to see this articulated with diagrams, or if you'd like to discuss this in your Bible study, please go to www.NoBlindFaith.com. In keeping with our goal, that we want to do more than just disseminate information, we want you to become disciplers of disciplers as well; this material is also available for free as a PowerPoint presentation for your use in teaching.

Fifteen

I'm not a Christian because I don't need all that guilt.
A security guard at Advanced Micro Devices (while I was working there in the 80's).

Heaven's Just a Sin Away.
Country Music Song: The Kendalls, 1996

Western religions have spent millennia inflicting shame, guilt, repression, and punishment upon human sexuality -- especially women's sexuality.
Council for Secular Humanism[261]

Why The Law Was Given: Introduction

The problem with you right wing fundamentalist Christians is that you want to force *your* close-minded intolerant morals down *our* throats! Why don't you mind *your own* business and keep *your* morals to *yourself*! What two consenting adults do in the privacy of their own home is none of *your* business and certainly none of the state's business."

I was doing one of my favorite things, debating non-Christians on line. I always make sure I'm in a controlled environment though, as debating on un-moderated sites is not worth the hassle. This person was quite angry because I'd been discussing same-sex marriage. Since we were moderated, he used no bad words but went on to attack my statistics, my motivations and my character.

So far we've been talking about morality and the laws of man and God. I've been saying Christians need to be part of the law making process of a secular government like that of the United States, but did my online nemesis have a valid point?

Does it even make sense for us to be imposing our Judeo-Christian moral values on non-Christians and non-Jews? Maybe we should just observe them in our families, and that would be enough.

To address this, we need to figure out a few things:

First, we need to figure out why the moral laws were given by God. Are they only applicable to Christians? What about social groups or cultures or even governments?

Second, we need to determine what the actual moral laws are – that is, is "don't eat pork" a moral law and if not, how do we differentiate?

---

[261] www.secularhumanism.org/index.php?section=library &page=haught_17_4

Third, if the moral laws are violated and we are imposing them on non-Christians, what sort of punishments should accompany them? Clearly, we don't think we should be stoning people who eat pork or work on Saturdays.

Fourth, we need to figure why societies made any laws at all to begin with. What were each society's purposes and goals for the laws?

In the next few chapters, we'll break all of these down and hopefully answer all those questions to your satisfaction.

Now I'm quite sure that once we start to talk about this in detail, all of us will immediately understand that it's obvious why the laws were given and why they are what they are. But for some reason we never seem to factor that into our discussion with non-believers or into our own thoughts about politics. And to tell the truth many of us have never really given it much thought. *I* certainly hadn't until someone challenged me.

Why did God give us the laws and why do most non-believers think God's laws are oppressive?

As can be seen from the quotes at the beginning of this chapter, most skeptics, non-Christians and many non-Christian Worldview "Christians" believe that the moral laws of God were made by some ruling class or sexually repressed priests to oppress us. And this may make sense if you view it from a non-Christian, non-God believing viewpoint. After all, if there is no God and we are being compelled to follow restrictive rules that seem to have been designed to prevent us from enjoying ourselves, what thinking person would not object? I believe I can show, however, that this is a close-minded and in fact small-minded view. These people are not looking at the big picture and are certainly not looking at it with maturity or experience.

If we put aside our biases and look at this rationally, we can immediately figure out, even from a humanistic perspective, why most moral laws exist. First, let's look at our *own* U.S. laws and see if we can glean anything that would apply to God's laws.

When a group of senators or representatives (or even misguided judges) come up with a new law, what is their motivation? It could be so that they can manipulate the nation to gain power or money. But, if we were to assume the best of our legislature, we would assume that they were making those laws for the *good* of society.

Mary-Katherine's first trip home

While I was writing this book, our own lovely daughter Mary-Katherine was born. Yet, before I could bring my own amazingly cute[262] daughter home, the hospital handed me a piece of paper. It looked very official and told me that I'd have to make sure that her very first journey in a car was in a state approved regulation car seat that had been installed to specific standards. If I failed to do this…well the consequences were ominous.

Now let me ask you this: Why did my state legislature decide that they needed a law requiring that babies be put in restrictive car seats – contraptions that in fact prevent you from seeing their itsy bitsy cute kissable little faces and

---

[262] Yes, she is indeed amazingly cute. Go to www.JesusIsInvolvedInPolitics.com to see a picture.

Neil Mammen

chubby cheeks while you are driving. Why would they be doing this? Is it to oppress me? To bother me? To force me to buy a car seat and thus give them sales taxes that they could spend on some ineffective state government program with a bloated employee pool? To give me a needless guilt trip? Obviously, it is not for any of these reasons. In fact, we know that thinking this would be illogical and immature. It is simply because they believe car seats protect babies, and protecting babies is important. They decided it was immoral to risk a baby's life in a car. Protecting babies was a moral value in the minds of lawmakers, and they believe it is okay to impose that morality on me, the baby's own father.

So why did the legislature make this law? To reduce the likelihood that parents would hurt or kill their babies in an accident or even a sudden stop. The legislature is interested in making sure our society and culture survives as long as possible. Why? Because we elected them to do that. It would be quite stupid for us to elect representatives to destroy our culture. In fact, this is the primary reason we create governments, to protect us and thus society. So first, the government has a vested interest in the survival of my daughter and second, the laws they codify are to protect me, her and our society.

So why did God give us the laws?

Clearly, all laws are given to protect us. So if there *is* a God and He gave us some laws, it would make sense that they were also given to protect us from ourselves and others. Let me rephrase that. All of God's commandments and laws are given to us not because God is a killjoy or because He wants to see us chafe under difficult rules and regulations, *but* because He loves us and wants us to be safe and have joy. His laws are the guidelines that will keep us that way. He has designed us and the world in a particular way. Accordingly, there are certain ways that we need to operate and if we reject that, there will be unpleasant physical and spiritual consequences. Some of these are short term; others are very long term, taking generations to become apparent. I will try to prove this to you decisively as we go along, but the commonsense of this should be apparent to you now.

Look through the Ten Commandments and ask yourself, would violating them have physical or spiritual consequences, and is that why they are commandments? That is are they commandments precisely *because* when disobeyed they have undesirable consequences for individuals or society?

Okay, you may ask, what about "Don't have any other God's besides me" or "Keep the Sabbath Holy?" While an polytheist may (invalidly in my opinion) contest the value of not having idols, I think anyone can easily argue that if God exists and has the characteristics described by the Bible, then worshiping dead stone and wood or anyone or anything other than the true God has serious consequences, physical and spiritual.[263] We should all realize that

---

[263] For the atheistic argument we have, "If God does not exist, all things are permissible" Dostoevsky has a character in his novel imply this about the violence done to man by those who may feel there will never be eternal consequences for their inhumanity. For the idol worshipper we can say that praying to piece of stone means that it's not real, and if it's not real, that means that someone is fooling you into blindly believing something that's not true. This usually leads to manipulated behavior.

taking a day's rest every seven days is healthy.[264] Note too that some laws are based on us maintaining a healthy relationship with God, the lack of which *also* has consequences.

So we can see that if there is indeed a God, then it is self-consistent and logical for the commandments and in fact all the laws to have been given for our safety and the safety of those around us. This, as discussed, is similar to our nation's laws.

When we argue with people who tell us that we are being intolerant or close-minded because we won't allow same-sex marriage or prostitution to be legalized, we have to say, "Wait. The issue is not whether I am close-minded, but whether those actions will cause damage to society or to the people engaging in them. Is it tolerant to let a person that you think is racing towards a bridge that is out, continue his race to death? Or is it more loving to warn him, put up barriers, and make it illegal to drive towards that bridge? Don't governments put up 'Keep Out' signs and build barriers in dangerous areas?"

Is this getting more obvious?

I hope it is getting more apparent why God's laws are important for all men, be they believers or not? I hope it is also getting more obvious why we would want God's laws codified into our nation's laws, especially if *our* kids are to live here safely. Do you see why Christians need to be involved in making those laws?

A reminder about morality

Remember: All valid laws have their foundation on moral values and a law without a moral foundation is tyrannical.

Imagine you are arguing with a non-Christian who claims that you are narrow-minded and a religious freak for wanting to ban, for example, same-sex marriage. Your job is to move the argument away from whether you are a religious freak to whether same-sex marriage has unhealthy physical and social consequences. Remember though that while your basis is the Bible, you cannot use that to convince them. The longer they try to typecast you as an unthinking, ignorant, brain dead religious freak who blindly follows some sexually repressive meaningless tradition, the harder our fight will be.

So step one: Explain that it's not that you are blindly following a meaningless tradition or even the Bible.

Step two: Explain why you think the laws were given to protect us. And ask them if you can explain to them why you think same-sex marriage has bad consequences. They needn't agree with you. They just need to understand how you came to that conclusion.

Step three: Provide real world examples of why your theory is true and why this action has negative consequences to all of society. In the next few chapters, we'll be able to provide you with some of these examples. We will also provide you with multiple sources for more facts and figures and analysis in the footnotes. I recommend that if you care about your unsaved neighbors you become a student of these facts and do enough of your own research to be

---

[264] I know some of you are thinking, "But should the punishment for working on the Sabbath be death?" We will discuss that in a future chapter.

Neil Mammen

able to rationally explain it.

Back to why the Law was given

Okay, so why was the law given? Not for God's sake. He needs nothing. Though there is a law about taking glory for ourselves, God is not afraid of *us* getting too powerful, despite the perceived anthropomorphisms at the Tower of Babel.[265] All of God's commandments and laws are given to protect *us* and enable us to live in joy. The laws are the guidelines that will keep us all safe.[266] The laws were made for us.

Christ himself clarifies this to us when he rebukes certain of the Pharisees in the Gospel of Mark:

> **Mark 2:23** *One Sabbath Jesus was going through the grain fields, and as his disciples walked along, they began to pick some heads of grain. 24 The Pharisees said to him, "Look, why are they doing what is unlawful on the Sabbath?"*
>
> *25 He answered, "Have you never read what David did when he and his companions were hungry and in need? 26 In the days of Abiathar the high priest, he entered the house of God and ate the consecrated bread, which is lawful only for priests to eat. And he also gave some to his companions."*
>
> *27 Then he said to them, "The Sabbath was made for man, not man for the Sabbath."*

"The Sabbath was made for man, not man for the Sabbath."[267]

Our Lord is clearly explaining why the commandment about the Sabbath was given. It was given to us for our *own* well-being, not for God's well-being, not because it was arbitrary or capricious, not because He was a killjoy and wanted us to force us to not do what we wanted to do. We were to rest on the Sabbath because it was healthy for us to rest on the Sabbath, not because the Sabbath would have its feelings hurt or that God would have *His* feelings hurt. Things are sacred for a reason. The Sabbath was made sacred to help men and women who needed a rest every seven days.[268]

This would be similar for all the laws that exist, including laws against fornication, homosexual indoctrination and divorce, which have real world, statistically verifiable physical consequences. I will prove this to you in this book.

---

[265] I.e. God wasn't really "scared" that we'd ever be able to compete with an extra-dimensional being. But if we were to take glory for ourselves, we can easily see that things wouldn't work. I also think God did this to limit centralized governments. Just like churches, God seems to like distributed groups with local control.

[266] For one, taking glory for yourself is a sure way to create strife with your fellow man. When we are vain and selfish it hurts our communities, it hurts others. We were created equal, and that's the way we need to be. God was not created and He's not equal to anyone so again we see it does not apply to Him. The laws are there to protect and serve mankind. Note that they also convict us.

[267] My Jewish friends tell me this is also the current interpretation of the Jewish Law.

[268] So when those particular Pharisees interpreted the law as an entity of its own and translated the picking of wheat as "work" when it obviously wasn't, Jesus was quick to lobby/criticize his legislators to tell them that they had missed the point of the law and had created a new law that made no sense. Remember we can't lump all the Pharisees into this because we know there were a few godly Pharisees like Joseph and Nicodemus.

"I don't need a guilt trip"

I'd just gotten my masters degree and at the age of 22 by the grace of God, managed to get a job at AMD (Advanced Micro Devices). I would often chat with a young security guard who worked at my building (yes okay, she was cute too). When she found out that I was a Christian she said, *"I'm not a Christian because I don't need all that guilt."*

To tell the truth, I'd never viewed Christianity that way. It had never been my experience that Christianity caused me to feel any *more* guilt. On the contrary it allowed be to be forgiven of my guilt. I communicated that to her, saying perhaps she needed to come find out what "my" kind of Christianity *was* – that is, the kind that actually frees people. Nowadays I also like to add, "Well you know one possible reason why laws were given to us by God, may be for our health and the health of our society? When our legislature comes up with a law, most of the time it is for our own protection. Seat belt laws are a good example. Do you think seat belt laws are made to give us a guilt trip? Or are they made rather to protect us? If you think of it, obeying the seatbelt law would actually *prevent* us from having a guilt trip in the event of an accident, rather than *giving* us one. My security guard friend had gotten the entire concept backwards.

The Law is made for Man, not Man for the Law

So in the same way do you think that the Creator of the universe and of mankind may be giving us guidance for our *own* good and His laws are *not* to saddle us with a guilt trip? After all, if there is a Creator, would *He* not know better than we do?[269] It may be worth our time to study why all of His law were given and not ignore them blindly.

As we can easily deduce, *all* of God's moral laws were made for man's benefit, not man for the law. The laws were made for our well-being. They are not made for God, and they are not made to ruin our fun nor are they made randomly (i.e. they are not capricious). A non-Christian who does not trust the "God of the Christians" and any "Christian" who thinks that we are at liberty to reinterpret the Bible, has no reason to imagine that this God's laws are good for him. Especially if some of the laws seem so restrictive – for example, no sex before marriage –most non-Christians see no reason why anyone would want to restrict their fun.

So the next time you argue about *any* moral issue especially if it relates to a political issue, like a law against abortion or same-sex marriage, it is critical for you to be able to discuss *why* a moral issue is good or bad for mankind. When talking to a non-Christian, it is *not* enough just to say "God says homosexuality and adultery are wrong." That claim may have worked in a day and age when science and rationality were reserved for people of great learning. But today "knowing why" is very commonplace requirement and rightfully so.

Imagine if you were sitting at In-N-Out Burger one day and a person from my hometown in India showed up dressed in a saffron robe with his head

---

[269] I wrote a book about this: Who is Agent X: Proving that science and logic show it's more reasonable to think God exists. Rational Free Press, 2009. Available at www.NoBlindFaith.com

completely shaved. He then sat next to you and pulled out the Baghavad Gita, a Hindu holy book.

And he said, "Ah, I'm telling you only, the Baghavad Gita says our soul reincarnates into bodies like a garment. Thus, eating that beef is evil. It used to be a human being."

How convinced are you going to be?

Not very.

In the same way, why should a person who does not believe the Bible is the Word of God care what *it* says about homosexuality or sex or anything; unless you can prove it makes sense?

Most people want to know *why* something is good or bad before they choose to not do it,[270] especially if it goes against their natural human desires. And while it is true that there are certain moral laws for which we don't fully comprehend the underlying reasons, many of God's laws have reasons that can be derived with a little bit of thought and research. In fact, there are moral laws that the world rejects as being old fashioned, but we can look at them statistically today and realize why they are still relevant and how they have tremendous social consequences. We will see some of these shortly.

The law showed us our failure

As we have shown, one purpose of the law was to protect us physically. A second purpose was to show us that we were incapable of following it and we are thus condemned spiritually. If we could follow the law perfectly we'd be sinless. But we cannot and we are incapable of keeping the law, so we realize that we need God to help us. He needs to save us.

But if no one can keep the law why then have a law?

A non-Christian friend of mine once asked, "What's the use of even having a law then? No one can keep *your* God's law completely; we are all doomed to fail. So why even have a law?"

To respond, I asked him this, "Tonight when you leave here, you'll drive home, won't you?

He said, "Yes."

"Will you keep every single one of the thousands of traffic laws on the books of this state? Will you adhere to every single speed limit especially the 25 mph residential ones? Will you stop fully at every single stop sign?"

He laughed, "Of course not."

I responded, "Then why have any traffic laws at all?

He said, "Touché."

Just because we are unable to keep the law, it does not follow that the law has no value. The integrity of the purpose of the law to protect you and show you your faults is maintained even if you do not or cannot follow it all.

Legalism

At this point, it is worthwhile to address the issue of legalism. Some people get the impression that if we insist on adherence to the moral values of

---

[270] Of course, we also know for a fact that this is not always the case. Just because someone knows that something is bad does not mean that they will not do it. Smoking is an example.

the Bible, we are espousing legalism. That is a misunderstanding of legalism. To a Christian, legalism is not adherence to the law. There are at least two types of legalism. The first is the idea that you *can* follow the law and be saved *spiritually*,[271] and this ignores man's sin nature and the role of God's grace. In other words, Christian legalism is any view that says that observing the law is possible and that, and not faith in Christ is what saves you from separation from God. Remember if you *were* able to follow the law perfectly you would indeed be saved. It's just that you *can't* because of your sin nature.

The second type of legalism is following the letter of the law but not the intent. A number of the Pharisees were famous for this.

This is important to understand. If you will notice, our Lord's attacks against these particular Pharisees focused on the fact that despite the fact that they claimed to follow the laws to a T, their hearts were not in line with God's compassion. His attack on them was directed to the fact that they did not interpret or care to understand *why* the law was given. Remember, he said, "The Sabbath was made for man, not man for the Sabbath." They thought observing the Sabbath and ignoring the plight of the crippled man would preserve their holiness. They forgot that there are *real* reasons why laws are given and they are all for the benefit of man, not for his oppression. This is equivalent to giving someone a ticket for safely running a red light on the way to the hospital while they had a critically wounded person in their car.

But, by now I hope we all see that, if the law is given for our protection, obeying the law then is not legalism, it's just *wise*. After all we don't call someone who insists on driving down the wrong side of the freeway "free from legalism" do we? We call them "dangerous maniacal fools," and throw them in jail. In the same way, we call people who observe the traffic and moral laws "kind, wise and considerate."

Jesus followed God's Law perfectly and never broke it. Do we call Him legalistic?

So when someone (especially a Christian) calls you legalistic for wanting to observe or enforce the moral laws of God, ask them why the laws were given. Ask him if Jesus was legalistic? After all He did say:

> Matt 5:19 Anyone who breaks one of the least of these commandments and teaches others to do the same will be called least in the kingdom of heaven, but whoever practices and teaches these commands will be called great in the kingdom of heaven.

If the laws were given for everyone's safety like a traffic law, isn't wise to observe the laws and foolhardy and dangerous to ignore them?

The opposite of legalism

By the way, the extreme opposite of legalism is antinomianism, the heretical view that moral laws are *not* binding. We won't need to discuss that.

---

[271] Note if we could keep the law, it would save us. But we can't keep the law, yet as we've said, obeying the law, in most cases can and will save you in many *physical* ways just not spiritually. And that too because you are incapable of following the law, if anyone were to follow the law perfectly and not rebel against God, they would be sinless. Only Christ was able to do that.

Neil Mammen

In summary: So why should we follow the law?

First, because we will suffer less. The more people follow the laws of God the less we will *all* suffer. When someone speeds down the wrong way on a freeway, more than the irresponsible driver suffers, all those who crash into him or the wall while trying to avoid him will also suffer.

Secondly, we obey God's laws because we love Him and trust His guidance, and realize His law is in line with His Character. The Law of God is part of the very nature of God. Blatantly ignoring His law is usually an indication that we do not love Him or do not trust his wisdom or we do not wish to honor him. There are many wise reasons to follow the law and calling that legalistic is pure ignorance.

So pastors, if your job is to guide us and protect us and be shepherds of the flock, does that not include protection of the innocent? Does that not include advice and reprimand? Does that not include some concern for what the moral laws of the land are going to be? Surely you don't think that God's laws only have *spiritual* consequences. Why would God give us moral laws to protect us *physically* and then expect us to ignore them in the creation of a government whose very job is to protect us *physically*? Remember that the government's existence is to protect those who created that self-same government. So if laws based on moral values are there to protect us, who better to know what these laws should be, than pastors and Christians?

Sixteen

God this! God that! That's all I hear about God! God wants this from us, God wants that from us, God is jealous, God wants us to worship Him; God does what He wants when He wants to. He sounds very selfish, arrogant, and proud – just who does He think He is?

Conversation in the Dish Room, 1980

Just Who does God think He is?
God the Spoiled Brat!

I'm going to take a little detour here because you will run into this argument now and then, and one of the goals of this book is to equip you.

Notice that none of the laws are given to protect God. No, not even the "Do not use the name of God in vain."[272] None of them apply to Him. It you look at the Ten Commandments, you won't see a single law that applies to God.

Occasionally when I'm in a friendly debate with an unbelieving friend, they'll make some sort of claim about God being a hypocrite because He does not follow His own rules. Well this usually indicates a complete ignorance of the concept of moral values or laws and a complete ignorance of the nature of the Almighty God.

---

[272] Naturally, you are going to ask if the "Do not use the name of God in vain" commandment has any physical consequences. Sure, I can't imagine being mad at God, the source of all goodness and joy could be good for you in any imaginable way. I've known very many "angry" atheists, though in truth technically they weren't really atheists since they were mad at the God they didn't believe in. A good example of an angry atheist is Madelyn Murray O'Hair, who hurt herself greatly by her anger. This is documented by her son, who ironically became a Christian evangelist. Get his story at www.wjmurray.com. And oh by the way, she is dead and is not trying to take "Touched by an angel"; reruns off the air. That was a fraud. Some of us Christians are way too gullible. However the so-called "Fairness Doctrine" will take many things off the air as they force Christian or conservative radio stations to give equal time to liberal viewpoints and hosts who can't make a dime in advertising (which is why Air America is operating under bankruptcy protection as I write this).

God in the Dish Room

Let me tell you a story about my first few months in the U.S. As you know, when I had first planned to come to the U.S. from the Middle East, my father lost his job at the University of Sana'a, and we were unable to afford my tuition, so I was not able to come. Yet God was gracious, and my dad got another job in South Sudan, and I was eventually was able to come to the U.S., but Dad's new job did not pay as well as the old one, so in order to be able to pay my expenses, I had to get a job in the U.S.

Now the law in the States was that I was not legally allowed to take a job *off* campus unless I got a work permit. Not having a permit, I naturally looked for a job *on* campus. It turned out that the only job I could find was in the dining room. And because I'd never held a real job before in my life, the only job I could get was at the bottom of the rung. So not only was I in the dining room, but I was also in the dish room, and not only was I in the dish room, but I was in the lowest level job in the dish room - slop.

The job was doing slop for breakfast every morning from 6 a.m. to 9 a.m. This means I sat next to this large conveyor belt and kids put their used trays on the belt on one side of the partition. My job on the other side was either to remove the silverware and trash from the trays or empty the leftover food into this monster garbage disposal. The disposal was so big my entire arm could have fit down it. The first few days I was so scared of it that I had nightmares. I think they eventually made a horror movie about it.

Anyway, I would get up at 4:30 a.m., shower and walk the three miles to campus (I didn't have a bike yet – yes, and you guessed it – it was uphill both ways, 105 degrees F in the freezing snow and I was barefoot and only had a ragged torn thin T-shirt! Anyway, you get the picture). I would work in the dish room till 9 a.m., and then go to my first class of the day. For those three hours, I was stuck across from this really cute gal also doing slop. So in effect, I had a captive audience, and I naturally used this great opportunity to …witness to her. No really! Okay, maybe I was a nerd. Or maybe that was just how I flirted. And yes, you can feel sorry for her, stuck for three hours a day across from some "know-it-all" Indian loudmouth computer engineer wannabe from the Middle East.[273]

Well, after a few months of this she said in frustration, "God this, God that, that's all I hear about God. God wants *this* from us, God wants *that* from us, God is jealous, God wants us to worship Him; God does what He wants when He wants to. He sounds very selfish, arrogant, and proud – *just who does He think He is?"*

And at that moment, I got chills down my spine. I turned to her and I told both her and myself. "Why, He thinks He's *God."*

"Oh," she muttered realizing what she had just said.[274]

Yes, He thinks He is God.

But let's go a step further. He doesn't just *think* He's God, He *knows*

---

[273] Don't forget and an economic liberal who was against guns and effectively pro-choice.

[274] The good news is that months later, after I'd been promoted three times to a cushy job checking meal cards, this gal came up to me and said: 'Thanks for all those talks in the dish room. I've decided that I do believe in God."

He's God. Because He *is* God.[275]

And being God, He can be as selfish as he wants.

And being God, He can be as jealous as he wants.

And being God, He can be as proud as he wants. Why? Because the rules that apply to us, don't apply to Him.

Now some of you might still say, "Why? Why shouldn't God be subject to the same rules that we are. How come God can be jealous, how come God can be selfish, how come God can be egocentric, how come God can do the very things he tells me not to do and I can't do those things?"

Doesn't I Corinthians 13 say, "Love is never envious or jealous or selfish?"

Isn't God supposed to be love?

But the Bible says he's a jealous God. He destroys people for disobeying him.

Don't we seem to be contradicting ourselves?

The answer still is "Because He is God."

You don't need no 'steenking' matches

Assume you have a kid. If that's hard, assume that you are babysitting a kid. While stumbling through the kitchen, the kid happens to find some matches and starts to play with them. He lights a couple and blows them out. That's fun. So he lights a couple more and blows them out, and then he does it again. This is pure fun, and then.... you catch him.

"Aaaargh" you say, "Maaaaaatches!!! Matches? Matches! You don't need no steenking matches, you can't play with matches" and you take them away from him.

Now a few minutes later, it being winter, it starts to get cold, so you decide to what? To light a fire in the fireplace. Guess what you use to light the fire? Right, the very same matches, in the very same matchbox, and you light them in the very same way that our little kid did.

Now in the eyes of the kid, what's the big difference between what you are doing and what he was doing? Absolutely nothing! How come you get to use the matches but he can't? In his eyes, it's just not fair. But in yours, it makes perfect sense. And what's worse, nine times out of ten, you could try to explain the reasoning to the kid, but he'd still think you were unfair because he has no intention of burning the house down and he knows that he won't burn the house down, he just wants to play with those matches. But still, he doesn't get to play with the matches, but you do! In fact, you could play with those matches before lighting the fire if you wanted to. Why? Because the rules that apply to him, don't apply to you. You are the adult. He's the kid.

The rules are for us, not God

God is the Creator. We are the created. Let's never forget that. God can do what He wants to, when He wants to and how He wants to as long as it

---

[275] Despite what Shirley MacLaine tries to preach about us "all being gods, we've just forgotten we are gods," only an idiot would think he was God when he wasn't. And no real God could forget that he's God. Look, if you are God, you'd know if you were Him or not. What sort of a feeble God forgets *anything*; much less, that He is God?

Neil Mammen

is consistent with His character, and let's not talk about fair or unfair.[276] If the minor difference between parent and child allows for different rules, how much more does it allow for different rules between a measly human and the Creator of all things and life and the entire universe with it's billions of galaxies and multiple dimensions (as many as 10 or maybe 26)? He made the rules, and He made them for us. In fact, as we said, He made the rules for our protection and *not* for His protection. He doesn't need protection. And in fact, the burden of proof is upon those who insist that God must never be vain or should never be jealous or should never desire or encourage our praising him. Sometimes you can destroy their argument by simply asking, "Why is being vain or being jealous wrong for God?" The footnote gives an example of one such argument I had.[277] In addition, when you say "God killed someone" you haven't said anything bad has happened. As we said when people die, all that has happened is that they've been moved from a limited four-dimensional existence to a multidimensional existence. God has merely moved them from

---

[276] By the way, if you are reading this and you believe in a God but have trouble with the first part of that statement, you may be portraying a sense of your own "godness" and rebellion. This could be an ego problem of yours. Think of the audacity of someone refusing to bow down to their Creator and the Creator of the entire universe. As we will see shortly, this was the first sin in time.

On the other hand, if you don't believe in a God and get angry with these concepts, then you may have some serious God issues. Perhaps you are angry at the God you don't believe exists, maybe because he did not give you something you felt you deserved. It is difficult to explain being angry about a God one doesn't believe exists. I can understand being angry at Christians who believe God exists, but not being angry at a God, an entity you don't believe exists. That's like being angry at Thor for what the Vikings did.

[277] Sometimes I end up in this sort of a discussion:

Me: Why is being egocentric or being jealous wrong for God?

Non-Christian (NC): Because it's wrong for everybody.

Me: That's not my question. Let's try this: Why is it wrong at all?

Non-Christian: Okay, because people will think you are a jerk.

Me: But why would they think you are a jerk?

NC. Because you are acting like you are all high and mighty and better than they are.

Me: But if you were God, you *would be* high and mighty and better than they are. So, that rule wouldn't apply to you.

NC. But they don't want to be reminded about that.

Me: Why not?

NC: Because then they feel smaller and more insignificant than you.

Me: But they *are* smaller and less significant than God. God is the infinite Creator of the entire universe and everything. They are a finite creation. This is the truth of the matter.

NC: They don't need to be reminded.

Me: But you still haven't given me a real reason all you've done is state that it's not right because it's not right for *you*. Why is it not right for someone who *is* greater than you? Think of it this way. Imagine if you were invited to a wedding and at the wedding, you fought to get all the attention instead of letting it all go to the bride and groom. Instead of making it an occasion to celebrate them, you try to twist it to be all about you. Would that be wrong? Yes. Is it wrong for the bride and groom to do things that celebrate themselves and not you? No.

NC: But that's only for a short time.

Me: All of creation is a celebration for the Creator. It's his wedding forever. It's his party.

NC: What if I don't want to be invited.....

Me: Now we've changed the subject....

Note: I don't think that we are insignificant, that is what the gospel message is about. But still no one can give me a valid reason why it's wrong for God to claim all praise and glory. I think it's a mind block for some people.

one place and time into another. You see you have to remember that God never actually kills anyone. Once God has created you as a soul, he never ever destroys you. All he's done is move you out of a temporary frail sick and limited physical body and freed your soul to exist in His presence, if you wish to. All he's done is destroy your body, because remember. You don't have a soul. You *are* a soul. You have a body. A body that will be replaced eventually.

The Westminster Confession

The Westminster Confession says that:

*As far as we are concerned, the chief end of **man** is to glorify God and enjoy Him forever.*

John Piper in his excellent book "Desiring God: Meditations of a Christian Hedonist" (Multnomah, 1996) expands this to the logical:

*As far we are concerned, the chief end of **God** is to glorify Himself and enjoy Himself forever.*

And He can do that because He not only thinks he is God, He *is* God. Here are some verses that show this:

Exodus 14:4 *...**I will gain glory for myself** through Pharaoh and all his army, and the Egyptians will know that I am the LORD."*

Isaiah 60:21 *Then will all your people be righteous and they will possess the land forever. They are the shoot I have planted, the work of my hands, **for the display of my splendor.***

Isaiah 43:6 *I [God] will say to the north, "Give them up!" and to the south, "Do not hold them back." Bring my sons from afar and my daughter from the ends of the earth – everyone who is called by My name, **whom I created for My glory** whom I formed and made.*

So remember the chief end of God is to glorify God and enjoy Himself forever.

It is logically and rationally necessary that God glorify Himself only

But let's go a step further. You see, it is not only acceptable for God to glorify Himself, but it is of utmost importance that God be for Himself; it is vital that He desires to glorify Himself only. It is not only a logical necessity that God praise Himself, it is also a logical *necessity* that God glorifies Himself *only* and not try to be sacrificing or self-effacing. (Yes, I know you are wondering about Christ – we'll address that shortly). God must be for Himself because if God wasn't for Himself, He could not be God for *us*. Think this through. If there were something else that God was to be glorifying instead of Himself, would not that something else then have to be greater than God? Let me repeat that. If there was some other being or some other thing, even if was just the concept of *love,* that was the focus of God's praises, then would not God cease to be God, and that thing that God was glorifying then be God instead? And if that is the case, should we not be focusing some if not all of our praises on that *other* thing that God was praising?

You see logically and rationally God has to be the greatest; there can't be anything greater than God. God has to praise Himself, or He would not then be the greatest. This can even be proven using set theory and equations.[278]

God the spoiled brat?

I was once arguing with an engineer friend. He had grown up in church but didn't consider himself a Christian anymore. At one point in the argument he blurted, "You know I have trouble taking the Old Testament seriously. Everywhere I read about God in the Old Testament, He's being judgmental, vain and selfish. He's acting like a big spoiled petty brat. How am I supposed to accept a God like that?"

Let me explain why God *must* act like that and why we can't. And how that does not make God a spoiled brat.

First, it is not wrong for God to act that way. For being selfish in itself is not evil. Being judgmental in itself is not evil; being arrogant in itself is not evil. It is only evil if we *humans* do it. You see the reason it is evil is because those things are reserved exclusively for God. For example, I can go for a joy ride in my own car, but that teenager down the street can't. He doesn't own it. I do. Driving a car isn't wrong. Someone *else* driving my car without permission is wrong. A judge can sentence you and imprison you, but I can't. It's wrong to be arrogant because you are not more important than another human. But God *really is* more important. So the rightness or wrongness of an act is not determined only by the act, but also by *who* is performing that act, what authority they have to perform that act, the rights associated with that act and if they are taking something that does not belong to them.

The greatest sin

Do you know what the greatest sin is? It is trying to make ourselves God. By being selfish, wanting glory or wanting praise, we are taking away from God what belongs to only Him. Do you remember what the first sin that occurred in *time* was? It's actually not in the Garden of Eden, nor is it in Genesis. It is in Isaiah 14:12. This is an allegory of the fall of Lucifer.

> *Is 14:12 How you have fallen from heaven, O morning star, son of the dawn! You have been cast down to the earth, you who once laid low the nations! 13 You said in your heart, "I will ascend to heaven; I will raise my throne above the stars of God; I will sit enthroned on the mount of assembly, on the utmost heights of the sacred mountain. 14 I will ascend above the tops of the clouds; I will make myself like the Most High." 15 But you are brought down to the grave, to the depths of the pit.*

So we see that the first sin in time is when Lucifer wanted what belonged to God, when he wanted to make himself just like the Most High. And in fact, this then explains why we are never to be arrogant or self righteous, or self-praising, for then what would we be doing? We would be trying to be gods ourselves and trying to take what belongs rightfully to God. And that is the primary sin. And that is what got Lucifer kicked out of heaven. In fact, it is what got Adam and Eve kicked out of paradise. They wanted to be like God, starting with knowing good from evil. Wanting to be just like God has severe spiritual consequences. At the root of it all, is rebellion.

---

[278] See "Can God Create a stone so big that He cannot move it?" at www.JesusIsInvolvedInPolitics.com.

Over the eons we have forgotten why being selfish is wrong, why seeking glory is wrong. We think it is wrong in *itself*. No. It is not wrong in itself. It is wrong for *us*. It was never wrong for God, just wrong for us. But over the years, we've thrown out the baby with the bathwater, so to speak.

God-like?

But you may complain, "Aren't we supposed to be God-like?"

No. We are supposed to be Christ-like, not God-like. We are supposed to emulate Christ in his incarnation[279], not in his deity.

Why the Diversion

This little diversion was important, because as we get deeper into the reasons the laws were given, you will run into people who will try to argue that the Bible is inconsistent. So it is important that we understand the entire background and the rational and logical consistency of the concepts as we move forward, especially when it comes time to defending God's morality and why we Christians have a duty to be in politics. Remember too that since the rules were given for our protection, God does not need to follow the rules He has made for us, because He does not need to be protected from anything.

---

[279] Yes "incarnation" means "in the flesh" same root word as in carnivore, chili con carne, and carne asada. I.e. God in the bod.

Neil Mammen

Seventeen

The puritan fathers knew that what a man did in the privacy of his own home could in time affect all of them. If a married man had a private affair, that would probably break up his family and his kids would eventually become a burden on the community. Broken homes would also increase the crime in the community. So it's not a matter of where something is done, but what is it that they were doing and what are its consequences? Does it hurt others?

My online response to the argument that "it's none of our business what adults do in the privacy of their own homes."

Politics is a moral enterprise from top to bottom.
Gregory Koukl, Stand to Reason

A Synopsis Of What We Know So Far

There are some conclusions we can make from the principles that we've discussed so far. Here's what we have:

Politicians make laws.

Laws are based on moral values.

Moral values are based on religious values.

The first conclusion

Anyone who says religion and politics should not be mixed does not understand the role of politicians and/or the source of moral values. Religion and politics *must* be mixed. There is no other option.

Here is another reason why it is meaningless to say politics should not or cannot be mingled with religion: If that were to happen, you would end up with people with no rational moral basis making laws. Worse, you may get those who actively hate God's Moral Law making our laws. And, as we will see in the next few chapters, this has had terrible social consequences in our country. Further if we were to allow immoral values to become law, and since laws change hearts, can you imagine what this would do the conscience of this nation? And since all sin is sin because it has a spiritual or physical consequence, an immoral, sinful law would be guaranteed to have woeful spiritual and physical effects. We will see these consequences shortly.

The second conclusion

The religious convictions of every lawmaker are of critical importance. Thus, how you choose whom you elect is critical. Note that I said "religious convictions" and not religion. This is because many politicians may claim to be Christian but may have no actual godly convictions. A person's convictions are reflected in his character. The character of elected officials is vital.

Note that this is completely contrary to what the media and many people were saying about Bill Clinton during his first campaign in 1992, when the evidence of his affairs with Gennifer Flowers arose[280] (long before Monica Lewinsky). I've always said that if a man is of such bad character that he is willing to cheat on his wife and then not ever ask for genuine forgiveness for it,[281] why would anyone want to consider him for an office in which he would be upholding laws? I asked the same about John McCain in 2008. Can we imagine that a man who cheats on someone as close as his own wife, whom he has known for decades and to whom he has vowed before God and man to be faithful, would hesitate to cheat or bring injustice to voters he hardly knows, just because they put him in office? I find that naïve.

In a republic, it is crucial that we elect only men and women of excellent character. Why? Because they are to vote their convictions, and if their actions which display their character, reveal shady inner convictions, we should never support them for office (unless the alternative is worse). What a legislator does in the privacy of his home *is* very important if it indicates a character flaw.

Forgiveness

On the other hand, our Lord commands us to forgive. If a man or woman has shown character or conviction flaws but has repented of them, asking for forgiveness from God and from the people he adversely affected, we are to forgive him. However, common sense says we should ask for verification of his convictions and behavior change. After all, trust is earned, and offending politicians need to re-earn the electorate's trust. No blind trust, no blind faith!

At times, a politician will have a complete turnaround while in the limelight. Some have been saved in office and consequently we've seen times when men have come clean, repented and have gone on to live godly lives and legislate with godly wisdom. (Though not a lawmaker, Chuck Colson as a public figure comes to mind.) So, if we believe they are genuine, we should give them the opportunity to prove themselves. But I would say nothing short of total repentance, a public agreement that what they did was sinful and immoral, and a promise never ever to repeat the behavior is required. Excuses, rationalizations, or complaints about fairness are unacceptable.

Always ask: Why do you hold that viewpoint?

At this point, I would like to encourage all Christians to ask their potential lawmakers how they came to have their convictions. Why? Because any conviction based on blind faith or mere preference is likely to disappear as easily as it came. A quick anecdote will illustrate.

---

[280] Lest someone claim this was never proven, in his autobiography *My Life*, Clinton documents that he testified under oath that he had sexual relations with Flowers.

[281] While we don't know if Bill Clinton ever did confess and ask his wife for forgiveness, at the time the very fact that he repeatedly and voraciously denied it, seems to indicate that it was unlikely that he confessed to anyone.

I have an Indian friend who, though a Christian by name and culture,[282] is not a Bible believing Christian. This is not a judgment call on my part. It was something he said himself when explaining his view that the Bible is a collection of human sayings, not the inspired Word of God. At some point in the 1980's, it became apparent that this man was staunchly opposed to homosexuality. When I talked to him about this, it became clear to me that his opposition to homosexuality was cultural as opposed to biblical or having a basis in scientific research. I "prophesied," if I may use that word, to my sister, that within a few years his opposition to homosexuality would change.

Sure enough; about 10 years later he did change his views. He started to argue that we should *not* be judgmental about people who practice homosexual behavior.

Why had I been so sure of that? Well simply because he had no real basis for his convictions. His view of homosexuality was purely a preference based on his and my Indian culture. While this is just one example, it indicates two things. First, we need to understand *why* a person has those convictions. If they are merely preferences, they may well change. Morality cannot be a preference. Second, and just as critical, if my friend had known the destruction to the body caused by homosexual behavior he would not have been so quick to change his mind. So, we need to educate the citizens of the U.S. and the world as to why certain convictions are valid, using scientific studies and statistical evidence. We should not rely on cultural traditions, blind faith or an unthinking acceptance of the Bible.

Does this mean Christians and Jews should vote only for each other?

Actually, while this may be the implication, it is a simplistic conclusion and it is incorrect. True practice is more complex. In a republic we should vote for people and parties whose platforms, morals, constitutional understandings and most important, their understanding of the *source* of all objective moral values are in line with ours. This is the only way we can ensure that the laws they make will be based on the values we share.

As I said in the introduction of this book, this book is fully inclusive of my Jewish countrymen and women who believe that God's Moral Laws are written in the Bible (the OT to Christians)[283]. There are many Jewish people whom I agree with because they fall in line with these principles. They have a Godly Worldview. "My" Rabbi (Rabbi Daniel Lapin[284]) and Michael Medved come to mind. However, if someone was Jewish in name only and not in convictions, or was a liberal, I would *not* vote for that person just as I would not vote for a politician who was only Christian in name and not in

---

[282] If you recall, the Marthoma Church in India is over one thousand nine hundred years old, founded by the Apostle Saint Thomas in AD51.

[283] Some may wish to argue that we Christians are not under the OT but only under the law of Christ. But surely, we agree that the Law of Christ did not invalidate a single jot or title of the law, it provided instead a path that allowed us to actually fulfill its requirements through Christ.

[284] www.rabbidaniellapin.com. Rabbi Lapin is the founder of the American Alliance of Jews and Christians (AAJC). A non-profit educational organization working to advance our nation toward the traditional Judeo-Christian values that defined America's creation and became the blueprint for her greatness.

convictions.[285] How do we tell? Well, since it is sometimes hard to know the personal life of any politician, the best way to determine this is to read his or her writings and to look at how he or she has voted in the past. Look at who their friends and associates have been. Then ask, "Do they portray a Godly Worldview?" The footnote will allow you to find information on what a Christian Worldview is.[286]

Similarly, I could *not* vote for someone who wanted to turn America into a theocracy or who wanted to impose the Ceremonial or the biblical Judicial laws on everyone, even if they were devout Christians. I'll clarify what these types of laws are shortly.

There are other requirements. We'll look at them shortly.

And for goodness sake, let's not have anybody say that we should *not* judge if people are Christ Followers or God-fearing Jews or not, or that we should not judge if they have godly moral convictions before we vote for them. Of course we have to judge. Using that sort of logic, we would have to conclude that it was wrong to judge if Hitler really was a Christian as he claimed, before the Germans voted for him in 1934.[287]

What if we don't have a choice?

On many occasions, especially on the coasts of the U.S., we won't always have the choice of voting for someone with our convictions, i.e. for someone that meets the above criterion. This was the argument that my previously noted discussion centered around. In these cases we need to be careful about the decisions we make. This is a true dilemma, about which many God-fearing men and women will disagree. Do we vote for the lesser of two evils, which is still an evil? Or do we *not* vote for them and let the "greater" of the two evils come to power. I don't know that I can answer this for the general situation. In 2008, I know that McCain was defiantly not my choice but was the lesser of two evils. I always say, "I didn't vote for McCain. I voted for Palin. McCain just happened to be on the ticket."

However, Christians must discuss, debate and analyze this at length and then use experience, conscience, convictions and knowledge of the consequences to vote whichever way makes sense. No one should vote blindly.

Here's the deal though, whenever we see ourselves in this situation, it is a real indication that we need *more* Bible believing Christians and Jews to get involved in politics so we can have more options. If we had more Christ followers and God-fearing Jews running and voting, things would take a rather positive turn. Perhaps we'll one day get to the point where we have to choose between two outstanding persons of constitutional knowledge, moral convictions and godly character. Isn't that a good goal to have?

"I can't believe you are saying only Christians and Jews should be in

---

[285] Naturally, there are other factors, such as whether I agree with their solutions.

[286] http://www.gotquestions.org/Christian-worldview.html also "Philosophical Foundations for a Christian Worldview" William Lane Craig, J.P. Moreland, 2002 Inter-varsity Press

[287] Hitler never had enough votes to win an election. He won some minor elections but was finally appointed to power by a weak president – an Aaron type of leader, to bring order to the chaos that Hitler had had his own people cause. www.historylearningsite.co.uk/Nazi_Germany_dictatorship.htm

Government!"

A liberal tried to attack me with this once. My response was, "Whoa! Whoa! Implied in that accusation is that I am *not* allowed to vote for or promote only God-fearing Christians and Jews. I didn't realize that we were living under a dictatorship with no freedom of speech! What is wrong with my preferring only certain types of people in government, and my encouraging other Christians and Jews to vote for them? Do you see me accusing *you* of being evil because you only want socialists, left wingers, and progressives in government? This is sheer hypocrisy! Your statement shows that *you* are the intolerant un-American one here." They quickly backed off.

If someone accuses you of this, don't take that monkey on your back. Mete it out deftly in return. This is America. We can vote for whomever we want and we can encourage and work to convince others to do so as well. Everything else is fascism. (OK, it isn't really fascism, but it's fun to say that).

So what can we add to our argument?

We know that politicians are the ones who make the laws, that all laws are based on moral values and that all moral values are based on religious values. Thus anyone who says that religion and politics should not be mixed is completely ignorant about the role of politicians or the source of moral values. Secondly, the religious convictions of any lawmaker you elect are of critical importance. Thirdly, anyone who encourages Christians to avoid politics is obviously ignorant of both the role of politicians and the origin of our laws. Pastors and elders, surely you agree that you have to lead and teach the flock in this regard. Should you do anything less?

Eighteen

Neil, you seem to be ignoring the Gospel here? The Bible is about forgiveness.
A friend complaining.

*Actually, the Bible is about repentance first, there's only forgiveness and mercy **after** repentance. Without repentance, the Gospel says justice will be served.*
My response.

Why The Law Was Given: What About Sin, Salvation, And The Law?

Lest you think that I've forgotten about sin and salvation. Let's take a three page Christian theological break here and clarify: Sin came about because we disobeyed the law. The law preceded sin (i.e. "Don't eat of the fruit of the Tree of Knowledge"). For you cannot sin if there is no law. But why was the law given? To force us to sin? Of course not! The law in the Garden of Eden about not eating from the tree was given to Adam and Eve for what purpose? It was to protect them and their descendents from great pain and suffering and keep them in harmony with God. Had Adam freely obeyed God, his life and our lives would have been a lot less painful. See the footnote if you want to know why the tree was put there in the first place.[288]

God said that if you eat of the Tree of Knowledge of Good and Evil, on that day you will surely die. But on that day when they ate, Adam did *not* fall over dead, did he? So what kind of death was God talking about? Spiritual death obviously (followed eventually by physical death).[289] What is Spiritual

---

[288] I know, you are thinking, "That doesn't make sense, why give Adam the option to rebel? If God had not given Adam the opportunity to sin then there'd be no problem." But that's not true. God has enough creations that obey Him and worship Him because they have no freewill *not* to. But God wished to have creatures love him freely and for Adam to have true freewill, he needed to have the opportunity to exercise that freewill and rebel. Without having that opportunity, Adam would never have had freewill. That's like saying, "You are free to go anywhere you want. Oh, all the doors are locked." That would not be freewill. To have freewill, one must have the opportunity to exercise that freewill and that includes the freewill to rebel against God. This concept of Adam's freewill is coherent even with Reform Theology.

[289] Note Adam's separation from God as far as we know was temporary, as we believe he did reenter God's presence after he died. So, he was never *eternally* separated from God.

death? Spiritual death is separation from God and that did indeed happen that day itself when God kicked them out of the Garden and His presence. It was a natural consequence of rebellion against God. Remember *Eternal* Spiritual Death is Hell. So clearly that law was for our well-being. But the law is now our curse because we are unable to keep the law due to our sin nature. And since it is now our very nature to rebel against God, it doesn't matter how hard we try to keep the law. We will eventually disobey what we know is good. We are all like the smoker who knows that cigarettes will kill him but rationalizes or purposely smokes in defiance against what he knows is true. Thus, we are under the same curse as Adam.

Galatians 3:10 All who rely on observing the law are under a curse, for it is written, "Cursed is everyone who does not continue to do everything written in the Book of the Law." 11 Clearly no one is justified before God by the law...

But if we cannot keep the laws given by God, (remember we showed earlier, all the laws have both spiritual and physical value) does that mean that the law is of no use and that our secular nation should ignore it? Absolutely not. Jesus tells us that the law will never be abolished.

Matthew 5:17-20 "Do not think that I have come to abolish the Law or the Prophets; I have not come to abolish them but to fulfill them. I tell you the truth, until heaven and earth disappear, not the smallest letter, not the least stroke of a pen, will by any means disappear from the Law until everything is accomplished. 19 Anyone who breaks one of the least of these commandments and teaches others to do the same will be called least in the kingdom of heaven, but whoever practices and teaches these commands will be called great in the kingdom of heaven. 20 For I tell you that unless your righteousness surpasses that of the Pharisees and the teachers of the law, you will certainly not enter the kingdom of heaven.

So then, how can we be saved? How can we be justified in front of God? We can't keep the law, and the law will not be abolished. So are we doomed? No. Not at all.

You see, God loves us and the law that condemns us also provides a way out. This same law that prescribes damnation for rebelling against God provides a scapegoat, a spotless lamb, a method of atonement that could be the substitution for that same curse. Someone who loves us greatly and is willing to suffer and die for us can become the curse for us and pay the price, the penalty for our sin.

Galatians 3:13 says that Christ is that substitution.

13 Christ redeemed us from the curse of the law by becoming a curse for us, for it is written, "Cursed is everyone who is hung on a tree."

So what Jesus was saying in Matthew 5 was that the law would never pass away. Why? Because it would be satisfied *fully*! What He was saying is that *He personally* was going to fulfill the law by paying the penalty, not that the law was cancelled.

So, now that Christ is the atonement, how do we avail ourselves of that?

Let's go back and fill in that missing passage from Galatians

Galatians 3:11 Clearly no one is justified before God by the law because, "The righteous will live by faith." 12 The law is not based on faith; on the

contrary, "The man who does these things will live by them."

So we avail ourselves of the atonement through faith. And that faith actually comes with a new law that encompasses (not cancels) the old law. This is the Law of Christ.

Having said all this, we can see that those of us who are saved are new creatures and are no more under condemnation by the law.

But does it not make sense that since the law was given for our safety, we should still use it as a wise and tested friend as we then evaluate our own nation's secondary laws, especially in a Republic. For as we've seen the law protects and guides all of us, Christian, Jew and even unbelievers. Now if that is the case, who is the most qualified to legislate the law? Someone who loves the law and respects it? Or someone who despises it and chafes under it?[290]

Moreover, currently many are attacking the basic Primary Transcendent Law of our Republic. If that falls we will end up like Rome and Germany in short order.

That is precisely why it behooves those of us who love God and love His Law to make our laws to protect our culture and our kids using the very same principles of the law that we love.

Pastors and elders let me ask you this: Is God's law of any value in instructing and guiding even those who hate God? Will an atheist and his children fare better in a nation that in a republican manner chooses to follow God's laws than they would in a nation that does not? If so then how can we refuse to try our best to do this?

Doubt my motives or goals?

Some readers seeing the focus here being mainly on political issues may doubt my zeal for and the importance of evangelization or my stance on the Gospel. Let me assure you that the focus of my Apologetics Ministry www.NoBlindFaith.com is purely about evangelization and teaching laypeople to witness to non-Christians in an easy non-confrontational way using facts, logic, history and reason. To find out my statement of belief please go to:

www.JesusIsInvolvedInPolitics.com/DoctrinalStatement.htm

---

[290] One could argue that since we are no longer under the law, we would have a tendency to ignore it and thus it disqualifies us as being good handlers of the law. But that is fallacious because the very fact that we realize that the law is good, and the fact that we realize that we should love the law, though it does not condemn us anymore, makes us far more qualified to handle it. Far more qualified that is than a person who rejects the law and claims it is unneeded or unnecessary. For you see those whose consciences were convicted by the law are now are no longer under the law and now love the law. Those who were not convicted are still under the law and either hate the law or see no value in it.

Neil Mammen

Nineteen

Socrates (to Euthyphro): "Is the pious loved by the gods because it is pious, or is it pious because it is loved by the gods?"
Plato, The Euthyphro Dilemma

Christian morality is based on pleasing or satisfying the whimsical capricious *God of the Bible, with only secondary importance for "doing unto others as you would yourself" and "loving your neighbor."*
Council for Secular Humanism[291]

Pointy Headed Boss (to Dilbert): "You are not allowed to have internal phone lists on your wall. There are excellent reasons for this policy, and I hope to someday know what they are."
Later - Pointy Headed Boss (to Catbert, Evil Director of Human Resource): "They're getting suspicious about the Random Policy Generator."
Dilbert Cartoon

Why The Law Was Given: Is God Capricious? Is God Good?

Did God arbitrarily make up the laws?

My Hindu friend who always argues with me about religion, had a smirk on his face. He'd been reading some atheist propaganda. Now, you must realize that he was only Hindu by name and by culture, not by conviction. He was a functional agnostic. The fact that we were eating at a vegetarian restaurant was because he'd grown up vegetarian and never developed a taste for meat. "Why is god good?" he asked with that smirk. "Is he good because whatever he does is good? If he said killing infidels was good would that make it good?"

When we try to argue that God's moral values are applicable to everyone and should be used as a basis for legislation, we have to first prove that God is not capricious. What my Hindu friend had been reading was the atheist claim that God *arbitrarily* decides what is good and what is bad. That, they say, makes Him capricious and His laws unworthy. Let me provide you with a definition of the word *capricious*.

> *Capricious adj.: determined by chance or impulse or whim rather than by necessity or reason; "authoritarian rulers are frequently capricious."[292]*

The quote at the beginning of this chapter from the Council for

---

[291] www.secularhumanism.org/index.php?section=columns&page=news
[292] www.thefreedictionary.com/capricious

Secular Humanism claims God is capricious and whimsical; He randomly decides what is good and what is evil for no good reason. This was Socrates' question to his student Euthyphro.

Bertrand Russell the avidly avowed atheist formulated the problem this way in his book, Why I Am Not A Christian:

> If you are quite sure there is a difference between right and wrong, you are then in this situation: Is that difference due to God's fiat [decree/command] or is it not? If it is due to God's fiat, then for God Himself there is no difference between right and wrong, and it is no longer a significant statement to say that God is good.
>
> If you are going to say, as theologians do, that God is good, you must then say that right and wrong have some meaning which is independent of God's fiat, because God's fiats are good and not good independently of the mere fact that he made them. If you are going to say that, you will then have to say that it is not only through God that right and wrong came into being, but that they are in their essence logically anterior to[prior to/separate from] God.[293]

In other words, Russell said that if good is good because God randomly decided what was good, then good is not *really* good. It is arbitrary. But if good is good because of something separate from God, then God is not sovereign because He's a slave to this goodness and thus goodness is greater than God. Is Russell right? Of course he is *not*, and I'll show you how to refute him completely in the next few pages.

Is whatever we do for God good?

Remember the Gestapo Captain and the liberal Rabbi in the Walter Martin story we described in an earlier chapter. The liberal Rabbi who believes there is no objective right or wrong is asked by the Gestapo Captain, "I'm going to kill you, is there any reason why I shouldn't?"

The liberal Rabbi can't say, "Because it's wrong or because it's inhumane or because it's bad."[294]

In many ways, the Gestapo Captain was a relativistic thinker just like the liberal Rabbi. The Captain thought that whatever he did for the Nazi party or the German people was automatically good and that morality was something that the Nazis, not the Jews, got to define. In the same way if we were to say blindly that whatever we do for God is automatically good, it could lead to relativistic thinking and the claim of capriciousness. So let's see how we can refute this claim.

Why God is not capricious

First, we must understand that it's important that the laws that we are given be non-capricious *real* laws with *real* consequences. If God were to give us laws that had no real consequences and merely order us to obey them because it was His whim, then He would indeed be capricious. And those laws

---

[293] Bertrand Russell, Why I Am Not a Christian (New York: Touchstone, Simon & Schuster, 1957), 12. As quoted by Gregory Koukl in Euthyphro's Dilemma on the Stand to Reason website. www.str.org/site/News2?page=NewsArticle&id=5236

[294] Yes, yes, I know you are thinking that he could say, "I have information that I can use to buy my life…" but let's assume like most of the Jews who were sadly killed, he doesn't have anything that the Gestapo Captain needed, that the Captain couldn't have taken anyway.

would be illogical, unnecessary, random and arbitrary.[295] Sadly many Christians don't seem to realize this. I personally didn't either until I had to respond to an atheist about it. (This is one of the reasons for my zeal for apologetics).

Take the first point: All the laws that God gave us must be real laws with real and negative consequences to humans (I will prove this with examples later). But that means when we sin, we are effectively committing a double crime – that is, doing two bad things. We are hurting ourselves and others, *and* we are rebelling against the Almighty God who created us. The latter being the more serious crime, but understandably not one that we wish to legislate.

Second, we have to understand that the secular atheistic humanists have phrased the problem based on their limited understanding of God. It's not that God is capricious or that He is beholden to a higher value. What will refute them and Russell is simply this:

God *is* good.

And that is our second point.

Huh? You ask.

Let me explain. It's not that God has arbitrarily determined what good is. Nor it is that He is beholden to a higher value than Himself. It's just that His *very* nature is one of goodness. God *is* good. God is by nature *good*. Goodness is who He is. God could no more decide tomorrow that torturing babies for fun was good than he could ever stop being God. Yes, God is enslaved but He is enslaved by His *own* nature. He is enslaved to *God*. He is enslaved to Himself. It's that vicious cycle similar to God having to be the center of His own praises. God could no more stop being good than He could stop being God.[296] Good is good, and God is good. Their sources are the same.

"Ah but," my atheist friends complain, "you've not defined good, you've just said that God is good, so your definition of good is God and your definition of God is good. That's circular reasoning, and you can't prove it."

But as we have already shown it is actually circular reasoning if you try to create a definition of good without a supreme moral giver. You need a standard and you need a standard giver.

Since my atheist friends cannot come to a definition of good without a standard, they are in a similar dilemma. At least our theory has explanatory

---

[295] Someone could argue that the command by God in the Garden of Eden, "Don't eat of the Fruit of the Tree of Knowledge of Good and Evil," was capricious. But that would be presumptuous. Whenever we are dealing with an intelligent agent like God, presuming you know all the parameters as a human is illogical. We can't argue from the lack of evidence. In addition as mentioned in an earlier footnote, if God did not give Adam the ability and opportunity to reject Him or disobey Him, He would not have truly given Adam freewill.

[296] Remember as we've said in a previous footnote, one of the things that we need to be clear about is that God cannot do *anything*. He cannot stop being God, He cannot sin, He cannot cease to exist, and He cannot be irrational or illogical. He cannot learn. He cannot make a round two- dimensional square. He cannot make 1+1 = 3. All of those actually are derived from "He cannot stop being God." For a full logical response to "Can God create a stone so big that he cannot move it" see www.JesusIsInvolvedInPolitics.com and do a search for "Stone so big."

power and is self-consistent.[297] Do note, however, that I do not use this methodology to prove the existence of God. There are enough other ways to do this (all outside the scope of this book, see "Who is Agent X? Proving that Science and Logic show it is more reasonable to think God exists," Neil Mammen, Rational Free Press, 2009).

Since the source of the definition of good is self evident, and the character of God is good, then it follows that God and the source of good can be the same. So there is no capriciousness in God.

But is it circular reasoning? It isn't, if I can show that God *has* to be good to be God. It's not circular reasoning then because being good *inherently* is a *necessary* condition for any god to be *the* God.

A bad god won't last long

Let's look at this. God could not be *anything* but good. In other words, there could not exist a god, who was bad, or a god who was irrational, or a god who was not loving? Why? Because it would not work. An irrational god would self-destruct and could not last for all eternity. An evil god would never survive. A deficient god who was in any way not self sufficient, or in any way destructive, or in anyway not 'just', could not last for infinity as his own shortcomings would destroy him.

How can I prove this? Quite simply: Bad cannot exist except as a privation of good, bad is a corruption of good. What I mean by that is that there is nothing such as "bad," bad only exists if good is corrupted.[298] If good ceases to exist, bad will cease to exist as well. A good example is a shadow (note, I don't mean darkness). A shadow cannot exist without light. If a shadow were to destroy all light, it would destroy itself. All that would be left is darkness[299], which is not a shadow.

That means infinite bad cannot exist, as it will cease to exist as soon as it becomes infinite. Since by necessity God is infinite[300] and by definition God is perfect in all things, He can never be infinitely or perfectly bad, as He will self-destruct (of course, the concept of God self-destructing doesn't make sense, and that's why we see that a bad god is impossible).

People can argue about it any way they want, but if they adhere to logic they'll end up coming to the same conclusion.

I would theorize that even Satan realized that if he *were* able to

---

[297] William Lane Craig, one of this century's best debaters and philosophers, has used this argument quite successfully in many debates against atheists. I.e. if objective moral values exist, then God exists. Objective moral values do exist, thus God exists. See www.williamlanecraig.com. I always describe Dr. Craig this way: He's the guy who, after he's done debating an atheist, you actually feel sorry for the atheist. In his winsome manner, Craig destroys every single one of their arguments. Most atheists don't know what hit them.

[298] One could try to argue that bad is a corruption of an amoral thing as well. For instance, a knife is amoral, for one can use it to kill instead of cut an apple. But the very existence of that knife is "good." It is good that the knife exists because it is useful and has purpose. Non-existence would be the only truly amoral thing, but non-existence is not an option if anything at all exists.

[299] Darkness would be amorality in this example, i.e. neutrality- neither good nor evil.

[300] This can be proved in one paragraph; science agrees that whatever caused the Universe to begin at the point of the Big Bang was outside of time and space. This can only be an infinite being, since you cannot create time if you are *in* time. For more on this go to www.JesusIsInvolvedInPolitics.com and look up "proving God exists."

survive without God (remember Satan was merely a created being),[301] he would inevitably destroy himself as he became fully evil. A deficient evil being like Satan could not become or maintain himself as a universal being. This is further exacerbated by the fact that evil has no definition if good does not exist; yet good, while not being fully appreciated, would still exist without evil. In all evil situations some good must exist. Even in Hitler's Germany, those who were Nazi's did good things. They loved their children. They cared for their elderly parents, (though who knows how long that would have lasted with their euthanasia programs?) It is impossible to imagine how the Nazis could have continued to exist if every Nazi was absolutely evil.[302]

So, as we can see, good can exist without evil. However, evil will destroy itself without good. Thus to exist, God must be good. Good must be a core characteristic of God. It's not separate. Bertrand Russell has been refuted.

Note too that "Good" as we see, is a transcendent value. Good existed long before a universe existed. Similarly $1+1=2$ long before any universe was created and it will still be true after all universes have died a heat death. There are no possible universes where $1+1$ is not equal to 2. Mathematics is a transcendent art. So are truth, justice, logic, rationality, love, reason and well, set theory among others.[303] They are all part of the very intrinsic nature of God. They are transcendent and eternal.

Okay now let's get back to the Laws.

---

[301] I have a trick question that I use now and then. I ask, "Who is the opposite of Satan?" The answer is *not* God. Satan is a created being not a creator. He is not omnipresent in time and space and all dimensions. He is not omnipotent or omniscient. The closest opposite to Satan may be one of the archangels. If you ask, "Who is the opposite of God?" The answer is "No one" No one can be the equal and opposite of the Almighty Eternal Creator.

This also means that Satan must be of such a mind that either he knowing that he can never destroy God wishes to be a thorn in God's side till he Satan is destroyed or thinking that he can destroy God is willing to destroy himself to do so.

[302] This is similar to the concept of Total Depravity. We humans are totally depraved, but we are not absolutely depraved. This means that while we have a depraved sin nature, not everything we do is sinful or destructive.

[303] Note that physical, atomic, and chemical laws are not necessarily transcendent because they did not causally (that's cause-ally not casually) exist before the universe was created and one could feasibly reason than a universe could be created with different laws.

Twenty

BARTLET: I like your show. I like how you call homosexuality an "abomination!"

JACOBS (Dr. Laura-like radio psychologist seated nearby): I don't say homosexuality is an abomination, Mr. President. The Bible does.

BARTLET: Yes it does. Leviticus!

JACOBS: 18:22.

BARTLET: Chapter and verse. I wanted to ask you a couple of questions while I had you here...Here's one that's really important, because we've got a lot of sports fans in this town. Touching the skin of a dead pig makes one unclean. Leviticus 11:7. If they promise to wear gloves, can the Washington Redskins still play football? Can Notre Dame? Can West Point? Does the whole town really have to be together to stone my brother John for planting different crops side by side? Can I burn my mother in a small family gathering for wearing garments made from two different threads? Think about those questions, would you?

The West Wing TV script (which was lifted from an urban legend email by the writers)

Which passages of Scripture should guide our public policy? Should we go with Leviticus, which suggests slavery is OK and that eating shellfish is abomination? How about Deuteronomy, which suggests stoning your child if he strays from the faith? Or should we just stick to the Sermon on the Mount - a passage that is so radical that it's doubtful that our own Defense Department would survive its application? So before we get carried away, let's read our [B]ibles. Folks haven't been reading their [B]ibles.

Barack Obama[304] repeating the urban legend.

Why The Law Was Given: Do We Need To Follow All Those Laws About Pork Or Stoning People?

"**A**h," the atheist arrogantly said to me, "Yes, you're the kind of person that wants us to listen to God's laws, the God who says slavery is good, who says we should stone people for working on Saturday and who thinks that gays should be executed."

I'd just sat through a debate at Stanford University watching Christopher Hitchens get decimated by Jay Richards of the Discovery Institute. Hitchens had spent his time on stage not responding to a single debate issue. Instead he'd spent his allotted minutes telling everyone what large male organs

---

[304] obama.senate.gov/podcast/060628-call_to_renewal_1/. Please note, this chapter was written at least a year before Obama was elected.

Neil Mammen

he had, how he hated Mormons and how all Christians were idiots and making a crude sexual jokes along the way. Jay had stuck to the topic and delivered a very systematic statement about why God existed and the ideas behind Intelligent Design. One of these arguments was the existence of objective moral values.[305]

After the debate, I'd gone up on stage to talk to Jay[306] and had gotten dragged into an argument with a very belligerent atheist. He was wearing a very faded "Silicon Valley Atheists" T-shirt and seemed primarily angry at Hitchens for doing such a lousy job. (Of course he used different language.) I'd made the mistake of asking him what Hitchens could have said to refute Jay. Instead of a response, he launched into attack mode. It seemed unrelated to my question, but later, on the internet, I found out that this was his standard spiel. It was obviously rehearsed. But don't think he's the exception; this is a standard issue that many non-Christians have when you start to witness to them. It would be unloving not to have a valid and logical response to them.

Whenever we talk about the law, we naturally run into these sorts of complaints. Many of my friends add "But wait, doesn't the Old Testament also have the weird dietary laws and even weirder laws about not patching old clothes with new cloth and so on?" Their conclusion is that the Old Testament does not apply anymore.

Or we get the ignorant ramblings of an email letter which was plagiarized by TV show writers of The West Wing to try and shame people who believe the Bible is God's Word as shown in this chapter's heading quote.[307]

Since we are not living in a Jewish theocracy, our country is not under the laws of Moses.[308] So, my non-Christian readers let me put your minds at ease. At no point are we insisting that the Old Testament laws are to be reinstated in our society or that they all have legal power today. Not even my God-fearing Jewish friends want this.

---

[305] If Objective Moral Values exist then God exists. Objective Moral Values do exist so God exists. See http://www.leaderu.com/offices/billcraig/docs/washdeba-craig1.html. Read all his debates. It's worth the time and will equip you to evangelize using facts and logic.

[306] I become friends with Jay when I'd hosted him for our August Apologetics Speaker Series at our local churches. Pastors and student leaders, if you ever need a great speaker on Intelligent Design or the concepts of the Free Market, let me heartily endorse Jay Richards. www.discovery.org. Say Neil sent you.

[307] For a point by point rebuttal of the nonsensical claims of The West Wing, see the response by Hank Hanagraaf of the Christian Research Institute (CRI) at:
www.mastershouse.org/issues_&_answers/homosexuality_hanagraaf2.htm

[308] Now we understand that we are now under the Laws of Christ. Gal 5:18 says… if you are led by the Spirit, you are not under the Law.
But does that mean we can do anything we want? Not at all. If we are led by the Spirit of God, then we won't do things of the flesh. And what are they? Paul tells us clearly:
Gal 5:19 Now the deeds of the flesh are evident, which are: immorality, impurity, sensuality, 20 idolatry, sorcery, enmities, strife, jealousy, outbursts of anger, disputes, dissensions, factions, 21 envying, drunkenness, carousing, and things like these, of which I forewarn you, just as I have forewarned you, that those who practice such things will not inherit the kingdom of God.
And what are the consequences if we are led by the Spirit?
Gal 5:22 But the fruit of the Spirit is love, joy, peace, patience, kindness, goodness, faithfulness, 23 gentleness, self-control; against such things there is no law.

However, as we said often in this book, there is a valid case for analyzing these laws and seeing what common sense guidance we can glean from them. So while they don't have legal power in our country, they do have great value in legislating "lesser laws. And I will propose some guidelines that we should and have indeed used to arrive at our "lesser" laws in a later chapter.

But now, let us look at the Old Testament laws, since the question is valid. As we do that, we first notice that God's commandments are targeted at four different groups: The Government, The Church/Temple, the Family, and Individuals. Each of these groups have specific laws that may or may not apply to the other. For instance, it is not the role of the Church or the family to imprison felons or enforce building codes. Similarly, it is not the role of the government to correct *or* teach the young. Some overlap. It is the Government and the Church's role to legitimize and enforce marriage vows. The roles are not to be confused and tragedy can befall a society that does mingle the commands. In addition, there are laws that apply to individuals *only*. We'll talk about that in the next chapter.

Besides the target audiences, we secondly notice, the laws are *further* divided into four types: Ceremonial laws, Judicial Laws, Regulatory/Civil Laws and Moral Laws.[309] Let's review these types.

The Ceremonial Laws

One breakdown of the description of the different types of the laws can be found on the Southfield Reformed Presbyterian Church website. Here is their description of the Ceremonial laws:

"The Ceremonial laws refer to the sacrificial rituals (the temple cults): the priesthood, the sacrifices, the Levitical holy days (i.e., the feasts), the temple, the music, the utensils, circumcision, ritual washings, and so on. The Ceremonial laws strengthened the faith of the Jews in the coming Messiah, by typifying both Him and the redemption from sin that He would bring. The Ceremonial laws were directed to those in Israel. They were restorative, for they reflected God's mercy and salvation. They were anticipatory, for they looked ahead to the perfect, final salvation wrought by the Messiah. And they were temporary, for as types and shadows they could not really remove the guilt of sin and bring perfection. God always intended to supersede the whole ceremonial system by Jesus Christ."[310]

So, we see that the Ceremonial laws described to the Jews are rules and ordinances that were to be observed in the worship of God. Many of my Jewish friends observe them out of tradition, yet none believes those laws should be the laws of this land. Why? Again, it's because we are not the theocratic nation of Judah. Moreover, these laws also don't apply to Christians because Christ has decreed that we do not need to worship at the Temple anymore. He has also told us that we already have a high priest (Himself) who supplants all other high priests. And we have an advocate who represents us before God the Father (the Holy Spirit). So, most Ceremonial laws do not

---

[309] Some scholars divide these into only three groups. See www.reformed.com/pub/law.htm for an excellent analysis of this. Last visited 3/6/07

[310] www.reformed.com/pub/law.htm

Neil Mammen

apply to Christians, and they certainly don't apply to non-Christians (we will see an exception though later). While many of my Jewish friends do adhere to them, they don't wish to impose it on you for they believe those laws were for the Jews alone.

The Ceremonial laws do however have symbolic value. Often these rules and regulations reminded the Jews that they were a chosen people, blessed by God and they were not to mix certain things together as an example of their uniqueness. And part of this was God's plan of how He was going preserve the Jews as a unique group from which His great love would be shown to all mankind centuries later. Many are the races and groups that merged[311] and lost their identities as time went by. But not so with the three tribes of Israel; Levi, Judah and Benjamin, because they observed the Ceremonial laws

While many of these Ceremonial laws, like the ritual dietary laws, are healthy or advantageous for us to follow, we don't want the punishments associated with all those laws to be imposed on people. So, while it would be wise for all of us to use some of them as advisories, it does not make sense to mandate every one of those that apply to our *own* health, as laws.[312]

The Judicial Laws

Next are the Judicial Laws. These were ordinances for the government of the Jewish commonwealth and the punishment of offenders. This is where most people get mixed up. Besides specific laws for the Jews in Israel under a *theocracy*, the Judicial Laws indicated the *punishments* that the people of Israel were to mete out to those who broke the *other* laws. It does *not* indicate what *non*-Jewish nations should do. Non-Jewish nations are to determine their own punishments for violating laws. Since we are representative democracy not a theocracy, our representatives are the ones to decide the punishments for us. So, sorry President Bartlet, (aka ignorant ABC writers), we don't need to stone our neighbors or our rebellious teenagers, we can choose other punishments or no punishment, or just stern warnings and the loss of Xbox privileges.

The Regulatory Laws

The Regulatory (also called Civil) Laws are the laws that God gave to his people as guidance for running their nation. After being slaves for 400 years, very few of the Jews knew a lot about farming or a building a free society. So God gave them certain laws, such as how not to plant certain crops next to each other (this also doubled as a Ceremonial Law), how to build homes with terraces that had a parapet so that people would not fall off the edge, and so on. Despite what "President" Bartlet said in his sophomoric rant,

---

[311] Note there were no restrictions on marrying those who were not Jewish by blood; the restriction was on marrying those who were non-Jewish by *belief* and adopted traditions. If a person became Jewish they were to be treated identical to any other Jew. E.g. Ruth and Rahab.

[312] There are those however, that involve the health of *others*, and in a public service setting it makes sense to mandate these into law. For instance, there are some ancient Ceremonial laws that we have made into a U.S. civil laws and with good reason, we'll hear more about that later. We could get into a heated debate at this point about the "Nanny State," which we find ourselves trending towards, where the government in getting involved in banning trans-fats etc. but I will leave that to others.

the punishments for violating these laws were not severe and certainly not death. Read it for yourself in Leviticus and Deuteronomy. Think of these laws as being like building codes that require balconies to have railings of a certain height. While these laws have great advisory value, no one in their right mind (except ignorant imbecilic mean spirited TV writers) would imagine that these were laws that we today would have to punish by death. That would be akin to the City Inspector coming to check your re-pipe permit and deciding you should be executed because you didn't install a backpressure valve. What pure rot! Did I mention that I think those ABC writers were idiots? I guess I did.

The Moral Laws

These are the Ten Commandments and other similar laws. These are the laws that this book is most concerned with. Moral Laws have both physical and spiritual consequences. They are given to protect us and to protect the weak and the innocent. They are transcendent and remain as a primary moral guide and a basis for our "Natural Laws," and there is value in having them taught publicly. Moral laws apply to everyone in every one of the four groups: Government, Church, Family, and Individuals.

Objective moral laws teach us principles that we can extrapolate to other laws. However, I would go a step further. I think every Christian needs to be able to publicly defend the value of the Moral Law and for that matter *any and all* of the laws if we intend to impose them on others.

Why?

We live in a post biblical nation. Most people don't know what's in the Bible, don't care what's in the Bible and don't agree with what's in the Bible. Thus, the burden of proof is upon us to be able to rationally and statistically defend the value of the Moral Laws that are in there. How do we do this? By utilizing the exceptional work that organizations like Family Research Council (www.FRC.org) have done to bring such research to the forefront. FRC has published many studies on the effects divorce, same-sex marriage and so on; we will look at some of them shortly.

Summary on the types of Laws[313]

So let's quickly summarize what we know about the laws:

We can take the Regulatory Laws as good sage advice when they apply, and the New Testament makes these plain to us.

We can ignore the Judicial Laws concerning punishments since the punishments listed there were for the people of a theocratic Israel, and not for our republic. It is logical that the punishments if any for not adhering to our

---

[313] One could argue that this is an arbitrary delineation into four groups but that is not the case, as I have laid out a logical explanation for the laws and their place and value in society. Thus, the onus would be upon those who would insist that we implement them *all* to justify why they *all* needed to be implemented. The second argument could be that: Well, in that case, why can't we say that the law against homosexuality was a ceremonial law and thus has no value today. Note they can't say it's a Judicial Law obviously, and if they said it was a moral or advisory law, they'd be agreeing with us, because we are the ones claiming the law against homosexuality is a moral and advisory law. The reason the law against homosexuality is not a ceremonial, is because the law against homosexuality was given to protect society. Homosexual behavior has measurable negative consequences to both society and those who practice it, unlike wearing two types of cloth. We'll discuss this in more detail in an upcoming chapter.

civil or Moral Laws in our nation are to be determined by our *own* legislature. Naturally, there will be few if any punishments for violating Ceremonial laws except perhaps for shame or shunning.

But unlike the rest, we should adhere to the Moral Laws because they are good for us and any violations have spiritual, social, physical and/or emotional consequences.

Some may ask, "Why should there be *any* punishment for violating the Moral Laws? Isn't there a physical consequence, and isn't that punishment enough?

Yes, there is a physical consequence to violating a Moral Law, which is why there was a law to begin with. However, the physical consequence may not occur to the one who violated the law and may not occur for generations, yet when it does, many "innocent" people will suffer. Or the physical consequence may not occur every time and, as with seatbelt laws, a punishment may be good negative reinforcement. In addition, if an immediate physical punishment is meted out, the one who committed the offense may learn their lesson quickly and perhaps others will see the punishment and be dissuaded from going down the same path. This is also why it is important that justice be quick and not delayed by years. However, it is up to the legislature and their conscience to determine which Moral Laws are to be punished and *what* those punishments should be.

So are there objective moral absolutes?

Absolutely (pun intended)! Is every law in the Bible a moral absolute? Absolutely not. As we've shown, some are. Yet, others like the punishments (stoning) or the dietary recommendations (pork) or the ceremonial rules (old cloth with new) are not. Is that an arbitrary decision? No. Look at the context, and you can logically determine if it is or isn't. Context and logic is king. Do rational people disagree on some of the peripheral (lesser) laws? Yes, they do, but they agree on the main ones. Do the disagreements indicate there is no objective morality? Not at all. Just because we do not know all the Moral Laws does not mean there aren't any. For years we didn't know or even agree on all the details about the laws of gravity or thermodynamics, did that mean these laws did not exist? Similarly, it just shows that we should be willing to discuss it and show the pros and cons of it, and determine the truth as with any law. However, I would say it is always better to err on the side of caution.

Twenty-one

But I tell you, Do not resist an evil person. If someone strikes you on the right cheek, turn to him the other also. And if someone wants to sue you and take your tunic, let him have your cloak as well. If someone forces you to go one mile, go with him two miles. Give to the one who asks you, and do not turn away from the one who wants to borrow from you.
Matt 5:39-42, The Sermon on the Mount

Or should we just stick to the Sermon on the Mount - a passage that is so radical that it's doubtful that our own Defense Department would survive its application? So before we get carried away, let's read our [B]ibles. Folks haven't been reading their [B]ibles.
Barack Obama, repeated[314]

But What About The Sermon On The Mount?

Jesus said: Turn the other cheek. Isn't there a tension between the Sermon on the Mount and all the Old Testament commandments?" A liberal friend was trying to show me that everything that Christ said in the New Testament should at best override all the Old Testament commandments and any judging and at the least make sure that Christians never support their nation going to war.

Barack Obama, in the quote above, implies that if we were to legislate from the Bible, our own Department of Defense (DoD) would have to be shut down.[315] Is he right?

So what about the Sermon on the Mount? Is there a tension? Can the DoD survive its implications?

Some people *do* indeed need to read their Bibles a bit more and in *context*. You see, in the introduction to the *very* same Sermon on the Mount, Jesus says that He didn't come to wipe out the law but to *fulfill* it.

Matthew 5:17 *Do not think that I have come to abolish the Law or the Prophets;* **I have not come to abolish them but to fulfill them.** *18 I tell you*

---

[314] //obama.senate.gov/podcast/060628-call_to_renewal_1/ Let me repeat, I know it sounds like I'm picking on a sitting president, but honestly, all this was written long before he won the 2008 elections. He just said a lot of things that attacked everything I believed in and were rich with fundamental errors in critical thinking. Do remember he fired the first shots in these quotes, I'm just responding to his attacks.

[315] I'm still not sure what his "solution" to this was? Was he suggesting we change our military or stop reading the Bible? After his "surge" of troops in Afghanistan, I think he must have meant we must stop reading the Bible.

the truth, until heaven and earth disappear, not the smallest letter, not the least stroke of a pen, will by any means disappear from the Law until everything is accomplished. 19 Anyone who breaks one of the least of these commandments and teaches others to do the same will be called least in the kingdom of heaven, but whoever practices and teaches these commands will be called great in the kingdom of heaven. 20 For I tell you that unless your righteousness surpasses that of the Pharisees and the teachers of the law, you will certainly not enter the kingdom of heaven.

What is "the Law and the Prophets?" Well to a Jew that would be the Torah and the Prophetical books. To a Christian that would be what we call the Old Testament. And that includes the Moral Laws[316] and the prophetical warnings and condemnations.

So why would Jesus precede the Sermon on the Mount with this statement. Obviously, there is *no* chance that He intends the Sermon on the Mount to eliminate anything from the Old Testament despite our liberal friend's claim.

So how do we resolve this seeming contradiction? Perhaps it's not a problem because it's not a contradiction. Here's how I teach this to others:

I ask the person this question, "So are you saying that based on the Sermon on the Mount, if someone assaults you or mugs you and they take him to a judge, the judge should turn to you and say, "Okay please let him assault your other side (slap the other cheek) and please go home and get another wallet full of cash to give this man."

The response I usually get is, "Huh? What has a judge got to do with the Sermon on the Mount?"

I ask, "Are you saying the Sermon on the Mount does not apply to judges?"

Their response, after a thoughtful pause, "Well now that you mention it, it would seem rather ridiculous to have a justice system that followed it."

Okay, we are getting somewhere. Because we now realize that what Jesus said was *not* a commandment to judges or on how to run a legal system. It was a "commandment" to an *individual,* not a government. It was not a commandment that allowed you to make a decision for anyone else. You could make it for yourself only.

Obviously, a judge making a decision for others who did not adjudicate justly would be an *evil* judge. We all know (or should know) that in the very same Sermon on the Mount, Christ says He Himself is going to judge everyone at some point even for things that the world considers minor, like lusting after a woman. We also know that the Bible is full of righteous judges punishing evil doers and un-righteous judges *not* punishing evil doers. So why is there no dilemma? Why do we not think Christ is being a hypocrite or inconsistent?

Well it's obvious then that Christ's Sermon on the Mount was not directed at judicial or justice systems. It was a personal and individual admonition. Not a judicial or governmental admonition.

---

[316] We should note that Christ also satisfied all the ceremonial and judicial law requirements through His life and death. I.e. He satisfied the Ceremonial laws by fulfilling the prophecies that their symbolism was pointing to and He paid the ultimate punishment satisfying all judicial laws.

In the Sermon on the Mount, the context makes it plain; it was *to* you, *about* you. It was personal not to a church or a government. Our Lord is talking to you as a Christ follower about what *you* should do voluntarily in your own private and personal life. If someone strikes you *personally*, you are to consider forgiving him. But if someone brings a rapist to you as a judge, you are *not* to consider forgiving him. He is to pay the legal price of his transgression or justice will not be served. And if justice is not served you are an evil judge.

Notice too that the purpose of government is to ensure justice is upheld and the safety of their citizens is maintained and that their culture will endure. None of this can be done if judges don't judge, policemen don't protect from enemies within, and armies don't protect from enemies without (i.e. outside).

The admonitions in the Sermon on the Mount are not to you in your office as a judge (if you were one) or to you in your office of governor or president or even senator. And certainly not to you in your office as a soldier or policeman. Perish the thought that soldiers or policemen would decide to turn the other cheek and not resist an evil person rather than protect the innocents in their nations. If this had happened with all Christian soldiers, most of you'd all be speaking German unless you were Jewish (in which case your culture and people would have been exterminated) and I'd be speaking Japanese and be considered a second-class citizen. If they decide to do it now, then all of our grandchildren will be Muslim in a few years, as half my classmates in Yemen assured me, was the eventual fate of the West, (the other half wanted to move here).

Note carefully, some commandments like the Moral Laws are to everyone, governments, churches, families, and individuals. Some commandments are to only individuals. Some only to churches and some only to families.

Pastors and Elders

So pastors and elders, perhaps you can see why we need men and women of wisdom and biblical knowledge to be the ones making the laws, judging righteously, and not getting confused between the need for corporate justice and the call for personal compassion. Obama's misguided, confused, ignorant, and mean-spirited statement also shows us that we need leaders who not only read their Bibles, but understand it and love it, not those who misinterpret it at will. Who better to do this than men and women of deep biblical knowledge and love that you have encouraged to become leaders in our government?

The Sermon on the Mount was directed to you as an individual,
not to a government.
Some people do indeed need to read their Bibles more, that too in context.

Neil Mammen

Twenty-two

If I believed that the God of the Bible exists, I would reject him. [Because he] punishes people for sins that their ancestors committed, reference Exodus 20:5
   Johnny Skeptic (web page)

Christians have this repressed sense of sexuality. They think fun is bad. This is why they are against any sort of sexual pleasure.
   Atheist friend in an email, unknowingly reflecting the Council for Secular Humanism's view

"But now, with the aid of modern neuroscience and a wealth of research, it is evident that humans are the healthiest and happiest when they engage in sex only with the one who is their mate for a lifetime.
   Hooked: New Science on How Casual Sex is Affecting our Children, McIlhaney and McKissic Bush, Pg 136,

The church's task is not simply to bind the wounds of the victim beneath the wheel, but also to break the wheel itself.
   Dietrich Bonhoeffer

Why The Law Was Given: Why The Emphasis On Sexual Sins?

I was talking to a relative about biblical Moral Laws, and she asked, "Why it is that sexual sins seemed to be condemned more than most other sins? Is it because Christians are so uptight about sex? Do they think sex is dirty?"

On the contrary, I explained, Christians think that marriage and sex are to be holy, meaning 'set apart'. We think that marriage and sex need to be protected and kept pure. In fact, Christians are shown in the Song of Solomon that sex is not only clean but it is meant to be a lot of fun as well. And contrary to common opinion, the so-called "Puritan" aversion to sex is one based on ignorance. The Puritans not only approved of sex (as long as it was between husband and wife), but there is documentation that they ruled for a women who brought her husband before the Puritan judges because he was not fulfilling his sexual obligations to her. He was sent home under threat of punishment if he did not meet his biblical obligations and fulfill her needs. Afraid of sex? I think not.[317] If they had been afraid of sex or considered it

---

[317] Of course, this is a Catch-22. Now everybody is thinking they were dirty old men. So, what is it? Are they prudes or dirty old men? Or are they repressed dirty old men pretending to be prudes? If one cannot think of an appropriate response that the Puritans could have taken that doesn't typecast them in some way in this scenario, it shows that the critics are being irrational.

dirty, they would have punished the woman, not judged in her favor, or they would never have documented the event. The Puritans thought sex was necessary, beautiful, sacred and holy. Think "Holy Sex" or "set apart" sex. And as the quote that we opened this chapter with indicates; now we are finding scientific reasons and statistical evidence for this. Don't short-circuit your future, your happiness and your health by compromising on "Holy Sex."

Christians and Set Apart Sex

Both my cute beautiful daughters were born during the writing of this book, and my whole outlook on life and sex and boys changed. It occurred to me that we Christians treat sex like healthy families treat their daughter. They don't want her out sleeping with anyone she meets, being abused by men, marrying a man not worthy of her, or being taken advantage of. Nor do they want her to be a lonely old lady who shuns romance and thus never gets married and never has any children. And they certainly don't want her to be a prudish lonely old woman hiding in her home, who despises men and is afraid of intimacy and who thinks sex is dirty. They want her to be courted and end up permanently married to a nice young man who will protect, cherish, love and adore her for all of his life and provide them with lots of happy healthy grandchildren.

I've never heard a preacher tell me that sex between a husband and wife is sick or evil or wrong. Back in the Victorian era this may have been so (but this may also be an urban legend), and maybe there are a few weird churches still out there. But this is never taught by any of the major denominations, and there is no biblical basis for it. In fact, Paul tells husbands and wives to never keep each other's bodies away from each other.

1 Corinthians 7:3 The husband should fulfill his marital duty to his wife, and likewise the wife to her husband. 4 The wife's body does not belong to her alone but also to her husband. In the same way, the husband's body does not belong to him alone but also to his wife. 5 Do not deprive each other except by mutual consent and for a time, so that you may devote yourselves to prayer. Then come together again so that Satan will not tempt you because of your lack of self-control.

So when the Old Testament blesses sexual acts between husband and wife as enjoyable and the New Testament says you should never deprive each other of sex, why does the world think they can twist this around and pretend Christians are prudes? We aren't! So stop with the stupidity already.

Greater condemnation

Still the Bible harshly condemns sexual sins and proscribes boundaries for sex. This may be why non-Christians perceive Christians as being anti-sex. So why do sexual sins receive greater condemnation than, say, lying. The reasoning is straightforward. Compare this to the laws of our land; if you commit an offense that has tragic and severe consequences, the fines and punishments are more severe. For instance, if you illegally burn down an empty barn, the state will punish you much less than if you were to burn down a hospital or a populated school. In the same way, God warns us *more* severely about sins that have *more* severe consequences.

Neil Mammen

So why are sexual sins[318] disapproved of in the Bible more severely than other sins? Because the consequences of those sins are greater! I don't mean only the spiritual consequences. Sexual sins, like adultery and divorce, have terrible physical consequences, some affecting entire cultures for hundreds of years, affecting millions and millions of people. Let's look at some of them, and as we do, we'll see the tragic role bad laws in America have played in hurting the weakest amongst us. In the end I hope you will see why saying, "We should not be involved in politics" is the most unloving, unkind things a pastor can say or a church can do.

We'll start with marriage and divorce, most sexual sins have a direct effect on marriage and the family; as we will prove.

Marriage and Divorce

In 1969 (many years before I came to the U.S.), one of the men I later learned to respect, Ronald Reagan, unfortunately did a terrible thing. As Governor of California he failed to veto the very first "No Fault"[319] divorce bill that came to him (called ironically enough, the Family Law Act). By 1985 almost every state in the union had followed California and instituted a form of No Fault Divorce. Prior to this, it was rather difficult to obtain a divorce even if both parties wanted it. As a result many couples ended up staying together[320], and as we'll see statistics show that they ended up better off. For years, a minority of Christians fought against "No Fault" divorce, declaring that it would have social consequences that we would be

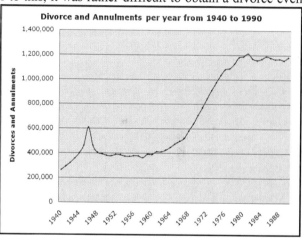

suffering for generations. Take a look *again* at the rate of divorces once the law was changed. They increased by 300% and stayed at that level.[321]

Still, for years, proponents of divorce claimed that divorce was good

---

[318] At no point am I suggesting that sexual sins lead to spiritual damnation any more than any other sin does. As we showed, all sin leads to separation from God (no one sin is necessary, but any one sin is sufficient), and at the root of all sin is simple rebellion against God. Yet, it is natural that sins of greater consequences would receive greater cautions.

[319] Interestingly, the collaborative online Encyclopedia Wikipedia claims that no fault divorce was a Bolshevik idea, first instituted in Russia in 1918.

[320] Or tragically accuse one another of abuse, which was one of few reasons for a divorce to be granted. However the no fault divorce law has not stopped this. Nowadays a parent may use this same false accusation to try to gain custody of their children. Some divorce lawyers even counsel their clients to falsify evidence and call the police prior to their leaving with their children, I have seen this happen in my very own extended family with a supposed "Christian" divorce lawyer in the Bay Area.

[321] http://www.cdc.gov/nchs/data/mvsr/supp/mv43_09s.pdf

for families, and "No Fault" divorce was even better. The idea was that it was better for kids to live between two homes and for their parents to divorce than to live in a family where their parents fought or hated each other. In addition, they claimed that it was better for women to be divorced than to suffer in a bad marriage. But finally, after enough time had passed to allow the consequences of divorce to affect our culture, statistics have come to our aid showing that the biblical injunction against divorce is for the good. It's tragic that it took us so long to learn it.

In 2000, Judith Wallerstein did one of the first in depth long-term studies of the effects of divorce on children.

By Marilyn Gardner Staff writer,
The Christian Science Monitor. New York, October 04, 2000

Thirty years after the divorce revolution first offered the promise of "freedom" to unhappy couples, assuring them that children are resilient and will quickly adjust, a quiet reappraisal is taking place. Several researchers now find that what might be liberating for adults can sometimes have unsettling long-term effects on children.

..."We've been wrong in thinking the main impact of divorce occurs at the breakup," says Ms. Wallerstein, who has followed the children of divorced families for 25 years. Noting that the major impact on children takes place when they reach their 20s, she adds, "That's when the ghosts rise from the basement."

It turns out that about a quarter of Americans have divorced parents. As a result many of these kids when grown are reluctant to marry, choosing instead to cohabitate and if they do marry, have a higher chance of divorce, thus feeding the vicious cycle. Sadly when these kids choose to have children out of wedlock, statistics show this can be even worse for *their* kids.

Wallerstein's book is a shocker. I recommend everyone reading this to buy her book even if it is to merely read the introduction by the author. Wallerstein talks about the individuals she's been personally following since the age of 3 or 4 when their parents went through a divorce. After reading her introduction about the trauma all the kids of divorce feel even as late at the age of 20 or older, I and most readers are stunned into a deep reflective horror at what we'd done to an entire generation of children. Apparently the trauma of their parents' divorce, even if it occurs *after* they have left the home as adults, psychologically, physiologically and relationally affect every *single* child for the *rest of their lives*. Read the entire book and you notice the tragic differences between children of divorce and non-divorce. In fact, buy the book for every couple you know who have kids and are considering divorce. *In light of that it takes a heartless parent to consider divorce or separation based on their own selfish desires.*

Note that neither Wallerstein nor I, suggest that divorce is never acceptable. Yet barring true physical abuse, if you love your kids, you will fight to protect them from divorce as long as you can and choose instead to unselfishly stay in your marriage.[322] This includes being very cautious whom

---

[322] I am not suggesting that divorces or separation should never occur for things like physical abuse. I am stating that the state and the culture should not make it easy or portray it as noble for any other reason.

you marry to begin with and how you nurture and care for your marriage after that.

Divorce and single parenthood have proved to have much worse consequences on society in general than we'd ever thought possible. As we'll show next, the shocking statistics indicate a correlation between the increase in kids from divorced and single parent homes and the increased incidence of rape, sexual abuse, drug abuse, loneliness, suicide and homicide.[323] If you want to see true social justice, increase the incidence of marriages and try to keep them intact. If you care about the innocents, change the laws. If you care about the future of marriage and innocents, ensure that those who *make* the laws love the Lord, *and* His Laws which keep us safe.

The consequences of single parent homes

Consider the following facts. This list is long, but please bear with it, as it will shock and sadden you. Where it discusses female-headed households it includes both out of wedlock children and divorced kids living with their mothers. Remember as you read it that despite widespread divorce and out of wedlock births, divorced/single parent household children are currently only 29% of the population. Remember too that *all* these statistics are consequences of our current laws. If this list[324] breaks your heart you can *never* say that politics is *not* the concern of the local church.

1. Kids are twice as likely to be juvenile delinquents or teen moms if their father does not live in their home.
2. Seventy percent of long-term prison inmates grew up without fathers.
3. Sixty percent of rapists grew up in female only-headed homes. This means kids from female only homes maybe four times as likely to commit rape as kids from healthy homes.
4. Seventy five percent of adolescents charged with murder grew up without fathers.
5. Fatherless children are three times more likely to fail in school, require psychiatric treatment and commit suicide as adolescents.
6. Fatherless children are up to 40 times more likely to experience child abuse compared with children growing up in two-parent families.[325]
7. Teenage girls from troubled families are more sexually active at earlier ages, and are more likely to become pregnant.[326]

---

[323] See also www.fotf.org for additional studies on this.
Also http://family.custhelp.com/cgi-bin/family.cfg/php/enduser/std_adp.php?p_faqid=1161 and http://family.custhelp.com/cgi-bin/family.cfg/php/enduser/std_adp.php?p_faqid=1065
[324] From iMAPP: New Research on Married Parents and Crime: Are children raised outside of intact marriages at increased risk for crime and delinquency? iMAPP's latest policy brief "Can Married Parents Prevent Crime? Recent Research on Family Structure and Delinquency 2000-2005" looks at empirical research from the United States published in peer-reviewed journals since 2000. September 21, 2005 MarriageDebate.com/pdf/imapp.crimefamstructure.pdf and DivorceReform.org/crime.html
[325] Source: Wade Horn and Andrew Bush, "Fathers, Marriage, and Welfare Reform," Hudson Institute Executive Briefing, 1997, Hudson Institute, Herman Kahn Center, 5395 Emerson Way, Indianapolis, IN 46226, (317) 545-1000. Quoted from http://patriot.net/~crouch/adr/kids.html
[326] Simpson, J.A. "Attachment theory in modern evolutionary perspective," in J. Cassidy and P.R. Shaver (eds.), Handbook of attachment: Theory, research, and clinical applications, (Guilford, 1999), 115-140.

8. Divorce, lack of support from their fathers, or "male bashing" mothers cause teenage girls to believe that men are unnecessary for raising children.[327] I'll show you why this belief is false in this very chapter.

9. Affectionate relationships between girls and their natural fathers delay puberty. The most important period for this effect is the first five years of the girls' lives, suggesting that the girls' brains are set up for relationship styles in this period. Close relationships with mothers are less significant in that regard. The opposite effect is seen when girls have close relationships with unrelated males, e.g., stepfathers. They reach puberty earlier.[328]

10. In general, teenage girls from divorced homes become promiscuous because they don't value men. Conversely, girls with secure attachments to both parents, who grow up in a low-stress home, delay sexual intercourse and choose long-term, stable mates.[329]

11. Seventy percent of those describable as 'violent' came from female-headed homes.

12. Eighty percent of those motivated by 'displaced anger' came from female-headed homes.

13. Of all the juvenile criminals who are a threat to the public, three-fourths came from broken homes.[330]

14. Even as far back as 1987 a study found that divorce – regardless of the economic status of the disrupted family – posed the strongest correlation with robbery rates in American cities with populations larger than 100,000. In other words it's not poverty that is associated with higher rates of robbery but divorce.

15. Young men who grow up in homes without fathers are twice as likely to end up in jail as those who come from traditional two-parent families.

16. Studies have shown that there is a strong correlation with the number of single parent homes and the crime rate in cities with a population over 100,000 regardless of the socioeconomics or racial composition of the city. *Yet another indication that it's not poverty or race that correlates to crime, but **single parent households**.*

17. A 1993 study showed that the rate of violent crime and burglary in a community is related to the number of single parent households with children aged twelve to twenty.

18. Delinquency rates are 10-15% higher in broken homes than in intact ones.

19. Among all possible contributing factors, "only divorce rates are consistently associated with suicide and with homicide rates."

20. Eric Anderson, a Yakima, Wash., anthropologist determined that most skinheads range from 14 to 27, *from largely middle-class neighborhoods* and broken, unstable families.

---

[327] Ellis, B.J., McFaden-Ketchum, S. Dodge, K.A., Pettit, G.S., Bates, J.E. "Quality of early family relationships and individual differences in the timing of pubertal maturation in girls: A longitudinal test of an evolutionary model," Journal of Personality and Social Psychology, 77, 387-401, 1999; referring to Draper and Harpending 1982, 1988.

[328] Ellis, B.J., Garber, J. "Psychosocial antecedents of variation in girls' pubertal timing: Maternal depression, stepfather presence, and marital and family stress," Child Development, 71, 485-501.

[329] Belsky, J., Steinberg, L., Draper, P. (1991). "Childhood experience, interpersonal development, and reproductive strategy: An evolutionary theory of socialization," Child Development, 62, 647-70.

[330] Ramsey Clark, Crime in America: Observations on Its Nature, Causes, Prevention and Control (New York: Pocket Books, 1970), p.39. Cited in Amneus, The Garbage Generation.

21. A recent study of 25,000 incarcerated juveniles made by the Bureau of Justice Statistics indicates that 72% of them came from broken homes. At the time 74% of the nation's children lived with two parents, only 26% with one parent.

What's worse about all this is that the cycle is self-feeding as children growing up with a single parent at home may see marriage as abnormal.[331] It's a downward death spiral. Pastors, can you honestly say that the damage done to society by these laws is none of your concern? Christians do you think that Christ really wants us to stand idly by as divorce destroys the lives, dreams and hopes of millions of children every year? What is our call to true social justice? What is our call to the second commandment? Love your neighbor? Is it loving our neighbor to let laws like this destroy them; when God has given us a way to stop them by getting involved in making good laws and removing destructive laws?

Note also that even liberals should want stable families and less crime. When these misguided kids do what they do, we *all* suffer. They're not just raping and stealing from their own. They're raping our daughters and stealing from you. This isn't contained. Liberals, even if you don't like the message, it's worth your time to investigate it. It's like a cancer; of course, we don't want to hear the news. But can we fail to investigate it in good conscience?

What about other countries?

This phenomenon is not limited to America. A study conducted by two sociologists, Robert J. Sampson and W. Byron Groves, analyzed data from hundreds of British communities and found that in neighborhoods with a high percentage of single-parent homes the amount of crime was significantly higher regardless of race or income. Yet another indicator that crime is not related to income but to single parent and divorced homes.

Poverty?

When I showed this to some of my liberal friends, they tried to claim that all this was due to poverty. But they were silenced when I noted that this increase in crime and problems cannot be explained by "poverty." Multiple statistics indicate that the problems exist in neighborhoods with middle class families. Many of these studies show that regardless of race or income, crime is directly correlated to the number of broken homes in the neighborhood. In other words, take a reasonably wealthy community with a high divorce rate and you'll see all these same problems i.e. gangs, drugs, violence, rapes, suicides.

In fact, divorce is what causes poverty and crime first. Then it feeds on itself.

Note too, that many of these studies show that having gay parents would result in similar situations to a female headed household or a single parent household, because the child will be missing either a male father or a female mother.[332]

---

[331] "Family Groups with Children Under 18 Years Old by Race and Hispanic Origin, 1980 to 2000," Table 54, 2002 Statistical Abstract of the United States, U.S. Department of Commerce.

[332] I know some of you are thinking, what about when one parent dies. But this is like asking, what if something terrible happens to the kid and deciding that if terrible things happen we should encourage

Ask yourself now. Is there a valid reason for Christians, or anyone of any religious view, to view some sexual sins as worse than other sins?

Pastors and Christians, do you want to reduce America's crime, poverty, suicides, depression, poor grades and sexually transmitted diseases? There's one simple answer: Get people to get married and stay married. Don't encourage unwed mothers to have more babies by subsiding them through an unloving entitlement government program. Next to abortion, this is the true social justice issue of our time. Do you care for the poor and suffering? Throwing money at them in new welfare programs will not help and exacerbates the problem. These studies show that money is not the problem, broken families are the problem. Preaching over and over again about marriage or holding marriage seminars is a good start and should be done, but it will barely if at all provide any help. And that too if it helps, it will only help those in your congregation and not the vast un-churched masses outside your doors. However, if you teach those in your congregation to take the next step and vote that way and get involved such that the laws are changed, the tables will be turned. The law is a great teacher and as long it directs our youth, it will have the final say.

So what is the solution?

Pastors, let me remind you that *every single one* of these statistics can be directly attributed to bad laws like No Fault Divorce, failed social programs and welfare laws that remove the father from the home or encourage out of wedlock births by rewarding it financially. ***All determinations made by politicians.*** Do you *still* think the Church has no business here? Do you think you have no business here? The laws must be changed. How heartless can we be to not do that?

A note to skeptics on Abortion

At this point skeptics will be saying, well how can you say we should stop abortion, when we see that 75% of these kids from divorced families, if not aborted, become criminals. This is *not* a Straw Man Fallacy on my part. I've had this question thrown at me far too often, usually in a snarky way. Especially since the book, Freekonomics came out. In that book, the authors say that crime has gone down because of how many unwanted kids have been aborted. But the answer is quite obvious, and I deal with it in detail on our website (see footnote[333]). Here's quick summary, if the fetus is human and morally equivalent to a 1 day old baby, (which I show is scientifically and morally true) then what you are saying is, "Yeah, this 1 day old baby *may* become a criminal, so let's kill it now." This is Hitlerian! Why stop there, why not kill all babies from single parent homes, since we know they have 400% higher chance of becoming rapists? What's the difference? If someone ever

---

them to happen more often. Of course, if one parent dies that's terrible, but just because parents occasionally die, that does not mean you make this the normative situation. This reminds me of the argument that some pro-choicers give me about miscarriages and abortions. They say, "Well what about miscarriages, fetuses die all the time." To which I answer, "Yes people slip off cliffs all the time too, but you don't see us trying to legalize pushing people off cliffs. Do you?"

[333] "How to win Abortion Arguments without appealing to the Bible or Religion" available at www.NoBlindFaith.com

makes this statement to you, reply as follows, "Yes, crime may be less because of abortion, but are you really suggesting we *murder* babies to reduce crime? You want us to perpetuate a worse crime to alleviate *potential* lesser crimes. Are you out of your stupid mind?" OK, you should probably skip that last sentence.

The solution is to *solve* the cause of the problem, not eradicate the *victims* of it. We can't let the killing of innocents continue just because we want less crime.

You've messed up heterosexual marriage so don't preach to us

It is important to note that in the battle to legalize same-sex marriages, many advocates of it have pointed to how we have failed at heterosexual marriages. They point to the possible 75% rate of divorce today and say, "Well it's not working anyway, so what's the big deal?" But whenever they try to blame us for failing at heterosexual marriage, some even pointing to the fact that the "Bible Belt" has a higher divorce rate than liberal areas, refuse to take that monkey on your back.

First, liberals don't marry as often as conservatives. Many of them just live together. So naturally their rate of divorce will be less, you can't divorce if you never got married. An accurate measure of this would be to count separations, find out how many people broke up after cohabitating for two years and count that and any divorce as a "separation." Suddenly the Bible Belt's "separations" will be insignificant. The liberal separations will go through the roof. And second, remind them that certain Christians (at least those who were wise enough to be involved in politics at the time) fought tooth and nail to stop No Fault Divorce. We warned that there would be severe consequences for everybody, including our *own* families and children, and we were right. The law changed the culture, the law changed society and the law changed *us*. We all have a sin nature and are also susceptible to bad laws. This is like a recovering alcoholic wisely saying, "Don't bring alcohol around me" and then you blame him for having trouble when you do tempt him with alcohol. Of course, the bad law affected Christians as well.

Finally, if you think about it, trying to justify same-sex marriage because we've messed up heterosexual marriage is illogical. It's like saying, "Some incompetent doctors have been practicing medicine, and killing patients, so let's let *anyone* practice medicine now, because you doctors have made a mess of it." What rot! The proper solution is to *tighten* the standards, not *loosen* them. I ask you, "What sort of stupidity is passing for logic these days?"

The Case for Marriage

The same article we looked at earlier in this chapter, discusses Linda Waite and Maggie Gallagher's book, The Case for Marriage: Why Married People are Happier, Healthier, and Better off Financially.[334]

---

[334] Doubleday; 1st edition (October 3, 2000)

Professor Waite, a sociologist at the University of Chicago, also challenges the widely held belief that divorce is usually the best answer for children when a marriage becomes troubled.

*"Culturally, Americans think it's morally wrong to stay together if you're unhappy," Waite says. "Every marriage has bad patches. **When people stay with the marriage, very often it gets better maybe a lot better.**" Among couples who stick it out, she finds, **permanent marital unhappiness is surprisingly rare.***

*...**Her large-scale study shows that simply viewing marriage as important for children ignores its wide-ranging benefits for adults. Married couples enjoy better health, make more money, and often live longer than their single counterparts.***

I think that speaks for itself. God it seems has some special ideas about why divorce is bad and marriage is good.

The Wheel and the Cycle

Now if you read those statistics about marriage and either got defensive, or thought "Oh my, how can we help those poor kids," you have missed the point.

"The church's task is not simply to bind the wounds of the victim beneath the wheel, but also to break the wheel itself."
Dietrich Bonhoeffer

Christians, we need to not only reach out to bind their wounds (which as I will show, we *already* do), but if we stopped there, we would not be acting responsibly. As Bonhoeffer so eloquently implies, we must break this wheel of destruction, the death spiral. How can we be so heartless as to let this continue without taking some action that will prevent this from happening to future generations?

Pastors, if you still don't think the church should be involved in averting this sort misery; may I ask what the Church's purpose is regarding the second greatest commandment? Is it just to bind the wounds that the wheel has and not bind the wheel that is doing the crushing? Are we to stand around and never lift a finger to stop *more* damage when God has blessed us by allowing us to live in a nation where we actually *have* the peaceful and biblically sound mechanism to stop the misery? Is this not one of the "talents" that God has given us? If we hide it in the ground and not use it, how will He deal with us when He returns?

As a pastor of a church, after looking at the destruction caused by one bad law on divorce, can you honestly say that it is not your concern what the laws of that land are? Can you honestly say that Christians should not be intimately involved in forming the moral content of any nation's laws? I would suggest that if pastors were to pay more attention to the lawmaking in this land, they would need to spend less time in counseling, supporting, helping and more time preaching the gospel and evangelizing. Pastors are the doctors, and doctors must surely spend as much time halting the diseases as they do treating the consequences of the disease. In fact, should they not urgently work to reduce the circumstances that cause the disease, so that fewer people will get sick? Isn't that their responsibility?

Neil Mammen

The cost to government i.e. us

For a casual estimate let's take just the cost of crime (for defense, police, incarceration, damage etc), which was supposedly around $1.7 trillion annually in 1999;[335] while this is not in anyway an exact calculation it gives us some sort of a feel for what one bad law has done in terms of costs. Since 29% of the population seems to result in about 70-80% of the crime, that could indicate that had No Fault Divorce never been made legal and if our families were still strong, our crime rate costs could reduce by at least 50% if not 75%. This is about $850 billion a year. And that doesn't count the suffering that we could have prevented.

Again, remember, this is not an precise number in anyway as I've not eliminated white-collar crime or other crimes that are less a product of broken homes. However, it also does not include the cost of welfare, schooling, social services and the myriad of other costs due to broken homes. So let's look at *those* numbers:

> ...*a single divorce costs state and federal governments about $30,000, based on such things as the higher use of food stamps and public housing as well as increased bankruptcies and juvenile delinquency. The nation's 10.4 million divorces in 2002 are estimated to have cost the taxpayers over $30 billion.*[336]

Even those who see themselves as "Just Fiscal Conservatives" and not morally conservative should realize that divorce is *bad* for *any* budget.

In the statistics, we see that though single parent children are only about 29% of the child population, they are the cause of a major portion of our crime, a major consumer of our justice system and counseling funds, and a major consumer of our welfare funds. Worse, it feeds on itself, causing more broken families (through crime, deaths, gangs, suicides and more divorce). One of the greatest reasons welfare and entitlement programs are going up in cost every year is due to divorce and the breakdown of the family, and throwing more money at the problem is *not* going to solve it. Let me say that again in a different way. Do you have a heart for the poor and downtrodden? Then let us start to take people out of poverty and welfare. You can't do that by giving them money because that is not what put them there and that has never worked in the past. They have broken families. Money will not solve that. In fact, this is also part of the reason why schools are having problems. It's because the family is failing. Spending more money on schools is not going to solve anything. You *have* to change the laws of the land to be more in line with God's Moral Law. It is after all why He gave us the law. If you do that, you will start to see a significant change in just a few generations. Ignore the problem, and the weight of welfare and crime will grow and sink us all. It's the death spiral of our country and culture. *If you care about true social justice, you have to care about God's laws becoming our nation's laws. If you care about God's laws and our nation's laws, you have to care about*

---

[335] New Crime Study Pegs Cost At $1.7 Trillion Annually
www2.davidson.edu/news/news_archives/archives99/9910_anderson.html
[336] Whitehead, B. and Popenoe, D. *The State of Our Unions.* July 13, 2004 from
http://marriage.rutgers.edu/publications as quoted inwww.divorcereform.org/soc.html

politics.

Turn the tide around

Slow down or discourage divorce, sex outside of marriage and cohabitation[337], encourage marriage and the reduction of single parent homes, reduce taxes and encourage one parent to stay home to raise the kids and be involved in their day-to-day lives (we show evidence for this in this chapter as well), and you start to heal many of our nation's ills. Encourage or pass laws that increase the breakdown of the family structure, separate parents from kids, and you create more problems and need more money for social programs. What is tragic is that many of the very social programs that liberal legislators have dreamed up actually exacerbated the problem by breaking up the family even more. For instance, if a social program like Welfare rewards women financially, only if there is no male in the home, this gives them an incentive, directly or indirectly, to abandon fathers. Guess what will happen over time and millions of families? Guess what *did* happen?

Second, as we saw[338] the presence of a father is required for a healthy home. Fatherless homes breed problems. This is particularly relevant when we consider lesbian marriage, premarital sex, extramarital sex and the other "sexual" sins.

Men who grew up with only a mother, rather than appreciate women, statistically tend to despise women and as we've seen, tend to be more often the ones who rape.

Third, we notice that allowing rampant divorce is not loving or caring for kids. It's not loving or caring for adults either. Divorce it turns out damages women more than men. Studies of the financial consequences of divorce usually indicate that years later, women end up much worse off than men, even if they initiate the divorce and get alimony. Why aren't feminists all over this?

Don't you see, if men and women of God who understood human nature; who understood why the family were so important and why Charity has to come from Churches not government; had been making the laws, we may never have gotten ourselves into this mess. And millions of kids would have been spared their current fate. If you care about true social justice and the suffering of children and women, you will care *about* the laws about divorce. If you care about the suffering of innocents, you will care *who* makes these laws.

Generational curses?

Exodus 34:7 Yet he does not leave the guilty unpunished; he punishes the children and their children for the sin of the fathers to the third and fourth generation.

Some atheists have accused God of being mean and cruel because of this passage. I suggest that they don't have the complete picture. Perhaps what

---

[337] By taxing unmarried partner benefits.

[338] Some friends, on seeing this data, suggest that I'm presenting an opinion. But as I stated in the introductory chapters, what we've presented is not an opinion but an argument. Divorce and single mothers cause social and emotional damage to kids and affect society negatively. The only way they can disprove this is to show specifically why our conclusions are incorrect. Merely saying "That's your opinion" is fallacious. It won't work.

God is telling us is *not* that He will necessarily lean forward and 'smite' those innocent children, but rather that those poor children will *naturally* suffer physically and emotionally due to the sins of their fathers.[339]

Pastors, do you really think we need not get involved politically? As Dietrich Bonhoeffer asked, when are you going to help us break the wheel? When will you take the responsibility to help change the laws that created the wheel? If you say you care for the poor and the abused, do you care enough to help get our laws changed so we don't create more poor and abused? If pastors all over the United States were to rise together with one voice and encourage their people to elect godly people and enact godly laws, the wheel will begin to be bound. How can we stay silent? How can we abdicate this great responsibility? Especially as I indicated at the introduction of this book, if Christians even just voted and voted biblically, we could *end* this all. The fact that we haven't is *our* fault.

Divorce's effect on Women

I was at a reunion of old friends from my college church group. I brought this topic up (fancy that). One of my friends said, "So are you saying that if a woman is in a miserable marriage she's just stuck? Tough luck!"

Is she stuck? Does she have to just consider her kids and tough it out? Is divorce the solution to a miserable marriage? Having looked that effect of divorce on kids let us now look at the effect of divorce on adults, women in particular. Divorce was supposed to free women. Feminists supported No Fault Divorce in droves,[340] not realizing that they were contributing to the overall disadvantage to women in society. For instance, a study done in 2006 shows that divorce makes women sick:

Divorce makes women sick
The Week page 22, Nov 17, 2006 Issue 285

Divorce makes women sick. For women, divorce can be so stressful that it causes physical illness, says a new study. For 10 years, Iowa State University researchers tracked 416 middle-aged women, 102 of whom had recently been divorced. At first, all of the subjects were in similar health, though the divorced women reported 7 percent more psychological stress. But after 10 years that mental state had begun to wear down their bodies—and the divorced women reported 37 percent more physical illness than those who had stayed married, ranging from simple respiratory infections to heart disease and cancer. Women are hit with a cascading set of problems when they divorce, study author K.A.S. Wickrama tells Newsday. They lose financial security, may move to a different and smaller home, and often have to manage child care alone. Having added responsibility for their kids, in turn, often means they lose ground at work, making their financial situation even more precarious. "It looks like they are trapped in this vicious circle of financial problems and other stressful life events," Wickrama says.

Other studies show that rather than being the "freeing" issue for

---

[339] You may at this point ask, "Why does he not protect those little kids? Is he heartless?" I will address this shortly.

[340] Although lately a few feminist groups are wising up. Apparently NOW, the ultra liberal National Organization of Women, is fighting against No-Fault divorce in New York state, the one state without a no fault divorce law. We can pray that one day they'll come out and admit their other past mistakes.

feminists, divorce has had the effect of lowering the average quality of life for women and lowering the median income for women.

Does Divorce Make People Happy?

Not at all, in fact statistical evidence shows that couples that *didn't* divorce ended up *happier* than couples that *did* divorce.

Findings from a Study of Unhappy Marriages[341]

Call it the "divorce assumption." Most people assume that a person stuck in a bad marriage has two choices: stay married and miserable or get a divorce and become happier. But now come the findings from the first scholarly study ever to test that assumption, and these findings challenge conventional wisdom. Conducted by a team of leading family scholars headed by University of Chicago sociologist Linda Waite, the study found no evidence that unhappily married adults who divorced were typically any happier than unhappily married people who stayed married.

Even more dramatically, the researchers also found that two-thirds of **unhappily married spouses who stayed married reported that their marriages were happy five years later.** *In addition, the unhappy marriages reported the most dramatic turnarounds:* **among those who rated their marriages as very unhappy, almost eight out of 10 who avoided divorce were happily married five years later.**

... Divorce did not typically reduce symptoms of depression, raise self-esteem, or increase a sense of mastery. This was true even after controlling for race, age, gender, and income. Even unhappy spouses who had divorced and remarried were no happier on average than those who stayed married.

So, as we can see, the evidence is rapidly building to allow us to prove that the Bible knows what it is talking about and the law against divorce was not given simply because God didn't want us enjoying numerous sexual partners but because it would be bad for us.[342] This adds credence to our statement that the laws are not capricious but are given for sound reasons. To show us the safe way to live, and to protect us. Divorce is not the "solution" even for the happiness of those in the marriage.

Thus, we have strong evidence that divorce, the breakup of the family and same-sex marriage have long-term generational consequences. Many of the nation's family organizations, including the Family Research Council and Focus on the Family, were formed to strengthen the family based on an understanding and foreknowledge of these consequences. "As the Family goes, so goes the nation."

---

[341] Linda J. Waite, Don Browning, William J. Doherty, Maggie Gallagher, Ye Luo, and Scott M. Stanley http://deltabravo.net/custody/marriagestudy.php

[342] We believe God designed us this way. While a skeptic could argue that God didn't have to design us this way and God only did so because he was a killjoy. The minute the skeptic made that argument he'd have to for the sake of the argument be conceding that God existed and then the argument would be merely one of who knows best. And if you posit that a God exists, you automatically concede that He'd know best. So, you can't argue that you know that a God wouldn't do it this way. Are you sure you know all the parameters? Science never makes that audacious claim. Why do you? William Lane Craig and Huge Ross argue that it may have been a logical necessity to make man and how they interact with the world a certain way because it was the only rational method available. More of this in my upcoming book: Gödel, Einstein, Darwin: ID and how all four-dimensional questions cannot be answered with four-dimensional answers.

What can we do about this?

We've seen that divorce is not just an issue between two individuals but a true social justice issue. Divorce creates injustice and causes great harm. If divorce were tougher, then fewer divorces would occur. People would be forced to work harder at keeping their marriages together. People will stay married longer and divorce will go down. How can I prove this? Quite simply, when No Fault Divorce laws were passed, divorce rates skyrocketed. Change the laws and people's behaviors will change.

I know you are thinking, "No it won't, now that the cat is out of the bag, people are not going to go back to the old ways just because the laws change." But history has shown that never to be true. When we change laws, habits change. They may change slowly but they *do* change. The most effective change as we've mentioned before is not in those who saw the law change, the most effective change is in the children who grow up under the new law. Children who know nothing better.

Pastors, will you not work with us to try to change the laws on divorce? Do you not see that it will reduce the pain and suffering of your *own* congregation in the generations to come? Do you care? Do you not believe me?

What adults do in the privacy of their own home

I want to discuss an excuse that people bring up all the time. They say, "What consenting adults do in the privacy of their own home is their own business." This standard statement is repeated by my liberal friends like a mantra every time I discuss sexuality. But the minute we look at this closely, we realize that it's not true at all.

First, let's start with something we can agree on. If a person smokes and reduces his lifespan by over six years, is it of any concern if he does it in the privacy of his own home? What if he never smokes in front of his kids? What about an alcoholic? What if he never drinks and drives? Is it affecting anyone else?

Hopefully you know the answers. Yes, even if he does only smoke or drink in the privacy of his own home, there are consequences. With smoking for instance, smokers die younger, they have more sick days, and they may contract lung cancer. All these have consequences to their family, employers, employers' insurance rates and so it goes. With alcoholics, there are consequences to their marriage, chances of violence, poor relationships with their family (making a family effectively a single parent family, abuse and abandonment of their children) and so on.

It's not the act that is the issue; it's the long-term consequences of the act that is in question. Evaluate every and all behaviors this way. It is logical.

At one point when I was discussing this, someone asked, "What if I know people who haven't suffer any of these consequences, can they do it?"

I laughed. "So you are telling me that because you found a few exceptions to the rule, the rule has no value? I can find many people who have run red lights and have not died or killed anyone. Does that mean that running red lights is acceptable or the red light law is of no value?"

The reason alcoholism and smoking are considered bad is that they have wide ranging and real consequences, moving these vices to the privacy of your own home does not make them any less of a vice. They are vices because they have consequences on humans. They are not harmless preferences. Let me say that again. If these actions had no consequences, we would not be calling them vices and we Christians and the Bible would not be against them.[343]

By the way, don't forget that Christians have been saying that smoking was bad for more than half a century. It's sad that it's only in the last 20 years that the secular world recognized it.

Now let's apply this concept to sexual sins. If a married man has an adulterous relationship with a woman (or vice versa), it almost always causes pain in the family and often causes the family to break up. And if the family breaks up, the consequences to society are enormous. They are not only emotional but financial (in the increased costs of welfare and crime control), physical (rapes, murders, crime), spiritual and psychological. Multiply this now by 350 million people. Arguing that there are occasional exceptions to the rule or that people need to get over it is ridiculous.

If consenting adults did something in their homes that *truly* had no consequences on society, then it would indeed be none of our business and we wouldn't care about it. *The problem is that the actions that most people are trying to justify **do** have consequences on society.* That's the crux of the matter. That's the argument we are making. That's the *only* reason we care.[344]

An upcoming law

Family organizations in Washington DC are working with representatives to pass laws that would allow a spouse to sue any person who had an adulterous relationship with their husband or wife. Why is this of value? Because it then behooves anyone who would want to have sex with someone else to personally ensure that they are not having an affair with a married person (despite any false claims the married person may make about being single). For instance, if a husband has an adulterous heterosexual or homosexual relationship with another person, the wife can then sue that other person in civil court and bankrupt them. This could extend to prostitutes presumably. The end result would be a lot less divorces due to adultery. Who in their right mind would want to risk having an affair with a married person? Now, I'm sure some skeptics can think of exceptions to the rule or problems with such a law. But first, remember these sorts of laws used to exist on our books and may in fact still exist in some states. Secondly, once these special cases are itemized and ironed out, such a law would be of a great teaching value to the hearts and minds of the younger generations. It's time once more to use laws to help families *not* hurt them. Go to *www.divorcereform.org* for

---

[343] Note that this does not immediately mean that we should regulate or prohibit these actions. We have to study each of these carefully and decide if it is worthwhile prohibiting them or if there are alternatives.

[344] Once during a FaceBook argument I explained this fact, to which a liberal said, "No, I don't buy that at all. You guys just blindly want to impose your fanatical ideas on us because you read it in your Holy Book." And sadly, he's right about that because many Christians indeed do not know the real reasons behind the laws. I offered to prove to him that that was not the case with me and directed him to our ministry site www.NoBlindFaith.com and invited to meet him to prove it. He refused to meet. The chicken!

Neil Mammen

more information on other ways we can start to fix our families. Also see the Objections Appendix for an answer to why the government should control marriage but not things like the "fat" content of burgers.

"Just" Fiscal Conservatives vs. True Conservatives

I'm often asked if I can recommend someone who is just a fiscal conservative, i.e. he thinks it's important to ensure we don't slouch towards socialism and is for lowering taxes, but he's a moral liberal and is pro-choice or cares nothing about adultery, cohabitation, divorce or homosexuality.

I can't recommend them, unless the other option is worse. Why not? Because a person who is only fiscally conservative (I call them a Just Fiscal Conservative, a JFC) is *only* dealing with the *symptoms* of the problem. He's ignoring the *cause* of the problem. The reason our schools spend more money than schools all over the world and are failing is *not* because we aren't spending enough money. A large part is because 30% of the kids come from broken homes[345] and as we've seen from the statistics, this has a direct impact on the child's educational abilities. Worse, it affects every other kid in the same classroom. Imagine if now we let our culture degrade even more, such that that number grows to 50% of all children. Obviously, throwing money at the problem will not help it. The Just Fiscal Conservative is going to fail eventually because he's not addressing the root of the problem. He will eventually be overwhelmed by social problems. It's like hiring an accountant to manage the cost of medicines for malaria. For a while he'll be able to reduce waste, but until you *stop* the malaria with mosquito nets and by killing the larvae your accountant is merely buying you a little time. Fix the source of the problem or you'll eventually run out of money.

Other sexual sins

"Sex is relatively harmless if it's between consenting adults and good for the soul. The oldest profession in the world should be legalized so that many people who do not have access to this would have a chance to have some fun."

This snarky comment was made to me by an ultra-liberal, universalist 60-year-old missionary kid who claims he's "more" Christian than us "mean-spirited" fundamentalists. He was and is a proponent of the sexual revolution. So let's look at other sexual sins, is he right? As we will go along, notice that most sexual sins lead to pain, divorce, single parent families or to same-sex families. In all cases, they lead to children not having *both* a father and a mother in a stable healthy relationship.

Cohabitation - living together before, or instead of, getting married

As most people now know, statistics[346] show that people who live together before marriage, rather than ensuring a strong marriage, actually have

---

[345] The other reason is the teacher's unions like the NEA only care about making things worse by spending millions fighting for immoral and completely unrelated things like same-sex marriage or fighting against meritocracy in education.

[346] Except were noted, information taken from www.citizenlink.org/FOSI/marriage/cohabitation/A000000888.cfm last visited 4/25/07.

an increased chance of divorce.[347] But there are numerous other problems.

1. According to a Penn State study in 2000, married couples who lived together before they got married show poorer communication skills than those who didn't live together first.[348]

2. Cohabiters have much higher incidence of violence and abuse than married people.

3. The National Institute of Mental Health (NIMH) found that women in cohabiting relationships had rates of depression nearly *five times higher* than married women, second only to women who were twice divorced.

4. The National Sex Survey reports that cohabiting men are nearly *four times more* likely than husbands to cheat on their partner in the past year, and while women are generally more faithful than men, cohabiting women are *eight times more* likely than wives to cheat.[349]

5. The National Marriage Project reports that while the poverty rate for children living in married households is about *6* percent, it is *31* percent for children in cohabiting homes, and closer to the *45* percent for children living in single parent families.

When children are born into this relationship as they invariably are, we get more broken homes, more messed up kids, more messed up and depressed women, more welfare, more crime, and more divorce. The vicious cycle repeats.

Cohabitation is a simply a stupid, mean & incredibly selfish idea when you look at the statistics. Why would anyone want to set themselves and their future kids up for pain? Yes, I know that you may know one or two cohabitators that have stayed together, but we also know a few 95 year old smokers. Why does this statistical deviation not convince you that smoking is beneficial and should be promoted by government and the media? Any law or policy that encourages cohabitation, like health benefits for partners, easier adoption laws outside of marriage, tax deductions for cohabiters and so on will hurt the innocent. If you want *true* social justice you will not support any law that encourages or rewards cohabitation or adulterous behavior. Even a "Just Fiscal Conservative" should realize that they are asking for high social costs by encouraging these things. The logic is simple and the facts cannot be refuted. Any claim for "equal" rights is selfish and indicates they don't care about kids or facts, only about their own desires. Societies must not reward behavior that will damage its very own foundation. But who will pass those laws? Not liberals. Not non-Christians. Do you really think we have no responsibility here? Should not this be preached in sermons in every church? Why is it not happening? And is just preaching sermons enough? Should we not act to change the cause of the pain? The law that encourages this behavior.

Sex before or outside of marriage

Statistics show that monogamous married couples have more frequent

---

[347] Cohabitation and Marital Stability: Quality or Commitment? Elizabeth Thomson, Ugo Colella. Journal of Marriage and the Family, Vol. 54, No. 2 (May, 1992), pp. 259-267 doi:10.2307/353057

[348] www.psu.edu/ur/2000/co-habit.html last visited 4/28/07

[349] Naturally, the word "cheating" indicates that the partners had agreed to be monogamous and one wasn't.

and more satisfying sex than all those sexually liberal folks out there who have sex outside of marriage. Remember, in their book "The Case for Marriage: Why Married People Are Happier, Healthier, and Better Off Financially"[350] by Linda Waite and Maggie Gallagher, the authors found that statistically:

> [B]eing married is actually better for you physically, materially, and spiritually than being single or divorced. Married people live longer, have better health, earn more money and accumulate more wealth, feel more fulfilled in their lives, enjoy more satisfying sexual relationships, and have happier and more successful children than those who remain single, cohabit, or get divorced.

Aside from this, what consequences can the sexually liberated expect? Only an idiot would not realize that sexually transmitted diseases would be almost non-existent if people were monogamous and had sex only within marriage. This would eliminate AIDS, Chlamydia (which causes cervical cancer), Gonorrhea, HPV, Syphilis, Herpes, and a host of other medical afflictions. Again the facts and the "stats" are clear and getting more exposure daily.

Catholic Answers[351] notes this:

> New scientific studies also suggest that if a woman has multiple sexual partners, this will lower her levels of oxytocin which in turn will damage her ability to bond. Oxytocin is a neuro-peptide most commonly associated with pregnancy and breast-feeding. It seems to act as a human "superglue," helping a mother bond with her infant. It is also released during sexual arousal and there, too, seems to work as a "superglue." Since estrogen enhances the oxytocin response, females are capable of more intense bonding than males, and are more susceptible to the suffering that accompanies broken bonds.[352] According to an article by Drs. John Diggs and Eric Keroack, "People who have misused their sexual faculty and become bonded to multiple persons will diminish the power of oxytocin to maintain a permanent bond with an individual."[353]

Is there any wonder why divorce and short relationships are getting more rampant? Despite my liberal friend's ignorant idealistic claim about sex; forty years after the "sexual revolution" its fruits are not looking so good.

And yet more evidence continues to roll in:

> In recent months, three new secular books have rolled off the presses that focus on just how rotten the fruit of the sexual revolution is: Dr. Miriam Grossman's Unprotected (Sentinel), Laura Sessions Stepp's Unhooked (Riverhead) and Dawn Eden's The Thrill of the Chaste (Thomas Nelson).
>
> Grossman, a psychiatrist at the University of California, Los Angeles, condemns politically correct campus cultures that encourage students to wear sunscreen and forgo fast food, but whitewash the consequences of promiscuity. Washington Post journalist Sessions Stepp echoes Grossman's thesis, chronicling the emotional and relational consequences promiscuity had on nine young women immersed in the culture of casual sex. And Eden, a

---

[350] "The Case for Marriage: Why Married People Are Happier, Healthier, and Better Off Financially" Published by Broadway; Reprint (October 09 2001)

[351] www.catholic.com/chastity/Q1.asp#top6

[352] Neural Oxytocinergic systems as Genomic Targets for Hormones and as Modulators of Hormone-Dependant Behaviors, Rockefeller University NY, 1999.

[353] Eric J. Keroack, M.D., FACOG and Dr. John R. Diggs Jr., M.D., "Bonding Imperative," A Special Report from the Abstinence Medical Council.

deputy news editor at the New York Daily News, recounts how she spent the years before her conversion to Catholicism trying to practice what the sexual revolution preached, only to end up frustrated and lonely.

All three books make it clear that women have paid a high price for the victory of the sexual revolution, a price that includes loneliness, plummeting self-esteem and even suicidal depression, not to mention skyrocketing rates of sexually transmitted diseases, abortion and divorce.[354]

Sex is relatively harmless if it's between consenting adults? Are you serious? How wrong can you be? How mean-spirited, ignorant and cruel can you be?

Pornography

Christ's admonition against adultery is quite clear here. Pornography destroys marriages and lives and in some cases leads men into pedophilia. Worse, like any addiction, the effects plateau requiring many porn addicts to need harder core and resort to sadistic imagery over time. Almost every single serial murderer has been an avid consumer of porn.[355] Most rapists are addicted to porn. Is there a connection? Porn does not blunt any desires, it may actually incentivize men to act out the fantasies they see.

TIME magazine (not a bastion of conservativism) reported the following (amongst a lot of other words that tried to down play this info):

In recent years, a number of psychologists and sociologists have joined the chorus of religious and political opponents in warning about the impact of pervasive pornography. They argue that porn is transforming sexuality and relationships—for the worse. Experts say men who frequently view porn may develop unrealistic expectations of women's appearance and behavior, have difficulty forming and sustaining relationships and feeling sexually satisfied. ...At the 2003 meeting of the American Academy of Matrimonial Lawyers, two-thirds of the 350 divorce lawyers who attended said the Internet played a significant role in divorces in the past year, with excessive interest in online porn contributing to more than half of such case. ...Recent studies show a correlation between increased aggressiveness in boys and exposure to pornography, and a link between childhood use of porn and sexually abusive behavior in adulthood.[356]

Furthermore, the porn industry oppresses the young impressionable girls who get lured into that so called "glamorous" lifestyle only to ruin their chances of happy marriages, families and committed love with sexual contentment.

Oh and don't buy the lie that just because many Christians are addicted to pornography there's any justification not to ban it. That's like telling a doctor, "Well you have malaria so treating malaria is hypocritical." If porn is out there Christians will be infected just like non-Christians.

Every day, across our country in every town, in your town, pornography laws are being eased, and good laws are not being enforced. These changes allow porn to be made available easier and easier, causing men

---

[354] http://www.catholic.org/national/national_story.php?id=23817

[355] http://www.forerunner.com/forerunner/X0393_Murder__Pornography_.html

[356] http://www.time.com/time/2004/sex/article/the_porn_factor_in_the_01a.html

Neil Mammen

to be enslaved and marriages to be destroyed. Why? Because Godly men and women are not in authority! Pastors who stand idly by as this happens in their communities are *not* being good shepherds. New laws are made even to the point of allowing libraries in your cities to be forced to allow porn to be viewed on public computers at all times with no limitations. Pastors and elders, can we honestly say this is *not* our concern? That this is not our job? Instead we choose to try and treat the suffering caused by these bad laws and ignore the causes? Do you wish we could stop spending so much time in counseling and instead preach the Word? How about trying to strike at the cause? How many have to have their lives ruined before Pastors agree to venture out and try to protect them? Whose job is this?

Homosexuality

Whenever I discus homosexuality I am always very careful to clarify up front that I have friends who are gay and ex-gay. I have no wish to cause them harm them in any way. Nor do I wish to make homosexuality a crime. When I discuss homosexuality with Junior High and High Schoolers, we always start with a pledge that we will not harm, insult or abuse anyone who is practicing homosexual behavior.

There are many gay people that I would sacrifice my life for, especially if they do not know Christ yet. Some sent me nasty emails and we ended up being friends. The reason I discuss homosexual issues is because I care about them and believe that the evidence shows that homosexual behavior is damaging to them. They need our help. They need to know this information especially if they continue in their behavior. The media will not tell them it. Remember we judge the morality of any behavior based on its consequences and we want the freedom to warn people without threat of prison as we are now facing. However, at no time do we wish to make homosexual behavior amongst single adults a punishable offence. This is *our* Judicial Law option.

The CDC's (Center for Disease Control's) studies show that the average gay male may have a reduced lifespan of up to 21 years due to HIV and other disease.[357] Statistical studies of gay diseases show increase tendencies in gay males towards drug use, alcohol abuse and a host of gastrointestinal and fecal oral diseases.[358] It's a damaging habit. For more information, I recommend Frank Turek and Norm Geisler's book, Legislating Morality.[359]

One thing I try to get teens to realize is that as they go through puberty, their hormones go crazy. Just as we don't expect them at as teens to have all the wisdom needed to make life's decisions; we don't expect them to have the wisdom to make decisions about their sexuality. This is especially the case because their hormones are going wild which makes them susceptible to making some very unwise emotional decisions.

"Just because you *think* you are gay or *feel* gay or are *curious* about it

---

[357] International Journal of Epidemiology, Vol. 26. No3. Table 2, page 659 also available at www.JesusIsInvolvedInPolitics.com search for "Mortality Gay"

[358] www.traditionalvalues.org/pdf_files/statistics_on_homosexual_lifestyle.pdf

[359] Legislating Morality: Is It Wise? Is It Legal? Is It Possible? Wipf & Stock (February 2003)

or are even *attracted* to someone of the same-sex," I say, "that does not mean you *are* a homosexual. These feelings happen to almost everyone, and statistics show that while 1.5% of *young* teens *think* they are homosexual, by the age of 18, only 0.8% think they are homosexual. That means over 50% realize for *sure* that they are 'straight.' Meaning that 99.2% of the youth population aren't homosexuals. So don't have sex, don't let yourself be recruited by homosexuals and don't make any lifelong decisions till you are older. You have plenty of time."[360]

Recently, the American College of Pediatricians sent a letter to school superintendents commenting on how schools were *unhealthily* promoting homosexuality and prematurely labeling teens. All of which they said would encourage immature kids to make bad decisions and engage in harmful behavior to themselves.[361]

Remember that School Boards are the ones who will control what your child sees and experiences in school. They determine if your school will have a pro-gay agenda or not this year.

Occasionally after I've spoken, ex-gay people have come up and thanked me to be doing what I do. Some like Kevin have even joined my ministry and now teach with No Blind Faith Ministries (www.NoBlindFaith.com).[362] I never stand in condemnation of individuals. I recognize my own sin. At the same time, I will stand in opposition to their legislation of immorality. For if Christians do not rise up to protect ourselves and our Bibles from the hate speech laws, laws that are currently in Congress, we will not be every able to speak out about the destruction caused by the homosexual lifestyle. Who will then speak the truth to them in love? If it becomes a crime to speak out, who will tell hormone raged confused teens that the emotions of the moment do *not* indicate that they are gay, just that they are hormonal. If a man is hurtling towards a bridge that is out, if a culture is

---

[360] For about 50 years, gay advocates have been claiming that 10% of the population was homosexual. This is absolutely false. This myth was started in the late 1940s by Alfred Kinsey. He published a book called "Sexual Behavior in the Human Male," after he did a survey on the sexual practices of men. The only problem was 25% of his men were prison inmates, and 5% were probably male prostitutes. But what's interesting is that even with this bias, he still came up with a result that does not support a 10% number. He found that only 4% of those men were exclusively homosexual throughout their lives, and 10% were homosexual for only 3 years of their life (perhaps while they were incarcerated).

In contrast, a 1989 study showed that among all teenagers only 1.5% of the males and 1.1% of the females thought they were homosexual. By the time teenagers turn 18, these numbers change: They both go down to 0.8%. In 1992 a study resulted in the following statistics: 2.7% men and 1.3% women were homosexuals or people who don't consider themselves homosexual but have had at least one homosexual experience. Remember that this number includes people who don't consider themselves to be gay but have had even a single homosexual experience. This is a far cry from the 10% that gay advocates claim.

The 1989 study and other recent studies show the falsity in Kinsey's studies. Taken from Five Lies of the Century, David T. Moore page 226. Quoting Gary Romafedi, et al., "Demography of Sexual Orientation in Adolescents," Pediatrics (1992): 714-21. More recent studies will be posted at www.JesusIsInvolvedInPolitics.com as I am made aware of them.

[361] "Just the Facts about Youth and Sexual Orientation." 2010 www.factsaboutyouth.com

[362] When those practicing homosexuality say, "Homosexuality must be genetic, after all why would anyone *want* to be gay and be rejected by their family and society?" Kevin tells them, "The same reason why anyone would *want* to be addicted to drugs or cigarettes? Because the *immediate* need and resulting high is compulsive."

passing laws that speeds up its journey to that washed out bridge, how loving is it of us to merely give them comfort as they continue on their ill-fated journey. A journey that we are fully aware will end in tragedy for them and for untold millions of innocents who buy into their laws and lies.

Pastors and elders, if we do not make a stand for the morally lost who may never show up in your church, we will be condemning them to a life of pain. If we don't get involved politically, those who make the laws in violation of God's Moral Will, will bring *more* pain and suffering to untold millions. They will start by constraining our freedom of speech. Do you not care? Do you not think this is part of your shepherding responsibility for your flock who *will* be affected by these evil laws? Are you not to guard against these? We must stand in the gap. Time is running out. Can you honestly and compassionately say it is not your battle? Can you in good conscience withdraw yourself and your flock from the frontlines of the battle? The battle invades your congregation's homes daily. The frontlines of this battle are in the making and enforcing of the laws. What is your role in it?

Same-Sex Marriage

A well-known pastor recently seemed to be backing off on his stance against same-sex marriage (SSM). On my FaceBook page, I admonished the pastor saying that this was a stupid move. Another pastor friend of mine reprimanded me, "You are just playing politics" he said, "How dare you attack a shepherd just because you don't like his *politics*?"

Was this a valid reprimand? Let's look at the same-sex marriage issue. Dr. James Dobson of Focus on the Family had an article that was published in Time Magazine. He writes the following:

The unique value of fathers has been explained by Dr. Kyle Pruett of Yale Medical School in his book Fatherneed: Why Father Care Is as Essential as Mother Care for Your Child.[363] Pruett says dads are critically important simply because "fathers do not mother." Psychology Today explained in 1996 that "fatherhood turns out to be a complex and unique phenomenon with huge consequences for the emotional and intellectual growth of children." A father, as a male parent, makes unique contributions to the task of parenting that a mother cannot emulate, and vice versa.

According to educational psychologist Carol Gilligan, mothers tend to stress sympathy, grace and care to their children, while fathers accent justice, fairness and duty. Moms give a child a sense of hopefulness; dads provide a sense of right and wrong and its consequences. Other researchers have determined that boys are not born with an understanding of "maleness." They have to learn it, ideally from their fathers.

... We should not enter into yet another untested and far-reaching social experiment, this one driven by the desires of same-sex couples to bear and raise children. The traditional family, supported by more than 5,000 years of human experience, is still the foundation on which the well-being of future generations depends.

Two Mommies Is One Too Many, James C. Dobson, Time Magazine, Tuesday, Dec. 12, 2006

---

[363] Kyle D. Pruett, Free Press (January 31, 2000)

Naturally enough, Dr. Pruett, who was quoted in Dobson's article, was immediately attacked by gay and lesbian activist groups. Sadly, Dr. Pruett tried to retract what he'd written. He even attacked Dr. Dobson, saying his views were taken out of context by Dobson. But if you read Dr. Pruett's book for yourself (I have, and I do recommend it), you will see that Dr. Dobson took nothing out of context. It's not hard to see right through Dr. Pruett's fright, yet, his whole book talks about the need of fathers including the title. After all, how do you take the title out of context: Fatherneed: Why Father Care Is as Essential as Mother Care for Your Child.

In fact, a website called FatherMag.com does a review of the same book and reports almost the same thing:

> Dads support kids' novelty-seeking behavior, and help children learn to master frustration... Good fathering also improves children's interactions with siblings. Father's presence helps a child to learn to form relationships with both sexes. Fathers like to stretch their kids' communication skills in preparation for worldly dialog. I learned that it is the closeness the child feels to Dad that is most predictably associated with positive outcomes. [364]

But we don't need to depend on the Dr. Pruett alone. A great many studies (see the footnote[365]) in addition to the ones I cited earlier show that children need both a male father and a female mother to be normal, well balanced and healthy. So if same-sex marriage becomes allowed by law, what will be the consequences to society 40 years from now? It's easy to start gauging this. Take a look at European countries that have legalized same-sex marriage. Marriage overall has stopped having any real significance. When interviewed about why they are not getting married the response has been "I don't need a piece of paper to tell me whom to love." You see if marriage is only about love then they are completely correct.[366] When same-sex marriage is legalized, marriage becomes only about love and not about the continuation of society or the needs of children. As a result the rate of marriages is going down in countries that have legalized same-sex marriage. More and more children are being born to couples who are merely living together. Cohabitation couples split at much higher rates than married couples, resulting in single parent families.[367] As we've seen, an increase in single parent families destabilizes a culture and causes more death and suffering.

There are numerous other reasons why same-sex marriage will destroy and hurt society. Frank Turek's book "Correct, Not Politically Correct; How Same-Sex Marriage Hurts Everyone"[368] itemizes a number of these.

While we do not wish to make homosexuality illegal, we do know that if same-sex marriage becomes legal, homosexuality becomes a Civil Right not

---

[364] www.fathermag.com/news/3772-fatherneed.shtml I decided that rather than quote my own opinions of the book (lest Dr. Pruett say I took him out of context) it would be better to quote other people's reviews, folks whom he has not accused of twisting his words.

[365] Studies that show Fathers are critical: www.fathermag.com/406/father-daughter/

[366] Of course, it's silly to say that marriage is about love only. Why then require a vow. If you love them stick with them, when you are not in love anymore then leave them. Why make a vow? The obvious reason is that marriage is not about love but a legal binding contract made to protect society.

[367] For more information please go to www.frc.org/get.cfm?i=if03h01

[368] CrossExamined (December 9, 2008) available at www.CrossExamined.org

a behavior. We've already seen churches and private individuals being sued in states where the courts have ruled that SSM is legal. Even that bastion of conservatism, NPR (I'm kidding) published an article that shows multiple situations of oppression against churches and private companies due to the SSM issue. For example, "When Gay Rights and Religious Liberties Clash" by Barbara Bradley Hagerty (June 13, 2008).[369] This article documents the legal battle faced by: Adoption Agencies, Catholic Charities had to close their doors in MA because they didn't want to violate the Bible and give up kids to same sex couples; Private Universities, an Orthodox Jewish University who didn't want same sex couples in their Married Housing was sued; Parochial schools, California Lutheran High School suspended two girls who were in a lesbian relationship and were taken to court; Private Medical Services, a doctor was sued for declining to do in vitro fertilization for a lesbian couple; Psychological Services, a counselor was fired for not wanting to counsel a lesbian because she couldn't in good conscience encourage her lesbian relationship; Civil Servants in trouble for not wanting to do same-sex weddings; Private Companies, a private Wedding Photography service was sued for declining the job and recommending a lesbian couple to another photographer; Wedding facilities, Ocean Grove Camp Meeting Association of New Jersey a Methodist organization was sued for not wanting a lesbian wedding on their site; Youth groups, for not allowing gay counselors. All these have resulted in expensive lawsuits designed to intimidate small businesses and churches. Will your church be next?

Adoption?

By the way, nobody can claim that allowing gays to adopt children will help the adoption rate. There are more than enough heterosexual married couples who want to adopt. In fact, almost 80% of all married couples say that they have considered adoption, even if they have their own biological children already. Many are even ready to adopt kids as old as 16. If adoption were easier and less expensive we'd see a lot more of it. That means that there are potential adoptive homes for as many as 40 million kids. Do note that some liberals have tried to accuse us of being racist in adoptions, but just in my own close friends, over half of the kids adopted have been African or African American. And while we are on the topic, why aren't 100% of adoption costs tax deductible? Representatives, are you listening?

Prostitution

My liberal Universalist missionary kid friend who was vainly trying to defend the sexual revolution also made the ridiculous claim[370] that prostitution was the world's oldest profession and should be made easily available. By glamorizing prostitution, besides the destruction of the relationships with the wives of the men who meet with these prostitutes, my friend completely

---

[369] http://www.npr.org/templates/story/story.php?storyId=91486340

[370] Anyway, you look at it, the oldest profession is hunting if you don't believe in God, or animal husbandry and farming if you do (Adam). If you insist that we are talking about women, then it would be motherhood in both cases since even evolutionary theory claims the females stayed home to feed and care for the young.

forgets the tragic lives the prostitutes end up living. Not to mention the immense current horror of sexual slavery. Women all over the world have been abducted, lured or even sold by their families into sexual slavery to satisfy the demand for prostitutes. For any one to assume that prostitution could exist without this continuous stream of innocent victims is ignorant, even if it were legal. There are numerous missionary outreaches to women and children caught up by this insatiable demand that grows greater each time wicked men are allowed to indulge in it. Even in the U.S., 50% of all prostitutes have been physically abused and 90% experienced violence in their personal relationships. 85% have STDs and pass it on to their customers and most have an extremely high rate of cervical cancer. Add to this the high rate of depression, suicide attempts, alcoholism, drug abuse and eating disorders amongst them. Prostitution is oppressive and it is despicable and mean-spirited for any liberal or libertarian to promote it. Legalizing it does not solve any of these problems but makes it worse in fact. [371]

Polygamy and Polyandry

Polygamy (multiple wives) is a natural extension of same-sex marriage. If marriage is about love then why limit it to two people. Surely, we can love more than one person. Yet, there are severe consequences to polygamy. If just 10% of the men in America were to marry three wives, there would be a 20% shortage of women for men to marry. This imbalance would severely destabilize our culture.

In fact, as we've seen in polygamous societies of the past, young males who cannot find or fail to successfully compete for wives become a threat to the dominant males and usually end being kicked out of the community or if that is not possible (if the entire culture practices polygamy) they end up in roving gangs of rogue males. Polygamy could destroy the United States if it became legal and even a minority of the population started to practice it.[372]

Polyandry (multiple husbands) on the other hand has rarely worked in any culture.[373] It is embraced by very very few men or women (less than 1%) and thus would not serve to balance the incidence of polygamy, even if both were instituted. Homosexuality despite claims of being 10% of the population is actually less than 2%, it would also not be sufficient to counter polygamy.[374] There are good reasons why God forbids these things. Pastors, perhaps you would consider studying and teaching these facts on a regular basis.

Statistics?

At one point someone tried to argue, "Neil, you can twist statistics to say anything you want." But that is simply false. It's precisely with such

---

[371] The University of Rhode Island: www.uri.edu/artsci/wms/hughes/mhvhealt.htm. This website also shows that legalizing prostitution will not reduce this oppression.

[372] Some authors have argued that the resulting excess of unmarried men requires leaders to wage wars to manage this population either by the capture of new women or the death of young men.

[373] A simple study of polyandry in Tibetan cultures will show that it has had significant problems.

[374] 2% gay + 1% polyandrous, removes only 3% of the males from needing mates. Compared to the 20% caused by polygamy. Remember you can't multiply the gays by 2 because they'd be marrying *each other*.

statistics that we decide if drugs work or not, if our advertisements are working or not, if our disease prevention is working or not. A number of my patents were based on statistical analysis of Internet surfing patterns, which I then used to design Internet Traffic Shapers. Police use crime statistics to protect you.[375] City traffic engineers use accident statistics to make intersections safer. You use statistics everyday yourself; if one road on your commute is often busy; you try to find a different route. If one type of ingredient bothers your daughter's stomach, you try foods with different ingredients. That's using statistics. The question to ask is: Were the statistics based on an appropriately sized sample, was the resulting conclusion correctly derived from the data, and can I make predictions based on these statistics that can be confirmed. In other words, if I can predict and then prove that the crime rate and the costs to government are less in areas with more intact families then, I know that my statistics are being correctly used. As our facts showed this was indeed true. I encourage all pastors when using statistics to go to the core data and review that as well.

Note too that while I've only quoted a few sources here (too many and your eyes would have glazed over), if you go to the web pages referenced in the footnotes, you will be able to find 100's of studies that confirm the few I referenced.

Wrap up

So, we see that all sexual sins have huge consequences in the physical and spiritual lives of people and can affect millions upon millions of innocent children. In addition, the effects and costs are multigenerational. Just look at the consequences in the U.S. alone. This is precisely why God and Christians view sexual sins as worse than other sins. God knew what He was doing when He stated the law and He was not being capricious. Governments should be *discouraging* divorce, adultery, cohabitation, casual sex, sex outside of marriage and same-sex marriage; they should give huge tax breaks to those who are married (with no income caps). To encourage staying together, as an incentive, every year you are continuously married you should get a slightly bigger tax break.[376] Because you are the backbone of society.

Remember too, that things like abortion and homosexuality and divorce deal with death and destruction and thus they are moral issues. Since they are moral issues, they are biblical issues. Being moral issues they are also issues of the law, for the law is the legislation of morality. Since politics is concerned with the law, they are thus political issues. Anyone who says we should keep the church out of politics is spouting nonsense. The church *has* to be involved with moral issues precisely due to the damage they cause to innocents. The church *has* to care about true social justice to obey the second commandment. The law is all about morality, and politics is all about the law, so how can the church *not* be involved in politics?

Can pastors, elders or any Christians claim to be absolved of the

---

[375] www.youtube.com/watch?v=RSJdB8hXOkA

[376] Note that there are still negative effects even if parents get divorced after their kids have left the home.

responsibility if they are not at least involving themselves in the effort to bind the wheel that destroys families, creates the need for welfare, creates rapists, murderers, criminals, causes suicides and worse, has generational consequences? We cannot turn a blind eye to these things once we realize that the laws of our country can and do prevent or increase all of these.

Remember my pastor friend who'd reprimanded me? I took him to lunch and gave him all this information. I concluded with, "This is not *just* politics. It is life and death. Life and death for millions of innocents. It is God's Law not a game. God's Law is given to protect us and others. We as pastors and teachers shirk from teaching this at our own risk. We will stand before God and be asked what we did with what we were given. Just politics? Surely you jest."

May God have mercy upon us when He comes to judge us!

Neil Mammen

Twenty-three

"go-ange yata loma tata sahasra vatsara, go-vadhi raurava-madhye pace niranta"

Translation: *Cow killers and cow eaters are condemned to rot in hell for as many thousands of years as there are for each hair on the body of every cow they eat from.*

> **Sri Caitanya Caritamrita adi lila, chapter 17 verse 166 Caitanya Mahaprabhu[377]**

But We Shouldn't Just Impose Our Laws Blindly On Others

Imagine that one day some of my old Muslim college friends from the Middle East came to the United States to settle down. Assume that they eventually became a majority in a particular city and decided that since the Islamic cultural and moral values indicate that women should cover their hair at all times, they wanted to make that an American law. How many of us would accept that?

None of us would, and we'd fight against it. Why? Because as far as we are concerned just because *their* religion teaches them to cover women's hair it does not mean that we should do so. It is not *our* moral value.

Now imagine a different scenario. It's the early 1800's, a Jewish man living in our European town tries to convince us that we should all wash our hands after touching sick or dead people.

"This is the law of Moses," he tells us. Yet we ignore them. It's not *our* moral value we say.

And lest we think that in the 1800's they washed their hands after touching dead people, we would not be up to date on our history of hygiene. They didn't.

Yet, the orthodox Jew is insistent and desires greatly to convince us Gentiles. So he decides to do a scientific and statistical study. Over the next few months he shows us in his study how washing hands reduces disease and

---

[377] www.bhagavad-gita.org/Articles/holy-cow.html

death. So even though we have yet to believe in parasites, viruses, or bacteria (not discovered till the late 1800's), we pass a law that says food preparers and medical practitioners must wash hands on a regular basis.

So, if you are reluctant to believe that covering a woman's hair is a moral issue, and as the Europeans in the example were reluctant to believe that not washing hands was a moral issue; how much less will someone who is not a Christian think that divorce, or abortion or same-sex marriage are moral issues, without evidence?

In other words, we cannot walk around expecting non-Christians to accept our moral values without question, or believe that we know what we are talking about.

But some of my Christians friends complain, "But it says so in the Bible."

Well back to the example we used before, imagine you are sitting at In-N-out Burger one day and an Indian guy with a thick Indian accent comes up to you. Half his head is shaved, he's wearing a saffron robe, and he's holding a very thin book. It's his holy book. The "Baghavad Gita" (the Song of God). He says this to you, "Sri Caitanya said eating meat is murder. You will rot in hell for eating that burger."

Now, how likely are you to jump up, ask for forgiveness, give your Animal Style Burger a good Hindu cremation and then eat just the tomato?

Not very.

Why not?

Because even if you respected other people who have different points of view, you couldn't care less what the Baghavad Gita says when it comes to your *own* moral values. You don't think it's the Song of God or even the Word of God. You aren't convinced it has any value.

So now ask yourself, in the same way why should any non-Christian put any value on what you claim to be the moral law given to us by God in the Bible?

We must prove our faith and our beliefs are true and we must prove our moral laws are wise.

We have no choice. Years ago when a majority of the United States accepted the Bible as the irrefutable, infallible, inerrant Word of God, we did not have to fight this battle. But that is no longer so. It is now critical that Christians know how to prove that Christianity is true. We have to do this using apologetics as commanded by the Holy Spirit in 1 Pet 3:15.

What is apologetics? I'm glad you asked.

It's the defense of the truth of Christianity using logic, reason, science, philosophy, history, archeology, philosophy and rationality.

Christians must dedicate much time, money and energy to proving that, like the ancient law of washing hands, God's Moral Laws really *are* wise and applicable. That means we have to do more studies and statistical analyses that show that divorce is bad and has a bad effect on kids; that same-sex marriage has societal consequences that are bad; that homosexual behavior reduces life-spans; that sex outside of marriage destroys and degrades lives and causes divorce; that socialism, while it may work for a few generations in a small homogenous country of 11 million, does not work in a large country of 300 million; and so on. We should be ready for every moral value that we codify into law to require an associated study or analysis that shows why that moral value makes sense, and we have to be able to do it without using the Bible.

If we can do this often enough, people will start realizing that the Bible knows what it is talking about. And what's better, they may start realizing that Christians are not the close-minded mean-spirited unthinking sheep that the media makes us out to be.

Fortunately, lots of Christians are doing this very thing. But we need more. We've already seen some of these studies when we studied the laws about sex.

But even with statistics and reason, people may still reject these wise laws

I had been invited to speak at Evergreen College in San Jose just prior to the California Proposition 8 Protect Marriage vote. The teacher named Clark who invited me to present, indicated that she would stay neutral on the issue and told me that she had invited an ACLU lawyer to present the opposing side. When the day arrived, there were about 100 kids present plus a few staff members. Not a huge crowd, but probably all that were interested. The ACLU lawyer presented her side first. When my turn came, everybody expected me to stand up and present a religious argument. I didn't. I presented a statistical argument using facts and figures showing how same-sex marriage in other countries has reduced Traditional Marriage almost by 50%. I also showed many of the stats on what single parenthood does to a culture. I told them to refute my argument they had to show that either my facts were wrong, or my logic was wrong.

After I was done speaking, the students had questions. Unsurprisingly barely any of them touched on my facts except for the Christian students from LiveActionFilms.org[378] who attended. For the rest, I kept bringing the issue back to the facts telling them that, no, I was not homophobic and that that implication was merely an ad hominem fallacy and even if I was homophobic, was it relevant? For even if a Nazi proved that $1+1 = 2$, it's still 2. His being a National Socialist is not relevant to the facts or the logic.

Then the teacher, who had invited us, decided that she didn't want me to respond to questions anymore and encouraged the students to "share their feelings," rather than ask questions. Which not surprisingly, tended to be feelings about why I was wrong. When I started to respond to correct their accusations, the teacher said, "That was not a question, the student was only sharing their feelings."

Needless to say, I was not deterred and kept interjecting responses, but one could feel the tension in the room. It was quite silly to say the least. I found it very irritatingly childish of the teacher to say the least. One student or

---

[378] Live Action is a group of High School and College Students who have video taped Planned Parenthood; counseling an underage girl to hide the fact that she was a victim of statutory rape; illegally given her recommendations of out of state abortion providers. They also recorded phone conversations about Planned Parenthood taking donations specifically targeted at reducing the African American population for racist reasons. Go to www.LiveActionFilms.org to find out more.

staff member (hard to tell as she was an older woman) said, "You have not given us any facts here today. I don't believe you."

I stood up to say, "All I've given you is facts and in addition all the evidence is available on our website at www.NoBlindFaith.com." But the teacher interrupted me shutting me down and said, "That wasn't a question she was just sharing her feelings."

Of course, this was really ineffective because I was wearing an X-Large T-shirt that had a bright red NoBlindFaith.com logo on it, which I merely pointed at. *But*, you see the problem.

After my talk, about 20 of the 100 kids came up to take my business card to find out more or emailed me for the data. Later that day two staff members who were present contacted me separately by phone to apologize for the first teacher's attempt at censorship. The point is that even with the facts in front of them, this teacher wanted to censor me and many of the kids did not want to listen to reality. Do we really imagine that this teacher was so twisted in her belief system that she could try and censor the truth and reason and still look at herself in the mirror? Sadly, yes.

Sin nature is such that though we may continue to show the wisdom of the Moral Laws in the Bible, using statistics and science and experience, many will still reject these guidelines.

It is at this point that we hope we can convince enough wise Christians who understand the value of God's Moral Laws to help us to impose our values on others. Is this wrong? Not at all, because, as we've shown, any law is an imposition of someone's values on another. The question you should ask yourself is: Is it better for your kids and your society to have someone else's ungodly moral values forced on them or is it better to have *your* proven, time tested moral values forced on your kids? Would you rather that their *ungodly* laws were forced on *you* or your *godly* laws were forced on *them*? In the long run, which will be better for your kids, your neighborhood, and your country?

Remember there are more than 60 million of us Christians in the U.S. and sadly we are not making our voices heard. The only reason America is where it is today is because of us Christians, who are not voting or affecting the culture and laws like we should. The blame has to lie squarely on our shoulders. God has given us talents and we are squandering it and hiding it in a hole. He *will* judge us for that, make no mistake.

Any decision to not participate or to even wait is a decision to accept *their* ungodly moral values. And sadly, that's what we as Christians have been doing, abdicating our responsibility to be salt and light to the world.

The very concept of not legislating a moral issue *is a moral decision* to allow it to continue. By *not* legislating against abortion and not ensuring we have strict constructionalists judges appointed, we are ensuring that legislation and judgments *for* abortion passes and it *has*. By *not* legislating against lowering the age of sexual consent to 13, we are de facto legislating *for* it to be 13. By not legislating against allowing teachers to take your daughter for an abortion without your permission, you are legislating to make that legal *and* common place. When are pastors and parents going to stand up and shout "Enough?"

Neil Mammen

When push comes to shove and we have to then impose something like a ban on same-sex marriage or abortion, it becomes fundamentally necessary to have Christians making those laws and imposing Christian moral values and not atheistic or secular moral "preferences." And as we showed, it's also critical to have the right people appointed as the judges, not those who decide that their own whims are to override the constitutional rights of the citizens.

But is it right to force others to observe God's laws, shouldn't we just love them?

Remember my pastor friend who was chastising me for calling out another pastor. "It's just politics," he claimed.

Imagine that you are part of a cannibalistic tribe in the Caribbean. You only go to battle to protect yourselves, and for centuries, your warriors have eaten your enemies whom they killed in battle. However, for centuries many of your greatest warriors have also tended to go mad and die. The more battles they win, the faster they seem to go mad. You realize that as your warriors continue to diminish, you will reach the point where you cannot protect yourselves, and your enemies will overcome, rape, and kill you all. They would not eat you however as that is not *their* tradition. One day some strange white medicine man shows up in your midst and tells you, "When you eat a human you eat prions that cannot be killed by cooking. This gives you "variant Creutzfeldt-Jakob disease" aka "mad cow disease for humans." The reason the warriors go mad is because the warriors eat the most human flesh. You must stop eating humans. It is immoral."

You believe him. Many of your friends believe him, you have a slight majority, but not *all* believe him. The witch doctor does not. You are personally worried about your sons becoming warriors and going mad. You are also worried that if this continues, your protection from your enemies will erode and soon your enemies will easily rape and pillage you and your family and destroy your entire culture.

Don't get caught up in the morality or immorality of killing the enemies in this example, because they were trying to kill you first. The question is: Now that they are dead, should you eat them or not?

You have a choice now: Vote to ban cannibalism for your entire culture or say "*It's just politics.*" How about "It's not *our* job to enforce, insist, or impose our morality on our government."

Let's say that the only way you can change the law is to become the chief of the tribe? Let's say your tribe has an established ethical way of allowing someone to become chief (i.e. you don't have to kill anyone) and you have the capability to *try* to be chief if you want. Do you try to do it? Do you try to become the chief and try to change the laws?

What if we were talking about slavery?

Did this suddenly become relevant?

At what point do we say, "We must protect the future of our society and the innocents with godly laws?" And we are agree we must do it the American way and democratically impose it on those who disagree with us. Remember, all laws are an imposition of *someone's* moral values on others.

The only question is: W*hose* laws will we choose to impose?

Is it *just* politics? Or is it in fact the survival of an entire people group?

Is it just politics? Or is it slavery and the prevention of one of the greatest evils imposed on our fellow man?

Is it just politics? Or is it divorce, abortion and same-sex marriage which has and will slowly destroy our family structure?

It's *not* just politics. It's life and death. It's pain and suffering. It's good versus evil. It's more maladjusted kids, more suicides, more crime, and more drugs. *Just politics? I think not.*

If you still think we are not to impose God's rules on others

Then you are claiming one or more of the following:

1. God's laws do not affect society and are not meant for non-believers.

Yet, this is refuted over and over again in the Bible when we see the physical consequences of sin and this is also refuted in the statistics presented in this book.

or 2. God's laws have only a spiritual effect and no physical effect.

This is the claim that our society will not be physically affected by same-sex marriage, a break down in the family structure, gambling or pornography or other such moral issues. Again this is refuted plainly by the facts.

or 3. If our society is going to die, let it die.

This is the view that this is God's plan. Our home is not on earth so we should not seek the welfare of our nation. This is refuted by Scripture and God's command to the Jews in exile in Jeremiah 29:4-7.[379] This also seems like a mean-spirited heartless view. We know that cannibalism is bad, yet with no compassion in our hearts or care for the suffering of others, we do nothing about it. Passively thinking, it's not our place to impose our moral values on others. "Let those poor wretches die in their pain without guidance." We plainly see how much damage divorce, same-sex marriage, the censorship of Christians and abortion is doing to this nation and yet we refuse to lead our country morally.

or 4. We are not going to insist on a safe future for our society and our kids, regardless of the facts.

We know that in the example, cannibalism leads to madness; in real life bad laws on: divorce leads to more suffering, crime, rape and welfare; pornography leads to more divorce, rape and child abuse; gambling leads to more divorce, suicides and welfare, and so it goes. Yet we refuse to act.

Do you see why there is no justification for us to *not* do our best to try and impose those moral values as laws? Laws that would stem the destruction on the poor and the children.

---

[379] Jer 29:4-7 "Thus says the LORD of hosts, the God of Israel, to all the exiles whom I have sent into exile from Jerusalem to Babylon, 'Build houses and live in them; and plant gardens and eat their produce. Take wives and become the fathers of sons and daughters, and take wives for your sons and give your daughters to husbands, that they may bear sons and daughters; and multiply there and do not decrease. Seek the welfare of the city where I have sent you into exile, and pray to the LORD on its behalf; for in its welfare you will have welfare.' "

When fellow Christians say, we should not impose our Christian values on others, we can rightly ask, "Why do you say that? Is it that you just don't care about the suffering of innocents due to the bad moral choices of others?" We impose our laws on those we love. Which is why we impose our moral values on our kids. We also impose them on the Mafia, on street gang members and everyone else. We impose moral values to protect the weak and lost. Can we do any less for our society?

If you care about loving your neighbor, you will care about true social justice. If you care about true social justice you will care about the immoral laws which are hurting people and shattering lives. If you care about the immoral laws you *must* be involved in politics. Or we are hypocrites, full of false compassion with no desire to fix the problem when we *actually can* fix it.

Pastors can you really say this is not your concern? If it isn't, then *whose* concern is it?

But is it effective?

What is the most effective way to achieve a healthy society? Fixing the problem at the source as well as at the grass roots, or letting the nation blindly suffer the consequences of evil or ignorant leadership and throw social services and money at the symptoms. If we merely try to influence the few people we know like our friends and those in our church, we will only get what we've been getting these last 50 years in the U.S., i.e. the continued moral decay of the country.[380] Surely you see it is madness to do the same thing and expect anything different. This decay came about because Christians divorced themselves from guiding the country. Let's not make it worse.

Someone *will* lead the country, why should it be at the worst, evil men and women, or at the best, morally ignorant men and women. Why should it not be men and women who use the wisdom of God, the wisdom of the Holy Spirit, the wisdom of the Creator of the entire universe to guide this nation?

Perhaps the real reason is that many of us aren't involved politically is that despite all the evidence shown in this book many of us don't really trust that these moral laws are indeed the wisdom of God or that they will be effective. If that's truly the problem, then we are lost.

Pastors

So pastors, will you be one of those leaders, or will you help groom a future leader in your church?

Are you preparing your flock to witness to the world by sharing with them the information from the large number of studies that have been done on social and moral issues? Or are you abdicating your God given responsibility to lead His sheep? This is all part of the outreach and political process.

But don't forget, we still have to be able to convince non-believers that our moral values are valid in the market place of ideas. We need to do this

---

[380] This is made worse by the fact that many Christians don't even have non-Christian friends to influence, and those who do have non-Christian friends are too scared to say anything to them. Don't get me wrong, if this method was working I'd be all for it. But it's simply not working, its failure is phenomenal. When was the last time you made any moral clarifications to your non-Christian friends? As an apologist, I do it whenever I can, but apologists are few and far in-between (which is why my main ministry is teaching apologetics and evangelizing to everyone I can hook into a conversation).

so when a Christian politician rules in a certain moral way, he or she can't easily be attacked for being a closed minded, mean-spirited fundamentalist. We have to show others that these values are moral because they are *good*. They should be made into law because they will protect us. Pastors, what are you doing to train your flock to think this way? Or are you only feeding them emotionally? When was the last time you used facts to prove to your congregation that God's laws have a real life value? How often do you do this?

Find out more.

There are consequences to all of the moral issues, like gambling, the lottery, abortion, embryonic stem cell research and euthanasia. Remember it's because there *are* consequences that they are moral issues.

To find out statistical and historical information about the consequences of these types of moral issues go to *JesusIsInvolvedInPolitics.com* and enter the keywords "Moral Statistics."

To find out more about apologetics, which is teaching the rational, logical and scientific defense of the faith go to www.NoBlindFaith.com.

𝕿𝖜𝖊𝖓𝖙𝖞-𝖋𝖔𝖚𝖗

Garbage in, garbage out…
Well known engineering saying

Don't let the consequences of your logic force you to abandon that logic.
My admonition to atheists.
Who is Agent X: Proving Science & Logic show it's more rational to
think God exists (Rational Free Press, 2009)

The Consequences Of Bad Laws:
A Quick Summary
&
Why We Must Elect Moral Conservatives:
The Elevator Pitch

In the '60s and '70s Christians "prophesied" that if we passed No Fault Divorce, we would reap the results in crime, welfare, suicides and suffering in the near future. And we did.

Now let's ask this: What if we'd had pastors and preachers in every congregation educating and preaching the dangers of this law? What if we'd had far more godly men and women in politics back then? What if their convictions were to seek the heart of God with regard to moral legislation and so prevented measures like No Fault Divorce from passing? Or, once that was done, what if the U.S. had Christians and Jews at the federal level who sought to stem the bleeding by creating a binding covenant marriage law option. What if they'd created a workfare system that did *not* break up families (by their policies against fathers)? What if instead they'd instilled a respect for hard work, entrepreneurship, employment and family?[381] Would not America and our people be better off? Wouldn't this have helped unbelievers and believers?

Of course it would have. In other words, if people – even those who are secular – obey God's laws, they will be far better off than those who disobey His laws. This is common sense.

The manufacturer's instructions

Here's a simple illustration. Assume that when I was a kid I got an electric train set for my birthday. Now assume that I read the instructions with

---

[381] A tragedy of the welfare system is that in sheer numbers it broke up even more African American families than the horrible slavery system did. How could we allow something that was supposed to help a group of people do something to their families that was worse than when they were enslaved?

contempt, they said I need to use it with a 12-volt adapter and should not plug it directly into the wall. Now, let's say that I wanted the train to go really really fast and thought that if 12 volts was good then 220 volts from the wall would be almost 10 times better. (Remember, I grew up in Africa, where wall sockets put out 220V, not 110V). So I believe I can use this gadget any way I wanted to with any power source. Then let's say my dad walks into the room and forces me to use the correct adapter. Will I benefit from being forced to follow the guidelines? Yes, of course. As long as I follow proper guidelines, even those I don't like, I will have an electric train and if when my dad leaves and I decide to abandon the guidelines, I'll have a mess of smelly melted plastic and risk electrocution. And *no,* I'm not going to admit if this is a real life example.

So we see that if laws are made to protect us, even if we don't agree with or accept them, if we adhere to them or are forced to adhere to them, they will still protect us. This won't save us from eternal damnation, of course. The Bible teaches that we are saved by God's grace combined with our faith in Christ, not by adherence to the law (for no one can hold to it fully). So adherence to the law will not save us spiritually, but it *will* protect us *physically.* And, to tell the truth, who can argue physical protection or lack thereof won't have some long-term spiritual consequences?

Why do I bring this up? Because I can't even count the number of mostly liberal Christians who have tried to argue with me that we should never hold non-Christians to God's laws. That idea holds no water and violates the plain scripture. Remember this verse?

> *I Tim 1:9 We also know that law is made not for the righteous but for lawbreakers and rebels, the ungodly and sinful, the unholy and irreligious; for those who kill their fathers or mothers, for murderers, 10 for adulterers and perverts, for slave traders and liars and perjurers ...*

If non-Christians adhere to God's laws, they will be saved from the physical consequences of doing stupid things. In fact, while they don't agree with us about the effect of the laws, they really should not argue that we don't care about them when we try to impose God's laws on them.

What are most "punishments" from God?

We can see now that many "punishments" from God are not really active curses but rather the natural and supernatural consequences of disobeying Him. As in the train example, it wasn't that the manufacturer of the train suddenly showed up and grabbed my train and melted it just because I decided to plug it into 220V. Nor was the manufacturer capricious in disallowing and warning against use of 220V. There was a real reason for that law.

I would argue that we are often protected from the full extent of our stupidity by God's protecting rather than punishing us.

But lest you think I am suggesting God never acts willfully, let's not forget that there are ample examples of where God does actively punish nations and people. For instance the Babylonians[382], the Israelites and the

---

[382] I must note here that there may be some validity to the argument that the only reason the Babylonians were able to take over the Jews was because the Jews had weakened their own nation by disobeying God. That is, one could argue that a God fearing, law-abiding nation would naturally be

Golden Calf event and Ananias and Sapphira, where God acted without waiting for the natural consequences to take effect over time. Imagine how much more amplified God's active and inactive punishments become if our laws don't align themselves with God's Moral Laws.

The skeptical view

Let us again consider the view of skeptics and atheists. They think there is no God, so all biblical rules were made by people in power who wished to control others through superstitious beliefs. Otherwise why create the rules? Is this true? Let's look at one such biblical rule.

The savior of pregnant women

Dr. Ignaz Semmelweis was a Hungarian-Jewish physician in the mid 1800s. At the hospital where he worked, pregnant women would come in to give birth to their babies, and 13% of them would end up dying of puerperal fever, which had nothing to do with pregnancy. Semmelweis tried to discover why 1 in 6 women who were healthy when they came into the hospital suddenly died of this fever. He noticed that in his ward every morning doctors would study the bodies of women who had died during the night then move immediately to attend to the new incoming patients. He concluded that doctors were somehow infecting the new patients with a disease they never had. So he decided to force all doctors to wash their hands with chlorinated lime after touching the cadavers and before examining patients. Almost immediately, the mortality rate dropped from 13% to about 2%. He then made them wash all their instruments as well, and the hospital's mortality rate went to almost zero.

Still, his theory went against the current scientific "consensus." The consensus of the time blamed diseases on an imbalance of the four basic "humours" in the body, a theory known as dyscrasia. The concept of "invisible" or tiny creatures that caused disease was considered superstitious. Dr. Semmelweis' peers rejected his findings. It was also argued that even if his findings were correct, washing one's hands after each patient would be too much work and just plain inconvenient. Also, as you can imagine, the other doctors were also not too eager to admit that they had caused so many deaths. They abandoned the logic because they did not like the consequences that it led to.

To be fair, Semmelweis could not fully explain why washing hands worked. Still, despite the physical evidence, a post-Enlightenment intellectual attitude dominated scientific circles at the time; Semmelweis' facts violated their consensus; so his peers told him his claims were Jewish, "religious" or "superstitious." They went back to their old practices, Semmelweis was mocked, and the tragic death rate returned with a vengeance. Like that teacher at Evergreen College the facts were to be censored and truth sacrificed because it didn't go along with their perceived values. It wasn't until many years later that Pasteur and Lister proved the existence of germs.

About 5000 years before all of this, however, another Jewish man named Moses declared that God told him to write a law saying that if you

---

stronger economically and militarily and would lose its might as it abandoned God's guidelines. However, unless we can prove this historically, it's only speculation.

touch a dead body, you are unclean and must therefore immediately wash your hands and anything that touched that dead body.[383] This washing included people's tents, clothes, and open containers. Additionally, the water used for hand washing was to have hyssop dipped in it. Hyssop has antimicrobial and antiviral properties, not something the ancient Hebrews would have known about.[384]

> **Numbers 19:14** *"This is the law that applies when a person dies in a tent: Anyone who enters the tent and anyone who is in it will be unclean for seven days, 15 and every open container without a lid fastened on it will be unclean. 16 "Anyone out in the open who touches someone who has been killed with a sword or someone who has died a natural death, or anyone who touches a human bone or a grave, will be unclean for seven days. 17 "For the unclean person, put some ashes from the burned purification offering into a jar and pour fresh water over them. 18 Then a man who is ceremonially clean is to take some hyssop, dip it in the water and sprinkle the tent and all the furnishings and the people who were there. He must also sprinkle anyone who has touched a human bone or a grave or someone who has been killed or someone who has died a natural death.*

As we can see, sometimes it makes sense to obey the commandments in the Bible *even* when we may not know why. In most cases, science has had to catch up to the Bible. Yet hopefully today these will be the exceptions rather than the rule. Now that hand washing is a legal requirement for food servers and preparers as well as medical providers, we see how at least one "ceremonial" law actually makes sense today as a civil law in secular society.[385]

The Semmelweis reflex

Interestingly, the experience of Dr. Semmelweis has given a name to the automatically dismissal or rejection of information despite the evidence, without thought, study, or evaluation. This is called the Semmelweis Reflex.[386] As Jonathan Wells indicates in his book, *The Politically Incorrect Guide to Darwinism and Intelligent Design*, we see many in the Darwinist camp suffering from this affliction. This is why as a scientist myself, I find the idea of "consensus" unscientific. You can "consensus" all day, but at the end of the day one side has to provide the evidence and the other side has to investigate it. The search for truth is not a popularity contest. It's an argument; and the only way you can refute an argument is to show the facts are wrong or the logic is wrong.

The Spiritual Consequence of Sin

In this context we should remember that sin has more than physical effects. Why? Because sin is rebellion against God. When all of us, including unbelievers, sin, we know inherently that we are doing evil, doing wrong and

---

[383] Leviticus 11:24-25, and Numbers 19:13-22 quoted.

[384] www.answers.com/topic/hyssop last visited 5/21/07

[385] As an interesting side note, apparently all those posters you see in restrooms telling you that workers need to wash their hands before returning to work are not required. Some company made a bundle by fooling restaurant owners into thinking they had to order and post these posters. That company has since been sued. Hand washing is required, but posters are not.

[386] www.answers.com/topic/ignaz-semmelweis last visited 5/19/07

as the Bible tells us, our own conscience convicts us. Yet we do it – in resistance and spite – and there is a far worse evil that we perpetuate when this happens. We sin in active rebellion against the Almighty God, creator of the universe. Apart from redemption in Christ, this rebellion has dire spiritual effects, separating us from God for all of eternity.

It is unloving to impose rules on others?

It is important to realize that it is not unloving to impose these laws on our society. We are all subject to the consequences of our society's actions. If we see that a certain moral failure would create *more* problems for our society and children, is it not important for us to be loving and attempt to help impose these values on others? In other words, it would be socially *unjust* to *not* impose these restrictions on society. Restrictions like the requirement to wash hands before preparing food or after touching a dead body. No one can say this is oppression or that we should mind our own business. Why? Because the consequences of bad laws *will* affect not only us but also our children and our nation. It seems to me that it would be more unloving and unwise *not* to act. If you care about true social justice, you will care about imposing God's laws on the public, even an unbelieving public. You just have to be ready to defend those laws using logic, facts, science, or reason.

Please don't think I am calling for laws to be adopted blindly from the Bible. I am not. In fact, that idea scares me scares me more than what we have now. I will propose a safe and secular approach to law making, all the while regarding carefully what we believe God's Moral Laws are and taking into consideration that sometimes we don't always know why God has commanded something. Rest assured too that we never want to use the Old Testament as a guide to punishments. Those were *their* Judicial Laws, not ours. Punishments for disobeying our laws must be determined by our legislature and electorate.

What can we can add to our argument?

Most valid human laws are created to protect us. All of God's laws keep us safe spiritually and physically. If unbelievers keep God's laws, they will also be physically healthy, and society will suffer less. Divorce and the breakdown of the family are the primary causes of our society' problems, which include child abuse, rape, gang violence, low grades and the increase in dependence on welfare.

What do we say to social moderates? The Elevator Pitch

I was at a Californian Republican Party Convention in San Jose. This book was in its final stages and I got into an argument with two people, one a Christian and the other a Republican gentleman who rapidly revealed that he was *not* a social/moral conservative. The opening salvo at me was, "How can you say you don't like so and so *just* because they are pro-choice. We can *only* get a pro-choice governor elected in California. We've got to stop thinking about what divides us and look at what unites us."

I started down the line explaining the moral laws, objective truth, the consequences of bad laws and I realized that there was far too much to explain and I'd never have enough time. I tried to speed it up and got my listeners very confused as I skipped things. When I tried to discuss the consequences of sexual immorality and divorce on a nation, the gentleman bristled. He'd been divorced. It struck me then that I needed an "elevator pitch," a quick systematic 10 minute summary as to why we need men and women with Christian moral values making our laws. It's not simple and note that each of these points have taken us many pages to prove, thus we should not imagine that people will blindly accept them. In fact most non-Christians will not accept all the points. But that's fine. I think the best way to present this is to tell them, "Here is my systematic reasoning for why we must elect Fiscal *and* Moral Conservatives. Once I've told you these points, I'd be happy to go back over them and try to defend them to you factually and logically."

Ready? Okay, here is my elevator pitch.

Why we need to vote for people with a Godly World View:

1. All laws legislate *someone's* morality. Thus, the moral values of any legislator will determine the morality of our nation's laws.
2. We are a republic not a democracy.
3. In a republic, we make decisions and new laws *not* based on mob rule like a democracy *but* based on a transcendent and fixed primary moral code. These new laws are to be guided by the conscience of the legislator in submission to the original moral code.
4. Yet, being a republic is no guarantee of success. There have been many republics like the Romans and the Nazis which have fallen apart. We can make the case that they failed because their moral code was not transcendent and was changed slowly by the masses, dictator or oligarchy until it destroyed the society.
5. It can be proved logically that the original source transcendent and fixed primary moral code must be *objective* and *cannot*[387] be determined by the masses (a mobocracy) or the elite (an oligarchy) or a monarchy (a dictator or king) or each individual (an anarchy), or a "thing" like DNA (stupidity). The objective moral code can logically only be determined by *a being* who has supreme authority over all mankind and is omniscient.
6. We can prove that logically, the Authority, who is the source of the objective moral code can *only* be the Supreme Law Giver, the Creator of mankind, i.e. God.
7. However, when we claim *that*, we have to be able to prove which God truly and objectively exists. To do that we need science, reason, history and objective truth. This proof is known as Apologetics. There is *only* one God that is proven by any Apologetics (facts and reason and history), and that is the Judeo-Christian God.
8. The United States was founded on Judeo-Christian principles. So the supreme law and authority that all our laws were based on, was always intended by the founders to be the laws given by the Judeo-Christian God. Not a "religion" but a system of natural unchanging moral laws. If you disagree with this then you render not only the Constitution meaningless but you create an unstable house of cards. Why? Because then you have no valid source for our unalienable rights. These rights are the justification for our revolution and the basis for our constitution and the freedom of our population.
9. The Judeo-Christian God's morals are conveyed to us through the Bible which can be statistically and historically proven to have been accurately transmitted (OT for the Jews).
10. In a republic, all laws that are derived from the transcendent moral code are to be

---

[387] I would use "cannot" and not "must not." Because it's logically fallacious to use the masses or DNA or a society etc to determine objective morality.

evaluated based on the conscience of the legislator (not on desire of the masses). Anyone who rejects that objective moral law written in the Bible has a misguided conscience and thus a faulty basis for his lawmaking. They do not understand the sin nature of man or believe that our rights come from God. Anyone with a faulty understanding of how we get there from here will have a faulty basis for his legislation. And this ends up being a disaster in the making. They will eventually erode our rights, lead us to either a mobocracy, an oligarchy, or monarchy and cause lots of pain and suffering in the process. Therefore, a social moderate is not fit to be a lawmaker or an executer of the Law. He will be dangerous.

11. We can statistically show that immoral laws about divorce have destroyed families, increased crime, rapes, suicides, gangs and welfare. Immoral laws like welfare promote the break up of the family and lower the productivity and tax base of the nation. Similarly, a pro-choice representative displays his rebellion to the transcendent moral code. Being only fiscally conservative i.e. a Just Fiscal Conservative is dealing with the symptoms (the high cost of bad governing) and not the cause (the bad moral laws that *cause* human suffering and the need for social programs). Why do you think social costs are rising not falling? It's like addressing the symptoms of malaria but not eradicating the cause of malaria. You can cost cut all you want, but eventually you will go bankrupt. And that's exactly what is happening today.

12. Thus we can conclude that Just Fiscal Conservatives are a bad idea and will cause pain to our nation and its people. They will legislate relativistic laws that will bring pain and suffering to all of us. We should only vote for them if they are the last resort.

Whew, did you get that all? Yeah, I know you are thinking, "Boy, that had better be an elevator in the Empire State Building." It's long but it is systematic.

(This list of points can be freely copied, printed and passed on to others as long as this book and the website link are referenced. Go to JesusIsInvolvedInPolitics.com and do a search for "Vote for people with a Godly World View" to download it).

Many people will disagree with one or another of the points, but then at least when you argue you can focus on the actual point that you disagree on, not the downstream consequence of that point. In other words, a moderate republican may disagree with electing only Moral and Fiscal conservatives, but it maybe because he disagrees with some fundamental issue like "there is a objective morality." So let's find out what *that* issue is and focus on that.

Twenty-five

Who will rise up for me against the evildoers? Who will stand up for me against the workers of iniquity?
    Psalm 94:16

If I profess with the loudest voice and clearest exposition every portion of the truth of God except precisely that little point which the world and the devil are at that moment attacking, I am not confessing Christ, however boldly I may be professing him. Where the battle rages, there the loyalty of the soldier is proved, and to be steady on all the battlefield besides is mere flight and disgrace if he flinches at that point.
    Martin Luther (not King), Weimar Ausgabe Briefwechsel 3, 81f.
        Luther is saying if we avoid the very conflict point that the devil is attacking, we are not confessing Christ. That toughest, most contested issue is precisely where we prove *our loyalty to God.*

But The Church Needs To Focus On Starving Kids And Not On Same-Sex Marriage Or Abortion!

The Church and the Moral issues: What the Prophets did.

Looking at some of the latest magazine articles from Christians on both sides of the political spectrum, there seems to be discontent with many about so-called "Christian Right Wing" organizations. I have seen this in magazines and in publications. Of special note are comments by Jim Wallis (the self-described member of the "Christian Left") who has written many books about Christians in politics (most of which I've read diligently). Interestingly, he and I agree on the idea that Christians should be involved in politics, but that's where the similarity ends. Wallis contends that Christians should focus on "social" issues, but not moral issues. He and others left-leaning Christians argue that we should follow Christ's lead and not try to impose our morals on America by trying to stop same-sex marriage, adultery, divorce, or abortion. Instead, they say, we should address hunger, poverty, injustice, and racism.

When I brought up this topic with my gorgeous wife,[388] she looked at me quizzically and asked, *"Is there a difference?"* That is a great question! Is there a difference between moral and social issues?

---

[388] She really *is* gorgeous. I'm not just saying this to gain favor with her.

What is Morality? Why were the laws given? Revisited

As we've already discussed, as Christians we realize that all moral issues are "moral" because they have *consequences*. God gave us moral laws not to take the fun out of life, but to provide instructions on how to live well[389] and not hurt others or ourselves. To drum it in: Sin is not sin *just* because God said so. There are *reasons* why He said so. He said so because when we commit sins, we will hurt ourselves and others. God told us what sin was because He loves us and wants us to be safe.

Remember *He is not capricious, and His Law is not capricious.*[390]

It is easy to look at trends like adultery and No Fault Divorce and see how they hurt our society. Broken families are one of the major causes of poverty, hunger, and violence.

It is a simple analysis. Moral issues, abortion, adultery, and divorce lead to the breakdown of the family, which leads to more of the above ills. Maladjusted kids have kids who get further messed up.[391] A vicious cycle feeds on itself. It takes only one generation to foul up a civilization, and it may take tens of generations to heal it, if that is possible.

This is why God said adultery and divorce are bad. His rules for living are not "old-fashioned moral values," just there for His pleasure or for tradition or to avoid us from having fun, that when disobeyed, have no consequences. When God said disobedience would result in generations of curses, this is what He was talking about!

The argument on the political left by Wallis and his ilk is that we Christians should be addressing hunger, poverty, injustice and racism, not same-sex marriage or abortion. But, as we've shown, godly laws and morals regarding adultery and divorce have a *direct* effect on the first three of liberals' favorite causes. *That is, there would be far less hunger, poverty and injustice if people respected God and obeyed His Moral commandments with regard to marriage and the sanctity of all life.* After all, if a pre-born human is of no value and can be aborted, why should one worry about a post-born human? Also, we have already clearly shown that it was precisely *Christians* who have done the most to try to eradicate the fourth issue, racism.[392]

In other words, Wallis does not want to fix the flawed laws that cause

---

[389] Remember that we've already established that God's laws apply to all men, saved or unsaved. If the unsaved adhere to his law, they and their societies will also be blessed physically.

[390] © 2007. This statement would make a good T-shirt, giving you many opportunities to witness when people ask what you mean by that. Just make sure you know why the law was given. "*God* is not capricious, and His Law is not capricious" also works but may intimidate someone from asking questions.

[391] Yet, it would be fallacious to assume that if no divorces occurred, none of these social ills would exist. We are fallen people. However, as we have statistically and rationally shown, the increase in divorce is tied to the increase in these social ills. Similarly, No Fault Divorce has led to more divorces and its subsequent consequences. Same-sex marriage is expected to decrease the number of married households, devalue marriage in general, and cause more social problems. All bad laws have large social and unjust consequences. The Bible articulates this often when it talks about rulers who do not fear God.

[392] Yes, this is historically true. Christians have been the most active in reducing and eliminating slavery and racism when you count the number of people who did not suffer under it but fought for it. And you can't argue that evangelical Christians have enslaved people more than any other religion. Historical evidence does not support that assertion.

all the pain. He wants to focus blindly on the consequences of those. My lovely wife was right. In the search for a compassionate solution, there is no fundamental difference between moral and social issues. One *causes* the other, and one can argue that removing the *causes* should be just as important as fixing the consequences, maybe even more so.

In other words, if you care about true social justice you have to care about society and government having moral laws about divorce, welfare, same-sex marriage, and abortion and other "moral" things like that. How interesting!

An Analogy

Consider a doctor out in the jungle who deals daily with malaria patients. Would we consider him good if he dealt only with patients' symptoms and not the causes of the disease? Should he not have some consideration for eliminating the cause of malaria as well? Should he or someone in his organization not be telling and educating his patients about standing water, mosquito nets and the lot? In a way one could say, in view of the long-term cost in repeated human suffering, that eradicating malaria is *more* important than merely treating symptoms. Because without treating the cause the symptoms and suffering will gets worse.

As I mentioned earlier, this example is actually extendable to people who are Just Fiscal Conservatives only but not Moral *and* Fiscal Conservatives. Just Fiscal Conservatives (JFCs) just want to fix the symptoms. Reduce taxes, spend less, and manage expenses. It's giving people anti-malarial tablets but doing nothing about *stopping* malaria. The truth of the matter is unless they are Moral Conservatives as well, those fiscal problems are going to grow and destroy them. You can't just reduce taxes, if the crime rate, rape rate, welfare rate is going up; eventually it's going to catch up with you and you can manage expenses all day and still fall behind.[393] Remember how divorce costs the United States 30 billion[394] a year?

But, if you address the moral problems at the core, divorce, abortion, homosexuality, same-sex marriage, fatherless homes, non-nuclear families, entitlement mentalities, broken families, lack of sexual moral teaching in schools etc, you can reduce the need for high expenses and taxes down the line. Do you see why these are all the conservative causes and their focus.

When I was Chief Technology Officer and VP of Engineering at one of my startup companies, I used to post a quote in my office. It said:

Don't sacrifice the important on the altar of the urgent.

In other words, sometimes we get distracted with the urgent (the symptoms) and forget the important (the cause). If we can deal with both, that's great, but never ignore or postpone the important.

Therefore, when a Christian organization or church confronts an

---

[393] In this malaria example, the liberals would be the witch doctor. He'll dance around a dead chicken, make you feel good about yourself, but end up destroying you. His dead chicken is well intentioned but it just doesn't work. In the final analysis, the liberal is the mean-spirited uncaring one.

[394] Whitehead, B. and Popenoe, D., *The State of Our Unions*. July 13, 2004 from http://marriage.rutgers.edu/publications as quoted inwww.divorcereform.org/soc.html

Neil Mammen

immoral law like No Fault Divorce, they are targeting precisely the *causes* of problems like hunger and violence. They are targeting the important! I would think even Liberals would want to change this.

Today's moral issues are *tomorrow's social problems.*

Believers who get involved in the fight follow in the footsteps of great men and women of God like Telemachus, whose sacrifice stopped gladiatorial fights and William Wilberforce, who halted slavery in England more than 70 years before it was stopped in the U.S. and many many others.

Does anyone seriously want to argue that Wilberforce should have focused only on feeding the slaves or improving their living conditions and ignored the law that put them there? That's exactly what Jim Wallis and most left wing Christians are arguing for. It's pure folly and uncompassionate.

We shouldn't ever focus on just a single thing, and we should never focus on symptoms alone. Therefore, we must to try to eradicate causes of the disease and focus on areas where we can be the most effective.[395] Wilberforce targeted the cause, the immoral law that allowed slavery. He did not spend all this time *only* trying to bring cushions and food to the slaves or salve for their manacled chafed skin, which would be the equivalent to what many of us are doing by only feeding the homeless and counseling the troubled and holding Divorce Care meetings and after school programs to keep kids off drugs. In the same way, we need to feed and comfort, but we must *also* go directly to fix causes: bad laws on marriage and abortion, governments creating dependants, socialism and bad values being passed into law. Anything less is heartless and unchristian.

Wallis fails again

"Ah but," you say, "even Wallis considers social issues as moral issues." True. But where his argument falls apart, is in the fact that evangelicals and Catholics *are* feeding the poor. As I will show you in the next chapter, conservative Christians and "right wing fundamentalists" give and donate **much** more than the liberals or the left wing folks.

Wallis is really a socialist – and an international one too, in that he believes American Government and taxpayers should solve the problem of poverty in America and address worldwide needs as well. We, he says, are responsible for alleviating world suffering, not as individuals or through voluntary charities as most Christians think it should be done and *are* doing it, but through mandatory governmental handouts to other nations. So, he favors *forced* involuntary higher taxes. Wallis wants forced international compassion at the point of an IRS agent's gun. Rather than realizing that the reason people are starving are because of oppressive central governments, he blames their plight on American free market entrepreneurs who work in the only system proven to alleviate poverty.

To conservatives this is foolhardy. We say, keep government out of this. Governments are corrupt, inefficient, top heavy and impossible to correct.

---

[395] I say this because someone may complain that the cause of the disease is unsaved people, and that's *all* we should focus on. However, we must to fight our battles on multiple fronts. Spreading the gospel is one front.

American individuals will give 130 times as much money to charity (that's not 130% but 13,000% as much) as what the government gives to anyone, and we'll do it more efficiently. I will substantiate this in the next few chapters. In addition, for every dollar given to a Christian organizations like World Vision, 85 cents or more goes directly to individuals in need. Yet, for every dollar given to government programs, in most cases perhaps less than 20 cents goes to the actual need. The rest goes to pay for government workers, office supplies, inefficient contractors, union dues, union benefits, incompetent workers, health care, overtime, pensions, dead people, cheats, lazy people, crooks and so on and so on. None of whom are actually producing any *real* goods. They are users not creators.

Worse, government employees never leave the system. How often have we seen a layoff of government employees, except in extreme budget deficient times and after some serious legal expenses to fight the unions? And when they retire, many collect 75-80% of their last salary as pension effectively paying them millions.[396] Is this fair? Who else gets this? Even during the 2009 depression, Obama and liberals made sure government was the only sector that was growing. What logic was that? That's the first thing that should have been cut. Government doesn't generate any income or goods. In fact, if you think about it, every government job requires about five private sector jobs just to pay for it (in taxes). Government jobs should only be allowed when they are absolutely required for *defense* infrastructure and no U.S. based private agency can compete for that function. When Obama announced that he'd created jobs but it turned out most of those were Government jobs, what really happened is that we were 5x that many jobs in the hole now. If they'd created 100,000 government jobs, it meant that we were now 500,000 more jobs in the hole because those jobs didn't create any wealth, they used up wealth.

Moreover, governmental agencies are always trying to grow their empires. There is the "Use it or lose it" rule. If an agency does not spend up to budget, its allocation is lessened the next year. So they make sure they "use it" for whatever harebrained new social welfare schemes they can come up with. Today's government is not our friend.

If you decide that a private charity is not handling your money correctly, you can just stop giving it to them. If they don't clean up their act, they'll stop getting money. Imagine what happens if a government program isn't using your money correctly. Do you think you can stop giving to them? Try it and maybe they'll give us a cell next to Wesley Snipes in tax jail.

A great example of government inefficiency was actually provided to us by a liberal. After Hurricane Katrina, $80 billon dollars was allocated by the Government to rebuild houses and provide aid, months later very few houses were rebuilt or even permitted to be built with all that money. Yet Brad Pitt, the actor went out there and with money from private donations, built 70 homes before the Government had built even one. All at no cost to the Gov-

---

[396] www.projo.com/news/content/top_pensions_06-07-09_RQEIQB5_v63.291cdce.html

ernment. See the link in the footnote for more information.[397] There are numerous examples of this, where private donations and people step in and solve the problems that government had taken years and millions if not billions of dollars to try to solve.

Secondly, we say to Wallis, socialism never works. An evaluation of socialism in the past shows its utter failure. Christians especially should understand this. As mentioned earlier, socialism presumes that humans are not sinful, lazy or greedy. But we are all that and worse. Wallis of all people, as a Christian, should reevaluate his stances in light of the base nature of man as described by the Bible. He violates his own theological basis.

Even the Bible refutes socialism. When the fleeing Israelites complained that in Egypt they'd been guaranteed food and work for their entire lives (Egyptian socialism), God doesn't agree with them. He punishes them for complaining and leads them to a land where they have to work for themselves and achieve their goals without a nanny state to provide for (and oppress) them. When the Israelites ask for a king in I Samuel 8, God warns them that the king will tax them heavily.

Additionally, many of Wallis' solutions result in higher taxes, and they have consequences, including reduction in the amount of money people can give to charities. Capital (i.e. money that can reduce suffering and provide jobs) moves from competitive industries to wasteful inefficient and unmotivated governmental bureaucracy, which never works efficiently. It just grows and stifles competition, becoming a hydra, a many-headed monster.

Socialistic thinking allows politicians to create terrible social catastrophes like welfare, as we have shown.

Higher taxes that Wallis endorses and is required by socialism also forces mothers to have to work outside the home to feed and clothe the family. This doesn't give them the choice of staying home and doing the most important job of all, molding the minds of the next generation of Americans and Christ followers. This is additionally bad, for numerous studies have shown that kids in daycare are more violent, less stable, and more troubled. For example:

Does Day Care Damage Your Child?
Major New Study Says Day Care Can Be Harmful
CBS News WASHINGTON, April 19, 2001[398]

(CBS) For working parents who are already riddled with guilt, it's the last thing you want to hear.

"We find clearly indisputably and unambiguously that the more time children spend in care the more likely they are to be aggressive and disobedient," announced Jay Belsky, who led what is being called the most comprehensive study on the effects of child care to date.

The study followed more than 1,000 kids in 10 cities from birth through kindergarten. The findings, which surprised many of the researchers, reports CBS News Correspondent Cynthia Bowers, appear to fly in the face of other studies that suggest day care has little or no negative impact on kids.

---

[397] John Stossel: Wal-Mart, Private Sector Moved Faster After Katrina Than FEMA. www.abcnews.go.com/Politics/Vote2008/Story?id=6031025&page=1
[398] www.cbsnews.com/stories/2001/04/19/national/main286594.shtml

...Belsky, a research psychologist ... added that children who spend more than 30 hours a week in child care "scored higher on items like 'gets in lots of fights,' 'cruelty,' 'explosive behavior,' as well as 'talking too much,' 'argues a lot,' and 'demands a lot of attention.'

*Even more surprising, the results are the same regardless of the type or quality of day care, the sex of the child, or whether the family is rich or poor. What seems to matter most is time. **More hours spent away from parents, the more likely the child to have behavioral problems.***

In fact, one could easily argue that Wallis' zeal for higher taxes will have immoral consequences and hurt the very people he is trying to help. *This is not true social justice.*

Worse yet. Since Wallis wants socialism, him and his kind would give us what happened in Greece in 2010. Riots on the streets as their government went bankrupt with all that they were spending and with little they were producing. People who'd gotten used to the state feeding them went on rampages. This is not loving!

What about Starving Kids though?

Does Wallis have a valid objection on this issue? No. As I will show in a few pages, he does not have a leg to stand on here. Christians and their churches feed and care for the poor, the starving and orphans far better and more extensively than any governmental program could.

But what about focusing on ourselves

Now someone may complain that we in America should address the problems of poorer nations and not worry so much about our own problems. But this is still incredibly faulty reasoning because if America continues its moral slide, it will end up being in the same situation as the countries we are trying to help. Coming back to our doctor analogy, would the doctor treating the malaria victims and trying to prevent future malaria cases be acting responsibly if he himself fell prey to malaria?

To paraphrase Hugh Hewitt: Ask yourself what type of administration and laws and moral culture in our country will help American Christians bring the "Great Commission" to fruition, especially in foreign countries. Would a United States that persecutes Christians be conducive to the Great Commission in Africa or India or the Middle East?

If Christians must focus on preaching the gospel, wouldn't part of that calling involve *preparing* the way for the gospel – that is, ensuring that the laws of the land did not oppress or limit them and would enable them to have time, money and resources to use for preaching that gospel?

We must not forget that our children and grandchildren have to live in the society we leave to them. If God judges our nation in the future, His wrath will fall on everyone. So pastors, elders and Christians in general, it behooves you to be involved in the moral direction of a nation at the political and national level.

Twenty-six

1 In those days when the number of disciples was increasing, the Grecian Jews among them complained against the Hebraic Jews because their widows were being overlooked in the daily distribution of food. 2 So the Twelve gathered all the disciples together and said, "It would not be right for us to neglect the ministry of the word of God in order to wait on tables. 3 Brothers, choose seven men from among you who are known to be full of the Spirit and wisdom. We will turn this responsibility over to them 4 and will give our attention to prayer and the ministry of the word."

Acts 6

*The church must be reminded that it is not the master or the servant of the state, but rather the conscience of the state. It must be the guide and the critic of the state. If the church does not recapture its **prophetic** zeal, it will become an irrelevant social club without moral or spiritual authority.*

Martin Luther King[399]

What Would Jesus Do?

You right-wingers are mean-spirited and care only about your rules and morals. I care about people."

I was on a debate site and a liberal "Christian" was attacking me for speaking out against social programs that didn't work.

Do Christians focus too much on moral issues and not enough on social issues? Yet, if we follow our Savior's lead, we notice that he focused on relationship with God before compassion. Forgiveness of sin, holiness and personal morality came before healing, in his priorities. Theology trumped social issues. An Old Testament version of this is seen in 1 Samuel 5:22, where we see that obedience to God and His commandments is more important than sacrificial worship.

In Mark 2:1-12 when Jesus healed the paralytic, he first forgave the man's sins (the spiritual/moral issue) before he healed the man (the compassionate/social issue). Almost always we see Jesus teaching before he performs miracles. Mark 1:21-45 provides a good example. This is the opposite of what most of us think should be done. We might say, "Do the miracle so the crowd gathers, then teach."

But our Lord's main concerns were moral. This makes sense because moral lapses can have terrible long-term consequences, not only for those who sin but for succeeding generations of their children as well. Interestingly, at no time, as far as we know from Scripture, did Jesus address ever-present

---

[399] http://www.mlkonline.net/quotes.html

injustices like slavery or the horrible treatment of his own people at the hands of the Roman occupiers. This is not to say that Christians should not address slavery or injustice. We just can't appeal to our Savior's known actions in asking that these issues be made priorities over other issues. It is probably significant that while the Bible mentions slavery in passing, many think it was such a key issue that it was worth our nation fighting brother against brother and killing more than 600,000 of our own in trying to solve the problem.

Yet, in comparison though the Bible has a clear and precise mandate against homosexuality, we see many Christians backing away from that topic. By the way, don't be bamboozled by the argument that "Jesus never talked about homosexuality." If you believe the Bible is divinely inspired then everything that Paul wrote about homosexuality comes from the very mouth of Jesus and the Holy Spirit. Jesus *did* talk about homosexuality, *through Paul*. And if you don't believe the Bible is divinely inspired or inerrant, then why do you care what a faulty error ridden book says anywhere *else*, like about things like equality and compassion? If you don't care what the Bible says about homosexuality why do you care what it says about the equality of man? That's where modern day society got the idea to begin with. If one is outdated, so is the other.

So assuming that we believe the Bible is God's Word (which I do, and I'm assuming you dear reader do as well), then if an indirect mention about slavery is vital, how much more important should the Bible's prohibition of homosexuality, and thus same-sex marriage, be? If your church focuses on racism or slavery, which are barely mentioned in Scripture, how much more importance should you put on the effects of divorce, which is explicitly mentioned? If we get involved and change laws and even get political parties to focus on eradicating slavery, how much more should we then be involved in politics to change laws about the homosexual indoctrination of our kids and divorce and other problems that affect the family? If God saw fit to be very specific about them, why do we think these issues are unimportant to God? If they are important enough to be in the Bible, shouldn't they be spoken of in the pulpit? Is not God's Word good for teaching and reproach? And shouldn't Christians work to change the laws in accordance to it?

How about the Apostles?

One could say Jesus had other things on His mind, but as followers of His, it would seem that we should make social issues a priority. Yet, when we look at the Apostles' priorities, we see that the feeding of the needy seems like an afterthought. Even after they realized it was something they should attend to, they recruited deacons to address it and did not do it themselves because, to put it in their words:

Acts 6:2 It would not be right for us to neglect the ministry of the Word of God in order to wait on tables. 3 Brothers, choose seven men from among you who are known to be full of the Spirit and wisdom. We will turn this responsibility over to them 4 and will give our attention to prayer and the ministry of the word.

This is not to say social issues like feeding of the widows are unimportant. They are important but not more so than the ministry of God's

Word. Remember the order of the commandments. First, "Love the Lord your God" and second "Love your Neighbor as yourself." Theology and the Law followed by true social justice. But, you may argue, "The ministry of the Word and Loving God does not cover moral issues. So, the church should not be involved in influencing moral laws." Oh really? I think it does. What was the message the Apostles were teaching? Did it not include "Turn away from your sin and repent and be saved?" Didn't it include behavior and lifestyle issues which the Old Testament prophets spent their lives hammering on? How can you repent if you don't understand what you are repenting from? How can you be sanctified if you don't know how to get there? How can you want to be saved if you don't think there's anything to be saved from? How can you love God if you love everything He hates and promote all that repulses Him? Why would Christ die to save you from sin then not care if you continued to commit the same thing i.e. the sin, which sent Him to the cross to suffer and die?

Objection: But organization XYZ never feeds the poor.

I was reading a critique by a Christian pastor. He wanted to know why Focus on the Family was not "focusing" on preaching the gospel. Was this a valid criticism?

How is the church arranged? Do we insist our teaching pastors operate on dying foreign children? Do we require our choir directors to be missionary pilots– flying medicines and doctors into remote areas and carrying sick people out? Did the early church force the Apostles to hand out food to the widows? No. We understand that each person in the body of Christ has specific skills and gifts. Just as the Apostles created the office of deacons to address people's physical and social needs so they could attend to teaching, the contemporary church also has delineation of functions. Christian organizations are composed of *individuals* with certain gifts *who have gathered together* to use their gifts.

So asking an organization that focuses on moral issues why they are not feeding the poor or preaching the Gospel would be like asking people in a church's Celebrate Recovery ministry why they aren't feeding the poor or why they don't have a political task force speaking out against female circumcision or child prostitution in the Thailand. Organizations can't and don't need to do everything. We don't ask Mission Aviation Fellowship to do the job of Teen Challenge, nor do we ask Teen Challenge to lead marriage seminars. As Paul asks: Are all a foot or an ear? Are we not all one body and each part of the body has its own function for which God has created them? Why is working against abortion or same-sex marriage or embryonic stem cell research[400] unwise? Is it wise for all Christians corporately to focus on only one issue or problem? Do we as a church feed the homeless outside our door but ignore and starve our own kids? Do we feed the homeless outside our door and become slack in giving our children moral guidance? Do we feed the homeless outside

---

[400] Do not confuse Embryonic Stem Cell Research (ESCR) with Adult Stem Cell Research (ASCR). ESCR kills an embryo and as yet has provided no cures. ASCR does not kill anyone and has resulted in at least 57 cures. Go to www.NoBlindFaith.com and do a search for Stem Cells.

our door and let the kids in our churches do drugs? May that never be![401] Each organization can focus on as small or as large a goal as they wish.

For instance, the Alliance Defense Fund[402] is organized to defend Christians from illegal and unjust legal action. You will not find them holding large Billy Graham type evangelistic rallies and frankly, they probably don't have the talent base in their organization to do so. In the same way, asking why FOTF isn't focusing on evangelization is inane.

But pastors, lest you think that this excuses you and the church from the need of speaking the truth in love about moral issues or being involved politically it doesn't. For the church *is* precisely where saints get equipped to learn God's law to fight evil men who make evil laws. Who's equipping *your* saints? Remember, if *you* don't teach them biblical values and guide them, MTV and NBC will happily do that for you. And if you do teach them and then tell them to hide that knowledge and light under a bushel you violate God's instructions and let evil continue.

Objection!

I know, by now you are thinking "But, preaching the Gospel was direct command to *all* of us." Yes it is, but to us as *individuals*. So while groups like Focus on the Family and Family Research Council may not as an organization be involved in preaching the Gospel, I personally know that individuals at FOTF and FRC make it a *personal* goal of theirs to witness to unsaved friends and family. Their corporation's goals are not evangelization but their *personal* goals are. This accusation just does not carry water. One may as well ask any private Christian company the same question: Why doesn't Chick-fil-A focus on preaching the Gospel instead of making a great chicken sandwich?

Glamour and the Prophets of Old

Perhaps the reason we don't hear about Christians speaking out more about AIDS ministries and homelessness ministries, as opposed to adultery, divorce, same-sex marriage or abortion and embryonic stem cell research, is similar to the reason why we don't see the lifelong missionary doctors[403] on the cover of Time magazine. It's not that those people aren't around. It's just that their jobs are not glamorous and so you don't see them featured in secular media except perhaps to shed a negative light on it.

It may be that people who don't have deep convictions are easily fooled into thinking that the symptoms (AIDS and homelessness) have no relationship to the real problem of creating more broken homes and the devaluation of life (adultery, divorce, same-sex marriage or abortion and embryonic stem cell research). I would contend that AIDS and homelessness

---

[401] One could argue that many of the missionaries that I grew up with did exactly this to their kids. They focused so much on their ministry that they forgot their homes, and many of their kids grew up hating Christ and the church.

[402] www.alliancedefensefund.org

[403] While secular media won't appreciate their missionary deeds, at least they could recognize their humanitarian deeds. They are doctors, after all.

are exacerbated by adultery, divorce, and homosexuality.[404] How many people really want to disagree with me on that?

Saying that divorce and adultery and homosexuality increase AIDS, crime and homelessness can be an unpopular stance. This is similar to the prophets of old, such as Elisha and Elijah, who predicted consequences of certain actions and were hunted or killed for it. Perhaps it is time that Christians see organizations composed mainly of individuals with exhortation gifts as "the prophets" of today. The ancient prophets' duties were mostly about calling for a change on moral issues and warning and prophesying about the consequences of not changing – with rare incidents of compassion like the feeding of the widow and her child and occasional incidents of prophesying *about* the future. Let me repeat that as it's is a critical distinction. Biblical prophets worried more about prophesying the future *consequences* of immorality than they did about prophesying the *future*. In fact, I argue that the "schools of prophets" described in the Old Testament were identical to the organizations today calling for moral change.[405]

Christians have been attacked because they claimed that one evil action or another was the consequence of immorality. Yet, any way you look at it, all suffering stems from someone's sin; starting with Adam's in the Garden of Eden. Let us not be naïve.

Conclusion

I call all Christians to play a role, financially or personally, in the work of Christian doctors and local and overseas missions, but I *also* call as many Christians as possible to take an active part in the prophetic ministry of organizations concerned about with the moral direction our nation is taking. After all, when the people did not listen to Jeremiah, they ended up persecuted and oppressed by Babylon. This may have more significance to it than we realize.

What can we add to the argument here? Christ and the ancient prophets addressed moral issues before addressing social issues. The prophets called for change in kings, commoners and the culture. Christian organizations calling for change in politics and culture are serving as prophets in our day.

---

[404] Yes, I know you may be thinking that AIDS is also caused by sharing of needles during drug injection. But as we've already shown, drug use is increased by divorce and adultery. Similarly, children from divorced homes are at higher risk of sexual molestation. This and not having a father figure in the house has been shown to increase the incidence of homosexual behavior.

[405] Of course, we can't expect anything less than to be treated similar to the prophets of old -- but hopefully without the killing part.

Twenty-seven

The Gateses spent the year giving more money away faster than anyone ever has.
   Time Magazine 2005 Person of the Year issue

But The Church Isn't Focusing On Social Issues At All, We Are Lacking In Compassion

You are all mean-spirited intolerant right wing fundamentalists!" retorted an anti-Christian, relativistic, *missionary kid* to me during an email debate. Are we really mean-spirited? Are we really intolerant?

As I noted, I'm an immigrant to this great nation and was fortunate to grow up in Africa, the Caribbean, India and the Middle East. A while ago, I was perturbed to see Bill and Melinda Gates and Bono portrayed on the cover of Time magazine as altruistic models for the rest of the world. While they are to be commended for their actions, the article seemed to imply that these extremely wealthy people were heroes for donating a portion of their wealth to help underdeveloped nations. Why was I perturbed? Don't get me wrong; I wasn't perturbed that Bill and Melinda gave a part of their income. They can give whatever they want, whenever they want to and however they want without judgment from me.[406] Their wealth does not bother me either. They worked hard for it and have created much wealth for others, including me (thanks Bill) by doing what they do. I wasn't bothered that Bono had spent much of his free time talking world leaders into forgiving 3rd world debt (money that had been mostly wasted by government or stolen by dictators and was now burdening those same countries). He can spend his energy anyway he wishes to and kudos to him and those he positively influences.

Here is why I was perturbed. While growing up in Africa and the

---

[406] Okay, okay one judgment: I believe it would have been wiser for Gates to give business micro-loans than handouts. We need to teach people to fish, not just give them fish.

Middle East, I was surrounded by missionary doctors and pilots who had given up cushy lives to help the starving, poor, sick and needy. They dedicated their entire *lives* to this ministry. Some even paid for their mercy *with* their lives. Missionary doctors killed in the Yemen Arab Republic, and people like Bonnie Witherall, killed in Palestine, are the true heroes in my estimation. Bonnie was a friend of my wife's family and a member of the church that my father-in-law founded and led for 29 years, before retiring. Why haven't real heroes like these people *also* been featured on the cover of Time magazine at least once in the last 10 years? Maybe I missed that issue. Note that these folks were not out there *only* to spread the gospel. They were doctors and nurses providing free care, food and supplies. Why is Time Magazine only admiring the Gateses and Paul Hewson (Bono) for their benevolence?

Before Band Aid

Notice the irony of an angry, now adult, missionary kid saying that Christians are mean-spirited; he's angry that he was abandoned in a boarding-school while his Christian parents brought medical and agricultural aid to India, the very thing he's claiming Christians aren't doing.[407] Long before Band Aid or USA for Africa in the 1980's (which were concerts to raise money for Africa), Christian organizations were working all over the world in places like Africa, India and the South America, rescuing orphans, feeding, teaching, training and healing. Even before secular musicians got into the act, Christian rock bands (such as Petra with the children of Biafra in the late 1970's), had already been raising awareness of starving children overseas. And now, long after music and movie celebrities tired of the cause d'jour, Christian groups continue their ministries of care, healing and feeding. They do this without fame or accolades. Who are the real heroes? Has Time Magazine ever thought of people like this for "Person of the Year?" Why not?

Before the feminist movement

What about Sofie Reuter and Anna Jakobsen? Do they count as heroes? In China's secular society, baby girls have no value, and abortions are performed to select boys. But this is not a communist invention. How can we prove that? Well in 1880, long before communism showed its ugly face, these two Norwegian missionaries, Reuter and Jakobsen wrote:

> It is an exception that a [Chinese] couple would have more than one or two girls. If there would be more born, they would be disposed of immediately. It was done in different ways. She could simply be put out as food for wild dogs and wolves. The father would sometimes take her to a "baby tower," where she would soon die of exposure and starvation and be discovered by birds of prey. Others again would bury the little ones under the dirt floor in the room where they were born. If there is a river flowing by, the children would be thrown into it.
>
> **Robin Lane Fox, Pagans and Christians, HarperCollins, Reprint Edition (January 1988)**

Reuter and Jakobsen went on to found one of the first safe havens for

---

[407] I'm not justifying missionaries dumping their kids off at boarding school but in those days, many expats did that.

Chinese baby girls. They would comb each of the abandonment places daily and rescue more babies.

Let's go a step further. What about the heroes in the local churches? As discussed earlier, naysayers and condemners of the conservative churches, such as Jim Wallis, say right wing Christians and Catholics have done a terrible job of compassion and that we need to have the government step in and step up care using our taxes. Is that true? Has he done any research on this? Or has he blindly bought into the anti-Christian worldview because it is convenient for him?

I have Hindu friends who condemn their own Hindu traditions and laud Christians because until recently everyone knew about Christian orphanages for non-Christian kids, but no one had ever heard of a Hindu orphanage, especially for non-Hindus. I'm sure there are one or two here and there, but the entire concept of orphanages all over the world in every culture and nation came from Christians, and most orphanages are *still* run by Christians. Kids in some rural areas of India can receive an education *only* because there are free Christian schools nearby.

Who Really Cares?

I want to introduce some shocking information revealed by Arthur C. Brooks in his recent book, Who Really Cares: The Surprising Truth about Compassionate Conservatism, Basic Books (2006).

Most liberals including Jim Wallis say conservatives are not doing enough to help the poor. They point to the measly 2 billion dollars a year that the U.S .Government gives to other nations for charity work. They say this is a tiny portion of our national GDP. They compare this to larger ratios of GDP amounts that other countries give. Usually they tout one European country or another over the U.S. But in this, they are speaking off the cuff. Brooks shows that, contrary to the mean-spirited drivel put out by liberal media, the conservative "Red States" are the biggest givers, the biggest donors and the biggest volunteers. Also, the American people donate not 2 billion dollars yearly, but 130 times as much. Yes, that is 260 billion dollars (in 2008 that number was up to 308B) – that's billions with a b – more than a quarter of a trillion dollars. And conservatives represent a large portion of that giving. Conservatives give 30% more than liberals do, according to Brooks, and overall, he says, Americans give 11 times as much Italians do and seven times as much as Germans.

So to say, that Americans give the least of all the nations is nonsense. My liberal friends need a reality check. The U.S. Government gives less than 0.7% of what individual Americans give. The problem is that many left wing Christians want the *government* to give people money. When Wallis says "we" are stingy he must either not know how much individual Americans give, or think private contributions count for nothing. He forgets that it is not government's role to be charitable to other nations. Usually when governments give money, 50% to 80% is wasted either in administrative bureaucracy or given to some corrupt foreign government official (especially since most liberals work hard to ensure that none of that money goes to any Christian organizations).

Liberals need to preach to their *own* choirs and ask them to give more. Conservative Christians are doing what Jesus told us to do. We simply want to do it *ourselves* and not have others who happen to be American citizens be forced to give without a choice.

But is the church slacking off?

No. Christians are working and making a great difference all around the world *including* their local communities. In 2003, Christianity Today presented an article that looked at a surprising study done by Professor Ram Cnaan, an Israeli-born secular Jew who directs the Program for the Study of Organized Religion and Social Work at the University of Pennsylvania. Professor Cnaan found that while churches freely provide social services, they and the communities they serve, generally do not have accurate measures of the effects. In his book "The Invisible Caring Hand: American Congregations and the Provision of Welfare," Cnaan assessed the dollar value of church-provided social services. He found that the net value of a congregation's social and community services averaged $15,307 per month or about $184,000 per year. This number includes the value of space, utilities, staff, and volunteer hours (calculated at a rate of approximately $11 per hour – what government worker do you know who gets paid $11 an hour after benefits, overtime[408], vacations, and pensions?) In his study, the average church was about 400 people. There are thousands of congregations all over the United States doing this (note while not all participate, there are over 300,000 churches in the U.S.). Cnaan says:

> *Although congregations can be viewed as being publicly subsidized because of their tax-exempt status, the value of their services to their communities far exceeds the value of the tax exemption, there is also the value of services that cannot be measured in dollars, such as informal help, pastoral counseling, value instruction, residents' representation, and community pride.*[409]

The most significant finding, according to Cnaan, is that nearly all congregations in the study provided some form of social and community service, most commonly for children, the elderly, the poor, and the homeless. Can you say "True Social Justice?" Besides formal programs, such as housing projects or neighborhood cleanup activities, churches provide pastoral counseling, care for the sick or bereaved, referrals of people to more specialized agencies and space for community groups to meet. I would add that churches provide drug counseling, keep teens off the street, give them a purpose, reduce teen pregnancies and STDs, and help keep families together.

Professor Cnaan suggests that were it not for congregations, about a third of children now in day care centers would have no place to go, most scout troops and 12-step groups would have no place to meet, and many

---

[408] Don't forget they can almost never be fired even if they don't work hard. So, while there are many hard working government employees, my friends and family who work for the government will tell you of the large number of slackers in their division. There are tales of teachers who "retire" on the job, one they'd named Scantron Dan. Yeah, I know Scantron Sam would be a better name, but his name really *was* Dan.

[409] Ram Cnaan, The Invisible Caring Hand: American Congregations and the Provision of Welfare, NYU Press, 2002.

homeless shelters and soup kitchens would disappear.

He has been asked if evangelism was the major reason churches provide services. His answer is "not really"…

> *I was expecting them to provide social services primarily in order to persuade people to change their religion and become members. [But] that assumption was simply wrong. Of course, everybody would like the people they help to join the congregation if they are not members already. But an overwhelming majority of congregations do what they do because to provide social services is for them to actualize their faith—to do the right thing. People said, "If you want to be like Jesus, you have to help the needy. That is why I'm giving so many hours a week to this."[410]*

Imagine now that you are in a church of 1000 or even 5000 people, which means you are providing 2.5 to 12 times the services that Cnaan calculated. Consider the magnitude of positive community impact in this.

Americans are the most giving people in the entire world! They give more of what they have than* any *other people group or nation!

Here's a list of some local church ministries. Some are minor, some are major, all are important. Note that in all cases these ministries are available to anyone without any requirements about them adhering to any particular set of Christian beliefs. If you are a Christian, none of these should surprise you. Feel free to just skim over the titles.

1. **World wide Medical Missionaries and Hospitals:** Financial, emotional, and manpower support for numerous medical missionaries around the world. Growing up in the Middle East and Africa, I found the best hospitals were always the free missionary hospitals funded by Christians. Most of them were funded by you Americans. The local socialized government hospitals were dirty, understaffed, crowded and you had to wait hours even if you had an appointment. *In Christian hospitals, doctors and nurses really cared about you. It wasn't a job. It was their purpose in life, their calling by their Lord.*

2. **Celebrate Recovery:** Christian 12 Step Recovery program designed to help people overcome your hurts, habits, and hang-ups, addictions, past abuse.

3. **Divorce Care:** Christian Divorce Recovery program designed to help you recover after a divorce.

4. **Divorce Care 4Kids:** Christian Divorce Recovery program designed for kids whose parents have gone through a divorce.

5. **Children's Ministry:** Includes classes for all ages. Children to share in services filled with fun, singing, teaching, and more.

6. **Hannah's Hope Chest:** A benevolence ministry, mothers who find themselves in need are invited to visit Hannah's Hope Chest to "shop for free" for needed items such as clothing, bedding, children's items, and household items.

7. **Homeless Ministry:** Every Saturday they distribute sandwiches, toiletries, and other donated items to the homeless.

8. **Hospital Visitation Ministry:** A team of volunteers visits those in the hospital to encourage and pray with them. Members of the church can ask the church to visit friends of theirs who don't have much family.

9. **Adopt-a-Hwy:** Cleaning the freeway as a service to the community.

---

[410] Ram Cnaan, The Invisible Caring Hand: American Congregations and the Provision of Welfare, NYU Press, 2002.

10. **Prayer Ministry:** Meets and prays for the needs of the community.
11. **Single Adult Ministries:** Include a variety of small groups, activities, and monthly meetings for single adults age 30 and up. Provides a social outlet for singles in a safe environment where they can develop relationships and family.
12. **Small Groups:** Meet throughout the month for relationship building, guided study, and serving opportunities and to provide people with a support structure.
13. **Athletics Teams:** Fun athletics opportunities for kids, youth, men, women, and co-ed teams throughout the year.
14. **Youth Ministries:** Jr. and Sr. High youth programs: Weekly services and a variety of special events, including concerts, youth rallies, paintball trips, mentoring, discipling and more.
15. **Christian Health Center:** Free health care to members of the community.
16. **Beautiful Day:** This ministry's motto is "Emptying Churches. Filling Needs." It works with local residents and businesses to reach out to the community, to fix the homes of those who can't afford to fix their own homes, clean up their yards, paint their houses, and plant gardens. It also includes working with local schools to encourage teachers with notes and "goodies" and provide volunteers to help school projects to clean up, replant, build play structures etc.
17. **Retirement Home outreach:** Youth and adults go to retirement homes to provide service and minister to the residents. It also teaches youth to respect and love the elderly as they develop relationships.
18. **Rake and Run[411]:** Junior Highers in the fall pick a street at random near their church and rake all the leaves of people's front yards for free. They don't witness, they just knock on the door and say "We are from XYZ church and we'd like to rake your lawn as a free offering to you."
19. **Education in Foreign Countries:** Many American Churches pay for building, staffing and teaching all kids in a local village for free.
20. **Microloan and Business center:** Christians provide microloans through a business center that provides Christian ministry to the locals. This is a hand up rather than a hand out.
21. **International Disaster and Emergency Services:** They meet the physical and spiritual needs of suffering people throughout the world through evangelism, medical care, housing development, disaster relief, and aid for the hungry.
22. **Living Alternatives:** A pro-life organization that provides confidential services to women in crisis. Services include pregnancy testing, education, Christian counseling, post-abortion counseling, and referrals. Young mothers can also receive assistance with housing, clothing, diapers, and other infant care supplies.
23. **Christian Children's Ranch:** Provide safe homes for abused, neglected, and troubled children. Their goals are to meet the spiritual, emotional, educational, social, and physical needs of each child.
24. **Prison Ministry:** Church members go to local prisons to have services, play sports and to counsel.
25. **Restoration Urban Ministries:** Various Urban Ministries for the homeless. Services include food pantries, clothing centers, transitional housing, drug and alcohol support groups, youth programs, and counseling.
26. **Car Repair Ministries:** Willow Creek Church in Illinois has a ministry to single mothers. The mechanics in their congregation hold a regular car repair workshop and all single mothers can bring their cars in for a checkup and repair.

---

[411] Dreamt up by Pastor David Underwood.

27. **Spokes to Folks:** Started by my friend Paul Leuty. Every Saturday, Paul and his now huge gang of volunteers take old bike parts and fix the bicycles of the homeless living in downtown San Jose. www.spokestofolks.com

28. **Homes for Unwed Mothers**[412]: Since the early 1980's, when the Rev. Jerry Falwell opened a home for unwed mothers at his Thomas Road Baptist Church in Lynchburg, Va., (Falwell would provide full healthcare and college tuition to these young mothers who did not abort their babies), organizations including the National Right to Life Committee and the Christian Action Council have built a network of alternative services for pregnant women contemplating abortion. My wife and I have been personally involved with a home in San Jose called Heritage Home. Unwed mothers who choose to not abort their babies can come and stay here, all their medical aid is provided and the staff finds jobs for women who have kept their babies, and current residents baby-sit for them. Food and infant formula are available for former residents who have fallen on hard times. Women who have been addicted to drugs or alcohol or been abused by male companions, as most have, begin to bring order to disorderly lives.

The list goes on. I'm sure Christian readers can add many more ministries to this list. Note I've only listed the "outreach" ministries, we could easily add another twenty "in reach/fellowship" and sustaining ministries that meet the needs of those who are within the church. These are just as important to local and state governments because they ensure that additional dependants aren't added to the state welfare or social roles.

Now, at no point do I think we should rest on our laurels. We can and *should* always encourage ourselves to do more, to give more, to sacrifice more, to love more. We can start by all truly giving at least 10% of our income to our church and missions.

So, what can we add to the argument?

Anyone who implies that Christians are not involved in social issues, locally and around the world, is either uninformed or disingenuous. It is nigh time for us to focus on the moral problems and related legislative issues to prevent *more* social issues from bringing our nation to its knees. After all, we are the ones who are and have been picking up the pieces. Surely, we owe it to ourselves and those who are suffering to try and reduce what is causing the suffering.

---

[412]www.nytimes.com/1989/07/23/us/anti-abortion-revival-homes-for-the-unwed.html

Twenty-eight

The state cannot get a cent for any man without taking it from some other man, and this latter must be a man who has produced and saved it. This latter is the Forgotten Man.
   William Graham Sumner

We can judge the character of a man by the way he is willing to take your money forcibly to give to the poor; but refuses to voluntarily give his own money to the poor.
   My admonition to Christian friends who were planning to vote for Barack Obama in 2008 after it was revealed that for years Obama made more than a quarter of a million dollars yearly but gave less than $1,050 to charity most times.[413]

A friend: I think we should take care of the poor and provide free healthcare.
Me: Of course, we should. So, how much money do you give to the poor last year? How much did you donate to hospitals locally or overseas?
Friend: (embarrassed silence)
Me: (laughing) You did not give any money to the poor, did you? You see, that's the problem. You personally don't want to give money to the poor. You want the government to take money away from others and force them to give it to the poor. I, on the other hand want Christians and the church to do it voluntarily. I don't want to force you to do it. You don't need to do it. Just reduce our taxes, and leave it to us.
   This was a lunch conversation, we are still great friends, by the way.

Is Jesus A Socialist?

I have a picture on my computer. It's of a group of protesters at a rally. One young lady is holding up a very large sign that says, "Jesus was a Socialist!"

While we may think the sentiment is admirable and Jim Wallis, Tony Compolo and many liberation theologians would like us to believe that it is true, the reality is it's a complete misunderstanding of what our Lord told us to do.

Remember how we discussed in an earlier chapter (*What about the Sermon on the Mount?*) how there is no logical way to apply the Sermon on the Mount to governments. It was directed to us as *individuals*. Imagine again how ridiculous it would be if you went to a judge because someone had assaulted and mugged you, and the judge insisted that we follow Christ's admonition so you were now legally obliged to let the mugger hit your other cheek and take your clothes. Those with a limited understanding of the Bible

---

[413] rhog.blogspot.com/2008/03/saint-barack-stingy.html

tend to make the same mistake when they look at all the other teachings of our Lord. The complaint that I hear over and over again is that Jesus told us to love our neighbors. Thus the conclusion they come to is that we should collect taxes and feed the poor with that money. We should then raise more taxes and give to the needy in the form of free healthcare and housing. It would be the most loving thing to do. It's what Jesus would want us to do.

Now I fully agree, Jesus did say, you and I should give to the poor, take care of others, sacrifice for our neighbors who aren't even related to us, provide medical assistance to the stranger, food to the hungry and shelter to the homeless, and we should visit the prisoners.

*But he said **you and I** should do it. He never said the government should do it.* He said, *"You,* the individual, follow me." He said, *"You* do as I tell you to do." He said, *"You* give money to the poor *yourself."*

He never said *force* the person next to you to do it. He never said force *others* to do it. That's stealing and coercion. It does violence to Christ's words, and I admonish Compolo and Wallis for twisting scripture in this way.

Our Lord did not say take money away from the selfish and give it to the poor, nor did he say take money away from the rich and give to the struggling. He never even said take money from the *filthy* rich. In fact, we'll prove shortly that forcing someone to give money (that is, goods) at the point of a gun (the IRS) to another is stealing.

I cannot find anywhere where Jesus said, "Take from someone innocent to give to yet another person." Jesus said, *"You* the individual should give sacrificially. You the individual should go into the entire world and preach the gospel. You the individual should take from what God has given you and freely give. But through an apostle He also said, "The Lord loves a cheerful giver." Not a *forced* giver. As far as I can tell, Compolo is confusing Jesus with Stalin or Mao.

If you think Jesus would approve of using the government to force charity and sharing with others (socialism), you should be consistent and say that Jesus would approve of using the government to force *evangelization.* Why aren't you promoting Missionary Soldiers? It's the logical conclusion, after all. Why do you balk at this? You can't logically get one without the other.

So when people say "the government should help the poor because the Bible says we should help the poor," you just reply, 'The Bible also says we should preach the gospel, do you want the government doing that too?" The point being that just like evangelization, the Bible actually commands us as *individuals* to help the poor through personal giving and charity and *not* through government force (at the point of an IRS agent's gun). No, Jesus was no socialist. He was into personal responsibility. To coin a word, he was a "personal charitist." If you can show me where Jesus ever said that the government must provide charity through violence, force or coercion, then you would have a case.

By the way, if you ever need to argue with someone about this, start with the Sermon on the Mount as we did earlier and show why Christ's words obviously did not apply to the government there. Thus, the burden of proof is

Neil Mammen

upon *them* to show that it *does* apply here. Then ask them why it doesn't apply the same way to the Great Commission.

Breakdown government to what it really is

Every time you think of the word "government" with relation to goods or services, think instead "other people." For instance: "*Government* must take care of the poor" becomes "O*ther people* must take care of the poor." "*Government* must provide me with welfare" becomes "O*ther people* must provide me with welfare." If you want to get even more personal, make it local. "*My neighbors* must provide me with welfare."

Who is the government? It's your neighbors and other people. But, you object, I'm part of the government too. Yes, but you can't use the word "we" because those "others" are not *voluntarily* participating. You are forcing them to participate.

But why did Jesus never promote socialism?

For one, humans are corrupt. The minute you bring a whole set of corrupt individuals into play who are not easily monitored or made accountable, things get lost, people get hurt, money and resources get wasted. Mini empires are built. Graft happens. Worse, people receiving this mindless free handout with no personal touch get used to getting something for nothing, which our Lord knew was bad for the spirit and well being of a person. As we'll show next, it is even bad for the intelligence of a child. Studies show a direct link between a reduction of IQ and the length of time a child's parent was on welfare.

It is also bad for the persistence of faith. We've seen that the more socialistic a country is, the less Christian it is. Look at the nations of the Netherlands and Sweden, countries that used to send missionaries all over the world. I grew up with many Dutch and Norwegian missionaries in Africa and Yemen. Yet today you'd be hard pressed to find the same density of Christ followers there as were there even 25 years ago. For Christians to crave socialism seems like a self-extinguishing death wish.[414]

God designed work and responsibility to be satisfying and compelling, goals to be hard to achieve and fulfilling, and work to be worth the effort. Can any Christian argue with this? God wanted healthy competition to be an incentive and discipline to build character. Imagine if collegiate or professional sports teams kept no score or ensured that all scores came out equal regardless of skill or effort. Do you think we'd have the kind of excellent athletes we see there? I'll elaborate on this in just a bit.

Impersonal, uncaring non-adjusting compassion?

Moreover, our Lord does not want a faceless, careless government dolling out feed. No. Christ wants there to be a direct connection between those sacrificing and those receiving. He wants His followers to be the personal bearers of the gospel message and of care and love. He wants those

---

[414] Is there a link or is it just that all nations have less Christians? Well, to compare, just look at the density of Christ followers among the Scandinavian immigrants in the U.S. The density is far greater here among them than in their home countries. There are two possible reasons, socialism, and state controlled churches.

who receive this love and care to look into the eyes of some of the ones who are sacrificing for them – the ones giving their time, passions, and life for them – and in doing so, the receivers would look into the eyes of Christ. Christ wanted His followers to discern what should be nurtured and what should be abandoned, just as the Bible has commandments to discern the truth and hold fast to what is good.

Growing up in the Middle East and Sudan, I was able to experience care from the missionary hospitals and from the socialized government hospitals. In the missionary hospitals, I was met with caring doctors and nurses whose life's ambition was to sacrifice what they had for the Lord and care for people according to His command. Many of these folks were risking their lives to present Christ's love to others.[415]

In the government hospitals I was met with people who had "retired at work," had a steady paycheck and could never be fired. Christ was not exemplified or glorified in the "government compassion" (or lack thereof). This doesn't mean there aren't compassionate government workers, but they were the exception and not the rule. If excellence is not built into the rewards system of the machinery, how can you expect it rationally?[416] The lowest common denominator will prevail.

When done right, compassion from a person or a group builds, teaches and strengthens, but compassion from a government always creates dependency, a spirit of entitlement and an expectation. Compassion from a person or a charity can change its mode of operation if it sees something is not working, but compassion from a government can never change without a myriad of forms and the mini dictators within the government and their tiny fiefdoms being threatened.

As we've shown, compassion from a charity usually provides more than 85% of every dollar given to it to the recipient. Compassion from a government usually goes to hire government employees, pensions, union dues, paper work, lobbyists, buildings and more employees. Then corruption seeps in, or money is given to people who don't really need it. Think of the examples we saw with Hurricane Katrina where millions were wasted and where the private sector and private charities actually got things done while the government efforts hurt everyone. What's worse with governmental departments is that the next year they'll need *more* money to achieve the little they *were* achieving this year. Don't forget too that politicians redirect money to their pet projects (usually things that are named after them). Government is not the answer.

Trying to stop corruption can make things worse

Add to this the sad fact that when well meaning officials try to stop corruption, the new checks and balances end up miring things in paperwork and force honest citizens to pay high prices to lawyers or consultants just to

---

[415] If you recall, as I mentioned, after we left Yemen some crazy Muslim fundamentalist shot and killed three of the missionaries in this hospital. Local Yemenis were outraged at the attack on the missionaries.

[416] Note that in private hospitals as long as there is meritocracy and competition and people can be easily fired for cause, quality can be assured.

Neil Mammen

work around the paperwork. You can't win with the government because it was never meant to work that way.

Did Christ expect the government to meet people's health or material needs? Never! You never see Him asking either the Roman government or the Jewish leaders to hand out money to the poor. He only asked that they provide equal justice to the poor and the rich alike. He didn't say one should have any special privileges over another. Notice that in the story of the Good Samaritan, which by the way was the impetus for all Christian missionary work, the Good Samaritan is not the government. He's a *private* individual who gives only of his *own* resources. Notice too that he is not a socialist and does not force the innkeeper to keep the wounded man for free, nor does he insist that any others help pay the costs. He does it himself voluntarily.

Think about it, what is one of the greatest tactics Satan could use to attack the Church and make evangelizing less effective? How about by replacing the Church's works of love and charity with a faceless government. By making Christians complacent so they do not give as much or care as much. By limiting Christians ability to be seen as loving and instead be seen only as legalistic moral enforcers. Our moral stances should go hand in hand with our works of charity. If evil one can disassociate those two, he knows we will be less effective. Note too how the US Government has been trying to do foreign works of charity now, something that has always been the task of the church and our missionaries. Remember, we do that task so much more efficiently than government today without it costing the taxpayer a dime and we give 13,000% more.

Should the government adhere to religious values?

What's funny is that often the same people who argue that Christ would never have been involved in politics so we should not be involved in politics or impose His moral commandments on others and are the very ones to argue that Christ was a socialist and that the ethical thing for the government to do is to impose His commandments about charity on others. Which way do you want it? Is the government supposed to be religious and follow Christ when it comes to handing out money but irreligious when it comes to moral values? What nonsense! They have flipped God's moral code on its head and taken a diametrically opposite approach. It's sheer silliness.

In addition, as we saw before, liberals have reversed the concepts of the Constitution as well. They want the government to enforce the assigning of *goods* by the point of a gun, but they want to leave the enforcing of *rights* (like the right to bear arms and fetal rights) as a voluntary exercise. We will lose our republic this way.

Christ would no more demand that you forcibly take someone else's money and give it away than he would make you force someone else to go spread the gospel when he or she did not want to. No, Jesus was no socialist.

Voluntarily Compassionate Christians

And this is why Christians for 2000 years have been the ones who voluntarily and *personally* fed the poor, *personally* cared for the orphans, *personally* brought medical aid and even today *personally* provide almost

$184K worth of free volunteer social services per church of 400 people within the U.S. And this is why America is the largest giving nation in the entire world, even when adjusted for GDP.

Sure, other religions have taught compassion, but nowhere is the mark of the missions, outreaches, orphanages and hospitals greater than those of the Christian church. When you think "charity hospital in the third world," do you immediately think, "Oh it's funded by a Hindu group or an atheist group"? No, you think, "Christian Missionary Hospital" and with good reason.

When you think of a doctor who could be making millions in America instead living in some small hut in Africa, raising his children among the natives and providing the locals with free medicine and free medical services including free air-support, you don't immediately think, "Ah, he must be funded by the Secular Humanists of America."

As we've noted, America is the greatest giving nation in the world. Last year we gave more than $260 billion to third world nations. In GDP this was 9 times more than the Germans and 11 times more than the Italians, the next closest nations. Conservatives gave the bulk of that. So much for socialist nations and their giving! So much for the kind-heartedness of liberals! None come close.

Recently, during the 2010 Haiti earthquake crisis, none of the socialistic countries donated anything of any real value to Haiti. The U.S. carried most of the burden. Socialistic countries talk a lot but do little when it comes to compassion. Socialism is not Christ-like!

Are we mean-spirited?

When my liberal friends accuse me of being mean-spirited because I want to take away government subsidies and convert welfare to workfare and stop socialized medicine, I say, "Look, guys, I don't want *you* to take care of the poor. We Christians will do it. I want you to get *out* of the compassion business and *now*. I want you to get the government out of it. Both of you are doing a lousy job. I want you to reduce our taxes and let *us* take care of the poor the sick, the suffering, the orphans and the widows. We've been doing it for the last 2000 years. You haven't. Send them to us."

You won't find Christians saying that taking care of the poor is bad, but you will find many saying that forcing someone *else* to take care of the poor is bad. You won't find Christians saying feeding someone is bad, but you will find them saying, "Be careful that you do not feed them till they forget how to feed themselves." That is why Christians have started schools and occupation training centers over the centuries.

So even if you are not a socialist but believe Jesus would condone the taxing of one person to pay for another, you would not have any biblical basis for this. All you would have is your unsubstantiated desire. Worse, this is a false compassion and doesn't work. Jesus was not a socialist. He made many personal sacrifices. And that's what you should be too if you care. And if history is any indication, that's what Christians have always faithfully been and continue to be.

Currently while there is a tax deduction for charitable giving, there are caps. This means that means if you make $200,000 one year and give it *all* to charity, you may still end up owing taxes on money you don't even have. Why is this just? If you want to see the need for government entitlements diminished, how about giving people a $1.50 tax write-off for every dollar that they donate to a charity – with *no* cap on the maximum amount? Add this to a reduction in taxes, and giving will increase tremendously. We will soon not need entitlements that destroy the family. We won't need an incentive destroying Universal Healthcare either. We Christians will be able to take care of all those who can't afford to insure themselves. (Of course, we need tort reform so our hospitals aren't sued every few seconds.)

Let's break down socialism to what it really is

Imagine that you live in cul-de-sac with 10 neighbors. The person on your right is a rich person. He's worked hard all his life, earned a lot of money and is doing well. He owns four cars. To your left is a poor immigrant who moved into the country recently. He has four kids and is the sole breadwinner for his family. They have one car that barely works. You do all right financially but are not extremely rich. You and your wife work, and you have two cars, which you need for commuting.

One day an unfortunate thing happens to your poorer neighbor. He loses his job, and his car breaks down. There's no way to fix it and no way for him to find another job without a car.

Now ask yourself, is it morally acceptable for you to go over to your poorer neighbor's house and give him your car?

Absolutely.

Okay, but that presents a problem because you need your car to take care of your family. So let's look at option 2. Is it morally acceptable for you to go over to your richer neighbor's house and ask him to give one of his cars to the poorer neighbor?

Of course it is. There is nothing wrong with that.

But then your neighbor says, "No, I like my cars."

Okay, let's look at option 3. Is it morally acceptable for you to go over to your richer neighbor's house with a gun and force him to give one of his unneeded cars to your poorer neighbor?

Would Jesus do that?

Absolutely not on both of these options.

Well okay, but you are an individual. What if you instead go to your seven other neighbors and have *them* all vote on the question of whether they want your rich neighbor to give the poor neighbor a car? The vote ends up being 9 to 1 against the richer neighbor. *Now* is it morally acceptable for you to take one of the richer neighbor's cars? Which way do you think Jesus would vote? Do you think He would approve of that?

"Of course not," you cry. "That's still stealing and oppression."

Well, what if you got the mayor and the entire city to vote that your richer neighbor must give his car to your poorer neighbor?

What if you got your entire country and your socialist president to rule that your richer neighbor should give his car to your poorer neighbor?

You know what we call that don't you? Indentured or forced labor, when the state unethically takes what you've worked so hard for. What's worse is that if the rich neighbor is making $300K a year, he's not being forced to give one car away at gunpoint; he has to give as much as 30% of his income or $100K. That's at least 5 decent cars per year. Per year! It may be legal, but it certainly is not moral. Then there are state taxes.

Do you see that if it's immoral for you as an individual to force someone to give up his property, it is still immoral for a group or any third party to do so as well? Renaming that group a "government' does not suddenly justify the actions. The Ten Commandments apply to individuals as well as groups or governments.[417] That car is a "good" not a right. And you *are* violating someone's rights by taking it from the one whose legal and moral labor produced it.

Jesus would want you to sacrifice *yourself* and perhaps help convince your neighbors to voluntarily sacrifice, but He would never be a socialist. It's a complete misunderstanding of everything Christ has asked us to do.[418]

This excellent example about the cars was borrowed from Mike Winther from the Institute of Principle studies, www.principlestudies.org. I recommend a visit to his website and attendance at his classes if you live in Silicon Valley or Central California.

I was once talking to an engineer, who said, "Well, I agree that socialism is wrong, but two years ago my father got very sick. If it wasn't for the free Medicare that the government provided he would have died." Now you have to understand, this sort of a statement is meant to imply that we *have* to have some sort of socialized medicine. After all, who'd want his father to die; *I* certainly don't want his father to die. But wait! Something is wrong here (and I really did this), I said, "Now *I* don't want your father to die and I would

---

[417] The objection some will now make is: Well what about imprisoning someone or execution? But this is not the same, is it? Remember that your unalienable rights are guaranteed by God only if you do not violate someone else's unalienable rights. In the case of criminals or murderers, those individuals have done something immoral and violated the unalienable rights of others. Thus, we are morally obligated and justified by God in the Old Testament context to restrain them and take due recompense. However, the rich neighbor has not done anything evil to your poor neighbor. So, what right do you have to violate his rights? Now if you think that he did violate the poor neighbor's rights, you need to itemize his crime and prosecute him for it. Simply saying, "You are rich so you are evil" is a lynch mob mentality. Others may object: But I can't just imprison someone. I need the community to do that. No, you can imprison someone, you need the community of his peers to convict him. If a convicted felon were to show up at your house, you could legally imprison him until such a time as you could hand him over to others.

If anyone reading this was then to say, "But the rich stole from the poor – that's how they got rich," they would be digging their own graves. You are saying that to someone who had grown up among the poorest of the poor in Africa and India. "You, dear reader, are filthy rich. In fact, you are richer than 90% of the population of the world. Will you be happy when I come to take away your shirts and cars and homes? Why do you have almost 300 square feet of house for every person in your family, when 30 square feet is more than enough? It is time to share your home with 10 times as many people. I can bring some of my childhood friends over. You sir, are a thief of the highest form. Return all you have right now." The hypocrisy of this view is made plain the minute you take it to its logical conclusions. Morally, you can penalize a man only when he has specifically violated another man's unalienable rights. You lose your rights if you take away another's rights. That's why we imprison felons.

[418] Yes, I know some of you are thinking: "But it's a social contract. If they don't like it, they can leave the country." But that is simply not true. It only works for immigrants who come into a country when it is already socialistic. It doesn't count for someone under whom the law changed and who probably can't afford to leave their country to go elsewhere. And it certainly smacks of oppression to force them to adhere to a system they never signed up for. No law can be just if it infringes on another man's unalienable rights. Remember, these were the reasons why we broke away from England.

have been happy to donate to his care, but" and I pointed to a fellow engineer, "can you explain why it is *his* responsibility to *involuntarily* make sure your father does not die, for no fault of his own? What if he has his own problems?" And why stop at just the car or healthcare? Why not equalize everything? If taking one person's hard-earned car or money is acceptable, why not take everyone's and pool it to give us communism, which is just socialism taken to its logical conclusion? What is the moral difference? There is none. Neither work.

Socialism is oppression, it's forced charity at the point of a gun.[419] Voluntary compassion is Christian. If God's law is absolute, a majority opinion for it does not make an evil act moral. God's moral commandment on stealing applies in full force to governments, churches, families and individuals. There is no exception. If the entire country decides to lynch someone, does that make that lynching moral? If the entire country decides that Jews are not human, does that make exterminating them moral? If something is immoral for an individual, it's immoral for a neighborhood, a town, a state and a country. Give me one rational and ethical justification for it? Let me repeat, we should not violate the unalienable rights of an innocent person! That car, the product of the neighbor's legal and moral labor is inalienably *his*.

But I think we Christians should be ready to give up some of our rights

I was in an argument on FaceBook and a Christian said this to me. But that's not the point, is it? Of course I'm ready to give up some of *my* rights, whenever I donate to charity, or whenever I give up some of my time in volunteer work, I'm saying, "I give you some of what belongs to me." But I do it *voluntarily*. Yet, we are not talking about *my* rights *only* are we? The issue is the rights of the neighbor next door. It's not just my rights that are at stake, it's other people's rights. What *right* do *I* have to force *others* to give up some of their rights? That's the question we are debating here, isn't it? Not whether I should be willing to sacrifice, but whether I should *force you* to *unwillingly* sacrifice. Remember, democracy doesn't not make immoral acts moral. This was precisely what the founding fathers feared when they condemned the "mobocracy."

Jesus also knew that Socialism doesn't work and can hurt

Imagine that you had a healthy able-bodied 25 year old son, that he lived in your home, that you fed him, paid his bills, provided his entire healthcare, bought him anything he needed and gave him an allowance to buy things he wanted. He could work if he wanted to, but he knew that he didn't really have to. How mature do you think he'd be? Do you think that he'd achieve his full potential? Do you think that he'd be prepared for battle against the evil one? Would it be love to treat him like this his entire life?

We all know that just doesn't work in individual cases. So how much

---

[419] Some may say, the rich person was only able to create that wealth because of the structure of society we'd assembled around him. But nobody is sacrificing to allow the rich man to create that wealth. It's all voluntary. We each participated in creating that structure because we wanted to. To penalize a person for legally working within that structure is a violation of his rights.

less will it work en masse? The very concept of socialism goes against a primary Christian concept – the obvious truth that humans have a sin nature. Socialism depends on people *working* as much as they *can* and only *taking* as little as they *need*. Yet, human nature is such that we *work* as little as we *need* and *take* as much as we *can*. The concepts of socialism violate the basic premise of the Gospel i.e. that man has a sin nature. Socialism says: Jesus you didn't need to die, because man is essentially good and never got Adam's sin nature. Anybody who advocates socialism is essentially ignoring the reality of human nature. And our real world experience shows that it won't work.

As they continue to give "goods" away as rights, socialism runs headfirst into reality. How does a socialistic government ensure that people work as much as they can and *not* take as much as they can without the government becoming a totalitarian regime? It cannot, if there is a large population. You may be able to control small populations with similar cultural values and ancestries and traditions or a small commune and the ability to kick people out. However, with a large population you are forced to end up with Big Brother and a massively corrupt, incompetent and intrusive government – a government run by sinful people. Socialism in a large population leads to an oligarchic fascism or bankruptcy and inflation. Sound familiar? For the former, think China, Russia and North Korea. For the latter think Greece and Europe.

Socialism hurts evangelization

Socialism also limits the opportunity to spread the Gospel, because it takes away something that is the role of the Church and makes it the role of the government. Worse, socialism takes away the stigma of having to ask for help, which encourages people to stop working towards being self sufficient, and it creates a mentality of entitlement.

Now it would be one thing if the government was doing a better job of it than we were. But they aren't.

Socialists are greedy and uncompassionate

Many people imagine that capitalists are greedy, selfish and uncompassionate. But remember as we've already shown, the reality is just the opposite. Capitalist countries and people give the most to charity. Socialist countries and people give the least. And you can't argue that that's because those socialist countries take care of the needy, because if you took up an offering amongst individual socialists for poor *foreign* nations, socialists would *still* give the least. Remember too that, if you took up a collection in America, you find that liberals and progressives give up to 30% less than us evil free-market conservatives. No, greed and selfishness is not associated with capitalism, it's associated with socialism.

Socialism has always been and always has to be "Big Government"

Hitler, Mussolini, Stalin and many of the Roman Caesars had socialism in common. Remember, in socialism, you have to control the output of "goods" to try and ensure sufficient supply. So you have to take control of industries, banks, production and trade. Some people think that to the left we have communism and to the right we have fascism. But that is simply not true. Hitler was a fascist socialist, so was Mussolini and Stalin. The two extremes are really "big government" or "no government". While we have no space to discuss this in great detail in this book, suffice it to say, that when society has "limited government" and people are incentivized by the fact that they get to keep the fruit of their own labor, they prosper the most. Centralized governments always mess up and end up being corrupt and inefficient. You will be unable to find one government program in the US that has not wasted money and has not spent much more than they originally thought it would and given us rotten results. Think of public schools, Medicare, Social Security and welfare. It simply doesn't work. It never has, and wishfully thinking that one day it will, is to be a mean-spirited idiot as you condemn future generations to pain.

In truth, most of the socialists I've met have either been elitists, thinking the masses are stupid and they must therefore control and take care of the people; or they have been selfish and lazy and feel entitled, they want someone else to take care of them.

Socialism usually lasts at the most three full generations before it falls apart by going bankrupt.

I wrote that last line in 2007. But just before this book went to publication in 2010, it seemed like the evidence of that prediction was being provided to us. Look, for instance, at the severe problems the Spanish, Swedes, British, Germans and Greeks are having as this is being written. This is because the first generation still retains the hard work ethic from before socialism was implemented. The next generation learns a bit from their parents, but they grow up in the welfare state system and the third generation knows only to take what they can. At this point (the third generation) the system breaks down because there are fewer and fewer people putting into the system and more people taking out of it. By the fourth generation capital dries up, entitlement is massive, people work reluctantly. The Swedes have calculated that a significant portion of their workforce is simply *not* working. There is no incentive to do so.

Our Lord was not a socialist because He knew that socialism only works for insects – creatures with no free will, ambitions, sin nature or competitive instincts apart from the colony.

Socialism is not social justice. Socialism is social oppression.

The Socialist Basketball Association

It's fun to apply any sort of socialist principle to professional sports and see if it would still be successful. What if the NBA were socialistic (the SBA)? Let's imagine that the SBA commissioner made it his job to ensure that no single team ever scored higher than other teams. His job and that of the referees was not to ensure that no illegal plays were made or no "unjust" acts committed (that is, rights violated). Instead, it was to spread the wealth (the scores or "goods"). Any time a team or player started doing extra well, they would be taxed in points – and would be forced to give points to teams who didn't have talent or didn't want to practice as hard. Or they'd give these points to players who had hurt themselves. After all, in basketball, unlike business, if you get a point or win, it's *always* at the expense of the opposing team. So, we level the *success* field. If we did this, what would happen to the excellence, the drive, the motivation, the thrill of achievement? How long would you watch professional sports? Do you see? It just does *not* work.

What could work?

Yet if you had a system that recognized and anticipated man's sinful greedy nature and leveraged it in a constrained manner, you could indeed find a workable solution. It's the same idea that the mathematical genius John Forbes Nash came up with, called Game Theory.[420] In this theory you anticipate that each person is out to get what they want based on their selfish nature. Then you compensate for that and act accordingly by providing rules to constrain unethical actions (but not unethical intentions, as we cannot manage intentions). The free market is like that. It will never be perfect because man is not perfect, but it works and would be much better than socialism.

A morally and legally constrained free market system is the only one that has ever worked reliably. "Morally constrained" means the government ensures that contracts are kept and ensures that no man is given an unfair advantage (it turns out that most monopolies like railroads were only monopolies because they've recruited Government to protect or subsidize them, read details in the reference below).[421] A free market is based on honoring of contracts and rights, not a forced equality of results. I call it "Morally Constrained Capitalism." There is no forced sharing of the fruits of other people's work. Remember, goods are not rights.

Can a Christian be a Capitalist?

Some people try to argue that capitalism and free market economics are not compatible with Christianity or Judaism. They say, "Look at the Ten Commandments. If Christians adhered to 'Do not covet your neighbor's goods,' capitalism would never survive! Capitalism is all about wanting a car as good as your neighbor's and wanting to buy better things." Those who take this line of reasoning, however, fail to understand the commandments or are purposely twisting them. Coveting your neighbor's car means you want to take *his* car. It does not mean you want to let him keep his own car and earn and pay for your *own* car, which just happens to be like or better than his. Coveting your neighbor's wife does not mean that you want to find and marry another beautiful woman; it means that you want to commit adultery with the wife your neighbor has. You want to take *his* wife! These folks are twisting what the Bible says. Capitalism is not coveting. Socialism, on the other hand, *is*. Why? In socialism you *do* want to take that neighbor's car or money away from him and give it to someone else. You covet his goods (money) for yourself or someone else. Don't be fooled.

Now of course this does not mean that Christians should try to "keep up with the Joneses." It does mean that Christians can justly and morally seek a better lifestyle. They can and should put in a smart and honest day's work

---

[420] Game Theory refers to zero sum game occasionally, but in this case, it does not apply to the market being fixed but to the actions of the participants. Look up "Nash Equilibrium in Economics" on a search engine.

[421] The Myth of the Robber Barons: A New Look at the Rise of Big Business in America, Burton W. Folsom, Young America Foundation (2007)

toward making their dreams and the dreams of their customers and neighbors come true. After all, look at the Proverbs 31 woman, who sees that her trading is profitable (verses 18 and 24). *The Bible encourages **profit** making.*

The Ten Talents

Can we tie this all back to Jesus in other ways? Yes. In the parable of the Ten Talents in Matthew 25:14-30, the man who works the hardest and accumulates the most *profits* gets the most rewards. Note that in this instructive story, God is the master, the Kingdom of Heaven[422] is the *current* church age and the man who chooses *not* to participate in the free market is punished. There is no equality of results – nor, for that matter, was there equality in the original dissemination of the talents.[423] He even takes the one talent from the bad servant and gives it to the *most* capitalistic servant. Jesus clearly was rewarding and encouraging the free market system both in financial as well as spiritual realms.[424] Jay Richards has written a great book on this. It is titled *Money, Greed, and God: Why Capitalism Is the Solution and Not the Problem*, (HarperOne, 2010). I recommend reading it.

Jesus was not a socialist!
He taught that you and I should personally sacrifice for others.
He never taught that we should force anyone else to sacrifice for others.
Socialism is stealing. It is also oppressive and unloving.
Socialism is immoral and unbiblical.

---

[422] We know the Kingdom of Heaven is not the New Earth or even Heaven, because Christ talks about the evil one being there and sowing etc.

[423] One cannot limit this parable to only being applicable to witnessing or holy things.

In addition, some may try to use the example of the parable of the Vineyard Workers in Matthew 20 as an example of socialism or worse communism. In this parable, the master makes a deal with some workers to pay them a day's wages for their work. But at various times during the day the master returns and hires more workers promising this time to pay them fairly. But at the end of the day he not only pays the ones he promised a day's wages that promised amount, but he also pays everyone else the same amount, even those who only worked an hour.

But this parable does not help the socialist in any form? Why? Because it acknowledges the capitalistic owner of the field as being above the workers. In true socialism, the owner of the field would have to share his field with the workers or be penalized by taxation or the government would own the field. Further this parable shows that the master is allowed to negotiate and pay whatever he sees is a fit wage to whomever he wishes at whatever rate they both deem as fair, as long as keep his word or contract. Imagine having that conversation with a union.

[424] Lest you complain that this was not about the free market but was about using your God given talents, you should know that theologians from the early church till this day, accept the fact that spiritual truths and physical truths are conveyed simultaneously. For instance, Peter's vision about the sheet with unclean animals in Acts 10 is universally accepted as telling us two things: The spiritual point – the Gospel is also for the Gentiles and the physical point – we can eat all animals without regard to their being clean or unclean.

Twenty-nine

...how about the Economic Opportunity Act of 1964 -The War on Poverty-which President Johnson said ..."strikes at the causes, not just the consequences of poverty."

[Yet] trillions of dollars later, black poverty is the same. But black families are not, with triple the incidence of single-parent homes and out-of-wedlock births.[425]

Star Parker, ex-welfare mother, ex-burglar, ex-drug addict, now President of CURE, Coalition on Urban Renewal and Education.

The Tragic Consequences Of Welfare

I was at a conference, chatting with a gentleman at my dinner table. I mentioned some of my research and he immediately sounded interested. I noted some of my conclusions on marriage and welfare and how "No Fault Divorce" was and is probably one of the greatest destructive forces in America. I didn't realize it at the time but I was talking to a man who had spent years on precisely that. His name is Patrick Fagan.

Patrick works with the Family Research Council's division called Marriage and Religion Research Institute (MARRI) and MappingAmericaProject.org. In the last few years, they've done enormous amounts of research, identifying trends related to family structure. Remember when I said that we need to have actual statistical data to convince non-Christians of the value of Christian morals. That is precisely what Patrick and his team do.

His organization provides us with charts and data on how broken families have serious consequences on society. A child's home life and just as interestingly his church life affects society's crime rates, suicide rates, educational levels, drug use, poverty levels and many others. Take any serious issue and you can see how it is tied to both the stability of his parents and if they took him to church as a child.

Patrick also works with the Heritage Foundation and this is where we find some very tragic information about how Welfare has destroyed our nation. *The simple fact is that children are suffering because the U.S. welfare system has failed. Designed as a system to help children, it has ended up damaging and abusing the very children it was intended to save. The welfare system has*

---

[425]www.freerepublic.com/focus/f-news/2204926/posts

failed because the ideas upon which it was founded are flawed. The current system is based on the assumption that higher welfare benefits and expanded welfare eligibility are good for children. According to this theory, welfare reduces poverty, and so will increase children's lifetime well-being and attainment. This is untrue. Higher welfare payments do not help children; they increase dependence and illegitimacy, which have a devastating effect on children's development.

How Welfare Harms Kids.[426] Robert E. Rector and Patrick F. Fagan Backgrounder #1084

The paper goes on to list the following facts:

a. Welfare plays a powerful role in promoting illegitimacy.
b. It triples the level of teen sexual activity.
c. It doubles the probability that a young woman will have children out of wedlock.
d. It triples the level of behavioral and emotional problems amongst kids.
e. It doubles the probability that a boy will engage in criminal activity.

In fact, the paper shows that higher welfare benefits have a decisively negative effect on children. Comparing children who were identical in social and economic factors such as:

a. Race
b. Family structure
c. Mothers' IQ and education
d. Family income, and
e. Neighborhood residence

Two researchers, June O'Neill (who later became the Congressional Budget Office Director) and Anne Hill[427] of Queens College, found that the longer a child was on welfare, the lower his or her IQ.

The researchers' study showed that it was not poverty but *welfare* itself that had this horrible effect on children. Children under five who had spent just two months a year since birth on AFDC (a welfare program) had cognitive abilities 20% below those who had received no welfare, even after holding family income, race, parental IQ, and other variables constant. Welfare creates the need for *more* welfare. This is not compassion! It's oppression!

Back on Uncle Sam's Plantation

We began this chapter with a quote from Star Parker; in that same article, she said this:

... I wrote a book called "Uncle Sam's Plantation." I wrote the book to tell my own story of what I saw living inside the welfare state and my own transformation out of it.

I said in that book that indeed there are two Americas. A poor America on socialism and a wealthy America on capitalism.

I talked about government programs like Temporary Assistance for Needy Families (TANF), Job Opportunities and Basic Skills Training (JOBS),

---

[426]www.heritage.org/Research/Welfare/BG1084.cfm

[427] M. Anne Hill and June O'Neill, Underclass Behaviors in the United States: Measurement and Analysis of Determinants (New York: City University of New York, Baruch College, August 1993). See also: M. Anne Hill and June O'Neill, "Family Endowments and the Achievement of Young Children With Special Reference to the Underclass," Journal of Human Resources, Fall 1994, pp. 1090-1091.

*Emergency Assistance to Needy Families with Children (EANF), Section 8
Housing and Food Stamps.*

*A vast sea of perhaps well-intentioned government programs, all
initially set into motion in the 1960s, that were going to lift the nation's poor
out of poverty. A benevolent Uncle Sam welcomed mostly poor black
Americans onto the government plantation. Those who accepted the
invitation switched mindsets from "How do I take care of myself?" to "What
do I have to do to stay on the plantation?"*

**Instead of solving economic problems, government welfare socialism
created monstrous moral and spiritual problems. The kind of problems that
are inevitable when individuals turn responsibility for their lives over to
others.**

**The legacy of American socialism is our blighted inner cities,
dysfunctional inner city schools and broken black families.**

*Through God's grace, I found my way out. It was then that I understood
what freedom meant and how great this country is.* [428]

A fix for welfare?

The tragedy of all this is when Newt Gingrich and conservatives first
tried to implement a fix, by turning welfare into a sort of "workfare," the news
media and many others called them baby killers, racists and claimed that they
wanted to starve the poor. Yet after the 1996 Personal Responsibility Act (also
known as Welfare Reform) was implemented, not only did the percent of
African American kids in poverty drop 10% but the number of unwed mothers
dropped.[429] As a telling sign, even Bill Clinton tried to claim responsibility for
this law that was forced upon him by a conservative congress.

The solution out of dependency and poverty turns out not to be by
handing out money but actually ends up being only through churches and with
a government that practices tough love. Charity must come from church
ministries and outreaches that also practice the tough love of holding people
accountable for their actions and the biblical command:

II Thessalonians 3:10 *"If a man will not work, he shall not eat."*

The fix for this is for people to obey God's moral laws about personal
responsibility, marriage, divorce, and sex; *and for the church* not the
government to be the solution provider. Do you see how true social justice is
not trying to put people *on* welfare, but trying to get them *off* it; because it is
bad for them and for their kids?

Yet, the church cannot be the solution provider to sufficient people if
it is over taxed, over restricted, repressed or oppressed. Do you see why
anyone who cares about the poor and the oppressed in America has to first care
about the laws of this nation? And has to make sure the church is free to do its
job unencumbered by regulations, censorship, red tape or the fear of capricious
civil suits.[430]

If you say you care about the suffering but then elect presidents and

---

[428] www.urbancure.org/article.asp?id=3141

[429] www.neoperspectives.com/welfare.htm

[430] Note that valid legal suits are necessary to protect society. As there will always be sinful people in
church.

congressmen who think the freedom of the church should be restricted or who think government would do a better job of ministry than the church, you are creating Bonhoeffer's dreaded wheel. If you say you care about true social justice but abandon moral values and moral laws, your false social justice will make things worse; and you yourself have then *become* Bonhoeffer's dreaded wheel crushing the innocent.

If we say we care about true social justice, but don't get involved in protecting the innocent by enacting moral laws, and providing solutions that work we are being hypocrites. Remember, if welfare actually worked we'd be all for it. But despite good intentions it simply doesn't work and instead hurts.

No society or individual ever improved their condition by only charity. Except in the case of the dying, the purpose for charity must be to get people to a point of self-sufficiency. *That* is the best thing for them. They can only get to that point if they participate in the free-market and exercise their individual liberties and rights (not take other people's goods). We should incentivize them to succeed.

> *Welfare is not true social justice; it is in fact social oppression.*
> *It violates the commandment to love your neighbor.*
> *The Church leading them to independence is the only solution.*

Thirty

Pharaoh: Joseph, it is obvious that God has given you great wisdom. I will make you ruler of all of Egypt so that you can use that wisdom to pass new laws and policies and bring great prosperity to Egypt, especially in the great famine that is to come.

Joseph: Oh no great Pharaoh, politics is so dirty, evil, and corrupted. I'll have nothing to do with it or you. How can I be the chief politician of Egypt and sin against my God? You guys stick to your evil morality, I repeat, I'll have nothing to do with it. I'll just stay in prison and pray for you. Prayer changes things, and if God wants to change Egypt, He'll do it Himself. Have a nice day, Pharaoh.

So rather than be involved in politics, Joseph went back to prison, and Pharaoh continued worshiping the Egyptian idols. A few years later, millions of Egyptians and most of Joseph's family in Canaan starved to death when the famine hit. Pharaoh made many sacrifices to his Egyptian gods, but it did no good.

My twisted view of how things would have been if people in the Old Testament had the same attitude towards politics as many pastors and Christians do today.

The New Testament, The Old Testament And Politics

Were New or Old Testament figures involved in politics? If so, that would give us further examples of why *we* should be politically active as well. We could also dispense with some arguments fellow believers have used to say Christians should *not* be involved in politics.

Well, as it turns out, the Bible is full of examples of people getting involved not only in the politics of their native countries but also, when circumstances took them there, the politics of adopted countries. As an immigrant to this great land, I have great biblical role models.

Think about this as well; imagine that you are in Israel while Ahab is king (remember he was not of the line of David). You've heard the prophets tell of the punishment that is to come to Israel for disobeying God's laws and for the oppression of the innocent that Ahab and his people are doing. Yet, somehow, you are given an opportunity to help influence some of Ahab's laws. Do you take that opportunity? What in your conscience allows you to abdicate that charge to try to achieve justice? What do we call the prophets who went along with Ahab? Why do we think we pastors and preachers will not be judged the same way especially when we *do* have an easy way to influence all our laws today?

John the Baptist

John the Baptist spoke out against the sin of the lead politician of Judea. King Herod, a man who wasn't Jewish, but whose father had smoozed his way into becoming appointed ruler of Judea by the Romans. Herod was committing adultery with his brother's wife. Herod's adulterous mistress did not take too fondly to John's admonition and made sure that his head rolled.

One is reminded of the many Christian pastors who were too wimpy to speak out against Bill Clinton's adultery. That was sin wasn't it. Surely, one can condemn the action and call him to repentance without condemning the man. Those pastors didn't have anything as serious as their heads to lose.

Remember as we said in the introduction to this book, you can't say "Oh, John was not involved in politics; he was just speaking out about sin." But it was the personal sin of a *politician*. If we are to speak out about the personal sin of a politician which may not even affect us, how much *more* should we speak out about the sin of a politician that condemns millions to death and suffering through a bad law? The reason we Christians *do* need to be involved in politics is precisely because immoral men are doing immoral things, immoral laws are being passed, and immoral men are being elected and they are appointing immoral judges all of which is changing the nature of this country. John spoke about a ruler sinning in his public and personal life. Jesus as we showed also spoke out against immoral men, immoral laws and the immoral application and execution of *moral* laws.

Are we suggesting that it's okay to speak out against immorality in our leaders when we can't do anything about it except lose our heads; but it's not okay to speak out against it and actually do something about it when we have the God given opportunity to do so under *our* Civil Authority (the Constitution)? Perish the thought that we actually do something effective. Remember James 4:17 says:

Anyone, then, who knows the good he ought to do and doesn't do it, sins.

Peter and Paul

Peter and Paul are asked to stop preaching. They are told it is against the law. But they instead of submitting to the local authorities, their rulers, they decide that God's Law is greater and continue preaching. They were practicing civil disobedience against their governmental authorities.

Joseph

Joseph, the son of Jacob, while in prison petitions the Wine Taster (which by the way was a powerful cabinet position and not just a sommelier) to tell the Pharaoh about him. Then he not only becomes involved politically in Egypt, he becomes the chief politician under Pharaoh. You don't see him saying, "Oh no Oh Pharaoh, I'm a follower of God, and we followers of God should *never* get involved in politics. We'll just let God do what he wants and stay out of the way." No. In fact, Joseph became a ruler and passed many laws that would later benefit the children of Israel.[431]

Years later the Jews shied away from politics and failed to maintain

---

[431] Genesis 41

their influence with the Egyptian leadership. The Bible says a new Pharaoh arose that did not *know* Joseph.[432] Then what happened? The Israelites became slaves for 400 years. Could that happen to our children or descendants? Why do we think we deserve any better treatment?

Nathan

The prophet Nathan went to King David after David had sinned with Bathsheba and had murdered her husband. Nathan had to confront the ruler of Judea. Why? Why did he not just mildly submit to the civil authority? Because the *final* civil authority is not the king, the final civil authority is the Law of God. There is no divine right to do evil, even for the king; how much less so for an elected official?

Nehemiah

Nehemiah was the wine taster to King Artaxerxes. There's that powerful position again. The wine taster got to hear and know all the intimate details of the king's affairs. Nehemiah uses his political connections to persuade the king to allow him to go back to Israel and rebuild the wall. In other words, laws were changed (that's legislation) and decrees were made stemming from the work of a godly man in the political arena.

Daniel and Civil Disobedience

How about Daniel? He not only becomes involved in the politics of all the kings of two nations he serves, but also sets a moral example and then leads by it, practicing civil disobedience to turn the king's heart. Here was a great opportunity for him to "honor" the authority set by God over him and merely submit. But in deference to God's greater Law, he does not do this, and his disobedience leads to new laws being made to allow prayer and reverence for God.

> *Daniel 6: 25 Then King Darius wrote to all the peoples, nations and men of every language throughout the land, "May you prosper greatly! 26 "I issue a decree that in every part of my kingdom people must fear and reverence the God of Daniel. For he is the living God and he endures forever; his kingdom will not be destroyed, his dominion will never end.*

Here's a man of God being involved politically. What's even more fascinating is that Daniel changes the laws for not *only* the Jews but for *all* the Babylonians, believers and unbelievers. Is it permissible to practice civil disobedience? Is it good to be involved in the legislation of new laws even in your adopted country? Is it our duty to fight for the removal of bad laws? Daniel and his friends show that it is. Pastors and Christians there is just no precedence in the Bible to avoid involvement in politics. If these are our Bible heroes, shouldn't we emulate them?

Shadrach, Meshach and Abednego and Civil Disobedience

Shadrach, Meshach and Abednego practiced civil disobedience by refusing to bow to the image of the king, and as a result of their courage (and God's grace) laws were changed:

---

[432] Exodus 1:8 Now there arose up a new king over Egypt, which *knew* not Joseph. (KJV)

Daniel 3:28 Then Nebuchadnezzar said, "Praise be to the God of Shadrach, Meshach and Abednego, who has sent his angel and rescued his servants! They trusted in him and defied the king's command and were willing to give up their lives rather than serve or worship any god except their own God. 29 Therefore I decree that the people of any nation or language who say anything against the God of Shadrach, Meshach and Abednego be cut into pieces and their houses be turned into piles of rubble, for no other god can save in this way."

Again, new laws were applied to everyone in the land.

If we look closely at Daniel and his three friends, we notice some other things about their civil disobedience.

They were commanded to do wrong by the law. They did not do wrong in God's eyes, but they disobeyed the immoral law. They did not complain when punished for their disobedience. They went willingly to what seemed certain death. Christians in our day can do the same by resisting socially commanded evils.[433] And then they did get involved in legislating new moral laws when given the opportunity.

Esther

Esther is one of my favorite examples of involvement in politics. Many people know the story. Esther is slave girl living in Persia. She is Jewish, but no one knows that. Through a sequence of events, in part due to her extreme beauty, she becomes the king's wife. She was not placed in a harem as is usually envisioned. She was replacing the earlier Queen Vashti as the king's *sole* wife. While she is in the palace, a plot unfolds to kill and execute every single one of her people, the Jews.

Her uncle Mordecai goes to her and asks for her help. Her first answer is, "It is not permitted for me to go to the king of my own accord. If I approach the king on my own, I could be put to death."

Can we read more into her answer? In other words, she is saying, "Is this really my place to get involved? It is so dangerous, it is so costly, and it is so worldly. I don't think there is much I can do. I don't we should be involved this way. We are to submit to the authorities. That's why they are there. After all, God is in control. He'll decide what the king does and does not do. He will choose the leaders. It is up to Him to decide. This is someone else's job. I just became queen, I would become unpopular. I have three new cats, four new dogs, all these new slaves that can't get my kosher breakfast right and that Persian women's meeting on Tuesdays. Oh and the king could put me to death. Besides, you can see that the king is surrounded by crooked politicians."

Is this your attitude toward politics today? Are you a pastor who thinks, "It is not permitted for me to be involved in politics? If I get involved, I could lose my tax deduction. I could become unpopular. Our congregation will shrink. I'm busy." Are you thinking that if God wants something to happen,

---

[433] Norm Geisler differentiates between two types of situations that call for civil disobedience, situations where you are commanded to do something evil – forced to pray to idols, for example, or forbidden pray to God – and situations in which you are allowed to do something evil but not forced to do it, abortion being an example. Geisler recommends different responses to each.

He will do it on his own? That politics is too worldly? Or that people will reject the gospel message?

What does Mordecai say to Esther?

Esther 4:13 "Do not think that because you are in the king's house you alone of all the Jews will escape. 14 For if you remain silent at this time, relief and deliverance for the Jews will arise from another place, but you and your father's family will perish. And who knows but that you have come to royal position for such a time as this?"

He is saying: What if this was *why* God put you here? What if this is the one primary reason for which you were created?

And her answer:

Esther 4:16 Then I will do it. And if I perish, I perish.

Esther says, "If the price is death, then so be it, I will do it." Esther was trying to save the lives of tens of thousands of Jews. Are we willing to do the same to save the lives of *millions* of children and poor? Children, who will end up criminals, commit suicide, join gangs? Are we willing to do something unpopular? Uncomfortable? Are we willing to step outside our comfort zone?

So, Esther appeals to the king. She lobbies him, actually. She gets involved in the politics of the situation. She is crafty, inviting her chief opponent to dinner, luring him to expose his evil plans. And God uses her to save the *entire* exiled population of Jews. She becomes a lighting rod for all Jews to stand up and advocate for themselves, to protect their rights, land and property. Esther gets many laws passed. The first said the Jews could protect themselves. The second said Haman's ten sons should be hanged. And as the book of Esther ends, we see Mordecai, a godly man in a position of authority, second in rank to King Xerxes, gets involved in legislation, passing laws for the good[434] of the Jews.

Esther 8:9 At once the royal secretaries were summoned—on the twenty-third day of the third month, the month of Sivan. They wrote out all Mordecai's orders to the Jews, and to the satraps, governors and nobles of the 127 provinces stretching from India to Cush. These orders were written in the script of each province and the language of each people and also to the Jews in their own script and language. 10 Mordecai wrote in the name of King Xerxes, sealed the dispatches with the king's signet ring, and sent them by mounted couriers, who rode fast horses especially bred for the king.

Esther 10:3 For Mordecai the Jew was second in rank to King Ahasuerus, and he was great among the Jews and popular with the multitude of his brothers, for he sought the welfare of his people and spoke peace to all his people.

Both Esther and Mordecai get involved in politics, attaining high political power, working for the welfare of the Hebrew people, and passing many laws.

Now some have argued that Esther only got into politics because she had to, because people would die. And how, I ask is that different from the issue of abortion where people *are* dying? How about the increase in suicides and crime due to divorce? How about when the Church starts being persecuted

---

[434] The word in the NIV is 'welfare,' but that makes it sound like free giveaways due to today's connotations of the word. Mordecai was passing laws for the 'well being' of the Jews.

and Christians like the Jews in Ester's time find their lives at stake. May I suggest, people *are* dying. What are we doing about it? Are we waiting for them to be stabbed in the streets before we take action? Surely, our compassion for the poor and the orphans and the needy requires us to take some action to stop divorce and welfare from destroying them?

Are there lessons here?

What can we learn from this? Would God use us in the workings of a government to save people? Should we seek worldly power in order to promote the welfare of fellow Christians (and in doing so seek the welfare of generation of families to come)? Should we be engaged in the political structure of a nation even if we are just immigrants and are only here for a short time? Could this be why God has put us into an influential position with a group of Christians who need to be guided to achieve great things? Could we be used by God to help those who would be oppressed by taxes or discrimination, deserted by their fathers, killed by their mothers, molested by their mother's boyfriends, forced into the destructive addictive bondage of welfare? Do you think the Old Testament doesn't apply today? Or do you think it applies *only* to the Jewish people?

Don't forget that the real-life drama of Esther and Mordecai took place in a secular nation, with a secular king, with secular laws. In fact, the analogy is perfect. They got involved where they were. This is true of a number of leading Jews in exile, from Daniel, to Shadrack, Meshack and Abednego, to Nehemiah and of course to Joseph. All were people of God in foreign lands, and He used them to guide and establish moral laws in their foreign homeland. Just as the Jews were in a country that was not their final home, Christians are in this world, a place that is not our final home. They become involved. They were commanded as we saw to become involved. Shouldn't we?

Can anyone say the Old Testament indicates that we are not to be involved in politics? On the contrary, it repeatedly shows how we *are* to be involved in politics, *especially* in a godless nation.

Leaders and Judges

Now let's turn our focus toward Israel and its leaders.

Moses is special, of course, since he was governor, judge, jury and pseudo-legislator to the entire nation. I say pseudo because he did not make up the law; he simply received it from God. He *was* a judge though.

The judges – Joshua, Samson, Debra and others – were lawgivers and decision makers, so we have to say they were politically involved. You might argue, "Well Israel was a theocracy, so they were justified in being involved since they were not only the civil leaders but the religious leaders." If this is your argument, you are still stuck with the fact that they dealt with both religious and civil issues. Remember too that Jesus dealt with both kinds of issues. And we agree Christians in politics should concentrate on passing moral laws, not stray into legislating theological, ceremonial, or religious issues.

What about the Prophets?[435]

Now let's look at the Old Testament prophets. You will be hard pressed to find prophets who did not advise or admonish kings. Here is a list of a few of the prophets, just to prove the point. As you read it, I want you to compare what the prophets did to what organizations like Family Research Council (FRC), Focus on the Family, American Family Association (AFA) and numerous other Christian family groups are attempting to do today. Calling out and warning people about bad laws and bad leaders. Trying to guide good leaders to good laws, trying to ensure we appoint godly leaders.

King making Prophets

Samuel was a king maker. God used him to appoint a king (King David). That was political wasn't it?[436]

Ahijah, like Samuel, was a kingmaker. On God's command, he appointed a rebel as king, to break Israel into two nations. (I Kings 11:29). But this rebel king refused to obey God's moral commandments, so Ahijah then condemned the king for being immoral (I Kings 14). And what was the king being immoral about? The very laws that he was enacting and enforcing.

Warning Prophets

Isaiah constantly reminded the people that if they continued in sin and follow their sinful leaders, God would wipe them off the face of the earth.

1:18 See how the faithful city has become a harlot!

*1:21... Your **rulers** are rebels, companions of thieves.... Israel's worship of me is **made up only of rules taught by men**.... I will turn my hand against you; I will thoroughly purge away your dross and remove all your impurities*

2:19... By the wrath of the Lord Almighty, the land will be scorched and the people will be fuel for the fire.... Each will feed on the flesh of his own offspring.[437]

Notice how Isaiah differentiates between *rules taught by men* and God's moral laws. Isaiah's political influence is apparent in that he enjoyed his greatest influence under Godly King Hezekiah, who reigned from 715 to 697 B.C.

Jeremiah denounced the sins of his countrymen and prophesied the judgment and destruction of Judah that was to come. And he didn't limit this to his own nation; he also condemned Babylon, Moab, the Philistines, and other nations about the wrath that was about to fall on them as well. So, we can't say that he limited himself to a theocracy. He was liberal with his warnings and condemnations. By that, I don't mean he was left wing. Rather, he was profuse, willing to warn anyone and everyone who deserved it.

Elijah and Elisha were always fighting with the kings, prophesying against them or to them, advising them, challenging them, condemning them,

---

[435] Since we do not want a theocracy or monarchy, it makes no sense for us to even discuss kings. So, we will not use them as an example except when we talk about prophets

[436] I'm waiting for someone to compare the prophets who appointed kings to Christian groups who work to appoint presidents. However, I think this falls apart in the comparison since we are not a theocracy. But there's something to be said there.

[437] We see this fulfilled as described in an earlier chapter.

showing them that their priests were wrong.

Civil or Spiritual?

While the prophets included kingmakers, they mostly included men who warned people that if they continued to disobey God, they would suffer the consequences. Now again you may complain. These men were dealing with the *spiritual* aspect of politics, not the secular aspect – that's why they were so involved. But remember they were not dealing with rituals or hand washing or even theological issues. Principally, they addressed moral questions. They warned about prostitution, child sacrifice and justice – matters we would consider secular today. They also advised kings on waging war. *Isn't this what politics is all about?*

Whatever one might say about them, the prophets were not shy about politics. The Bible is replete with political activity.

Do remember we are not talking about nor do we care who likes who, or who gets invited to a state dinner, or if a freeway was named after someone (unless they use tax money to do so). We are talking about *laws*, laws are based on morals, morals are based on your religious values and that is what John the Baptist and all these other prophets were talking about and that's what got many of them killed. I hope it is apparent to you by now what the difference is. We are talking about who makes our laws and what they are to be based on and what causes are worth standing for and maybe even dying for.

Some pastors say there is no evidence in the Bible that godly men imposed their laws on others. That is false. First, remember the verse from I Timothy about how the law is specifically for evil men.

*We also know that law is made not for the righteous but [it is made] for lawbreakers and rebels, the ungodly and sinful, **the unholy and irreligious**;*
1 Timothy 1:8-11

Unholy and irreligious? Surely, that covers everyone.

Second, what I've shown in this chapter is only the tip of the iceberg of laws made by godly men and imposed on others even foreigners. What is the entire book of Judges about? What are all the fights in the wilderness against Moses about? There you have Dothan and others, ungodly men chaffing against God's representative and God's laws. God condemned both the Jews and Gentile nations because they did not honor Him or keep His laws. So, should not pastors be calling their flocks to emulate the prophets? Should not pastors be emulating the prophets?

So what can we add to our argument?

Old Testament prophets took moral stances, advising or castigating those who made and enforced the laws. They were men of God influencing public policy for the good of both godly and ungodly people. Isn't that what this is all about?

Thirty-one

Hanna More (Abolitionist): Mr. Wilberforce, we understand that you are having trouble choosing whether to the do the work of God or the work of a political activist [i.e. a politician in parliament].
Wilberforce: (pensive silence)
Thomas Clarkson: We humbly suggest that you can do both.
From the Movie, Amazing Grace, Bristol Bay Productions, 2007
Clarkson was the founder of the Committee for Abolition of the African Slave Trade.

We are called to care about those who are being oppressed in Christ's Second Commandment. Yet, it seems irrational to argue that we must just preach the gospel and hope that Christians (and perhaps non-Christians) will live moral lives and stop hurting others. If that methodology supposedly worked, how do you explain the existence of Slavery in both England and the Southern United States? Both were Christian cultures and yet those fine believers seemed to have no kind intentions toward willingly abandoning this great evil.
Conversion to Christianity does not automatically create a moral society. Moral societies are influenced heavily by legislating moral laws like the banning of slavery. And moral laws are only legislated when moral men and women actively get involved in their legislation through the political process not by an accident of luck. Are you really suggesting that we should never have fought against slavery in England or the US and let millions continue to die on slave ships? After all, that is the natural conclusion of your argument.
My rebuttal in an online debate with a Christian.

Politics And Christians Of History

W

hy stop with the Bible? History is full of Christians who were political activists or politicians. Theodore, Bishop of Cyrrhus in Syria, tells us of the martyrdom of Telemachus[438], a monk who grew up in the east, far from Rome. But when he heard that Christianized Rome under a Christian Emperor Honorius still held gladiatorial contests, he was upset at the horrible moral lapse of an entire society. In AD 404 he traveled to Rome, to the then named Flavian Amphitheater (renamed the "Coliseum" in the 7th Century[439]). Seeing the horrible immoral spectacle of gladiator killing gladiator and the bloodthirsty crowd cheering, Telemachus clambered over the stands and dropped onto the arena floor. Running out in

---

[438] Ecclesiastical history: a history of the church in 5 books from A.D.322 to the death of Theodore of Mopsuestia, A.D.427 by Theodoretus bishop of Cyrus. A translation, published by Bagster & sons, 1844. Page 326
[439] Interestingly, the name "Coliseum" comes from the "colossal" statue of Nero that once stood there. www.sacred-destinations.com/italy/rome-colosseum.htm

Neil Mammen

between the gladiators, he beseeched them and the crowd to stop. Indignant, the people started to throw stones and objects at the monk. Tragically, he was felled when one of these objects dealt him a mortal blow. Yet, he continued beseeching the crowd to Christ like piety and love, even as he died.

The Christian Emperor Honorius was moved by this act and his conscience was so pricked that he issued a law banning gladiatorial fights that very same year. Telemachus, a pastor, priest, man of God, did not hesitate to act morally against a legal but immoral law, and through his actions, convinced the politicians to change the law and the face of Rome.

Even before this noble monk's martyrdom, we see Christians in the early church either getting involved in politics or if they became Christians while politicians, staying involved in politics. All of them working to bring about a just society, based not on the ancient barbaric traditions of their culture, but on God's Moral Law. Examples include Christians like as Flavius Clemens, brother of the emperor Domitian. Even Bishop Ignatius of Antioch on his way to his martyrdom in Rome, tells those Christians in government and politics not to "pull any strings" to save his life. Obviously there were Christians in politics that were powerful enough to have tried to do something. Eighty plus year old Ignatius wished instead that his death be a testimony to unbelievers.

As Christians started getting more and more involved in politics, the Romans started to retreat to their temples, trying to shore up their religion. It even prompted a Christian Apologist to mock them with this:

> ...we [Christians] have filled every place among you—cities, islands, fortresses, towns, market places, the very camp, tribes, companies, palace, senate, forum—we have left nothing to you but the temples of your gods.
> **Quintus Septimus Florens Tertullian.**[440]

Do you see, how Christians were starting to permeate the government and the culture; and note how the tactic that the Romans tried, i.e. running to hide in their temples failed miserably at the end of the day.

Modern Day Political Activists

How about Corrie Ten Boom? When her Christian family realized they could not stop Hitler through the normal channels, they hid Jews. The price they paid for this was death. Only Corrie survived.[441]

Remember too that while Hitler[442] was not truly a Christian, many Germans were. This is even more alarming in light of the concept most American pastors espouse – that the church should stay out of politics. In the late 1930's, Germany had an anti-Christian government controlling a predominantly Christian nation and a church that mostly stayed out of politics. The name given to these Christians who turned a blind eye to Hitler? "Useful Idiots" or "Good Germans." Good indeed. They are saved and are our sisters and brothers in Christ, but will Christ call them good and faithful servants in the final days?

---

[440] Apologeticum, Tertullian, Chapter 37. Sadly, Tertullian was ensnared by the Montanist heresy later in life.

[441] The Hiding Place, Corrie ten Boom, John Sherrill, Elizabeth Sherrill (Author), Chosen Books, 1971

[442] Hitler was most probably an occultist.

Ah but you complain, "Corrie and Telemachus were all activists, they didn't become politicians or run for office!"

Notwithstanding the fact that I *am* calling us all *to be* political activists, let's then look at William Wilberforce. Appalled, as a Christian, by the very idea of slavery, Wilberforce worked for over 40 years in the British Parliament to abolish it. He started in 1787 and he finally got the first law passed in 1807, (yet it took till 1833 for all slavery to be abolished). Notice too that it was only by getting many other Christians elected to Parliament that he were able to succeed. The British Government, once masters of the slave trade, now sent their vast armada of ships to do what? To *stop* slave traders. All because Wilberforce was a Christian who was not afraid to engage in politics to change the Law. Remember there was no other way to change this horror.

The Wilberforce movement later came to the U.S. through Christians. Suppose Wilberforce had said, "If God wants to stop slavery, *he'll* do it. It is not for me to get politically involved. I should just preach the gospel to change hearts and hope things change." Is that your attitude today? What if Wilberforce and every Christian after him had had the view of many pastors today, staying at an arm's length from politics and concentrating on spiritual matters? Can you imagine the continued cost in human lives? Do you think change would have taken place in England? Do you think it would come in America? What precedent or justification do pastors and churches have *not* to be involved in politics?

Look at the rest of the history of change in this country

It was religious people including the Quakers, who realized that slavery is wrong, and who actively worked to abolish it in the United States. A law was written and passed against it precisely because of the pastors and believers who labored for years for it. But was slavery against *man's* law? *No.* Slavery was legal. The reformers realized the practice was against *God's* Law! They knew it had to be changed. It was and will never be enough to *just* try to change hearts, because even Christians and their children can be influenced by bad laws. Just think about the Christian kids who grew up with gladiatorial combats, slavery and racism.

The entire Civil Rights Movement was brought about by religious people. Black ministers were joined by thousands of white preachers and pastors and churchgoers – people who were persuaded first and then got involved in the political process to pass new and godly laws. Their plea was religious, not legal. Discrimination is wrong because it violates God's law. Here again is a prime example of how if we keep religion out of politics, we'll end up with racism and other evils. Pastors and Christians is this resonating with you? Do you realize that many who have discriminated against African Americans over the years have been Christians – uneducated Christians who grew up under evil laws and did evil things, yet still were saved by grace? Just preaching salvation in church didn't do the job did it? Many of the slave owners were already saved but seriously misguided.

Similarly, if abortion is going to be stopped, it will have to be stopped by religious people. If the cloning of humans for spare parts is going to be prevented, religious people will need to make the effort. If same-sex marriage will be halted, it will be by the initiative of religious people. Who are these religious people? They are you and I and other Christians, led by pastors, deacons and elders. People who care for the innocent. Will we take a stand?

Where should we train for this? Where else but our Sunday schools, our Bible studies, our small groups and prayer meetings? Where should we learn about this? Where else but our sermons and mentoring? If we don't do it there, where else will we do it? Who will preach God's heart concerning this? Will pastors? Who will be the prophets pointing out the sin of the people and exposing evil leaders.

I'm not ever saying that that's the *only* thing we should focus on. But if we don't focus on it there, where else exactly will we do it? That's where we started the fight against slavery. That's where we should preach the defense of true "God given unalienable rights" for the oppressed. That's where the battle for true social justice (not the immoral redistribution of wealth) begins.

Since history shows that the only true moral change occurs when Christians and the church get involved with the legal and political systems, why is this not considered more important? Can we continue to let our society race toward Gomorrah as we remain smug, binding up the wounds of those destroyed by what *we* are allowing to happen.

If *we* personally do not bring about change, we will see another three or four generations of kids suffer the consequences of bad laws that split up their families, lead them to depression, abuse, more divorce and suicides. Do we care? Are we satisfied that as long as *our* kids are okay, everything is fine? Yet, don't forget that our grandkids will *not* be okay. We can no longer sit idly by.

So, what can we add to our argument?

Throughout the history of the world and this country, we see men and women of faith standing up to change or make the laws of their nations, bringing health and justice to the people; and wisdom to the national debate. If justice is ever going to come to this world, we Christians will need to roll up our sleeves and make it happen. *We* are God's agents of change. Who will lead us?

Thirty-two

Every person who shall be chosen a member of either house, or appointed to any office or place of trust . . . shall . . . make and subscribe the following declaration, to wit, "I _____, do profess faith in God the Father, and in Jesus Christ His only Son, and in the Holy Ghost, one God, Blessed for evermore; and I do acknowledge the holy scripture of the Old and New Testaments to be given by divine inspiration."

Delaware Constitution, Art. 22 (adopted Sept. 20, 1776)

Our laws and our institutions must necessarily be based upon and embody the teachings of the Redeemer of mankind. It is impossible that it should be otherwise. In this sense and to this extent, our civilizations and our institutions are emphatically Christian.[443]

U.S. Supreme Court, 1892

Congress shall make no law respecting an establishment of religion, or prohibiting the free exercise thereof; or abridging the freedom of speech, or of the press; or the right of the people peaceably to assemble, and to petition the Government for a redress of grievances.

The First Amendment to the Constitution

What About The Separation Of Church And State? What Can Churches Legally Do?

We've all heard of the "requirement" that church and government be separated. Most of us believe that the Constitution says somewhere that the church must not be involved in politics. A successful businesswoman I know who claims to be a Christian[444], has even said, it is morally wrong for a church to accept tax deductions and then ever make any sort of political commentary or moral condemnation of any law.

I hope this book as answered the silliness of the idea that the church should not be involved politically. The church cannot fail to be involved. It would be *immoral*, heartless and wicked for the church *not* to be involved. The church must be the conscience of the state.

Now let's see if it is constitutional or legal for the church to be involved. Jefferson, wrote the phrase:

"building a wall of separation between Church and State."

---

[443] Church of the Holy Trinity v. U.S., 143 U.S. 457 (1892); cited by Barton, America's Godly Heritage, pp. 10-11

[444] I say "claims" because I grilled her once and it was revealed that her beliefs were really Universalist.

This phrase was used by a Supreme Court Justice in 1963 to halt prayer in schools. Since that time (and here is a great example of how laws change hearts), a majority of people think that the government and the church cannot and should not mix. If we knew our history, however, we would realize that the First Amendment was a restriction on the federal government. It was never a restriction on the states and it was never a restriction on the Church. In fact, most states at the time of the founding of the country had official denominations.[445]

Secondly, if we look at the background of this statement by Jefferson, we see it was not written in the Constitution. Nor was it law anywhere. The phrase comes from a letter written by Jefferson to the Danbury Baptists. Even if *Jefferson* wanted that phrase to be in the constitution, it wasn't and they never voted it in, or signed it like they did the Declaration of Independence. It was not their original intent as the debates reveal.[446] So judges should not be treating it like it's the law, and they should certainly not be making judicial decisions based on that.

Historian Dave Barton of Wall Builders argues:

Thomas Jefferson had no intention of allowing the government to limit, restrict, regulate, or interfere with public religious practices. He believed, only with the other Founders, that the First Amendment had been enacted only to prevent the federal establishment of a national denomination...

Jefferson committed himself as President to pursuing what he believed to be the purpose of the First Amendment: not allowing the Episcopalians, Congregationalists, or any other denomination to achieve the "establishment of a particular form of Christianity.

Since this was Jefferson's view, in his short and polite reply to the Danbury Baptists on January 1, 1802, he assured them that they need not fear; the free exercise of religion would never be interfered with by the government.

David Barton www.wallbuilders.com/LIBissuesArticles.asp?id=123

But I've been told the founding fathers were not Christians

People commonly say America was not founded by Christians. They point to eight men, Thomas Jefferson, Thomas Paine, Ben Franklin, George Washington, Ethan Allen, Sam Adams,[447] John Adams and James Madison, who they claim were "deists" as opposed to traditional Christians. Atheists love to point this out, but I find it odd that those who do not believe in God try to bring to their side of an argument, men who *still* acknowledge God and His moral law but argue that He just doesn't interact on a daily basis with us. Of the eight men listed, the most "atheistic" ones, i.e. Thomas Paine and Ethan

---

[445] Note this does not mean that I recommend having state churches. It's just an indication that these same men were not worried about banning state churches.

[446] Yes, and I'd be happy to argue "original intent" about this phrase. Because I don't think you'd be able to defend the "original intent" to separate all religion from the state. It was designed to protect religion from the state, not protect the state from religion.

[447] I know, you are thinking that one of them went on to create a furniture store (Ethan Allen) and the other to create a beer company (Sam Adams). By the way in this list, based on their writings, Sam Adams and Washington were definitely Christians, Franklin believed enough in God to ask everyone to pray for His Guidance. Both Jefferson and John Adams believed in an active God but were a non-Trinitarians so we may not consider them Christians, Madison called Christianity "the best and purest religion." Leaving only Allen and Paine.

Allen had very little input into the Constitution and the Declaration of Independence. Note the DOI was not signed by either; I'm not sure if the reason was because of its attribution to the source of rights being from God. But even with those eight, why are we ignoring the fact that the huge majority of the rest of the founding fathers, who were the *actual* framers of the Constitution, were indeed Christians.

Gregory Koukl's from www.STR.org[448] notes:

> Back then church membership was a big deal. In other words, to be a member of a church back then, it wasn't just a matter of sitting in the pew or attending once in a while. This was a time when church membership entailed a sworn public confession of biblical faith, adherence, and acknowledgment of the doctrines of that particular church.
>
> Of those 55 Founding Fathers, we know what their sworn public confessions were. Twenty-eight were Episcopalians, eight were Presbyterians, seven were Congregationalists, two were Lutheran, two were Dutch Reformed, two were Methodist, two were Roman Catholic, one is unknown, and **only three were deists**--Williamson, Wilson, and Franklin.
>
> To heap more fuel on the fire of my point, of the 55, the Episcopalians, the Presbyterians, the Congregationalists, and the Dutch Reformed (which make up 45 of the 55) were Calvinists, for goodness sake! In other words, these weren't just Christians, these were among the most extreme and doctrinally strict Christians around. Of the 55 delegates, virtually all of them were deeply committed Christians. Only three were deists. Even Franklin is equivocal because, though not an orthodox Christian, Franklin seems to have abandoned his deism early in life and moved back towards his Puritan roots. Indeed, it was 81 year old Franklin's emotional call to humble prayer on June 28, 1787, that was actually the turning point for a hopelessly stalled Constitutional convention. We have his appeal on record thanks to James Madison who took copious notes of the whole proceeding. His appeal contained no less than four direct quotations from Scripture. This does not sound like a man who was hostile to the Christian religion.

Religious men involved in Politics?

Note too, of the 55 men, a *full* 29 of them held Bible Seminary degrees. For some of their quotes go to: www.scribd.com/doc/3817371/Founders-on-Faith

Yet we all agree that even if all the founding fathers were Christian, that would not necessarily make the country Christian today. At the end of the day, America is as "Christian" as its current legislators are. *But remember as David Baron says, "the legislators don't reflect the country, they only reflected who **voted** in the last election," if they voted biblically that is.*

However, I hope that by now you are convinced that most of the founders were Christians; our nation could not have been founded the way it is without Christians. Don't forget the atheists tried their attempt at a constitution, it ended up killing thousands in the French Revolution and that constitution lasted a very very short time.

As I've shown, in the Declaration of Independence the very concept of human rights and the basis for our Constitution falls apart if there is no God.

---

[448]www.str.org/site/News2?page=NewsArticle&id=5097

Recall that if we remove God from the Declaration of Independence and from the basis of the Constitution, we end up with a piece of nonsense that grants meaningless rights and has no rational standing. This means we are knowingly playing with fire if we continue to elect legislators who don't understand this fundamental basis for all laws. Furthermore, any system of government that does not anticipate and recognize mankind's sin nature in the making of its laws and plans will end up in anarchy or tyranny.

But what about the Law that's says that we shouldn't talk about politics in Church?

This is actually another great example of how laws change hearts. The idea of preventing churches from speaking out about political issues is a recent invention. Prior to 1954, no pastor would have thought that it was a bad idea to mix politics and religion. In 1954, however, Lyndon Johnson fell afoul of certain non-profits (they weren't even churches) who claimed Johnson had gotten elected only due to massive voter fraud.[449] When these non-profits spoke out against him, he managed to pass a law to amend the IRS code to indicate that non-profits would lose their tax deductions if they became involved in politics.[450] Sadly, most Christians were sleeping at the wheel when this attack came, and like the urban legend frog in the boiling pot, we were cooked as we slumbered. Till today, we actually think it's wrong for churches to be involved in politics.

The law wasn't even intended to apply to churches, yet here we are decades later and everyone believes in their heart that it is morally wrong for a church to be involved in politics. Talk about laws changing hearts. Even some God-fearing pastors think that this law is one of God's laws. When you ask them why they think that, they say, "Well isn't it obvious?"

No, it isn't obvious and it's false, and what's more, Jesus would never have put up with it as we saw. He was out there naming names, condemning the king, his individual senators and representatives, and many times doing it to their face.[451] Pastors and Christians should we be doing any less?

But we can't *afford* to lose our tax deduction!

Yes, I know and here's the beauty about all this. You can still talk about politics in church and *not* lose your tax deduction. The only limitation is that you can't promote or disparage any particular individual or political party. However, you are free to speak out against that candidate's stances without naming him. You can and should promote propositions that enact biblical principles and encourage your congregations to call their senators. You are free to speak out against moral issues. In fact, I believe God commands us to do so.

---

[449] For more information: www.afa.net/pdfs/pastorsandpolitics.pdf

[450] The current IRS rule says: 'Currently, the law prohibits political campaign activity by charities and churches by defining a 501(c)(3) organization as one "which does not participate in, or intervene in (including the publishing or distributing of statements), any political campaign on behalf of (or in opposition to) any candidate for public office."' www.irs.gov/newsroom/article/0,,id=161131,00.html

[451] Of course, you may object, "But Jesus had no tax deduction to worry about." But surely, Jesus would have spoken the truth regardless of any tax deduction? Can we agree that we should not let the government dictate what we do or do not say when it comes to moral issues?

On the other hand, you are always privately allowed to speak out against individuals like Jesus did, as long as you clearly state that you are speaking as an individual yourself and not speaking for the church.

Here's what the Liberty Counsel legal opinion states:

Outside of express endorsement of or opposition to candidates for political offices, pastors and churches may engage in many other permissible activities. Churches may host voter registration drives, be a host site for balloting, or host a forum where candidates address the congregation or answer questions from a moderator. Candidates visiting the church may be introduced, and political candidates may even preach in the pulpit so long as the pulpit is not used as a political forum to urge the members to vote in favor of the candidate. Churches may also distribute objective voter guides that address the candidates' views on a broad range of issues.

Pastors can preach on biblical, moral and social issues such as homosexuality and abortion. Pastors can urge the congregation to become involved in the political process, urge them to register and vote. Pastors can acknowledge visiting candidates. Pastors can personally endorse or oppose political candidates, personally work for political candidates, and personally contribute to them. Also, a pastor's name may appear in a published ad or letter signifying the pastor's endorsement of the candidate, and the pastor's title and affiliation with the church can also be listed with the notation, "Title and affiliation for identification purposes."

Pastors, Churches and Politics: What May Pastors and Churches Do? www.afa.net/pdfs/pastorsandpolitics.pdf

But is there a limit to how much time you can spend on political issues? Yes, but you'd probably never reach that limit. According to the same legal opinion of the Liberty Counsel the IRS has ruled that a church can spend up to 5% of its time or more on political activities but can't spend 15% of its time. Understand how this is calculated though. The above legal opinion states:

Take, for example, a church that opens its doors on Sunday morning for worship from the hours of 9:00 a.m. to 12:00 p.m., and then again on Wednesday evening for a midweek service from 7:00 to 8:30 p.m. Assume that the church engages in absolutely no other activity and has no volunteer or paid staff. Thus, the church engages in worship and teaching activities for only 4½ hours per week and does nothing else. Four and a half hours amounts to 270 minutes, and 5 percent amounts to 13½minutes. Thus, a church that only operates 4½ hours per week could devote at least 13½ minutes each Sunday to lobbying activities.

Thus, every Sunday this church could urge its congregation to contact their Senators and Representatives to vote in favor of the Federal Marriage Amendment, or any other local, state or national law, including state and federal constitutional amendments.

As you can see, when you consider all of the activities a church engages in throughout the week, it will certainly be more than 4½ hours. To determine this amount, you would need to calculate the time of all the volunteer and paid staff throughout the entire year. The substantial part test is not determined by merely looking at a particular event in isolation of others, but in conjunction with the church's overall activities. Thus, a church could devote a significant amount of time to lobbying activities during part of the year and a small amount of time during the remainder of the year.

I recommend every pastor take a look at the complete brief at the

Neil Mammen

Liberty Counsel (www.lc.org) and American Family Association website, (www.afa.net). One thing you should notice is that since the inception of this rule, not a single church has ever lost its tax deduction, despite numerous "complaints" by organizations like Americans United for Separation of Church and State.

But my congregation won't go for this.

Yes and therein lies the rub. The only way to lead your congregation into a more Biblical Worldview that includes politics is to start from the basics. Much of what is in this book has been written with an eye to that. The material can be used for Bible studies and sermons. Additional resources on the www.JesusIsInvolvedInPolitics.com website are available. Tools like "The Truth Project" series from Focus on the Family (www.FOTF.org) are invaluable. If you lead people logically and gradually to the conclusion by laying a foundation of reason and facts, I would imagine that most people will come to the inescapable conclusion that we as Christians have to be involved politically and the churches are the best places to start. If you start now, within a few years, you'll see a change in the attitudes of your congregation. In fact, it may grow your congregation, as much of this information is excellent for evangelization. Many unbelievers do not realize the wisdom and coherency of the law. And when they learn of it, it usually attracts them. I would also recommend you do something equivalent to a "40 days of Apologetics" so that your congregation has a solid foundation of why their faith is factually, historically, and objectively true. More ideas are provided on our website.

On the other hand, if we ignore this, we may all suffer the consequences, the first of which will be the successful removal of all church tax deductions, already in the courts thanks to atheist Michael Newdow. Let me ask you pastors, "Which president's appointed judges do you want on *that* case? What Worldview do you hope he has?"

Thirty-three

Man's greatest fear is "extinction without distinction."
"Why everyone needs to be in ministry" No Blind Faith Sermon, 1992

The fact that people respond badly to the truth is not a reason for us to stop speaking it. It is a reason however to find better ways of communicating it.
My response online to a Christian attacking me for how we've messed up telling people about Christ; and why she doesn't witness anymore, 2007

But You Will Turn People Away From The Gospel!

After much prompting and many years of prayer by a Christian friend, a young homosexual man finally decides to visit his friend's church. They walk in and the gay man immediately feels out of place. He notices singles groups and married groups and feels there is no group for him. He manages to sit through singing, announcements and a skit or two. Then in the middle of his sermon the pastor turns to a passage in scripture and goes into great detail on the theme that homosexuality is a sin and condemned in the Bible. Turned off, the young man leaves discouraged, and never again sets foot in a church.

If we start to address issues like homosexuality and abortion or even politics from the pulpit, the common fear is that we will turn people away from hearing the gospel. How do we deal with this issue?

I would say first, that if a pastor wants to teach on homosexuality, he should do so in a compassionate way. As we've shown, each law was given to protect us. I believe it's the pastor's job to figure out whenever possible, *what* the law is protecting us from, using time tested real world statistics and information. He should not use hearsay or shoddy science. He should study literature on the subject himself and discuss it with others. Then, knowing the facts, he should teach it in a loving way with the primary purpose to protect those who practice the behavior, those who may be influenced into doing so and those who may vote on the issue. The pastor is after all the shepherd of the flock.

When dealing with topics like these, I would strongly suggest that a

Neil Mammen

pastor *never* appeal to the Bible alone, for he cannot know if unbelievers are present or may listen to a recording of the sermon at a later time. If you appeal only to the Bible, you lose a chance to equip the saints and you lose everyone who does not take the Scriptures to be the Word of God. This is as effective as a Hindu telling you to not eat meat, because the Baghavad Gita teaches the transmigration of souls. Are we teaching the truth for effect or for some self-righteous reason? Do we really care about reaching people and helping them?

If I am personally witnessing to someone who says he's homosexual, I do not focus on his homosexuality, he doesn't need to stop his homosexual behavior first, he needs to be saved first. Once he's saved and respects me as someone who cares about him *then* we can talk about why his homosexual behavior is damaging. When teaching the entire flock however, we *must* teach the dangers of homosexual behavior, anything less would be irresponsible. Not teaching it due to the chance of someone who disapproves being in the audience has never been a valid reason to not teach the truth.

When passing laws we must pass laws that protect society, not condone, promote or reward various destructive behaviors. Note, that I do not wish to outlaw homosexuality, but I also do *not* wish for pastors and Christians to be censored and punished by laws like ENDA (Employment Non-Discrimination Act).[452] Pastors, you *should* be worried about this.

When I speak about homosexuality to teens or adults, I hope to convince people that the reason Christians oppose the behavior is not that we fear or are disgusted by it. It is because we love people and believe there are physical and spiritual consequences to the behavior. We hope homosexuals will stop for their *own* sakes as well as our children's.[453] As I've indicated, whenever I am asked, I invite a formerly-gay friend to co-preach on this topic and give his testimony. His compassion for those in the "gay lifestyle"[454] comes from experience. Then he goes on to talk about life-span reduction[455], addiction, pain and broken lives. We cannot stand silent and let those we love blunder blindly along in self-destruction.

When I talk about this with teens I make them stand and vow with me not to make fun of those who are gay – never ever. This is important. The promise is never to call those practicing homosexuality names or be mean to them. When they question the morality of gay behavior, they must promise to do so in the same way they might question a friend who has sex outside of marriage. They must deal with them in love and with sensitivity. I tell teens that they are commanded to care about homosexuals just as much as they love themselves. "Now that Christ has died for our sins," I say, "I don't believe we can ever say that the sin of homosexuality is any worse than the sin of adultery, the sin of sex before marriage or any other sexual sin, and none of

---

[452] http://www.citizenlink.org/enda/

[453] Remember we already showed that you *can indeed* love the sinner and hate the sin. How many of us have known and loved a son or a sibling with a drug or alcohol addiction? Did you have to love their alcoholism to love them? Absolutely not! You loved them, but hated their addiction.

[454] Many of my gay friends argue that there is no "gay lifestyle," but I use this phrase because it does have descriptive power.

[455] When we teach, we always focus on compassion and use facts that we get from the CDC and pro-gay websites. There is enough information there that we don't need to use anti-gay information.

these sins separates a person permanently from God. Rejecting Christ is what determines that."

Over the years, I have had a various ex-gay people come up to me and tell me that they wish they had had this information years ago. They tell me that they had to find it out the hard way. Isn't it our duty as pastors, teachers and people who care for others to get this message across in a loving way?

But they may still be insulted

True, some may still be insulted. However, every pastor has to deal with this catch in the situation. Suppose, in the story at the beginning of this chapter, that we replace "gay friend" with "racist friend." Someone invites a racist friend to church, and that week the pastor is speaking from a particular passage in the Bible. He goes into great detail about how racism is bad and how it was condemned in the Bible. The racist friend is turned off and never sets foot in church again. What now? You see, it is the same scenario and many claim that there are far more racists than there are gays (only 2%) in America. Why stop there? What about gossip or even adultery? Someone invites an adulterous friend to church, and that week the pastor is speaking from a particular passage in the Bible. He goes into great detail about how adultery is bad and how it was condemned in the Bible. The adulterous friend is turned off and never sets foot in church again. What about gluttony, greed, anger or alcoholism? How about wife abuse? Someone invites a friend who abuses his wife to church, and that week the pastor goes into great detail about how wife abuse is bad. The wife-abusing friend realizes this is referring to people like him and is turned off. He never sets foot in church again.

Do you see the silliness of this statement applied to homosexuality when we take it to its logical conclusion? And here's the kicker. Homosexuality is clearly addressed in the Bible. Wife abuse and racism are not. Why then do we feel that we should *not* address homosexuality but it's okay to address wife abuse and racism? Where do you draw the line? Do you say it's all right to address something that we culturally disapprove off like racism, but we should never address something that the culture *approves* of, such as homosexuality, abortion or adultery? Something that the world is at this moment attacking?

Remember Luther's quote?

If I profess with the loudest voice and clearest exposition every portion of the truth of God except precisely that little point which the world and the devil are at that moment attacking, I am not confessing Christ, however boldly I may be professing him.[456]

Don't forget, when the Church was preaching against slavery, it was considered socially offensive to speak out that way. It was politically incorrect, and deemed to be offensive to teach the *equality* of man.

Put yourself back in the 1800s. Would you be justified by refusing to speak out about slavery lest slaver owners reject Christ? Seriously? These issues are precisely what the world and the devil are attacking right now. What's the difference? Will you teach the flock about these very issues? Will

---

[456] Martin Luther, Weimar Ausgabe Briefwechsel 3, 81f.

you confess Christ? The core teaching of the Bible is about human failings and how because of them we all need Christ. Yes, the entire Bible is about sin and salvation. Without sin, there is no need of salvation or a savior. All cultures sin and all sinners strive to justify their sin. So speaking out against sin is not taken too kindly in *any* culture. It never will be. In fact, the more a culture attacks the truth the more you realize how much they need that message. There will never be a good time.

So the question is: Do we stop just because our message is not welcomed? Many churches *have* stopped. They think it's too mean-spirited to tell the harsh truth. Is it wrong to think that these maybe the same type of men and churches who would not have spoken out against slavery? But is that the kind of church you want to be the pastor of or attend? Is that the kind of church you want your church to become? Let me issue a warning. The day you do that your church will become irrelevant. Look around. Churches like that are losing attendance all over the world. We call it syncretism and universalism. Once your church becomes slightly syncretistic, your members will either leave to find a conservative church or will leave to find a fully syncretistic church. "Why not go whole hog," they ask themselves?

Teaching the basics

In addition, since we all agree that one of the duties of a pastor is to teach Christians how to live their daily lives and become Christ followers in both word and deed, surely we see that it is the pastor's role to disciple believers. If we stop discipling i.e. teaching them about what we should and should not do, how will believers learn? If we do not teach about homosexuality, abortion, adultery, greed, racism and all those things called sin *in church*, when and where do we teach it? If pastors do not teach about it, who will? The next generation of Christians will not learn this if we do not teach it. How will your kids learn their moral values? From MTV and sitcoms? Pastors, are you a disciple maker or just an entertainer? If you do not emulate the Bible and teach what sin is, how can you call yourself a Bible teacher? Will we breed, in a few generations, Christians who have never known that the Bible speaks out against homosexuality or other politically incorrect sins because their pastors have ignored those portions of Scripture, so "new-gen" Christians think those parts of the Bible are wrong or inconsequential or misinterpreted?

Since we know that God's moral laws were given to protect us, who will protect these Christians? Do we doom them to the painful consequences of their ignorance? Is it more loving or less loving to force children with diabetes to painfully inject themselves with insulin daily? Is it more loving or less loving to never tell a child that he does not have to be homosexual? Is it more loving or less loving to tell gay men and women that there are ex-gays out there? If you don't tell them, who will?

And lest we forget, if we Christians are not involved politically, it will become illegal to speak out against these moral issues everywhere.

Teaching the reasoning – teaching them to fish

Yet, if you just teach the application of moral values but never the rational reasoning or principles that brought us to that application, you short change your flock. If you never teach your flock the way to reason, or how to process and interpret the Bible themselves independently from you, you will create a generation of people who cannot think for themselves. Pastors, is that what you want your congregations to be? Or do you in fact want to duplicate yourself, training (discipling) a few hundred such that they can each teach 10 or 20 and those teach 10 or 20 more, resulting in an exponential duplication of yourself to hundreds of thousands? Or are you going to be like most pastors, once you are gone, those who liked you leave because you are no longer around to give them that emotional high or to tell them what to do in each and every situation. As a result, your legacy lasts less than one generation. That's what you'll get when you teach only based on emotions or teach only answers to specific situations.

Man's greatest fear

Psychologists say man's great fears are falling and loud noises. I say my greatest fear is of making a loud noise when I fall. Okay, okay. The truth is I think "man's greatest fear is of extinction without distinction." By this, I mean that we are afraid that we will die and no one will know or care that we ever lived. Pastors, I'm sure you know this, if we want to be remembered, we must create disciple *makers*, not just disciples. It's what Jesus did. Make sure you develop in people, the ability to reason, think, defend, contend for the faith and, most important, create other disciples who can teach others. Don't just feed them. Don't even *just* teach them to fish. Teach them to teach others to fish. Teach them to be teachers.

My soapbox

Let me step up on another of my favorite soapboxes here for just a moment (not that I haven't been on one this whole time). Pastors, if you want to be able to leave a church and have it continue to grow without you (after you die or retire), then teach your flock to reason theologically, rationally and scientifically. Teach them about non-superstitious "Decision Making and the Will of God."[457] Help them learn to defend the Christian faith with Apologetics and teach them to teach others to do the same. Teach them to think. In doing this, you'll create a church that is strong in its beliefs, not just dependant on you or its current emotional state for its beliefs.

My dad was a great example to me in this. For years, he was a teacher *of* teachers. He worked at the Higher Teacher Training Institute in Sudan. Whenever I asked him what he did, he would say he teaches teachers to be good teachers. When I asked why he did that, he said it was important that there were teachers and that they were able to teach others properly.[458] He said the same thing when he co-founded the Sudan Theological College[459] in South

---

[457] Decision Making and the Will Of God: A Biblical Alternative to the Traditional View, Garry Friesen & J. Robin Maxson, Multnomah (January 1, 2000). I also recommend the audio teaching series from Stand to Reason, www.str.org

[458] He said this was the way that Africa would grow and become self-sufficient.

[459] The Sudan Theological College was founded as the theological education for the Sudan Pentecostal Churches. It prepared students for pastorships with a B.Th degree and was associated with the Assemblies of God. Major funding came from the Swedish Free Mission. Each student family was

Sudan, which was a training school for pastors.

I made that my goal. Whenever I teach a class, I want not only to impart knowledge but also to impart the zeal, goal, drive and skill people need to be able to teach *others*. I want them to become teachers of teachers. This is one way to ensure that I have a legacy – that I do not come to "extinction without distinction."

But do we teach this in the main service

Now we come to the real issue. If we have to teach about these tough topics, should we teach them to "seekers?" Do we teach these in main Sunday worship services? Or do we teach them in the middle of the week or Bible study settings? For the Apologetics part, *of course* you should teach it to the seekers. Who better to teach it to? For some issues like abortion and homosexuality and current controversial laws, each church body has to figure this out for themselves. Some churches have a "seeker" service that does not deal with controversial moral issues and focuses instead on the Gospel. These churches must make sure that they have another service for their flock and an active program to "graduate" people over. Otherwise, people's views and understanding will be superficial (milk instead of meat). A congregation that knows little or nothing has no reason to be Christian, and it certainly does not know the heart of God on moral issues. These churches may end up skin deep with no real convictions. Their people will seek teachers with words that tickle their ears. When the charismatic leader dies, leaves or stumbles, the congregation disappears.

Other churches deal with these tough issues right in the main service. They are "seeker friendly" but don't think that excludes tough issues biblical teaching. Many of these churches still have a high growth rate. Part of these pastors' philosophy is that if you do not preach the law, how will people realize they are sinners? If you do not preach sin, how can you preach salvation? If you do not preach salvation, you are not a church. You are a social club. The law is meant to be a tough master – to convict and chafe, to scare and condemn. Without the law, there is no gospel. Without the gospel, we are wasting our time on Sunday and wasting our tithes. If there is no perceived need for Jesus, why is anyone wasting time and money in church? It's cheaper and far less work to belong to the Rotary Club.[460] It does not require giving 10% of your income and does not require as many hours a week in volunteer service.

But Democrats need a place to worship as well

When I heard this objection the first time, it made me laugh. Of course they do. And who says they shouldn't do so in the chair right next to me? Any Democrat who loves the Lord is welcome next to me anytime. Any Democrat who hates the Lord is *also* welcome for that matter. In fact, anyone is welcome next to me at church, especially those who don't love the Lord or don't believe He exists. I'd rather they were in church next to me hearing the gospel,

---

given a traditional Sudanese Tukul hut and electricity produced by solar power, for students to study at night.

[460] Which is a great organization; a few years ago, they even gave me a Paul Harris Medal.

learning apologetics and learning a Biblical Worldview, than anywhere else. But what does that have to do with anything in this book? Absolutely nothing!

Now to be fair, the comment was made in the context of abortion. The theory being that if we speak out against abortion in church then Democrats won't feel comfortable there. But I have not said anything about Republican versus Democrat versus Green Party or Tea Party regarding what churches preach. We are talking about biblical moral values and common sense laws. If a Democrat holds to biblical moral values, nothing should chase him away from church. *If the church preaches something from the Bible that the Democrat party disagrees with and it makes a Democrat uncomfortable, it's the Democrat party that should change its stance not the church.* I would think the Democrat should realize this and stop being a Democrat. Note I'd say this if it were the Republicans too. Since when are we called to compromise God's Word or His Moral principles? What audacity!

Democrat or Republican, I don't care what they call themselves. It's what they stand for that decides it for me.

But all are welcome to sit next to me at church. I would love it. I'll save them a seat and we can go out to lunch afterwards. As one pastor said: Our church is not a country club for saints, we are a hospital for sinners. We are *all* in need of a Savior.

The Gospel is offensive

We Christians need to be able to rationally and logically present why we believe what we believe. Blind faith is unbiblical and actually condemned in the Bible. So whenever a pastor teaches on a political issue, he must teach it in love, not out of arrogance, and just as important, he must clearly and rationally explain *why* we hold the stances we do.

I believe that anybody who is interested in spiritual things, anybody who is seeking or in whom the Holy Spirit is working to bring them to a saving knowledge of Christ will be open to a reasonable, gentle and loving explanation of any issue. This is true whether it is adultery, wife abuse, racism, same-sex marriage, abortion or slavery. If the person listening gets angry or upset about a message preached in this loving manner, I would suggest that it would have made no difference what you had focused on. The very second you address the exclusive gospel message this person will be upset and leave anyway. The message of Jesus Christ, its exclusivity, and the biblical teaching of damnation will be the stumbling block to a heart that has not been opened by the Holy Spirit. You don't need to worry about a gentle teaching about the physical consequences of homosexuality being the issue that turns him off. The Gospel is offensive enough.

There are thousands of churches in the U.S. that teach all these controversial things and on the other side there are thousands that are afraid to teach this or do not believe these conservative positions. Do you know which of these churches are growing rapidly day-by-day? I'll tell you. It's the conservative churches. It's the churches that aren't afraid to preach the truth in love and compassion. Look around at the liberal churches; they are dying on the vine. After all, when a church never teaches you anything different from what you would get at your local health or social club, why join it?

Look at the hard-core Bible churches, and you notice that they are getting larger by the day. They have a huge number of ministries that show that they care, and when their pastors speak, they speak God's politically *incorrect* truth in genuine love. People crave that kind of guidance. Someone *will* lead them. Who will it be?

People want to be led. Who will lead them?

Thirty-four

"People who put economics over moral values are generally known as prostitutes, drug dealers or thieves."
Anna Mammen, 2001

The purpose of government is very, very narrow scripturally. It isn't to help the poor. It isn't to redistribute wealth.
Gregory Koukl, Prostituting the Vote[461]

You call this job creation? Are you serious? A government job is negative job growth. It's five times worse than job growth. Because for every government job you create, you have to create five private sector jobs just to pay that salary. If Obama created 100,000 government jobs, that means we are half a million more jobs in the hole than when we started.
Me, on a rampage on FaceBook

How Then Shall We Vote?

I had just graduated from college with my Masters degree in Electrical Engineering and Solid State Physics. I had just moved to Sunnyvale, CA. I was young, Christian and a headstrong liberal. Then I got my first paycheck. The shock of seeing Uncle Sam, Mother California, Sister Santa Clara County and numerous other entities I could not fathom, take away 40% of my pay, nearly made me a conservative overnight. You know how it goes. But I was not a U.S. citizen then. I didn't even have a green card. (They're not green, by the way; they're pinkish). I was an H1-B. That meant I had a visa that lets you work in the U.S. But I couldn't vote, so I was experiencing what is commonly known as "taxation without representation."

Now you may well be thinking, "The reason you became a conservative was because you were greedy and mean spirited and didn't want poor people taking your money." But this would be far from the truth. I'd been brought up in a giving family, so synonymous with my getting a paycheck was the habit of giving. But *I* wanted to decide who to give to, not let some government official do it for me.

Over the next few years, while attending an evangelical church, I started looking at moral issues, looking carefully at social issues, getting into big long discussions with my conservative and liberal friends, reading and arguing passionately. I came kicking and screaming due to the overwhelming logic and reason into the conservative camp. The only thing conservative about me before that time were my clothes and my belief in Christ. Tony Compolo

---

[461] www.str.org/site/News2?page=NewsArticle&id=5510

would have loved me. And in fact, it still wasn't until the early 90's and after I lost about three long and involved arguments about guns that, I finally became a believer in the 2nd Amendment. Prior to that, I was actually anti-gun and thought the 2nd Amendment was stupid.

Every year or so, my roommates received thick election booklets in the mail. They usually ignored them. One day I decided to read one and almost had a heart attack. Government officials were trying to pass some sort of bond. The more I read, the more I realized that a bond was worse than a credit card debt. You borrow money now and pay almost three times the amount later. That meant more of my hard-earned money being spent by a group of folks who made four times what I made. Any way I looked at it, it sounded like more taxes to me. I told my roommates they had to vote against it. They then asked me what I thought of the other propositions and how they should vote on them. They created a monster.

Within a few years, I had started writing "Neil's Biased Voting Recommendations." Although he had invented the Internet and I worked for a company with Internet access, Al Gore had not made email easily available to my friends yet, so I'd make a few printouts for them, and they would make copies for other friends. For over six years while I could not personally vote, my voting recommendations were being read and presumably followed by many voters. I'd get phone calls from folks I didn't know, asking me how I thought they should vote. When email became commonly available, people began forwarding and printing my recommendations for others. The secondary effects were not huge but it seemed that my opinions were being parlayed into about a hundred votes.

I also got a few critics. One guy blasted me for trying to create sheep who blindly voted as I told them too. He told me I should not be imposing my ideas on other people. (I asked him if he was imposing *that* idea on me. That ended the interaction for some reason.) But as a consequence, I always had disclaimers that said, "I would rather you did your own research, but if you don't have time, here is my research." I also always told people why I recommended something, so they could freely decide if they agreed with me. I am not interested in blind faith voters any more than I am interested in blind faith Christians.

So how *should* we vote?

Here are some biblical, logical and Christian worldview guidelines that you can apply to almost all arenas. If you agree with and act on them, I believe we can effect some great changes in our nation. You'll notice that some of these repeat various overlapping themes.

1. Vote biblically.
2. Vote for morality over economics (morals over money). For example, do not vote for someone who will generate jobs but is pro-choice or socialistic. You are hurting society and your kids and violating God's laws.
3. Remember being just fiscally conservative is self-defeating as we showed. The moral issues will soon become unsolvable fiscal issues. We want a Fiscal *and* Moral Conservative. Vote for the former only as a last resort.

4. Never vote for any law that would "stick it" to a group of individuals who are not doing anything immoral. It's mean-spirited, ungodly, and reminiscent of what the Nazi's did and eventually it will bite *you*. Remember, when income taxes were first sold to the Americans in 1913, they were told, only the filthy rich would pay them. They started at 3%. Yet, in a few short years, tax rates were as high at 90% and everybody was forced to pay taxes. This has been repeated many times in the last few years. Think luxury taxes, or recently "Cadillac health plan taxes" or even unfair taxes on an isolated group of people like doctors. The National Socialists did this to any group of people they did not like, like the Jews.

5. Vote for long term results over short term results.

6. Do not vote for the public to pay for a ball park. If ball parks were such good investments then private venture would have paid for it. Imagine if it was Toyota trying to force the government to buy them a bigger factory because they would hire more workers which would need more stores and homes etc? Where do you draw the line? When governments get involved in private enterprise they mess things up.

7. Vote for lower taxes, as higher taxes put a burden on parents and force them to have to both work. This, as we have seen unfortunately increases crime, anger and dysfunctional kids. They also reduce the money that goes to churches for the work of God and churches are who should providing welfare for the needy. High taxes kill jobs. Recently a medium sized company in California decided to move their headquarters to the Netherlands (how ironic). Why? Because the Dutch government promised that their tax rate would go as low as 10% compared to the over 35% it is here. This would move about 300 jobs to the Netherlands for the company's finance and administration departments not to mention all the rent and tax money from those 300 jobs and entertainment budgets and so on. The US and California need to incentivize these folks to stay, not chase them away.

8. Do not vote for bonds. They are just an expensive way to borrow money. If your government cannot afford something critical, like any responsible company or person, it has to cut its spending somewhere. In a company, if you have to spend more on R&D you spend less on the Christmas party. In a family if you spend extra for medicine, you eat out less.

9. Don't blindly believe the stories the media tells about people. Remember Dan Rather who blindly parroted a false story about Bush, because the ignorant idiot Dan never did any research? Remember all the nonsense that was said about Sarah Palin wanting to ban books or about her son not really being her son? These were all totally made up. The media is supposed to investigate and dig out the truth *after* they've researched it. But they don't, because they have an agenda. So don't be manipulated. There are a lot more lies and half-truths in the media today, especially since they have no moral values themselves except their agenda. They lie knowingly. By the way it was Tina Fey on Saturday Night Live who said she could see Russia from her back door not Sarah Palin. Make sure you do your own research. The Media lies. For evidence of this see Bernard Goldberg's book, Bias: A CBS Insider Exposes How the Media Distort the News, Regnery Publishing 2001. By the way, Bernie is a liberal, so you *are* getting an inside view.

10. Do not vote to give any powers to a "good" person or administration that you would not want a "bad" person to have. Any power you give to a President that you like will be a power that a President that you don't like, will also have. Remember that all men have a sin nature and eventually one will be elected who will use that power that you gave good men, for evil.

11. Vote for Christians or Jews who have a *voting* record that coincides with the moral heart of God not the charity heart of God, because justice, not charity is the

job of government. However, it is of great value to watch what each person has *personally* done charitably in their own lives. For instance, Obama while greatly propounding government charity (that is other people's money) gave less than 1% of his high *own* income to others. As I've said, it is a true test of the character of a man to see how he proposes to take and use *your* money for good works but refuses to use his *own*.

12. Remember, and this is ever so important: We all know fakers, and hypocrites. Anybody and I mean, *anybody* can use "Christianese" and sound like a Christian. What you have to do is look at their *Worldview*. Do they have a Christian/Godly Worldview? How do they view the world? How do they live their lives? Do they speak the words but not live the life? Do they really believe? It will be obvious in their lives. Bill Clinton and Barack Obama were very good at using Christian language and terms, but a simple survey of their past actions would have immediately revealed that they did not really believe what God-fearing Evangelicals, Catholics and Jews believe. They did not have a Godly Worldview. As a result, when they took office they immediately appointed anti-Christian individuals and took actions that were immoral and unbiblical. Appointing men who were tax cheats to run the IRS and Treasury Departments and men who were promoters of homosexual pedophilia to be in charge of schools. Obama's School Czar was responsible for pushing books to kids that were sexually graphic.[462] Do not presume that a man will govern any differently than what he truly believes.

13. Look to see if they fail any of the litmus tests i.e. are they:

a. Pro-abortion or pro-choice

b. Pro-homosexuality or heterosexual immorality in any of its guises

c. Pro-socialism

d. Pro-income redistribution

e. Pro handouts vs. Tough Love

f. Multi-cultural to the point of hating America: While they should respect other cultures, do they believe in preserving the American culture and its Judeo-Christian traditions or are they at the core anti-American and anti-Jew or anti-Christian? Remember I'm an immigrant saying this. I came to America because it *was* America. I don't want it to become India or Sudan or even Switzerland.

g. Anti-founder: Do they despise our founders? Do they even believe America was founded by Christians who believed in the Moral Law (even if they are Jewish)? If they don't, then they are a threat to the traditions and future of America as a great nation. This includes the English language. Again, remember that I'm saying this as someone of East Indian origin born and brought up in Africa and the Middle East. I've lived in other countries, some that have split over or are killing each other based on cultural divides defined by language. You *don't* want to emulate them.

h. Anti-History: Do they try to rewrite the history of this nation's foundation?

i. Have they cheated on their wives and have not genuinely repented?

14. Do not vote for any person who will *not* vote his own conscience, or who cannot articulate the difference between a democracy and a republic and why a democracy is so dangerous.

15. Remember the sin nature of man and tough love. Do not vote for anything that allows people to indulge their sin nature without consequences– be it laziness,

---

[462] 'Sex acts between preschoolers' among subjects of books backed by openly 'gay' Obama adviser. http://www.wnd.com/index.php?pageId=117978

sexual immorality, or whatever. True love will be strong and stern and move people out of codependency on the Government and handouts.

16. Remember that biblically, the purpose of government is not to redistribute wealth but to protect citizens from evil people and provide justice. There is no way to biblically support socialism, you can biblically support your own donations, but you can never biblically support the concept of forcing others to donate. So never vote for government handouts in any form. If you see starving people, take up a voluntary donation or work with existing organizations. Do not subsidize a bond or raise taxes on others.

17. Do not vote or support any politician who has ever added "earmarks" into a proposed budget, even if they helped your state financially. That politician has stolen from other people to pay you. This is not just.

18. Make sure the person you vote for knows the difference between God given unalienable rights and "goods." A right is something that we are given from God and is *not* based on someone else's sacrifice. Goods are things that are the product of someone's work. You have a right to your own goods, but not anyone else's. For instance food, healthcare, clothing and a house, are all goods. No one has a right to these. The only right they have is the freedom to strive to gain these goods without unfair rules regulations or oppression.

19. Make sure they believe that it's the church's place and the voluntary giving of kind individuals to provide goods to those who are unable to get those for themselves, not the governments'.

20. Make sure they love the Constitution of the United States, and will protect it and observe it. Do not vote for anyone who does not understand how the Constitution is to be interpreted or why it is "living" through amendments not through unelected judges.

21. Make sure they are proud to be an American and love this country. This is obvious. Governments are created to preserve the nation. Any election of a person who would destroy the nation will hurt us all and violates the very reason we created that government to begin with. Don't vote for anyone who wants to equalize or diminish America in *any* way.

22. Make sure they are for smaller government and for reducing the size of government and giving more power to the states and individuals.

23. Make sure they are not past members of any sort of socialist party. Unless they've publically recanted all their stances, explained why they changed their mind and you see evidence that they have written and legislated in a different way since then.

24. Make sure you know whom their friends are and what their friends believe. Remember the old proverb? A man is known by the company he keeps.

25. And finally and most importantly, do they understand what the primary moral code of our republic is? Do they believe it is the Judeo-Christian moral code as documented in the Bible? Do they know what Natural Law is?

May I be so bold as to suggest that you copy and paste this list on your refrigerator every election season? If you want an easy to print and email version, that is being updated regularly go to

www.JesusIsInvolvedInPolitics.com/HowThenShallWeVote.htm.

Democrats vs. Republicans

A question that naturally comes to mind is whether one should vote Republican or Democrat or Libertarian or whatever. This is an interesting question. God is not a Democrat or Republican. The real question is which party comes closer to biblical principles. So let's look at how a follower of Christ should vote when it comes to parties. In this section, I have listed some of the commonly perceived areas of moral disagreement between the two major parties.

Most liberal candidates gravitate to the Democrat Party because it has a liberal platform, and most conservative candidates go to the Republican Party because it has a conservative agenda. This does not mean Democrats are exclusively liberal or vice versa. There are liberals among Republicans and conservatives among Democrats. So right off the bat we realize that one can't easily vote straight down party lines.

What do the parties stand for?

So, as a first step we should evaluate the moral standards of each party's platform. Let's look at the 2004 Democrat and Republican platforms.

Abortion –

Democratic Party: Democrats start by taking an unethical and unbiblical position of supporting abortion on demand. The platform language is *"Abortion should be safe, legal, and rare."* See footnote for a full rebuttal of this.[463]

Republican Party: Republicans, on the other hand, declare that unborn children have a fundamental individual right to life that cannot be infringed. *"We support a human life amendment to the Constitution and we endorse legislation to make it clear that the Fourteenth Amendment's protections apply to unborn children."*[464] This is in line with moral, ethical, and biblical principles.

Marriage Amendment –

Democratic Party: You'll notice again that the Democrats start by taking a stance contrary to the Bible. *"We repudiate President Bush's divisive effort to politicize the Constitution by pursuing a 'Federal Marriage Amendment.' We support full inclusion of gay and lesbian families in the life of our nation and seek equal responsibilities, benefits, and protections for these families."* This violates principles of many of the major religions like Judaism, Islam, Christianity and Mormonism. And one must ask, "What do you mean by Politicizing the Constitution?" It was only because *others* were trying to change the laws on marriage that we needed to step in. This sort of language is disingenuous.

---

[463] www.democrats.org/pdfs/2004platform.pdf I always ask Democrats this when given a chance? If abortion is not the killing of a human being, why do you want to make it *rare*? I don't see you wanting to make plastic surgery rare. So obviously, you think abortion is the killing of something we shouldn't kill. In which case how can you logically want it to be safe or legal? In the 2008 interview with Rick Warren, Obama said that the question of when life begins is "above his pay grade" Rick Warren should have asked, "If you aren't sure when life begins, how can you kill it? Isn't the appropriate response to "not being sure if something is human" to *not* kill it? What kind of heartless cruel evil person shoots at something or kills something that he's not 100% sure is not human? As Ronald Reagan said about abortion: If you aren't sure, you can't shoot.

[464] www.gop.com/media/2004platform.pdf. Contrary to "Blue like Jazz" author Donald Miller's ignorant mean-spirited claim, that John McCain was a recent convert to the Pro-Life cause, McCain has been pro-life for over 30 years -since the day then governor Ronald Reagan sat him down and explained to him why abortion was murder and he had to protect life. While I am not a McCain fan, McCain had a 100% approval rating from the Pro-Lifers during his entire tenure in Washington. It was only the Stem Cell issue that seems to have confused McCain.

Republican Party: *"We strongly support President Bush's call for a Constitutional amendment that fully protects marriage, and we believe that neither federal nor state judges nor bureaucrats should force states to recognize other living arrangements as equivalent to marriage."* This is in line with moral, ethical and biblical principles.

Gays in the Military-

Democratic Party: *"We will enact the bipartisan legislation barring workplace discrimination based on sexual orientation. We are committed to equal treatment of all service members and believe all patriotic Americans should be allowed to serve our country without discrimination, persecution, or violence."*

Republican Party: *"We affirm traditional military culture, and we affirm that homosexuality is incompatible with military service."* This again is in line with God the Holy Spirit's commandments to us through Paul.

Embryonic Stem Cell Research (ESCR)-

Democratic Party: *"President Bush has rejected the calls from Nancy Reagan, Christopher Reeve and Americans across the land for assistance with embryonic stem cell research. We will reverse his wrongheaded policy. Stem cell therapy offers hope to more than 100 million Americans who have serious illnesses – from Alzheimer's to heart disease to juvenile diabetes to Parkinson's."*

Republican Party: *"We especially welcome and encourage a stronger emphasis on adult stem cell and cord blood stem cell research, which has already provided benefits to hundreds of patients and provides real promise for treatments to help millions of Americans."* This again is in line with the biblical concept that life begins at conception. By the way, Adult Stem Cells (ASC), taken from things like nasal passages and bone marrow have been used for actual cures for over 73 different diseases.[465] ESC, which the Democrats have not only been pushing but forcing us to fund, has been shown to cause tumors and have been used for cures in exactly zero diseases. It saddens to me to see that Democrats want to use people's hard earned tax money to fund the unethical and unsure science of Embryonic Stem Cell Research with not even a single cure, while not even mentioning Adult Stem Cells.

What is most irritating to me is that whenever the media talks about stem cell cures, they never differentiate between successful *Adult* Stem Cells Research and the failing science of *Embryonic* SCR. Leaving their viewers thinking there is no difference and that conservatives are against *both*. For more information on Stem Cell research including information and proof of Adult Stem Cell Research cures (including paralyzed people walking again) please go to www.JesusIsInvolvedInPolitics.com and look up "Stem Cells."

Tax Cuts-

Democratic Party: *"[Cancel] tax cuts for those making over $200,000."* It is safe to say that the Democratic Party wishes to spread the wealth and is generally socialistic in its approach. It is immoral to target one class of people. The idea that those who make more money must have stolen that money from the poor or oppressed them to make that money is not only unethical but it violates their civil rights. They have been accused, convicted,

---

[465] www.stemcellresearch.org/facts/asc-refs.pdf also see www.stemcellresearch.org

and punished for the crime of oppression and coercion without *even* a trial. This is not justice, and Jesus would never have stood for it.

What's worse, even Democrats and Liberals agree time after time that tax cuts are what boost the economy. Why do you think Clinton, Pelosi, Reid and Obama all wanted to give people a "tax stimulus" check? Of course, this single check was the right direction but the wrong implementation (yes even when Bush did it) and it didn't work. You want people to see that they are getting to keep more of their *own* money *long term* to stimulate investment in their own businesses, not throw them a bone. It's the difference between showing someone that he can grow food vs. buying him a meal. One is an investment attitude, the other is a handout.

Republican Party: *"Making the tax cuts permanent is a crucial first step toward expanding ownership and ensuring that America turns economic growth into lasting prosperity."* While Christ commands us to pay our taxes, at no point does He encourage us to force others to pay more taxes. And to tell the truth for every dollar that you allow Americans to keep, the more they give to charities that achieve so much more than any governmental agency. Christ was not a socialist. Many times Democrats will accuse conservatives that they wish to starve the poor and oppress and take advantage of them. Yet when you look at which principles are both more godly and more successful as far as allowing people to grow independent, self sufficient and not starve, we constantly see the conservative principles help bring about true social justice, while the liberal or Democratic ideals bring about dependency and cultural, economic and mental slavery. Remember too a government job is not something that creates wealth; it sucks up wealth that others have made. It's easy to talk compassion but tough love always seems to work better. In addition, time after time, we've seen that anytime taxes are reduced the economy improves and unemployment goes down and the poor get the opportunity to work themselves to self-sufficiency. See the objections appendix where I cover the false Zero Sum Game concept.

Moreover, as the Laffer Curve[466] shows us, when taxes are reduced not only does more prosperity occur but also more tax revenue is generated. I recommend Tom Del Beccaro's book "The New Conservative Paradigm" that details this relationship with facts and charts.

Summary of the platforms

So, from just what I have shown, there are four areas where the Democrat platform goes directly against biblical moral values. In the area of taxes, Democrats appear neutral, but they seem to have an interest in imposing a redistribution of wealth, which is not at all biblical. Democrats and Liberals think the government should replace the Church for works of charity, which we've shown, has been a recipe for disaster. They also feel the government should baby-sit their citizens and remove individual citizens of personal responsibility. They want the government to be the great equalizer of talents and results, and which flies directly in the face of the parable Jesus gave us of the 10 talents, where God is the master and distributor of talents.

Note too that as far as war is concerned Democrat Presidents have taken the US into more wars than Republican Presidents.

So leaving the tax and war issues aside, I still conclude that with their

---

[466] The Laffer Curve, www.heritage.org/Research/Taxes/bg1765.cfm

current platforms there is no ethical way a Christian can vote for a Democrat candidate in good conscience. You would be voting for either murdering humans or sanctioning evil or as we've shown, things that can be proven to hurt the poor and the innocent. Even if a Democrat does claim to go against their party's platform (known sometimes as Blue Dog Democrats), it becomes foolhardy to vote for them. Why? A great example was Senator Ben Nelson from Nebraska during the Health Care reform debacle in 2009 and 2010. Senator Nelson is supposedly a "pro-life" Democrat and said that he would not vote for any bill that included government funded abortions. As a result, his own Democrat leadership immediately threatened to close down a large military base in Nebraska, which would have resulted in a loss of jobs in his state, and forced him to sign the bill. To sweeten the deal, they gave him lots of *our* money to spend in his state for pork.[467] Guess what, Nelson's "pro-life" stance vanished quickly.

Similarly, for the House bill. About six supposed "pro-life" democrats with Representative Bart Stupak as their leader were blocking the health-care bill because it would allow the federal funding of abortion. Yet, with a few promises of money for this or that and a symbolic presidential executive order that said that money could not be used for abortions (which will be overthrown by the courts in a few years), they all quickly rolled over. Thus writing the obituary for the "pro-life" Democrat. There can be none with their platform of death.

So you see, in reality it's very difficult or impossible to validly justify a vote for someone whose *very* party platform violates the heart of God's laws given for our safety. Today, voting for a pro-life Democrat is like voting for a pro-civil rights KKK member. Yes, there may be a few good cookies at the bottom of the garbage bin, but is that where we should be going to get our cookies? Nelson and Stupak voted for money over morals, I wonder how they look themselves in the mirror at night. I'd call that money they were promised "blood money."

When people run as a candidate for one of the parties, they in essence agree to be under the authority of the party. If they buck its policies, they tend to be marginalized in the party and lose influence. So there is a lot of pressure to conform. In other words, as much as a Democrat claims to be pro-life, his party's platform is for killing babies, and they have never passed any pro-life laws, so this casts a doubt on the person who would embrace any such platform. Is he being authentic? By electing a Democrat, you automatically allow that party to leverage its numbers and if they achieve a majority, they can prevent pro-life bills from ever seeing the light of day. As we've explained, the pro-life issue is just the tip of the iceberg. Do not be deceived.

Moreover, if someone says, "I'm a Democrat because of their economic principles but I don't agree with some of their moral principles." They're no different from a prostitute, drug dealer, or thief. They are putting economics over morality. If they then claim that they "care" about the poor, which is a moral issue (implying the Republicans don't care about the poor and

---

[467] amerpundit.com/2009/12/19/ben-nelson-caves-on-abortion/

that it's the government's job to provide for the poor), you know that they do not understand the Constitution or the difference between goods and rights. They should not be in office. Their solutions will cause more pain for all.

This does not mean you can vote in good conscience for *all* Republicans, but at least you can agree with the party's platform.

But the Republicans are fiscally as bad as the Democrats

The Republicans were in control of congress for 12 years (1995 to 2006). Toward the end of that period, despite hard work by real conservatives in the ranks, the party as a whole violated every one of its fundamental fiscal principles. Republicans increased special boondoggle earmarks. They wasted money and supported morally liberal Republicans like Arlen Specter over true conservatives who were running against them (probably because they were afraid the conservative would lose). The tragedy of waste brought upon us by the Republicans is even more shocking when you realize that under Bill Clinton the national debt was only $3.5 trillion. Yet, in the 12 years under Republican congress before Democrats took over in 2007, the national debt grew more than 100% to more than $7.5 trillion. In view of the huge wastage of money, no one can legitimately argue that this was because of the war in Iraq. Here is a brief list of items that made up the over 7000 special earmarks per year. [468]

- $1 million for the study of DNA in bears
- $7.8 million for the study of Hawaiian sea turtles.
- $6 million to study sea lions in Alaska
- $3 million for a Florida Golf clinic for teenagers
- $500,000 to the International Coffee Organization
- $100,000 to a World Food Prize in Iowa
- $750,000 for the Baseball Hall of Fame in Cooperstown, NY (Are baseball players really that badly paid? Why can't they pay for their own museum?)
- $700,000 for the Silver Ring Thing Museum in Sewick, PA

Ask yourself, why is it the taxpayer's job to pay for any of these projects or causes? Why are we paying for museums or Golf Clinics or sea lion studies? These are goods not rights.

If you want to read more about how the Republican party was betrayed by its own leaders read Joe Scarborough's scathing book "Rome Wasn't Burnt in a Day: The Real Deal on How Politicians, Bureaucrats, and Other Washington Barbarians are Bankrupting America."[469] Joe was a Republican Congressman in the class of 1994, the year of the "Republican Revolution." Another excellent book is "Breach of Trust: How Washington Turns Outsiders into Insiders"[470] by Tom Coburn. Senator Coburn documents the culture of Washington and what really goes on and what needs to change.

These two books are must-reads. They will make everyday Republicans sick and ready to toss the rouges that perpetuate this nonsense out of office and go with the Tea Party.

---

[468] All taken from "Rome Wasn't Burnt in a Day" Joe Scarborough, Harper Collins, 2004.
[469] Harper Collins, 2004
[470] Thomas Nelson, 2003

It's easy to find out who these rouges are. Just go to the Citizens against Government Waste website at www.cagw.org. When you know who they are and if they are your representative, send them an email telling them that if they ever *ever* add any such earmarks in another budget you won't vote for them and will work against their candidacy.

In addition, let it be known that any Republican who cheats on his wife or commits adultery will never ever get our vote.[471]

The Democrats

Yet, for all the accusations against the Republicans, the Democrats were no different when they took over in 2007 and then when Obama became president they destroyed all previous records in wasteful spending.

The Democrats specifically pledged to limit spending increases and employ pay-as-you-go (PAYGO) budgeting to keep the budget deficit in check. Yet, within a year they broke every one of their promises. In just 10 months the Democratic Congress passed legislation that increased federal spending by a combined $454 billion over 10 years; raised taxes and fees by $98 billion over 10 years and passed a budget resolution to increase taxes by $2.7 trillion. Although they pledged to halve the number of earmarks to 6,746, that year Congress included 11,351 earmarks in the spending bills, almost 4000 more than the Republicans did.[472] When Obama came into office, they passed seven plus Trillion dollars of earmarks under the guise of economic incentives. Not only did no economic improvement occur as we conservatives warned everyone, but unemployment went up to 10%. In the 9 months they raised the debt from 7.5 Trillion to almost 12.5 Trillion. Wow! So, not only were less people working and paying taxes, but now the debt was even greater and the government had hired more un-fireable people making government costs higher. Nice going. But what do you expect from an administration run by a man who's never run a business or made a profit in his life? In fact, less than 7% of his administration had any private sector business experience. You can't vote in people with no experience and expect them to perform. It's idiocy. We got what we voted for. Christians could have changed that outcome had we gotten involved. But we didn't or we sadly were duped into voting for a party that has the killing of innocents in its platform.

We should understand what national debt really is. When congress creates debt, what it really is doing is diluting the value of our money. When we went from $7.5 Trillion to $12.5 Trillion in debt all we really did was devalue the dollar by that much more, i.e. we added 5 Trillion more dollars to what was already in circulation. What this is, is really, stealing from everyone. It especially hits those on fixed incomes the worst. Why? Because their saved dollars are not worth as much and they are unable to earn new income at the inflated rates. Secondly, if someone bought an investment for $10,000 ten years ago and sold it today for $20,000, the government will want taxes on the

---

[471] If they have done so in the past, until we see full repentance we aren't interested. Unless we are forced to compromise because they are the lesser of two evils (e.g. in 2008 we were forced to choose between an adulterer, McCain or a baby-killing enabler Obama). But we will do so holding our noses.
[472] www.heritage.org/Research/Budget/bg2081.cfm

$10,000 that he supposedly made. But that *same* government diluted the value of our money through debt, such that the $20,000 today is worth less than $8,500 ten years ago. So not only did the government steal $1,500 from the man in inflation but they now want him to pay 40% of his vapor paper gains as though it was a real profit. So in the end the man has lost $1,500 plus about $2000 more in taxes. So his net gain is negative $3,500, or a loss of 35% on his initial investment after 10 years. Does anyone wonder why no one is investing as much anymore? Every time you see a deficit, think inflation that is hurting you personally and is stealing from the poor and those unable to help themselves.

Obama and the Democrats promised total transparency and the broadcasting of the healthcare debate on CSPAN, eight times during his campaign.[473] He promised that the public would get to see every bill for five days on the internet. Yet we saw them have most of the meetings in secret and then force bills to be voted on before even their own Democrat *representatives* had a chance to read them. When asked about this, the Democratic leadership laughed. This is an oligarchy not a republic.

Many earmarked measures are monuments to themselves. Charlie Rangel took $2M to create the Charles B. Rangel Center for Public Service at City College in New York.[474] There should be a law that says any edifice named after any living person has to be funded by private funds only. Of course, the Democrats have always claimed they want to increase taxes and add programs, that being the way to redistribute wealth. They only made a fuss about the earmarks because they realized that most Americans didn't really want a tax and spend Congress.

We need to realize is that both parties are sick. It is going to take men and women of God who are committed to certain principles and refuse to violate them to change the face of politics. That means we need true moral *and* fiscal conservative Christians to be placed in office and then to vote their consciences. The Tea Party approved candidates come to mind (as long as they are morally conservative as well). But we can't make that happen unless the church and Christians in general get behind them.

How do we determine which candidates for public office hold to our moral values? We have to wade through propaganda and look at how they actually voted in the past. That is all there is to it.

Conservatives are mean, Liberals are immoral

Here's a headline directly from the DNC webpage[475]

Republicans Block Health Coverage for Children: *Democrats in Congress tried to override Bush's veto of children's health coverage on Thursday, but Republicans stopped them from reaching the needed majority. The bill would have brought health coverage to approximately ten million children in need.*

The implied claim here is that George Bush and the Republicans hate children and want them to get sick. Yet, when you look at the reasons why

---

[473] A few are shown here: www.youtube.com/watch?v=QuGXs2sm02M

[474] www.townhall.com/columnists/JacobSullum/2007/12/26/entitlement_mentality

[475] www.democrats.org/a/2005/09/the_2004_democr.php visited 11/10/07

Bush vetoed the bill, you realize it was because it not only cost too much, but the bill actually ended up providing health care to kids whose parents weren't exactly poor. But what is tragic is that the entire conversation seems to have forgotten to discuss if it is even government's role to *provide* healthcare to begin with. Entitlement programs will bankrupt America and just don't work.

You see, when liberals complain that conservatives are doing something wrong, they don't argue the issue that the conservatives are arguing. They argue Straw Man fallacies most of the time. That is, they argue against something that is not the targeted conservatives' issue. For instance, when conservatives tried to reform welfare, liberals characterized conservatives as wanting to starve poor people. Conservatives said, "No, that's not true. The real issue is that we think welfare is set up in a way that hurts the poor because it takes away their self-confidence and independence and forces the family to break up." That is, a mother will not get money unless there is no father in the home. This encourages the mother to kick the father out if he has trouble providing as much as the government can. We see the conservatives were correct about revamping welfare.

Yet, you don't see this done as much in reverse. Sure, many conservatives claim that liberals want to allow the killing of babies through abortion. But if you look at the issue, at the core it *is precisely* whether a woman has the right to kill the fetus, which we believe science has shown *is* as human as a baby is. So, the argument the Republicans are claiming is correct at the core and is consistent. They believe what they are saying. In fact, we believe that killing a fetus is morally equivalent to killing a baby. So, whenever you look at an argument, you need to get down actual issues, ignoring vindictive words that are being thrown back and forth. And remember the news media are not there to tell the truth. They are there to sensationalize and sell ads. They are not your friends.

Therefore, it is not that conservatives are mean spirited. They *do* care about the poor but think it's their personal responsibility, not government's at the point of a gun. As the data we showed earlier indicates, conservatives give more of their time and money than liberals give toward alleviating poverty. Democrats want a government fix. They do not want to face the problem themselves. Conservatives want to be personally involved, and they know that for every dollar the government takes in, probably only 20 cents makes it to needy people. If government were a charity, we'd stop giving it money and arrest the lot for fraud.

Liberals are unethical

Democrats have also taken to a new strategy; they now target key conservatives and file thousands of frivolous ethics violations against them. Forcing the conservatives to pay for their own defense and slowing down the real work that needs to be done. This is the reason why Sarah Palin quit as Governor of Alaska; she was hit with a large number of malicious unfounded lawsuits for things like wearing an old jacket with a logo that she'd worn for years, (no one complained about it before she became a VP candidate), or taking a question from a group of reporters milling in their lobby. All this forced state employees to have to spend time filing papers going through emails and scraps of paper rather than making things happen. It was mean-spirited to the people of the state if anything. Palin quit to allow the state to function as it needed to.[476] This is similar to what happened to Newt Gingrich[477] and Tom DeLay.[478] Perhaps Conservatives need to play this game in return until Democrats realize that they need to change the law to requiring the loser to pay the costs or come up with a better solution which will put an end to this lousy unethical tactic. [479]

The Tea Party and Conservative Party

I have to mention the Tea Party and the Conservative Party at this point. Though the TEA Party focuses on fiscal issues, many of their members are true moral and fiscal conservatives and don't mince their words or compromise their actions. I recommend all Christians and God-fearing Jews seriously consider the candidates that stand by the Tea Party and the Conservative Party principles (as long as they are *both* Fiscal and Moral Conservatives). The Republican Party would be wise to work with them and adopt their principles. Today, a third party in the elections would give power to those who hold immoral values, but the Republican party adopting the these Parties' principles would give conservatives a sure win every time.

Can we always vote Republican?

No, never! Republicans actually started as the Big Government party. Christians should only vote with the party that aligns itself with biblical principles and who wants the *least necessary* government interference in our lives. Remember nothing else will work. Everything else will cause pain and suffering.

Don't ask "whose side is God on?" Ask instead "Are they on God's side?" You can tell by how closely they believe His *entire* law.

The parties' stances may change over the years. But currently the Democrats have godless sinful evil stances in their platform.

---

[476] Going Rogue: An American Life, Sarah Palin, HarperCollins (2009)

[477] Compare Hillary Clinton's book deal to Newt Gingrich's
//edition.cnn.com/TRANSCRIPTS/0012/15/se.01.html

[478] en.wikipedia.org/wiki/Tom_DeLay_campaign_finance_investigation.

[479] I know some reading this will complain about Bill Clinton's impeachment. Yet Clinton was under investigation for a *rape* charge with ample of evidence and at least 4 victims were complaining. This was *not* a frivolous issue. His actions with Lewinsky when he lied was an indication of his past behavior and dishonesty. //en.wikipedia.org/wiki/Bill_Clinton

Thirty-five

A voice sprang up, "Every day, 9,000 children under the age of three die because of AIDS," a voice said. "How can you vote any other way?"
Another voice, "Every day, 30,000 children die from preventable causes, like lack of proper nutrition, clean drinking water or basic medicine. How can you vote any other way?"
A Jim Wallis meeting

Can A Christian Be A Single-Issue Voter?

Y ou can't be a single-issue voter! It's close-minded," said my friend.

How many times have you heard someone say this? Maybe you even believe this yourself. I find this to be a bit of a red herring. The reality is that it is almost impossible to find a candidate who violates biblical principles in *only* one area. I've found that most candidates will have unbiblical principles in at least five areas. In fact, just by listening to a candidate's views on some of the stricter moral laws in the Bible, one can immediately judge his or her heart as being rebellious or submissive to God. You want a man or a woman with a Godly Worldview and sold whole-heartedly to God. Never ever, vote for a candidate with a rebellious heart to the Bible. For instance, if a candidate bristles at some of the laws provided by the Bible, you are seeing the tip of the iceberg. His actual rebellion is far far greater and as a politician, he may hide it so it lies below the surface. Yet, if he interprets the Bible differently enough from you, most evangelicals, Catholics, and those who led you to Christ, you can bet that he will continue to misinterpret the Bible. Putting this man or woman in office will result in tragic consequences to the well being of our nation and the culture that our kids will grow up in.

Of course, there are numerous other influential factors, but if you have chickens with diseases that you need to treat, bringing a fox into the hen house not going to be inconsequential and will make your disease treating and death prevention efforts harder, if not worse. We have enough existing problems without us having to fight the one who steers the government.

Christians know that all of us have a sin nature. They of all people should know that people lie and that the evil one is always waiting to deceive us. So never trust what a politician says, watch what he's done all his life. Anyone can say anything, or act any way during an election season. Look at what has he done in the past, Look at how he has voted in the past. Read what

Neil Mammen

he has written. Look at who his companions have been. That'll tell you what he *really* believes.

Yet the concept is worth discussing

Can we be single-issue voters? The single "issues" on most people's mind are abortion or same-sex marriage. Let's see if we can figure this out. Here's a blog from a pastor friend of mine who admires Jim Wallis:

> *Wallis was speaking at a Catholic school, and a young lady said, "I am a single-issue voter. I vote on abortion and the candidate that takes the strongest stance against abortion. Every day, 3600 children are killed because of abortion. How can I vote any other way?"*
>
> *Wallis didn't say anything. He just waited to see what her peers would say. A voice sprang up. "Every day, 9,000 children under the age of three die because of AIDS," a voice said. "How can you vote any other way?"*
>
> *Another voice. "Every day, 30,000 children die from preventable causes, like lack of proper nutrition, clean drinking water or basic medicine. How can you vote any other way?"*
>
> *...What Wallis is saying is that if you're going to be pro-life, you have to be pro-life everywhere you find life threatened. And the unborn aren't the only children whose lives are being destroyed...If you're going to call yourself pro-life, you better look to protect all life.*

Hopefully dear reader, you have immediately seen that this objection is a Straw Man. If you recall that is where someone creates an argument that is *not* yours but resembles it loosely and then attacks the creation.

Yet, here's why this is a Straw Man. Find me one politician who is pro-life and thinks we *should* allow the 30,000 children to die from lack of proper nutrition. Show me one politician who thinks that we should not do anything about the 9000 children who die because of AIDS. No such conservative politician exists. That kind of person is a straw phantom existing in the mind of Jim Wallis, my pastor friend and others who have not been thinking clearly or who have bought into the lies promulgated in the news media. Why are there no politicians like this? It is because if public figures tried to be this way, they would not receive campaign money. They would not get votes either, because they would have no traction with the thinking public. They certainly wouldn't get my vote. In addition, the issue is not really whether they *care* about starving kids but whether they agree on the *solution* to *prevent* kids from starving. It's a Straw Man and a red herring (a false trail to distract you).

In reality, there are only two kinds of politicians in this situation:

a. Those who *do* care about the children in Africa and *want* to keep the killing of unborn children legal,[480] or

---

[480] This is a footnote worth repeating. You will hear politicians say that they want to keep abortion safe, legal and rare. I always ask them, as Scott Klusendorf suggests, "If abortion is not the killing of a human, why do you care if it is rare? We don't see you wishing that plastic surgery was rare. Yet, if Abortion is the killing of a human or if you aren't sure, couldn't that be murder?" What they are saying is, "I want to keep the killing of humans, safe, legal and rare." We don't hear them saying I want to keep plastic surgery safe, legal and rare. Safe and legal yes, bur the "rare" shows their self-deception and shows where their argument falls apart. Why do you want to keep it rare? Secondly, imagine if a politician were to say, "I want to keep slavery rare but legal." Or "I want to keep racism rare but legal." Would we even tolerate that for an instant?

b. Those who *do* care about the children in Africa and *don't want* to keep the killing of unborn children legal.

The only difference between them is the issue of *abortion*. So, can one be a single-issue voter? Absolutely! Because in this case there is only one moral issue that differentiates the two candidates. Abortion.

Those other issues are distractions created by lies and misrepresentations from either the media or the politician who wishes to use ad hominems against his opponent because he has no real defense.

Still, is it really a single-issue?

Yet, as I mentioned earlier, abortion and same-sex marriage are litmus tests for almost every other moral issue. They are the tip of the iceberg. Any politicians who would actively seek to create laws that violate biblical principles are not politicians who Christians should ever support. In fact, we should actively work *against* them. Don't get me wrong, this is America and those politicians can take whatever stance they wish to take on these moral issues. My concern is with Christians who would have the gall to vote for a man or woman who takes a diametric opposite stance to what the Bible clearly and plainly says; and think that they will be able to stand in front of God one day without remorse. God is not mocked. Whatever a man sows that will he also reap (Gal 6:7).

But you ask, "What about politicians who won't commit to spending taxpayer funded billions on AIDS or nutrition? This shows they don't care." Well, many smart politicians think that the way to solve those issues is not through inefficient governmental involvement, but through what been *proven* to yield better results, i.e. private enterprise and charities. So while you may find politicians who think there are better ways to solve these other problems, you won't find any who think it's good to have people dying of malnutrition. However, this is not true about abortion; they can't argue that there is "another" compromise solution to abortion. Imagine if some senator had stood up and said, "I'm against slavery, but freeing the slaves is not the answer, we should come up with a compromise." To which you'd ask, "And how is any compromise short of freeing the slaves anything *but* slavery?" In the same vein, I ask, "Tell me one possible compromise to stopping abortion that is *not* killing a human being?"

Add to that the question of locality, responsibility and effectivity. What if someone stood up and said, "How can you worry about freeing the slaves while 30,000 children are dying of malnutrition in Africa?" Would we consider this valid? The representative *can* do something to free the slaves, but he probably can't effect much change on evil foreign *political* regimes that are the actual cause of those children dying. *Note that voluntary charities can feed them, but that's not the government's job, it's your job!*

Again, here is the rock bottom question: Is the person running for office someone who upholds biblical moral values? Are they rebelling against the values I as an evangelical or a Catholic or a God-fearing Jew believes God has ordained for the health of His children? That's the *single* issue I vote on.

Neil Mammen

But even with all that, you can still be a single-issue voter

I just spent a few pages arguing that this is *not* a single issue. But I never answered *whether* we can or should be single-issue voters. Let me answer that by asking a question. If there was a man or a party running for office whose platform included ideas that had worked in the past; ideas that provided more jobs for everyone; more food for everyone; healthcare for everyone; an assurance to improve the economy; a promise to advance the nation technologically and so on; let us say he agreed with you on a majority of issues. He was the ideal candidate for you, *but he also wanted to kill the Jews.* Could you based on that *single* issue decide logically, rationally and morally that you would *not* vote for him?

Of course, you could! Especially since that describes Hitler.

So, the issue is not whether we can be single-issue voters. Yes, we can![481] The only question is *what* are those single issues that qualify as worthy single issues? May I propose that one of those "sufficient" single issues is the murder of innocent human beings? Would you agree?

So of course, we all can be single-issue voters.

The next question you have to ask this, "If you are willing to ignore the murder of innocents in your zeal to vote for someone, it can only be because you *don't* really think that unborn children are really human or you truly *want* to kill babies. It's like voting for an 'anti-racist' person who just happens to be a member of the Klan? Either you *are* a racist or you tolerate racism in others. Both are unacceptable. There is no in-between. How can a Christian vote for the murder of what both science and the Bible indicate is innocent human life?"

What about economic issues or same-sex marriage?

Okay, we have to admit that some people oppose abortion but not same-sex marriage. Some may be against abortion but favor some other immoral value. But, these cases are exceptions and need to be evaluated individually. A warning though, as I've already said, disagreement on one biblically mandated moral issue is usually just the tip of the iceberg. You are seeing *their* Worldview. Most people don't violate the moral values that God has described in the Bible because they just happen to interpret the Bible differently; they violate it because they do not *wish* to submit to His leading. Often, it's *rebellion* that is at the root of their refusal. It is critical that you as a voter carefully analyze *why* this candidate disagrees with your moral values. Never give them a pass on it.

At no point, however, should we vote for a candidate with whom we agree economically but disagree morally. Why? Because people who put economics over morals can lead our nation to Hitler-like values. Imagine an electoral race in which one candidate would help people economically by ensuring that jobs grew in the United States but wanted to keep slavery legal. However, the other candidate who doesn't have a plan to grow jobs, opposes slavery. Which way should you vote?

Not voting is the same as voting for slavery. You decide.

---

[481] To mimic an abused phrase. Actually, I think the Obama campaign stole this from Bob the Builder.

Thirty-six

Legality alone is no guide for a moral people. There are many things in this world that have been, or are, legal but clearly immoral. Slavery was legal. Did that make it moral? South Africa's apartheid, Nazi persecution of Jews, and Stalinist and Maoist purges were all legal, but did that make them moral?
Walter Williams[482]

All [laws], however, may be arranged in two different classes. 1) Divine. 2) Human... But it should always be remembered that this law, natural or revealed, made for men or for nations, flows from the same Divine source: it is the law of God.... Human law must rest its authority ultimately upon the authority of that law which is Divine.
James Wilson, a signer of the Constitution and U.S. Supreme Court Justice[483]

To instance in the case of murder: this is expressly forbidden by the Divine... If any human law should allow or enjoin us to commit it we are bound to transgress that human law... But, with regard to matters that are... not commanded or forbidden by those superior laws such, for instance, as exporting of wool into foreign countries; here the... legislature has scope and opportunity to interpose.
Sir William Blackstone, *Commentaries on the Laws of England* [484]

How Then Shall We Legislate?

We *have* to legislate morality. We've proven that over and over in this book. In addition, if we care about justice and our grandchildren we have to have laws based on God's moral values.

But how do we do that? Do we legislate from the Bible or from the Koran or some other religious document? Should we come at it from the other side and abandon all religion, appeal to only secular humanism? Do we legislate every single moral value and create a totalitarian state? Let's look at these.

What is the primary moral code of our republic?

As we have logically and carefully proven, the primary moral code of our republic *must* be the fixed Laws of Nature and Nature's God. It is God's immutable, transcendent moral law. There is no way to budge on this. It

---

[482] http://www.freerepublic.com/focus/f-news/1195301/posts

[483] James Wilson, The Works of the Honorable James Wilson, Bird Wilson, editor (Philadelphia: Lorenzo Press, 1804), Vol. I, pp. 103-105, "Of the General Principles of Law and Obligation." As quoted by Dave Barton at www.wallbuilders.com/resources/search/detail.php?ResourceID=4

[484] Blackstone, Commentaries on the Laws of England (Philadelphia: Robert Bell, 1771), Vol. I, pp. 42.

logical and rational and cannot be changed for cultural or social reasons. It cannot be changed due to precedence. The source for this law is the Judeo-Christian Bible. The portions of the Ten Commandments that deal with man's interaction with man comprise much of this foundational code. Unsurprisingly though, this moral code is shared on numerous (though not all) of its points by many people and cultures today and in past history. The influence today is due to the compelling nature of the Law and the work of Christian philosophers over time; *and* the very bad experience of history when nations and cultures have abandoned these laws. In addition, the Bible says the law is written in our hearts, so many people hold these values without realizing the source. Even some atheists like Bertrand Russell see value in the Judeo-Christian law and many other atheists believe in the unalienable rights of human beings. However we must not sleep as there are many movements today to strip certain individuals of rights or to give animals the same rights as humans or worse, to reduce humans to the value of animals.[485]

But what about the lesser laws, the ones that our representatives are allowed to legislate? How do we come up with these laws?

Though we see that the primary moral law cannot be changed, there seems to be leeway on the lesser laws. The ones that our founder James Wilson said in the quote above was "Human Law," or as Blackstone says in the laws about "the exporting of wool." Let us spend some time understanding how to legislate these "lesser" laws.

Option 1. We should legislate these Human Laws *directly* from the Bible.

It may shock some readers (especially skeptics) to learn that I do *not* think we should be legislating these lesser laws *directly* from the Bible. Wait a minute! Am I contradicting myself? Didn't I say earlier that we should use the Laws of Nature and of Nature's God? Didn't I say the "Authority" can be proven to be the God of the Bible? I did indeed but here's the problem: it's not constitutional and it's dangerous.

I don't think there is a constitutional or biblical case for legislating these Human Laws *directly* from the Bible. And there is no logical or constitutional basis to legislate the Ceremonial, Civil or Judicial laws from the Bible, though they are useful as advisories. Nor is there any validity to be legislating those laws that were directed *not* to the government but to one of the other three groups i.e. the church, the family, or the individual.

The Theocracy

Remember too, that the United States is *not* a theocracy, and we don't ever want it to be one. We have seen what can happen under a man directed theocracy, such as during the Spanish Inquisition, and worse. Many people,

---

[485] Earlier revisions of this book had a quote purportedly from George Washington or John Adams that said "The government of the United States is not in any sense founded on the Christian Religion." But on further research, it was revealed to be a line supposedly in the Treaty of Tripoli but was written by neither and it was only *signed* by Adams. Yet, both Adams and Washington's numerous *other* quotes indicate however that they did not believe this. See www.eadshome.com/JohnAdams.htm and christianity.about.com/od/independenceday/a/foundingfathers.htm. This casts doubt on if they indeed intended to convey this or shared this conviction.

who came to America in the beginning, came fleeing religious persecution. They would no more want to be ruled by a Baptist theocracy than you or even most Baptists would. Even when Christians legislate through religion, you can get twisted excesses.

We need a layer in between (I said *layer,* not lawyer), to protect both Christians *and* non-Christians from Theocrats. But this does not mean Christians should *not* be politically active. They should be very active because they are in tune with the moral law of God.[486] Christ calls us to be "salt and light" to the world and so, we must winsomely defend our positions with logic and reasoning (I feel we are just in extending 1 Pet 3:15 to this).

The Bible does *not* command us to try to set up a "Christian America," just a moral one. This does not mean governmental leaders who are Christian should not, as individuals, take guidance from the Bible when voting on moral issues. We believe that God's character determines an objective morality and our Republic is logically based on His immutable code, so it is natural that we should turn to Him to find it. Remember again, morality is not religion, though all of us are informed about our morality by our religious paradigm. Note too we all can come to certain moral truths independently of religion (since God has written the law in to our hearts), but these should be validated by facts and we should not depend on feelings as emotions can mislead us.

Nor should we blindly impose these lesser moral values on non-Christians without any rational justification, we can and should try to convince people that our reasoning is valid. If we can persuade our representatives to think and vote morally and constitutionally, all of us will benefit. We need to engage with people, including our lawmakers, civilly in the marketplace of ideas.

Then when we do constitutionally legislate and impose our moral values on others who disagree with us, they cannot fault us for getting there in the way a republic is to operate. We can remind them that we are tolerating the imposition of *their* moral values on us, right now.

Later in this chapter, I will propose a methodology to derive the laws, i.e. the lesser laws, *without* becoming a theocracy, without legislating directly from the Bible.

Option 2. We should legislate directly from the Koran or other religious books?

Clearly, for some of the same reasons why we should not legislate directly from the Bible, we should not legislate from the Koran or any other

---

[486] Remember though morality is not religion, we all come to our understanding of morality, and to common moral values from our religious paradigm even if it's atheism – for unbelief is still a religious system. However, if a person claims to be religious then his or her morals will be determined by that religion. If a person is irreligious, his or her morals will be determined by that lack of religion. Note, if a person were to object to this, saying that they adhere to a particular religion but do not adhere to its moral guidelines, we would have good reason to doubt that they adhere to that religion. Logically we would know that they merely give it lip service or have a cultural adherence to it but do not "believe" it. Normally when people lose their belief in a religion they only cling to its traditions until it becomes popular to abandon those traditions or it becomes inconvenient to adhere to those traditions.

Secondly, what one believes about God (or does not believe) and what one believes about man affects one's moral values.

"holy book." The world has seen the effect of legislating from the Koran. Today it's known as the Taliban. But what of using the Koran as our primary moral code? There are already many "true" Muslim Republics that legislate Sharia law. I doubt we wish to emulate them. Additionally, most Islamic states tend to be dictatorships or oligarchies and this fits with the Islamic desire for the "Caliphate." Remember, just like Christians and Jewish are to take direction from the Bible, Muslims are to take their direction from the Koran, and that is our fundamental problem. Unlike Christianity, where no person is to have lesser rights whether they be Christians or non-Christians, the Muslim holy texts clearly articulate that non-Muslims are not to have equal rights with Muslims.[487] There are many Christian republics and states that people would love to "escape" to. But there are probably no Muslim republic or states that people want to escape to.[488] As you can see, we don't really want to legislate from the Koran.

Option 3. Should we legislate from the humanist perspective?

No. Secular humanism is based on faulty premises. First, it abandons the fixed primary moral code concept and thus is self destructive. Second, assumes that human beings are good and do not have a sin nature. It believes that personal worth *and* rights come from and are defined by humans, not God. Not withstanding that, as we showed, a humanist's view of the absence of God invalidates our Constitution and makes the concept evil merely a preference.

If people are essentially good, why is the world situation getting worse? Why did we kill more people in the last century than we've killed in all previous centuries combined till now?[489] If people are naturally good, why do we have to spend time teaching our kids to share and obey and be kind and respectful? How many parents say to their two-year-olds, "Now, Sally, you need to learn to be a bit more selfish?" What does a kid that age say when she has something and another tot wants to share it? She says, "Mine!" Human nature being what it is, we have to train children to share and be polite, to say thank you, to respect and obey their parents and not to cheat or lie. Why do we have to teach kids to be good if they are inherently good? You tell me. Why do some 2 year old kids, who have never been spanked or abused, aren't allowed to watch TV and have no role models for violence, instinctively try to strike others when angry?

People are not essentially good, we have a sin nature, and we see the effects of this truth in any system making that faulty assumption. Atheistic or even Theistic Communism is such an example. Its basic idea is great. People work as hard as they can and take only what they need. Everybody shares. But communism has failed horribly with terrible consequences. Why? Because communist leaders found out that human nature is the opposite of what communism needs. People in communist societies worked only as much as they needed to and took as much as they could until the system went bankrupt.

---

[487] Surah 9:29 see also "Unbelievers in Islam" www.islam-watch.org/Shabana/RealIslam/Chapter6.htm

[488] Note that some states like Kuwait in their oil rich heyday did attract people from poorer *Islamic* countries with their extremely rich socialistic policies. Something they could do as long as someone *else* was drilling their oil and buying it. But it's not sustainable.

[489] USSR: 40M killed, Communist China: 80M killed. //users.erols.com/mwhite28/warstat1.htm

People were starving. Corruption was everywhere. To fix this the leaders had to add control through fascism; they had to force people to work, piling yet another failed concept to the mix, tyranny and fascism. It has failed in Germany, China and Russia and everywhere else. As Dinesh D'souza says, "True believers in communism can only be found in American Colleges today." Everyone else has had to face reality except them. The irony of it all is that Russia and China are rapidly becoming more capitalistic that the U.S. and as a result succeeding in many areas.

Secular humanism has traditionally assumed that you can avoid absolutes

In fact, one signer of the Humanist Manifesto II, Joseph Fletcher (author of Situation Ethics: The New Morality) claims that there are no absolutes. Yet, the manifesto he signed insists that there should be total sexual freedom for consenting adults, legal abortion and euthanasia. Are those not absolutes? Of course they are. The declaration that "absolutes should be avoided" is itself an absolute. It's self-refuting. It is a "suicide statement," it kills itself the minute he states it. This illogic permeates humanist philosophy, so everything falls apart. Now that would be a fun debate to have.

Secular Humanism assumes human beings are the origin of personal value and rights

A few years ago, I was in a debate with a friend of mine on abortion. He said that while he agrees that fetuses are human, he believes they have less value than babies so we should be able to abort them. To him this position is logical and morally acceptable.

Remember the earlier chapter on rights? What is the problem if mankind gets to determine the value of other humans? Slavery. Racism.

The funny thing is that my friend is an African American. So, I asked him if he thought it was morally acceptable for the KKK to determine *his* value. He didn't seem to get it. Any time a human determines the value of another human and we accept that as moral, we have slipped back into Hitler's eugenics. Hitler decided that the mentally retarded had less worth than the mentally fit. Then he decided that the Aryan race had more value than the Jews, gypsies, homosexuals and Christians. Some people will see the word "Hitler" in that statement and assume that they can immediately object and say they are insulted. But that's a fallacy. You have to show me why this is not a good comparison. Merely saying you are insulted is not a refutation.

As discussed extensively earlier, mankind's inherent value has to come from somewhere outside of man. It has to come from the Creator of and Authority over mankind. If it does not, all we get is "Might is Right," a philosophy far from morally acceptable. Rights must come from the Creator or they are fleeting and remain granted at the mere whim of those in power.

So what is the origin of the morality we need to legislate when it come to these lesser laws?

If it is not directly from the Bible, not from the Koran or any other religious book, and not from secular humanism, where does it come from?

We should legislate the law that is written on our hearts.[490]

The Bible tells us that all men and women have the moral law written in their hearts.[491] But how do we know what that is? The Declaration of Independence answers this question quite well, saying, "We hold these truths to be self-evident." Exactly! We should make laws from commonly understood self-evident truths.

Christians believe an objective morality is "written" in on all hearts, even the hearts of non-Christians and atheists. Note, that this is just one of the steps in the process. I'll itemize all the steps shortly.

If the law is written on our hearts, why is there so much disagreement on it then? [492]

There are multiple possible reasons for this. Like indulgent parents, some people want to be loving and understanding and end up being permissive, which results in bad laws and pain. It is not loving to allow someone to destroy themselves. Or they have no idea of the consequences of certain actions and blindly want to be "positive." Some may just wish to rebel against the "rules." Some really want to do things that are bad for them like sex outside of marriage or adultery. Others may have seen situations where one moral law seems to conflict with another, and assume there is no objective morality and never realize that there is a moral hierarchy of laws.

Given all of this, how do we determine these lesser laws in a secular society?

How too does a *non-Christian* determine moral law? There are basic principles for discovering moral laws. I've listed them below and I believe that if we apply these diligently, doing our best to avoid personal biases, we will end up with laws and values similar to those that Christians desire for the safety and health of society. Remember though, as we go through this methodology, we must not limit our testing to one method. If we did that, we could end up with bad laws. Every proposed law must pass *each* of the tests.

---

[490] Romans 2:14 Indeed, when Gentiles, who do not have the law, do by nature things required by the law, they are a law for themselves, even though they do not have the law, 15 since they show that the requirements of the law are written on their hearts, their consciences also bearing witness, and their thoughts now accusing, now even defending them.

[491] First, we need to deal with a couple of objections. If man is inherently evil, how can we say the law is written in his heart? Second, if man is inherently evil, how can we *trust* him to reveal the truth of the law which we claim is written in his heart? Won't he lie about it?

Let's answer the first objection. Man's evilness is not due to the fact that he has the law written in his heart. It's that he knows the law and willingly and purposely rebels against it. Once men beat their consciences into submission as a slave of their desires, they become callous to the law in their hearts. The response to the second objection is that man is not absolutely depraved. He still has a good conscience and influences of good. He just tends to want to do evil. So, you may not want to trust some men about the law in their hearts but since we all have the same law, we can tell if someone is lying.

[492] I've done a fair amount bit of research on this topic but have borrowed heavily from Frank Turek and Norm Geisler's book: Legislating Morality: Is It Wise? Is It Legal? Is It Possible? Wipf & Stock Publishers (February 2003). I strongly recommend readers add this book to your library.

1. The first and basic principle is simple: Human lesser laws should be based on the Golden Rule. Do unto others as you would have them do unto you.

But we need to go a step further. Lesser laws should also be based on our reactions to others doing the same thing to us. Is it okay to cut in line? Well ask yourself, how would you feel if someone you did not know cut in line in front of you? That's the determination. It is not whether we want to cut in line that is important, but how we would feel if someone did that to us.

The same holds for abortion. We don't set our stance on abortion based on whether *we* want to have one. We try to imagine someone aborting *us*. How would I vote on abortion if I were the one being discarded? But we must not use *only* this principle for a moral law. We need to look at the others as well. If we used this principle alone, we could argue that it is good for the government to give us free food and medicine because everyone would like that. This brings us to the next point.

2. The long term consequences of each law should be studied.

If a law results in bad habits, destructive behavior, reduction of motivation, increased incidences of disease, death, or increased emotional or physical pain, this is a good indication that moral principles are being violated.[493] In other words, if an action causes death and disease, it's probably immoral. If it causes the breakdown of the family or loneliness or insecurity, it's probably a bad law.

This means Christians should pay/donate for long-term social and statistical studies (as done by www.FRC.org) and use the information to inform non-Christian legislators. Christians should never ever say, "Well the Bible says that X is wrong and that settles it, so we should legislate that way." While I believe the Bible is infallible and inerrant as originally written, and that any legislation that lines up with it will be good for the country, that belief carries no weight with the man on the street. This is why we find so much resistance to Christian ideals. We need to be able to explain and defend our concepts rationally and logically in public discussion.

3. Lawmakers must recognize a hierarchy of moral laws.

When I teach this concept to college kids, I introduce it by saying, "I'm going to teach you how to legally run a red light." Too many people have abandoned the principle of moral absolutes because they had a dilemma in seeing two moral laws that seemed to collide. Rather than realize that whenever two moral laws appear to conflict, you apply the higher law, they abandoned the entire principle, throwing the baby out with the bathwater. We should not abandon the principle just because we don't understand the methodology.

Is it okay to run a red light? Of course not! So we have a law. It says,

1.Don't run red lights.

Hopefully you are saying to yourself, "Well yes, but there are

---

[493] Certain cultures, for example, reportedly held festivals where sex was not reserved to a man and his wife. Does this result in emotional pain or disease? If it does (and despite the myth of the noble savages we see now that it did), then it is immoral regardless if it is acceptable in that culture.

exceptions to that rule." In which case ask yourself "Are the exceptions less important than the original rule?" If you were to run a red light just because you were impatient, would that be acceptable? Obviously not. We'd say that is wrong. But that's not the example you were thinking of, was it? You were thinking that it's okay to run a red light, for example, when you have a medical emergency and need to get someone to the hospital. Right? So, the valid exceptions to the original rule have to be more important than the reason for the original rule. So let's say there's someone in your passenger seat that needs medical attention immediately. To simplify, we have two laws here…

1. Do what it takes to save a person who is dying, or whatever dire situation prevails.
2. Don't run red lights.

Hopefully you agree that it would be silly to abandon traffic laws in every situation just because we have identified a condition in which a higher law supersedes a traffic law. Also, just because an issue is complex does not mean the basic principle should be abandoned. The decision we just came through can be complicated and require an even higher moral that overrides the first two. Let's say there is a man in the crosswalk at the red light. Should we risk killing someone in a crosswalk while running a traffic light in a medical emergency? No! So, now a higher law supersedes the "medical emergency" law. That is the law of "don't kill. "

In simple terms we now have

1. Don't kill anyone
2. Do what it takes to save a person who is dying.
3. Don't run red lights.

Despite the complexity, I hear no sane people clamoring that we should abandon traffic laws, and we don't eliminate them because the occasional exception to the rule.

Do you want to complicate it even more? Let's say that the man in the crosswalk has a gun. He just shot your friend in the passenger seat, which is why you need to get your friend to the hospital. The gunman is about to turn that gun on you and shoot you. The intersection is crowded with people fleeing in panic, and the light is red. How do you make your decision? Clearly, if you can think fast, you try to figure out which laws work first. How about this:

1. It's okay to kill someone in self-defense or the defense of others by hitting them with a car.
2. Don't kill anyone **innocent.**
3. Do what it takes to save a person who is dying.
4. Don't run red lights.

So you hit the murderous thug with the gun, thus protecting other innocents, you cautiously negotiate the intersection to ensure you don't kill anyone else fleeing the maniac with the gun. Then you run the light and drive to the hospital.

As you can see, the list grows. Moral absolutes still stand, but "lower" moral imperatives give way to laws that trump them. No one abandons the law of gravity or disbelieves it just because we know that there are complicated exceptions that override it in certain cases, such as the principles of aerodynamics. Similarly, we should not abandon absolutes just because a situation is complicated. We just need to understand these principles and apply them. That's what the Wright Brothers did when they figured out how to fly a plane.[494]

Some may argue that this is "situation ethics." But that is simply not true. In the actual situation ethics classes taught in the 1980's, students were told there were no moral absolutes except what they came up with as a consensus, (does this remind you of a democracy/mobocracy?) They were not told that there *is* a transcendent unchanging moral hierarchy, and if that was mentioned, no one taught them how to identify the hierarchy. From what I've heard (I was not in the US at the time) in the "lifeboat, situational ethics" classes, kids were trained to think that someone who was sick or with a handicap or was elderly was of less value than a young, healthy or able person. I don't think any one can argue that someone's life is less important than the need to observe red traffic lights. Naturally, we can and should debate the placement of laws in the hierarchy, but we must recognize that there is one. I think most people would agree that saving the *life* of an innocent person is the highest law, saving the *rights* of an innocent person would be lower, and so on.

4. Governments must take great care to balance personal rights with personal responsibilities.

God gives us rights. So, when someone comes along and says, "I have a right to free food," we must sit back and ask, "Is that obvious?" The answer is no. That is a "good." It's the product of someone's labor. You only have rights to your own goods. If it isn't a real "right," it will probably end up hurting us or others. Of course, some things that are not rights are indeed good ideas. Those should *not* be made into laws. Rather, they should be voluntary suggestions. An example of this is giving money to the poor. It should be voluntary, and in the same way, poor people cannot think they have a right or entitlement to it.[495]

Here's an interesting dilemma for liberals. Many liberals say they have a right to abortions, a right to health care, a right to welfare, a right to paid leave, a right to arts funding, a right to same-sex marriage, a right to a certain wage, and at the end of life, a right to die. Then they claim they don't believe in absolutes or that nothing is black and white. Who are they kidding? And of course I then ask, "Isn't that statement that 'nothing is black and white', a black and white statement itself? Where's the gray in that statement?"

---

[494] An atheist once tried to argue saying, "But Neil, aerodynamics is a physical law. You can't change it. We are stuck with that. You can't equate physical laws with moral laws." That therein was the crux of his misunderstanding. You see we *do* equate physical laws to moral laws. Both these types of laws preexist and need to be discovered. In fact, we think moral laws are *more* permanent and transcendent than those measly physical laws. After all, physical laws didn't exist before the universe existed and will end when the universe ends, which science tells us it will. Yet moral laws never began and will never end, thus they are far more permanent that physical laws. Moral laws are like mathematical laws, logic, and set theory. They are transcendent and never ending. Moral laws are part of the very nature of God. Physical laws are limited to this particular universe.

[495] I know what you are thinking, "But what if we all would like there to be free food." The problem here is you can't take just one item out of context. The law must meet all the requirements not just one or two. Free food for all just doesn't work in practicality, and requires a totalitarian government that ensures that every one works as well and when they don't, the government has to become intrusive.

Others think that morals should never enter the discussion but believe that free healthcare is the right thing to do. I always ask why they are imposing their morality about the right or wrong thing to do, if we should keep our morals out of the discussion. It's pure hypocrisy on their part.

5. Moral laws cannot be written solely with the extreme exceptions in mind.

We can't write laws to legalize all abortions just because we can think of exceptionally rare cases where the procedure might possibly be justified. This is like arguing that there should be no speed limits, because somewhere someone who is allergic to bees may get stung by a bee while driving, and need to drive at 110 miles an hour to an emergency room. If absolutely necessary, specific exceptions can be written into laws. For example, ambulance drivers are allowed to run red lights, but everyday motorists are not; except in an emergency.

6. Ambiguity over "where you draw the line" is not an argument for not drawing a line.

Simply because many states disagree on whether the drinking age should be 18, 19 or 21 does not mean there should be no drinking age laws. We should draw the line somewhere while searching for the optimum.

7. Lawmakers who believe and live by moral law themselves will be better legislators than those who do not live by morals.

Bill Clinton was a very bad president. Why? Because he did not live under the moral law of "no sexual harassment," but he expected everyone else to. He violated the law, thinking he was above it. Crooked politicians regardless of party should be ousted. Why? Because if they don't believe they need to live under moral codes, how can we expect them to come up with ones that are valid? The best way to determine a moral code is in our reactions to it. If crooked people never stop to consider what they would do if the tables were turned, how could you expect them to devise truly moral laws?

When Clinton was running for president, the common mantra was, "Character doesn't matter – it's the economy, stupid!" This was a claim that a politician's personal morality should not be used to gauge how they would do in lawmaking. But then why were all of these people up in arms when a racist like David Duke, a former KKK member, tried to run for office?

This is a critical point. Since our understanding of the moral law for a situation is based on how we personally react to it, if we elect a crook, he will react to all situations wrongly, and we will end up with bad laws. Ravi Zacharias says, "One can no more reconcile immorality in private with a call to public integrity than one can reconcile being a racist in private with being unprejudiced in public." Wasn't the primary problem with Idi Amin, one of the most corrupt and murderous dictators in Africa, one of character? Amin was a liar, a cheat, a thief and a murderer. Why does character matter, indeed? Do you think that had Amin's character been upstanding it would have made no difference? You tell me.

8. Laws with a long history should not be discarded lightly.

One of the laws of the old west was: One should never remove a fence until one has thought long and hard about why it was put there. Most of our laws came about for a reason. And while some need to be abandoned, we should understand why they were enacted before voting them out of existence. Sometimes, as with laws that discriminated racially, they needed to be done away with because they were immoral. In addition, the onus is upon the one who wishes to remove the fence to prove it is in the wrong place. If someone wants to change an old law, they should offer extensive proof as to why it needs to be changed and what the social, financial, emotional and other consequences will be. The current debate about same-sex marriage comes to mind.

9. Laws that promote our traditional morality and religion can only be good for the country.

As long as we don't legislate religion; laws that promote it, yet separate it and protect it from the state, can only be good. As said, most laws derived from religion can be categorized as Moral, Ceremonial, Civil and Judicial. We should not force the ceremonial or Judicial Laws of any religion on anyone. We *are* saying, however, that we should protect the Biblical Ceremonial laws if people want to practice them as long as they adhere to the other items in this list. We should learn from their Moral Laws and consider them as a basis for our laws, but we always leave the Judicial Laws out. Criminal punishments which are the Judicial Laws are set by our *own* lawmaking bodies. This applies to all religions. For instance, we should feel free to take the cue from Muslim law that stealing is not allowed, but we should pay no attention to their punishment for stealing – the felon's right hand being chopped off. Similarly, we should consider the value of taking one day a week off from work, respecting the Sabbath, because it is good for us to rest, but we should not be stoning anyone for not observing this.

At this point, someone may bring up the idea of men having multiple wives, practiced in various religions. When we run this concept through the points in this list, we see it falls short on many fronts. So, it is not really a value that we should enshrine in law. Similarly for other Laws like forcing women to wear veils.

10. Before a controversial law is passed, an unbiased long term double blind study of the effects of the law should be done.

This is almost self evident from previous discussions, but it's worth repeating. Other nations or states and their responses to the law should be studied. Has this law been effective? What were its consequences? If possible, it should be applied to a smaller population of people or region and evaluated.

11. Is it necessary?

Is this a law that replaces common sense? Is it a nanny state law? Too many unnecessary regulations even if they are well meaning can hurt a culture.

The 11 recommendations

So there you have them, eleven recommendations on how we should

Neil Mammen

arrive at the Human Laws. I do believe we can refine this further, so do not feel this is the final say on this. Note that, at no time did we recommend legislation *directly* from the Bible, nor did we suggest blind adherence to existing laws. Even so, at the root of this discussion we see that while morality is not religion, personal standards of behavior usually derive from religious views or the absence thereof. That is why we really want representatives who have a Godly World View making our laws. You will also notice that there are numerous moral values that should *not* be legislated for or against, yet those bad behaviors should not be subsidized or endorsed by the government. Think of "smoking." The government should not subsidize it, nor should they make it illegal.[496] Naturally, it would behoove the media and the arts (think Hollywood) to *not* promote bad moral values for the health of the country (but since they continue to promote certain unhealthy values like sex outside of marriage and homosexuality we have to vote with our wallets).

You want to legislate Morality!

It's funny but some of my liberal friends have tried to accuse me of wanting to legislate every single moral value. I quickly turned the tables on them by asking them what their recommendation was. "Are you saying that we should not legislate *any* moral values?

When they hum and haw, I say, "Of course, we must legislate *some* moral values. Isn't the question '*what* should we legislate' and 'where do we draw the line'? And don't tell me that I want to legislate more moral values than you. I'm not the one trying to legislate the forceful giving of money to the poor through socialism. I'm not the one saying that we should make it a law that every home recycles or uses less energy or be punished. I could go on and on. Don't try to pin this silliness on me. You are the one who wants to control the masses. Not me. You are the one going overboard on legislating morality with punishments, not me."

Have I contradicted myself?

In a previous chapter, I said elected officials should vote their conscience. In this chapter, I have repeatedly said we should not legislate the lesser laws directly from the Bible and should have valid reasons for all laws. In fact, I berated Obama for saying he wanted valid non-biblical reasons against certain abortions before he would oppose them. Have I contradicted myself?

Not at all. You see, though Blackstone notes we have no choice on the primary or Divine laws, one does not really even need a biblical reason to stop murdering babies. The argument against partial birth abortions and babies born alive in a botched abortion is *not* religious. It is a moral, ethical and biological argument. There is only one question about these abortions that we need answer. Is the 21-week-old fetus human? That is the fundamental question. It has its own unique human DNA and can even survive outside the womb. Those facts make the answer clear. The burden of proof to show that *even* fetuses and zygotes are not human and thus have no rights is upon those who

---

[496] Note that this does not easily extend to legalizing Marijuana, but that's a longer discussion and not in the scope of this book.

want kill it, not those who express caution like me.[497] My argument was that Obama was either ignorant of the argument, unable to comprehend it, being disingenuous or a bloodthirsty baby killer. You tell me which is worse.

As Christians, the Bible and the Holy Spirit inform our conscience. But, we need not legislate the Human Laws from the Bible directly. Legislators in addition to their conscience can take various biblical moral principles, do some research on them and come up with ample scientific and statistical evidence as to why those moral values should be the law. Obama was doing *none* of these.

Find out more

This chapter borrows heavily from Turek and Geisler's excellent work titled "Legislating Morality. Is It Wise? Is It Legal? Is It Possible?"[498] As space does not permit a complete discussion on how to legislate in this book, I encourage to you get a copy of their excellent book for more details.

The other book that will reward you greatly is written by the French classical liberal theorist, political economist, and member of the French assembly Frédéric Bastiat. What was known as a classical liberal theorist[499] in the 19th century would today be considered a conservative. His small book is simply titled "The Law."[500] He talks about what the law can and cannot do morally and effectively.

---

[497] To defeat abortion arguments without using the Bible go to www.JesusIsInvolvedInPolitics.com/Abortion.htm

[498] Wipf & Stock Publishers, 2003.

[499] Recall that the phrase Classical liberalism in standard academic sources means early liberalism, which is the liberalism of Jacksonian democracy in the 19th Century. They stressed laissez-faire economics and strict constructionism. Classical liberalists believed in a form of liberalism in which the government does not provide social services or regulate industry and banks. Obviously, the language has changed and today they would be considered conservatives or libertarians.

[500] Available from the Foundation for Economic Education www.fee.org.

Thirty-seven

The effectual fervent prayer of a righteous man availeth much.
James 5:16b (KJV)

Where there is no vision, the people perish: but he that keepeth the law, happy is he.
Proverbs 19:18 (KJV)

*Pastors are afraid that they **may** lose their tax deductions and their congregations if they speak out in church about laws and politics. But the sad truth is that if pastors don't do exactly that, they **will** lose their tax deductions and eventually their congregations as courts rule against them.*
What they fear the most will happen to them if only as a consequence of their inaction.
Email to a Pastor friend.

The Call To Action:
What Pastors, Christians And
The Church Can Do Right Now!

P**RAY!**

What can we do right now? We can pray. We can fall on our faces and petition God to forgive this nation and not deal with us like He dealt with His own people. Yet, even as we say that, we realize how foolish it is, for why do we deserve to have it any easier than God's own people?

So, I also ask you next, to pray that God uses *you* and your church greatly to *change* this land and change its laws before we get to that point.

Pray that God raises up real men and women of God from within your congregation to lead this nation.

Pray that everyone sitting in pews who loves God will get out and vote and work towards more moral and more just laws.

Pray that everyone sitting in pews will realize that if they love their neighbor and care about the poor and oppressed, they will work towards ensuring moral and wise legislation.

Then I urge you to *do* something physical about it.

Teach the Law

Pastors, we must teach the law. The entire law. We need to teach on all the moral issues. Why each law was given, what the physical consequences are on each individual and on society when we violate them. This requires pastors to work closely with people like Patrick Fagan of the Family Research Council (www.FRC.org). For that we must also fund them. Churches *can* do that.

Do you think that anyone in your congregation have ever been hit with the President Bartlet type questions? i.e. Do I need to stone my son if he dishonors me or kill my brother for working on the Sabbath? Do you think that hampers their witnessing when they seem inconsistent?

If I may be so bold, why not teach the principles in this book. Teach the differences between the four types of laws, so people are not confused. Pastors, can I challenge you to ask 20 people in your congregation to tell you the difference between the laws that apply to individuals only and the laws that apply to individuals *and* governments? Does your congregation know the difference between the Ceremonial and Moral laws? I'd bet 90% of us are clueless about this. I was, until I started trying to answer Bartlett's questions and started doing research.

Perhaps pastors could spend four weeks every year on "The Consequences of Sexual Sin on Our Culture." Cover especially the consequences of divorce, every single person in your congregation should know what they are choosing to do if they decide to get divorced and weigh the consequences on their kids and how divorce does not improve lives, especially for women. Immunize them against divorce. Vary the way you present it each year and over time you may get folks inviting un-churched friends for this special month.

Pastors, we need to preach the moral values of the Bible in love. We need to preach about the consequences of sinful acts on society and about the sin nature of man. We should not fear preaching about the "dangerous" topics like abortion, adultery, cohabitation, same-sex marriage, homosexuality, divorce, gambling, greed, gossip, sexual immorality. I'm not saying we should preach on these topics exclusively, but we should preach on it more than we have been. We should look at the old sermons given by the stalwarts of the faith; the ancient preachers like Spurgeon, Augustine, Edwards, and the Puritan fathers and preach the dangers, as well as salvation by faith in Christ, as they did. We cannot consider ourselves loving if we *never* warn our flock about danger and always speak of "good" things as they charge headlong into pain and destruction.

Pastors, we need to educate our flock about what is happening in the legislature and town halls around us and how the laws they are making will affect our children and our society. We need to speak out against bad laws that violate biblical values and speak up for good moral laws. We need to teach people what to vote on and the principles behind it. People are perishing, but blessed are those who keep God's moral law.

Teach your congregation how to judge a politician's moral character, to look beyond the politician's words to their past actions, their past votes and their past writings. Teach them how to evaluate a politicians Worldview. Does this politician have a Biblical Worldview? Teach them what a Worldview is.

But you ask, is this "Sunday Sermon" material? Yes it is, since the wrong man or woman in office will cause pain and suffering for innocents. Where else do you teach compassion and love for your fellow man? Keep emphasizing this point. Be bold. Remember, there are biblical answers to almost every aspect of life. Answers that work. Surely it's time we started teaching it again.

By the way, many pastors think that we are blindly stumbling in the dark when it comes to governmental systems that work. But the truth is that there is a system of government that actually works and provides answers to almost all objections. Let me assure you it's not a "socialist" model, but surprise, surprise it's a *biblical* model. There's no space in this book to provide details beyond the smattering that we have, but why not invite Mike Winther from the Institute of Principle Studies to give his ten week Biblical Principles of Government Class (www.principlestudies.org). This will educate your congregation on what a biblical government that is *not* a theocracy should look like. It's not new, nor is it unique to Mike, it's just taken from the Bible and no this government won't oppress non-believers, and guess what, it works. Use his DVD course for small groups if you can't fly him out often enough from Central California.

Invite me to speak; I'll take the heat.

Teach the Controversial issues

Part of teaching the Law is to teach the controversial issues. Why not spend at least two weeks a year on abortion? Show your congregation what an aborted fetus looks like? Show them what each type of abortion results in. Show them the information and how to argue against abortion without using the Bible (see JesusIsInvolvedInPolitics.com/Abortion.htm for details). What are you afraid of? That you may become unpopular? Seriously? Invite Scott Klusendorf (prolifetraining.com) or myself to teach this.

Teach them all the consequences of divorce, teach them why Same-Sex marriage is unbiblical, and teach them the consequences of Homosexual behavior. If you don't educate them on these things who will? Exactly…MTV!

Teach them why politics is related to the law and why the law is related to compassion. Teach this book.

Preach the Gospel of Salvation, use Apologetics.

With over 75% of all youth leaving the church when they get to college because they have only a blind emotional faith, it's time for the Church to teach apologetics to give them a rational faith. It's also important for the Church to reach out to unbelievers. See www.NoBlindFaith for more information.

Get involved politically

We can't just pray and sit on our laurels. Imagine if the Children of Israel had said, "Okay we're just going to pray about this land of Canaan occupation thing, and then wait in our tents for God to strike them dead. After all they are giants and we'd lose miserably." Imagine if they had not marched around Jericho? So, we can't just sit around.

I am asking, pleading, requesting, pastors, Christians and the church in general to get involved in politics, just like Jesus was and is. What does this mean? What does this look like?

Registering to vote

There are 60 million evangelicals in America
Some 24 million (40%) evangelicals are not even registered to vote.[501]
Of the 36 million who are registered to vote, not all vote, only 20.5
million evangelicals voted in 2006.

Imagine if tomorrow just about a 1/5th of those God-fearing men and women not yet registered, did so. Then what if these 5 million more God-fearing men and women decided to vote their biblical values? How would that change this nation? We could stop abortion; halt same-sex marriage; bring back our freedom of religion; bring back sanity to the courts; reduce taxes; stop euthanasia and its abuses; allow mothers to stay home to bring up our kids; reduce the incidence of single family homes; reduce divorce; discourage adultery; reward marriage; reward hard work and entrepreneurship; encourage charitable contributions; reduce crime; reduce government costs; reduce government payrolls; get rid of bad teachers; bring back morality to schools; bring in school vouchers (or better still return education to private charities); stop the homosexual recruitment and brain washing of the young; reduce sexual molestation; reduce murder; reduce gangs; stop the banning of spanking; reduce the amount of time you pastors have to spend on counseling; and pastors we will save your jobs and perhaps your freedom. Whew! Need I go on? Do you think none of these are worthy goals? Do you think Jesus does not care about them? Do you not think this will bring about a mutually prosperous America (at least until what your eschatology predicts will occur).

So, I'm calling pastors to assist in registering believers, making sure they vote and encouraging their flock to be involved in the political process on an intimate basis. Some pastors I know do something called the 5-minute miracle. They have everyone stand up one Sunday morning.

Then they say, "If you are not registered to vote please sit down." Followed by, "Those of you who are standing, if someone is *sitting* next to you, wave your hand and an usher will get you a voter's registration form for them." May I suggest you do this at least twice a year?

These are all non-partisan actions. No one can accuse you of taking sides with individuals and you won't lose your tax deductions. But, if you *don't* do them, the laws may change and you *will* lose your tax deductions and start being taxed on your housing, gas and tuition allowances, as well as your church property. Even as I write this, various atheists groups are trying to pass laws and get judges appointed who will eliminate all religious charitable deductions including the option to opt out of social security. Think it can't happen? With anti-Christian judges appointed by non Biblical Worldview presidents, it's inevitable. Pastors, please don't think you can hide your heads in the sand. As mentioned before, go to www.JesusIsInvolvedInPolitics.com and look up "What Churches Can Do" and you'll get an up to date list of all the activities you can do legally.

---

[501] As compiled and quoted by Dave Barton www.wallbuilders.com/LIBissuesArticles.asp?id=3930

Neil Mammen

Voter guides

Pastors, may I suggest you ask for and allow non-partisan voter guides to be distributed at your church before every election. These guides take Christian moral issues and describe where each candidate stands on them. Candidates are asked to send in their responses and if a candidate doesn't send in a response, it is selected based on the candidate's past votes or their party's platform. They make no recommendations on how to vote, nor do they say what the biblical stance on these issues are. Pastors, we are expecting you to be teaching your flock what the biblical stances are on a regular basis.

Go to www.JesusIsInvolvedInPolitics.com and lookup "Voter Guides," we'll get you a source to get these or guidance to make your own. I'll bet there are lots of people in your congregation who would love to take on this task.

Signature Gathering

Pastors, your help is critical in gathering signatures to put moral propositions on the ballot box. Talk about the importance of the issue from the pulpit then have a table in the back for people to sign, or if you feel comfortable enough, pass out the signature sheets in the bulletin and walk them through signing it. Imagine it was banning of slavery on the table? Imagine it was the destruction of families that would lead to suicides, homicides, depression and gang violence? Again, I bet there are lots of folks in your pews every week who'd love to do this for you.

Give financially

If you are a layperson, may I recommend you auto donate (i.e. schedule your bank to do it automatically) a small or large monthly donation to at least one of *each* of these organizations

Give to legal organizations that defend Christians against laws against speaking out against homosexuality or defend against school principles that forbid 6 year olds from doing a Christian show and tell at school. These include the Alliance Defense Fund (alliancedefensefund.org), Pacific Justice Institute (PJI.org), the American Center for Law & Justice (ACLJ.org) and Liberty Counsel (lc.org). These organizations also provide free legal support to Christians who have been oppressed or discriminated against. Some recent cases include school kids who were forbidden to have a Bible club on campus even though an Islamic club was allowed. There was also librarian at Ohio State University who was discriminated against and threatened with a sexual harassment suit simply because he recommended conservative books along with the left wing academic department's liberal books as reading materials for freshmen.

Give monthly to family organizations like Focus on the Family (FOTF.org) and Family Research Council (FRC.org). They fund studies like the Mapping America project as well as engage with the news media and talk shows and cable news shows. These are all critical to getting the message out there to the public and the legislators.

Give monthly to PACs like FRC Action (FRCaction.org) that accepts non deductible donations and is allowed to work to influence legislation directly by talking to lawmakers.

All these and other recommended organizations can be found at www.JesusIsInvolvedInPolitics.com/RecommendedOrganizations.htm

Invite local candidates to speak at your church

I recommend that pastors consider inviting candidates who are running locally to come speak at their church. As you approach the elections, invite one local candidate each week to speak for ten minutes after a service. If pastors did this, we would see a surge in informed voting. One pastor of ours did this, and it was a tremendous service to the community. In fact, many non-members and people in the community came when they heard that each local politician would be there. I recommend that you inform each candidate that they have to attend the entire service in order to speak afterwards. This will expose them to some good biblical preaching. Plan your sermon topic accordingly. An apologetics sermon seems appropriate, a sermon based on moral laws, how Jesus was not a Socialist, and the difference between goods and rights would be even more strategic.

In the invitation, tell the candidates that you ask all your candidates 7 questions and you want them to answer what they truly believe. Then send them the questions ahead of time:

1. Do you believe in objective moral values?
2. What do you base your morality on?
3. Where do you stand on the issue of homosexuality?
4. Where do you stand on the issue of abortion?
5. Do you know the difference between goods vs. rights? Do think it's the government's job to provide goods? What's the difference between governmental socialism and personal charity?
6. Which law do you think our republic is founded on? Is it changeable?
7. Have you repented and accepted Jesus Christ as your Lord and God and follow the *entire* Bible as your moral guide? Or if they are Jewish: Do you accept the *entire* Law and the Prophets as being from God and will you legislate with that as your moral compass?

They can respond in writing or in their ten minutes up on stage (bad idea). Anything they write is posted on the Church's website for all to read. If they feel awkward answering any of these, then it's very telling to your congregation. Candidates who decline your invitation to speak, are appropriately identified to the congregation. People in the congregation can then make up their own minds on how to vote.

School Boards

School boards have great influence. In recent years, some have forced the teaching of homosexual doctrine, new age mantras, Islamic prayers and other questionable course content. If a majority of the board members were Bible-believing Christians or Jews, this would stop immediately. School Boards hire the principles and superintendents of schools. These are the folks who determine if the homosexual agenda will be pushed in schools – if gay friendly books like Heather Has Two Mommies, will be used in class and so on. Even as I write this, Texas school boards are trying to remove any mention of Christianity from every school book. If they are successful all publishers will be motivated to follow and every state will end up with the faith that founded this nation censored from our children's schools and thus minds. In San Diego, a school board tried to remove a teacher's 25 year old poster that said "In God we Trust." They said that it would insult Muslim students.[502] They seemed to forget that even Muslims believe in God. Next door were posters with Lennon's "Imagine there's no Heaven" and the Dalai Lama, both of which *are* very offensive to Muslims. As you can see, school board seats are powerful positions.

What's even more surprising is that most school board members are elected by a tiny fraction of the voters. This is mainly because no one knows who these people are, and they have no budget with which to obtain publicity. I have seen school board members in San Jose, the 10th largest city in the United States, get elected by margins as small as a few hundred votes. If school board candidates who are God-fearing could post their statement of faith and the fact that they are running for office in local churches and synagogues; and if pastors and rabbis could impress upon their people the importance of this position, just imagine the changes we could effect. The way a pastor would do it is to include the offices that are being sought along with the candidates' name and a one-paragraph testimony of their faith. The pastor should invite all candidates to post their testimony. Those that are not Christ followers or God-fearing Jews, will appropriately have nothing to say but will have had an equal opportunity.

City Boards, Aldermen and County Supervisors

Pastors, of all people should be concerned about who is on the city boards. These are the people who will decide if you can increase the parking density on your church owned private parking lot. These are the folks who fought one of our churches and cost us almost a million dollars in legal fees just so we could move out of one office building into another. Recently, certain city boards decided to declare properties as blighted and forced them to be sold below value to developers so the developers can build new structures and the city can raise more tax revenues. Are you sure that you want your church sitting on some prime real estate to suddenly be declared blighted, forcing you to move? Though this is a gross violation of the constitution, we have a few liberal Supreme Court judges who ensured that this law was not overthrown. The conservatives are still the minority in the Supreme Court, because 25% of Evangelicals voted for Obama in the last election. Obama promptly reappointed a socialist to the next vacant post. Had we been able to put a strict constructionalist in that post, not only would this have been overthrown but even Roe V. Wade (Abortion) could have been overthrown.

So, pastors since today the courts are not on your side, the people *on* that city board are your only chance. I would recommend as a pastor you make it a habit to go down to city hall and get to know these people personally. Ask if you can pray for them. If you have a church of even a 1000 and most of them live in the same area, at election time your church can decide who gets on that city board if you are proactive about it. If you don't have that big a

---

[502] http://www.citizenlink.org/CLtopstories/A000012238.cfm

church, consider banding together with neighboring churches to make a difference.

Pastors can help Christians take control of the unions they are forced to join

Many Christians are forced to pay into unions that have philosophies that they don't agree with. For example, public school teachers in California are forced to pay union dues just to be able to work. Yes, that seems un-American, but it is the status quo. For example, the California Teachers Association (CTA) and the National Education Association (NEA) are not just pro-homosexual; they promote other immoral agendas that have nothing to do with teaching kids. Many Christian teachers pay their dues and then tolerate the immoral stances their unions take. While many states have alternative professional organizations, most teachers don't know about this and they don't have much choice. I believe that if Christian union members were to identify themselves in church or in a secondary organization, they could then band together and start taking control of their local chapters of their unions. Why not leverage the numbers we have? In some areas of the country, a majority of union members may be Christ followers. As with local politicians, pastors could allow teachers to post their testimonies and the fact that they are running for union offices. Let both sides speak so there is no issue of partisanship.

Why don't we try to take back the unions and bring some balance to them? I realize that we may not be successful, but if you are paying dues anyway, why not see if you can get equal representation? Meanwhile, if your state allows it, petition the union to refund the portion of your dues it uses for purely political purposes or join an alternative union. In many cases, there are alternatives. You can search online. For one alternative to your union, see www.aaeteachers.org. Their dues are around $180 a year. Better still; let's elect representatives and a president who will appoint judges who ensure that no state can insist you join a union to work anywhere. The freedom from oppression while you work is also an unalienable right.

Pastors can help start Values Advocacy Councils

In San Jose, a group of churches joined together to start the Values Advocacy Council (www.vac.org). It is funded and run by churches and lay people, and its charter is as follows:

The Values Advocacy Council was formed in 2003 to be a voice for Christian values in public policy matters in Silicon Valley. We work to help elected and non-elected officials to make values based decisions and take values oriented actions. www.VAC.org

What does that mean? It means we work with local pastors and individual Christians to bring to attention to what's going on politically and administratively. For instance, when a school board recently planned to teach sexual "tolerance" material in grade school, we were able to inform parents in the district so they could show up and put an end to that.

We advise and guide local politicians and inform people to show up en-masse whenever there's a critical issue in city hall or a school board meeting at which people are planning to do stupid things. All this is done through the help of local pastors. At this point, on many issues, city officials realize they need to talk to the pastors before making major decisions. If you think about it, if 50 pastors having an average church of 400 adults each, banded together, that would be 20,000 potential voters. Numbers like that change the equation so that elections and policy formation falls more closely in line with God's Moral Will. Being a 503c corporation, churches are allowed to donate to VAC type organizations if approved by their elder boards. Elders, are you with me here? Why not suggest to your pastor that he help start such an organization or help fund one. VAC was founded by pastor David Sawkins of Venture Christian Church and Larry Pegram, a layman.

If you are interested in forming a VAC type organization in your community, visit www.VAC.org and email them for a VAC "starter kit."

What can Christians do?

That was a summary of what pastors can do. What can Christians do? Well, besides running for office at all levels (especially school boards), we can band together to get many things done. We are a powerful voting block. Here are some ideas.

Boycotting Magazines, Movies, TV shows, TV sponsors and Companies, Newspapers

There are probably over 100 million Evangelicals of all ages in the US (60 million of voting age). We are a huge powerful force. Why are we not using that power to change our culture? Christians can stop subscribing to liberally biased newspapers. Let them die on the vine. Over and over again we see cases where TV and newspapers have deliberately lied about things, slanting or twisting words out of context. One remembers how Katie Couric took Sarah Palin's coherent answers and edited them to make her look extreme and incoherent in pure deceit.[503] Remember they have no objective moral values so they feel free to do what they think is "best" for society. They are their own moral standard.

Choose instead to subscribe to newspapers that are not slanted against you and will give you both or all sides of a story. Why are you putting money into the coffers of people who hate your values and give you only one perspective? Whenever my local San Jose Mercury News calls me up to get me to subscribe, I say, "Thanks for calling. I realize you are just doing your job, but if you will, tell your boss I think the paper is too liberal and biased, so I'm not interested." Sometimes they try to argue with me. It doesn't work.

Most newspapers and magazines are on their last legs. It's our duty to make sure the ones that want the whole truth to get out, stay alive, and those that skew stories and issues one way, the liberal way, are not supported by our subscription dollars. Let those who agree with them support them. Let me recommend a good conservative magazine to replace the dying Newsweek or liberal Time, try www.TownHall.com. In the meantime, if you want to find out what the liberals are saying about something, use the Internet. It's free.

Some may point out that many Christians work at liberal newspapers.

---

[503] This is just one example patterico.com/2008/09/25/cbs-has-horrible-transcript-of-palin-interview

Yes, that is true. Two good friends of mine work at the Mercury News. I'm glad they are there. Unfortunately, neither are in a decision-making position, so we can't put economics over morality. In fact, one could argue that if this country moves toward more godly laws, there will be more prosperity and lower taxes. Lower taxes have always spurred the economy. Jobs will come. Christians could also consider an employee buyout of their papers if they align themselves with savvy Christian investors (be careful though as spirituality is not a valid replacement for good business experience).

Get together in your Bible studies and write letters to the editors of local newspapers. If enough of us did it, we'd overwhelm the paper with truth, facts and reason.

We can boycott companies that give or fund organizations that promote unhealthy or blatantly immoral activities. For instance, businessmen can refuse to stay at hotels that show X-Rated movies, see www.cleanhotels.com for a list.

TV shows: did you know that if you have a digital set top box, the cable provider can tell if you are watching a show? I designed this technology *myself* into our settop boxes and headends. We know what you are watching and when. This determines if a show gets advertisers and stays on the air. Recording it to watch later is no different. We know what you record and even when you play it back. This statistic then becomes the incentive to make more shows like that and to charge advertisers more money. With more than 100 million Christian viewers of all ages, this is in our hands folks.

Become a member of the American Family Association. www.afa.org. Donate to them. Support them. AFA is one of the most influential Christian organizations that alert Christians to write to and boycott companies that make anti-Christian policies. They've made a difference in our culture. I recommend you subscribe to and read the AFA magazine.

Buying TV Affiliates

This battle has two fronts. Politics and new laws will change the hearts of those in coming generations, but there is another important scene of skirmish: the culture. Worldly and sinful excesses in American life exert tremendous pressure on our youth. The culture changes, and gradually over time, laws are also changed by those who were changed by the culture – unless the process can be stopped by godly men and women.

As you can guess, one of the strongest influences of culture is the media. Mainly television – ABC, NBC, CBS, and Fox. These networks reach millions of Americans every hour of every day, and in addition to entertainment, there is the news. News outlets are not your friends. They constantly misinform and provide one-sided approaches to news events. They ignore stories that might show them to be wrong.

If I had a few billion dollars, maybe I could buy an entire network and make sure the right kind of stuff was shown. But I don't, and while I'm sure they are around, I don't personally know any Christians who have that kind of money. Yet, if believers were to band together in groups of 20-100, however, they could start to buy up affiliates. A small affiliate in a small market can be as low as $5 million. With a business loan, a group of Christian investors could probably buy it with as little as 30%, or $1.5 million dollars, down.

When I suggested this idea to Fred Barnes of Fox News, he said "That's a great idea, these stations are cash cows." The Internet has not destroying the affiliates. It is ruining newspapers and perhaps the newsrooms of these affiliates, but TV shows are still making money. If groups of Christians were to start buying television network affiliates, they could gradually get control of programming. Affiliates can refuse to broadcast offensive entertainment and ensure that local newscasters (appropriately hired) provide accurate and balanced information despite what network news airs. Over time, Christian owned affiliates could band together and make serious changes, even at the network level. I suggest that we start immediately. Form a group of interested investors and start looking into buying affiliates. Make sure you do your due diligence before you buy anything and try not to bid against fellow Christians. That last thing we want is a price war. Again don't invest blindly, don't think that theological know how is any substitute for business know how. And avoid anything that smells like a ponzi scheme. Invest only the money that if you lost, would not force you to change your current or future planned lifestyle.

Funding Movies with Family Values

As said, there are multiple fronts in this battle. The most important, actually, is culture. We have to engage the culture, and the best way to do this is to help fund and produce family value movies. Opportunities will be posted as they occur on the JesusIsInvolvedInPolitics website. These movies usually make lots of money and beat R rated movies in profit almost every single time. Note, I'm not just talking about going to see the movies I'm talking about being part of the production funding.

On the converse side, stop going to secular movies that promote immorality. Stop subsiding the promotion of immoral values. If 100 million Evangelicals and Catholics stopped watching family destroying adultery promoting movies (and TV shows) tomorrow, we'd see a shift in the culture *and* we'd get better movies. We are funding our own destruction. Make the sacrifice. To find out which movies have family values look up Ted Baehr's www.MovieGuide.org.

Urge Congress to stop supporting PBS and NPR

Sesame Street is a huge moneymaker. If it were to go private and require advertising revenue, I know of few companies that would not get in line to be able to broadcast their shows. Byproducts of Sesame Street characters like Tickle Me Elmo and such toys make billions. Sesame Street does not need tax dollars. In fact, little else on NPR or PBS does. Years ago, when the technology was expensive and community networks did not exist, there was a need for PBS and NPR. Today these networks are a drain on public resources. Much of their programming is aggressively anti-Christian. Or actively promotes other religions and worldviews. We have no problems with people doing this. We just don't think taxpayers should be paying for it. In fact, with a few million dollars and a license from the FCC, you could create a radio or television station in your garage today. You can do it on the Internet without needing any licenses. Just post it on Tangle.com for free and create your own "channel." Digital audio and video equipment including HD cameras are inexpensive. These networks can continue to ask subscribers for money. That's okay. They can even keep the spectrum they already have if they want it. But leave the forced-payment tax base alone.

Stop donating to PBS and NPR yourself. Send that money to the Family Research Council instead. They'll fight to uphold your values, not break down the family and create more pain.

Join and help fund organizations that act as prophets in Washington DC and your local and state governments

Participate in their calling and letter writing campaigns, donate money on a monthly basis. They are the prophets of our times. They keep a pulse on the laws and politicians and the corporations and call them out by name.

Family Research Council: *www.FRC.org*

American Family association: *www.afa.net*

Focus on the Family Action: *www.citizenlink.org*

I recommend subscribing to their Citizen magazine.

To find a local or state organization, please visit www.JesusIsInvolvedInPolitics.com and do a search for "VAC." We plan to have information on local groups there. In the meantime, if you live in the California Bay Area, especially Santa Clara County, please join the Values Advocacy Council (go to VAC.org to sign up) and help us make things happen. You can join as an individual. Other counties, contact us if you want your group posted on our website.

Please also join our mailing list, send an email to: JesusIsInvolvedInPolitics-subscribe@yahoogroups.com.

Visit your Senators and Representatives

One year, I was in Washington D.C. for a Family Research Council "Watchman on the Wall" conference. This is a yearly meeting for pastors. FRC helps with your lodging costs if you are a pastor from a small church. My friend, the founder, and chairman of the Values Advocacy Council, Pastor Dave Sawkins invited me, as well as a number of other pastors, to visit the office of then California Senator Barbara Boxer. It was an off the cuff idea. You can just walk into Congressional offices. So, we did just that.

The lawmaker was not there, but we talked with her aide. We asked if we could pray with her. She stiffened. "No, thanks," she said. We respected that, then told her we disagree with Boxer's stances on basically everything (we itemized them). The aide listened. When we were done, we asked "How many other people tell Boxer and her staff this."

"Actually, you are the first ones," the aide said.

What struck me then is that Christians have gotten tired. We have said, "It is of no use to express ourselves to such a Senator. She is liberal and anti-evangelical." So, we've given up. Now let me ask you this. What if Christians in numbers visited each of their representative's office and spent ten minutes telling their aides that they disagreed with these lawmakers' thinking and positions. What effect would that have? None? I don't think so. At least it would make a ruckus.

So, let me ask you to do this to your senator, whatever state you live in. Be nice. Be polite. It's a no stress situation for you. You after all are the customer in this situation. Do it even for the conservative senators. Remember you don't have to wait to go to D.C. to do this. Your representative has a local office. Why not make this one of your church ministries. You visit the local representatives, give them a piece of your mind and/or offer to pray for them. Organize groups and do this. Home Schoolers; why not go visit your liberal or conservative representatives. Give them a piece of your logic. They may learn a thing or two.

Let no elected official be able to say, "No one has told us this." And don't bunch up. That is, if twelve of you are going, make separate trips to the senator's office. Four visits of three people are more powerful than one trip of ten. While we still have strength, let no one say that nobody objected! If anything, this will keep them busy and prevent them from doing more mischief. Senators have told me that the most influential action is for people to visit or handwrite a note to them. The next most influential is a fax. They've said that they make decisions on as few as three hand-written letters or faxes.

Blogs, FaceBook, and Sunday School classes

Start writing blogs on the ideas in this book and share with your friends. Join our Facebook page and post our comments on your Homepage.

If I may be so bold, buy this book for your friends and challenge them to refute it. Download the free presentations on our website and teach it at your Church or host a Bible Study at your home. Suggest your men's group use this book as their study. Get involved, get educated.

But we must not leave the table

A few years ago, pastors and Christians in Silicon Valley gathered together to move city hall and make their presence know about a key moral issue. They were successful in stopping bad legislation; however, within a few months of this event, these same pastors abandoned all things political. This had the unfortunate effect of leaving those politicians who'd sided with them hung out to dry with no support. They were reviled and attacked in the media and discouraged at every town hall meeting. No pastors showed up to support them. Imagine being the lone voice for godly values against a room full of liberals who call you names and reporters who twist your words the next day in the paper.

One day one of those politicians approached Pastor Dave Sawkins and said. "When are you Christians going to come to the table and stay?"

You see, we can't engage and disengage at will. We have to *stay* engaged. We have to be in it for the long term. We have to be the moral guide to politicians and legislation. Many politicians are in politics for the wrong reasons; many politicians have no moral compass. However, we can guide these folks with consistent engagement, rational dialog, and a healthy explanation of how to logically get from statistical studies to moral values to legislation. Dave Sawkins went on to found the Values Advocacy Council as a result of that meeting (www.VAC.org), perhaps you can start an equivalent one in your city).

Pastors, they should know you at city hall because you and other pastors are having individual or group lunches on a regular basis with the City Councilmen and women and the mayors and the supervisors. Then when you show up for a moral issue, there's already a precedent of respect and friendship.

Let's not leave the table anymore!

Neil Mammen

Thirty-eight

The situation in the churches is characterized by weariness with the struggle, by uncertainty of purpose and by lack of courage.
   Author revealed below.

Looking at the lack of Christian involvement in politics, seeing that many of us don't even vote, we come to the terrible terrible realization that the only reason the massacre of unborn babies is still legal in America is because of us Christians. The blood of these innocents is really upon our hands, because if we wanted to change it we could, but we haven't.
   My response to a self proclaimed pro-lifer who hadn't bothered to vote.

...we [Christians] have filled every place among you—cities, islands, fortresses, towns, market places, the very camp, tribes, companies, palace, senate, forum—we have left nothing to you but the temples of your gods.
   Quintus Septimus Florens Tertullian.
   A Christian Apologist mocking the Romans.

Conclusion: We Can Indeed Win This Battle

Many years ago, at one of my first startup companies, we were asked to bid on a large project for a TV Head End (where channels are aggregated and distributed). As a young 32 year old, recently promoted Chief Technology Officer, I was given the RFQ (request for quote). That's a document that describes the product the customer wants. We are to read it, understand it, create architectural documents and give them a quote for designing and building it.

Reading it, I was startled. The requirements for the project matched, feature for feature, an architectural document I had personally written a few months earlier, when *we* were coming up with our *own* product idea. Every feature I'd put in that document was a feature the customer wanted. I turned to our marketing vice president and said, "This is an amazing coincidence."

He laughed, "Where do you think they got the feature set from?" They had obviously gotten it from *our* document. They wanted a quote on what I was *already* designing. Our VP then turned to the executive staff at the table and said, "Gentlemen, this is ours to lose!"

Do you get that? The deal was "ours to lose." Our competitors had a high "barrier to entry," in other words. They would have to work hard to win this deal. We were the only people who could "lose" it. Failure to win the contract would be solely our responsibility. "This is ours to lose!"[504]

---

[504] Yes, we did *win* the contract.

It's ours to lose

I started this chapter with a quote about the church becoming weary. Do you know who said this?

In the late 1930's, the Nazis had waged a campaign to convince the pastors in Germany that Romans 13 indicated that God wants the Church to submit to those in authority even when the authorities are evil.[505] Sadly, they were successful with almost all churches except for the "Confessing Church."

So, who said that the church was growing weary? It wasn't a Christian. It was Reinhard Heydrich, head of the Gestapo. He said this in 1938[506] when the church fell silent about the way Germany was slowly changing. He said it as he saw the church give up the fight and meekly align itself with the National Socialist party. He was saying this was a *good* thing for the Nazis.

Do you see? This is what people who oppose Christian values want you to believe – that the fight is no longer worth the effort. It is a lost cause. It's not worth going out to vote. Or it's not worth voting based on Biblical Principles. That we should submit to any and all governmental authority, good or evil.

But be encouraged, the truth of the matter is that a large majority of Americans, even those who are not evangelical or Catholic or God-fearing Jews *do* agree with our values. For instance[507]:

1. 89% believe religion and morality are important to them and their *family*.
2. 79% believe religion and morality are important to this *country*.
3. 64% believe there is not enough religion in schools. Only 8%, a small minority, believe there is too much religion in schools.
4. 87% approve of the reference to "The Creator" in the Declaration of Independence. Only 6% disapprove (This minority, clearly, do not realize that if you take out the Creator, the entire Declaration and Constitution falls apart.)
5. 88% approve of the reference of "One Nation under God," in the Pledge of Allegiance. Only 7% disapprove.
6. 78% approve of the Ten Commandments appearing in court houses across America. Only 12% disapprove.
7. 81% oppose removing crosses and other such monuments from public parks and other public property. Only 8% strongly approve.
8. 94% approve of a moment of silence allowing children to pray silently if they want to in public schools. Only 3% strongly disapprove.
9. 90% approve of a Christmas tree or Menorah being placed on public property during the holiday season. Only 5% strongly disapprove.
10. 82% oppose banning all prayer in public schools. Only 9% approve.
11. 79% oppose forbidding high school children from saying thanks to God in a graduation speech. Only 14% strongly approve banning it.
12. 83% oppose the left's model that the best way to protect religious freedom is to make sure no religious expression is permitted in public buildings.
13. Over 51% of America is pro-life, with almost 86% agreeing that abortion

---

[505] I deal with this Rom 13 passage in the Objections Appendix and show how it's been twisted.

[506] The Nazi Persecution of the Churches, 1933-1945 John S. Conway. Regent College Publishing (February 1, 1997) pg 220.

[507] Unless indicated, statistics from AmericanSolutions.com, 2009

should be either illegal or should be restricted compared to the almost no restrictions currently.[508]

14. More than 57% of Americans are against same-sex marriage.[509]

15. New studies show that Abstinence Education works[510] and parents are now insisting that all health sex education include teaching abstinence.

16. 80% of Americans say it is the responsibility of parents to teach their children about sex. Only 11% say schools should explain sex to children.[511]

The features Christian and other conservative activists want, are what the "customers" want. Their "feature requests" are from our "documents." Do you see? We can win this battle. *It is ours to lose.* Why are we hiding? Because we believe the liberal media? Will you stand up and be counted? Hear it again. It's ours to lose!

People are asking to be led. Even unsaved people listen to good ideas and follow. People are asking for sound moral leadership. They are seeking guidance. Who will lead them?

Add to this the fact that we can win this even without the rest of America; if we God-fearing men and women would just register and vote our moral values, we'd win *every* major election. Pastors, you are the key to doing that.

Yet time is running out

Older generations are dying, and as we have demonstrated, laws change hearts and younger people are influenced by current laws and culture. If pastors aren't training them in the law they will not know or love the truth. And there is a feedback effect. Like an microphone and amp getting into a feedback loop and giving you an unpleasant high pitched whine, bad laws yield unpleasant and evil social consequences, which lead to more bad laws and bad moral values, which in turn lead to worse social consequences, and so it goes, a spiral of destruction that is almost impossible to stop. Of course, the left will always suggest more governmental welfare and control to solve each problem that they have created themselves, until our enemies *without,* can easily destroy us because of the weaknesses *within* (of our nation and culture). This is the lesson from the history of civilizations far larger than ours that have died.

A few years ago, even liberal California passed a constitutional amendment to limit marriage to be between a man and a woman. Every year more and more of the younger untrained generation, get old enough to vote, pundits predict that in a few years that same proposition will not pass.

It may be too late for California, but it isn't for the rest of America. Yet in a few decades it may be. This is ours to lose. Will you help stem the tide?

We opened this chapter with a quotation from Tertullian. Tertullian was a Christian. He was mocking the pagan religious Romans who believed

---

[508] www.msnbc.msn.com/id/30771408/

[509] www.gallup.com/poll/118378/majority-americans-contine-oppose-gay-marriage.aspx

[510] http://www.lifenews.com/nat5950.html

[511] http://www.rasmussenreports.com/public_content/lifestyle/general_lifestyle/january_2009/80_say_parents_should_teach_their_children_about_sex

they could defend themselves by retreating from market places into their religious temples. They hid behind their faith. We all know what happened to them with the onslaught of Christianity in the marketplaces, the forum and the culture. Sadly, today we may be seeing the tables turned and are starting to hear:

> *"...we anti-Christians have filled every place among you – cities, islands, fortresses, towns, market places,* art, theatres, *philosophy,* universities, newspapers, magazines, TV shows, movies, popular music, *the very camp, tribes, companies,* governorships, *palace, senates, forum – we have left nothing to you but the* evangelical Bible churches of your God. *"*

Is this the mocking message being sent *to* Christians instead of from them? It's time to turn the tide, to take back the marketplaces and the palace, the senate and the forum. It's time to go back to the methodology of the early church and Tertullian. It's time for churches and individual Christians to take a stand in politics and culture, just as Jesus and his followers and the Old Testament prophets did.

If we don't act, we will be persecuted. In January of 2007, two men were arrested on public property for merely handing out Gideon Bibles.[512] Something the Gideons have been doing for at least a century. They were not trespassing as that charge was thrown out. Why were they arrested? Because the arresting officer did not like Christians. He said, "Now you can pray to Jesus all the way to jail." That's the sort of thing you hear in China not the U.S. Do you realize what is happening? America is becoming Yemen. It's illegal to witness to someone who is not a Christian in Yemen.

If we don't do anything America will change and one day like my father once told me, I may have to tell my son.

> *Son, we have to leave America, because it's illegal to give a Bible to a non-Christian in... the United States of America.*

The courts are biased. What kind of judge do you want to have adjudicating your crime of being a Christian? Who do you want to have appointed him? Which president? Which governor? Whose votes? And where will we go? As Ronald Reagan said, "If freedom is lost here, there is no place to escape to."

Don't imagine that you and I won't be next. Remember in my life I've seen that when they come, they usually start with the pastors.[513]

> ***But we can win this battle! If we make a stand!***
> ***Will you make a commitment to stand with us?***
> ***Will you say, "Not on our watch!"?***
> ***If so, email me[514] and spread the word.***
> ***Let's start by convincing just the non-voting Christians***
> ***why they need to vote biblically in the next election.***
> ***Let's get your pastor on board!***

This is OURS TO LOSE!

---

[512] http://www.wnd.com/news/article.asp?ARTICLE_ID=55304

[513] Like they have done in China, India, the Middle East and Sweden.

[514] Stand@JesusIsInvolvedInPolitics.com

Neil Mammen

APPENDICES

AND

NOTES

Q: Your type really makes me puke, you vacuous, coffee-nosed, malodorous, pervert!!!

M: Look, I CAME HERE FOR AN ARGUMENT; I'm not going to just stand...!!

Q: Oh, oh I'm sorry, but this is Abuse.

M: Oh, I see, well, that explains it.

Q: Ah yes, you want room 12A, just along the corridor.

M: Oh, Thank you very much. Sorry.

Q: Not at all. I'm sorry. Arguments are 2 doors down, this is Abuse.

The Argument Sketch, Monty Python

1+1 = 2 is a true statement even if a Nazi were to state it.
No Blind Faith, "Objective Truth" Sunday School Class

Afterword:
This Has Been An Argument, Not An Opinion

It's been quite a journey and I hope it has been a learning and transforming experience. In these pages, I have presented a number of arguments. By this, I don't mean I'm being contentious and mean-spirited. What I mean is that I am providing rationally thought out theses along with logic and facts that attempt to prove them correct.

As I have said before, I might be wrong. Only a fool would think it is impossible to be wrong on issues like this. However, if you remember what we learned in our College Logic 101 classes: There are only two ways to refute an argument, you have to do either one of the following:

a. Show that the facts are wrong or incomplete or
b. Show that the logic is faulty.[515]

Either of these must be shown to refute the entire argument, not just a small issue within it. There is no other way to disprove an argument.

Remember this, dear reader, if you are ever caught in such a situation, especially if you are trying to argue for the ideas presented in this book: Name calling and abuse –i.e. "You vacuous, coffee-nosed, malodorous, pervert" or "You are intolerant" or "He is an idiot," also known as the ad hominem fallacies, may give temporary enjoyment to some, but fortunately they do nothing to defeat an argument.

As the quote at the beginning of this chapter says, "1+1 = 2 is a true statement even if a Nazi were to state it." In on-line debates I've gone as far as

---

[515] Part of showing that logic is wrong is showing equivocation of terms – that is, the way I use a word in one part of the argument is not way I use it elsewhere. Thanks to Gregory Koukl of Stand to Reason (www.str.org) for this.

to say, "Okay, so let's assume that I am mean spirited, intolerant and oppressive. You still need to explain why my argument is wrong."

The fact that the person making the statement may have an ulterior motive or is cruel or is mean is irrelevant unless you are planning to accept their statements on blind faith.[516] If anything, when your opponents call you names, it may point to the strength of your argument because they don't know how *else* to defeat it. Or it may indicate their ignorance – show that they have done no research and are going by feelings. It may also suggest lack of intelligence. The opposing party may be incapable of logically processing what you have told them. However, I doubt you will make many friends by pointing out the latter.

Just my opinion?

Scott Klusendorf is an excellent and winsome pro-life debater who travels around the world teaching people cohesive rational arguments against abortion.[517] According to audiences, Scott always wins his debates against prochoicers.[518] Apparently Planned Parenthood will not let anyone in their organization debate him anymore, (if this is not so, please contact me and I will personally set up a debate with Scott at a local university). In the introduction to one of his talks, Scott discusses an interesting event on Bill Maher's now-cancelled show "Politically Incorrect." On this particular installment of the show, supermodel Kathy Ireland (trained by Scott and Gregory Koukl from Stand to Reason) presented a scientific, rational and philosophical case as to why abortion is morally wrong. At the end of the argument Bill Maher, said, "Yes, Kathy, but that's just your view." But this makes no sense. Ireland had presented an *argument*, not a view, not a preference, not an opinion. Maher was either unable to refute her argument or ignorant about what an argument is. As we know, his response to Kathy is *not* how one refutes an argument.

So, you may run into this after presenting the argument in this book to others. The person you are talking to may say, "Well, that's just your opinion."

Yet, that's not true. You did not provide an opinion. You provided an *argument*. This is very different from an opinion. The only time this would be an opinion is if the facts and the logic don't lead to a conclusion and some sort of hypothetical jump has to be made. However, *even if that is the case,* the onus is upon *them* to show that the argument is wrong. In fact, if they can't disprove your argument but still disagree with it, it is *they* who have an unsubstantiated blind opinion and not you.

Some folks may say, "I guess we'll have to agree to disagree."

But that is still silly. They can't "agree to disagree" without some

---

[516] By the way, I don't recommend this to anyone, as even well intentioned people can be mistaken and mislead others. Haven't we seen this happen many times in history?

And yes, of course, it also applies to everything I say as well. Be kind enough to check it, test it. Email me and correct me if I am wrong at Errors@JesusIsInvolvedInPolitics.com

[517] Scott can teach you and your church these winning arguments as well. Go to www.prolifetraining.com to schedule Scott.

[518] In polls of the audiences, both pro-choicers and pro-lifers repeatedly agree that Scott presents a better, more rational, scientific, and ethical argument.

Neil Mammen

valid rational basis to disagree. Unless the argument has left them with some room for multiple conclusions, it's silly to say "let's agree to disagree." And if that is the case, it's up to them again to show that multiple valid conclusions can be derived from the same facts.

Once while arguing on a mailing list with a liberal about the Just War Doctrine, he said, "Well, I don't buy it!"

When I asked "Why?" He just repeated, "I just don't buy it."

But that's ridiculous. If you are going to argue, you have to present a counter argument or a rebuttal. Merely saying that "you just don't buy it" is as good as saying, "I know you presented a logical argument with facts; but I can't refute your facts or show your logic is invalid so I'll ignore them."

Refuting parts of the argument

In this book I have at times provided information facts and arguments which, though useful knowledge and perhaps interesting points, may not be germane or vital to the central argument. On occasion, I also provided extra material that I believe augment my primary thesis. It would be fallacious for someone to bring up a new fact that counters one of these side arguments and assume that it negates *all* the arguments or the fundamental argument made in this book. To defeat the previous arguments, you would have to show why this new fact specifically invalidates *all* the arguments presented previously.

In doing additional research for this book,[519] I read a number of books on politics and religion. One of them, naturally, was Tom Minery's "Why We Can't Stay Silent," Tyndale House Publishers (March 2002). Minery has an excellent and easily readable book, which I recommend to all who are interested in more arguments to support this cause. I also ran into a website by a pastor and brother in Christ who disagrees with the premise Minery and I are arguing for. He uses one Bible verse (Gal 2:21) and a Straw Man (Politics is all about compromise) as a rebuttal to the Minery book. The pastor seems to think that his one interpretation of this "new" material is enough to rebut Minery's book in its entirety. But that is simply illogical. He may have had a good point (he doesn't, as I show in the objections appendix), and it may appear to address one or two of Minery's points effectively, (again I show it does not in the objections appendix). To refute Minery's entire case, however, the author of the website would have had to show why Minery's *entire* set of arguments is wrong or refuted successfully by this one verse. As explained, it is not enough to bring up a new issue or make a single assertion.[520]

---

[519] Occasionally I've heard what I call the "preconception" complaint. People say, "Well you wanted to prove this point, you had a preconception of it, so you went looking for facts and writings, such as Tom's book, that supported you. Or you read into these facts your conclusion."

However, having a theory that you think fits the facts and then seeking additional facts to back up the theory does not invalidate the theory on its own. We do this often as engineers and scientists. We call if predictive confirmation. Many great scientific discoveries were first preconceived theories. To invalidate a theory, you have to show that the facts do not support it or the logic is wrong. When coming up with theories, we usually add another requirement, that the theory is falsifiable. In all these arguments, I've done my best to evaluate whether conclusions proceed logically from the facts. But we can all make mistakes. If you disagree, email us: disagreements@JesusIsInvolvedInPolitics.com

[520] I have dealt with this verse in this book and shown that it has no bearing on the argument I presented even if you interpret it the way the web page author did.

People who don't hold to the validity of the Bible

This book was written for Christ followers and Jews who believe the Bible (the OT for the Jews) is the infallible and inerrant Word of God as originally written by the apostles and prophets. However, this book was not written *to* defend the accuracy or the inspiration of the Bible. If you do not believe the Bible is inspired or accurate, I encourage you to check out the many resources we have at www.NoBlindFaith.com. There we will provide you with a rational argument to show that the Bible (specifically the New Testament) is within a 99.8% accuracy of the original autographs,[521] and we have 100% assurance of the content.

Apologetics

I've referred to apologetics often in this book. Apologetics is the defense of Christianity using facts, logic, reason, science, history and philosophy. Using apologetics we can prove it is most reasonable to believe:

1. That God exists
2. That the Bible has been accurately transmitted (mentioned above)
3. That Jesus historically existed and claimed to be God
4. That the Apostles died for their claim that they saw Jesus die and saw him *physically* risen from the dead
5. That Jesus actually rose from the dead *physically*, proving He is God and the Bible is true.

Apologetics is critical for the youth of today. Our pastors spend all their time developing an *emotional* faith in our kids. Yet, tragically anywhere from 93% to 75% of all kids who are in Sunday School today, will leave the faith when they get to college. One of the main reasons the kids cite is that their faith based only on *emotions* could not stand the *rational* scrutiny of their professors and their peers when they got to college. By teaching your kids apologetics, you can reverse those statistics from 75% *leaving* to 75% *staying*.

However, you cannot count on the Church teaching your kids. For the church only has a 17% influence on your kids. Their peers, the media and their teachers have a 28% influence. The good news is that *you* parents have a 57% influence. So parents, you have to develop a culture of apologetics in your home, where you, the parent are doing the research and answering your kid's questions. He will get answers! Make sure they are rational and historical and come from you, not his atheistic professor. Imagine if one of your kids had a disease, would you not become an expert on the disease and it's cures? Well your kids *have* a disease, it's called a sin nature and the world is trying to constantly keep them ill. When will *you* become an expert and participate in their cure?

May I recommend you visit NoBlindFaith.com and using the links and information provided there become your child's best Apologetics Teacher.

Develop a Culture of Apologetics in Your Home!
Apologetics, Theology, Relationship
Rational Faith!

---

[521] We have all the options for the 0.2% variance, so there are 0% unknowns.

Neil Mammen

Attack: People who think they are right, bother me.
Rebuttal: Do you think you are right about that? (Unsaid: Do you bother
   yourself?)
   "How to detect self-refuting suicide statements"
   No Blind Faith Sunday School class

Appendix II:
Burning The Straw Men

As I mentioned in the opening chapter of this book, many people have preconceived ideas of what I am trying to say when I say that Christians should be involved politically. This appendix attempts to answer those objections to clear the way to a mutual understanding.

Objection 1. You are just arrogant to think you have all the answers.

I was debating with a Christian friend on FaceBook. At one point she responded with an "I'm glad you think you have it all figured out Neil." Her point when pressed, was that she thought I was being arrogant to think that I'd found "all" the answers.

I found that amusing because I had never made any claims to having found "all" the answers to anything. I'd logically and carefully been able to derive *some* answers to a *few* particular issues. And to tell the truth, I hadn't really come to any different conclusion that millions of other Christians before me had already come to, in the 20 centuries before I was born.

Her so called refutation, was simply an ad hominem fallacy, it was also invalid and a suicide statement. I'll explain what that is in a second.

It's an ad hominem fallacy, because she was calling me names and accusing me of being arrogant rather than dealing with the facts and the argument I'd presented to her. Maybe I *am* arrogant, but what does that have to do with whether I'm right or wrong. Are arrogant people never right? I do hope I am not arrogant. It is not my wish to be and it is not what I strive to be, but at the same time it is not a rebuttal of my argument.

Second, any accusation about figuring it *all* out is like rejecting something a physics researcher is working on by saying, "I'm glad you've figured it *all* out." No, he hasn't figured it *all* out, but his research has led him to certain conclusions that you may not like. Yet, being disparaging about his efforts to create a cohesive understanding does not contribute to the discussion and only mocks the effort. It's actually invalid, intolerant and mean spirited.

Thirdly, it's a suicide statement because when my friend made this particular claim, she was automatically presuming that she had "it all figured out" about me being wrong. A suicide statement is a statement that refutes itself the minute you state it. We go into detail about suicide statements in this book. To show the hypocrisy of this question we merely ask, "Have you gotten my being *wrong* all figured out?" Which is followed by, "If you have figured it all out, why doesn't your question apply to yourself? Why don't you consider *yourself* arrogant to have figured *that* out? And if you aren't sure of *all* the answers yourself, how do you know that I am wrong?"

As you can see it's pure silliness.

Of course, I could be wrong. I have been before, and I will be again. But then let's discuss the particulars of why and where you think this book may be wrong, I'm all for that. Hopefully you can see why calling people arrogant for providing facts and conclusions is not really a mature or valid response.

Objection 2. Aren't you suggesting that we should create a United States with the Christian equivalent of the Muslim Sharia Law – that is, take Biblical Laws and legislate verbatim from them?

Horrors! Absolutely not! Despite many alarmists who try to imply that that is what Christians want to do, we are not trying to create a Christian version of the Taliban. We would never want to do that. Never ever! I *do* think we should use the Bible as a guide, but I do *not* recommend legislating directly from it. We talk about this in great detail in this book. I do not want to experience any new version of the Spanish Inquisition, nor do I want to see us legislating biblical Ceremonial, Judicial or Regulatory laws (these are itemized in this book).

One reason we do not wish to legislate from the Bible is an obvious one that should strike fear into all Christians' hearts. It is the idea that we'd have a group of men who feel that they have the divine authority to interpret the Bible for the rest of us and write laws on that basis. This idea scares me, and it struck fear into the hearts of our founding fathers. That is why this book articulates clearly how we think laws should be discovered.

Second, state run churches turn people away. Look at Europe and we see what governmental churches did to those nations. People started to associate the inefficiencies, impersonal-ness and all the negative connotations of the government with the church. In fact, as Os Guinness implies in his speech at the Veritas Forum,[522] if you look at the Scandinavians, the number of Christians and Church goers amongst the Scandinavian American immigrants is far higher than the Church attendance in any of the Scandinavian countries today. Why? Culturally they are the same. So, what is different? It is their state-run churches (and perhaps socialism). So, at no point do we want the government to be associated with the church or vice versa. What we want instead, as this book describes, is to have godly men and women as representatives within the government directing its paths. There is a significant difference. In one, there are Christians *in* government, elected by the voters, in

---

[522] Os Guinness, The Veritas Forum, A World Safe for Diversity: Living with Our Deepest Differences in a World of Exploding Pluralism, speech given at Georgia Institute of Technology April 2009. Note I don't completely agree with all of Guinness conclusions regarding Right Wing backlash, but his facts I trust are accurate.

the other, which we do not want, the government *is* Christian. In addition, we note the requirement of defending the value of each moral law before we recommend it as legislation, never suggesting that is should be imposed by fiat or by the decree of the church.

Objection 3. Christians talking politics will scare non-Christians away from the Gospel.

Nothing in this book should scare non-Christians who think rationally and seek the truth. Nor at any point do I suggest that we do anything unreasonable. At no point do I suggest that we subvert the Constitution or violate the concepts on which this great nation was founded. And I never want any Christian to resort to using the Bible as the *only* justification for political or legal action.

In fact, I argue consistently that though we may have a biblical basis for certain actions, when it comes to convincing non-Christians, we should be ready to support those actions using science and statistical analysis. These approaches should comfort a non-Christian much more than the way many Christians have acted in their experience so far.

Secondly, I am calling Christians to do their constitutional duty and exercise their constitutional rights. That is all. It is simple and basic citizenship. Indeed, I am trying to show Christians that they have not only a duty to the United States but a moral and godly obligation to carry it out. If I refer to the Bible in this process, it is because in those cases I am appealing to Christians only.

Many years ago, I got into an argument with non-Christian friend. She was telling me that it was wrong for me to go around trying to convince people that abortion is wrong. I looked at her and asked her this, "Are you saying that I do not have the right to give people my opinion or try to convince them to vote a certain way? Are you saying I don't have the right to try to encourage people who agree with me to register and vote?"

She looked at me for a long second and then nodded. "I guess that is un-American, isn't it?"

Yes, it is.

Truth

*John 18:37 [Jesus said:] "...In fact, for this reason I was born, and for this I came into the world, to testify to the **truth**. Everyone on the side of truth listens to me."*

Non-Christian readers, please be assured that I am interested in the truth. This may sound trite, but it is not. I really am interested in rational thinking, logical conclusions, and real world solutions. Christianity is meaningless unless it has a real world, 4-dimensional, time and space effect. So, if you can show that my facts are wrong or my logic is flawed, I am willing to listen and change my mind. It would be idiotic not to.

Christians in general are not here to win under any circumstances. Twisting the truth is not what we are "about." We fundamentally believe that only the truth will set us free, so why would we want to believe a lie? What would we gain? It would be self-defeating. True, some Christians are self deluded and would rather hang on to traditions and the familiar even if it is false. I call these folks "Superstitious Christians." Thinking Christians want to explore all the facts and come to valid conclusions. You may not agree with us, but you do not need to be afraid of us because all we are doing is seeking the truth.[523]

If you fear the truth, that is another matter. Then you may need to fear us. If you are reading this book, however, I doubt that you fear the truth. But remember to read it with an open mind. Maybe you've been wrong so far. Only completely close-minded people think they can't be wrong. Don't get me wrong. I'm close-minded about some things (like that fact).

Logic

So let us dialog rationally and see where it leads us. As you read this, *do not let the consequences of your logic force you to abandon the logic*. Let me explain.

Often I have explained things to both Christians and non-Christians and found, to my dismay, that when we started the discussion they agreed that my facts and logic were sound, but at some point, they realized that that conclusion was disturbing. So, they abandoned their reasoning. One lady, for instance, said, "Wait, this means if what you are saying is correct, then my family is not going to heaven." She then abandoned all what she'd derived and been happy with up till then. Unable to disprove what she'd just been agreeing with, she let blind emotions take over.

Objection 4. Right Wing Christian involvement in politics has created a backlash.

What is funny about this statement is that it's partially right. But first, I'd argue that Right Wing Christian involvement only arose as a *consequence* of the attacks that were *already* taking place on Christian values and attacks on the poor and defenseless. Where was the Right Wing when Roe V. Wade was passed? I'll tell you where, it was sleeping or didn't exist. How about the gay indoctrination movement which started in the 1970's, the sexual revolution which has damaged millions of children and lives, the cultural attacks by Hollywood which eroded the family, taking God out of school which eliminated morality. Note I'm not even talking about prayer here.

There was no "Right Wing Christian movement" when those things started. The Right Wing movement was specifically started by people who were worried about the direction our country was taking; a worry validly arrived at due to all the anti-Christian movements. I would say they woke too late and too slowly. Yet had they not gotten involved, one can honestly say that Ronald Reagan would not have been elected, the Soviet Union would still be around oppressing Christians in every continent, and abortions would not have gone down 22%. Not only would prayer not be allowed in schools but by

---

[523] Of course, you could argue that some people wish to be self-deluded so they can be psychologically comforted that they know the truth. But today with the great growth of apologetics -- the historical, rational, and scientific evidence for the truth of Christianity -- these folks are rapidly decreasing in numbers. We are on the side of the truth seekers. It's important to note that Christianity is the only religion whose founder and Holy Book condemns blind faith and emphasizes physical proof and verified evidence.

now Christian clubs would not be allowed in schools, churches all over the country would be forced out of their towns by zoning laws, crosses would be removed from National Cemeteries (it's being tried as we speak) and preaching from Leviticus would be banned, the list goes on. Saying that a backlash was created by Christian involvement seems rather silly when Christian involvement itself *was* the backlash created by the attacks on our values.

Secondly, we must ask, why is a backlash wrong or unexpected? What was the backlash caused when William Wilberforce wanted to free the slaves? Have you done any research on that? If you have you'd realize that the social and political backlash was enormous. Wilberforce and his team of abolitionists were made into pariahs. What about when child labor laws were first attempted by the Lord Shaftesbury, Anthony Ashley Cooper?[524] Do you think there was a backlash? Of course there was. Why is this considered unacceptable? Do we not think that selfish and sinful men and women (even if they are also Christians) will not fight to maintain their sinful ways and ignore the plight of the poor and oppressed? Does this mean that whenever there is a backlash, we Christians should back off, become passive and let it happen? Any movement to impose or enforce a moral law will encounter a backlash. Ever tried this with your kids? How about a roving mob? Sometimes the backlash *will* result in your persecution. Did the fight for equal rights create a backlash? Blacks and whites were killed for that. Welcome to persevering for your faith, morality and true social justice. Will we stand or are we unprincipled wimps?

Objection 5. You are implying that politics is the most important thing facing our world or our country today.

Oh no. Absolutely not. Our first commandment is to love God. Our second commandment is to love our neighbors. The biggest problem facing our world today is that some of our friends and fellow humans are going to be separated from God from all eternity. This is the most urgent concern. If we love our neighbors, besides feeding them (which we do) and sending doctors to heal them (which we also do), the most loving thing to do is to make sure they don't spend eternity away from God. To do that, we must make sure they have an opportunity to hear the gospel presented clearly in a kind and loving way.

This imperative is even more poignant when you realize there are about 2 billion Christians in the world today. Let's assume that only 25% of those are real "John chapter 3 born again Christ followers." If each one of us in that group would see fit to focus on the calling of evangelism; and manage to lead just two people to Christ in the next year; within four years the *entire world* would have come to the saving knowledge of our Lord Jesus Christ.[525]

---

[524] Alvin J. Schmidt, How Christianity Changed the World (formerly called "Under their Influence"). Zondervan, 2004

[525] Here's how the math works. Year 1: 0.5B lead 1B to Christ. Year 2: 1B lead 2B to Christ. Year 3: 2B lead 4B to Christ. Year 4: We've run out of people to lead to Christ because 0.5B + 1B + 2B + 4B is already greater than the population of the earth. Of course, we realize that not everyone will accept Christ, but one of my classes had fun with this, imagining that towards the end, finding non-Christians would be so hard, that people would be scrambling to find and witness to at least one non-Christian. It's a great thought -- if only we could be used by God to do that!

Just four years? Wow!

We must realize, of course, that not everybody will be saved. In fact, until now there has never been a time in the earth's history when a majority of the humans alive were saved. But that does not mean we should not try to achieve that goal.

My point, in short, is that I firmly believe that our greatest focus should be on presenting the message of salvation to those around us in such a way that it reaches them effectively. This may require debating with them in the marketplace as Paul did, or traveling the world over and preaching the gospel, as all the apostles did. It may require feeding the poor and healing the sick, as everyone including the early church did, or it may involve other approaches and methods. My favorite strategy is to teach apologetics and provide a rational defense of the faith and move people away from any superstitious beliefs. In this way, we can show them that blind faith is unbiblical. Christianity is not a blind faith. It is a rational faith built on a solid historical and logical foundation.

We are called to communicate the Gospel and make disciples, and for this very reason we should be involved in politics. If we ignore politics for even a few years, we won't be able to do the most important thing we have been asked to do. Let me say that again. If we ignore politics for even a few years, the face of America and the world will change, and we will be prevented from communicating the Gospel and evangelizing as we do today and will instead be spending our time trying to survive, as Russian churches did in the 1970's and Chinese churches are today.

It is because we need to maintain the freedom of the church to obey the Great Commission that we should be involved in politics.[526]

Objection 6. But all Politics is nasty and dirty and Christians should not be involved in it?

Politics is not nasty or dirty in itself. It's that way because nasty and sinful people are involved in it to gain power or wealth or fame.

I think we can summarize that there are three kinds of people who get involved in politics.

The first kind, I call them Fame Seekers, seem to crave attention, money and power. Many times these individuals have no real foundational principles. They feel their way through morality, voting whatever provides them more power or more popularity. They are happy to compromise. These individuals are dangerous in that they go along with whatever principle is popular and they are very hard to pin down. They are who we commonly think of when we think of compromising politicians. In the text of this book, we called them Aaron leaders. Martin Luther King called them thermometers (instead of thermostats). They usually end up being moderates, because they have no fundamental core values except the value that says get reelected and

---

[526] You may object saying: But what about the early church, they obeyed the Great Commission while being persecuted? Here's what's different. If America and the Church do not stand strong, Islam will take over the world. Churches have not grown very fast under Islam ever, except when God moves supernaturally. Second, the early church escaped to other countries. But that's not possible anymore. If freedom is lost here, where will we escape to?

Neil Mammen

gain more power or fame. They speak enough "Christianese" to lure the ignorant Christian voter, and they are liberal enough to lure the liberal voters. Usually you can identify them in that they are the ones who flip flop on their stances without good justification. For instance, I'm always happy if a previously pro-choice politician becomes pro-life. Yet, if he cannot explain in *definite* terms what his reasoning for becoming pro-life was, I think we can immediately realize it was a switch of convenience and we can point to them as an Aaron leader. We've seen this with politicians on both sides. Remember a moderate conservative is really a liberal and will manage to compromise conservative and biblical principles to death. You see left wing ideology is pure compromise so compromise is fine for that agenda. But conservative and biblical ideology is about principles, principles that work, and if you compromise a little, you end up with left wing ideology. It's like saying this glass of water is pure, it just has a few drops of sewage.

The second kind of person who becomes involved in politics is what we could call the Principled Politicians; they see a problem and then run for office to solve the problem. These include Christian politicians, Liberal politicians and Libertarian politicians. They have an agenda; they are there to execute that. They stand for their values regardless of the popularity of that value. I respect these kinds of people for their steadfastness, even when they are liberal and adhere to principles that I strongly disagree with. You know where you stand with respect to them. I call these folks the Joshua leaders. They are the thermostats. That is they are the ones who decide when the heat should be turned on or off. There are very very few of these today. Sadly, without support from those who agree with them, after a few years in power, these folks tend to end up becoming Aaron leaders. With Christian Joshua leaders, the only way to ensure that their flame continues to burn brightly is to constantly engage with them, teach them, strengthen, and remind them of the rational thinking and facts behind those core values.

The third kind who become involved in politics are what I call the Fanatic Unprincipled Ideologues. These politicians are dangerous. They have core values, but they realize that revealing their core values maybe disastrous toward their being elected, so they pretend to be moderates or worse they say all the right Christian buzzwords. They are willing to lie or pretend for the "greater good" of their core values. They pretend to be moderates to get elected. The good thing about these folks is that the minute they are elected they attempt their agenda and their true motivations are revealed.

So how do we solve the problem? One solution to this problem is to elect rational thinking God-fearing honest men, and women with a cohesive Godly Worldview who will transform the process. But after they are in office it becomes our responsibility to keep them accountable every single day. Yes, it's true that politics can corrupt all involved. It may do so in the long term and it's human nature to fall to temptation, but that's why we should always evaluate the people we vote for and "un-elect" them when they become corrupt or useless. And they need to live in fear of that.

Objection 7. You are recommending involvement in politics as a way of evangelization. You suggesting that we use political legislation to change

the wickedness of man vs. preaching the gospel to achieve that end.

This objection was presented by a pastor as a rebuttal to James Dobson and Focus on the Family's involvement in the political arena. But this is not what Focus or I am suggesting. I'm suggesting that we use political legislation to protect the poor and the oppressed, something we are commanded to do. How else are we supposed to protect them? By hiding them, like the Jews were hidden by the Christians? It may yet get to that.

Blindly hoping that by preaching the gospel and never changing the laws, we'll one day be able to stop the wickedness of man is sheer shortsightedness, theologically unsound and it has never worked in the past. Take a look at the history of slavery in the predominantly Christian South. It wasn't until Christians took political action that this wickedness of man was halted. Our view is that political legislation can and should do only what the Declaration of Independence says it is supposed to do – make government protect the God-given rights of man.

You cannot force anyone to become a Christian, and involvement in politics is never a substitute for personal evangelization. Nor does it absolve any follower of Christ from the Great Commission. This book suggests what you need to be doing *in addition to* witnessing to the lost. And at no time do we ever recommend that we speak or act in any way that is not loving.

More importantly, I'm arguing, among other things, how moral laws in the United States make it easier to evangelize both in the United States and throughout the *entire* world. If we don't keep the laws of this land friendly to the spreading of the gospel, we will severely limit the ease in which we *do* share it. And I believe that since our secondary mission on earth is to spread the gospel,[527] it is critical that we are involved in politics to ensure that we remove and prevent obstacles to evangelization.

If you think evangelization is important, you need to be concerned that soon you won't be able to evangelize. "Hate speech" laws are already on the books to prevent Christians from being able to question homosexuality. Soon it may become illegal to tell someone they are a sinner. Slowly but surely Christians are losing the right to even talk about Jesus on school campuses and at their work places. Yet, lest you say "but God is sovereign and will always do what he wants to do," remember the Old Testament shows us the severe consequences to those who slow down the purposes of God's Moral Will through sins of omission or sins of commission.[528]

Objection 8. You are recommending laws as a way to force people to convert to Christianity.

This is a slight variation to the previous objection. But again, my

---

[527] Our primary mission being "to glorify God and enjoy Him forever" a la the Westminster Confessional.

[528] I always put it this way: Did God need the Israelites to take over Canaan the first time when the spies went in? Or could he have merely done it Himself and let the Israelites just walk in the front door? Did God need the Israelites to march around Jericho 13 times to make the wall fall down? Or could he have merely toppled the walls Himself? Obviously, He didn't need the Israelites to do anything, yet when they balked He gave them 40 years in the wilderness. I don't know about you, but I have no desire for 40 years of my own personal wilderness. Oh and yes, it was 13 times, once a day for 6 days and 7 times on the last day.

answer is, "certainly not!" No one can be forced to become a Christian. The concept is ludicrous. Not only can it *not* be done, but anybody who tries to do so immediately shows that he himself is not a Christian and does not really understand the gospel message. You cannot force anyone to be in love with Christ. You as an individual or as a government cannot force anyone to have a personal relationship with our Lord.

Objection 9. Christians should focus on changing themselves and their churches and not focus on changing the world or the culture.

Change ourselves? Yes absolutely. But focus *only* on changing ourselves or focus only on God? We see no precedent for that in the Bible. Only a few monks felt that way, and most of Christendom disagreed with them. If you recall, Jesus said we should love not only God, but also our neighbor as ourselves. In fact, you can gauge the truth of a person's claim that they love God by how much they love their neighbors.[529]

I had a friend who kept telling me that as soon as he got his life together he'd get into a ministry. First, he said he needed to get into shape physically. Then he said he needed to become more disciplined in his prayer life. Then he needed to finish his degree. Meanwhile he needed to get his car fixed. After that he needed…and so it went. Finally, I confronted him. "You are human," I said. "You'll have 'everything together' when you are *dead* and in our Lord's presence. Until then you'd better get your butt into gear and get involved in a ministry *now*. Ministry is not about perfect beings helping some poor souls. It's *imperfect* humans helping *other* imperfect humans. And if anything perhaps God will refine you in those ways while you are in ministry." Yes, he's still my friend.

If we wait until we've changed ourselves completely before we do anything else, we'll be waiting until we are resurrected with new bodies. We need to focus on many tasks now. In fact, we need to focus on *others* first. I've always said that we should not pick a church by finding the church where we learn the most, or the one that welcomes us the most, or the one that loves us the most, or one in which we feel most comfortable. I believe we should go to the church where God can *use* us the most, and while there we should start learning and teaching ourselves and others (in Bible studies) and not wait for the pastor to spoon feed us. Strangely enough, if we do that I believe we'll find that in time, this will become the church where we learn the most, where we feel most welcomed and loved, and where we feel most comfortable. This applies almost all the time, except perhaps for a season when we need healing or recovery.

Finally, suppose people in history had been required to wait until they were "in a better place" before taking action. Can you imagine someone saying to William Wilberforce, that he should wait to free the slaves until he had this or that shaped up or taken care of? Can you imagine someone telling him, *this* time in history was not right for social change, that he should wait until England turned her heart back to God? When Wilberforce first became a

---

[529] Note this does not work in reverse. Obviously, if people love their neighbors but reject God, it does not mean they still love God.

Christian, most of England mocked him for his ardent faith. You could say the same thing to the men and women behind the movement to free the slaves in the United States, or to Telemachus, who sacrificed his life to stop gladiatorial games in Rome. Then there's Martin Luther King, Lord Shaftesbury and thousands others. Try telling them to focus on changing the church or themselves and not the laws oppressing children and other humans.

To summarize, we absolutely need to change ourselves, but at no point should we ever wait until we or our society are "totally changed" before knuckling down on the tasks at hand.

Objection 10. But when I meet non-Christians should I really be talking to them about politics? Shouldn't I be witnessing to them?

Of course, you should be looking for witnessing opportunities. I don't propose that any time you meet non-Christians you should start pushing politics. In fact, as far as I'm concerned, you could get away with never talking to non-Christians about politics. This book is about *you* and *your Church* getting involved in politics. It's about Christians getting involved in politics and encouraging more Christians to vote. It's about Christians being able to explain cohesively and rationally why they vote the way they do. This book is not really about Christians arguing politics with non-Christians. Explain, yes. Argue, no. It's a subtle difference. When you explain, you say, "This is why *I* believe what I believe." When you argue you say, "This is why *you should* believe what I believe." I enjoy doing both, by the way.

Objection 11. All politicians are human, if we endorse one candidate and he turns out to be a bad apple or loses, or messes up, then the church will be marred.

At no point are we talking about the *Church* endorsing specific political candidates or parties. We are standing behind *principles* not people.

While we want to encourage Christians to be involved politically and run for office, the Church should not endorse individuals. After all, anyone can claim to be a Christian and spout the right verbiage, and even if someone *is* a Christian, that does not mean that God has blessed him or her with a *brain* that is capable of rational and logical thought or the ability to govern.

The churches and our pastors must educate the people about moral issues and the people can then vote accordingly by judging which individual will uphold those values. Those positions will always be valid as long as they really *are* moral values. There is great value in churches working *with* candidates and politicians, advising them on moral issues, but not endorsing them. The Church must be the conscience of the government.

In fact, even if the tax restriction is ever lifted and churches are allowed to endorse individuals, I don't think the Church should endorse anyone. They should align themselves with godly *principles* not individuals. However, you may be able to make a case for the Church coming out against a candidate. Imagine if more churches had come out against Hitler. He may not have been able to do what he did.

Remember though, that *not* endorsing individual candidates is a limitation only for the church. Individual Christians should certainly feel free to endorse politicians that they believe are of good moral character, have sound biblical principles and are very intelligent. However all politicians should realize that if they act immorally or codify bad laws, we will desert them. Christians should readily retract their personal support for immoral politicians. They should personally forgive them if the politician has repented, but politicians should remember that if they've misused our trust, it will take a long time and evidence of a change before we trust them again. Character counts and what a politician does in private is a reflection of his character and of key concern to us. Character is not only what you do in public, but is especially what you do in private when you think no one is watching or will find out. Imagine if we appointed a politician who decided that no one would find out and secreted away millions of public money. Character counts despite what Bill Clinton admirers kept saying.

Objection 12. God is not a Republican or a Democrat![530]

Of course, God is not a Republican. This is obvious. The statement makes no sense. God does not vote, God is not up for election. Just as Monty Python says "You don't get to vote for king," in the same way you don't get to vote for God. Creation is not a democracy, and God is not a president. God is the Omnipresent, Omniscient, and Omnipotent Creator of everything (and I wrote a book that allows you to prove that scientifically to your atheistic friends[531]). However, God does care if you are appointing men and women who have a heart after the things that He cares about. For this He will, I believe hold us personally responsible one day. Remember, those who enabled the wicked Kings of Israel to do their evil, were severely punished by God.

Jesus is not a Christian

Saying God is a Republican (or Democrat) is like saying Jesus is a Christian. Technically, he is not a Christian, and He never was. He never sinned, so He doesn't need to repent to be saved. We need redemption. He needs no redemption. He did not have to accept Himself to have eternal life. We follow Him. He does not need to follow anyone. *We* need to be Christians. He does not.

This is also similar to saying "God is on our side." God is not on anyone's side. Remember just before the battle of Jericho, Joshua is out looking at the walls when suddenly he sees a man standing before him with a drawn sword (Joshua 5:13-14). Joshua recoils and asks him, "Are you for us or for our enemies?"

"Neither" says the man "but as commander of the Army of the LORD I have now come." He then proceeds to tell Joshua what to do to take over Jericho, *if* Joshua wishes to obey God.

God, are you on our side or their side?

---

[530] Technically the name of the party is "The Democrat*ic* Party," so the right noun would seem to be "Democratic." Some "Democratics" have complained that Republicans are trying to call them 'rats' when they call them Democrats. I think this is silly, especially since their own website is www.democrats.org. In this book, I have used the words each party uses to describe themselves i.e. Republicans and Democrats.

[531] "Who is Agent X: Proving Science and Logic show it is more Rational to think God exists," Neil Mammen, Rational Free Press, 2009

"Neither" says the Lord. The question is: Are *you* on *God's* side? So, the issue is to determine what God's side is. What is God's heart concerning these things? You tell me, what is God's side when it comes to the legalization of the murder of babies? What is God's side when it comes to divorce, or homosexuality or the promotion of things the Bible clearly calls immoral? When we discover that, we'd better be on that side. But, we are not left to discover that blindly. He has given us the Bible, and He has demonstrated a way to rationally and logically process it.

We Conservatives are not automatically Republicans or Democrats or whatever. If one party adheres to God's moral values and principles, we will support it. If a member of one party is not a person of moral fiber and character, we won't vote for him. If we realize that it is fruitless to work with one party or the other, we should toss them out faster than they can blink. We affiliate ourselves with the party that follows God's and (thus our) principles, not vice versa. Some right-leaning people ask how anyone can be a Christian and a Democrat because of the party's stances on abortion and homosexuality. Some left-leaning people ask how anyone can be a Christian and Republican because they seem to want to starve the poor and destroy the environment. What are their actual platforms and achievements? We cover that in this book.

Objection 13. But when people come to church, if the pastor is talking about a political issue that they disagree with, they won't come back.

This is a key question and a valid concern. But I think there is more here than what meets the eye. Thus, I've dedicated an entire chapter of this book to responding to this question; see "But You Will Turn People Away From The Gospel!"

Objection 14. Are you promoting Liberation Theology?

This is not a book about Liberation Theology,[532] and does not promote Liberation Theology. We reject Liberation Theology. See the footnote for more details. For our statement of faith which clearly rejects this faulty theology please go to www.JesusIsInvolvedInPolitics.com and do a search for "Statement of Faith."

Additional Objections
Objection 15. The Bible is not a book about economics or politics; it is only concerned with salvation.

You can't be serious? It would be the height of misrepresentation to say that the Bible is *only* concerned with the afterlife and salvation. That, in fact was considered a Gnostic heresy in the early Church. Christ is concerned

---

[532] Some of you may not have been exposed to Liberation Theology and may ask what it is. Liberation Theology (LT) focuses on Jesus Christ as not only the Savior, but also as the liberator of the oppressed. Emphasis is placed on verses like Matthew 26:51-52, and Jesus' mission is interpreted to be one of physical liberation, not spiritual. The emphasis is that our Lord was only a bringer of earthly justice (despite the fact that he never spoke out against common social injustices that he was surrounded by). Yet, to Liberation Theologians these passages are considered to be a call to arms to carry out this mission of justice. Sadly, sometimes the call to arms is taken literally and involves violence. A number of Liberation Theologians, though not all, also add certain Marxist concepts such as the doctrine of perpetual class struggle, equality of results regardless of effort and so on. LT originated in the Catholic Church, yet both Popes John Paul II and Benedict XVI have rejected it harshly.

with the here and now as well. The physical as well as the spiritual. There is no artificial separation from the physical and the spiritual. That's why we feed the poor, worry about orphans, are concerned about widows and the defenseless. That's why we are to fight for justice and protect the innocent. For us to be so crass as to say the Bible speaks nothing to the plight of the unjustly treated would be to twist the Bible out of recognition and ignore the second great commandment. Love your neighbor as yourself.

God cares about economic and political situations because we have seen that there is really no physical oppression that can be greater or more widespread than that of an economic or political one (i.e. one caused by bad laws). Millions of people did not starve in Ethiopia (something that we are called to care about) because neighbors were selfish. In fact, the world was *selfless* and gave billions. The Ethiopians starved because of an oppressive political communistic regime. Millions are starving in North Korea because their economic system cannot survive reality and just does not work, and it's their political regime that keeps them in this plight. This does not necessarily justify us going to war against these regimes but it does justify ensuring that the conditions for these regimes gaining control is prevented, especially in our country. As we show in this book, millions of children in the US are suffering because of faulty political decisions and the bad laws that were passed on divorce. Millions more will suffer if more bad laws are enacted and the old ones are not repealed. We are called to prevent this from happening; we can do that by voting correctly.

For anyone to say the Bible is not concerned with starving people is to ignore Christ's compassion and His acts of healing the cripple, feeding the masses and caring for the sick, and is in direct contradiction to what the early church did. If you care about the poor and the widow and orphan, you *have* to care about the economic systems. If you care about the oppressed, you *have* to care about the political systems. The only way the Bible could be unconcerned about these things or not discuss these things is if the Gospel was like Hinduism; wherein you have to suffer your own karma and so should not be helped; or Asceticism wherein you are to divorce yourself from the world. This is not an interpretation of Bible that any rational person can defend.

Objection 16. But Christians should not be focused on politics; we should be concerned with what Jesus was concerned about: The poor, the sick and the oppressed.

Actually, we agree on the goal, yet as this book shows, it is precisely bad or ignorant people in politics and bad laws that cause the poor and the sick to suffer and allow oppression. If we Christians do *not* get involved politically and instead let evil men and women create the laws, we will see much more of the suffering that Jesus was concerned about. We will create more poor and more sick. In this book I show and I hope you can easily see that laws that break down the family; validate same-sex marriage; force higher taxes; prescribe universal healthcare; create welfare instead of work fare and dictate socialism; will create more poor and orphans and sick and help to turn the hearts of people against God. This is precisely why we care. And when we elect men and women who do not have a heart after God *and* a Biblical

Worldview we will have these evils forced upon us and our children.

Objection 17.   I don't have any problems with *Christians* being involved politically; I just don't think *churches* should be involved politically.

At first, this may sound like a valid argument, but here's the problem. The abolition movement started in the *churches*, the fight against racism and segregation started in the *churches*, most of the laws we consider *just* laws today, started as sermons in *churches* by pastors moved by the Spirit. Even something as simple as the addition of the words "Under God" into the Pledge of Allegiance, started as a sermon. So, the history of change refutes your claim. Change only occurred when the Church *and* the *churches* got involved.

Objection 18. I don't know any of this stuff; I just know that I'm supposed to love Jesus.

At one point, I heard this twice in as many weeks. It's one of those surreptitiously *arrogant* statements, because it implies in many ways the following, "I love Jesus and so I stay out of the fray, but you, *you poor schmuck,* who is all involved in politics, obviously don't love Him as much as I do." But what would have happened if William Wilberforce had said, "I don't know about stopping slavery using politics and the law, I *just* know I'm supposed to love Jesus?"

What if Christians had said that during WWII and no Christian joined the army?

What arrogance and ignorance. The point is, nobody is arguing that you should not love Jesus. We *are* supposed to love Jesus, but we are *also* commanded to go into all the world and make disciples of all nations, *and* we are commanded to love people and care if we are passing laws that will make more of them suffer. What we are discussing here is; how do those commandments translate into *action* in our daily living and our moral laws. Laws, which will teach and train our next generation.

I'll tell you one thing I *do* know; not doing *anything* to bring about true moral social justice to the suffering does not qualify as loving Jesus or loving people. And letting America change so that no missionaries are sent from here and our nation instead oppresses Christians, certainly doesn't qualify as responsibly going into all the world to preach the Gospel and making disciples.

In Summary

While moral laws will not save anyone, as I have shown in response to the last question, this book asserts that a strong evangelical-friendly United States with religious freedom and godly laws, is crucial for sending missionaries and money to the lost and needy in other nations. It is also critical for providing a haven for persecuted Christians like Abdul Rahman, the recent Christian convert from Afghanistan who was sentenced to death for becoming a Christian, and many other Muslims who become Christians. Many choose to stay in their home countries to spread the word, but others are forced to leave under threat of death. Imagine if you will, a United States administration that did not welcome any more pesky persecuted dangerous Christians. It's not hard to imagine, is it? Under the wrong administration and a 60% majority

Congress, this will slowly become a reality. Does your congress have a Christian Worldview?

Ask yourself this; what kind of administration, laws and moral culture in the United States would be the best for Christians who trying to follow Christ's call, the call to go into all nations and make disciples?[533] Would it be a United States that persecutes Christians? Not only *no*, but resoundingly so, and that is an issue to which we must pay close attention. Especially so for pastors and elders.

---

[533] If you are reading this as a non-Christ follower and are not familiar with the Great Commission, it is from the Gospels of Mark and Matthew. It is the commandment by Christ stating that He is the only way to be saved from condemnation and that we as Christians are to go out and evangelize the entire world. Mark 16:15 [Jesus] said to them, "Go into all the world and preach the good news to all creation. 16 Whoever believes and is baptized will be saved, but whoever does not believe will be condemned.

Matt 28:18 Then Jesus came to them and said, "All authority in heaven and on earth has been given to me. 19 Therefore *go and make disciples of all nations*, baptizing them in the name of the Father and of the Son and of the Holy Spirit, 20 and teaching them to obey everything, I have commanded you.

This is of critical importance because no one can validly claim to be a follower of Christ and condemn or not participate in the Great Commission. Because if they did condemn this command, they would *not* be following him, would they?

And lest someone object too strongly, remember Muslims, Baha'is, Hare Krishna Hindus, and even atheists like Dawkins and Hitchens spend their time and energy trying to convert others.

And if you ask, "What right do you have to go tell others that their religion is wrong." I'll just ask you, "Why you are telling *me* that my religion which commands me to tell others this, is wrong?" You have just refuted yourself with a suicide statement.

One of Rev. Barry Lynn's editors to me: Are you saying that people who believe in abortion are like Hitler?

My Response: No, I'm saying that people who realize the fetus is fully human and still want to kill her are acting like Hitler. (Pause) Now tell me why my logic is faulty?

Editor: (Shrugs in agreement)

Bystander: (grabbing my hand and shaking it) Thank you for that. Thank you!

A conversation at the FRC Values Voter's Conference. Barry Lynn is the founder of American United for the separation of Church and State. An "anti-Christian" organization that completely disagrees with most of what I've stated in this book. When I met him at the above conference, I told him what I was writing about. He was very cordial and immediately invited me on his radio show to discuss it.

Notes I:
Non-Christian Objections

My *non-Christian* friends constantly toss objections at me regarding my views on politics and Christ. I've identified and answered a few here, they may help you.

Objection: You think people who don't believe exactly what you believe are going to hell. That's close-minded.

You are right. It is close-minded. But let me ask you this; are you right about me being wrong? Aren't you being close-minded about me being right? Can you accept the fact that I could possibly be right?

You see you've caught yourself in a sort of dilemma here. If you say that I could *never* be right then you are being just as close-minded as I am. Which must mean that you think it's okay to be close-minded about *some* things. On the other hand, if you agree that I *could* be right, then you have again admitted that it's okay to be close-minded, at least on some issues. You refuted yourself the moment you thought it. After all, isn't it okay for a doctor to be close-minded about the fact that Cipro (a drug) is the antidote to Anthrax and a witch doctor's dead chicken dance is *not* the antidote? Is it okay to be close-minded about the National Socialists? So, the real issue is not that it's *not* okay to be close-minded, but *what* is it okay to be close-minded about?

Furthermore, this statement may show that you have a total miscomprehension of the real world. 1.3B Muslims, 2B Christians, hundreds of millions of Buddhists, 0.8B Hindus[534] all think that they have the exclusive truth about Nirvana or the way to Allah or God. Frankly, when you start adding up those numbers, you realize that I'm close-minded just like the vast majority of mankind. So I am close-minded, and your point is what? In other words, okay so what?

Being close-minded is only wrong if you are wrong about what it is you are close-minded about. And isn't that exactly what we are arguing about, i.e. who is right? I'm actually open-minded about being close-minded. You can't presuppose the conclusion. Even if I was right you would continue to be close-minded, it seems. Which is more rational? Which is more open-minded? I actually think I could be wrong. Which is why I base my beliefs on facts, reason and logic. Go to www.NoBlindFaith.com for details.

---

[534] Yes, even Hindus think that non-Hindus are wrong about how to get to Nirvana. So, the minute you think you are right, you are saying someone else is wrong in their beliefs. That's the problem with being a non-exclusivist. The minute you are exclusive about your non-exclusivism you have ceased being a non-exclusivist.

Objection: You talk about how single parent raised kids are so destructive, then why are you against abortion. If you allowed abortion, we'd reduce the problem because fewer of those kids would be born. You're contradicting yourself.

Actually, I'm not contradicting myself. It all revolves around whether the fetus is human. If it is, killing a fetus to solve the problems like juvenile delinquency and crime is akin to just killing the *juvenile delinquents* to solve the problem. Is that clear? Let me rephrase it. If the fetus is ethically, morally, and genetically as human as a baby, then your solution to the problem caused by broken homes is to go through town and kill the babies from those broken homes. Since I can show that the fetus is human, show me why my logic is wrong.

This is horrendously "Hitlerian" when you think about it. We are against abortion for only one reason. We think the fetus is human and there is solid scientific, ethical and moral proof of that. This proof is independent of the Bible or religion.

If you think the fetus is not human, *you* have the challenge of proving that fact. You need to provide scientific and rational evidence. And as Scott Klusendorf and Gregory Koukl put it, you can't use Size, Level of development, Environment, or Degree of dependency (the "SLED") as an indication of something not being human. Why? Because those characteristics are not morally, scientifically or biologically relevant to whether someone is human or not. You can apply any or all of those standards to the late actor Christopher Reeves or a 1-day-old preemie who is mentally retarded and in the ICU and they remain human. A fetus is not part of the woman's body. He has his own unique human DNA and does not even use his mother's blood. If you still claim he is, then you need to tell us why a male fetus' mother has 2 heads, 4 hands, 4 legs, 2 hearts and both male *and female* sexual organs?

So clearly, if you can't go around killing kids who were born in single parent homes, what can you do? You can encourage giving them up for adoption as soon as they are born. There are millions of couples who would like to adopt. Studies show that more than 50% of married couples have considered adoption *even* if they already have children of their own. Why? Because they love kids. There is no shortage of parents to adopt babies of any race.[535]

Further, as Scott Klusendorf notes, it shows how illogical or incompetent a politician is when he says, "I wish there were no abortions, I'm personally against it, but I wouldn't want to force my morals on someone else. I want it to be rare but legal."

We deal with the stupidity of the latter part in this book, "I wouldn't want to force my morals on someone else." But it's worth a review:

In a representative democracy like the U.S., you *are* supposed to vote your convictions based on a moral code and not the mob's desires. If you can't do that, then get out of office. You aren't qualified, and we don't need any "Aaron Politicians." (We discuss what that is in this book). A politician who says this obviously doesn't even have a sliver of understanding about the U.S. Constitution and the difference between a republic and a democracy. But, the first part of the statement is what shows that politician is disingenuous or incompetent. At best, it indicates that he or she is incapable of logical thought. At worst, it shows the person is disingenuous and trying to fool us. Here's the question you should ask them, "You said you personally are against abortion, can I ask *why* are you against abortion? After all, if abortion is not the killing of human life, then why are you against it? Why do you want it to be rare but legal? We don't see you taking such a moral stance on the removal of a tumor or liposuction. It is illogical to take this stance on something of this importance if there is no reason to do so.

"On the other hand, if abortion *is* the taking of human life, how can you let anyone *else* do it? What you have said in effect is, 'I think abortion is a terrible thing that I would never do, it maybe even equal to killing an innocent human, but who am I to stop you from

---

[535] No one can complain that Americans are racist about adoption. Look at the rush to adopt Chinese, Indian, and African kids. I know eight couples in our Christian community who have adopted over 15 kids from various nations including African American kids in the US.

Neil Mammen

doing that?'"

Think about this statement. It is disgusting. A politician who would say this would be the kind who during the slave era would have said, "I'm personally opposed to enslaving Africans and classifying them as non human, but I can't impose *my* moral values on others? If the people want to have slaves, we should let them. Having a slave is a personal matter and should be between the slave owner and his God. I'm running to be Senator of Mississippi not Minister of Mississippi!" (Okay that last part was just too tempting).

For a fuller answer to this and to decimate other such silly statements, I refer you to "How to win Abortion Arguments without appealing to the Bible or Religion" at NoBlindFaith.com.

Objection: You just want to take over America and are suggesting we only vote for Christians.

Here's how this objection came up and how the conversation went:

Liberal: I can't believe you are telling people to *only* vote for Christians.

Me: And God-fearing Jews.

Lib: Yeah, whatever.

Me: It's not just any Christian; it's those with a Biblical Worldview. But what's wrong with that?

Lib: It's un-American. It's wrong.

Me: Why?

Lib: Because you are implying that only Christians are Americans…

Me (interrupting): …And God-fearing Jews.

Lib: Yeah, whatever… and that America should be a Christian Nation.

Me: Judeo-Christian.

Lib: Yeah, whatever.

Me: I never said only Christians are Americans. People should vote for whomever they want, but let me ask you this, what is it wrong with telling others *whom* to vote for?

Lib: What?

Me: Why is it wrong for me to tell others whom to vote for? How come you haven't told others to vote for me?

Lib: Are you crazy? Why would I do that? Nobody should vote for you.

Me: George Bush?

Lib: Or him, he's evil.

Me: (smirk).

Lib (suddenly realizing what I'd done): Wait, no, that's not what I meant!

Objection: You talk about objective moral values, but we see many priests, pastors, and Christians who are hypocrites.

Let me answer this in the same way I respond to all my friends who make this claim: "Yes, you are right all Christians *are* hypocrites."

"Huh?"

Oh yes, all Christians are hypocrites. It is a logical necessity. Here's why: Christians hold to a standard that is impossible to attain in this lifetime. We fully know that, but we do have a standard, to be pure. We will always mess up something or the other, and never be perfect. Atheists or irreligious people self declare that they have no absolute standards and no objective moral values. So, it's easy to achieve nothing. If you have no target, you'll hit it every time. It's difficult to achieve a standard. So, logically and rationally, you'll find that all Christians are hypocrites.

But you may be tempted to ask, "If no one can meet the standards, then why have them?" We've already answered this earlier in this book. Nobody can or does keep all the traffic laws, yet we don't advocate anarchy on the streets, do we?

But, just as with traffic laws, this does not mean we should give Christian hypocrites (ourselves or others) a pass every time they mess up. When we mess up (sin), we must ask the forgiveness of whomever we have wronged. We must ask God to forgive us for rebelling against Him, and we must willingly accept any physical or legal consequences to our actions. We must make a firm commitment to never repeat that sin again. Then we will be forgiven. And no, we can't just pretend to be sorry. You can't fool God.

Some sins have more severe consequences than others, and these will require more severe physical punishments than others. While none of these sins will separate us from God, we may need to be separated from our flock, from our family and so on as punishment and to protect others.

Many times the sin we commit is caused by our weakness. Just because we ask for forgiveness does not mean the sin is not still tempting to us. In these cases, it is incumbent on those who love us to ensure that after we have paid the consequences, we are kept far away from the opportunity to repeat this offence.

So yes, we are hypocrites, and in each case, depending on the nature of our sin and the consequences to those around us, certain actions should be taken. Failing to take them would then extend the negative effects and perhaps the influence of the sin to others.

A good example is pedophiles. If there is a civil or legal penalty for any sin, it must be justly judged and the consequences should be meted out. After that, the offending person should not be allowed near kids again.[536]

Objection: You Christians want to take control of everything.

Actually we don't. Christians have been so reluctant to get involved and take control that it necessitated a book like this. Remember the gal who said, "Jesus said render unto Caesar so we should not be involved in politics either"? That's the prevalent attitude. A Jewish friend who did an extensive review of this book, on reading that comment said, "Oy! I can't believe someone would actually say this."[537]

We don't want control. We want an America that is strong, safe and the kind of place that would allow Christians to continue to spread the saving message of God throughout the world. We want an America where our kids would be able to grow up and uphold their moral values, which as we've shown are common sense values. Yes indeed, we do want God-fearing lawmakers and presidents but there are some Christians that scare me. In fact, I want the most competent person executing the jobs that they are competent in. For instance, I don't want Christian Supreme Court Justices. I want strict constructionalist justices. They could be atheist or Muslims or Scientologists for all I care, as long as they have a long documented *history* of ignoring their own biases and focusing on the original intent of the Constitution and of the laws that our lawmakers made.

Objection: I'm a libertarian. I think the government should stay out of moral issues like same sex marriage (SSM), divorce, and abortion.

Why stop there? Why not stay out of murder and stealing? They are moral issues too, let them self regulate. Ah, you were going to say because those actions hurt others. Well so does abortion, divorce and SSM. So, you obviously want to regulate *some* moral issues. In which case what we are now arguing about is degree of damage. If I can show you that abortion is the murder of a human being (which I can), can we regulate it? If I can then show you that SSM and divorce causes destruction to the entire nation and hurts innocent kids, can we regulate it? Isn't that the entire point? We only want to constrain those actions that cause damage, *because* they cause damage. Not because we have some twisted sense of wanting to control the masses. Moreover, mankind has a sin nature and just as we cannot have capitalism unconstrained we cannot have moral issues unconstrained. We can argue about where the constraints should be, but we cannot argue that no constraints are needed.

Furthermore, if you've read this book, you'll have seen the logic of why moral values are the very basis of *all* our laws, and you read the facts on how abandoning them has been the cause of most of our ills. Thus anybody without a firm moral foundation is standing on shifting sand and is not fit to govern or make our laws.

Objection: You want to control marriage because it hurts society, but where do we draw the line? Why not control the fat content in hamburgers then, it can cause

---

[536] I say this with caution as often-overzealous prosecutors can mete out justice unfairly. I'm thinking of a case I heard about on the radio where a young college student was arrested for streaking and as a result was branded a sexual predator for the rest of his life. This then needs to be compared to those cases where real sexual predators were allowed to return to society to molest again.

[537] She's also the friend who so wisely said, "When people tell me all religions are basically the same, I say, 'One word. Moloch!'" Moloch, if you recall was the God of the Philistines, they sacrificed babies to him. Can you seriously say all religions are the same.

obesity? You'll end up with a Nanny State! Don't you want government off our backs? Why not ban adultery, lusting, and cussing then?

The primary goal of marriage is to create a stable environment for kids. It has always been the function of government to protect the culture by ratifying marriage, both legally and morally. This is of critical importance to the future of any society. Marriage is an institution. Remember, we created governments to protect our society; especially the future of our society, i.e. our kids. Making divorce easy or allowing SSM violates the fundamental goal and interest of government as it does not provide any viable alternatives that are good for kids. Divorce and SSM can be proven to be self destructive to any government.

Secondly, as a Christian and this maybe hard for a non-Christian to accept, we believe that God has indeed commanded us to ensure that marriage is kept holy (for all the reasons we've mentioned). Thus we believe it is our job to convince enough others that a law protecting marriage is good for everyone. All laws are a legislation of someone's morals, so we are just doing what we believe is best for society. Surely we have the right to do that as Americans.

On the other hand, the primary goal of burgers is to provide nourishment. It is not supplied by the government. It is supplied by a private party. Burgers, much though some would like it to be, are not an institution. We do however regulate meat very carefully, how it's handled and how it's labeled. To control the fat content would be the equivalent of the government dictating "how" and "where" you got married, not how easy it is to divorce. We can and do require that restaurants publish the fat content of the burgers they sell. Note too, that there are numerous other alternatives to burgers that are just as viable and easily available. There are no other viable alternatives to marriage. If there was a monopoly on food in the US or there was a valid government mandate that someone eat only a particular food then government should regulate it, like we do (or should be doing) for food in the military.

Without marriage, society would collapse. Without burgers…well you tell me.

As to adultery, we actually did have laws against adultery. If you read the chapter on Sexual Sins, I discuss how we think laws that would allow a person to sue someone who had committed adultery with their spouse would go a long way to protect the disintegration of the family. Cussing is a personal admonition in the Bible and not one for the state, however there are standards of civility that are enforced in all governments. Don't forget that Judicial Laws, i.e. punishments for any and all of these are to be decided by the legislature not derived from tradition.

Remember any argument about "where do we draw the line" is invalid. For I could just say this, "Punish thieves? Where do we draw the line? Next you'll want to punish kids for spitting." The minute I say this your immediate response is, "You are taking it too far. Of course we should punish thieves, but that doesn't automatically mean we should punish kids for spitting." And you are correct. Just because we want to protect marriage, that does not automatically mean we wish to punish a man for lusting in his mind or people for spitting in public. Each and every law must be analyzed on it's own and then it's validity decided and if it is to be made a law what the consequences of violating that law is. It's irrational and a strawman to make the jump to something I have not said.

Objection: Christians claim that the idea of equality came from the Bible. But for centuries you Christians claimed this only meant spiritual equality not legal. So you can't claim that the idea of equality only comes from Christians.

Once you understand that rights cannot be only spiritual but must have a legal component to make it a reality, it becomes very hard to pigeon hole it as "only spiritual." So those Christians were just plain wrong.

I was reading an atheist's blog and he proceeded to complain that we Christians can't claim equality as our idea. Oh yeah? Well whose idea was it? Were Wilberforce and the abolitionists atheists? No, they weren't. Just because it took a while for Christians recognize this and then fight and win this battle does not suddenly make it an atheistic ideal. What silliness! It was germinated because of numerous Bible verses on it (e.g. Gal 3:24-29) not because of any atheistic or pagan creed.

Objection: You Christians want to convert the entire world.

Yes. Indeed we do.[538] We don't want anyone, not even you, to be spiritually separated from God for all eternity. That would be Hell. To prevent that, we want everyone to recognize their own need, for the one and only Savior that God has provided, His Son, Christ Jesus. We want people to accept and be grateful for Christ's atonement on the cross for their sins; and to walk with him in faith and dependence through the challenges of this life. We want Hell to be empty. Why is that such a bad desire? If you really believed that your friends were going to Hell, would you be content to let them continue on their way? We want people to be saved!

We want to be free to present the joy of this spiritual opportunity for them using logic, rationality and truth, not force.

Remember God has no grandchildren, either you love God or you don't. I can't make you love God with laws or force.

In addition, since when has it been a bad thing to want to convince someone that you are telling the truth? Don't be too quick to object, as you are liable to fall into the suicide statement trap. If you say it's wrong to try to convince someone of something, your very act, shows that *you* want to convince me of what *you* are saying. You are doing exactly what you object to. Isn't that hypocrisy? And you should not think you can escape this logic just because Christians hope people everywhere will come to see the awesome benefits of belief in Christ.

Let me close with a quote from the Atheistic Magician Penn Jillette of the Penn and Teller team. He and I may disagree about God, but we agree about warning others if we believe that they are about to be run over by a truck or are going to be eternally separated from God.

Penn's Commentary about a Christian who gave him a Bible.

I've always said, "I don't respect people who don't proselytize." I don't respect that at all, if you believe that there is a heaven and hell, and people could be going to hell or not getting eternal life or whatever, and you think its not really worth telling them this because it would make it socially awkward...And atheists who think that people shouldn't proselytize -- "Just leave me alone, keep your religion to yourself."

How much do you have to hate somebody to not proselytize?

How much do you have to hate somebody to believe that everlasting life is possible and not tell them that?

I mean, if I believe beyond a shadow of a doubt that a truck was coming at you and you didn't believe it - that truck was bearing down on you - there is a certain point where I tackle you. And this is more important than that.

This guy was a really good guy. He was polite and honest and sane and he cared enough about me to proselytize and to give me a Bible.[539]

That's why we want to convert the world. Not because we gain anything. There is nothing in Christian theology that says we get any sort of reward for leading others to Christ. I do it because the thought of my friends spending eternity apart from God, terrifies me.

---

[538] And so do the Muslims, Buddhists, and many Hindus for that matter.

[539] You can watch it on: www.youtube.com/watch?v=7JHS8adO3hM

By the way, if you know Penn, tell him I extend a friendly challenge. I'll show him the scientific and rational arguments for a non-mechanistic, extra dimensional, fine tuning creator. All without using the Bible. The challenge is to see if he can logically refute it, I'm saying he can't. See "Who Is Agent X: Proving That Science And Logic Show It Is More Rational To Think That God Exists" Neil Mammen, 2009, Rational Free Press. Available at www.NoBlindFaith.com

Maybe what the American church really needs is some good persecution.
A Christian friend responding to my alarms about our free speech rights
eroding.

Notes II:
Maybe Persecution is Good for The Church!

One of the more inventive and distressing objections I've heard in my discussions with Christians is the statement that "persecution is good for the church." The conversation has usually gone like this:

Me: If Christians don't start getting involved in the making of laws, soon the gospel will be banned, and we will be arrested for speaking it. In fact, in Sweden,[540] a pastor was thrown in jail for teaching about homosexuality from Leviticus. Even today in Canada, when Focus on the Family broadcasts, they have to modify their programs for that country because it is illegal to broadcast anti-homosexual remarks there.[541]

Them: Look what persecution did to the church in China. It grew and grew. Look at what persecution did for the early church. Maybe the church in America needs persecution to make Christians more serious about their faith. I'd say we need a bit of persecution.

This may be a well-intentioned statement, but it's illogical and the raw reality of true persecution is not being fully considered. First, if you remember why persecution came to Israel and if you read what Eusebius the early church Historian says, about why the early church was persecuted, both indicate that persecution was always the consequence of turning *away* from God's laws. Not from turning away from a relationship with God, but from turning away from *observing* his laws. Many probably had fooled themselves into thinking they had a *great* relationship with God.

I would think that the indication that a culture has turned away from a relationship with God is when the culture turns away from His Moral law. You cannot separate the two.

Persecution is consequence of exactly what we are doing now and rather than fix the problem you want to exacerbate it. What logic is that? Why not fix the problem?

That's like knowing that the consequence of smoking is lung cancer, yet rather than work to stop the smoking, you pine for lung cancer to fix the smoking. Yes, lung cancer and death do indeed stop people from smoking. But is that what you want?

---

[540] The pastor jailed in Sweden was 70-year-old Ake Green. He faced between 30 days and six months in jail. When the prosecutor was asked by a reporter, "What about the pastor's rights?" he was told, "When he started reading Bible verses about homosexuality, he crossed the line." www.citizenlink.org/CLFeatures/A000000129.cfm Last checked on 12/18/06

[541] "Already, Focus on the Family has to change its broadcasts for Canada when those programs deal with the issue of homosexuality, or it faces heavy fines from the CRTC, the Canadian Radio-TV and Telecommunications Commission." www.citizenlink.org/CLFeatures/A000000562.cfm

Also from the Canadian Broadcast Standards Council ruling, "By contrast, the Council considered a similar complaint in CKRD-AM re Focus on the Family (CBSC Decision 96/97-0155, December 16, 1997) ... referring to the CRTC's Religious Broadcasting Policy, which provides specific indications of the limits of religious broadcasting, the panel found that the Focus on the Family broadcast on CKRD-AM had stepped beyond the boundary of acceptable comment.

www.cbsc.ca/english/codes/cabethics/clause8.htm Last checked on 12/18/06

See also:www.cbsc.ca/english/codes/cabethics/clause8.htm

Moreover, those who say this seem to have no concept of what persecution really is. It usually comes from some Christian who has never been persecuted personally. Or has never seen their young daughters persecuted.

While I have many close Muslim friends who detest violence and wish that persecution did not take place in their homelands, it is worthwhile to look at what Muslim and atheistic persecution of Christians looks like.

Islamic Persecution

Imagine that the persecution of Christians in the U.S. begins to take place as it does in Egypt. Picture a young Egyptian girl named Mary. She displays her fragile wrist. It is encircled by a bracelet of scarred flesh, the disfigurement bearing witness to her abduction, rape, and nine-month captivity in the hands of her Islamic kidnappers. As part of their program to transform Mary into a Muslim, they poured sulfuric acid on her wrist, obliterating the tattooed cross she wore as a statement of her faith. She had grown up among Egypt's six million Coptic Christians, a minority community facing increased mistreatment from Islamic zealots. At the age of 18 when she was visiting a friend's home, she was kidnapped by a group of radicals from Gamat Islamaiya. After they raped her, they moved her from one hideout to another, and along with continuing sexual abuse, she was required to fast, pray, and memorize portions of the Koran. At first, she refused to wear the traditional Islamic robe, but they warned her that if she tried to remove it, they would pour acid on her face. Eventually, unable to resist her captors' demands, she signed official papers of conversion to Islam.

While Mary was being held hostage, her father went to the Cairo police. They told him to forget her. She was safe in the hands of Islam, they said, ordering him to sign a pledge that he would stop searching for her. He and other family members were warned by the police that if they interfered in the situation and Mary was harmed, they would be held responsible. This is a true story.[542]

This is the *real* persecution facing followers of Christ. It is not fuzzy discrimination. Now imagine your 70-year-old father or grandfather has a nice house in a nice city that he worked all his life to be able to afford. Imagine too that someone wants that house. All a person would have to do is to say, "This man blasphemed God," and he would be dragged into the streets, with you helplessly standing by as a mob bludgeons his brain to a pulp, and you would see the hands that loved you and hugged you and tenderly cared for you as child shatter in many places. You would see the pain in his eyes as he slumped to his death, his blood flowing onto the street. His main assailant now enters the house he has legally taken possession of because it was owned by a blasphemer. Then you watch as your grandmother is dragged out on the street and all her cherished belongings and memories are destroyed.

Do you want something like this for the church of Christ? Think carefully. What I have just described actually happened in a Muslim country, and there is more to the picture around the world.

Persecution in Indonesia

During the Christmas season in 2000 in Indonesia, the world's largest Muslim country and one known for religious toleration, terrorists bombed churches in 18 cities, killing scores, wounding hundreds. Catholic Archbishop Charles Chaput of Denver observed, "Violence against the Christian minority has steadily continued over the past decade." As an example, he cited beheadings of three Christian teenage girls in Sulawesi. The girls' heads were left at a church, each with a note that vowed, "We will murder 100 more Christian teenagers, and their heads will be presented as presents."

Persecution in China

China manufactures and exports Christmas lights and ornaments, but its government arrests and imprisons Christians who lead worship services, preach or

---

[542]www.ransomfellowship.org/Article_Persecution.html

otherwise operate without state approval. Richard Land, director of the Southern Baptist Convention's Ethics & Religious Liberty Commission, gives the example of Catholic Bishop James Su Zhimin of Hebei, who has spent more than 27 Christmases in prison. Similarly Cai Zhuohua, a Protestant pastor in Beijing, was sentenced to three years in the gulag, or laogai as it's called in China. His crime? Printing and distributing Bibles. His defense lawyer, the prominent civil rights attorney Gao Zhisheng, also a Christian, has been disbarred and now worries he may become his own next client.[543]

Other Persecution around the world

In 1998, the Portland Oregonian (not exactly a conservative paper) published an entire series on the persecution of Christians around the world.[544]

The following is an excerpt:

A Presbyterian pastor overlooks threats and builds the first Christian church in his region of Pakistan. A mob destroys the church. Masked men invade the pastor's home and stab him to death.

A man leaves Islam to become a Christian. Egyptian secret police arrest him without a formal charge and torture him with an electric probe to make him inform them about other converts.

A Roman Catholic boy in southern Sudan plays in the trees with his friends. Soldiers waging a holy war capture him and send him into slavery, where he is given an Islamic name and beaten with sticks by his masters.

...Around the world Christians are being tortured, beaten, raped, imprisoned, enslaved, forced out of their homes and killed -- in large part because of what they believe.

Of course, we would be remiss if we did not mention one of the best sources of information on persecuted Christians: The Voice of the Martyrs (www.persecution.com) has a newsletter detailing the current persecution of Christians.

The U.S. an Islamic Nation?

But, you may argue, "Who said anything about the U.S.A. becoming an Islamic nation?" Well here is the reality. Nature abhors a vacuum. While Christians are keen to disengage from politics, Muslims are not. In fact, most Muslims believe they have a holy duty to be involved politically. Having personally lived in a few Muslim countries (Sudan and Yemen) and having visited a whole lot more, I can confidently say that the concept of the separation of church and state is alien to most (though not all) Muslims. Islam is a religion of traditions and rituals and actions, not relationships. So, if you force an entire nation of people to adhere to the five pillars[545] of Islam, in their eyes they are doing you a favor. You will all be saved, and your kids will become devout Muslims.

Christians don't have this luxury. We know you have to have a personal relationship with Christ to be saved, and you can't force that on anyone. When we pass moral laws, it is not to force spirituality on anyone. It is to help them and us who have to live with them have a healthier life and more joyous life. It is to help the poor and the oppressed and just as important, our *own* grandkids.

The U.S. may not be becoming Muslim, but it is not becoming atheistic either. Atheists find themselves in a slowly shrinking minority. While Christianity is growing by conversions and Islam is growing by births, atheism is slowly but surely shrinking. In 1970, there were about 165 million atheists. By mid 2000's, this number had dropped to 150 million, and it continues to decline.[546]

---

[543] www.nationalreview.com/comment/shea200512190809.asp

[544] This article used to be at: www.oregonlive.com/special/christiansundersiege but has been moved.

[545] The five pillars of Islam are: Confession that there is one God Allah and Mohammed is his prophet; Praying 5 times a day; Giving alms to the poor; Fasting during the month of Ramadan; Going to Mecca on the Hajj pilgrimage if you are able.

[546] World Christian Trends AD30-AD2200 Barrett, Johnson, William Carey Library, Pasadena, CA 2001, Part 1, Table 1-2. Note this number obviously does not take into account "functional" atheists or state determined atheists like the Chinese who show up as Chinese folk-religionists or Confucianists, but rather self-proclaimed atheists. I.e. the ones who are proud of their atheism.

However, the truth is that many people are becoming syncretistic not atheistic. Syncretism is where you believe almost anything, using no discretion even when your beliefs contradict each other. Syncretistic people are not unified enough to affect political change against a driving, no holds barred force like Islam. Muslims don't have such apathy, and syncretism loses the battle. Meanwhile, Muslims who want Sharia Law are very effective against Christianity because Christians don't seem to want to unite and take a stand for godly healthy laws. Generally, they remain passive, hoping God will come to their aid.

Would you like to see proof of this? Look at what has happened in Europe, where Islam is making great strides amongst the syncretistic Europeans. Not so much by wining over the Europeans, but by immigrating in and replacing them. So if Christians leave the political arena, it will leave only one group to enter the vacuum: Radical Muslim Fundamentalists.

Is this being too alarmist?

I think not. When I first came to the U.S., I was shocked at the dearth of world news available here and at the ignorance of most Americans about world history. If you think I am being alarmist, it's probably because you have not been reading the history lessons of the rest of the world. It's useful to note that Christianity spread by appeal to facts and reason from the resurrection of Jesus until around 700 A.D. into northern Africa and Europe. But around 700 A.D. Islamic raiders took up the expansion of Islam. The major centers of Christianity used to be in Tunisia and Egypt. (Do you remember Augustine of Hippo? Well Hippo is in Tunisia). After 700 A.D., Islam spread by the sword to all of northern Africa, Asia and even parts of Europe. During that expansion, the Muslim raiders destroyed over 3000 churches and killed over 300,000 Christians.

On a side note: Don't apologize for the Crusades

Many Christians who have not studied history want to go around apologizing for the Crusades; I don't try to justify the actions of the Crusaders. They were not biblical. They did many stupid things. But I refuse to have a guilt trip about them after learning European history. We should ask these "crusade apologizers" when Islam will be apologizing for the 300,000 Christians who were massacred prior to the Crusades. Then we should ask them why the very first act of the Crusaders was to push the Muslims out of Spain. Why were the Muslims in Spain? And since they were in Spain did not the Europeans have a right to defend their own land? What sort of logic is this? Both sides have done their share of atrocities. Yet I find it odd that people complain strongly about the Crusades while appearing oblivious to the fact that the Muslims came in and slaughtered Christians a few hundred years earlier. If anything, Tunisia was a Christian land first. Its people voluntarily became Christian centuries before the Crusades. What about Spain? It was Christian until Moors took over parts of it in the 8th century. Why, I wonder, aren't Muslims held responsible for destroying Christians first?

Through violence Islam has taken over Christian centers like Constantinople, now Istanbul; Egypt, formerly the center of the Coptic tradition; Nigeria, currently fighting a losing battle with Muslim fundamentalists; Sudan, where southern provinces are Christian and animistic, and the north where I grew up, though Muslim, used to have churches on every street corner. Yet today, as everyone knows, it is dangerous to be a Christian in Sudan. Note that none of the original Christian inhabitants of those lands left or converted to Islam voluntarily.

Need I go on? The Crusades were not biblical or Christian; they were a tragedy of errors. But Christians should not feel guilty about a government's response to the wars of Islamic aggression.

This won't happen in our lifetime!

Sure, an Islamic takeover it may not happen in the United States in *our* lifetime, but can anyone guarantee it won't happen in our *children's* lifetimes? Will my daughter Mary-Katherine be safe? Will your grandchildren?

People may glibly say persecution is good for the church, but are they visualizing their children being raped, tortured or killed? Yes, God's Word will go forth despite persecution, but let us not be misguided and foolish enough to wish it upon our own children and our children's children. And if we should not wish it upon our *own* children, how *dare* we wish it upon *other* people's children? How heartless, careless and cruel can we be?

The only time the church has not grown!

Here is the alarming truth. Till recently the church had grown under every type of persecution except one. It grew under Roman persecution. It grew under communist persecution. It may even grow in the face of New Age persecution. But until the advent of Satellite TV and ministries like SAT7.org and IranAliveMinistries.org[547], Christianity had never grown under Muslim persecution – not in 1,400 years. The only time Christianity or any sort of freedom of religion made a comeback in a Muslim-dominated society was when external political forces violently removed the Muslim control. For example, Spain. Note the converse, Christianity has allowed Islam to flourish within its borders.

Of course, God can do anything he wants, but frankly the only other way for Christianity to grow in Muslim dominated lands is when God decides to give Muslims visions, and I have met a few of these converts. Yet, these converts are immediately persecuted. No nation has gone from Muslim to Christian or any other religion, while many nations and cultures have gone voluntarily and willingly from pagan, animistic, Viking, Buddhist or even Confucian to Christian. You can't argue that it's because Islam is so voluntarily compelling like Christianity.

So let me ask the question again, "Are you really sure you think it's a good idea for the church to experience persecution? How many millions will be born under that system and be damned to Hell?"

And what you are also saying is that we should stand idly by and *let* things progress to that point in this great nation, especially when we have a legal and constitutional way to prevent that from happening. Are you saying that we should *let* it happen to our children and aged parents? One day Armageddon may be upon us, but regardless of what your eschatology is, let *us* not be the ones responsible for bringing it on because we stood idly by when we could have done something.

Are you sure you want this legacy?

Is this the legacy you want to have when you stand before the Lord God Almighty? Do you really want to say, "Yes, Lord, you gave us a great nation, a great missionary nation, a great sending nation, a great giving nation, and we watched idly while it went to purgatory in a handbag. We let it turn into a nation that needed so much internal help and welfare that it couldn't reach out to other nations. We let it become a nation that isn't sending missionaries out and now needs missionaries to come *here*. We let it turn into a nation that persecuted Christians and as a result, we've become too busy surviving *ourselves* to be able to take the gospel of love to the rest of the world. We let it turn into a nation that persecuted the most innocent of all, the unborn, and we stood by idly.

Yes, Lord, we understand that all we had to do was vote and get involved earlier on, but we were too comfortable re-preaching the gospel to our own congregations to worry about maintaining the laws of our nation. We were short sighted and irresponsible. We hid our talents in the ground, and when people did come to faith in Christ, we encouraged them to abandon the government of the people, by the people. Yes, Lord, despite the great Constitution, which you gave this nation, we let it be eaten away and eroded by those who did not love you and hated your law given for our protection."

God did not take kindly to the Israelites when they and their kings turned away from Him. I doubt that He will be happy with us if we do the same. Is this being too dramatic? I don't think so.

---

[547] May I urge you to support these types of ministries. Our family does. They are effective and are building forbidden churches all over Iran and the Middle East.

Even if Islam does not take over

Let's say, on the other hand, that Islam is unable to seize the opportunity to take over the political structure. We will still have to deal with syncretism and the Homosexual Agenda. We have seen the beginning of persecution of believers in countries that used to be Christian. It starts with that and then progresses. If you know World War II history, you will recall how Hitler did it with the Jews. First, the Nazis blamed Jews for little things. Then they went to bigger things. Then they restricted the Jews' freedoms. Finally, in the confines of their twisted socialistic minds, they were able to "justify" extermination. The state needed it. Again, is this too dramatic? I don't think so.

Islam is stronger than syncretism, but unless Christians take a stand, Christianity will prove to be weaker than syncretism. So, while Islam will most probably take advantage of syncretism's failures, syncretism[548] on its own will pose a threat to the freedom of religion as long as Christians don't respond to the challenge it poses.

Let's take a closer look at formerly Christian nations in Europe, such as Germany. WorldNet Daily posted this on December 26, 2006 by Olivia St. John talking about the United Nations.

> *"A case in point is the European Convention on Human Rights, an offshoot of the U.N. Universal Declaration of Human Rights, which is currently being used by the German government to ban home schooling and to indoctrinate public and private school students into fully embracing a socialist state. Recently, almost 40 German families have endured imprisonment, heavy fines, state seizure of children, and in some cases the serious hardship of seeking asylum in neighboring countries, all because they have chosen to home school their children due to concerns over hedonistic exposure to sexually explicit materials in the German public school system. Incredibly, Sven-Georg Adenauer, a Christian-Democrat governor joined at the hip with the Socialist Party, demanded the prison sentences.*
>
> *...the European Court utilized Article 2 of the European Convention on Human Rights and concluded that "Parents may not refuse the right to education of a child on the basis of their convictions," adding that the right to education "by its very nature calls for regulation by the State."*

So a once-Christian country is imprisoning Christian parents just for home schooling their kids. Am I overly worried here? If you think so, you may have the unreasonable expectation that God will *not* allow this to happen in the U.S., when you yourself have said, "perhaps God *should* let it happen." Just remember this will affect your daughters and sons. In the opening of this book, I related a number of legislative bills that are poised to become the law of the land should Christians grow lax. One is a proposal by a Democrat representative from Mountain View, California (in my home of Silicon Valley) to pass a law that would punish parents with $1000 fine and a 1-year in prison for spanking their children. Do you really think I'm being an alarmist? You'll know that I wasn't when they haul you off to prison because your next-door neighbor saw you swatting your 2-year-old daughter's hand. Laws change hearts. Wait until spanking is reviled, and people are shocked by it as we are when Britney Speers drives on freeways with her child in her lap, an act that was legal and commonly done 15 years ago.

Remember too, all the examples I've provided about Christian freedom of speech being suppressed. How pastors in Sweden have been arrested for reading from the Bible, Christians in Britain arrested just for having pamphlets with Bible passages. Remember the NPR article "When Gay Rights and Religious Liberties Clash"[549] that discussed all the various suits brought on private individuals, companies, and charities by gay activists?

Look at countries where Christians were a minority yet were allowed to practice their faith. Persecution slowly grew over time there too. Why is this relevant? Because it

---

[548] I classify any belief system that tries to absorb multiple cultures and beliefs without any basis in fact as syncretistic.

[549] http://www.npr.org/templates/story/story.php?storyId=91486340

Neil Mammen

will be similar to what happens in the U.S. once Christians become a super minority. First, the U.S. will becomes an ex-Christian country like Germany, then, in time, other religions will replace Christianity.

The slippery slope is real

In Sudan, Eritrea, Pakistan, Egypt, Burma and Indonesia persecution of Christians has grown so slowly that today we mistakenly assume it has always been that way. When I was growing up in Sudan, Christian worship and evangelization was legal and unrestricted even though the country was run by a military dictatorship. However, Christians did not see the point or were not allowed to get involved politically and one fine day the Muslim Brotherhood took over the country, and today we have the massacres in Darfur.

In Eritrea, where I attended a Christian boarding school for six months and was airlifted out by the U.S. Marines during their civil war, we see a disturbing trend as well:

July 19, 2006 Around 1800 Christians have been jailed without trial in Eritrea as a result of their religious affiliations. Many face severe mistreatment for refusing to sign statements denouncing their faith. Reports indicate that some Christians have been sentenced to hard labor or held in underground cells in total darkness for days. Others have been held in solitary confinement in metal ... containers.

In May 2002 the Government ordered the immediate closure of all churches other than those affiliated with the Orthodox, Roman Catholic and Lutheran denominations, rendering all other Christian activity illegal. Those who continue practicing their faith, even in the privacy of their own homes, face persecution and imprisonment.

Eritrean Christians who fled to neighboring Ethiopia, Kenya and Sudan have described being beaten and tortured. Some refugees were forced to leave their families behind and fear reprisals will be taken out against them. Many who fled to the United Kingdom are reluctant to speak openly of the lack of freedom in Eritrea for the same reason.

Despite increasing reports of persecution and imprisonment since 2002, the Eritrean government has claimed 'no groups or persons are persecuted in Eritrea for their beliefs or religion'.

www.cswusa.com/Reports%20Pages/Reports-Eritrea.htm

Note how it starts by "outlawing" non-traditional churches and allowing only the older churches. Eventually, however, even these favored churches lose their rights.

The Patriarch of the [permitted] Eritrean Orthodox Church has been forced out of office and officially placed under house arrest, according to reports received by the Eritrean website, Asmarino.com.

Going back to Indonesia, remember this quote we saw earlier by Catholic Archbishop Charles Chaput in July of 2006, "violence against the Christian minority has steadily continued over the past decade."

In all this, one is reminded of the famous saying: [550]

First they came for the Communists but I was not a Communist so I did not speak out; Then they came for the Socialists and the Trade Unionists but I was not one of them, so I did not speak out; Then they came for the Jews but I was not Jewish so I did not speak out. And when they came for me, there was no one left to speak out for me.

Pastor Martin Niemoller, 1892-1984

Like the legendary frog in the boiling pot, persecution always starts slowly. Real frogs may be too smart to let it happen to them. But are real Christians?

A persecuted American Church?

If America should fall and its churches and Christians fall under persecution, what would happen to freedoms elsewhere? If America's moral decline continues, its social work will cease and the impact will be global. Thousands of American and indigenous

---

[550] There are several variations of this quote, but the message is still the same. Note that I do not necessarily condone all of Pastor Niemoller's other stances.

missionaries will lose their funding, and millions of people, who once depended on American missionary doctors and pilots, will have nothing and no one to care for them. One might argue that Christians in counties like Korea may take over that missionary role (since in many cases they have already). But that argument also applies to the Korean political scene and the African political scene as well. What sort of hypocrisy allows anyone to think that American Christians should shy away from politics but Korean Christians should not? What happens when Christians all over the world shrink from taking part in politics and become persecuted in their homelands? Persecuted Christians cannot afford to support much in the way of missionaries since they have no income, no money, and no base to work out of. Who then will lead the fight to stop the slaughter in Darfur? Who will lead the fight to stop sex slave trafficking in third world countries? Who will step in to protect Indonesian Christians or Burmese Christians? Who will provide the $260 billon a year in giving?

A short look at the past

Suppose England was persecuting Christians at the same time as they were sanctioning slavery in the 1800's. How effective do you think William Wilberforce would have been? Imagine if Wilberforce was in fear of his own life? Either being hunted down for being a Christian or being an undercover Christian, vary of being arrested if he ever revealed his true beliefs? Do you think he'd have time or the ability to fight against slavery? Do you think he would have been successful?

Similarly, how effective would the effort to abolish slavery in the U.S. have been if Christians were underground, afraid of persecution and not allowed to speak publicly – much less involved in the political process?

People who make these sorts of statements about the "goodness" of persecution are being extremely shortsighted. In what international ministries did persecuted Christians in Stalin's Russia or Mao's China participate? Even in Rome, the only reason the gospel spread is because God used the oppression of the Christians to disperse them throughout the world. However, that won't work today in our world of borders and passports. No non-Christian nation will take Christians in. Will you escape and move to Saudi?

Christians and conservatives account for most of the $260 billion given to charity yearly, and every church of around 400 people provides $184,000 in voluntary city services each year. If the U.S. Census Bureau is correct in saying there are more than 200,000 churches of *conservative* denominations in the country (and this does not even include conservative *non-denominational* churches), imagine the impact of a *persecuted* church on the rest of the United States. There would be no more outreach, and the well of charitable giving would go dry. How much of the total social services load would cities be able to handle? What would the cost be in lives? This is not true social justice! Do you care about the poor to build and protect the church? Saying that the American Church needs persecution and then letting it happen is heartless and cruel.

Recommended Reading, all available at www.ransomfellowship.org

- Their Blood Cries Out by Paul Marshall (Dallas, TX: Word Publishing; 1997).
- Atrocities Not Fit to Print, Nina Shea in First Things (November 1997) pp. 32-35. A report on the failure of the press to cover the greatest human rights story of our age.
- Candles Behind the Wall: Heroes of the Peaceful Revolution that Shattered Communism by Barbara von der Heydt (Grand Rapids, MI: William B. Eerdmans; 1993).
- A Fragrance of Oppression: The Church and Its Persecutors by Herbert Schlossberg (Wheaton, Il: Crossway Books; 1991).

There is an urban legend that says if you put a frog in very hot water, it will quickly jump out.

But if you gradually heat the water, the frog will adapt to the change and eventually boil to death.

Fortunately for frogs, they aren't that stupid.[551] Unfortunately, for frogs, some cruel humans have actually tried this experiment.

Unfortunately for humans, sometimes we aren't as wise at the frog and tend to ignore gradual changes, until we are "cooked" and it's too late.

Notes III:
Additional Objections

There are numerous objections that have been brought up by readers like you in discussions I've had since the first few drafts of this book. Rather than include them in the main body of the book, I've added them here. If you have an objection and think I have not covered it, please review these. Some may overlap various points I've made in the book. If after reading this you *still* think I have not addressed your objection feel free to email me at

Objections@JesusIsInvolvedInPolitics.com

Objection: But the Bible says we should be focusing on feeding the poor, not on making laws.

James 1: 26 If anyone considers himself religious and yet does not keep a tight rein on his tongue, he deceives himself and his religion is worthless. 27 Religion that God our Father accepts as pure and faultless is this: to look after orphans and widows in their distress and to keep oneself from being polluted by the world.

I addressed the issue of feeding the poor when I called all of us to be involved in social issues. We can do both. Taking care of orphans and widows, staying uncontaminated by worldly ways, and controlling the tongue are not the *only* components of true religion. James did not address foundational matters like belief in Christ, so we immediately see that this is not meant to be an exhaustive or complete list. James was speaking to Christians; addressing a virtue he saw lacking in those particular ones whom he was writing to. All Christians *are* to personally be involved in some way with those who need help, but one cannot read any exclusion into this passage. It can't be used to say *no* prophetic or moral issue ministries should be established. For if you did that then you'd eliminate salvation as James never talks about it here.

All it says is that Christians should *also* be involved in social issues. And indeed we the church have always been the first to address this matter. Moreover to paraphrase Bonhoeffer: If we merely bind up the wounds of those who have been broken by the wheel we are failing in our purpose. We must also bind the wheel that is doing the damage. We must change the laws of the land to prevent the creation of more widows and orphans, i.e. broken and single family homes, which lead to suicides and homicides.

Note too that there is a tendency to confuse individual responsibility with ministerial responsibility. Each person is called not only to care for orphans and widows but also to evangelize and preach the gospel. And let's not stop there. Followers of Christ are to visit those in prison, bless the sick, comfort the dying and so on and so on. As we said it would be unreasonable to assume, however, that every Christian ministry needs to do all these things. As we noted, we don't expect the Sound Ministry at our church to replicate the Junior High ministry, and it would be silly to expect a Christian Political Ministry (read

---

[551]www.snopes.com/critters/wild/frogboil.asp

"right wing Christian organization"), one trying to influence or incline the culture toward Christ, to be involved in feeding the poor. Yet as the statistics show, most members of these "right wing groups" in all probability, are *personally* involved in feeding the poor; reaching out to the needy and preaching the gospel in other ministries at their local church, as they are commanded to be.

However as we've also shown, the Church cannot use this excuse to abdicate its responsibility to teach about morality and to urge it's members to take action to alleviate suffering due to bad laws. Where else would they learn this?

Objection: How about Romans 13?

A friend of mine recently sent out an email critical of the president. Someone on her mailing list immediately responded with this:

> *Do I need to remind you that no government on Earth exists but by the permission of God. So, if you don't have anything to say about our president besides praying for his protection, well being, and spiritual growth, don't be saying it to me!*

This is wrong on so many counts that it's hard to decide where to start. The most complete but slightly harsh response to this would have been. "I'm a bit confused, are you saying that if you had lived in Nazi Germany you would be saying the same thing. Not that I am comparing our president to Hitler, but the principle is the same and let me remind you that the Nazis *did* use this verse to stifle any criticism of Hitler. If I cannot be critical of this president for any reason, then I cannot be critical of Hitler, Mao or Che Guevara; even less so for a citizen suffering under one of those evil men." Of course, you may get the old, "Are you saying our current president is Hitler? I'm shocked!" To whit you should reply in just as snooty a voice, "We are talking *principles* here, are you capable of understanding how *principles* can be applied to both extreme and general situations?" OK OK, say it nicely.

Jesus called His politicians snakes, hypocrites and cowardly rats, why can't we? I have to say this seems like a very un-American viewpoint. The founders of this nation banded together to give us the freedom of political speech to speak out against any bad leader, so can I ask why you are saying it's wrong? The founders did a lot more against their leader (George III) than pray for his protection, well-being and spiritual growth. They condemned him, overthrew his reins and usurped his tyrannical authority. Are you saying they were wrong? Would you say this to them? Even the Declaration of Independence, condemned George III and says, if a ruler starts to violate our rights we are to replace him. Have you read it lately?"

Many individuals including Christians it seems have a very myopic view of the world and are forgetful of history. But we do have to deal with this since this person was referring to Romans 13.

> **Romans 13:** [1]*Everyone must submit himself to the governing authorities, for there is no authority except that which God has established. The authorities that exist have been established by God.* [2]*Consequently, he who rebels against the authority is rebelling against what God has instituted, and those who do so will bring judgment on themselves.* [3]*For rulers hold no terror for those who do right, but for those who do wrong. Do you want to be free from fear of the one in authority? Then do what is right and he will commend you.* [4]*For he is God's servant to do you good. But if you do wrong, be afraid, for he does not bear the sword for nothing. He is God's servant, an agent of wrath to bring punishment on the wrongdoer.* [5]*Therefore, it is necessary to submit to the authorities, not only because of possible punishment but also because of conscience.* [6]*This is also why you pay taxes, for the authorities are God's servants, who give their full time to governing.* [7]*Give everyone what you owe him: If you owe taxes, pay taxes; if revenue, then revenue; if respect, then respect; if honor, then honor.*

We must remember that Paul while writing this was living under one of the most anti-Christian governments of all time. The question is: Is Paul referring to *every* decree of the government? The answer can only be no. Why can we say that? Because when commanded to stop preaching by their Jewish government:

> **Acts 5:29** *Peter and the other apostles replied: "We must obey God rather than men!*

Don't forget, that at times all citizens of Rome were commanded to turn in

Christians to be executed. How many Christians did that, turn themselves and their brothers and sisters in? How silly to think we must obey all commandments? It is thus obvious that we are to obey the governments when they do *good* but not when they command bad or try to limit good from being done.

Chuck Baldwin puts it this way:

The apostle clearly states that civil government is a "minister of God to thee for good." It is a not a minister of God for evil. Civil magistrates have a divine duty to "execute wrath upon him that doeth evil." They have no authority to execute wrath upon him that doeth good. None. Zilch. Zero. And anyone who says they do is lying. So, even in the midst of telling Christians to submit to civil authority, Romans Chapter 13 limits the power and reach of civil authority.[552]

One could even argue that there are two commandments here. One is for governments to do good. Remember too governments were formed by the people to provide protection for them, their families, their livelihoods, their culture, and their way of life.

And while governments on earth exist only through the enabling of God, the Bible has multiple instances where God condemns evil kings and sends prophets to instruct his people to reject their king's evil ways and stand in defiance against those ways lest they be punished (see the book of Micah). So while we may disagree if our current president or government is in violation of God's moral law we cannot say that it is wrong to stand in defiance against a government if that government is acting immorally.[553] Given all that, there are certainly no grounds for anyone to say we cannot condemn a government or its actions. This objection is simply irrational and indicates feeble thinking or worse blind repetition.

However, there is an even more overriding reason why we can condemn the actions of our presidents and legislators. In America, who is the "governing authority?" It is *not* the president nor is it the government worker nor is it the policeman or the soldier or the general, it is *only* the Constitution. Every president and lawmaker is commanded to be subject to the *Constitution* and swore an oath to uphold it. So to the American citizen, Roman's 13 reads:

[1]*Everyone must submit himself to the **Constitution**, for there is no authority except that which God has established. The authorities that exist have been established by God.* [2]*Consequently, he who rebels against the **Constitution** is rebelling against what God has instituted, and those who do so will bring judgment on themselves.* [3]*For the **Constitution** holds no terror for those who do right, but for those who do wrong. Do you want to be free from fear of those who enforce and uphold the **Constitution**? Then do what is right and it will commend you.* [4]*For those who obey the **Constitution** are God's servants to do you good. But if you do wrong, be afraid, for the **Constitution** does not bear the sword for nothing. Those charged with upholding the **Constitution** are God's servants, agents of wrath to bring punishment on the wrongdoer.* [5]*Therefore, it is necessary to submit to those who protect, uphold and enforce the **Constitution**, not only because of possible punishment but also because of conscience.* [6]*This is also why you pay taxes, for the authorities who uphold the **Constitution** are God's servants, who give their full time to governing.* [7]*Give everyone what you owe him: If you owe taxes, pay taxes; if revenue, then revenue; if respect, then respect; if honor, then honor.*[554]

Now that puts everything in perspective. When we condemn the actions of a sitting president or a lawmaker, if we are condemning them because they are failing to uphold the Constitution we are *obeying* God.[555] As long as the constitution is moral, they are God's

---

[552] http://www.newswithviews.com/baldwin/baldwin521.htm
I would recommend subscribing to Chuck Baldwin's regular emails.
[553] In addition, if you say that, you are saying that America is an illegal nation for it was founded by men who stood in defiance of *their* British Government.
[554] Thanks to Chuck Baldwin (www.NewsWithViews.com) and Gary DeMar (AmericanVision.com) for their work in clarifying this concept.
[555] Note we can also freely disobey the constitution if it were to be immoral. Fortunately it isn't. But the constitutions of other nations can be.

servants when they uphold our constitution and disobedient when they do not. Go do likewise.

For a complete and thorough exposition of this passage, see "The Establishments and limits of Civil Government" by James Wilson written in 1853.

Objection: We are not called to impose our morals on an unbelieving world.

Actually, I don't know why people think this is true. As we have comprehensively showed, laws are based on moral values. So, one has to ask, if our country's laws are not based on our Christian values, then whose values should they be based on? If Christians remove themselves from the voting or legislative pools, then whose ethics will be represented? It will be those of everyone *but* Christians. Is this the kind of country you want? I don't think so. Laws will be made based on cultural fads. Can you imagine the damage that will be done to the nation and to your kids and grandkids? Do you care?

Secondly, our Constitution allows for every person to vote their conscience, and it also makes provision for people trying to influence others in the way they should vote. (This is known as campaigning and freedom of speech.) Our conscience is dictated by our moral values, which happen to be our religious values as well. We are asked to speak and vote our conscience and thus our most cherished values. Surely, you cannot object to Christian organizations trying to influence other Christians to write to their lawmakers. Or are you objecting to Christians trying to influence their elected representatives? Isn't that their constitutional right? Christ spent a lot of time and energy to influence and teach *His* lawmakers – telling the Pharisees and other members of the Jewish ruling council why their laws were either applied incorrectly or just plain wrong.

Remember too, how God's law works. If an unbeliever keeps it, he will be physically (though not spiritually) blessed, because these laws are instructions in how to live successfully in this physical world. We can bless the unbeliever through our laws. Our morals which are God's laws save lives and reduce suffering. Isn't it heartless to keep them to ourselves and let the innocent and defenseless suffer?

Remember if you continue to insist that we Christians should not impose our moral values on others, you would have to say we were wrong to fight against slavery, racism, forced marriage, prostitution, or child abuse. Similarly, are we then wrong to try and stop the current killing of Christians in Darfur by Muslims? Who are we to impose our Christian morals on these Muslims? It's their government. They claim one of their moral values is to kill infidels. Shouldn't we just let them in that case?

And of course what about the verse in 1 Timothy that says the Law *is* for the sinner and irreligious?

Were we also wrong to try to stop the practices of the Chinese in abandoning their baby girls in the woods – or, in ancient times, the Romans who left unwanted babies to eaten by wild animals? Or how about the British, imposing Christian values on Hindus by preventing them from throwing widows onto their husband's funeral pyres. This list is endless. People in some cultures eat enemies they have killed, were Christian missionaries wrong to appeal to them to stop this practice? In other cultures, it was considered noble to abandon the elderly in the wild. Was it wrong of missionaries to try to stop this practice? Where do you draw the line? We can impose our rules on *other* cultures but not on our own? What logic is that? At what point, do we become complicit in evil deeds? Does a Christian merely *not* go to gladiatorial fights? Or does he try to stop them? Tell Telemachus that.

Objection: We shouldn't try to convince the world to hold to Christian values because they don't need to obey God's laws to be saved.

This is a variation of the previous objection. Those who raise this objection tend to believe people just need to be saved. One does not have to obey God's laws. Or one needs to obey them only *after* being saved.

I believe this is a Straw Man fallacy. That is, you are arguing against something that is not my position but loosely resembles it. In this case, the fallacy is assuming that I am proposing that we use Christian moral laws in government to evangelize or bring people

Neil Mammen

to Christ. But I have never advocated that. I have spent many years reaching out to atheists, agnostics, and people from other religions by giving them rational proof of the historicity and logical foundation of Christianity. I always try to combine this with genuine personal relationships and caring works. The motto of our ministry named No Blind Faith is "Apologetics, Theology, Relationships – Rational Faith" I have never used politics to lead someone to Christ. Nor have I said people can be saved by living "moral" lives. Salvation comes only by faith in Christ. At the same time, I believe it is reasonable to think and verifiable in experience that adherence to the "instruction manual," the Word of God, helps people live in healthy ways. If more people kept to God's laws about divorce, wouldn't the social mess we are in be less serious? Wouldn't there be fewer disorders, suicides, and drug abuse among kids? Wouldn't there be more resources, money and time available for solving other problems?

Here's my challenge to anyone who says that, "Are you suggesting that God's moral laws have no value to a non-Christian? Are you suggesting that if non-Christians disobeyed God's moral laws it would make no difference to their daily lives? Are you suggesting that if non-Christians *obeyed* God's moral laws it would not make their lives better and reduce the suffering of innocent children?" Do you see how ridiculous the opposing position can sound?

So when someone says we *can't* hold the world to Christian values, I feel he or she should explain why this is a bad idea. Why is it wrong to teach and try to convince a society that the "Manufacturer" of the world actually knows the best way to operate it? In other words, God's laws make for healthier and happier people. How can we even think of keeping it away from those who need it the most?

Objection: Forcing Christianity or godly laws on people will drive them away from God.

To tell the truth, I agree with the first part of that statement. I don't want to force Christianity on anyone. But I disagree with the second part. I will advocate for forcing godly laws, because I believe they have life and pain saving value as I show in this book. Besides, healthy discussion of the reasons behind the laws, may pique the interest of unbelieving people in discovering the "Source" of such laws.

"But look at the 1960's when we had godly laws and people turned away from them," someone might say. I would argue that the laws were not why people turned away. They turned away partly because Christians ran and hid in their churches and stopped engaging with the culture. I know of no one who blames the social and moral deterioration that began in the country during that period directly on laws. In fact, there may be a good argument that the deterioration began because people did not insist on adherence to God's laws. There is no evidence that building a nation on moral laws drives people away from God.

Objection: We just have to love people, not force them to obey laws.

This is a shortsighted objection. I would argue that having strong moral laws *is* a loving approach to the organization of society. Preventing moral laws from passing is *less* loving. Is it more loving to a child, or less loving to be forbidden to plug a fork into a light socket?[556]

Let's look at some real world examples. Is it more loving, or less loving to allow No Fault Divorce, which has resulted in so many single parent homes which in turn has been statistically proven to be one of the greatest causes of crime, suicides, rape, the growth of welfare and mental depression? How loving is it to allow a nation to have laws that encourage all that? How loving are we if we just let it continue to happen?

Is it more loving or less loving to enslave people under welfare, which we've seen causes a reduction in IQ, depression and increases out of wedlock births?

---

[556] We don't formally forbid that as a society, but we do have *laws* requiring sockets to be designed so it is not easy to put forks into them. That socket law would be considered a Civil Law.

Objection: We are not called to change the world politically, just spiritually. We should just preach the gospel and enough lives will be changed to change the world.

This objection is also a variation of previous objections, but it is well worth addressing in detail because it results in terrible conclusions. Christ engaged people on both the political and spiritual level. A church that does not change culture and government will become a church under persecution, and Christians will become inwardly focused and less influential in the world. Consider how few missionaries are being sent into other nations by nations that have a persecuted church today?[557]

In addition, if people start becoming Christians and follow your advice to immediately pull themselves from active political involvement,[558] you'll end up with a small portion of the country (all non-Christians) controlling it politically, and there will be no support or moral guidance from Christians. Or if you are merely passive about it, the culture will change and ensure no Christians are elected. This is not what the founding fathers envisioned. If you don't care about that, you still have to deal with the fact that you are promoting an oligarchy, that is a rule by elites, and your grandchildren will suffer under that legacy. All actions and inactions have consequences. Is this really what you want?

But most importantly what would you have done about slavery? Would you have let the horrors of the slave trade continue, let families be torn apart, tortured and killed in horrible conditions on slave ships because you were not called to change the law politically? How heartless a principle do you adhere to? What would Jesus wish us to do?

Objection continued: We should preach the Gospel instead

Some pastors say that we should preach the gospel to change the wickedness of man as opposed to using political action and legislation. However, this is a dangerous Straw Man fallacy. No one is saying we want to use political legislation to change the wickedness of man. We are saying we want to use political legislation to protect our children and other innocents who would otherwise suffer terribly as a consequence of bad social programs; or who would be killed or enslaved due to the increase in crime or drugs use and the degradation of society. We are saying we want to use politics and legislation to protect our rights to free speech including evangelization. These rights are rapidly eroding as Christians are being hauled into jail for handing out Bibles or witnessing, yes even in America, the land of the Free. It is precisely because of the wickedness of man that we need legislation to protect these rights.

What is more critical for us to understand is that if we don't act now, pastors may not be able to preach the gospel from their pulpits in a few years. It may become illegal to be a free-speaking spiritual shepherd. Look at what is happening in Sweden and Canada, where Christian clergymen are being arrested. Consider what pastors had to do in the USSR in the old days. In a sense, it is the pastor's very own job that we're trying to save. Let me reemphasis, if you *just* focus on preaching the gospel soon *you* will not be able to preach that very same gospel.

Let me repeat an important point. If Wilberforce and the Emancipation movement folks had just stuck to preaching the Gospel, slavery may still exist. Why? Because Christians were slave owners. They already had the Gospel. Preaching alone didn't help stop slavery in the England. Preaching that mobilized Christians to vote accordingly and get involved politically is what stopped it. Same for the myriad of laws that Christianity has

---

[557] Note that this was not the case with the early Church, as persecution caused the Christians to flee to new lands and expand when they started churches there. This worked because Christianity was not well known. Today if you try to flee, where would you go unless you move to an already Christian nation? You certainly can't move to a Muslim or Hindu country and not expect to be persecuted even more. Of course, we could colonize space.

[558] Ah but you say that you are not talking about complete dis-involvement in politics. Well in that case what are you talking about? If you agree that we should have some involvement in politics, then the question becomes: How much involvement is necessary? Are we involved only to the point of voting? As I've shown, this is nonsensical in a republican form of government. Where is the point of disengagement?-We have to be the lawmakers. There is no other conclusion to make.

Neil Mammen

changed or codified over history.

Objection: The Bible says we should be in the world but not of the world. This means we should not be involved in politics.

This is a peculiar objection. Why? Because this saying, "be in the world but not of it," is not in the Bible. You should look for it online. If you do this, you will see that the only verse that comes close to the idea is this:

John 17 14 I have given them your word and the world has hated them, for they are not of the world any more than I am of the world. 15 My prayer is not that you take them out of the world but that you protect them from the evil one. 16 They are not of the world, even as I am not of it.

Now all of a sudden we realize that the passage means something completely different. Jesus said that we are not of the world but He doesn't say anything about not *participating* in the world. Further, even if this saying were in the Bible, would it mean that you should not get a job or be president of a company? Does that mean you shouldn't buy a house? Once we start looking logically at these things, we realize that a lot of perceptions we have aren't at all biblical. And at what point do we say to the oppressed, yes we will let bad men make bad laws that will bring terrible suffering upon you and our children and we won't care. What part of the love your neighbor command should we ignore?

Don't forget too, the commandment to the Jews to live in Babylon and participate fully in it while they were in exile there. We are in exile here.

Objection: Paul said "righteousness doesn't come by law."

The passage that is being quoted is

Gal 2:21 I do not nullify the grace of God; for if justification comes through the law, then Christ died for nothing.

The implication here is that we should not be involved with the law because no one is saved through it. But this is yet another Straw Man fallacy. Nobody is arguing that we or anyone will get saved by adhering to the law. We all know that we can't because of our sin nature (Romans 7:14-18).

What Paul is saying is that the law reveals to us what sin is (Romans 7:7-9) and that the law could not save or justify us because of our sin nature (Galatians 2:16, Psalm 143:2). This then leads us to see our need for and believe in Christ. The Law is what required Christ to die for us, but at no point are we ever claiming that we can adhere to the law and be saved from God's justifiable wrath against sin. Rather, we are saying that requiring people and societies to adhere to God's moral law is loving to both saved and unsaved because it results in healthier lives and enables people in our great country to continue to obey the Great Commission. Moreover, the concern for the poor, innocent or young in society is all part of the second greatest commandment "Love your neighbor as yourself." Godly laws will protect them.

But let's take it a step further and presume that the Christians who disagree with involvement in politics by Christians or the church are right. Then the question is, "How far should we retreat?" Today we are asked by fellow Christians not to be involved in law making. What happens when tomorrow the laws are rewritten to make all churches illegal? Don't think it can't happen here. It happened in Rome before Constantine. Many people mistakenly believe that Christians were persecuted constantly in ancient Rome. But that could not be further that the truth. For years, the churches survived next to the Roman Senate. Suddenly a new Caesar would arrive and decide to ban churches, at this point Christians would begin to be persecuted. Then another Caesar would take over, who had some Christian influences in his life and the persecutions would stop. More churches would be built and the cycle would repeat. Even during Constantine's rule some of his co-Augustus's tried to revive Christian persecution. It was only through the state law brought about by Christians who were politically active and close to Constantine that it became illegal to persecute Christians. And when this happened Christianity was able to expand throughout Europe and Africa. Do you think it was wrong for those Christians to influence Constantine to not persecute Christians? Do you think it was wrong for them to get involved?

So, do we still not get involved? What happens when the law that says any pastor who teaches from Leviticus will be imprisoned? If you consider this unlikely, think again. It is a real bill in the Senate even as I write this (HR1532), which severely punishes hate speech, saying that anyone who incites anyone to violence by condemning any group of people can be arrested. How hard would it be for a group of individuals to claim that a pastor's reading from Leviticus incited someone else to kill a gay man? If you are still skeptical, let me remind you *again* about what happened in Sweden, where a minister was imprisoned simply for reading from Leviticus.

Objection: But Politics is a business of compromise

Remember, we are not talking here about self promotion or jostling for position. We are talking about making sure that *moral* laws are legislated. One can be a politician and choose not to compromise on key moral values. One can also be a politician and realize that there is a hierarchy of moral values. I am not advocating something like lying to stop abortion, but in the case of abortion, I may be convinced to allow an exception for rape and incest (only 0.6% of the cases of abortion) to save the 99.4% of abortions done for convenience. Don't be fooled, however, once we have the 99.4%, we'll come back for the other 0.6% later.[559] Remember William Wilberforce stopped slavery gradually because he was unable to get the votes to ban it directly. For instance, one of his first successes was banning any dealing with French slavers during the English French war. Since most slavers were French, this cut into the finances of those members of Parliament who were being funded by the slave trade. As a result, Wilberforce was able to mount a campaign and get Christian abolitionists elected to Parliament. Consequently, slavery was banned a few years later. Wilberforce was not a fool and did not say, "No either we stop slavery or nothing." He realized the incremental path *was* the path to stopping slavery.

Similarly many of our battles to stop abortion have been incremental, i.e. we've reduced abortion by as much as 25% in minors by implementing limitations like parental consent laws[560] (a minor must have a parent consent to the abortion). Anyone who tries to argue that we've failed at the abortion battle because we have an all or nothing mentality is either an idiot or speaking from pure ignorance. We've never had an all or nothing mentality.

Objection: Government can't save you.

I agree. Government can't save anyone. But no one is claiming it can. This is yet another Straw Man. The law can provide physical protections and be used to encourage good and healthy behavior. Government can't save us but, as Martin Luther King, said, "the law cannot make a man love me, but it can keep him from lynching me,"

Objection: "You are such a hypocrite! Spouting nonsense that you love the sinner but hate the sin is just an excuse for hate. You can't do that. You are intolerant!"

Does it make sense that God or we could love the sinner and hate the sin? It sure does. There are many examples of this. Here's one. Imagine that you are the creator and manufacturer of a hair dryer. You lay down the 'hair dryer law.' "Do not immerse this hair dryer in water." You have this law to protect people. Imagine now that someone accidentally put the hair dryer in water. Would you hate that person? No. But you would hate and be grieved at the fact that they were electrocuted when their hair dryer hit the water. So, you hate the "sin" (the hair dryer being immersed) but not the sinner (the person who immersed it).

On the other hand, if there was a group of people who ran around purposely

---

[559] Imagine if you ran into a one day old baby that was born from a rape, could you kill it? Of course not. In which case how can you kill a fetus that was born from a rape? There is no scientific, moral, philosophical or DNA difference between a one-day-old baby and a fetus. To see this full argument see "How to win Abortion Arguments without appealing to the Bible or Religion" at www.JesusIsInvolvedInPolitics.com/Abortion.htm

[560] http://www.jstor.org/pss/146045

promoting throwing hair dryers into water and telling others that nothing bad would happen, I'm sure you can see that you'd be justified in condemning them.[561] In fact, it would seem that these people are the ones who love the sin (watching people get shocked) but hate the sin*ner* (the poor folks who are dying). If they cared about the sinner, they would want to stop them from the sin that is destroying them.

Whenever someone tries to disparage the saying: Love the sinner but hate the sin. I ask them if they can imagine the situation if their brother became a drug addict. Could they hate the drug addiction, the drug and the drug pushers yet still love their brother? Of course, they could.

Objection: What about Global Warming?

Democrats and liberals complain that the conservatives want to destroy the environment; while conservatives contend that Global Warming, even it if existed, is not caused by humans. The issue is not whether we want to destroy the environment. It is whether we can reduce the rate of warming by any significant amount by throwing money at it. Fortunately, recent emails released from some of the key Global Warming scientists, have revealed that they have been manipulating the data and lying in order to fool the public.[562] India for one has withdrawn from the Intergovernmental Panel on Climate Change citing that they are tired of the lies and manipulation. Make sure you get Brian Sussman's book "Climategate" as well (WND Books, 2010). It's not about climate but about control.

Worse still for the cause, the liberal Copenhagen Consensus[563] has determined that every dollar we spend on stopping Global warming could have gotten 100 times the benefit if we'd used that money for other things like eradicating malaria or building dams.

Objection: You confuse morals with ethics in your diatribe on morality.

To tell the truth, I never thought there was much of a difference. Let me quote the Stanford Encyclopedia of Philosophy:

"The term 'morality' will be used more frequently than 'ethics'. Philosophers have drawn various contrasts between 'morality' and 'ethics' at various times... But etymologically, the term 'moral' comes from the Latin mos, which means custom or habit, and it is a translation of the Greek ethos, which means roughly the same thing, and is the origin of the term 'ethics'. In contemporary non-technical use, the two terms are more or less interchangeable, though 'ethics' has slightly more flavor of theory, and has been associated with the prescribed practice of various professions (e.g., medical ethics, etc.). In any case, no distinction will be made here. Morality is regarded here as a set of customs and habits that shape how we think about how we should live."[564]

---

[561] Ah, but you say, "If God exists, why can't He design the hair dryer so that we can safely immerse it in water? Why can't He make a waterproof hairdryer?" While all analogies have limitations, in this case any designer of equipment knows that that every feature you add has a consequence. For instance, a waterproof dryer, while easily possible, may be too big or too bulky or too expensive, or require batteries instead of 110V, which would be too heavy or require additional circuitry that would raise the cost and make it non-competitive, etc. And in reality, it's just not needed if you are willing to just be a bit careful. Now expand this from this simplistic example to the human body and the entire physical world. And don't forget, at the end of the day, God is also an artist and has an eye for beauty as well as function. Remember too that God cannot do *anything*. He cannot sin, He cannot stop being God, He cannot learn, He cannot make 1+1 = 3 as we commonly understand 1 and 3 to be. He cannot make a round square in two-dimensional space. The latter few are irrational, and it is fallacious to try to argue that the source of all rationality being could be irrational. In other words, God cannot create a universe where everyone has freewill, if they don't *really* have the freewill to sin and the sin has no real consequences. It's like saying "You have the freewill to disobey me. Oh by the way, there is no consequence to disobeying me." This means either God is capricious and morality and immorality are random differentiations by God, or you never really had the freewill to disobey God.

[562] http://blogs.telegraph.co.uk/news/jamesdelingpole/100017393/climategate-the-final-nail-in-the-coffin-of-anthropogenic-global-warming/

[563] www.copenhagenconsensus.com/

[564] From plato.stanford.edu/entries/religion-morality/ last visited 5/3/07

Whew! Did you get all of that? It is long winded, but the point is that morals and ethics are interchangeable words. So, I have just used the word "morals."

Personal Morals vs. Public Morals

Now I must admit that one could distinguish between *personal* morals and *social or public* morals. For example, I may *personally* decide that I will not drink alcohol because that would be wrong for me (especially if I were prone to addiction). But I would not impose this on society in the form of legislation. However, this immediately implies that I *know* that drinking a glass of wine[565] now and then for my digestion is not as Paul the Apostle tells us, inherently wrong. Thus, when confronted with a proposed law to ban alcohol, my conscience would be clear if I voted *against* any ban, since I know the problem is mine and not society's in general. However, if I *did* think that all alcohol is immoral, then my convictions would be that I should legislate against it, or I'd be a hypocrite. And in this case, if this was one of the critical issues of the times, then people should know that either they should not vote for me because they don't agree with this issue, or they should not vote for me because I am not true to my convictions.

Objection: You talk about bringing morality back to school. Schools are not supposed to teach morality, they should stick to academics.

Years ago during my seven-year tenure as a junior high counselor at Los Gatos Christian Church, our junior-highers were invited to a discussion about schools in a cable public access forum in downtown Los Gatos.[566] This was a tiny event. You have to understand that probably fewer than five people were watching the show on cable at the time, and it was filmed in a tiny studio. It was meant to be something like an Oprah talk show[567] with the junior-highers participating.

Bad idea. What junior higher has the guts to discuss things when adults are around? Anyway, it ended up with the two guests doing all the talking. Back then I wasn't as opinionated as I am now. (What a minute...what are you laughing about?) Anyway, halfway through the discussion, one of the teachers said, "Well, [public] schools aren't here to teach kids morality!"

That stuck in my craw, but despite being a counselor, I did not have the boldness to speak out at the time. However, after the half hour show was over and after they turned off the camera, I piped up, asking the teacher as nicely as I could, "You said that the schools aren't meant to teach kids morality. Are you saying that you don't think the schools should teach kids not to cheat on their tests? How about stealing their neighbors' watches[568]?"

He turned red and to his credit sheepishly said, "Okay, I guess that *was* a very foolish statement, *wasn't* it?"

You bet it was. Of course, schools have to teach morality and character. What could be worse than us churning out a school full of intelligent, mastermind criminals, or a bunch of well educated thieves, rapists and murderers? The sad thing is that this seems to be exactly what we are doing these days. True, schools aren't supposed to teach *only* morality, but they'd better be teaching kids that it's wrong to cheat as well as that 1 plus 1 equals 2. To provide credence to my argument, here's a quotation from Martin Luther King on this very issue.

"We must remember that intelligence is not enough. Intelligence plus character--that is the goal of true education."
Dr. Martin Luther King Jr., 1947

What is sad is that today these same liberals seem to want to only focus on

---

[565] Some have tried to argue that Paul was not referring to wine here but grape juice, however since other passages use the same word and indicate that we should not get drunk it seems to me that he has to be talking about wine and not grape juice. After all, it's hard to get drunk on grape juice.

[566] Los Gatos, California is a quaint beautiful little town in Silicon Valley.

[567] Do you remember when Oprah's show really was a "talk show" with members of the audience expounding their ideas and all too often their ignorance?

[568] iPODs hadn't been invented yet. Otherwise, I would have used that.

Neil Mammen

teaching our kids moral values and ignore academics. Sadly, their moral values are all values that we disagree with. Like it's evil to think homosexuality is harmful or it's evil to think Christianity is exclusively true.

Objection: You said that we shouldn't vote for "Just Fiscal Conservatives" (those who are socially moderate). While I understand that a person's view on marriage may affect financial issues when the family breaks down, but why would a person's pro-choice position make any difference?

Remember the entire basis for all laws is morality, which is tied inexorably to the Creator. You cannot separate the two. Anyone who does not comprehend that foundation has their feet planted firmly in mid air and will legislate incoherence and confusion. Abortion is also just the tip of the iceberg. I've never met a person who was pro-choice who did not also rebel against many of God's other laws. If a person is pro-choice, it can only mean one *or* more of the following:

1. They are ignorant about what abortion is and are pro-choice based on feelings not facts.
2. They are unable to logically deduce that abortion is murder despite the scientific evidence.
3. They cannot logically deduce that even if they don't know if the fetus is human, as long as they are not 100% sure that it is not, they cannot kill it, nor can they allow someone else to kill it. Imagine going hunting and not being 100% sure if what your friend was about to shoot at was a deer or a 4 year old child – would you let him shoot it?
3. They know it's murder and don't care.
4. They are willing to compromise the murder of babies in order to achieve other goals.

Note it could also be a combination of all of these, but all these point to the kind of person you do *not* want to be codifying your laws. These people at the end of the day do not have a Christian or Godly Worldview. They are rebelling against the plain facts and adjudicating with their feelings not facts or logic. This is critically dangerous and is precisely what has led to so much pain being inflicted on the helpless. In a sense that's like voting for someone who wants to protect marriage and is fiscally conservative but believes Jews are not fully human. We really should vote for someone with a *Godly* Worldview.

Objection: Capitalism is greedy and evil. Anytime one person makes more money than another, they are stealing from others. This is unchristian. We should equalize results.

Wallis, whom we introduced earlier in this book, and other liberals seem to have the mistaken idea that all economics end up in a zero sum game (also known as the zero sum gain). But this is not true. Zero-sum describes a situation in which one person's gain or loss offset by the losses or gains of everyone else. In other words, if someone does well, someone else must suffer equivalently. There is no net gain. Chess or Checkers are examples of zero-sum games. In them, it is impossible for both players to win. There's only so much to go around. Cutting a cake is zero-sum or constant-sum because taking a larger piece reduces the amount of cake available for others.

Yet, this is not necessary in commerce. People can gain or suffer together, as when a country with an excess of bananas trades with another country for its excess of apples. Both countries benefit. One country does not suffer because they other came out well. This is called *non*-zero-sum, when in the end both parties in the transaction benefit.

In fact, this is why commerce was started. There was a farmer. He grew wheat, but next door was a rancher who raised cows. Is it evil for the farmer to trade some wheat for some cows? Note, the first farmer could have raised his *own* cows, but he found it more efficient to focus on what he did best and then trade the results of his expertise with the products of the rancher's expertise. He would have lost time and energy and gotten worse results if he had not participated in the free market. With the free market they all won, as long as the trade was not coerced and the prices were based on the free market not artificially set by a government hack.

Wallis seems to think that standard economics is zero sum. But, it is not. Individuals create new value, and each new idea has new uses and consequences.

No country or community has ever improved their lot through charity. The best thing careful charity can do, is grow people till they can participate in the free market. But in the end capitalism is what frees people, not charity. Continuous charity hurts people.

Moreover, government messes things up. For instance, in the past, large manufacturing facilities were dedicated to making things like buggy whips for horse carriages, and any concept of moving to automobiles would immediately mean all the buggy whip employees would lose their jobs. However, by the nation going towards the automobile, immense new fields of commerce were created, nullifying over a period any downfall in jobs suffered by buggy whip makers. The new technology created a much larger market for automobiles and made efficient transportation available to ordinary people and allowed the gospel to be spread faster. Had a senator passed a law preventing automobile manufacture to preserve horse and buggy riding because his friend owned the buggy whip company or just because he felt compassionate toward all the buggy whip company employees, you can imagine the economic consequences. There would have been technological consequences too. The automobile has revolutionized the manufacturing process, the car-radio business (Motorola), the machine business, the assembly business, ambulances and even the health and medical industries – and so it goes. Rarely do technological advances limit themselves to their field of origin. One would have to be a Luddite[569] to not appreciate this.

You may say, of course, that had we restricted the development of the automobile we would not have the pollution problems or the global warming Al Gore claims comes from automobiles (now shown to be a farce[570]). But this is fallacious. First, I bet horses put out more carbon dioxide per mile than automobiles. Second, even if the American government had somehow suppressed development of the automobile, other counties which were already developing them would have left us in the dust and still be contributing to carbon dioxide emissions. Third, imagine an America with no automobiles or the technological advances related to them. Imagine then during the Second World War, America without this technology, without the ability to carry troops rapidly into battle and the Japanese finding a huge nation with a population riding horses and pulling carts. Now imagine being forced to speak Japanese or German and being forced to treat an emperor as though he were a god. Is that far fetched? Not at all. The Japanese did it to the Chinese. The point is that you can't suppress technology in one country and expect another country to not develop and use it. The communists and Nazi's were far worse for the environment than any other group. But again, let me remind you, Anthropogenic Global Warming is a farce!

The world economy is not zero sum because people by nature seek expansion and growth. Rather than taking away from someone else, as each person's part of the pie shrinks, markets grow, new technologies are invented and the overall pie grows. Even the "moderate" prince of the liberal left, Bill Clinton, realized this, saying:

> *"The more complex societies get and the more complex the networks of interdependence within and beyond community and national borders get, the more people are forced in their own interests to find non-zero-sum solutions. That is, win-win solutions instead of win-lose solutions.... Because we find as our interdependence increases that, on the whole, we do better when other people do better as well - so we have to find ways that we can all win, we have to accommodate each other."[571]*

Let me recommend the book by my friend Jay Richards, "Money, Greed, and God: Why Capitalism Is the Solution and Not the Problem," (HarperOne, 2010).

In Summary

Is not the United States government a government of the people, by the people and for the people? Yes. So, it is crucial for us, the people, to make sure that it remains a government for our children and their children. Voting alone does not cut it. At most, it

---

[569] A Luddite is someone who hates any new technology. They were named after the leader of the vandals who destroyed looms, thinking that the looms would put mill workers out of business. Instead, the looms created more jobs by reducing the cost of goods, thus increasing the demand.

[570] blogs.telegraph.co.uk/news/jamesdelingpole/100017393/climategate-the-final-nail-in-the-coffin-of-anthropogenic-global-warming/

[571] http://www.wired.com/wired/archive/8.12/clinton.html?pg=3&topic=&topic_set=

makes you a casual director with a two- to four-year say on the aims of the country. To be a real part of government, one has to be deeply engaged in its working parts. If I want to keep America safe for my Christ-following children, I am going to have to be actively involved.[572] Perhaps you feel the same way now? Email me if you do: *Stand@JesusIsInvolvedInPolitics.com*

---

[572] This does not mean we *all* have to run for office. Other ways of being involved are discussed in here.

A full Electronic Index of this book will soon be available online at www.JesusIsInvolvedInPolitics.com/electronicindex.htm

Neil Mammen ∽ WHO IS AGENT X?

PROVING SCIENCE & LOGIC SHOW IT'S
MORE RATIONAL TO THINK GOD EXISTS

How do you *start* to witness to an Atheist?

How about, by first proving God exists *without* using the Bible.

Once you prove God exists, then believing that Jesus rose from the dead becomes academic;
Miracles, creation/evolution etc.,
become minor issues.

If you enjoyed this book, you will enjoy Neil Mammen's conversational and easy to follow apologetics book.

Contains over 70 pages of responses to objections from actual atheists.

Order at NoBlindFaith.com

Are you a blind faith Atheist?

Have you looked at the facts logically?
Can one intellectually and scientifically derive the existence of God?
Is it really irrational, superstitious, or unscientific to think that an Eternal Agent is the cause of the Universe?
What are the reasonable conclusions we arrive at when we apply LOGIC to what we've discovered about the Big Bang?
Are the 4 'natural' dimensions the only ones that exist?
Current science requires even atheists to believe in at least 6 super-natural dimensions. Thus, aren't atheists really being irrational & unscientific to demand that nothing exists beyond our 5 senses?

Without using the Bible, Neil investigates the facts to derive the 7 characteristics of the cause of the Universe.
The rational and logical conclusion may surprise and will challenge you.
Give this book to an Atheist. It proves that contrary to "Dawkinism", one CANNOT be an intellectually honest Atheist or Agnostic.
Will they meet your challenge?

Turn the tables on your neighborhood atheist.
Put them on the defense.
Easy to follow! Great for Junior High and College students!

About the Author

Neil Mammen, a non-hyphenated first generation American immigrant is an Engineer during the day and an Apologist at night. As an engineer, he spends his time architecting and designing networking & video delivery systems, computer chips, boards, and FPGAs with **TentmakerSystems.com** and other US and international engineering companies. He received his BSEE in Computer and Electrical Engineering at the age of 20 and his MSEE in Solid State Physics and Computer Engineering at 22. Neil has co-founded four startup companies in Silicon Valley. He has about 20 issued and pending patents in areas varying from Networking, Traffic Shaping, and Packet Processing to LED Local Dimming TV methodologies.

Neil is the founder of **NoBlindFaith.com**, an Apologetics and Evangelization ministry focused on training everyday people to use apologetics in evangelization without awkwardness. Apologetics is the investigation and defense of the truth of Christianity using facts, reason, science, history, archeology, and philosophy. Neil is a speaker at various venues and Apologetics and Missions Conferences around the US teaching Apologetics, Theology and the defense of Christianity as a Rational and Logical Faith. Neil has been featured on: NPR debating Eric Rothschild of the ACLU and Eugenie Scott at the Commonwealth Club; KFAX Radio (with Stand for Truth Ministries speaking about Stem Cell Research); and on various other radios shows including the Lars Larson Show, American Family Radio with Frank Turek, and KKLA with Frank Pastore. He is on the board of the Values Advocacy Council and has spoken at local churches for the Family Research Council.

Some of Neil's blogs can be found at **CrossExamined.org**.

Neil can be scheduled as a teacher/speaker for conferences, church services, universities or retreats, anywhere in the world. Topics include Apologetics and Theology as well as concepts from this book:
speaking@NoBlindFaith.com

References for Neil Mammen as a Speaker

Neil's messages not only reflect professional and Scriptural integrity, but his sense of humor adds the well rounded touch that keeps our congregation anticipating his next visit or series.

David Underwood, Senior Pastor, Liberty Ridge Church

Neil has a gift that spans all age groups. This is because I can name none that exceed Neil's preparedness when he takes the pulpit. Neil has sound Doctrine and Theology. His style is relevant yet it remains biblically sound. You can expect dynamic visuals and creatively enhanced teaching that pulls each hearer in!

Chuck Aruta, Senior Pastor, New Beginnings Church

Neil is both dynamic and exciting to listen to. He is able to captivate an audience of any age from Jr. High to adults! Neil has a unique ability to take deep and sometimes complicated spiritual truths and communicates them in a relevant way. He speaks both to the mind and the heart. Not only can I speak to his ability as a speaker, I can also speak of his character (and his love of gadgets). Neil lives his life with integrity and his love for God is evident. He is generous, hospitable and faithful, both in his relationships with people as well as with God.

Adam Miller, Youth Pastor, West Gate Church

I love Neil's passion to communicate truths that matter. Whether he is speaking of the rationality of the Christian worldview, or the mandate for Christians to engage culture with a broad and winsome presence in all fields and vocations, whether speaking to students or adults, his thought is clear, his presentation entertaining and compelling, and his authentic and whole-hearted commitment obvious to all who interact with his prophetic message.

Jeff Reed, Senior Pastor, Hillside Covenant Church

Neil is a committed follower of Jesus Christ and an enthusiastic, gifted communicator. He is a wide reader and a keen discerner of culture. He knows the contemporary, as well as the historic challenges to the Truth of God's revelation found in the written word and the Living Word, Jesus Christ. He knows how to expose the lie and to expound God's Truth in a convincing, winsome way. Neil is articulate and courageous in presenting his convictions and he helps others to follow his example. I recommend him as a speaker for church services, seminars, and retreats.

Galen Call, Senior Pastor,
Los Gatos Christian Church/Venture Christian Church

5621393R0

Made in the USA
Charleston, SC
12 July 2010